ANIMAL ANATOMY
FOR ARTISTS

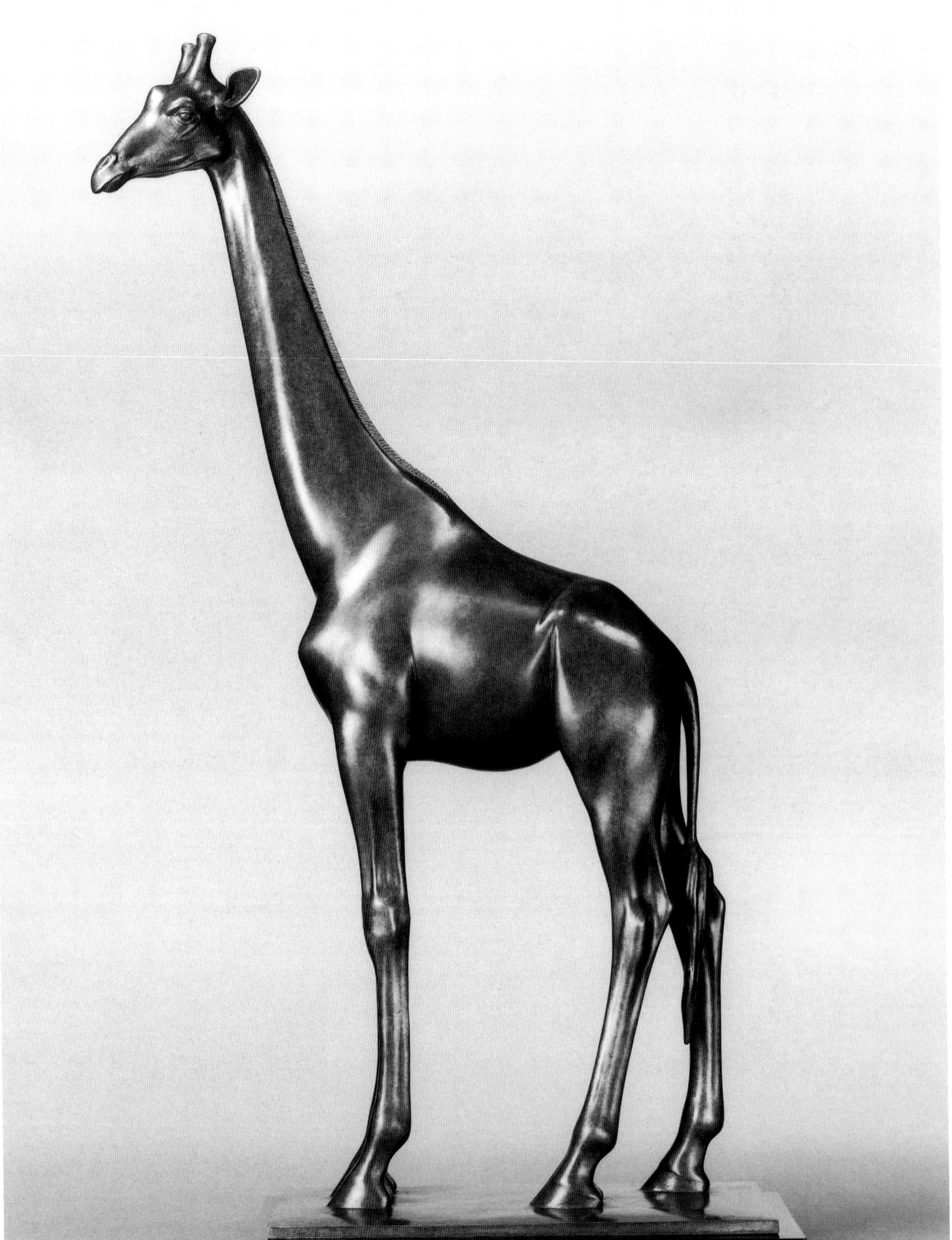

Eliot Goldfinger

Animal Anatomy for Artists

The Elements of Form

OXFORD
UNIVERSITY PRESS

2004

Frontispiece: Giraffe, 1983. Bronze, 18.5 inches high

OXFORD
UNIVERSITY PRESS

Oxford New York
Auckland Bangkok Buenos Aires Cape Town Chennai
Dar es Salaam Delhi Hong Kong Istanbul Karachi Kolkata
Kuala Lumpur Madrid Melbourne Mexico City Mumbai
Nairobi São Paulo Shanghai Taipei Tokyo Toronto

Published by Oxford University Press, Inc.
198 Madison Avenue, New York, NY 10016

www.oup.com

Library of Congress Cataloging-in-Publication Data
Goldfinger, Eliot
Animal anatomy for artists: the elements of form/Eliot Goldfinger.
p. cm.
Includes bibliographical references and index.
ISBN-13 978-0-19-514214-3
1. Anatomy, Artistic. 2. Animals in art. I. Title.

NC780.G65 2002
743.6—dc21 2003053586

Designed and typeset by Scott and Emily Santoro, Worksight.

All drawings, photographs, and sculptures are by Eliot Goldfinger.

9 8 7 6 5 4 3

Printed in China on acid-free paper

CONTENTS

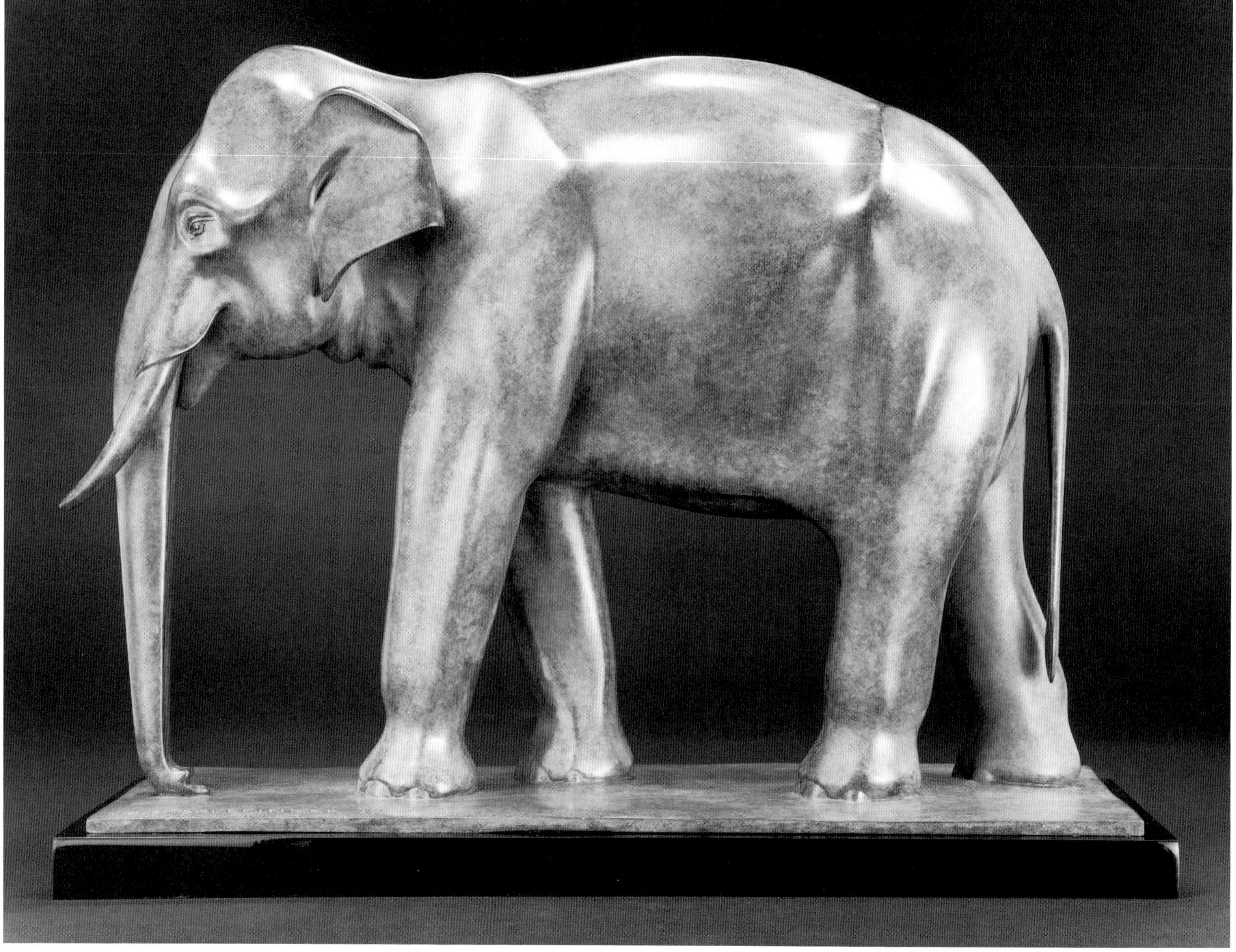

Indian elephant, 1983. Bronze, 13 inches long

To Louise, Gary and Evan

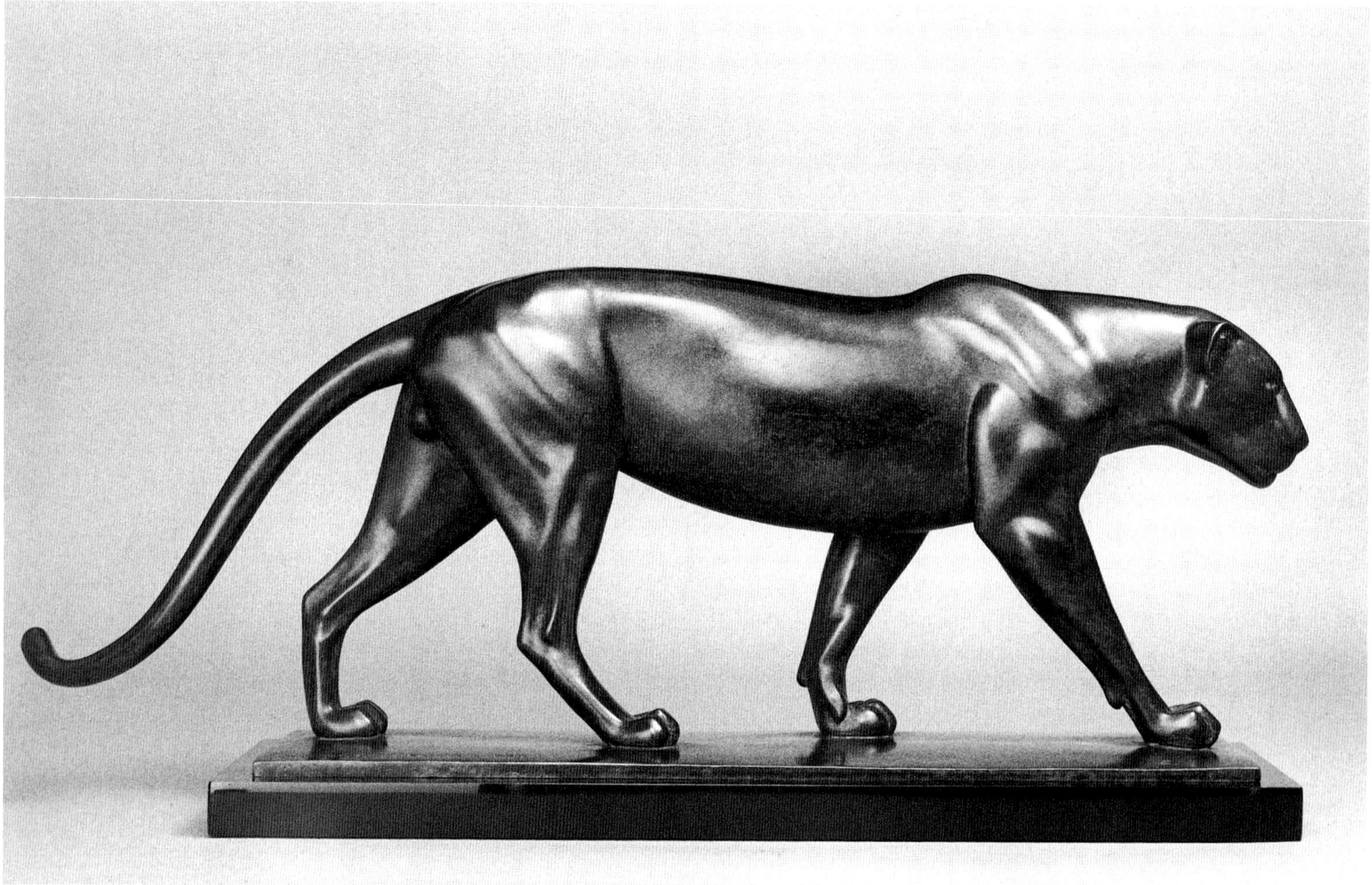

Leopard, 1984. Bronze, 18 inches long

ACKNOWLEDGMENTS

The strength of this book lies in the fact that so many people have been so generous with their time, knowledge, resources, and collections. I thank Stuart Pivar, founder of the New York Academy of Art, who provided an environment for me to teach animal and human anatomy to artists. He strongly supported the acquisition of an anatomical collection of comparative skeletons, related artwork, anatomical models and charts, and the use of dissection as part of the curriculum, which allowed me to create an anatomical teaching facility of the highest caliber with the best students. My two books on anatomy are a direct outcome of that experience.

I am indebted to the late Dr. Emil Dolensek—a great veterinarian, a remarkable man, a friend, and, to my great honor, my student—who taught me much about anatomy and made the animal hospital at the Bronx Zoo available to me to dissect some incredible animals. Jim Doherty, general curator at the Bronx Zoo, has been enormously helpful to me for many years in my study of live animals, and I am truly grateful for his generosity and his friendship, and for reviewing the animal silhouette drawings.

I offer heartfelt thanks to Henry Galiano, owner of Maxilla & Mandible in New York City, for his participation in the development of the content of this book from beginning to end, for reviewing parts of the manuscript, and for providing a great deal of anatomical research, reference material, and skeletons. I would also like to thank Deborah Wan Liew of Maxilla & Mandible, and Gary Sawyer of Ossa Anatomical.

Thanks also to sculptor and art historian Oscar C. Fikar for sharing his extensive knowledge and resources on animal anatomy; to Michael Rothman, natural history illustrator, for his comments, assistance with computer issues, and loan of reference material; and to sculptor Bill Merklein for arranging and assisting with the photographing of the cows, for making molds and casts of my small skeletal models, and for the loan of books. Special thanks to Dr. Corey Smith, veterinarian, for posing for the photograph in the "human anatomy" section.

I offer enormous thanks to Dr. Nikos Solounias, paleontologist, anatomist, and ungulate anatomy expert, for his assistance, for access to his anatomical library and human cadaver lab, and especially for generously reviewing the entire manuscript and all the illustrations for accuracy, consistency, and clarity. I am grateful to Michael Anderson of the Peaboby Museum of Yale University, for sharing his anatomical photographs and arranging access to the Peabody's skeleton collection.

I also thank the following people who have graciously (and most generously) allowed me to take and use the photographs of the animals for this book: Linda Corcoran of the Bronx Zoo, Kathie Schulz of the Catskill Game Farm, Lisa and Dr. Michael Stewart of River Meadow Farm, Dennis Brida, trainer of the thoroughbred "End of the Road," Amanda Moloney of Anstu Farm, Robert Deltorto of Westchester County Parks, and Gretchen Toner of the Philadelphia Zoo. A special thank-you to Chris Schulz of the Catskill Game Farm, who dodged a charging rhino in order to set up a perfect side view, in full sun, of an adult male white rhino.

From the American Museum of Natural History, my thanks to Mary DeJong, Tom Baione, and Amanda Bielskas of the main library for their assistance with my research; to Barbara Mathe of the Special Collections at the library for permission to reproduce my photographs of the skulls in the Department of Mammalogy; to Bob Randall and Eric Brothers of that department for their assistance and patience in selecting excellent specimens to photograph; and to Dr. Joel Cracraft, of the Department of Ornithology, for reviewing the bird text. Thanks also to Melissa Mead of the library at the University of Rochester for the loan of the photograph of the skeleton of "Jumbo" the African elephant and to John Thompson for access to the library at the New York Academy of Art. My thanks to Joe Ruggiero and Sal and Mike Perrotta of Sculpture House Casting, who did some of the moldmaking of my small-scale skeletons.

For the study and photography of animals from life, I would like to thank the Goldenbergs and their Visla dog, the Fridoviches and their German Shepherd dogs, the Finemans and their dogs, the Ricevutos and their rabbits, and the River Ridge Equestrian Center and their horses. Thanks to LJ, of Lion Country Safari in Florida, for arranging for me to photograph their animals.

Many thanks to Drs. Zita Goldfinger and Jay Luger, my sister and brother-in-law, both veterinarians, for their books, for X-raying a dissected rabbit, and for their assistance in the photography of their cats at the Forest Hills Cat Hospital; to my brother, Dr. Steven Goldfinger, for reviewing the manuscript and for his very helpful suggestions on consistency, organization, and presentation of the material; to sportswriter Vic Zeigel for sharing his connections in the world of horseracing which provided access to study and photograph thoroughbreds; to Lewis Gluck, for a particularly good piece of advice; to Dr. Mark Finn, for his help in clarifying many items and for his masterful guidance; to Dr. Ron Spiro, for his assistance in the digital photography of a bear skull; to Laura Orchard for her contribution, and to Christine Cornell for her valuable comments.

I thank my mother, Dorothy Goldfinger, for her love and support, and for bringing back a wildebeest skull (which I photographed and drew for this book), from her trip to Africa with my late father B. Sol. Heartfelt gratitude to Dr. Stanley Edeiken, most especially for his daughter. Thanks to the wonderful team at Oxford University Press—Joyce Berry, Elda Rotor, and Susan Hannan; and to Scott and Emily Santoro of Worksight for the exceptional work they did in designing this book. Very special thanks to Helen Mules for expertly navigating this book through the complex editing and design processes, and to Laura Brown for putting my ideas and drawings into the Library of Congress for a second time.

My sons Gary and Evan deserve special thanks for inspiring me with their love of each other and family, their humor, their creativity, and their passion and fascination with nature. Finally, I offer my love and gratitude to my wife Louise Edeiken for her patience, assistance, and support; for putting up with strange packages in the freezer and bizarre things boiling on the stove; and most especially for her love.

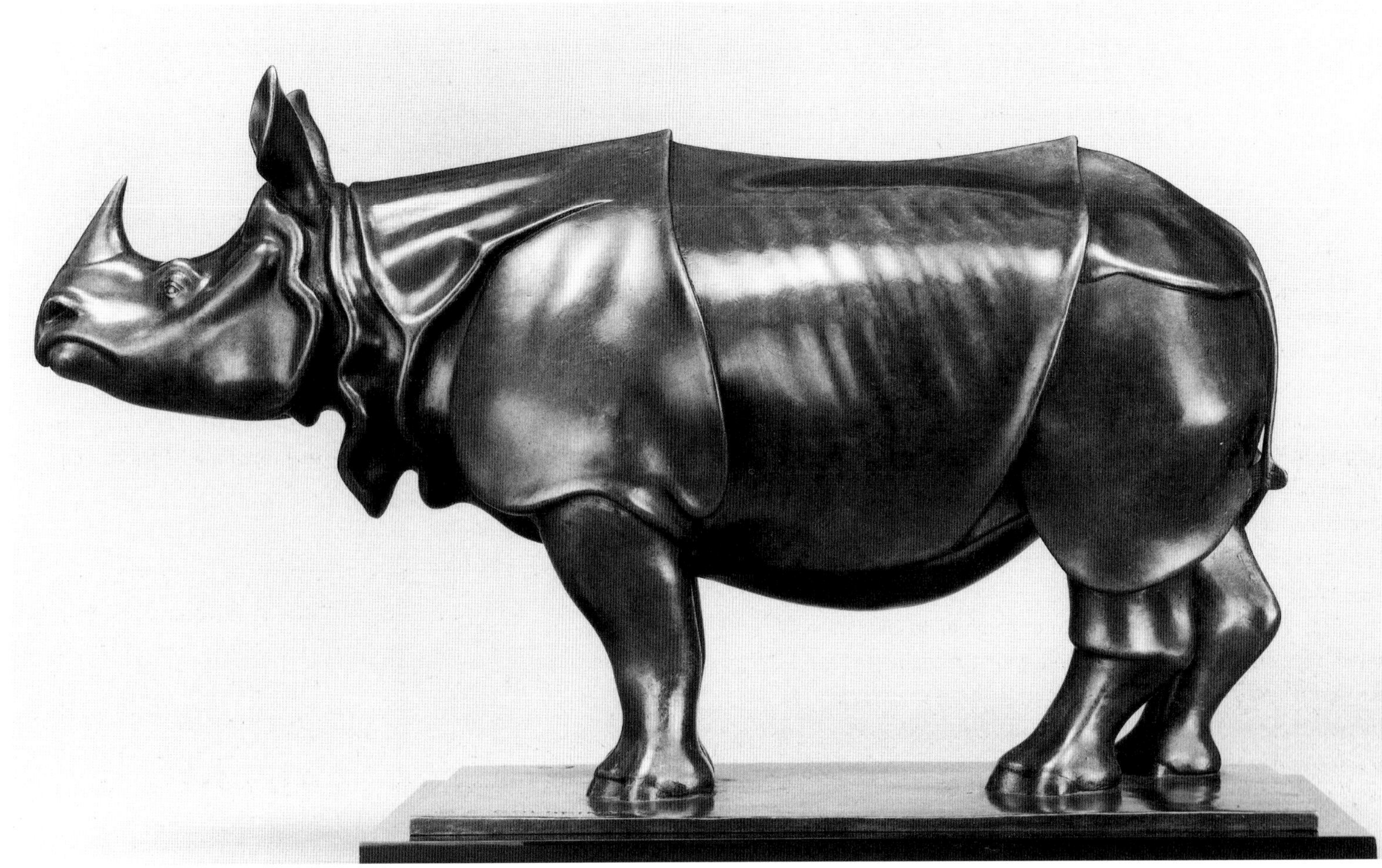

Indian rhinoceros, 1983. Bronze, 14 inches long

INTRODUCTION

The animal body can be visualized as a three-dimensional jigsaw puzzle, made up of distinct, interlocking pieces. These pieces all have very specific volumes that begin and end at very specific places.

This book is about these volumes. *Because all volumes in the body are created by anatomical structures*, we must study the individual anatomical components and how they relate to one another. Muscles and bones are responsible for most surface forms seen in life. Fat, fur, skin, glands, veins, cartilage, and organs also contribute to the creation of surface form.

In drawing, painting, and sculpting animals, one must begin with a general, understanding of the entire animal (shape, proportion), and then concentrate on its specific parts and details. This is called working from the general to the specific. For example, rough-out the shape of the entire animal first, define the shapes of the torso, the individual limbs, the head, and the neck, and then finally add the details of the individual muscles and tendons. Artwork can be embellished with the most numerous of details, but it must conform to a greater concept of larger shapes and volumes.

This book explores those features common to all the animals presented here, and presents a basic body plan that applies to all. Although each species is unique, with its own shapes and proportions, there are very close similarities between species because they all share a common ancestor. Important variations or exceptions to the basic body plan are discussed when appropriate.

In most cases, technical terminology has been replaced with more common usage, such as "front and back" instead of "anterior and posterior," or "deltoid" instead of "deltiodeus." Regions of the body are named based on anatomical structure, so the term "knee" for the front limb of the horse is not used, and that structure is called the "wrist." This unambiguously refers to the carpal bones of the front limb, and the term "knee" is reserved for the anatomical knee of the rear limb. Similarly, in the rear limb, the term "ankle" is used instead of "hock."

Classification of Animals

The animals presented in this book are grouped as follows:

The hoofed animals, or **ungulates**, are divided into two groups—the "even-toed ungulates," or artiodactyls, and the "odd-toed ungulates," or perissodactyls. The **artiodactyls** include: the bovids (cattle, buffalo, bison, antelope, goat, sheep, and pronghorn antelope—with permanent horns, commonly unforked, covered with a sheath, and present in males and usually in females); the cervids (deer family, including elk, and moose, in which only the males have annually shed, forked, bare bone antlers, and the caribous and reindeer, in which both sexes have antlers); the giraffids (giraffe and okapi, with permanent bony "horns" covered with skin); the camelids (camel, guanaco, llama, alpaca, and vicuña); the suids (wild and domestic pigs); the peccary; and the hippopotamuses. **Ruminants** are a suborder of the artiodactyls that have a multi-chambered stomach and chew their cud. They include the bovids, the cervids, and the giraffids. **Perissodactyls** include the equids (wild and domestic horses and asses, and zebras), the rhinoceroses, and the tapirs.

Carnivores ("meat eaters") include the canids (wild and domestic dogs, wolves, and foxes), felids (large and small cats), bears (including the giant panda), the raccoon, sea lions, seals, and the walrus. **Proboscideans** include the Indian and the African elephants. **Rodents** are a diverse group and include the mice, rats, squirrels, chipmunks, beavers, and porcupines. Rabbits and hares belong to the **lagomorphs**. **Marsupials**, probably the most structurally diverse group, include kangaroos, the opossum, the koala, and the probably extinct Tasmanian wolf. The **Primates** include monkeys, apes, and humans. The **Cetaceans** include the whales, dolphins, and porpoises. The giant anteater belongs to the **Edentates**, and the fruit-eating and insect-eating bats belong to the **Chiroptera**.

Method

All silhouettes (for the proportions) were drawn from photographs of living animals (ideally in the wild, rather than zoo animals), to capture the "essence" of the shape of an adult animal in profile. These are compared with other evolutionarily related animals to appreciate their similarities and differences. The goal was to present a "typical image" representative of the species, keeping in mind that for a "single type of animal" (wolf, rabbit, squirrel) there may be more than one species, subspecies, or breed; that there are differences (or no difference) between males and females and that characteristics vary between individual animals. What is presented here is a reasonable "norm."

In obtaining photographs of animals for the profiles, there was the problem of the lack of *absolute* side view photographs of an entire animal, especially photos showing the feet when an animal is standing in vegetation. Zoo photos usually show the feet, but the trade-off is that the bodies of captive animals may not be typical of animals living in the wild. If an animal is photographed even slightly off the absolute side view, foreshortening comes into play, and one end on the animal appears larger and the other end diminishes. Adjustments were made to these outlines to achieve an accurately proportioned side view.

The skeleton drawings of the animal, derived from drawings from the anatomical literature or from photographs of specimens, were then made to fit within these accurate silhouettes. Drawings and dry articulated skeletons are notoriously incorrect, whereas the skeleton inside a healthy, living animal is always correct. In producing the skeleton drawings, some limbs were shifted only slightly; in other cases, virtually every bone, including the individual vertebrae, was redrawn in a new position. Occasionally bone lengths were changed, and at times the skull was drawn from another source. The outline drawings placed around the skeletons indicate the surface in life. This surface is made up not only of muscle and bone, but of skin, fat, fur, and cartilage.

The muscle drawings were drawn over the skeleton drawings, generally "attaching" each muscle between its origin and insertion. Reference was made to illustrations and verbal descriptions in the literature, dissected material, and study of the animal in life. Animals dissected (entirely or in part) for this project, or for research in the past, include horses, dogs, cats, rabbits, pigs, a tiger, a wildebeest, a blesbock (antelope), a giraffe, a squirrel, an orangutan, and numerous human cadavers.

The drawings in this book, especially the individual muscle drawings showing the origins and insertions of the muscles, have been *slightly* stylized or simplified for the sake of clarity. Often in life, a tendon of insertion, whether narrow or wide, expands to attach into several places as it inserts—it can fuse with other tendons, muscle bellies, ligaments, fascia, and joint capsules. Here, the attachments have been "cleaned up" to give a sense of a single, ultimate, and accurate point of insertion, which is much easier to comprehend than an expansive area that wraps around and attaches to numerous structures. This is especially true of the tendons of the limbs that insert into the toe bones.

The black-and-white photographs accompanying the anatomical drawings were mostly taken at zoos. Priority was placed on three criteria: absolute side view (or as close as possible), visibility of the entire animal (especially the feet), and definition of anatomical features. Background distraction and lack of sharpness may detract from the quality of some of the prints, but the selections were made based on anatomical and proportional concerns.

Goal

With direct observation from life, combined with the study of anatomy, we can achieve a valuable in-depth understanding and appreciation of nature, as well as develop a sense of design and esthetics. This knowledge and sensibility, united with the inspiration generated from these studies, is transferred into our art, and with it we express ourselves in our time.

TERMINOLOGY

Anterior toward the front of the body.

Posterior toward the rear of the body.

Cranial toward the head.

Caudal toward the tail.

Dorsal toward the upper side; toward the back; "above."

Ventral toward the ground; the underside; toward the belly; "below."

Superior above.

Inferior below.

Medial toward the midline, away from the outside of the body.

Lateral toward the outside of the body, away from the midline.

Internal deep, away from the surface.

External toward the surface.

Proximal toward the center of the body; "near."

Distal away from the center of the body; "distant."

Deep away from the surface, or covered by other structures.

Superficial toward, or at, the surface.

Subcutaneous just below the skin; related especially to bone (bony landmarks).

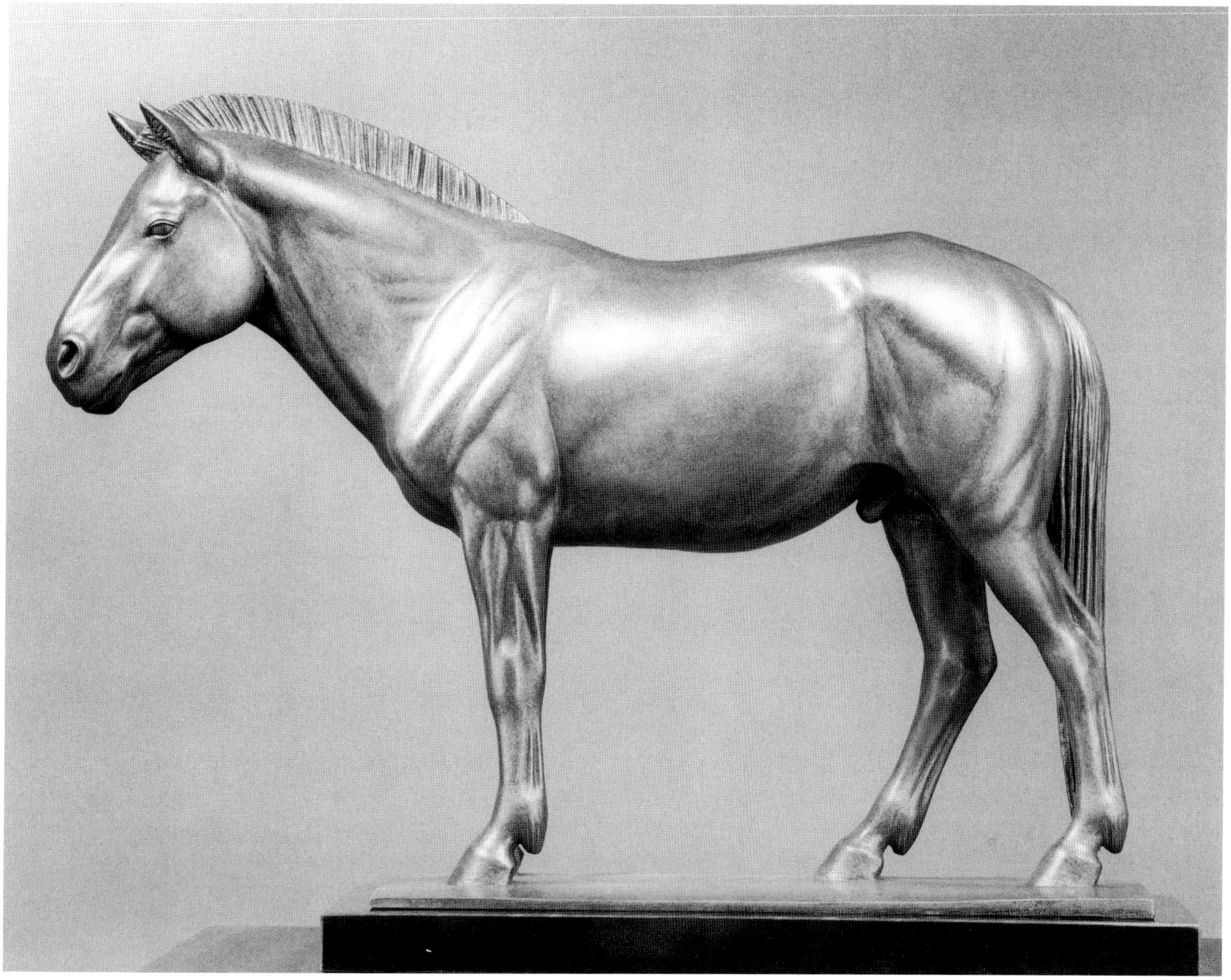

Mongolian wild horse, 1985. Bronze, 14 inches long

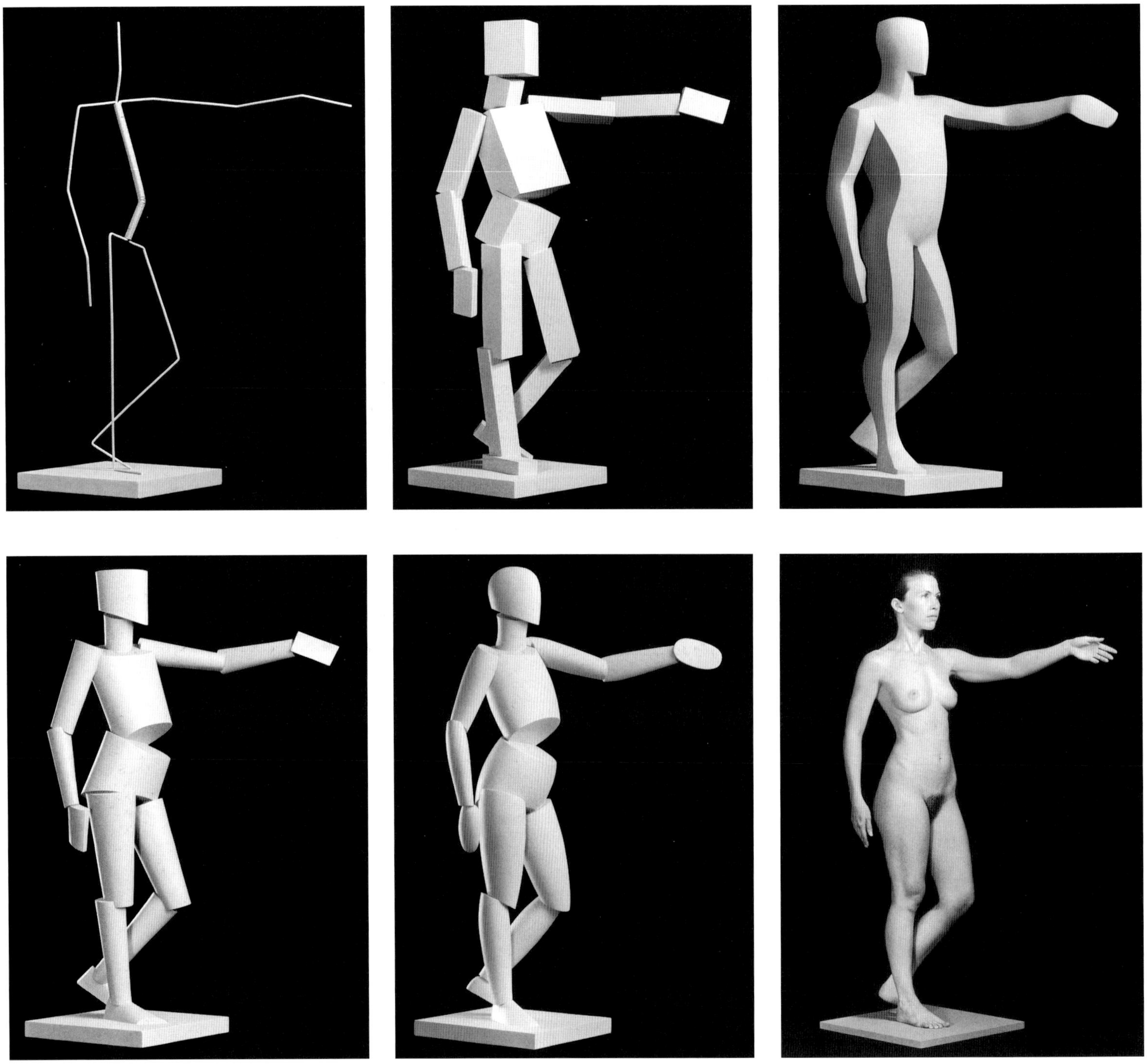

AXES AND VOLUMES OF THE HUMAN FIGURE: **FROM "HUMAN ANATOMY FOR ARTISTS"**

Basic body plan

There is a **basic body plan** common to most of the animals presented in this book. At its most obvious, they all have a head, a body, and four limbs. Most are four-legged and stand on all fours, and are described as having front limbs and rear limbs. The front limb is anatomically equivalent to the arm and hand in humans and primates, and the rear limb to the human lower limb. The animals in this book are surprisingly similar in many ways. The head is connected to the rib cage by the neck vertebrae and the rib cage is connected to the pelvis by the lumbar vertebrae. The two front limbs are connected to the rib cage, and the two rear limbs are connected to the pelvis. These units move in relation to one another, establishing the stance, or pose, of an animal.

Animals differ primarily in the shape and relative proportions of these structural units, in the position of the wrist, heel, and toe bones when standing and walking, and by the number of their toes.

Axes

An animal can be visualized as being constructed of a series of simplified, three-dimensional, somewhat geometric volumes (head, forearm, thigh). Each of these volumes has one dimension that is longer than the others. A line projected through the center of the mass of this volume on its longest dimension is called its **axis** (plural, axes). For the most part, especially in the limbs, these axes follow the skeleton, so that a line drawn through the long dimension of a bone is on, or close to, the axis of the volume of that region (for example, the position of the radius is close to the axis of the forearm).

One of the more confusing regions of the body is the volume of the upper arm. The humerus (upper arm bone) is mostly deeply buried in muscle, and lies toward the front of this muscle mass, with the massive triceps muscle located at its rear. Therefore, the axis of the humerus does not coincide with the central axis of the upper arm volume. It is important, though, that the actual position of the humerus be clearly understood, because its upper end forms the point of the shoulder, and its lower end is an important site for the origination of the forearm muscles.

Volumes

The axes indicate the *direction* of the volumes of the body. The **body volumes** themselves are created for the most part by the muscles and bones, and the separate body volumes define the various regions of the body (head, chest, forearm). Individual muscles often group together with muscles of similar function to create masses that attach to, surround, and are supported by the skeleton. As an animal changes position, the body volumes are redirected, and the shapes of the individual volumes are subject to change—a muscle or group of muscles becomes thinner as it is stretched and elongated, and thicker and more massive when it shortens.

The volumes of the head and chest are basically determined by the skeleton, and are covered by relatively thin to medium-thickness muscles.

An important body volume not created by bone or muscle, and therefore one that is highly variable, is the abdominal volume. This region contains the intestines and other soft abdominal organs held in place by a sling created by the thin abdominal muscles and their wide tendinous sheets. When the spine is flexed and the rib cage and pelvis approach one another, the abdomen shortens, becomes compressed, and bulges. When the spine is extended, straightening the body, the rib cage and pelvis move apart and the abdomen is stretched and narrowed.

Application of concepts

Conceptualization of body volumes is highly subjective. There are no hard-and-fast rules, but rather each artist, through a knowledge of anatomy and direct observation from life, creates a set of volume conceptions.

By conceiving accurately shaped, directed, and articulated body volumes, which then have the details of anatomy "engraved" upon them, the artist can create dynamically rendered and convincing animal art.

The following drawings show the axes and major volumes of various animals. The head, chest, and pelvic region are drawn as forms. The axes of the limbs are represented by lines. When the animal is in the standing pose, the axes are relatively simple and straightforward, as shown. In attempting to depict the frozen action of an animal in motion, knowing the exact position of all the axes of all the volumes of the body becomes crucial. The sculpture shows the volumes of the body; each volume, of course, has a directional axis, which must be visualized as passing through the center of its mass.

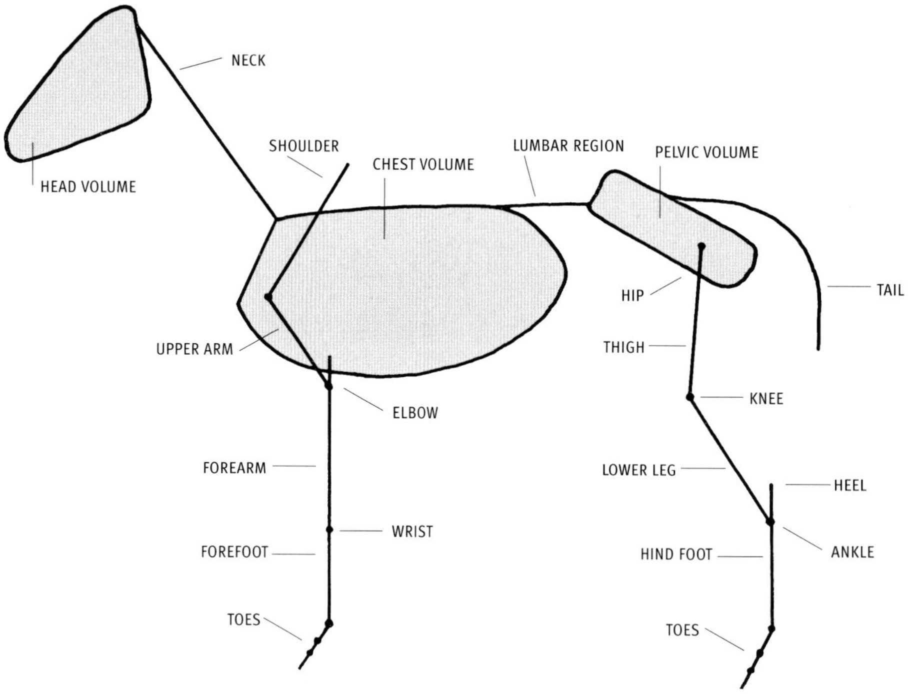

HORSE

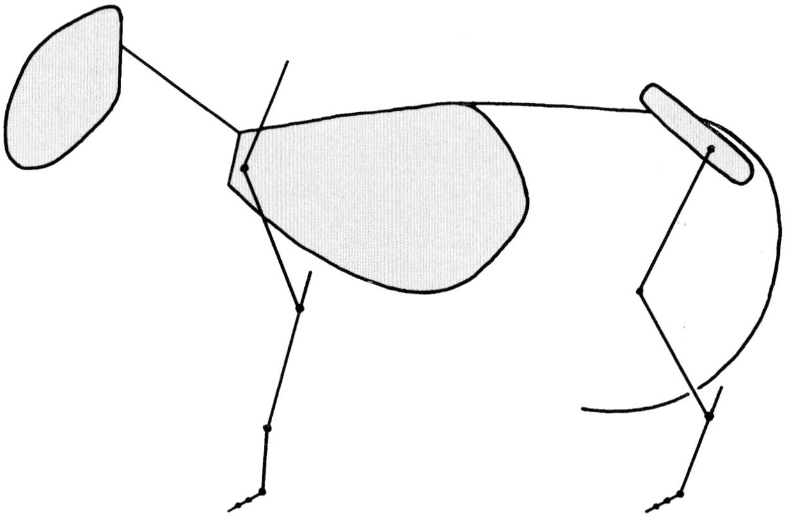

LION

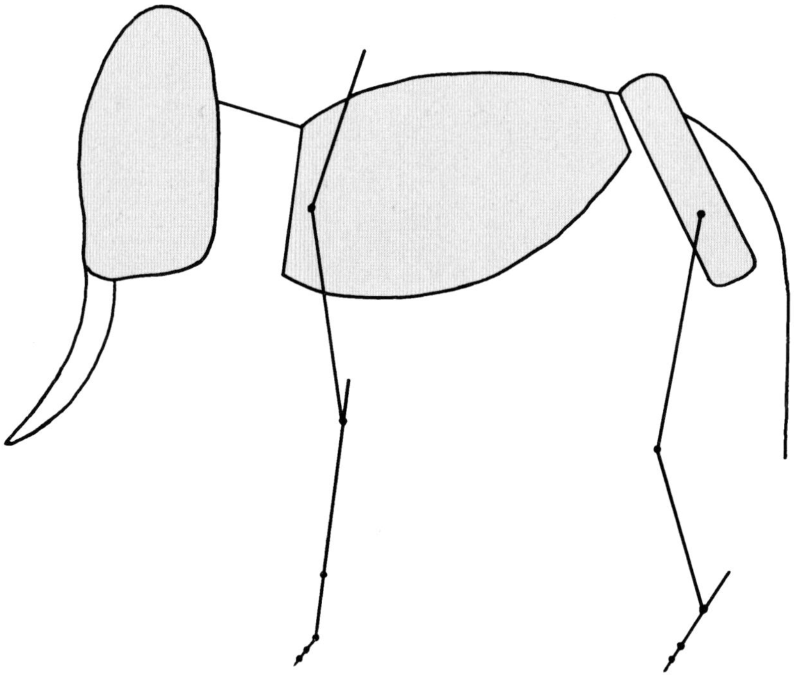

ELEPHANT

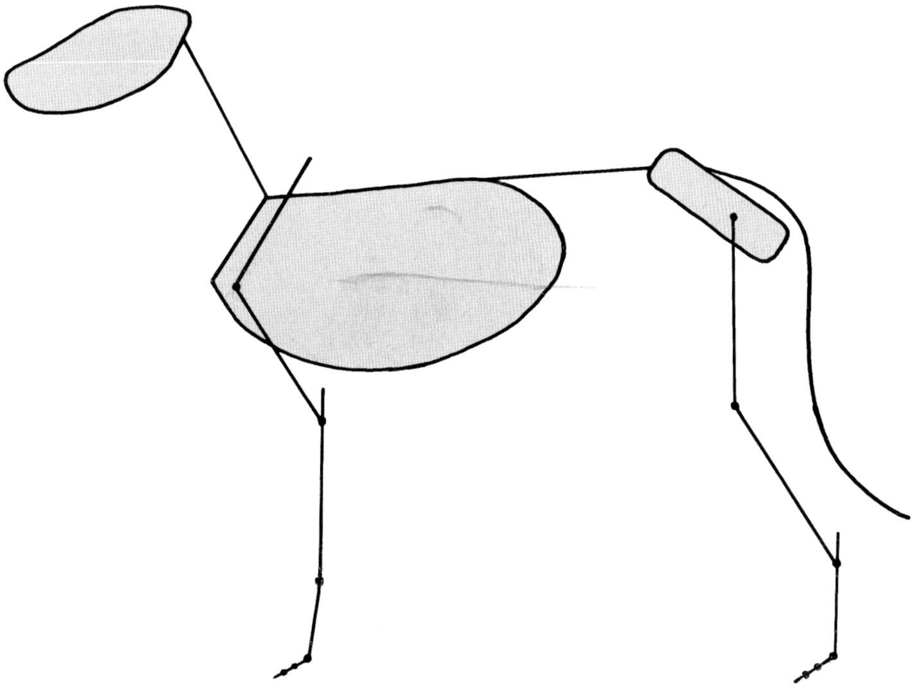

DOG

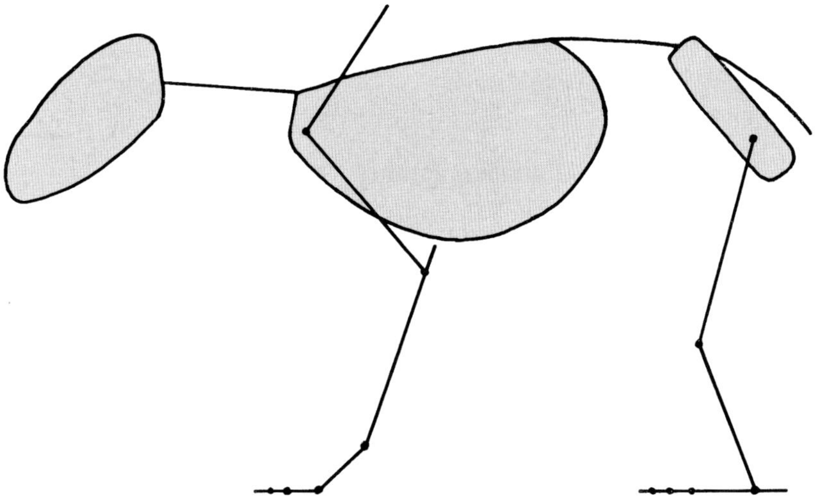

BEAR

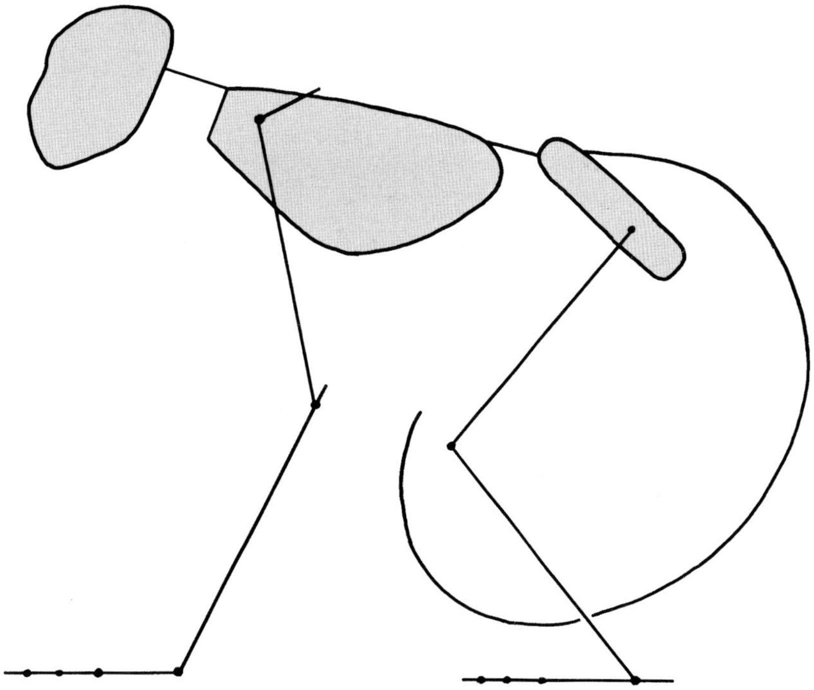

MONKEY

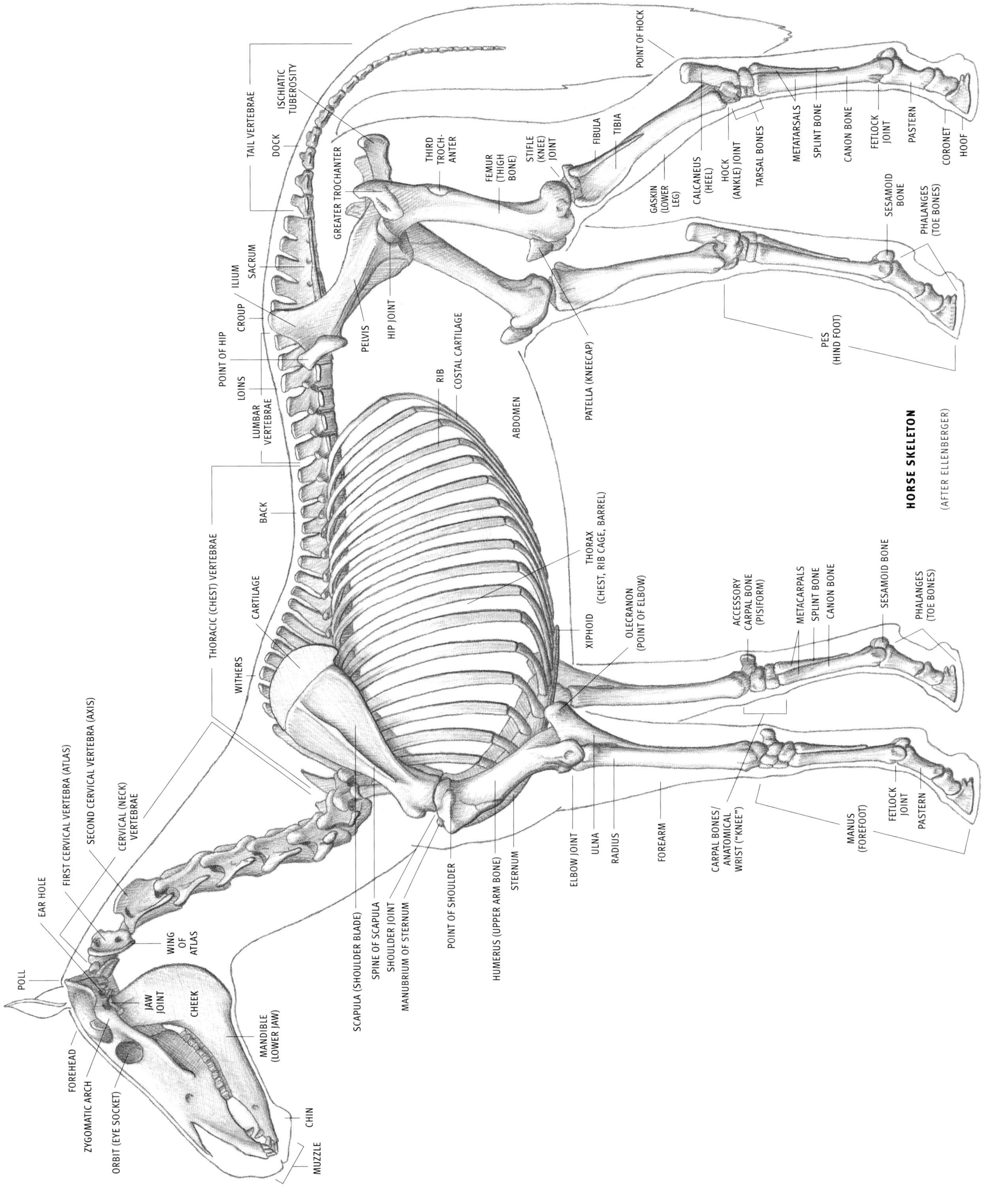

HORSE SKELETON
(AFTER ELLENBERGER)

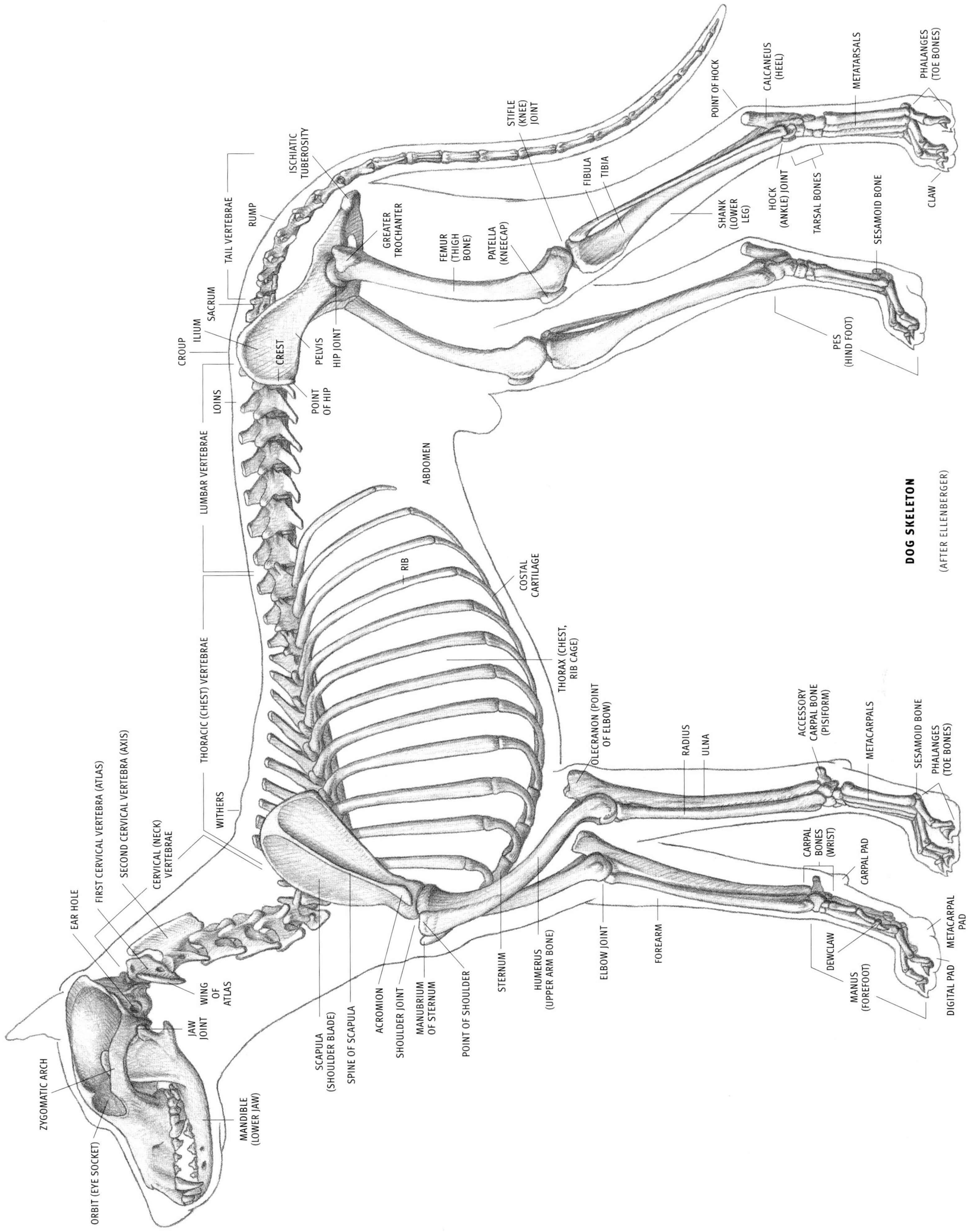

DOG SKELETON

(AFTER ELLENBERGER)

General

The **skeleton** is the internal framework of the body and is made up of bones and cartilage. **Bones** provide *support* (when they are locked in position by the muscles and ligaments) and *protection* (the skull, rib cage, and pelvis protect their contents). Bones also produce *motion*, acting as levers when pulled by the muscles. **Cartilage** is a hard, yet elastic (resilient) tissue, and can be found in the ears, the nose, and at the ends of the ribs, where they directly create surface form.

Bones move against one another, or **articulate** with each other, at **joints**. Their articulating surfaces are covered with **articular cartilage**. Bones are held in their proper relationship to each other at the joints by strong, fibrous, nonelastic bands called **ligaments**, which keep them in contact yet permit normal motion. A ligament connects bone to bone (a tendon connects muscle to bone).

Relating to bone, a **spine** is a projecting point or a raised ridge (the entire vertebral column is also called the spine); a **process** is a projection of varying shape, a **protuberance** is a bony projection or bump, and a **tuberosity** is an enlargement. A **crest** is a high ridge. A **long bone**, such as the humerus, femur, or tibia, consists of a **shaft** with an expansion at either end. The rounded, regularly shaped expansion is called a **head**. Large prominences at the ends of bones, which articulate with other bones and are covered by a thin layer of articular cartilage, are called **condyles**. Small, nonarticulating prominences found on the condyles are called **epicondyles**.

Bone may directly create surface form (elbow, forehead, medial surface of the tibia, outer point of the hip), strongly influence it (rib cage, sacrum, back of hands and feet), or be concealed deep in muscle (neck vertebrae; most of the humerus, femur, and pelvis). Areas of bone just below the skin are **subcutaneous** and can be felt and often seen at the surface. Prominent subcutaneous points of bone are called **bony landmarks**, and may serve as important proportional measuring points of the body. *Locating the bony landmarks in the living animal is the key to understanding the exact position of the entire skeleton*, most of which is embedded in the soft tissues of the body. In muscular individuals, subcutaneous points and ridges my show as depressions surrounded by bulging muscles. In thin individuals, these same bony areas may appear as raised points and ridges. The proportions of an animal are created by the relative lengths of the bones. Proportions are usually best measured from these bony landmarks.

The skeleton can be visualized as a combination of **volumes** and **axes**. The skull and rib cage are three-dimensional volumes that greatly affect surface form. The bones of the pelvis make a rigid volume, which is for the most part deeply buried in musculature. The limb bones—long and thin—are axes, or lines of direction passing through the form of a fleshed-out limb.

A series of adjacent, somewhat parallel bones, such as the metacarpals of the hand or the individual ribs, can create a **plane.** Large, single bones, such as the braincase of the skull, also create planes. Planes are often very evident on the surface, and can be flat or curved. The shoulder blade is a plane with a raised ridge on its surface. The muscles that lie on the shoulder blade maintain a planar quality, reflecting the flatness of the underlying bone. It is important to note the orientation of a plane (which way it is facing).

When studying the live animal, the first, and perhaps most important step is to accurately visualize the skeleton inside the body, for onto this internal scaffolding are attached the numerous convex forms of the musculature.

The skeleton is divided into an axial (longitudinal) skeleton and a limb (appendicular) skeleton. The **axial skeleton** consists of the skull, the rib cage, and the spine (vertebral column). The **limb skeleton** consists of the four limbs. In primates, such as humans, apes, and monkeys, they are called the **arms** and the **legs**. In four-legged animals, the limbs in front are called the **forelimbs**, and include the scapula or shoulder blade, and the clavicle when present. The limbs in back are called the **hind limbs**, and include the pelvis.

Skull

The **skull** is the skeleton of the head, and determines the overall shape of the head in life. It consists of the cranium or braincase in the back, the face in front, and the lower jaw. Major structures overlying the skull and influencing its form are the nostrils, the lips, and the chewing muscles (two on each side—four total). The **cranium**, which houses the brain, is a rounded form. It can be covered to a greater or lesser degree by the encroachment of the chewing muscles of the temple (the temporalis muscles) toward the midline on the top of the head. The muscles are farthest apart in animals with horns and antlers and in most primates (with the cranium exposed), and they touch on the midline in horses, domestic cats, and some breeds of dog. When the muscles are very developed, a raised bony ridge forms on the midline of the cranium, toward the back, which provides additional surface area for attachment of the temporalis muscle. This feature is typically seen in some dog breeds, large cats, and the male gorilla.

The back (or base) of the skull has a transverse bony ridge, the **occipital ridge**, with a protuberance on its midline called the **occipital protuberance**. The ridge can occasionally become prominent and define the separation between the back of the head and the neck, especially in carnivores. The protuberance may also be prominent, forming an important bony landmark. Other subcutaneous areas of the skull that directly create surface form are the bones of the forehead, the top and back of the cranium (when not covered by muscle), the **zygomatic arches** (cheekbones), the bones of the **orbit,** which surround the eye, and the top of the ridge of the snout, descending to the nose. The zygomatic arch, often the widest part of the head, is continuous with the orbit. In carnivores, the zygomatic arch is large and projects outward considerably. The back edge of the orbit in carnivores is missing in the skeleton, but it is formed by a ligament in life.

The **mandible**, or **lower jaw**, hinges at the back end of the skull, just in front of the ear hole. Therefore, when the mouth is opened, the entire bottom half of the head is involved, not just the mouth area. The convergence of the two sides of the lower jaw toward the front (the chin) is the key to understanding the shape of the bottom of the head. Also, note whether the lower edge of the lower jaw is straight or curved (in side view).

The **teeth** vary in number, size, and their absence or presence according to the different animal groups. They are, when all are present (from front to back), the incisors, then sometimes a space, the canines, then sometimes a space, the premolars, and finally the molars. Some of the more dramatic variations on this pattern are the absence of the upper incisors and all the canines in most of the hoofed artiodactyls (bovids and deer), and the extreme development of the upper incisors in the elephant (the tusks), the upper canines in the walrus, the self sharpening incisors in the rodents, and the canines in the warthog.

Horns and antlers are sometimes found in both males and females of the same species, and sometimes only in the males. **Horns** are present in the bovid group of artiodactyls, and consist of a **bony core** (an extension of the skull) covered by a horny **sheath,** similar in material and origin to fingernails. They are permanent and grow throughout life. **Antlers** are present in the cervid, or deer, group of artiodactyls. They are bony structures but are shed every year and new ones are regrown. While they are growing, they are covered with a soft skin called **velvet.** The velvet dies when the antlers are fully grown for that year and is then scraped off by the animal. The pronghorn antelope is notable in that it has a true horn with a bony core and sheath, but the sheath is shed every year (a new sheath grows under the old one before it is shed). Horns and antlers typically arise from the skull either directly above the eye, or more commonly from above and behind the eye. The giraffe has a unique arrangement of its three horns, with a horn above and behind each eye and a single one on the midline in front of them. These horns consist of bone permanently covered with skin and fur. The rhinoceros, related to the horse group and not the artiodactyls, has one or two horns, made up of densely compressed hair with no bony core.

Vertebral column

The **spine**, or **vertebral column**, is made up of numerous individual vertebrae, and extends from the back of the skull to the tip of the tail. It is most flexible at the neck, made up of the **cervical vertebrae**, and somewhat less flexible in the region located between the rib cage and the pelvis, made up of the **lumbar vertebrae**. The **thoracic vertebrae**, located between the cervical and lumbar vertebrae, have the ribs attached to them. There is some movement possible in this region of the spine, but much less than in the cervical and lumbar regions. The **sacrum**, located between the thoracic vertebrae and the tail, is actually several vertebrae fused together. It is rigidly locked in place between the two sides of the pelvis. The tail, when present, is extremely flexible. It is made up of the **coccygeal**, or **caudal vertebrae**. Mammals commonly have seven cervical vertebrae, twelve to eighteen thoracic vertebrae, and five to seven lumbar vertebrae.

At its simplest, a typical **vertebra** can be visualized as a drum-shaped **body** with three projections above. Projecting upward is the **spinous process**, and projecting out to the sides are the **transverse processes.** At the base of these projections is a hole in the bone through which the spinal cord passes. Other bony projections are present which allow a vertebra to articulate with adjoining vertebrae. Fibrous, elastic **intervertebral discs** are located between adjacent vertebrae (except for the joint between the first and second cervical vertebrae).

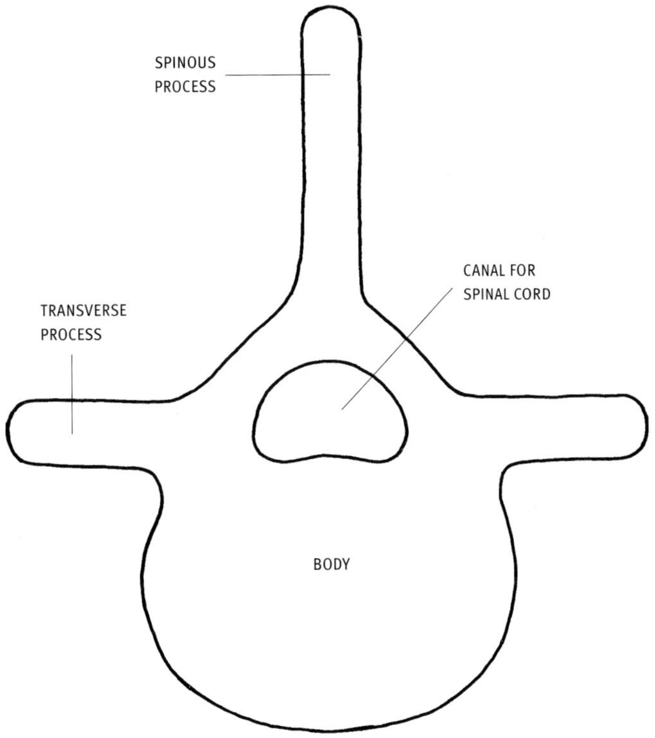

STYLIZED VERTEBRA

FRONT VIEW

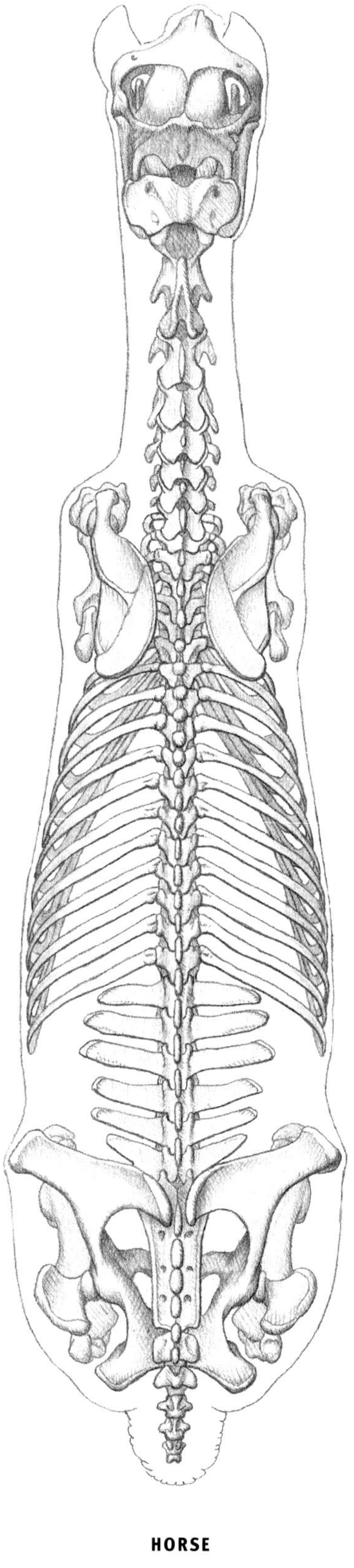

HORSE

TOP VIEW

(AFTER ELLENBERGER)

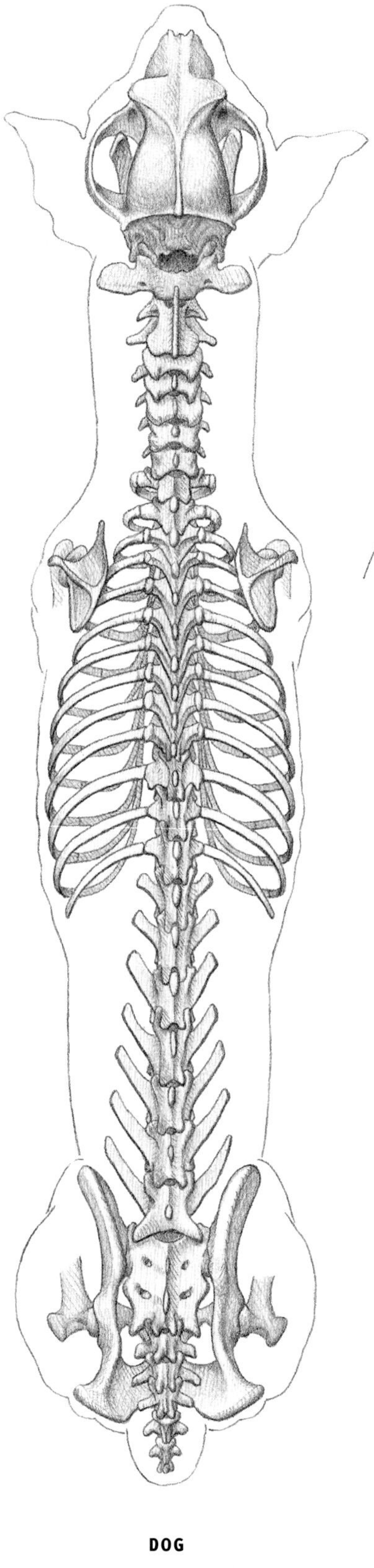

DOG

TOP VIEW

(AFTER ELLENBERGER)

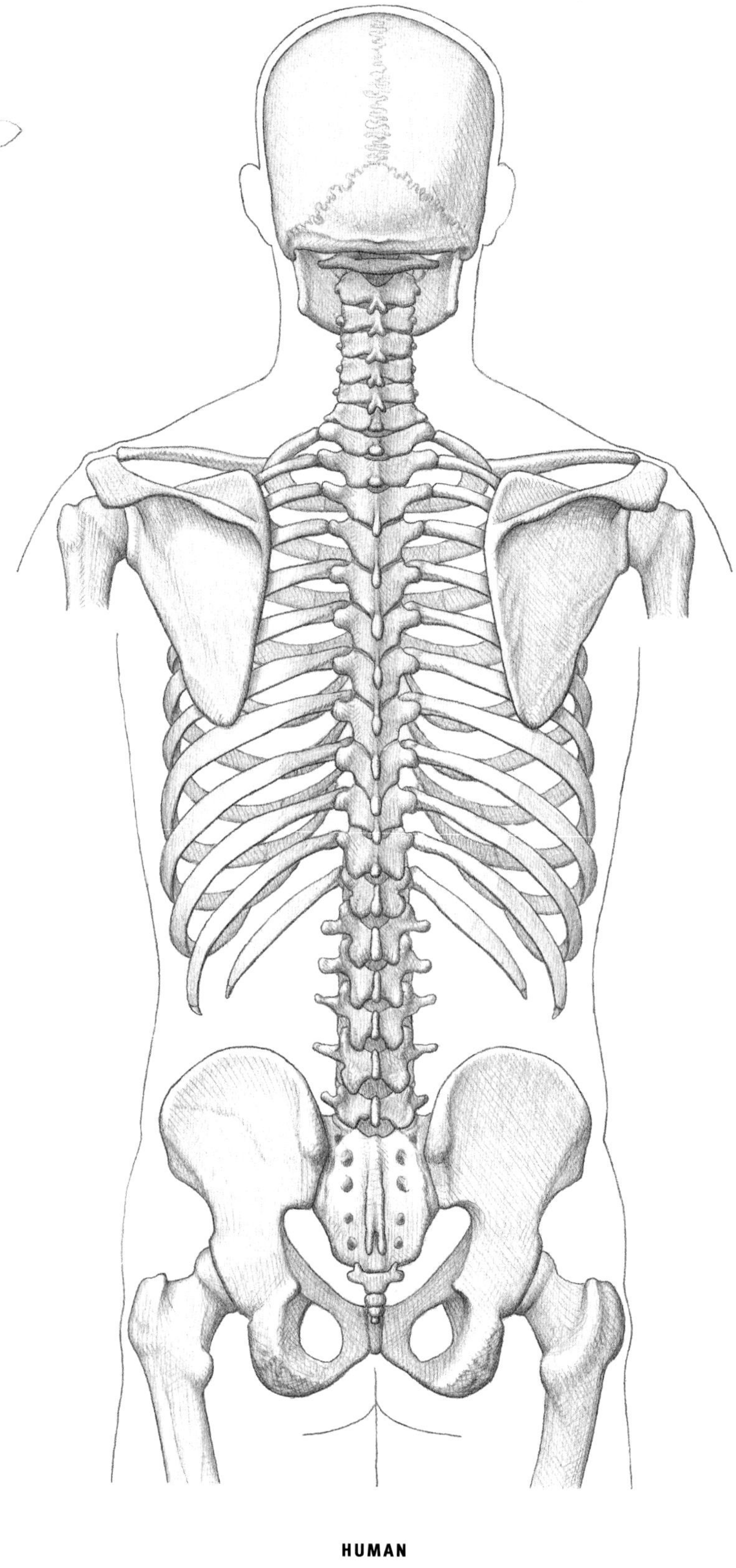

HUMAN

BACK VIEW

The first two **cervical vertebrae** are different from the other vertebrae, and they function in ways that have a substantial effect on the surface. The first vertebra, the **atlas**, is the shortest. It articulates with the back of the skull and allows for *only flexion and extension* of the skull. This permits the head to tip up and down without the use of any other neck vertebrae, which means that the head can be tipped exclusively at the skull/atlas joint with out any change in form taking place in the rest of the neck. The atlas expands into a bony wing on either side, making it almost as wide as the head—its edges can be felt below the surface, and vary in orientation (obliquity) among the different species.

The second cervical vertebra, the **axis**, is the longest of all the vertebrae. It permits *only side-to-side rotation* of the atlas (and therefore the skull) in front of it. This allows the head to rotate side-to-side without the use of the remainder of the neck vertebrae and without changing the form of the rest of the neck. This is most dramatically demonstrated in the giraffe. The axis has a very large spinous process which expands into an upright bony plate that is aligned with the long axis of the body. While not actually sitting below the skin, but rather embedded in muscle, it nevertheless affects surface form on the back of the neck by virtue of its size.

The **thoracic vertebrae**, especially the front ones between the shoulder blades, can have extremely long spinous processes. For most of them, their tips usually lie just below the skin and create the profile of the animal along its back. In the horse, the spinous process of the fourth vertebra, and those behind it, are all subcutaneous; the fifth is usually the longest. The spinous process of the fourth vertebra is where the nuchal ligament of the neck attaches, and is therefore the point at which the outline of the back of the neck meets the outline of the top of the thorax. Where the neck meets the thorax is an important point to take note of, in all animals, when the head and neck are both raised and lowered. In the ox, the neck profile meets the back profile at the first thoracic spinous process; however, when the neck is lowered, the prominent spinous process of the seventh cervical vertebra in front of it becomes visible.

In the horse, the spinous processes in the shoulder region extend beyond the top edge of the shoulder blade (and its cartilage). They are level with the shoulder blade in the dog, and lie below it in the cat. In the ox, deer, and goat, they are generally at the same level; however, in the bison, the extremely developed spinous processes extend well above the top edge of the shoulder blade.

The **lumbar vertebrae** have well-developed, horizontally projecting transverse processes. They project outward across the body more than the other vertebrae, and their tips can be quite conspicuous in the ox. The spinous processes above can occasionally be seen on the midline. In the horse and ox, there is limited motion in the lumbar vertebrae. In the carnivores, however, because there are more vertebrae and they are longer and narrower, this region is very flexible. In the ox, the lumbar vertebrae, as well as the thoracic vertebrae, are oriented in a more or less straight line, which gives the animal a fairly straight profile along its back. In contrast, the lumbar region of the carnivores, along with the posterior thoracic vertebrae, arches upward.

Except for the upwardly projecting spinous processes of the front tail vertebrae of the ox, which can be seen on the surface, the individual **tail vertebrae** of the various animals are buried in muscle and not noticed. Tails are absent in apes and humans, but present in monkeys. Tails can be prehensile (grasping) and hold the entire weight of a moving individual.

Rib cage

The **rib cage**, which forms the chest wall, is an important volume. Shaped somewhat like a cone, it is created by the individual ribs connecting to the spine above and to the sternum below. Its gets smaller toward the front and, in four legged animals, is flattened side-to-side. The back end is wide and open. The rib cage is wider at the top (near the spine) and narrower below (at the sternum).

The individual **ribs** lie approximately parallel to each other and are directed downward and slightly backward. The lower end of each rib attaches to a flexible **costal cartilage.** This junction may occasionally be seen on the surface in carnivores. The ribs and their cartilages at the front portion of the rib cage attach directly to the sternum, and are called the **true ribs**. The costal cartilages of the ribs in the rear portion of the rib cage angle forward to overlap the costal cartilages in front of them. Because they don't connect directly to the sternum, these ribs are called the **false ribs**. The cartilages of the last ribs do not attach to the cartilages of the ribs in front of them, and are referred to as the **floating ribs**. Carnivore ribs are slender; those of the ox are wide.

The **sternum** is an elongated, segmented bone located on the midline of the bottom of the thorax (front of the chest). The costal cartilages of the true ribs articulate directly with it. The sternum in dogs and cats is roughly cylindrical. In the horse, it is keel-like and flattened side-to-side in its front two-thirds. The midline of the sternum, whether flat or raised into a ridge, may be subcutaneous between the pectoralis chest muscles originating on either side of the midline. The projection at the rear end of the sternum, the **xiphoid process**, does not affect surface form.

The front end (or top) of the sternum is called the **manubrium**. It may be bony or predominantly cartilaginous (called the **cariniform cartilage**). The first pair of ribs articulates with it. In four legged animals, it is either pointed or flattened side to side, and may project forward beyond the articulation with the first ribs. In primates, the manubrium articulates with well developed clavicles; it, as well as the rest of the sternum, is wide, flat, and faces forward. Some of the neck muscles descending from the head attach to the front (or top) of the manubrium (or its cartilage). This junction becomes the point at which the front profile of the neck meets the profile of the chest. Called the **point of the chest**, it remains fixed in space regardless of the position of the head and neck, as long as the trunk remains stationary. This point is approximately level with the point of the shoulder in horses. The depression found above the manubrium and between the descending muscles on either side of the midline at the base of the neck is called the **pit of the neck.**

DOG
LEFT REAR LIMB
OUTSIDE VIEW
◂ FRONT

PATELLA MOVES BACK RELATIVE TO FRONT EDGE OF LOWER LEG WHEN KNEE IS FLEXED; LENGTH OF PATELLAR LIGAMENT REMAINS THE SAME.

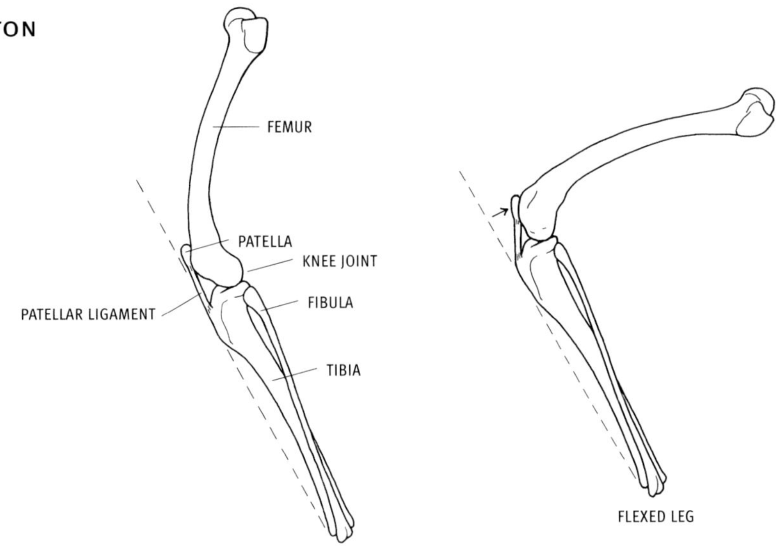

(FROM SPECIMENS)

Lower leg

The tibia and the fibula make up the bones of the lower leg. The **tibia** is a large bone that supports the weight of the body. Its lower end forms the entire ankle bone in the horse and ox, but only the inner ankle bone in dogs, cats, pigs, and primates, where the fibula reaches the ankle on the outside. The inner surface of the entire tibia is subcutaneous. The bony prominence at its upper end, to which the patellar ligament is attached, is called the **tibial tuberosity**. The front edge of the upper portion of the tibia rises into a subcutaneous ridge, called the **tibial crest**, or **shin**.

Two bumps may be seen on the surface on the front of the knee, especially when the knee is flexed. They are always the same distance apart, are formed by the patella above and the tibial tuberosity below, and are connected by the patellar ligament. The tibial tuberosity is continued downward into the tibial crest.

The full **fibula** is a slender bone that lies on the outside of the tibia. Its expanded upper end, the **head**, is an important bony landmark and does not articulate with the femur at the knee joint. Its lower end reaches all the way down to the ankle joint and forms the expanded outer ankle bone in dogs, cats, pigs, and primates. In the horse, the fibula doesn't reach the ankle but rather tapers to a point halfway down the lower leg. In the ox, only the upper and lower ends of the fibula are present. At the upper end, the head and a very short length of the shaft are fused to the outside of the tibia. The small lower end is fused to the underside of the outer portion of the tibia. These two fibular extremities are connected by a fibrous cord, which is a remnant of the missing shaft of the fibula.

Hind foot

The **foot** (pes, hind foot, hind paw) skeleton is made up of the tarsals, the metatarsals, and the digits, or toes. The **tarsus** contains from five to seven bones. The most prominent tarsal bone is the **calcaneus**, or **heel bone**, which projects backward and upward, beyond the ankle joint, to receive the Achilles tendon of the gastrocnemius and soleus muscles. Primates and bears stand and walk with their heels on the ground; this is called **plantigrade locomotion**. Most four-legged animals stand and walk with only the tips of their toes on the ground and their heels raised quite high up off the ground, never touching the heel to the ground while walking; this is called **digitigrade locomotion**.

ALL LEFT REAR LIMB
OUTSIDE VIEW
◂ FRONT

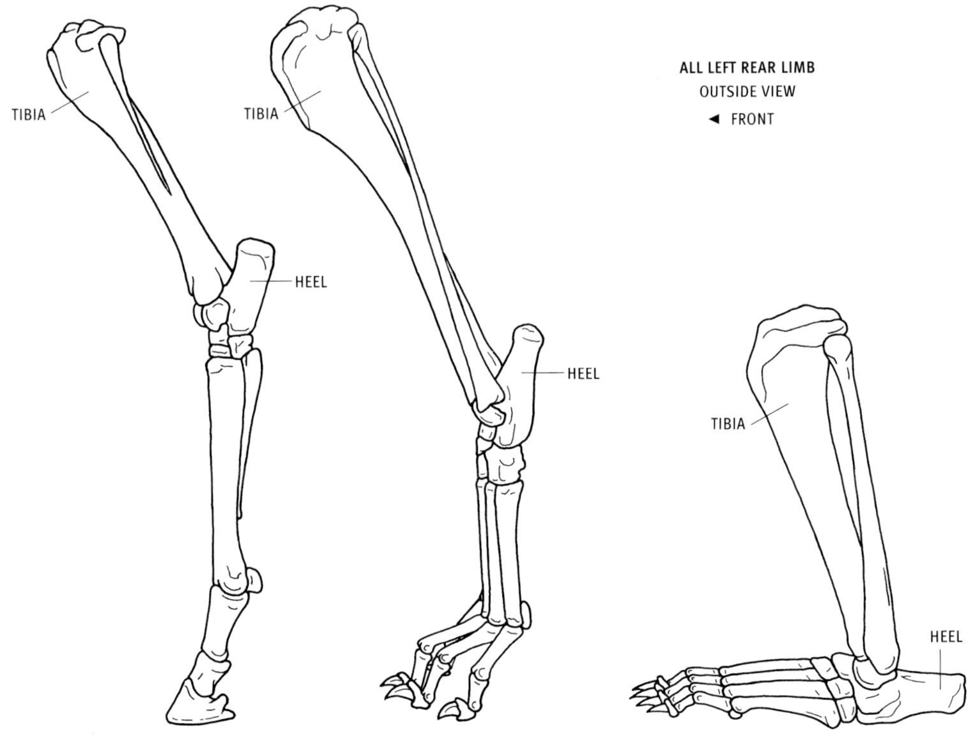

HORSE WALKS ON TIPTOE — **DOG** WALKS ON TOES — **BEAR** WALKS ON SOLE OF FOOT

(FROM SPECIMENS)

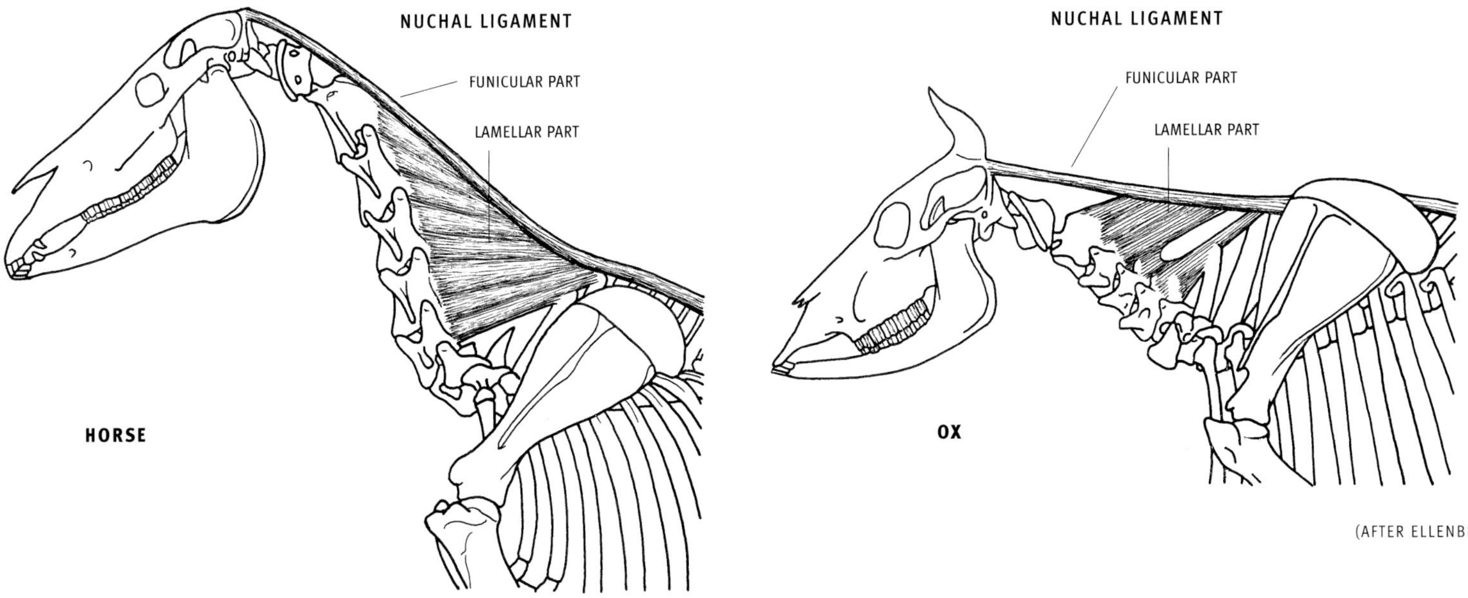

(AFTER ELLENBERGER)

The **metatarsals** and **digits** of the hind limb are similar to those in the forelimb, with some notable differences. In the horse, the single metatarsal of the hind limb is longer that the metacarpal of the forelimb. Dogs may have a very rudimentary first metatarsal; occasionally, especially in the larger breeds, a couple of attached small phalanges form a much reduced digit, complete with a claw, called the **dewclaw**. Cats often have a tiny, rudimentary first metatarsal only, or may have a fully developed dewclaw. Because these first digit bones are usually either absent or quite small and insignificant, carnivores are typically seen to have five digits in front (with a reduced first digit) and four in the back.

Primates have two phalanges in the big toe, and the usual three in the other four digits. The big toe is the thickest toe, and is opposable (it can touch the other four toes) in monkeys and apes, but not in humans.

Ligaments

The thick, strong, elastic, **nuchal ligament** is made up of the cordlike funicular part and the sheetlike lamellar part. The **funicular part** consists of a double cable (lying side-by-side) that connects the back of the skull to the top of the rib cage. The **lamellar part** lies deep in the neck. The elasticity of the nuchal ligament assists in lifting and then supporting the weight of the head. Muscles pull the head down; the nuchal ligament, along with muscles, helps raise it.

In the horse, the rear end of the nuchal ligament attaches to the tip of the spinous process of the fourth thoracic vertebra, and in the ox, to the first thoracic vertebra. This makes the neck of the horse appear relatively longer and its trunk shorter, whereas in the ox the neck appears shorter and the trunk longer. In the horse, the nuchal ligament can be seen on the surface. An elongated fat pad and the mane run along its upper surface. Covered by muscle and not directly visible in the ox, the presence of the nuchal ligament can be detected by the taut upper profile of the neck, between the head and the shoulder. In carnivores, the nuchal ligament is thin and has no effect on the surface. It can be seen and felt on the top of the back of the neck in humans when the head is tipped down.

The **sacrotuberal ligament** is a sheet-like ligament in the horse and ox, and cordlike in the dog and feline. It connects the sacrum and the first one or two tail vertebrae to the ischiatic tuberosity of the pelvis. The rear part of its posterior edge can occasionally be seen in the ox and the dog, passing downward and backward toward the ischiatic tuberosity.

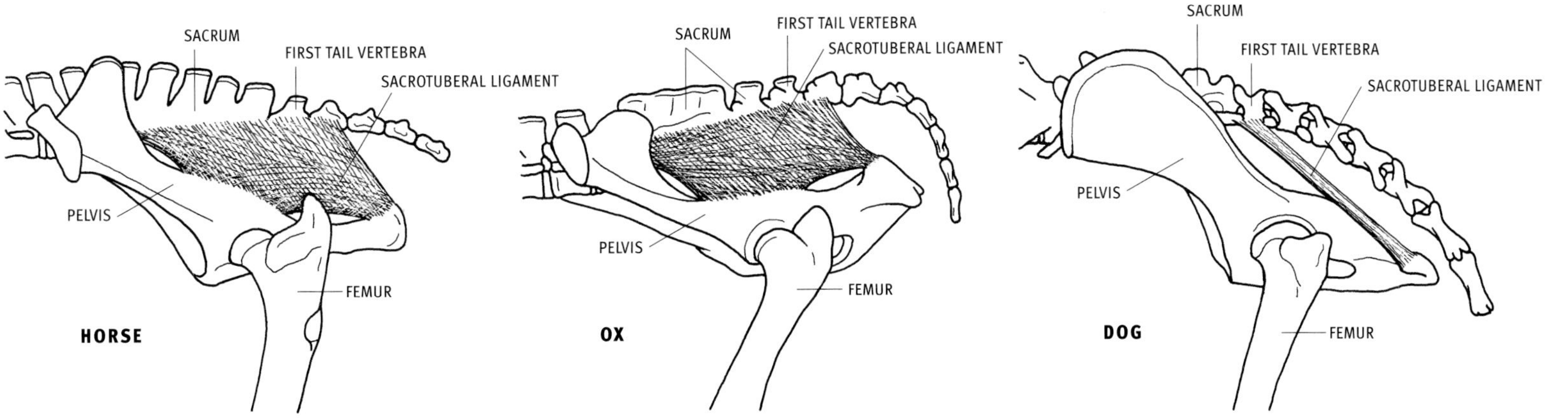

SACROTUBERAL LIGAMENT
PELVIS
LEFT SIDE
◂ FRONT

(AFTER NICKEL)

Joints and Motion

A **joint** is the place where two bones **articulate**, or touch, and usually move against one another. The articular surfaces are usually covered with lubricated cartilage. **Motion** takes place at joints. The motion may be slight, for instance, at the joint where a rib articulates with its vertebra or among the small wrist bones, or the motion may be extensive, such as at the hip joint, where the thigh bone can be flexed forward, extended backward, abducted outward, adducted inward, and rotated. Some joints have virtually no motion, such as where the pelvis articulates with the sacrum, or between the various bones of the skull. Bones are held together at joints by **ligaments**. They permit only the desired movement to take place while restricting undesired movement. Muscles and their tendons pull on the bones and create movement.

Flexion takes place when two bones are brought closer together, as when bending the elbow joint so the radius comes closer to the humerus (decreasing the angle between the two bones). **Extension** takes place when two bones are moved further apart, as when straightening the elbow so that the radius moves away from the humerus (increasing the angle between the two bones). **Abduction** involves moving a bone away from the centerline of the body, whereas **adduction** brings the bone toward it.

Rotation takes place when a bone is rotated around its long axis. Rotation occurs in the radius when the forearm is **pronated** and **supinated**—the upper end of the radius rotates in place on the outside of the elbow while its lower end glides around the lower end of the ulna. This motion takes place only in animals with a complete ulna and with a radius that is capable of rotation around the ulna, such as felines and primates. Rotation also takes place at the joint between the first and second neck vertebrae (the atlas and axis), permitting the head to rotate side-to-side without participation of the other neck vertebrae.

In four-legged animals, motion in the limbs is primarily flexion and extension, for the purpose of locomotion. Abduction, adduction, rotation, and gliding take place to a lesser degree.

The illustrations show the most important, most conspicuous movements of the skeleton. The degree of motion illustrated is based on photographs of animals in action. The left side of the body is illustrated. In most cases the horse is used, and these movements are similar in the various species. Other animals are illustrated where appropriate. *Each limb illustration shows only one joint moving, for the sake of demonstrating that particular joint. However, in some species, some joints always move in conjunction with others, which will account for the skeleton appearing unnatural (impossible) in some of the illustrations.* For example, in the horse, the ankle joint must flex when the knee joint is flexed, and conversely, the two joints extend simultaneously.

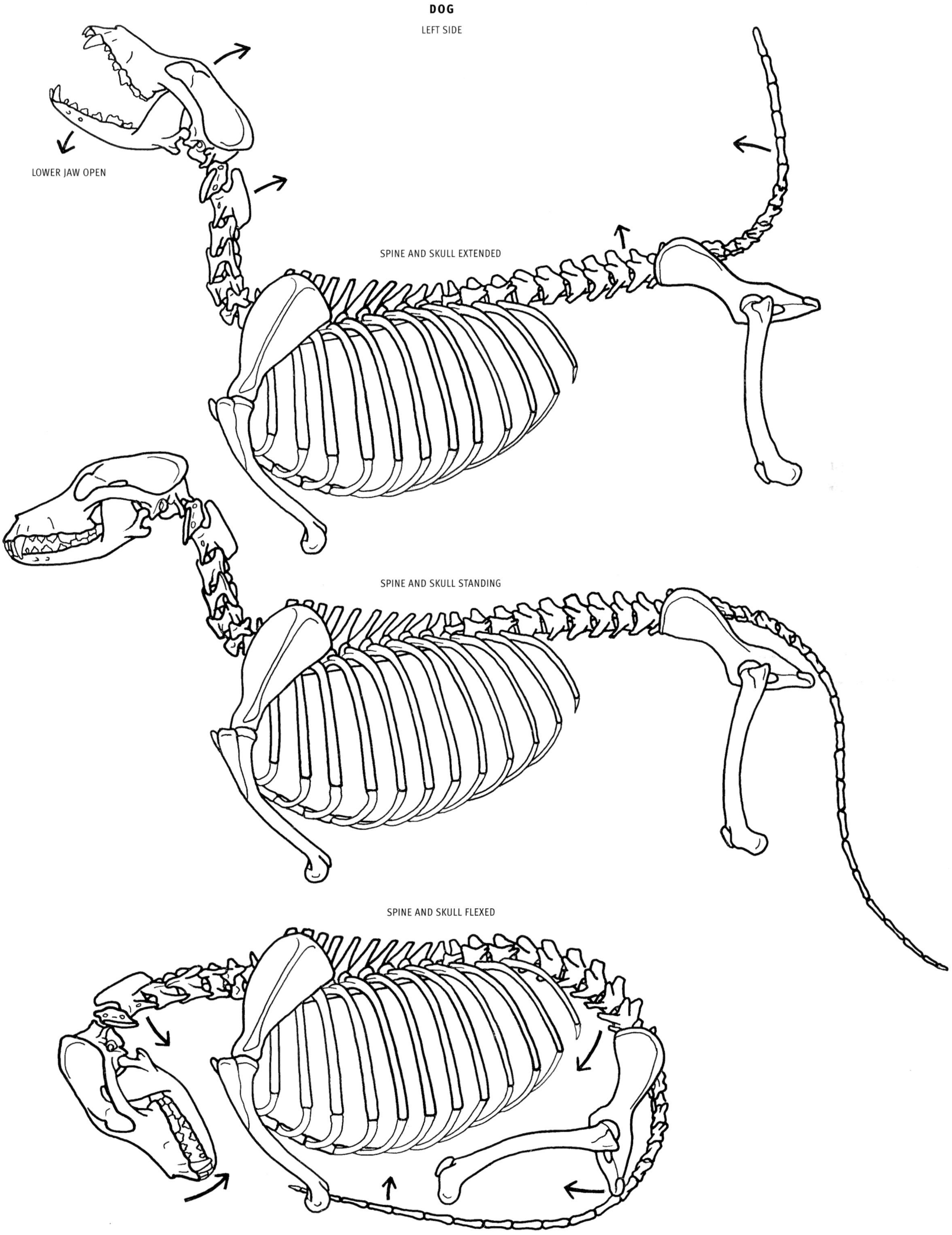
DOG
LEFT SIDE
LOWER JAW OPEN
SPINE AND SKULL EXTENDED
SPINE AND SKULL STANDING
SPINE AND SKULL FLEXED

WRIST JOINT

HORSE

LEFT FRONT LIMB
OUTSIDE VIEW
◄ FRONT

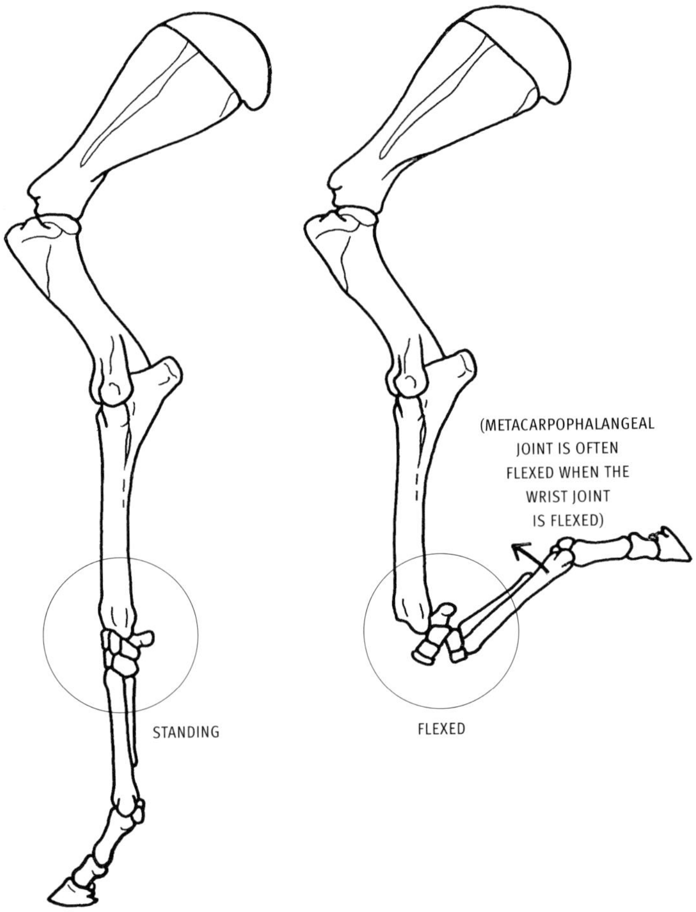

TOE JOINTS

HORSE

LEFT FRONT LIMB
OUTSIDE VIEW
◄ FRONT

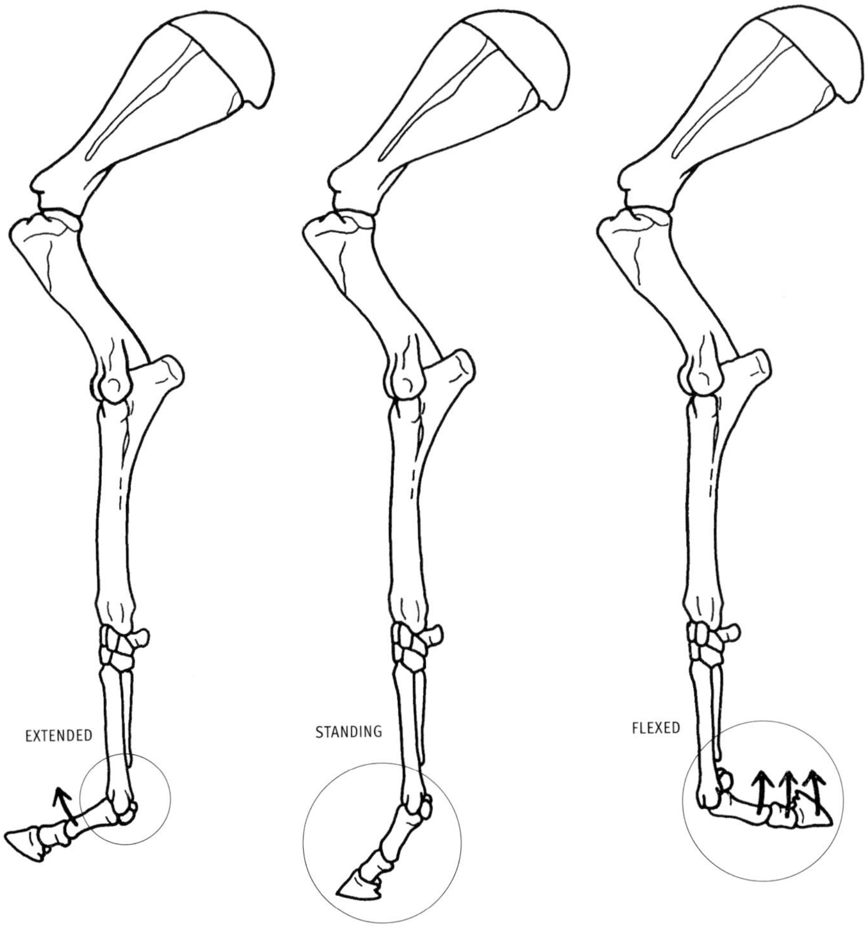

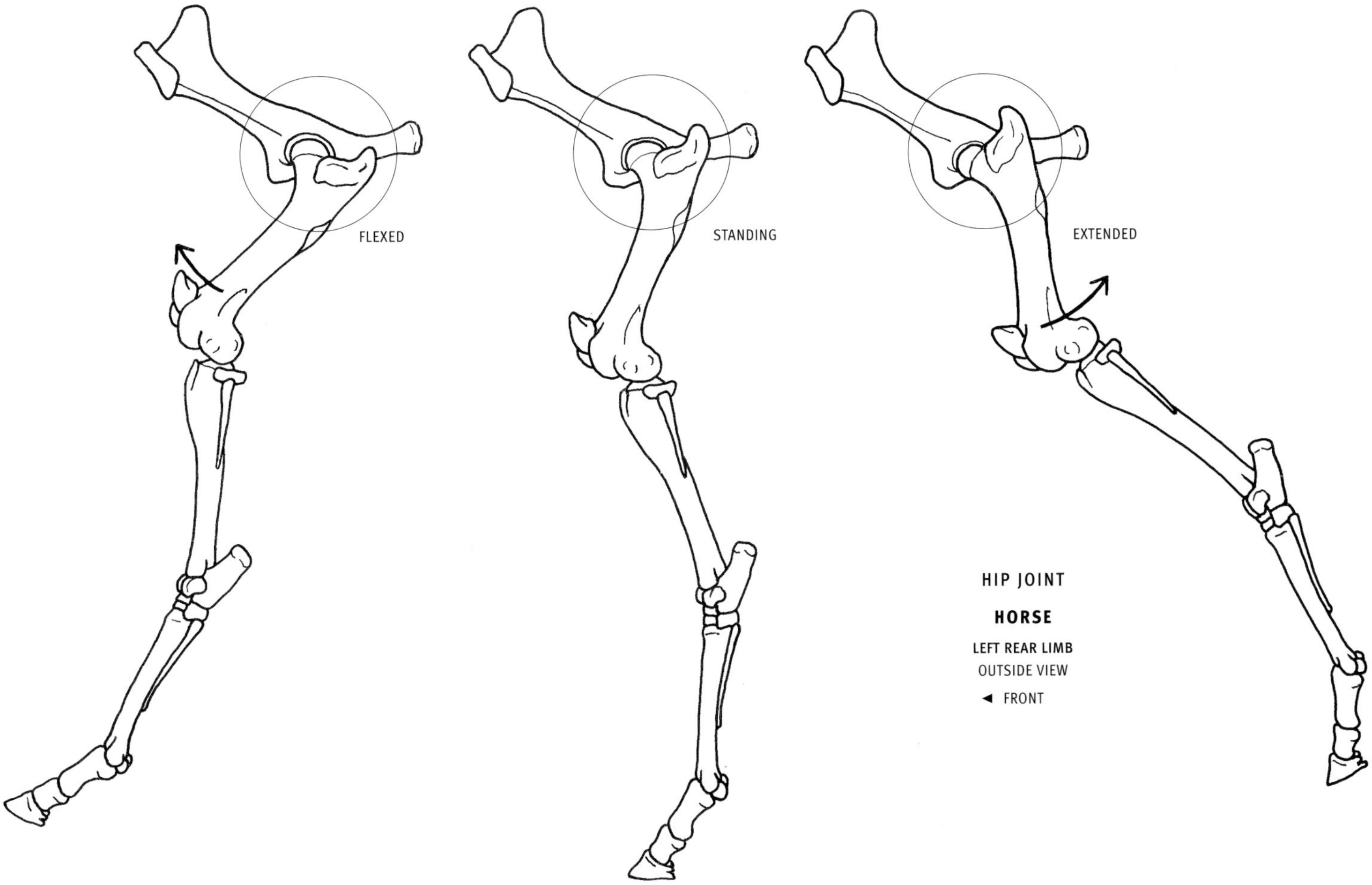

HIP JOINT

HORSE

LEFT REAR LIMB
OUTSIDE VIEW
◄ FRONT

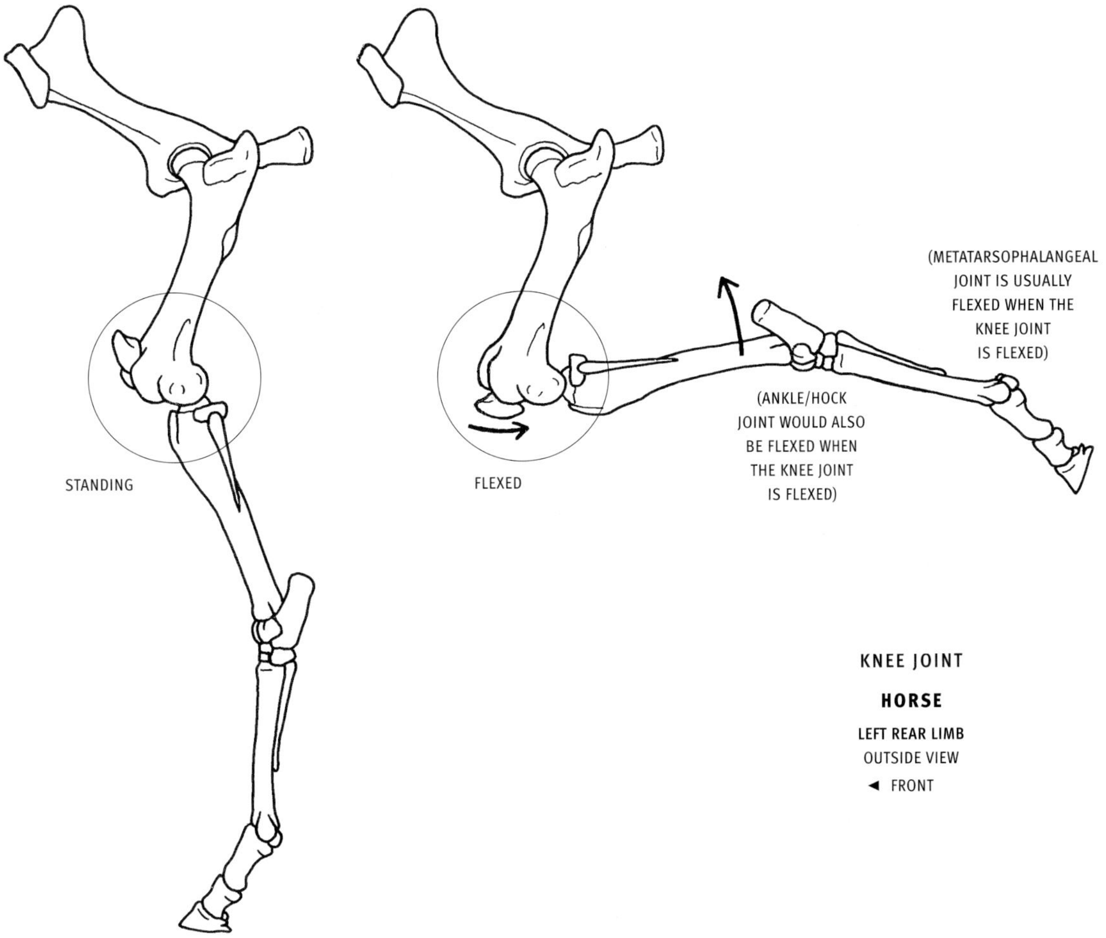

KNEE JOINT

HORSE

LEFT REAR LIMB
OUTSIDE VIEW
◄ FRONT

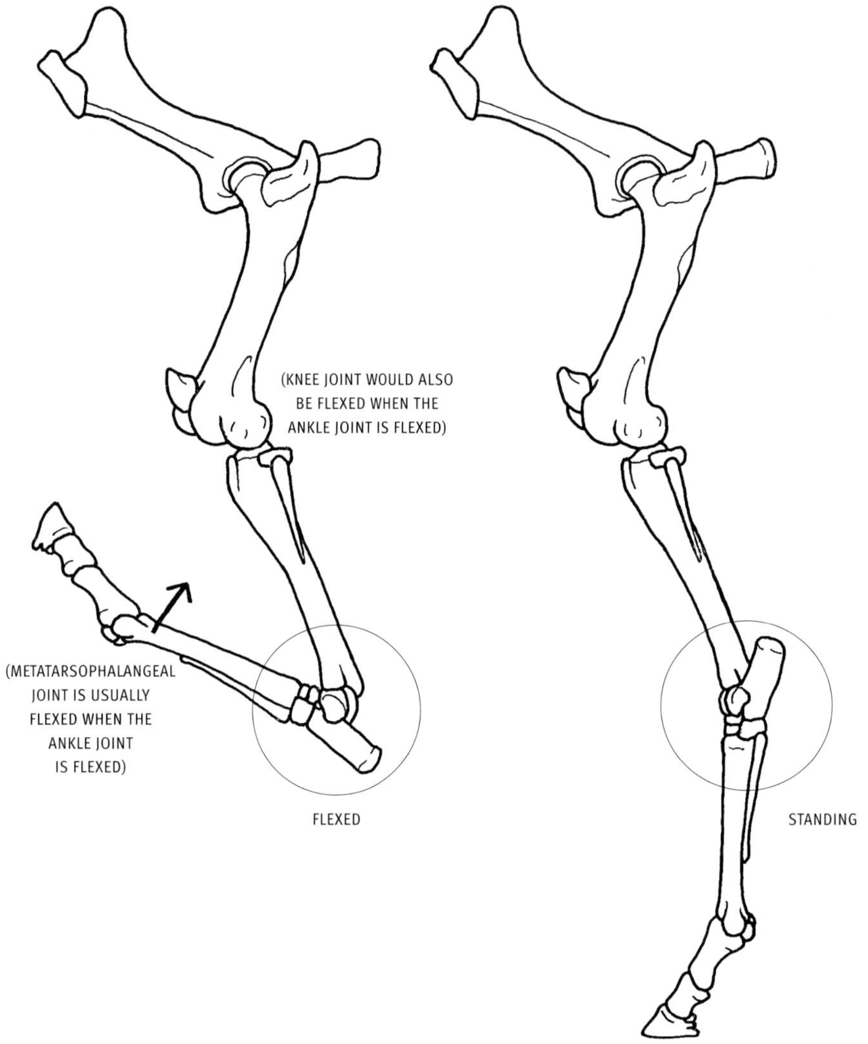

ANKLE (HOCK) JOINT

HORSE

LEFT REAR LIMB
OUTSIDE VIEW
◂ FRONT

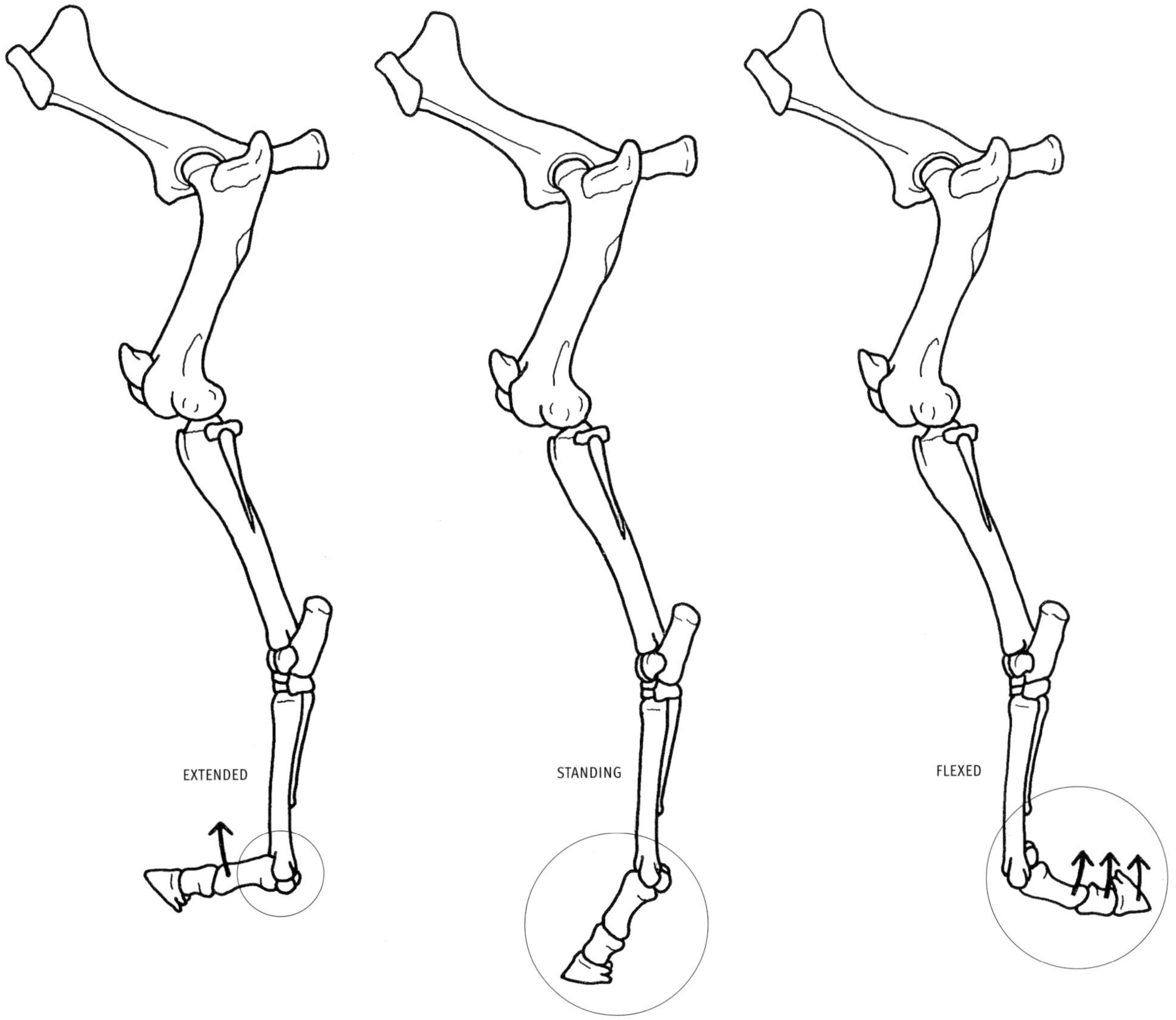

TOE JOINTS

HORSE

LEFT REAR LIMB
OUTSIDE VIEW
◂ FRONT

The **skeletal muscles** of the body are the organs of voluntary motion, and by their contraction they produce movement, stabilize body segments, or lock the joints as required.

These muscles attach to the skeleton and create most of the surface form of an animal. The two most common types of muscles are the **volumetric muscles**, with full volumes, like the triceps, calf muscles, or long narrow forearm muscles, and the **sheet muscles**, like the thin latissimus dorsi or the trapezius. The volumetric muscles create most of the body's forms. The sheet muscles cover the volumetric muscles and bone, whose forms may be either seen underneath or concealed. Sheet muscles can also produce form directly, especially at their edges where they appear in relief. A **muscle belly** is the total fleshy mass of a single muscle. It may consist of one or more **heads**, which are distinct muscle forms that usually begin separately yet have a single insertion after they fuse together.

Muscle fibers attach either directly to the skeleton or cartilage, or by means of a **tendon**, which may be cable-like or sheet-like. Muscles also attach to the surface of other muscles. **Fascia** is a connective tissue which, among other things, forms dense, fibrous, sheets that surround the individual muscles, the limbs, and the body as a whole, forming sheaths around them. Fascia holds the muscles in position, and yet allows adjacent muscles to glide past one another as they contract. Fascial surfaces also provide attachment areas for muscles.

When a muscle contracts and shortens, its origin and insertion get closer together and the belly becomes thick and full. When stretched, it becomes thin and elongate. One can think of the muscles of the body as a cluster of balloons attached to a rigid skeleton, all covered with a thin skin. Regardless of whether they are volumetric and bulging, or sheet-like and flattened, they all produce *convex forms*. This yields a complex, undulating surface created by a series of adjacent, yet distinct, anatomical forms.

Not all surface forms conform to the delineations of the muscles as described in an anatomy book. When a muscle pulls on its tendon or on a wide or narrow fascial sheet that lies on top of other muscles, the tension across the surface can create new forms by separating the underlying muscle belly into two or more forms. For example, the tensor fasciae latae muscle of the leg will pull on a narrow band of fascia on the outer surface of the thigh and compress the underlying vastus lateralis muscle, creating a vertical furrow. Also, a single muscle belly can at times separate into several basically parallel bundles as it contracts.

It is important to understand the shape and location of each muscle and muscle group in relationship to the skeleton, as well as how muscles change when they are contracted. This understanding is the basis of artistic anatomy.

Muscle groups

Muscles can be grouped into functional assemblages, which are often also visually distinct. Throughout the regions of the body there are **flexor groups,** which *bend* the joints, and **extensor groups**, which *straighten* them. Such muscle masses usually lie on opposite sides of a bone. For example, the thigh muscles on the front of the femur together form the extensor group of the knee joint, whereas the hamstring muscles behind the femur form the flexor group of the same joint (the hamstring group also functions as a hip extensor). There are also muscle groups that **abduct**, or pull a limb *away* from the body, or **adduct**, pulling the limb *toward* the centerline of the body. Functionally opposing muscles, whether single or in groups, are called **antagonists**. When a body is active, one muscle group will usually be contracting and become defined on the surface, while the antagonist tends to be relaxed and less defined, or even sag.

Some muscles (and muscle groups) cross only one joint and perform a single action (brachialis). Other muscles cross two or more joints, and can, for example, flex one joint and extend the other (biceps brachii).

The next section, on individual muscles, shows each of the muscles that create or influence surface form. For each of these muscles, an illustration shows where it begins on the skeleton (usually at the less mobile bone), called the **origin**, and where it ends (usually at the more mobile bone), termed the **insertion**. The positions of these **attachments** are quite consistent across the various species. In general, the horse is illustrated, and it is usually very similar to the ox (with the major exception of the toes and the overall proportions). When the ox or the dog differ substantially, they too are illustrated. The feline (cat, lion) is very similar to the dog. Noteworthy differences and variations are shown or described.

The origin, insertion, action, and structure are listed for each muscle. Important differences in the other species are listed, but the common features are not repeated.

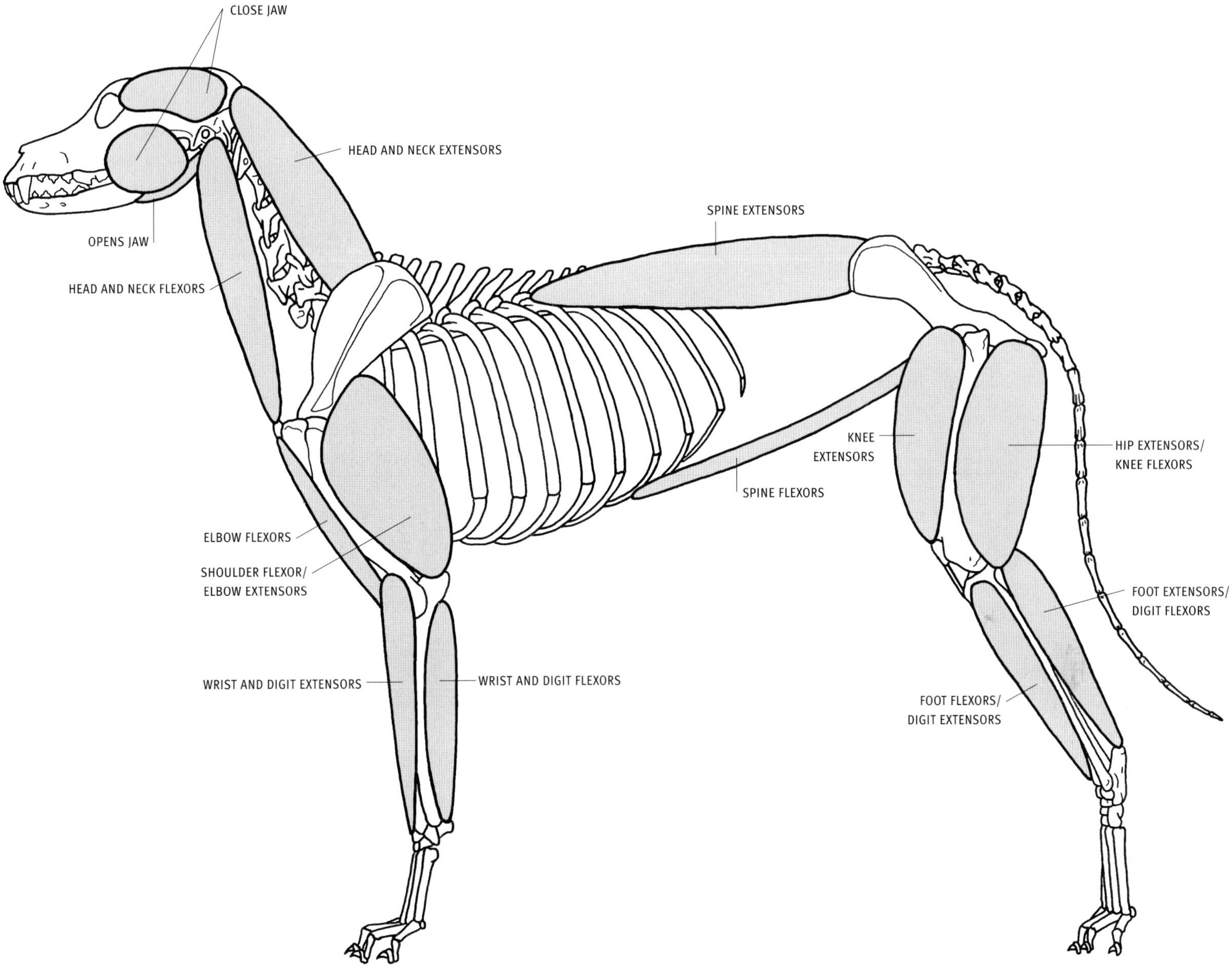

DOG

MAJOR ANTAGONISTIC MUSCLE GROUPS

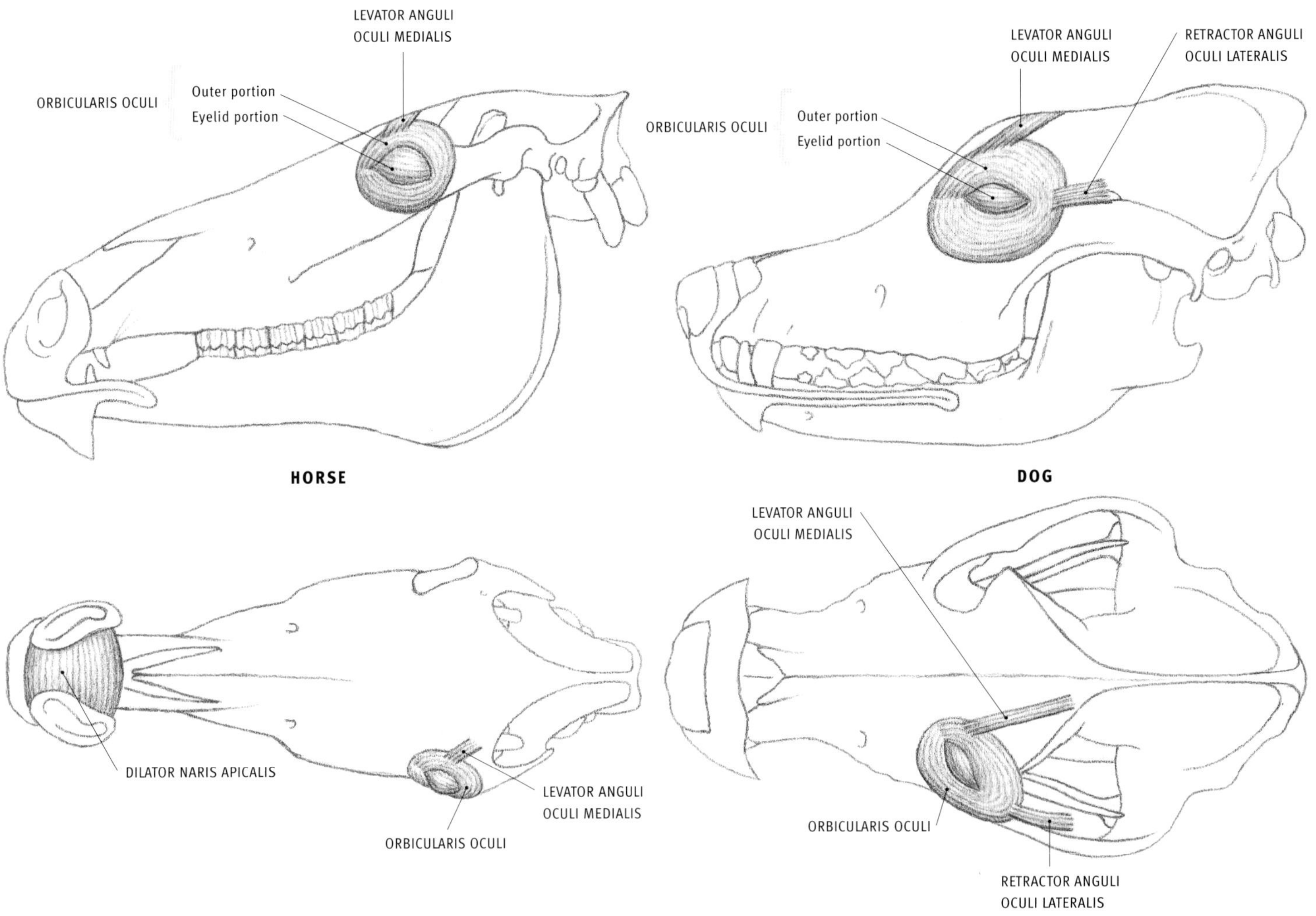

Orbicularis oculi

• Attachment: A short ligament at the inner corner of the eye, whose inner end attaches to the skull.
• Action: Eyelid portion: closes eyelids (blinking), primarily by depressing the upper eyelid. Outer portion: tightens and compresses the skin surrounding the eye, protecting the eyeball.
• Structure: The orbicularis oculi is a flat, elliptical muscle consisting of two portions. The eyelid portion lies in the upper and lower eyelids, and the outer portion surrounds the eye and lies on the skull. The eyelid portion in the upper lid is larger than that in the lower lid. The muscle begins and ends from a ligament at the inner corner of the eye, passing uninterrupted around the outer corner of the eye. This ligament in turn attaches to the skull, which is the only bony attachment of the muscle.

Levator anguli oculi medialis (Corrugator supercilii)

• Origin: Upper surface of the skull, above the eye (horse), or to the rear of the eye (dog).
• Insertion: The top of the eye region, merging into the orbicularis oculi.
• Action: Pulls the skin above the eye (the "eyebrow" region) upward, rearward, and slightly inward, creating wrinkles in the skin.
• Structure: This narrow muscle is an important muscle of "facial expression" as the effects of its contraction are conspicuous on the surface. This muscle in the feline is much wider—it spans the forehead from eye to eye; a small bundle of fibers separate and insert above the inner corner of the eye, similar to the dog. There is no levator anguli oculi medialis in the ox; fibers of the frontalis muscle insert along the entire upper edge of the orbicularis oculi and perform a similar function by raising the skin above the eye.

Retractor anguli oculi lateralis

• Origin: Side of the head to the rear of the eye.
• Insertion: Outer (rear) corner of the eye region.
• Action: Pulls the region of the outer corner of the eye rearward.
• Structure: The retractor anguli oculi lateralis is a short muscle. It is not found in the horse or the ox.

Dilator naris apicalis (Transversus nasi)

• Attachment: Horse: Upper, inner, and lower edges of both nostrils (from cartilage). Ox: Origin: Front end of the forwardmost (incisive) bone of the upper jaw, and from a tendinous band on the midline; Insertion: Inner edge of the nostril.
• Action: Dilates the nostrils.
• Structure: In the horse, the dilator naris apicalis is a single, rectangular muscle that spans the front of the snout from nostril to nostril. In the ox, it consists of a muscle on each side of the body that fuses on the midline. It is not found in the dog or the feline.

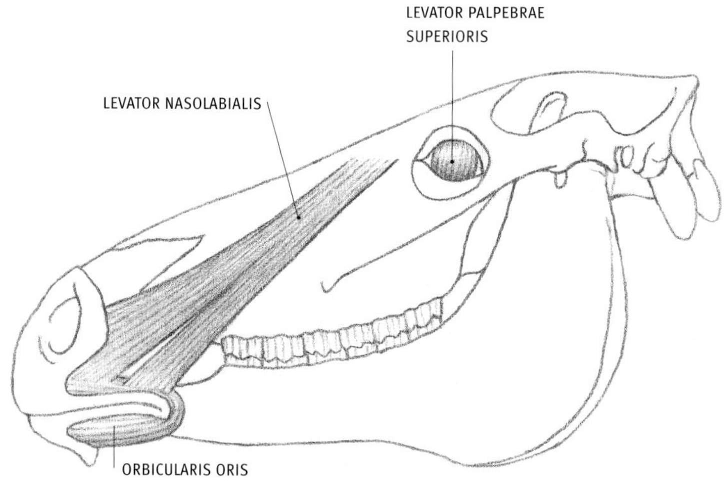

HORSE

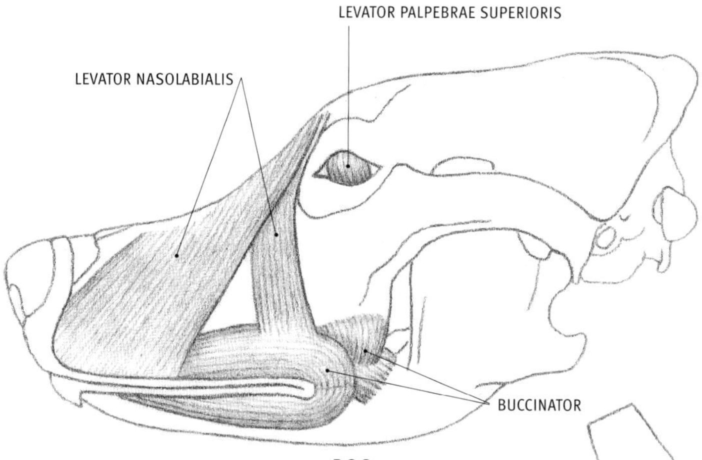

DOG

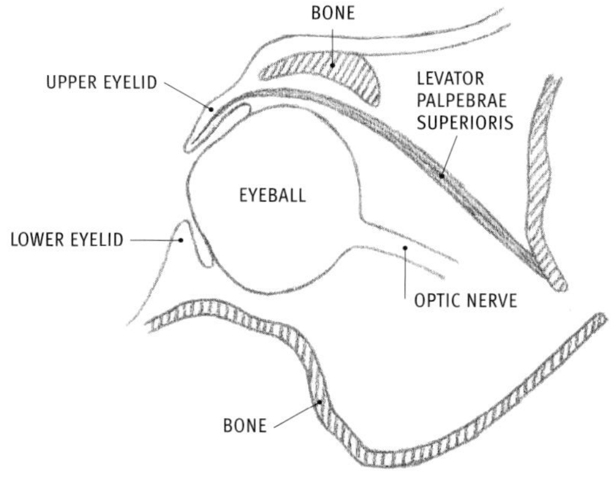

VERTICAL SECTION THROUGH EYE (HORSE)

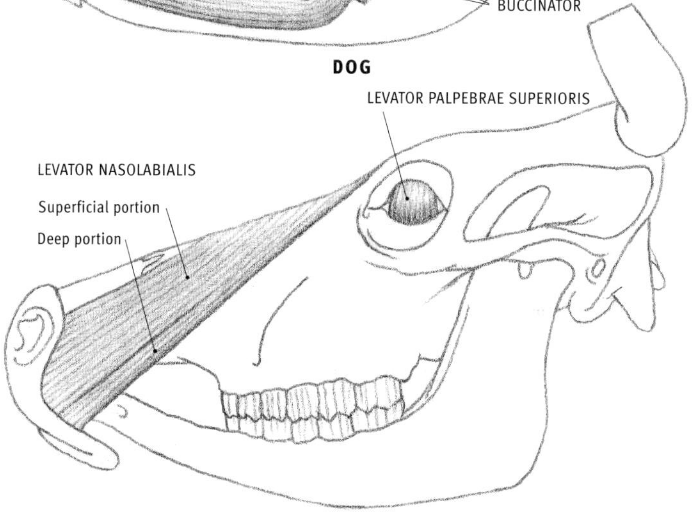

OX

Levator nasolabialis (Levator labii superioris alaeque nasi)

• Origin: Horse: Surface of skull in front of the eye. Ox: Midline of snout region, beginning at the level of the eye. Dog and feline: Snout region, just off the midline, beginning at the level of the eye. Feline: Also from in front of the eye.

• Insertion: Horse and ox: Outer edge of the nostril and the edge of the upper lip. Dog and feline: Side of the nose and the front of the upper lip, and into the buccinator muscle.

• Action: Horse and ox: Lifts the upper lip and dilates the nostril. Dog and feline: Lifts the upper lip, exposing the canines, and wrinkles the skin of the snout.

• Structure: In the horse, the nasolabialis divides into forward and rear portions. The caninus passes between them, first passing under the narrow rear portion and then over the wider front portion. The muscle is wider in the ox; it divides into superficial and deep layers. However, the rear edge of the deep layer is exposed. The caninus and also the levator labii maxillaris pass between these layers, first passing over the exposed deep portion and then under the superficial portion. In the dog and feline, the muscle divides into a wide front portion (directed downward and forward) and a narrower rear portion (directed downward and rearward in the dog and downward and forward in the feline).

Levator palpebrae superioris

• Origin: Small area of the skull deep in the back of the eye socket.

• Insertion: Lower edge of the upper eyelid.

• Action: Lifts the upper eyelid.

• Structure: The levator palpebrae superioris is a flat muscle that originates deep in the eye socket. It gets wider and thinner as it passes over the eyeball. The muscle ends in a thin tendon in the upper eyelid that passes among the fibers of the orbicularis oculi on its way to the edge of the lid. Lifting the upper eyelid beyond the normal open position has a dramatic effect on facial expression.

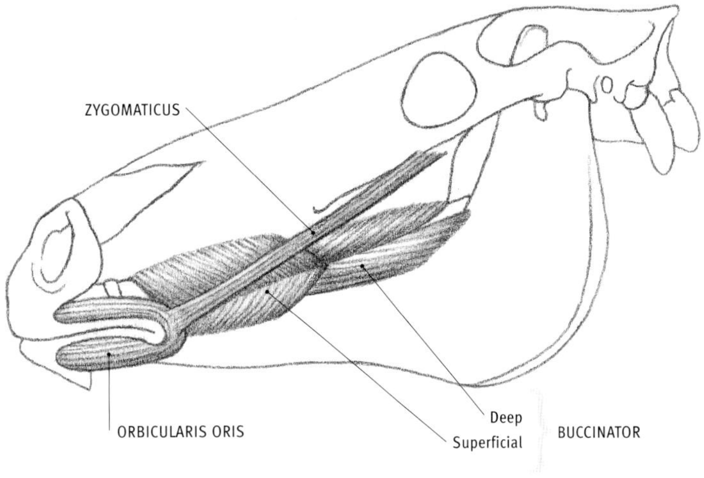

HORSE

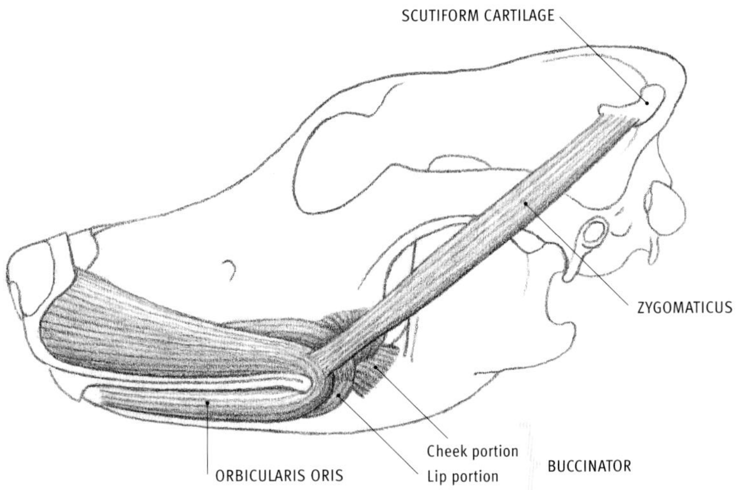

DOG

Orbicularis oris

• Origin: Corner of the mouth.

• Insertion: Into the lips as it surrounds the mouth. Dog: Also into the nasal cartilage on the side of the nose.

• Action: Closes the mouth by pressing and tightening the lips. Dog: Fibers to the nasal cartilage pull the nose downward and enlarge the nostril opening.

• Structure: The orbicularis oris surrounds the mouth, lying in the upper and lower lips. It is continuous with the muscle of the other side (in both the upper and lower lips) in the horse; absent in the front of the upper lip in the ox, and separated slightly in the upper and lower lips in the dog. The uppermost fibers reach the nose in the dog. In the horse it consists of two parts—a wide portion surrounding the lips, and a narrow portion in the margin of the lips. This allows for greater control of lip movements in the horse. The orbicularis oris is well developed in the horse and ox, which use the lips for grazing, and less developed (less mobile) in the dog and feline.

Zygomaticus

• Origin: Horse: Surface of the masseter muscle at the bony facial ridge, below the eye. Ox: Zygomatic arch and surface of the masseter muscle. Dog and feline: Cartilaginous plate (scutiform cartilage) lying on the surface of the temporalis muscle, located near the rear end of the upper surface of the head.

• Insertion: Corner of the mouth (slightly toward the upper lip), merging with the fibers of the orbicularis oris.

• Action: Pulls the corner of the mouth upward and rearward. Dog and feline: also pulls the scutiform cartilage forward.

• Structure: The zygomaticus is a long, narrow straplike muscle. In the horse, it can be seen where it leaves the surface of the masseter and also just before it attaches to the corner of the mouth. It is larger in the feline than in the dog.

Buccinator

• Origin: Horse: Lower edge of the upper jaw between the canine tooth and the molars, continuing along the tooth sockets of the molars; upper edge of the lower jaw between the canine tooth and the molars and an area to the rear of the last molar. Ox: Edges of the tooth sockets of the upper and lower jaws. Dog: Cheek portion: edges of the tooth sockets of the molars of the upper and lower jaws; lip portion: corner of the mouth.

• Insertion: Corner of the mouth, merging with fibers of the orbicularis oris. Dog: Also into the upper and lower lips (lip portion).

• Action: Flattens (compresses) the cheek, pushing food against the molars for chewing. Also pulls the corner of the mouth rearward.

• Structure: In the horse, the buccinator consists of deep and superficial portions. A tendinous band running the length of the superficial portion creates a furrow that separates the belly into upper and lower bulging forms, lying between the corner of the mouth and the masseter muscle. In the ox, the buccinator is divided into a superficial portion with vertical fibers, and a deep portion, the fibers of which are directed forward; it can be seen as a bulging form on the surface. In the dog, the buccinator consists of a cheek portion that is divisible into upper and lower parts that fuse together at the corner of the mouth, and a lip portion that passes forward from the corner of the mouth and passes deep to the orbicularis oris.

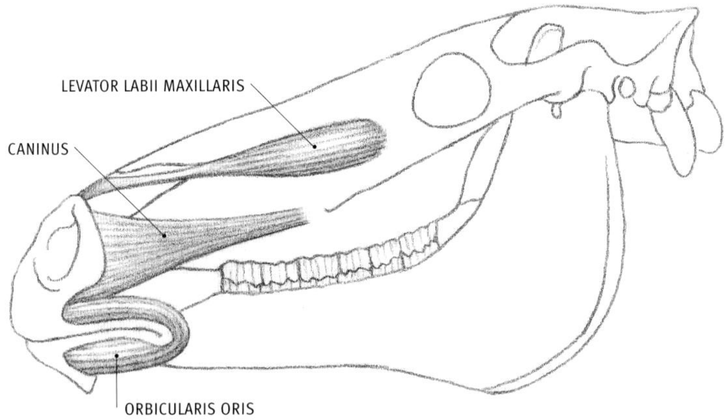

HORSE

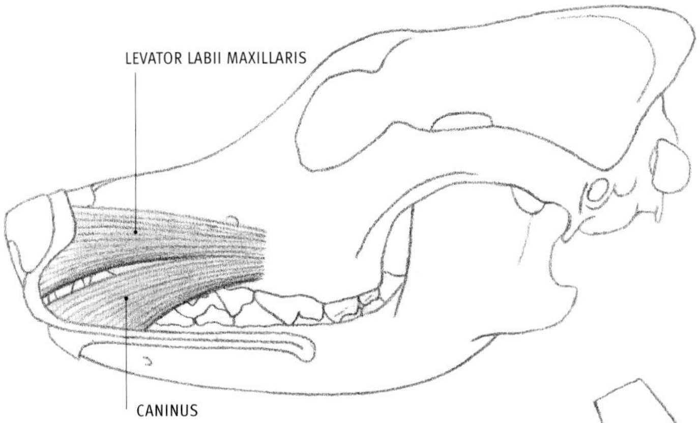

DOG

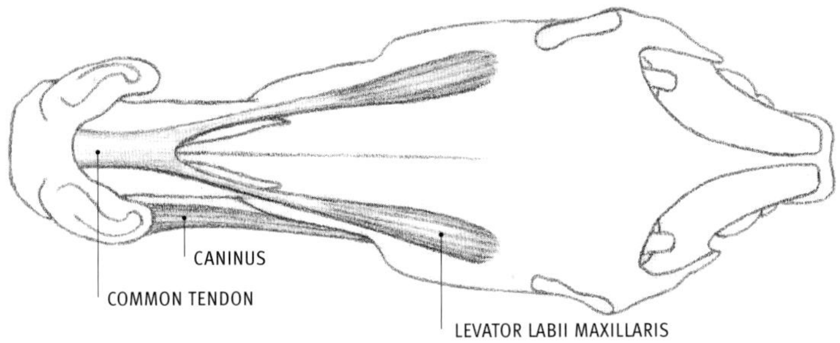

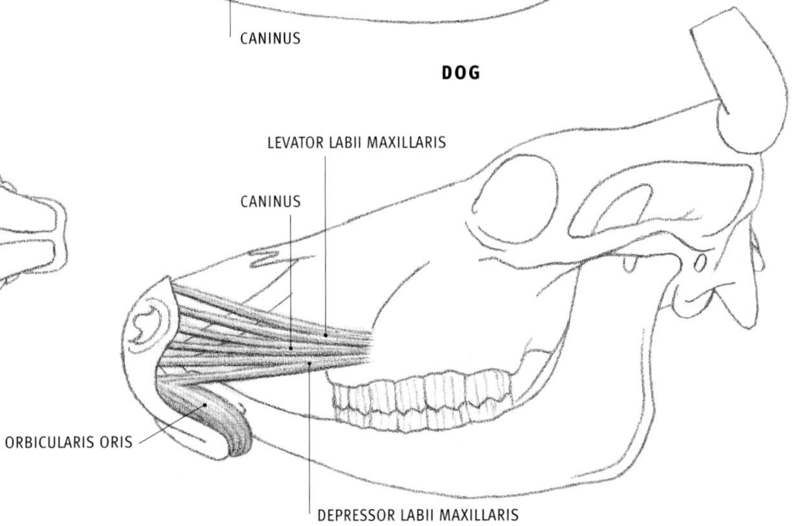

OX

Levator labii maxillaris (superioris) (Levator labii superioris proprius)

• Origin: Bones of the side of the face (in front of the eye in the horse; lower, at the end of the facial crest in the ox; above the large molar in the dog).

• Insertion: Horse and ox: Skin on the front of the upper lip, by common tendon with the same muscle of the other side. Dog: Front end of the upper lip and the side of the nostril.

• Action: Horse and ox: Muscles of both sides: Lift the front of the upper lip; by continued action, evert the lips, exposing the front teeth. One side only: Lifts and pulls the upper lip slightly to that side. Dog: Lifts the upper lip and widens the nostril opening.

• Structure: In the horse, the levator labii maxillaris is a long, teardrop-shaped muscle. It begins wide and thin, then narrows and thickens, develops a round tendon, meets the tendon of the same muscle of the other side, expands into a wide tendinous sheet, and finally inserts into the skin of the upper lip on the front of the snout. The belly and the tendon can be seen on the surface and are directed upward, inward, and forward. In the ox, it is a flattened muscle that passes between the two divisions of the levator nasolabialis and develops several tendons. It lies lower on the face than in the horse but still passes inward, upward, and forward over the nose to meet the tendons of the other side before expanding into the wide central tendon and inserting. In the dog, the levator labii maxillaris lies deep to the levator nasolabialis. In the feline, descriptions of this muscle vary among authors:it is described either as lying parallel and above the caninus, or as the rear portion of the nasolabialis, as described in this text.

Caninus (Dilator naris lateralis)

• Origin: Side of the face—in front of the facial crest in the horse; at the end of the facial crest in the ox; just above the large molar in the dog and feline.

• Insertion: Side of the wing of the nostril in the horse and ox; upper lip in the dog and feline.

• Action: In the horse and ox, the caninus pulls the side wall of the nostril rearward, dilating the nostril; in the dog and feline, it lifts and retracts the front of the upper lip, exposing the "canine" tooth.

• Structure: In the horse, the caninus is a thin, flat, triangular muscle. It begins with a thick tendon, and widens as it inserts into the edge of the nostril. It passes between the two branches of the levator nasolabialis, first passing under the rear portion then over the front portion. Its lower fibers blend with the orbicularis oris; the lower edge of the muscle may be visible on the surface. In the ox, the caninus does not diverge as much as in the horse, but rather develops two or three tendons that attach to the side of the nostril. In the dog, it lies just below, and parallel to, the levator labii maxillaris; they both pass under the levator nasolabialis.

Depressor labii maxillaris (superioris)

OX

• Origin: Side of the upper jaw, at the end of the facial crest, above the molars.

• Insertion: Front end of the upper lip and the lower portion of the nostril.

• Action: Pulls the front end of the upper lip and the lower end of the nostril rearward.

• Structure: The muscle splits into two bundles before inserting. It is not present in the horse, dog, or feline.

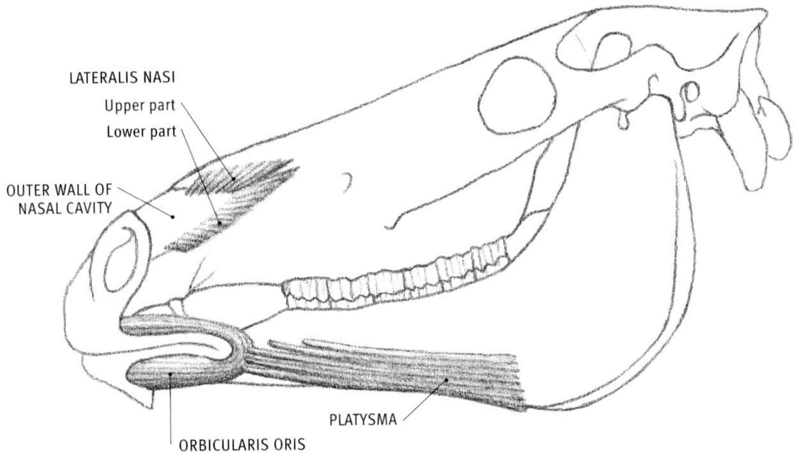

HORSE

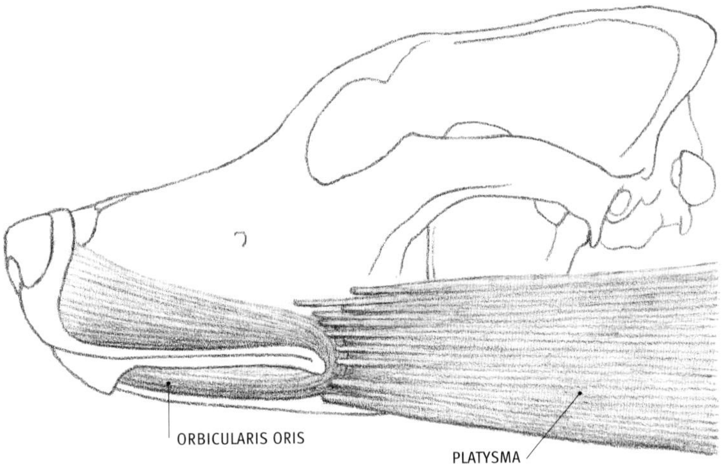

DOG

Lateralis nasi (Dilator nasi, Dilator naris alaris)

HORSE

• Origin: Upper part: From the nasal bone, along the upper edge of the large notch at the front end of the bones of the snout (to the rear of the nostril). Lower part: Along the bone of the lower edge of the notch of the snout.

• Insertion: Both parts insert into the surface of the outer wall of the nasal cavity.

• Action: Dilates the nasal cavity by pulling the soft, outer wall of the nasal cavity outward and rearward, and assists in dilating the actual nostril opening. It does not dilate or expand the "false nostril" (**nasal diverticulum**), which is a narrow, elongated, dead-end pocket that lies above the true nasal cavity.

• Structure: The lateralis nasi surrounds the bony notch of the snout and converges on the surface of the outer wall of the nasal cavity. It consists of upper and lower parts. The upper part passes under the tendon of the levator labii maxillaris. This muscle is not present in the dog or feline.

OX

• Origin: Upper part: From the edge of the top of the cartilage of the snout (in the front of the nasal bone and just behind the nostril). Lower part: Along the edge of the forwardmost projecting bone of the upper jaw (incisivus bone) and the adjacent cartilage.

• Insertion: Upper part: Upper part of the inner wing of the nostril. Lower part: Outer wing of the nostril.

• Action: Assists in dilating the nostril.

• Structure: The lateralis nasi is less developed in the ox than in the horse. It inserts directly into parts of the edges of the nostril, rather than into the outer wall of the nasal cavity.

Platysma (Cutaneous faciei & labiorum)

The platysma is the facial part of the **cutaneous muscle** ("skin muscle"), a thin muscular sheet that covers various parts of the body (see page 65). The platysma passes over the side of the lower jaw in the horse and inserts into the corner of the mouth, fusing with the orbicularis oris. It pulls the corner of the mouth rearward and has a strong effect on the shape of the mouth. It is least developed in the horse.

In the ox, the platysma is more developed. It pulls the corner of the mouth rearward (and also slightly downward by several inclined fibers designated the **depressor anguli oris**). Some fibers of the cutaneous muscle of the head transversely cross over the snout and insert into the upper part of the lateralis nasi. They assist in dilating the nostril.

The platysma of the dog is quite wide; it begins on the midline on the back of the upper neck and inserts into the corner of the mouth. The platysma of the feline is the widest and most developed of the species described here. It remains wide at its inserting end on the side of the face where it attaches to several facial muscles, yet, as in the other species, its importance is in its retraction of the corner of the mouth.

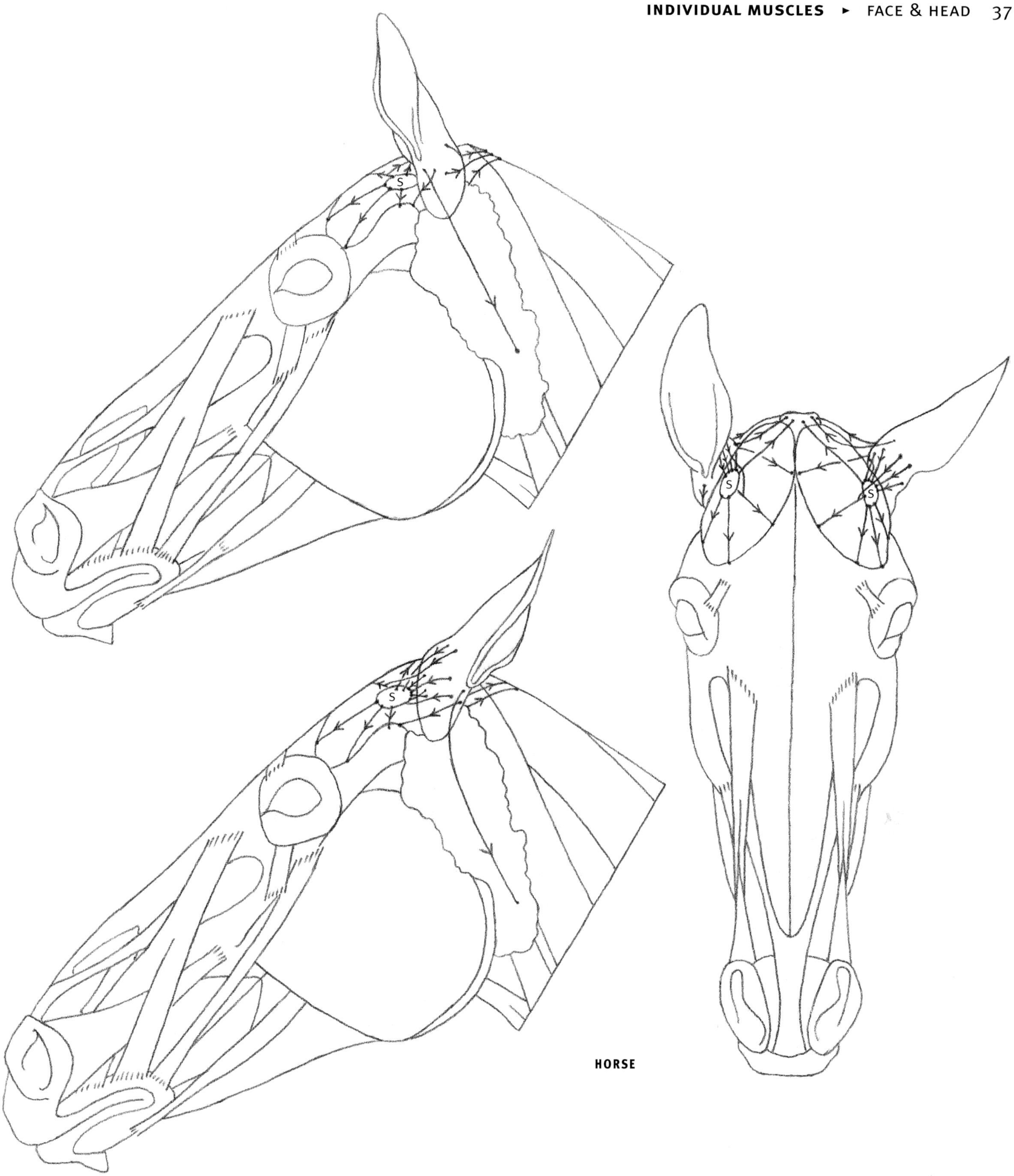

HORSE

Ear muscles

Numerous muscles surround and attach to the ear, moving it forward, backward, inward (toward the midline), and outward (away from the midline), with the ear pivoting at its lower end. They also rotate the ear from a forward-facing position to a rear-facing position, directing its concave, sound-gathering "cup" outwardly as it rotates. The muscles insert directly onto the ear, or insert onto the movable scutiform cartilage, which provides origin for other muscles that then insert onto the ear.

According to Sisson and Grossman (*The Anatomy of the Domestic Animals*, 1975), there are 17 ear muscles in the horse, and according to Miller (*Anatomy of the Dog*, 1979), there are 19 ear muscles in the dog.

Because the ear muscles are so numerous, do not create surface form, and lie in layers, they are depicted here as linear axes, with an arrow indicating their direction of pull. The ear of the ox tends to be directed horizontally, rather than upright, as in the horse, dog, and feline.

S *Scutiform cartilage*

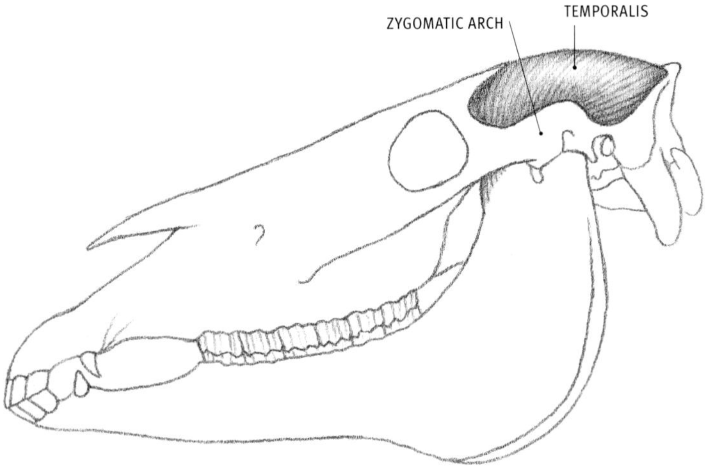

HORSE

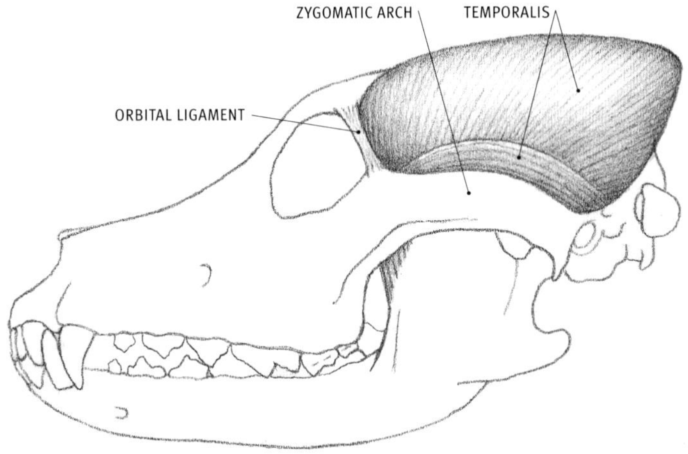

DOG

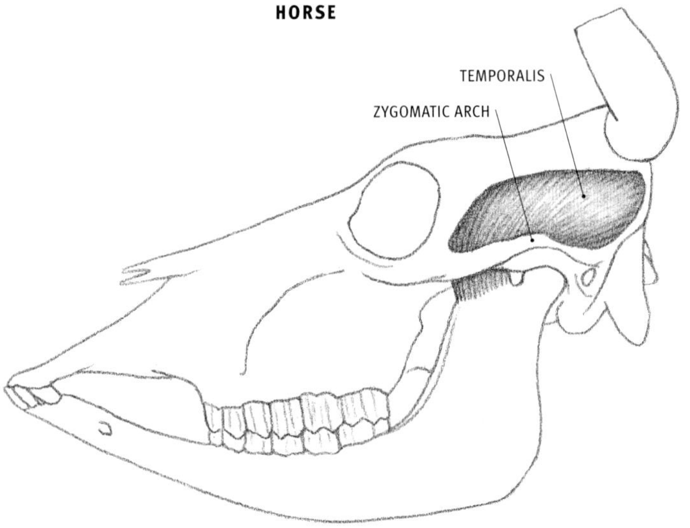

OX

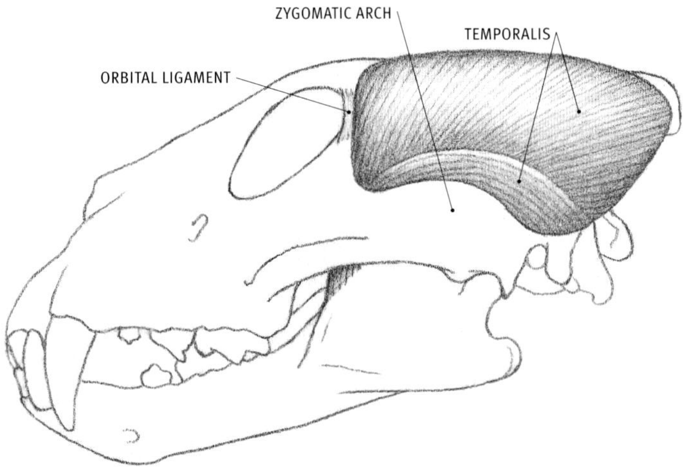

LION

Temporalis

• Origin: Upper rear part of the skull, on the rounded braincase and the surrounding bony ridges.

• Insertion: Top of the upward projection of the lower jaw (continuing down the front edge of the jaw in the horse, dog, and feline).

• Action: Closes the mouth, for biting and chewing, by lifting the lower jaw up and pulling it back.

• Structure: The muscle fibers begin from a wide origin and converge deeply onto the upper tip of the lower jaw. Except for the ox, the rounded form of the muscle fills out the upper back portion of the head, especially in the dog and feline, where the muscle is well developed. In the ox, the temporalis is small and lies on the side of the cranium. In the horse, a conspicuous hollow can be seen on the surface of the muscle behind the orbit. It is called the "salt cellar."

In the horse and feline, the muscles of both sides meet at the midline toward the rear. In the dog, the muscles of both sides may or may not meet at the midline, depending on the breed. In the dog and feline, an upright bony ridge of variable development may be located between the muscles of both sides. In the dog and feline, a small band of muscle fibers arises from the rear end of the zygomatic arch and curves upward, forward, and then downward to the lower jaw, deep to the zygomatic arch, where it fuses with the rest of the muscle.

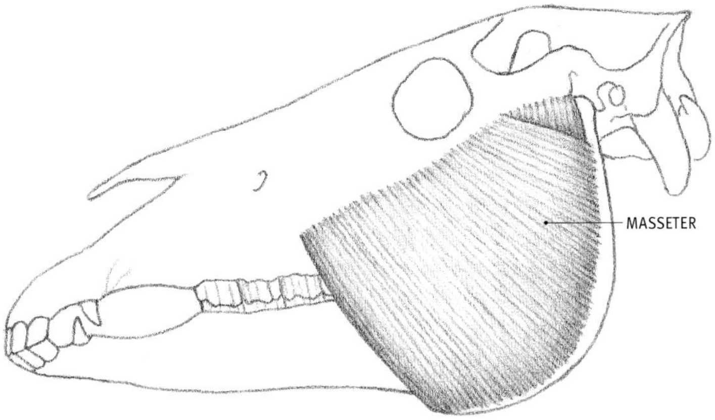

HORSE

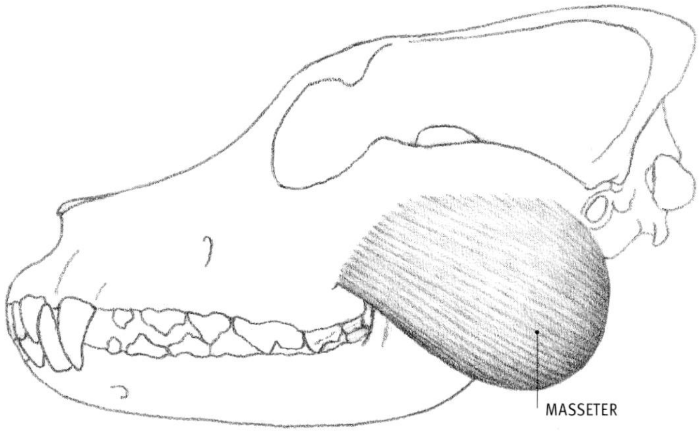

DOG

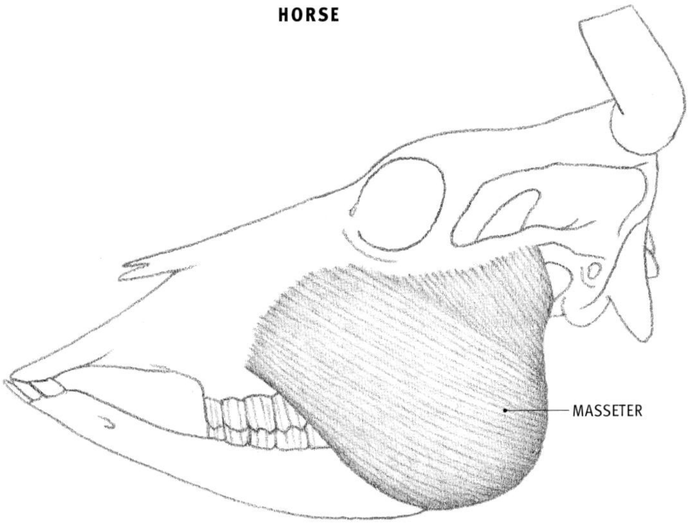

OX

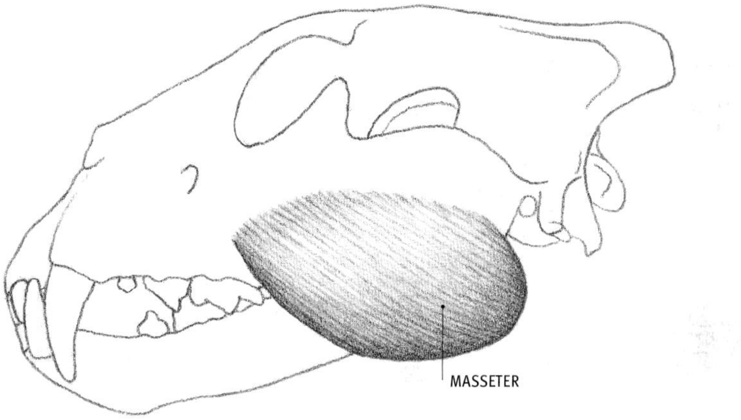

LION

Masseter

• Origin: Lower edge of the zygomatic arch (continuing forward along a bony ridge of the side of the face in the horse and ox).

• Insertion: Side of the broad, upright portion of the lower jaw—up to the thickened edge in the horse, to the rear edge in the ox, and into the lower and rear edges of the lower jaw and onto the surface of the deep pterygoid muscle (beyond the rear end of the lower jaw) in the dog and feline.

• Action: Closes the mouth, for biting and chewing, by lifting the lower jaw. In the horse and ox, it also pulls the lower jaw sideways (outward) and forward for grinding food. Because the jaw joint has a flattened upper articular surface, some gliding can occur here. The dog and feline have a more tightly hinged jaw joint, permitting basic opening and closing, with limited side motion.

• Structure: The masseter is a strong, flattened muscle in the horse and ox, bulging in the dog and feline. In the horse and ox, it stops at the edge of the lower jaw. In the dog and feline, it projects substantially beyond the lower and rear borders of the jaw. Composed of two or more layers, only a small portion of the deep layer of the masseter comes to the surface in the horse, just in front of the jaw joint.

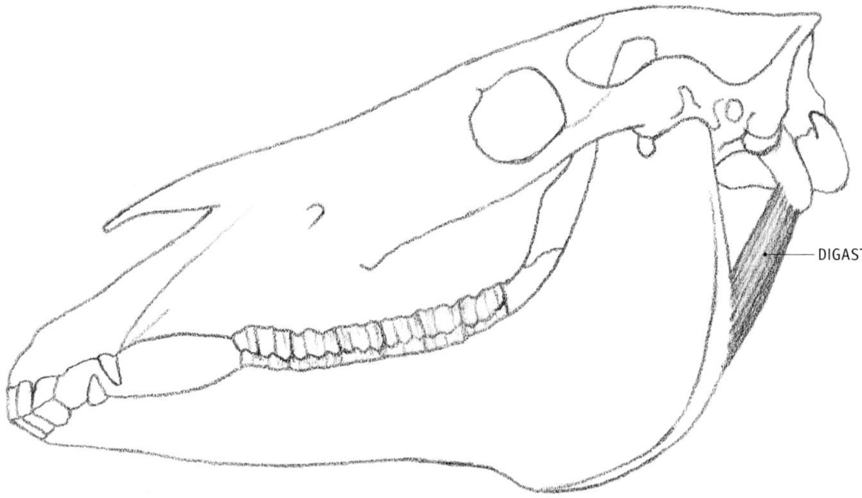

HORSE

DOG

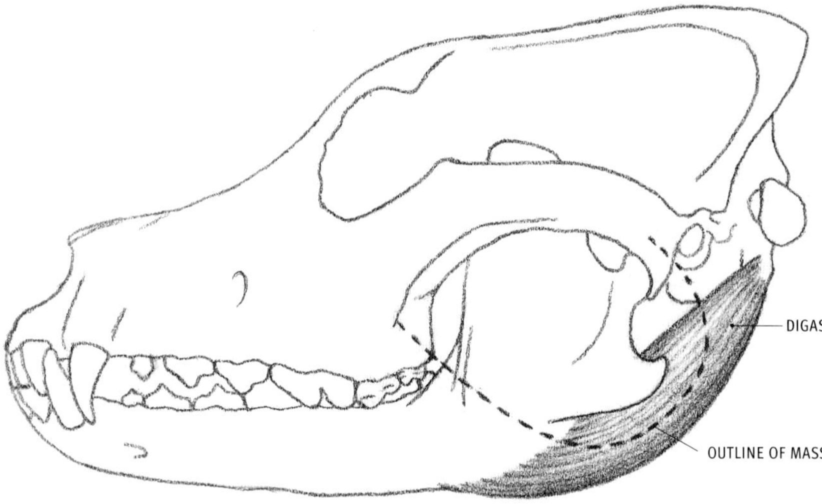

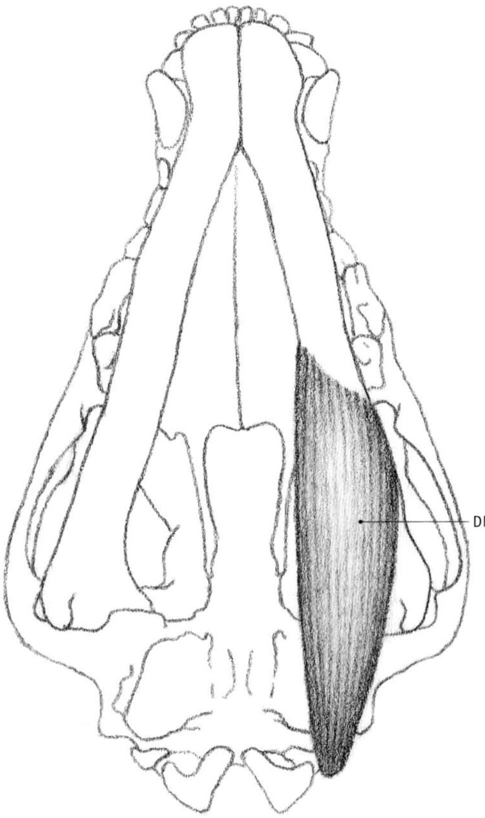

BOTTOM VIEW

Digastric

HORSE, DOG, AND FELINE

• Origin: Bony projection on the bottom of the rear part of the skull.

• Insertion: Horse: Rear edge of the lower jaw. Dog and feline: Lower edge of the rear end of the lower jaw.

• Action: Pulls the rear end of the lower jaw backward (pivoting the lower jaw at the jaw joint), which opens the mouth.

• Structure: In the horse, the digastric consists of a deep portion (not illustrated) and a shorter, more superficial portion called the **occipito-mandibularis**. The occipitomandibularis contributes minimally to the rear profile of the lower jaw. In the dog and feline, the digastric is a relatively thick muscle. Its front half usually projects downward beyond the lower edge of the masseter muscle to create the profile of the lower jaw in this region. In the feline, the muscle inserts farther forward than in the dog, sometimes reaching the chin. The digastric is not visible on the surface in the ox. The parotid gland lies on the side of the neck to the rear of the lower jaw, and covers the upper part of the digastric muscle.

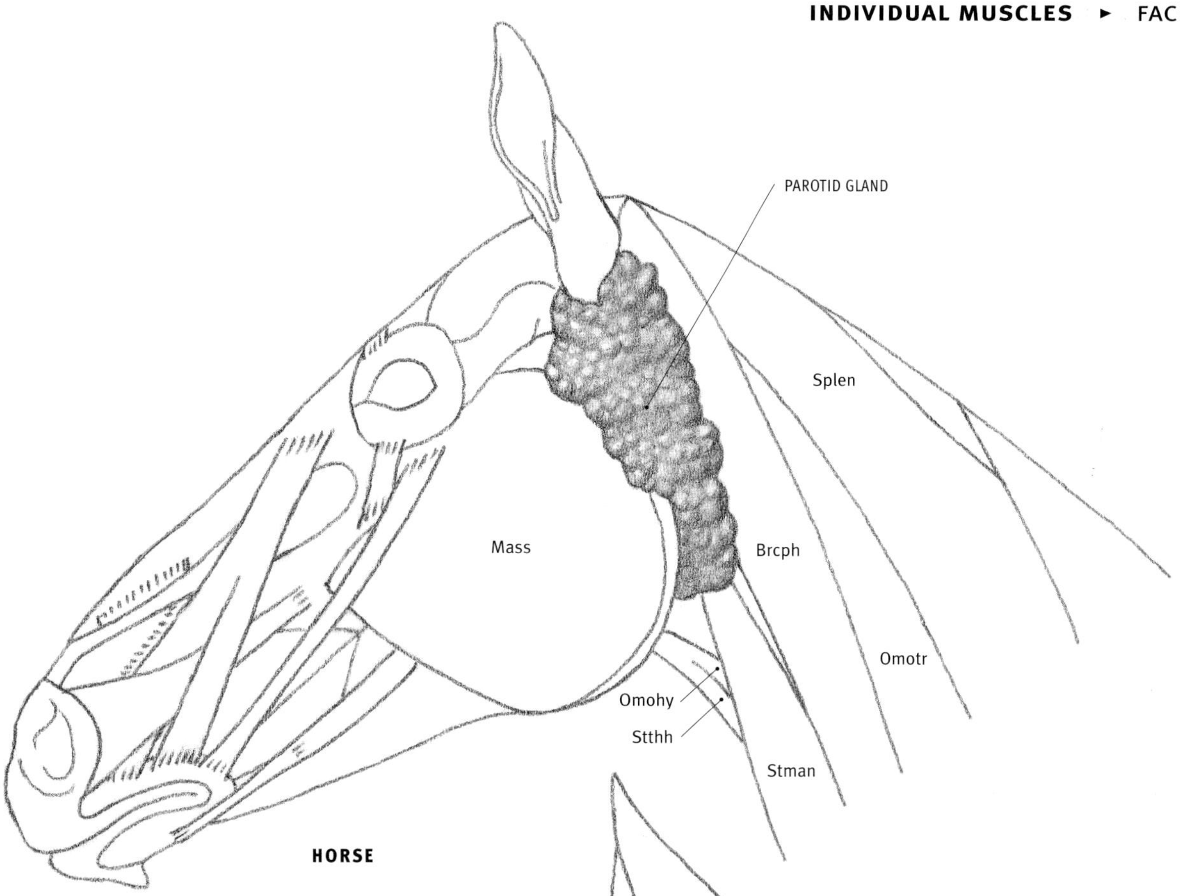

HORSE

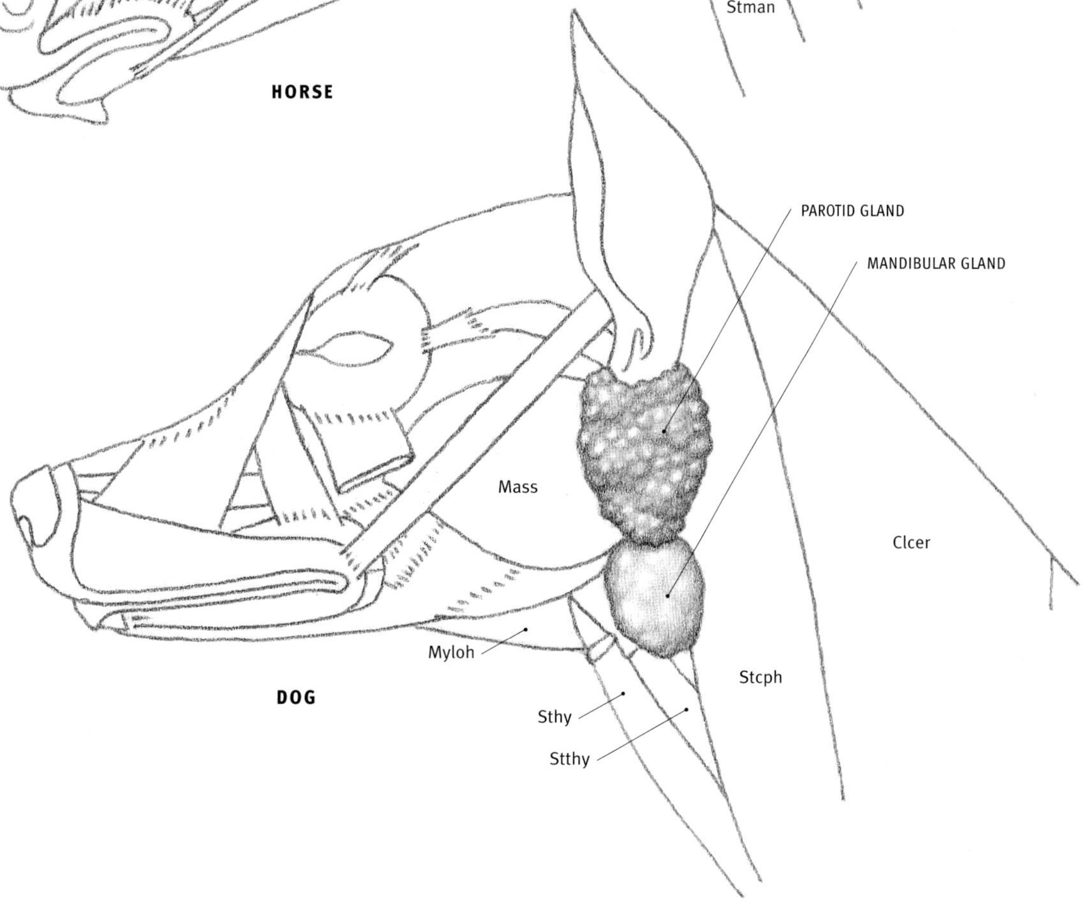

DOG

Salivary glands

The **parotid gland** is a soft, sponge-like form sitting in the hollow between the back of the lower jaw and the side of the neck (wing of the atlas). It extends up to, and surrounds (except in the ox), the base of the ear. The gland spreads over the rear edge of the lower jaw and softens the definition of the anatomy in this region. When the head is extended up, the parotid gland sinks in; when the head is flexed down and the neck is arched, it bulges out. In the ox, the parotid gland is narrower and reaches up to, but does not surround, the base of the ear. The parotid gland is elongated in the horse and ox, and shorter and relatively rounder in the dog and feline.

The **mandibular gland** is a separate, elongated gland that lies along the rear edge of the parotid gland in the ox. In the dog and feline, the mandibular gland is an ovoid body, approximately half the size of the parotid gland, and is located below the parotid gland. It is in contact with the lower end of the parotid. The mandibular gland of the horse is mostly concealed by the parotid gland.

Brcph *Brachiocephalicus;* **Clcer** *Cleidocervicalis;* **Mass** *Masseter;* **Myloh** *Mylohyoid;* **Omohy** *Omohyoid;* **Omotr** *Omotransversarius;* **Splen** *Splenius;* **Stcph** *Sternocephalicus;* **Stman** *Sternomandibularis;* **Stthh** *Sternothyrohyoid;* **Stthy** *Sternothyroid.*

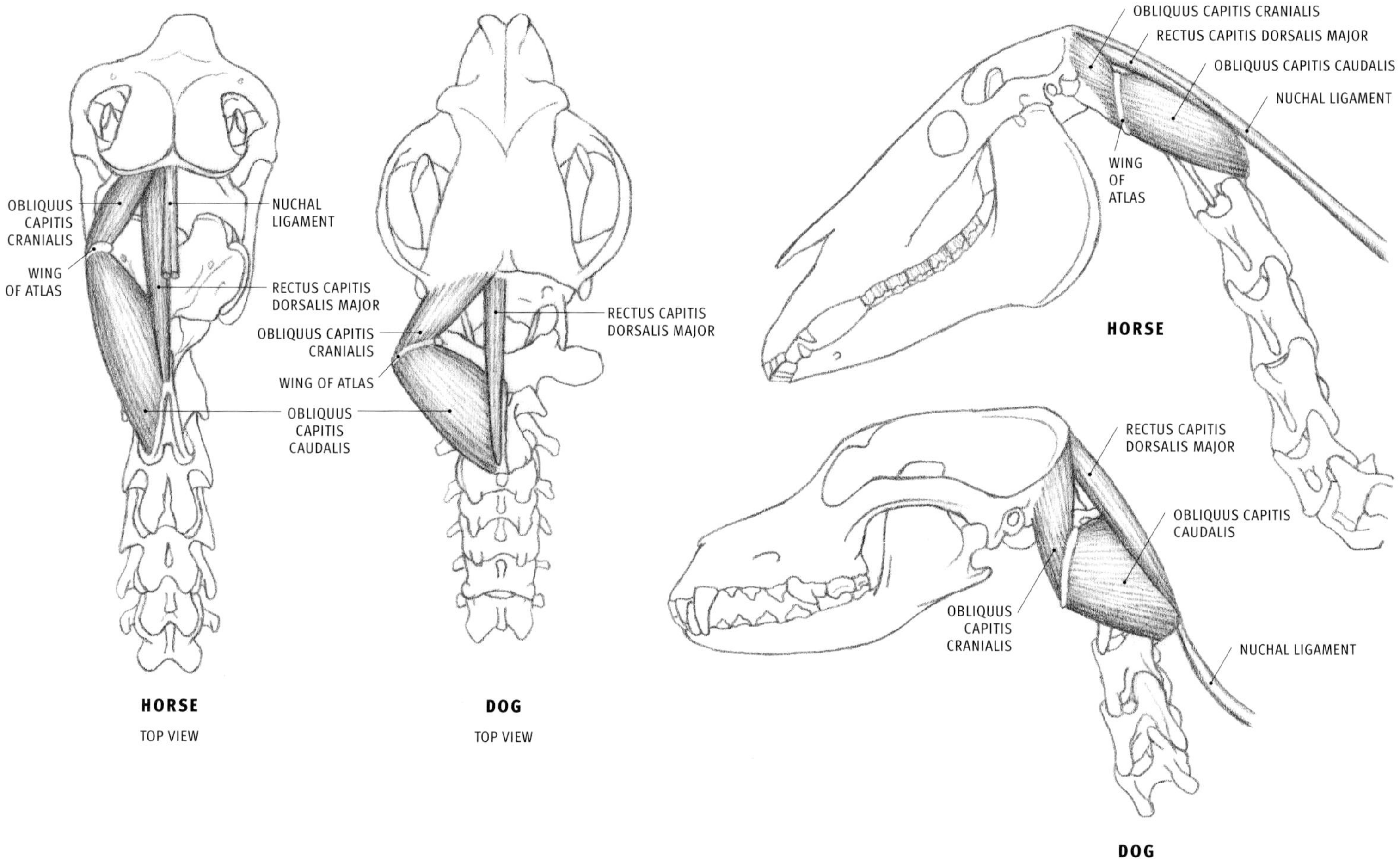

Short Neck Muscles

The following three muscles are located on the back of the neck, just behind the skull: the **obliquus capitis caudalis,** the **obliquus capitis cranialis,** and the **rectus capitis dorsalis major**. They are covered by narrow and wide tendons and thin muscles, yet they help create the fullness on the back of the neck, determined in large part by the width of the atlas (the first neck vertebra) and the vertical projection of the axis (the second neck vertebra).

Obliquus capitis caudalis (Large oblique muscle, Axoido-atloideus)

• Origin: Entire side of the expanded upright spine of the second neck vertebra (axis).
• Insertion: Rear surface of the expanded side projection, or wing, of the first neck vertebra (atlas).
• Action: Rotates the first neck vertebra (which pivots on the second neck vertebra) to the side, thereby turning the head to the side.
• Structure: Largest of the group, this thick muscle is directed forward and outward. Its rear portion is buried in muscle, but as it advances, it approaches the surface.

Obliquus capitis cranialis (Small oblique muscle, Atloido-occipitalis)

• Origin: Front surface of the wing of the first neck vertebra (atlas).
• Insertion: Rear part of the skull.
• Action: Both sides together extend the head.
• Structure: This is a short muscle which fill the space between the skull and the first neck vertebra. It is directed forward, upward, and inward.

Rectus capitis dorsalis major (Posterior straight muscle, Axoido-occipitalis)

• Origin: Upper edge of the upright spine of the second neck vertebra.
• Insertion: Rear end of the skull near the midline.
• Action: Extends the head.
• Structure: This narrow muscle lies just to the side of, and partly under, the nuchal ligament of the neck in the horse and ox. In the dog and the feline, it lies against its fellow of the other side on the midline; the nuchal ligament begins at the rear of the second neck vertebra.

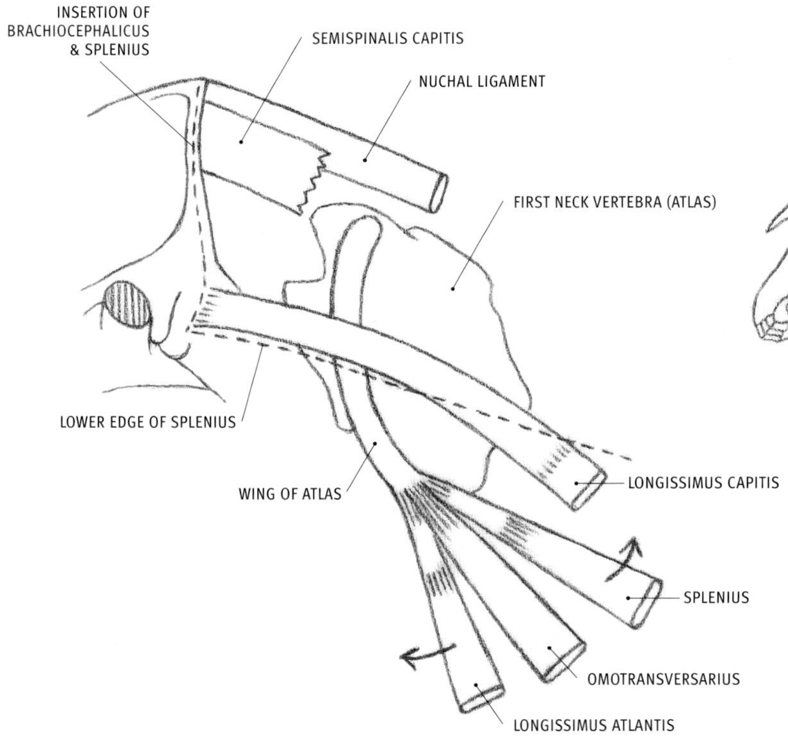

HORSE

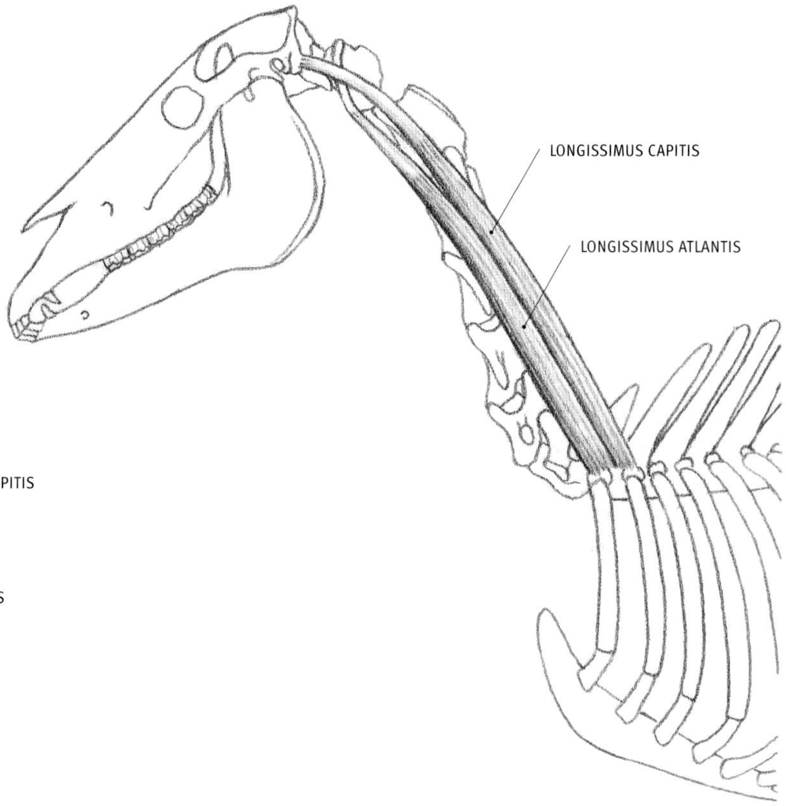

HORSE

Longissimus capitis and Longissimus atlantis

HORSE

• Origin: By tendinous fibers from the region of the sides of the first and second thoracic vertebrae, and by successive attachments from the upper sides of the seventh through the third neck vertebrae.

• Insertion: Longissimus capitis: base of the skull behind the ear hole. Longissimus atlantis: lower end of the expanded side projection, or wing, of the first neck vertebra (atlas).

• Action: Muscles of both sides of the body: extend the head and neck. One side only: pulls the head and neck to that side, or rotates the atlas, and therefore the head, to that side.

• Structure: The longissimus capitis and longissimus atlantis are two elongated, parallel muscles, part of the longissimus system of the vertebral column. They lie deep to the splenius. The upper (rear) muscle, the longissimus capitis, inserts into the skull by a flat tendon, in common with the splenius. This tendon may occasionally be seen on the surface passing over the wing of the atlas, as well as on its way to the skull. The lower (forward) muscle, the longissimus atlantis, inserts into the lower end of the wing of the atlas by a strong, round tendon, which can become quite prominent on the surface. This tendon inserts in common with the splenius and the omotransversarius.

The longissimus capitis and atlantis in the dog and feline do not affect surface form, but their tendons may be seen in the ox.

Several narrow or wide tendons and thin muscle pass over, or attach onto the lower end of, the wing of the atlas. The deeper structures (splenius to the wing of the atlas, omotransversarius, longissimus atlantis, longissimus capitis, and semispinalis capitis) may show through the more superficial structures (the wide, thin tendon and thin muscle of the brachiocephalicus and the wide, thin tendon of the splenius, both of which attach to the rear end of the skull). The key to understanding this region is to *isolate each visible form and follow it toward its origin and insertion*.

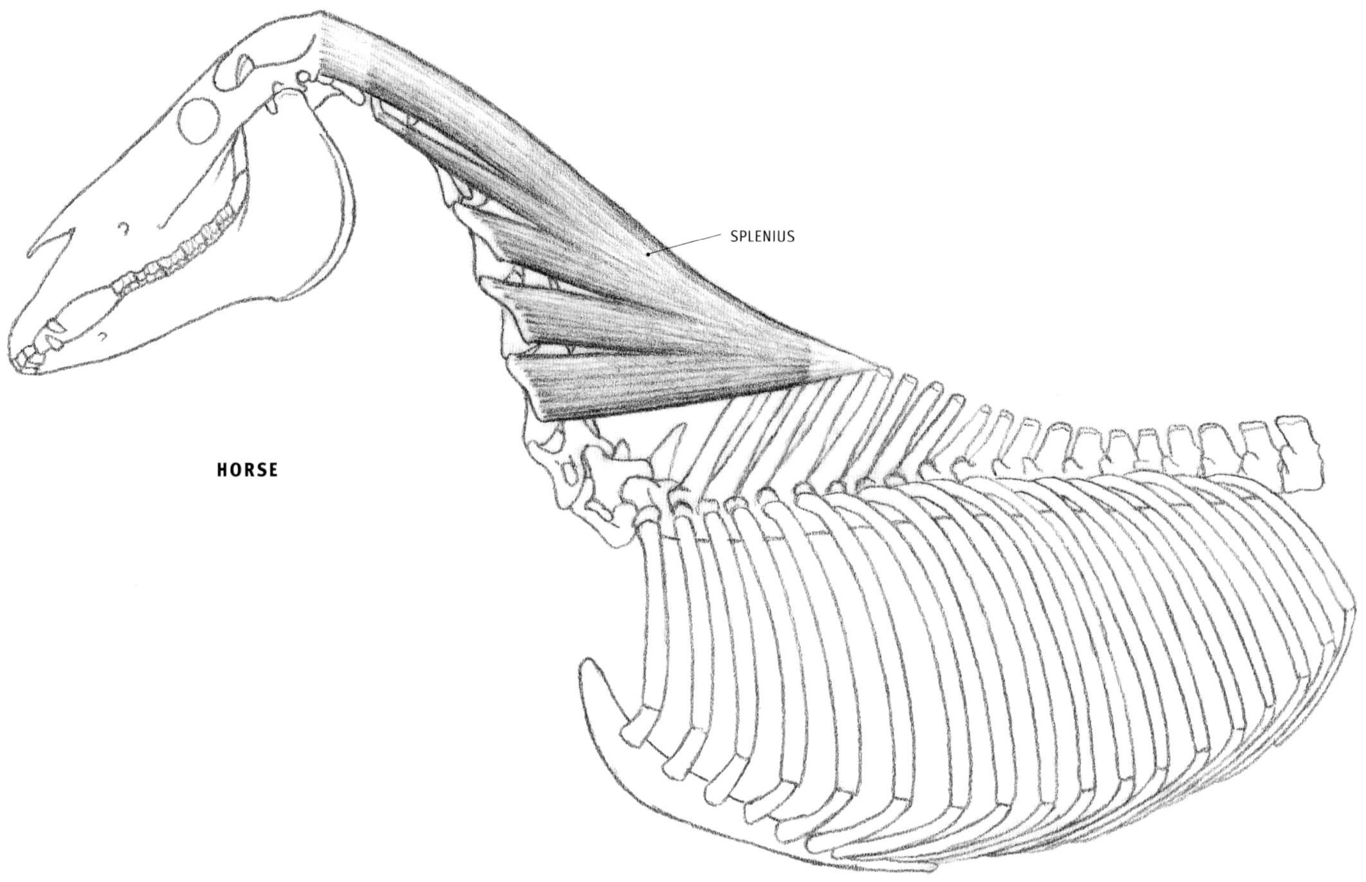

Splenius

HORSE

• Origin: Rear end of the cord of the nuchal ligament, and the tips of the upright spines of the third, fourth, and fifth thoracic vertebrae.

• Insertion: By five separate and distinct insertions into (1) a line on the rear end of the skull (from the midline above down to the mastoid process behind the ear hole), (2) the lower end of the expanded side projection of the first vertebra (atlas), (3) the sides of the third, fourth, and fifth neck vertebrae (not the second).

• Action: Both sides of the body together: Extend the head and lift the neck. One side only: Pulls the head and neck to that side.

• Structure: The splenius is a large, flat, triangular muscle located between the head, the top of the shoulder, and the neck vertebrae. It comes to the surface in an irregular rectangular window bordered by the brachiocephalicus in front, the trapezius and a small portion of the rhomboid behind, and the neck portion of the serratus ventralis (cervicis) below. The splenius develops into five segments—the uppermost segment attaches to the skull by a wide, thin tendon, the next to the first neck vertebra by a strong tendon, and the remaining three to the sides of neck vertebrae three, four, and five directly by fleshy fibers. The lower portion of the splenius is covered by the neck portion of the serratus ventralis, whose elongated segments are oriented in a direction very similar to the segments of the splenius.

In the ox, dog, and feline, the splenius is completely covered. However, it adds a layer of muscular thickness that participates in forming the volume of the neck. It is thicker in the dog and the feline than in the ox.

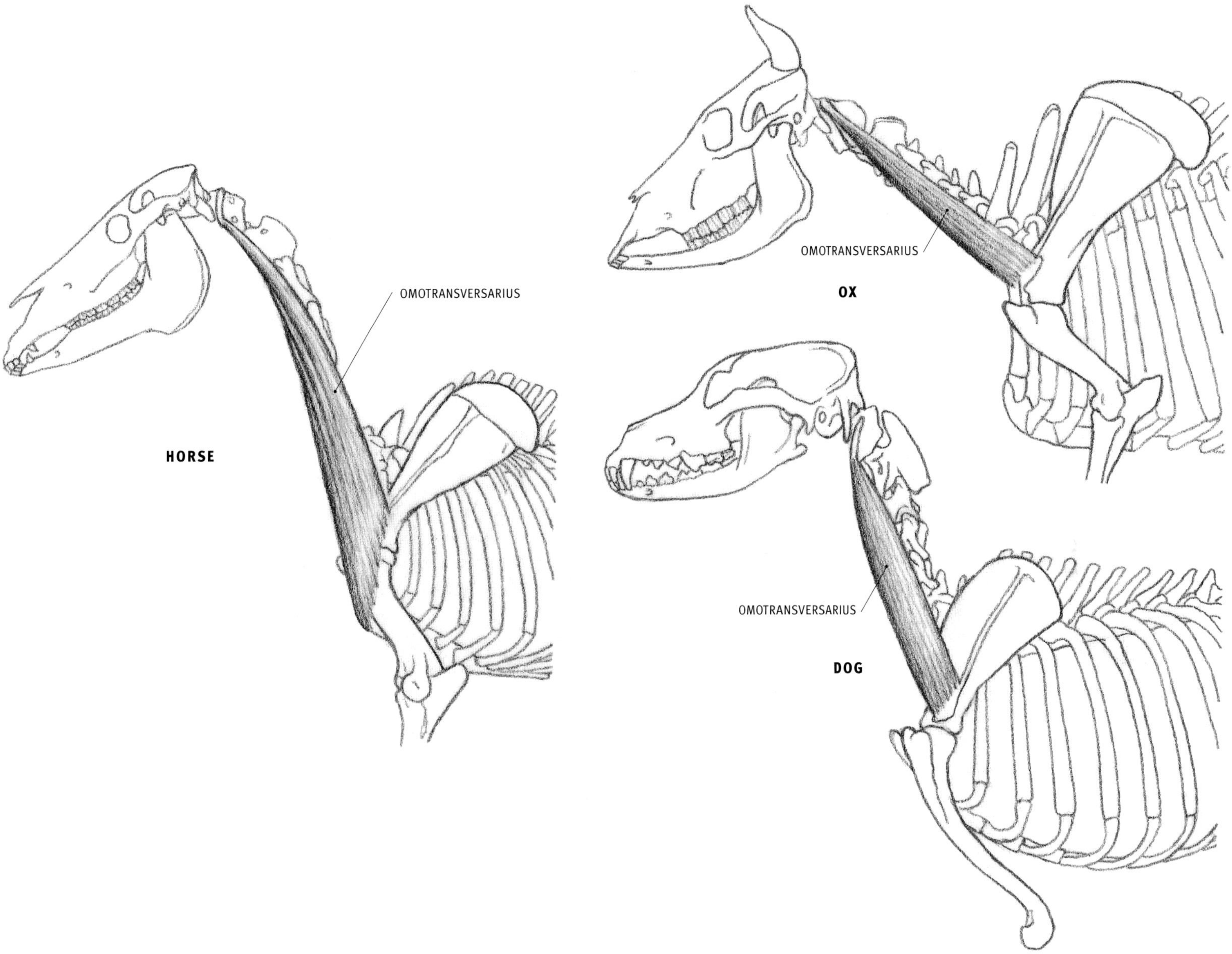

Omotransversarius (Trachelo-acromialis)

HORSE

• Origin: The sides of the first four neck vertebrae.

• Insertion: Fascia on the surface of the shoulder region and outside of the upper arm toward the front of the elbow.

• Action: Pulls the neck to the side when the limb is fixed; pulls the limb forward when the neck is fixed.

• Structure: The omotransversarius is thick and muscular on the side of the neck. It widens as it descends, then it thins as it passes over the shoulder, where it fuses with the fascia on the surface of the shoulder and upper arm. The omotransversarius used to be called the cleidocervicalis of the brachiocephalicus.

OX

• Origin: Side of the first neck vertebra.

• Insertion: Lower end of the spine (bony ridge) of the shoulder blade, and the fascia of the shoulder.

• Structure: The omotransversarius is a narrow, straplike muscle, tapered at its upper end, located on the side of the neck. It extends from the upper end of the neck behind the skull to the shoulder blade. Its upper portion is covered by the brachiocephalicus, which crosses it on a strong diagonal line. This leaves an elongated triangular portion of the lower end of the omotransversarius exposed at the shoulder.

DOG AND FELINE

• Origin: Lower end of the side of the first neck vertebra. Feline: Also from the base of the skull.

• Insertion: Lower end (excluding the tip) of the spine of the shoulder blade, and the surface of the deltoid. The origin and insertion are often reversed in the dog and the feline when the shoulder is considered the more fixed point of attachment.

Brachiocephalicus (Mastoido-humeralis, Cephalo-humeral)

The **brachiocephalicus** ("arm-to-head" muscle) is a long, wide, straplike muscle that passes from the head and neck down to the front of the elbow region. It can be separated into upper and lower portions by a horizontal tendon, which represents the missing clavicle (a vestigial clavicle may also be present). The longer, upper portion, the **cleidocephalicus**, ("clavicle-to-head") is further divided in some species into two parts—the **cleidomastoid** ("clavicle-to-mastoid bone") and the **cleidocervicalis** ("clavicle-to-neck") or **cleido-occipitalis** ("clavicle-to-occipital bone"). The smaller lower portion, located between the shoulder and the elbow region, is called the **cleidobrachialis** ("clavicle-to-arm").

The clavicle is absent in the horse and the ox and is represented by a tendinous line (present in the ox, variable in the horse). In the dog and the feline, the tendinous line is present and more distinct, especially in the feline. A small, vestigial bony clavicle, lying deep to the brachiocephalicus, is fused to the inner half of this tendinous line. The clavicle does not articulate with the skeleton.

HORSE

• Origin: Continuous line on the rear of the skull, beginning on the midline, passing downward and forward, and ending behind and below the ear hole (on the mastoid process).
• Insertion: Line on the humerus that begins halfway down the outside of the bone and passes downward and inward on the front of the lower half of the bone.
• Action: Pulls the entire forelimb forward and extends the shoulder joint when the head and neck are fixed. Both sides of the body: Pulls the head and neck downward. One side only: Pulls the head and neck to that side.
• Structure: The brachiocephalicus is a simple, long, straplike muscle passing from the head to the arm. Its upper end develops a thin, wide tendon that attaches to the skull and allows deeper structures to show through. It descends in front of the shoulder joint. The lower end of the muscle passes between the biceps and the brachialis (completely covering the biceps) and then inserts on the humerus, in common with the pectoralis descendens. The brachiocephalicus lies in front of the omotransversarius, which used to be considered part of the brachiocephalicus, and was called the cleidocervicalis.

OX

• Origin: Cleido-occipitalis: upper rear end of the skull and adjacent nuchal ligament on the midline of the neck. Cleidomastoideus: Base of the skull, just behind the ear hole.
• Insertion: Diagonal line on the lower part of the front of the humerus, passing downward and inward, beginning halfway down the bone toward the outside; fascia of the surface of the upper arm and the forearm.
• Structure: The upper portion of the brachiocephalicus is divisible into the cleido-occipitalis and the cleidomastoid. The two portions are distinctly separate, with their upper ends separated by a narrow interval. The upper end of the cleido-occipitalis widens as it approaches the top of the neck. The muscle as a whole narrows at the shoulder and passes in front of the shoulder joint.

DOG AND FELINE

• Origin: Cleidocervicalis: Midline on the back of the front half of the neck. In the feline it also attaches to the edge of the base of the skull for a short distance from the midline. Cleidomastoid: Base of the skull behind the ear hole.
• Insertion: Dog: Vertical line on the lower half of the front of the humerus. Feline: Inner surface of the upper end of the ulna, just below the elbow joint, in common with the brachialis.
• Structure: The upper portion of the brachiocephalicus is divided into a superficial part, the cleidocervicalis (**cleidotrapezius** in the feline), and a deep part, the cleidomastoid. The cleidocervicalis begins wide and thin on the back of the front half of the neck and covers a considerable portion of the neck. The cleidomastoid is deep and covered by the cleidocervicalis and the sternocephalicus. The overall muscle narrows as it descends, crossing in front of the shoulder joint. Because of its insertion past the elbow joint onto the ulna in the feline, the form of the brachiocephalicus is directed lower on the limb than in the other species.

TERMINOLOGY OF BRACHIOCEPHALICUS
LEFT SIDE OF NECK
◂ FRONT

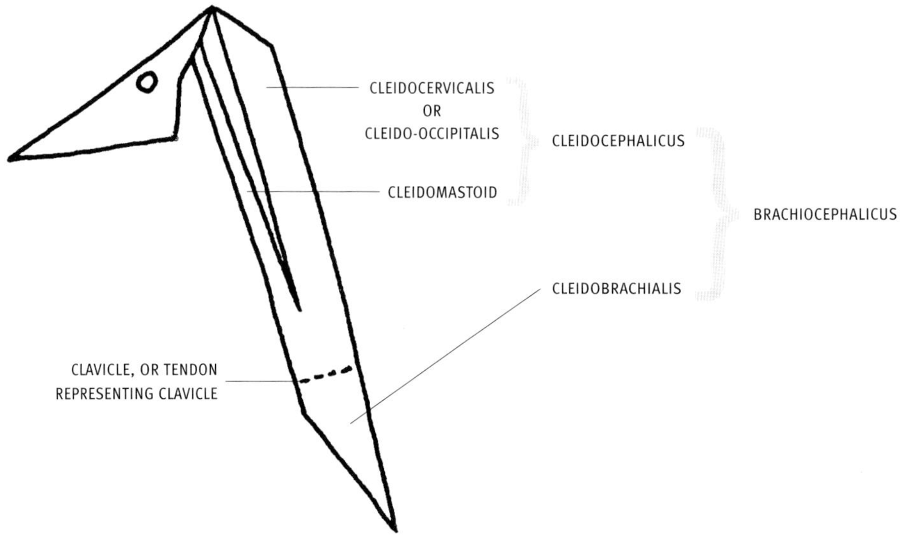

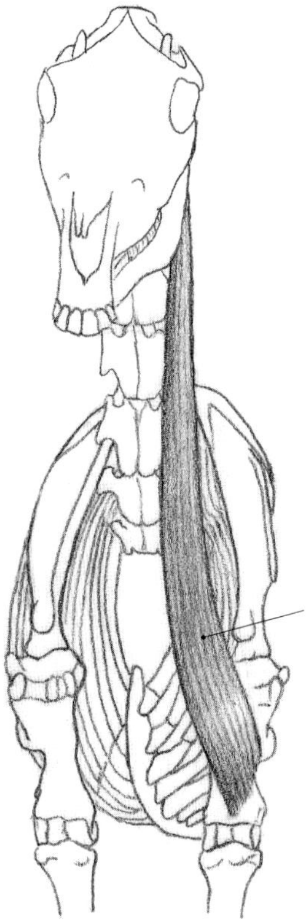

HORSE

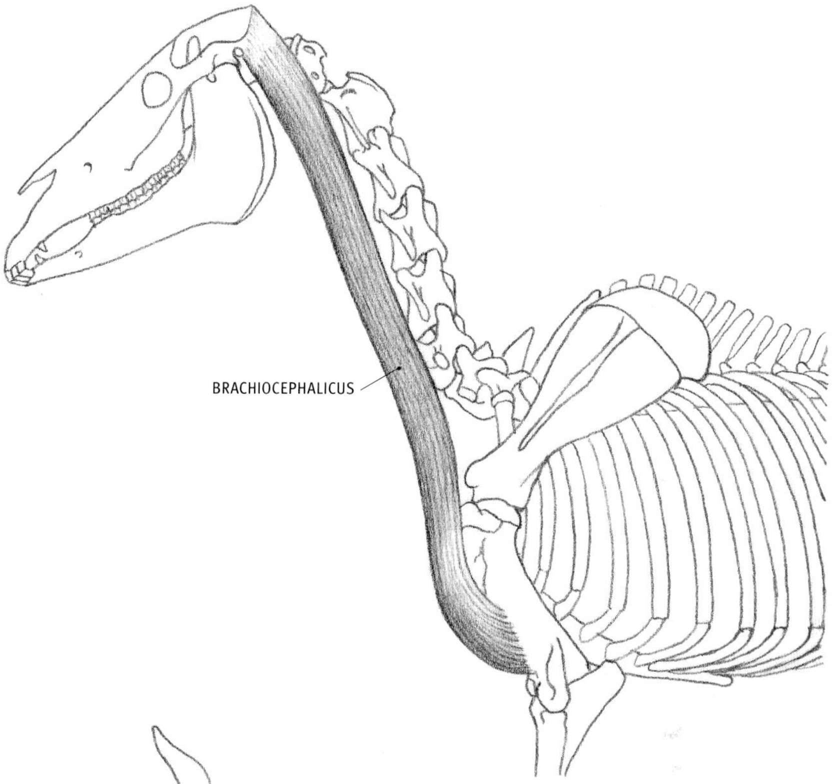

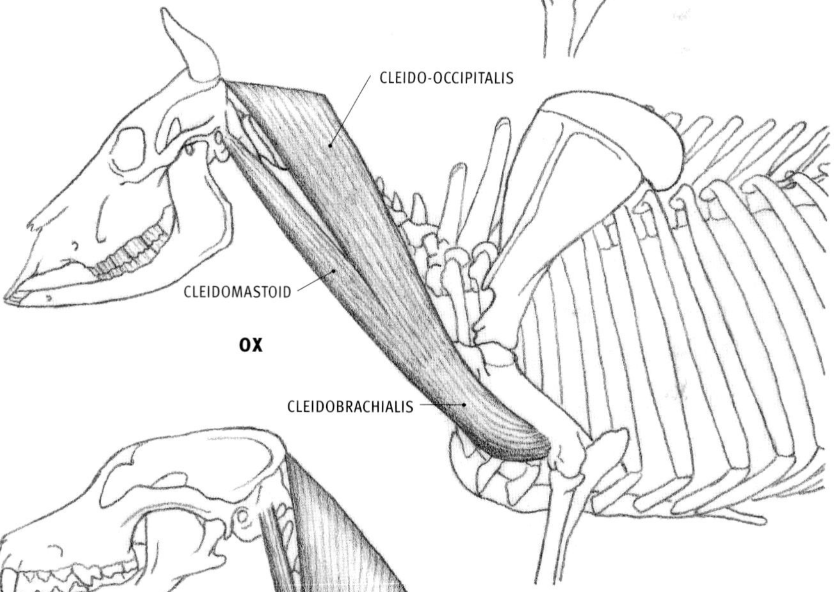

OX

BRACHIOCEPHALICUS SEPARATED INTO ITS COMPONENTS IN THE OX AND THE DOG

DOG

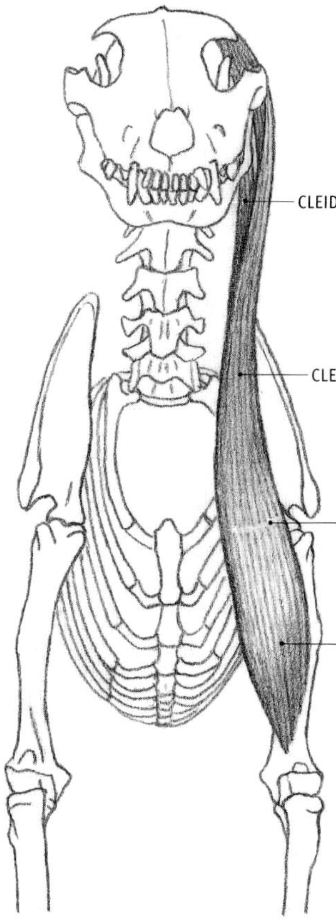

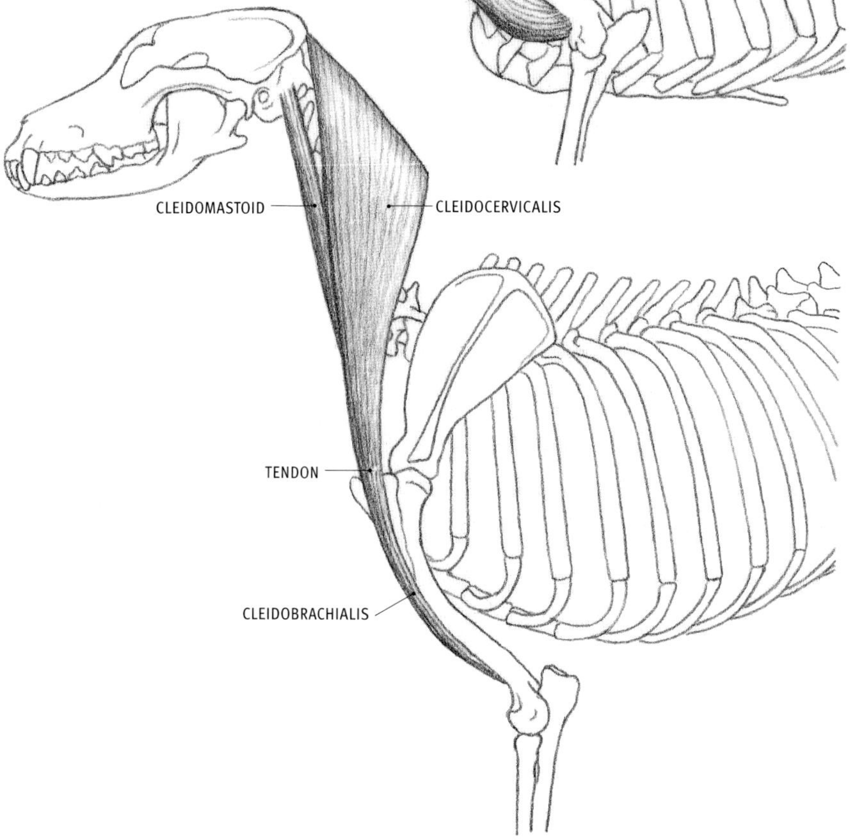

Anterior Neck Muscles

The sternohyoid, sternothyroid (together combined as the sternothyrohyoid in the horse and the ox) and omohyoid are long, narrow, straplike muscles that lie on the front of the neck and converge at the upper end of the front of the throat. These thin bands of muscle lie on the **trachea** (windpipe) and pass over the **thyroid cartilage** ("Adam's apple")

The **hyoid bone** is composed of a number of thin bones that are suspended from the rear end of the base of the skull. The sternohyoid, omohyoid, and mylohyoid attach to a roughly "U" shaped portion of the hyoid bone that wraps around the upper end of the throat. The hyoid bone is hidden from view behind the lower jaw in the horse and the ox, but it is seen in the dog and the feline in the side view. Loose skin folds on the front of the neck and the bottom of the jaw often obscure the hyoid bone and its attached muscles.

Sternothyrohyoid

HORSE AND OX

• Origin: Cartilage at the front end of the sternum.
• Insertion: Hyoid bone, thyroid cartilage.
• Action: Pulls the hyoid bone, and the tongue which is connected to it, downward and rearward.
• Structure: The sternothyrohyoid passes from the throat to the sternum, and consists of the combined sternothyroid and sternohyoid. It remains in contact with its fellow of the other side of the body, on the front of the neck, throughout their lengths. The lower end of the muscle at the sternum begins as a single belly, and is covered by the sternocephalicus. Near the throat, it splits and sends a narrow side branch to the thyroid cartilage (the sternothyroid). The larger inner branch (the sternohyoid) inserts onto the bottom of the hyoid bone in common with the omohyoid.

Sternohyoid

DOG AND FELINE

• Origin: Deep surface of the front end of the sternum and the front edge of the cartilage of the first rib.
• Insertion: Hyoid bone.
• Structure: Only the sternohyoid comes to the surface; the sternothyroid is deep. The bulge of the thyroid cartilage may be seen through the muscle at the upper end of the neck, when not obscured by loose skin folds.

Omohyoid

HORSE

• Origin: Deep surface of the supraspinatus and the subclavius muscles, just above the level of the shoulder joint.
• Insertion: Hyoid bone, in common with the sternohyoid.
• Structure: The omohyoid begins deep to the shoulder and only comes to the surface on the side of the throat. It emerges from under the brachiocephalicus, crosses the trachea on a diagonal line, and inserts onto the hyoid bone. This muscle is not superficial in the other species.

Mylohyoid

DOG AND FELINE

• Origin: Inside surface of the lower jaw, just below the tooth sockets.
• Insertion: Into the same muscle of the other side, along the midline, and then into the hyoid bone.
• Action: Raises the floor of the mouth and the tongue; pulls the hyoid bone forward.
• Structure: The mylohyoid forms the downward bulging floor of the mouth. Both sides together form a sling under the lower jaw. This sling drops down below the level of the lower jaw and therefore forms part of the profile of the throat when not obscured by loose skin folds.

The mylohyoid of the ox may drop slightly below the lower edge of the jaw, whereas in the horse is does not, and therefore does not participate in creating the profile.

HORSE

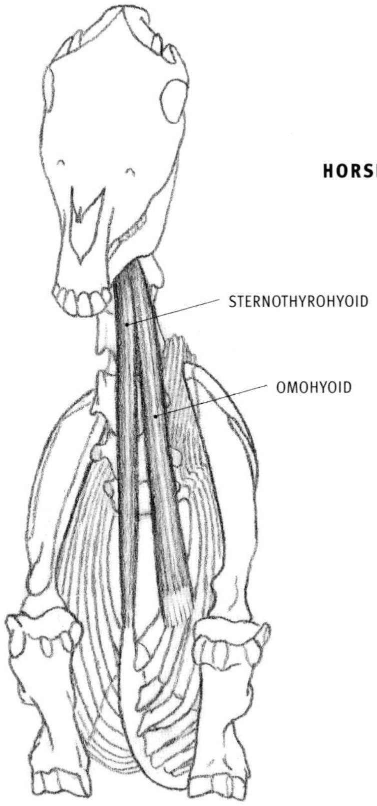

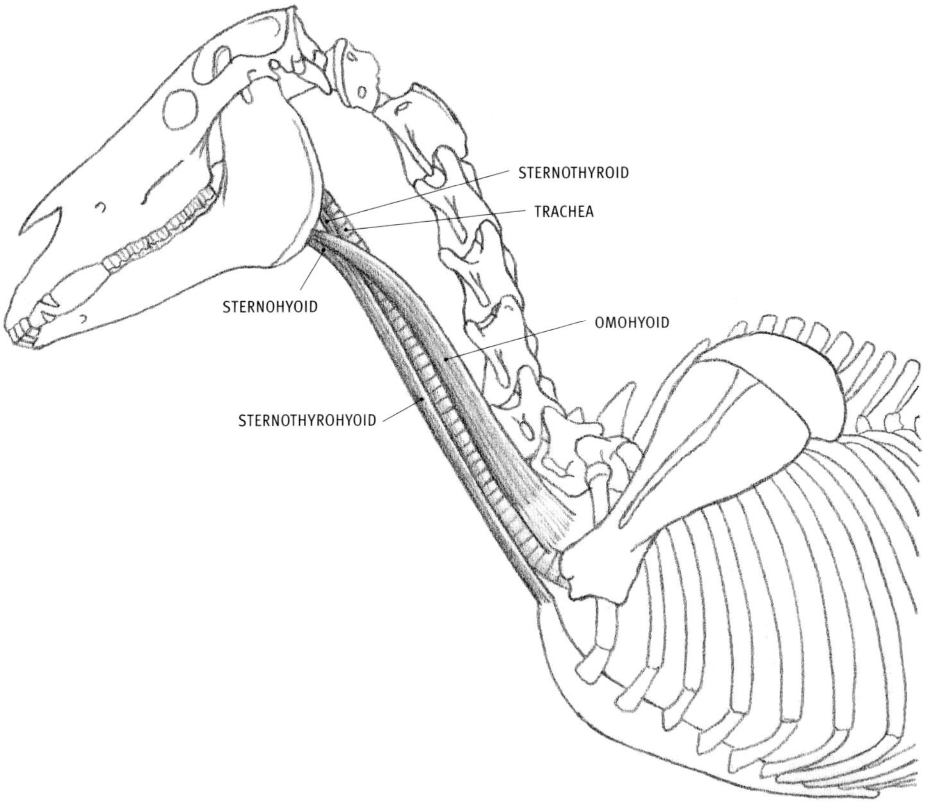

DOG

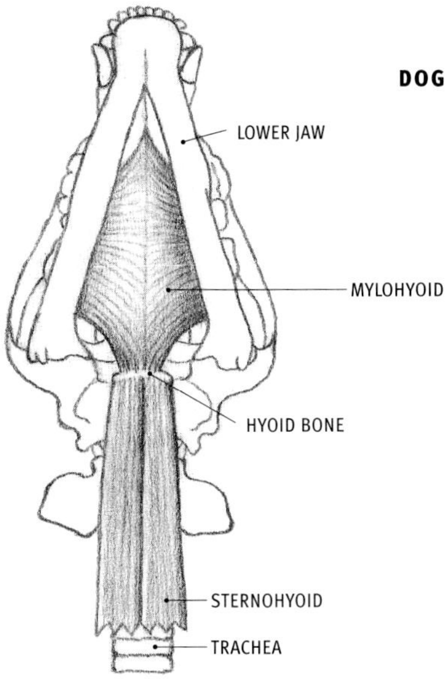

BOTTOM VIEW

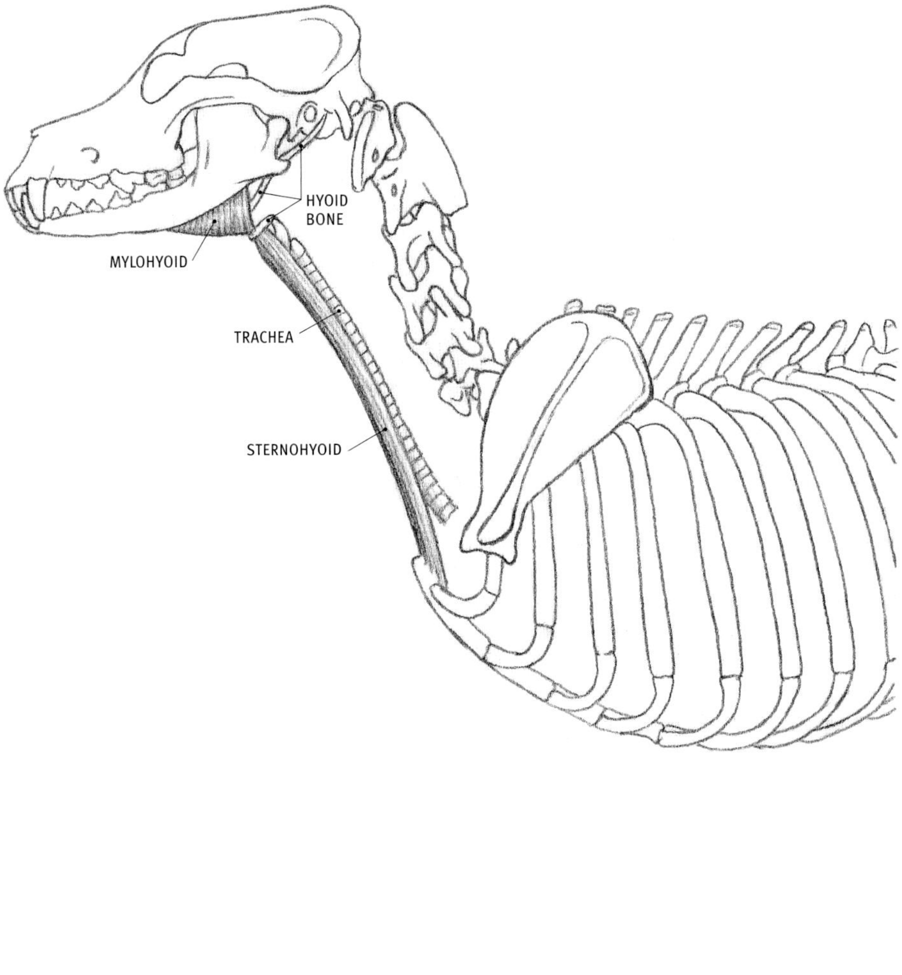

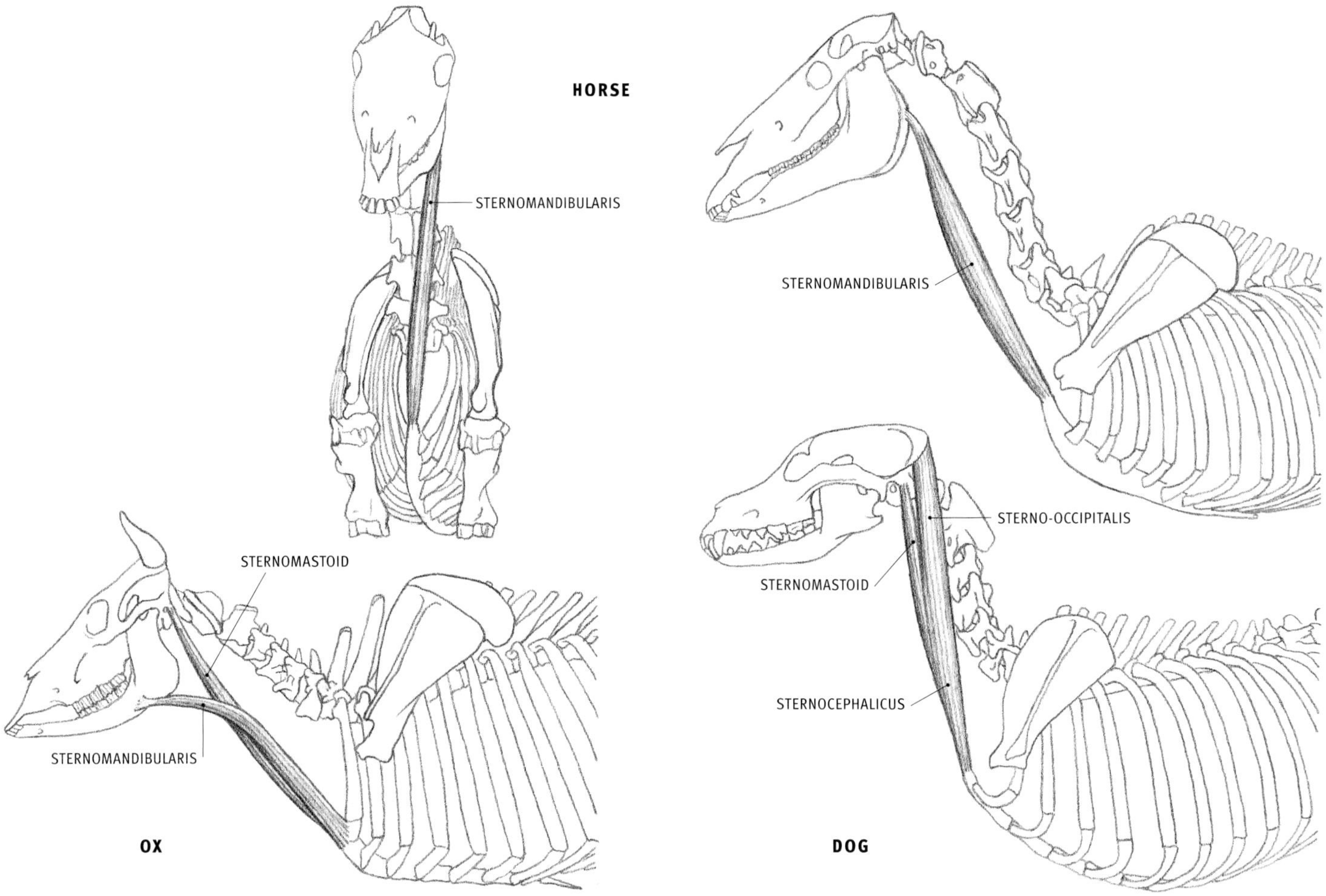

Sternocephalicus

The sternocephalicus ("sternum-to-head" muscle) is the general name for the muscle that begins on the front end of the sternum (the manubrium) and ends on various parts of the skull. When it inserts onto the lower jaw, or mandible, it is called the **sternomandibularis**; onto the mastoid process on the base of the skull, the **sternomastoid**; and onto the occipital bone on the upper rear edge of the skull, the **sterno-occipitalis**.

HORSE **(Sternomandibularis)**

• Origin: Cartilage at the front end of the sternum.
• Insertion: Halfway down the rear edge of the lower jaw.
• Action: Both sides together: Pull the head and neck downward. One side only: Pulls the head and neck to that side.
• Structure: The sternomandibularis is a long narrow muscle that passes up the neck from the midline on the front of the chest to the rear edge of the lower jaw. The muscles on each side of the body are initially in contact with each other beginning at the sternum; they then begin to separate and diverge one half to two thirds of the way up the neck. At its upper end, the muscle narrows and then disappears under the parotid gland, which lies on and behind the rear edge of the lower jaw. The jugular vein is located between the sternomandibularis and the brachiocephalicus. At a level just above the bottom of the lower jaw, the jugular vein sends a branch forward, which lies on the upper end of the sternocephalicus. This venous branch can appear as a furrow on the surface.

OX **(Sternomandibularis and Sternomastoid)**

• Origin: Front end of the sternum and the cartilage of the first rib.
• Insertion: Sternomandibularis: Lower edge of the lower jaw and the surface of the front edge of the masseter muscle. Sternomastoid: Base of the skull in the region behind the ear hole.
• Action: See above. Also opens the mouth by pulling the lower jaw downward.
• Structure: The sternocephalicus consists of two *separate* muscles—the sternomandibularis, which attaches to the lower jaw, and the sternomastoid, which attaches to the base of the skull. For most of the neck, the two muscles parallel each other; the sternomastoid lies to the inside of, and is partly overlapped by, the sternomandibularis. Below and behind the angle of the jaw, the sternomastoid continues upward, passing under the sternomandibularis on its way to its higher and deeper insertion on the base of the skull. The sternomastoid muscles of both sides of the body are in contact with each on the lower third of the front of the neck, where they come to the surface. Here they lie between the sternomandibularis muscles, which are not in contact with each other.

DOG AND FELINE **(Sternocephalicus)**

• Origin: Front end of the sternum, in common with the muscle of the other side of the body.
• Insertion: Sterno-occipitalis: Upper edge of the rear end of the skull. Sternomastoid: Base of the skull behind the ear hole (mastoid process).
• Structure: Most of the sternocephalicus, from its origin upward, is a single belly. Near the head, it separates into the wider, thinner sterno-occipitalis, and the tapering sternomastoid. The sternomastoid lies to the front of the sterno-occipitalis; it inserts on a deeper plane onto the base of the skull behind the ear hole. The sternocephalicus muscles of both sides of the body are in contact with each other for a short distance above the sternum before they diverge.

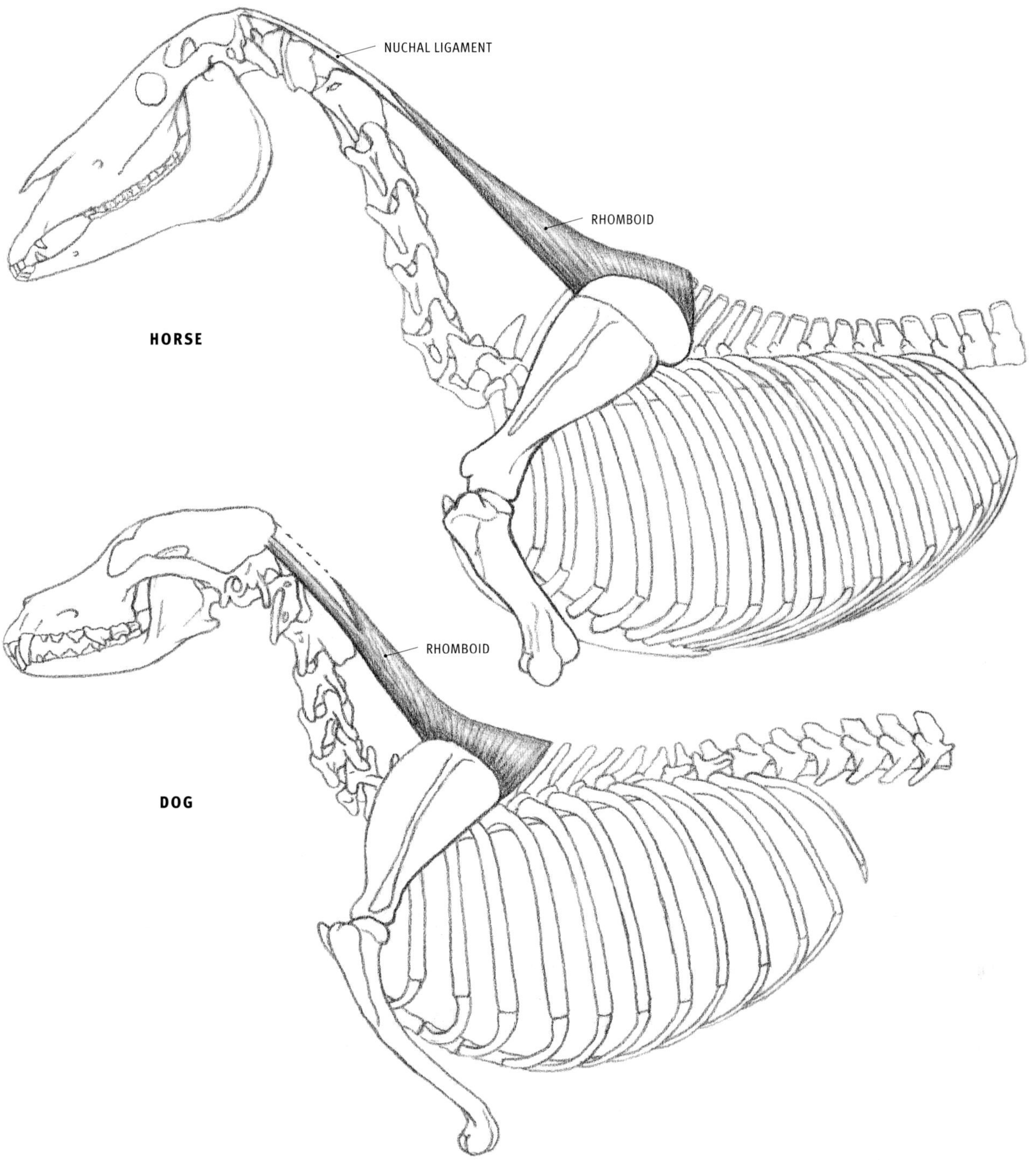

Rhomboid

HORSE

- Origin: The side of the lower two thirds of the nuchal ligament and the tips of the upward projections of the thoracic vertebrae and intervening ligament to the seventh thoracic vertebra.
- Insertion: Inner surface of the cartilage of the shoulder blade.
- Action: Pulls the upper end of the shoulder blade upward, forward, and against the body. When the shoulder is fixed, it lifts the neck; one side only pulls the neck to that side.
- Structure: The rhomboid is an irregular four-sided muscle with an extremely pointed front end. It consists of two parts (neck and chest parts), which are continuous, and is here treated as a single structure. The portion on the neck is long and narrow. Its tip is superficial—the remainder can be distinctly seen under the trapezius as an elongated triangular form, widest where it meets the shoulder blade.

OX

- Origin: The side of the rear two thirds of the nuchal ligament and the tips of the upward projections of the thoracic vertebrae and intervening ligament to the fifth thoracic vertebra.
- Structure: The rhomboid is completely covered by the trapezius. Its form can be detected as an elongated triangle on the side of the neck, under cover of the trapezius.

DOG AND FELINE

- Origin: Midline on the back of the neck and shoulder from approximately the second neck vertebra to the sixth thoracic vertebra; base of the skull.
- Insertion: Upper edge of the shoulder blade.
- Structure: The rhomboid is also covered completely by the trapezius. It is thicker in the dog and the feline than in the horse and the ox. The neck portion sends a separate outer muscular band to the base of the skull, attaching a short distance away from the midline. The rhomboid is not seen under the trapezius as a distinct form, but rather adds a muscular fullness to the back of the neck in front of the shoulder.

HORSE

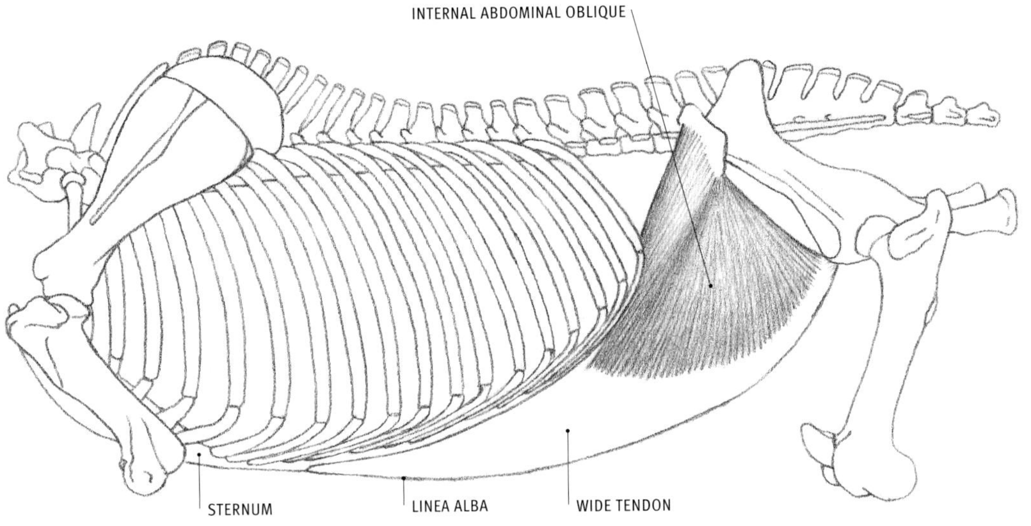

OX

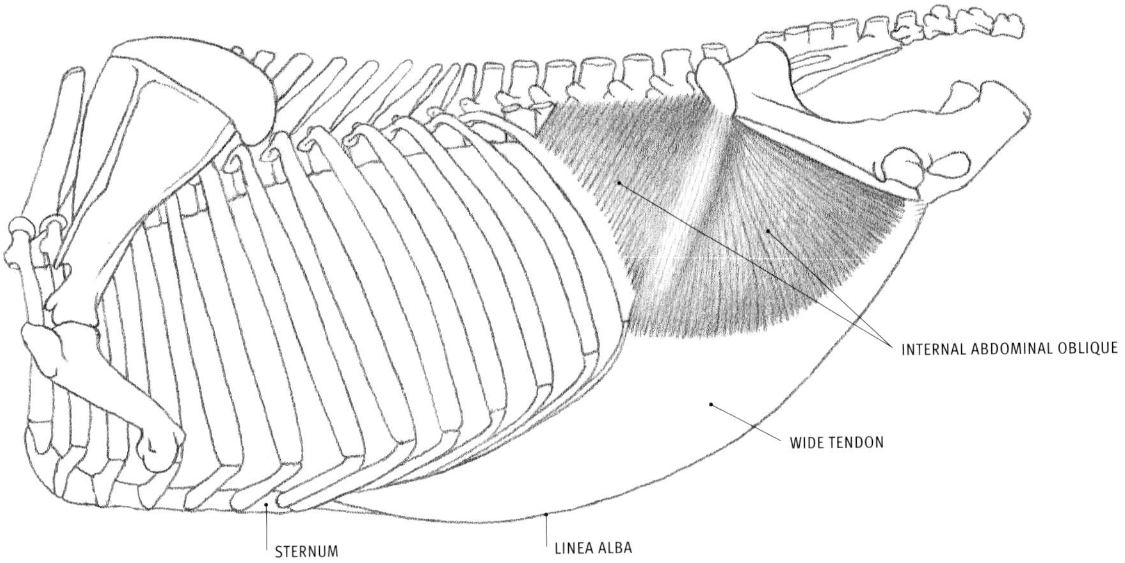

Internal abdominal oblique (Obliquus internus abdominis)

HORSE

- Origin: Outer expansion of the front of the pelvis ("point of the hip")
- Insertion: Inner surface of the cartilage of the last four or five ribs, and by its wide tendon, into the midline on the bottom of the abdomen (linea alba) and the front end of the bottom of the pelvis.
- Action: Compresses the abdomen and supports its contents; assists in bending the spine to one side.
- Structure: The internal abdominal oblique is a triangular, fan-shaped muscle that develops a large, wide tendon. The muscular portion is located on the upper portion of the side of the abdomen. The muscle and tendon of both sides of the body form a continuous sling that passes under the abdomen and passively supports the abdominal contents when relaxed, or compresses them when the muscle is tensed. The wide tendons from each side of the body fuse on the abdominal midline, contributing to the linea alba. The **linea alba** is a tendinous thickening of the midline of the abdomen that passes from the rear end of the sternum to the front of the bottom of the pelvis (pubic bone). It is formed primarily by the fusion of the wide tendons of this muscle and the external abdominal oblique.

OX

- Origin: Also from the surface of the lumbar spinal muscle (longissimus).
- Insertion: Most of the rear edge of the last rib and its cartilage, and by its wide tendon into the midline on the bottom of the abdomen (linea alba) and the front end of the bottom of the pelvis.
- Structure: This muscle is irregular in shape rather than triangular. Muscle fibers descending downward and forward from the point of the hip form a raised relief, called the **"cord of the flank."** This ridge borders the rear side of a triangular depression, the **"hollow of the flank."** The lumbar spinal muscles border the top of the hollow, and the last rib defines its front border. The cord and the hollow are usually subtle or absent in the horse, but they can be quite prominent in the ox, with the cord separating into two or three separate forms radiating from the point of the hip. Muscle fibers of both the internal and external abdominal obliques are present in the hollow, filling the space between the rib cage and the pelvis. This distance is greater in the ox than in the horse.

DOG AND FELINE

- Origin: Side of the spinal muscle in the lumbar region; lower end of the crest of the ilium at the front of the pelvis.
- Insertion: Lower end of the last rib and the midline of the abdomen via the wide tendon.
- Structure: The internal abdominal oblique lies inconspicuously on the side of the abdomen, mostly under cover of the external abdominal oblique. It does not produce the cord of the flank or the hollow of the flank.

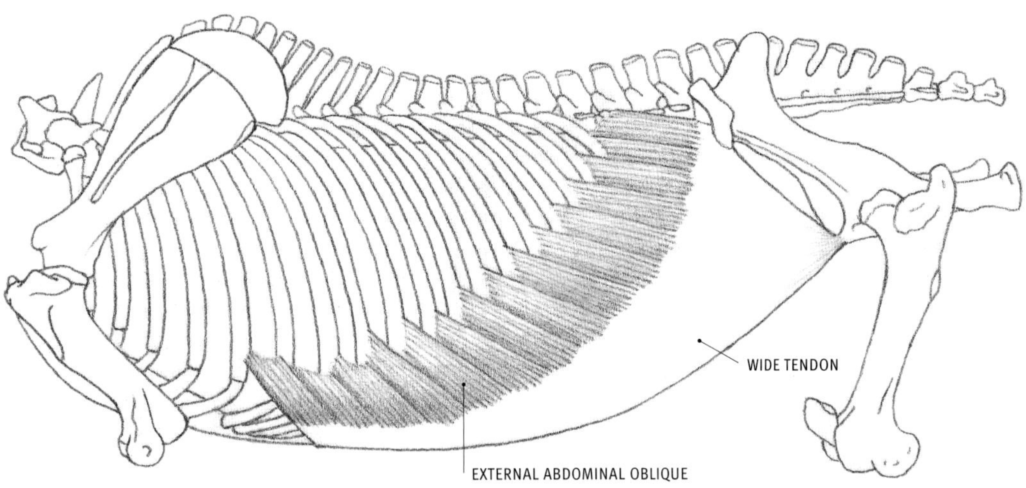

HORSE

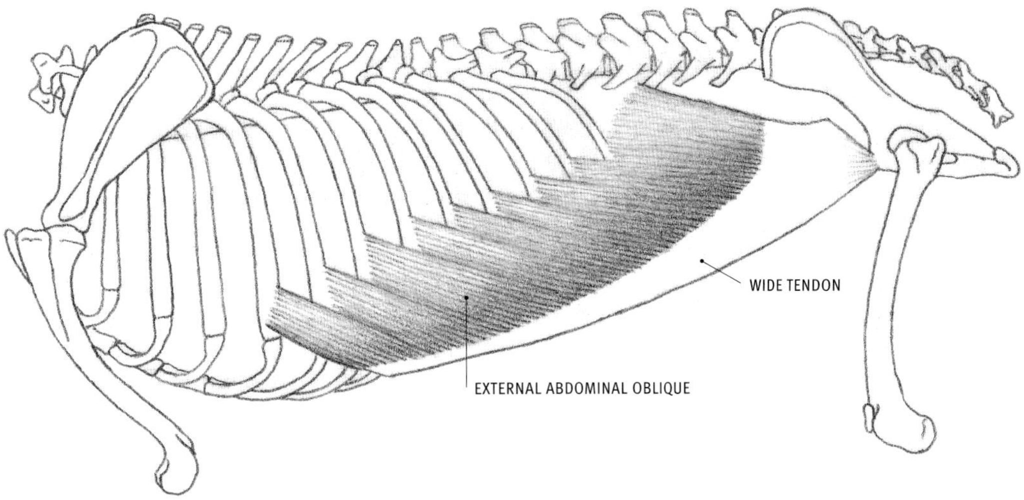

DOG

External abdominal oblique (Obliquus externus abdominis)

HORSE

• Origin: Rear edge of the outer surface of the last fourteen ribs, the fascia between the ribs, and the side of the surface of the spinal muscles in the lumbar region. The position of the origin gets progressively lower on each rib toward the front of the body.

• Insertion: The midline of the abdomen (linea alba), from the sternum to the front end of the bottom of the pelvis (pubic bone), and the outer expansion of the front end of the pelvis (point of the hip).

• Action: Compresses the abdomen; flexes the trunk (primarily at the lumbar vertebrae); one side only bends the trunk toward that side.

• Structure: The external abdominal oblique is a large muscle composed of a muscular band, that curves upward on the side of the body, and an extensive tendon. It embraces part of the side of the rib cage and the entire abdomen. The lower edge of the muscular portion curves upward toward the point of the hip. The front of the muscular portion forms four units whose ends alternate (interdigitate) with the forms of the serratus ventralis thoracis; the forms of both muscles are oriented in roughly the same direction. The remainder intersects with the forms of the ribs, where they meet at a wide angle. The location of the insertion of the muscular fibers into its wide tendon on the side of the abdomen may be seen on the surface, especially during exertion. The wide tendon of the external abdominal oblique fuses to the wide tendon of the underlying internal abdominal oblique; the combined tendon passes over the rectus abdominis muscle to reach the midline of the abdomen. The front portion of the muscular portion of the external abdominal oblique overlaps the flat belly of the rectus abdominis.

OX

• Origin: Rear edge of the outer surface of the last eight ribs and the fascia between the ribs.

• Structure: The upper edge of the muscle in the lumbar region lies just below the level of the point of the hip, but its wide tendon reaches up to insert into it.

DOG AND FELINE

• Origin: Last nine or ten ribs, the fascia between the ribs, and the side of the surface of the spinal muscles in the lumbar region.

• Insertion: The midline of the abdomen (linea alba), from the sternum to the front end of the bottom of the pelvis (pubic bone), and from a short ligament passing upward and forward from the pubic bone.

• Structure: There is no insertion into the upper front end of the pelvis. In the dog, the tips of the originating fibers of the front portion of the muscle (on the side of the rib cage) are covered by the latissimus dorsi muscle. In the feline, the entire origin from all the ribs is covered.

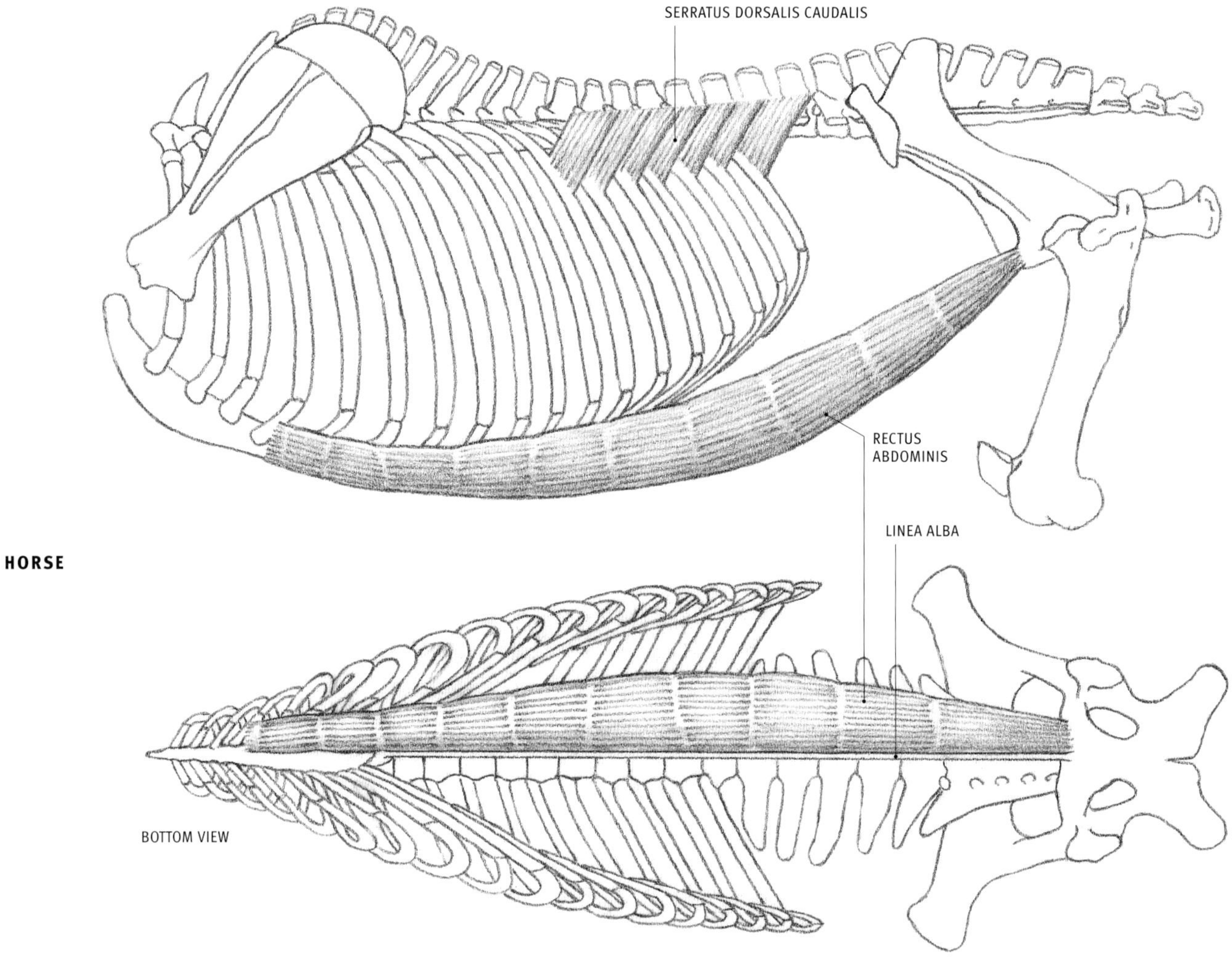

Rectus abdominis

HORSE

• Origin: Cartilage of the fourth to the ninth ribs and the adjacent area on the sternum.

• Insertion: Front end of the bottom of the pelvis (pubic bone).

• Action: Flexes the trunk, primarily in the lumbar region; compresses the abdomen.

• Structure: The rectus abdominis is a long, straplike muscle, lying on the bottom of the abdomen. Widest at its middle, it passes from the bottom of the rib cage to the bottom of the pelvis. Several tendinous bands are embedded across the belly, functionally separating it into a series of short muscular units, rather than one long muscle. The muscle bellies of both sides of the body are separated by a narrow, fibrous band called the **linea alba**, which is formed primarily by the fusion of the wide tendons of the abdominal muscles that pass over and under the rectus abdominis.

OX

• Origin: Outer edge of the sternum, from the level of the third rib cartilage continuing rearward.

DOG AND FELINE

• Origin: Dog: First rib and its cartilage, and the sternum. Feline: Cartilage of the first and second ribs, and the sternum.

• Structure: The muscle belly is widest toward the front, more so in the dog than in the feline.

Serratus dorsalis caudalis

• Origin: Surface of the spinal muscle in the region of the middle of the back.

• Insertion: Upper ends of the last few ribs, ranging from the last four to nine ribs, depending on the species.

• Action: Pulls the ribs rearward, assisting in exhaling.

• Structure: The muscle is insignificant in its effect on the surface. It is included here because its rear portion lies just under the skin.

HORSE

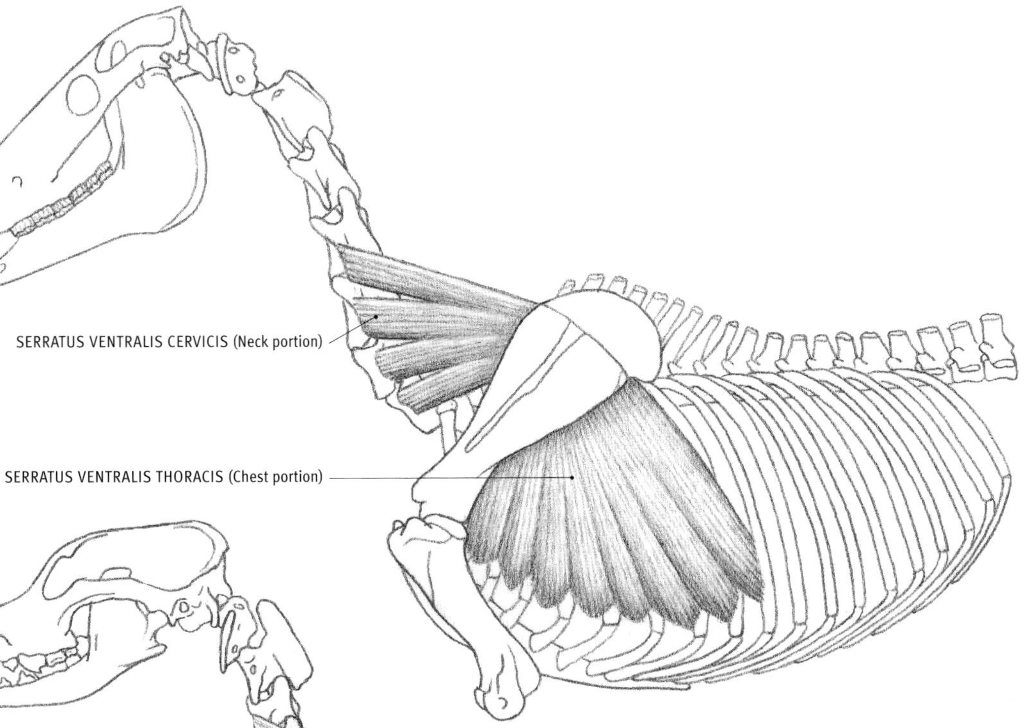

DOG

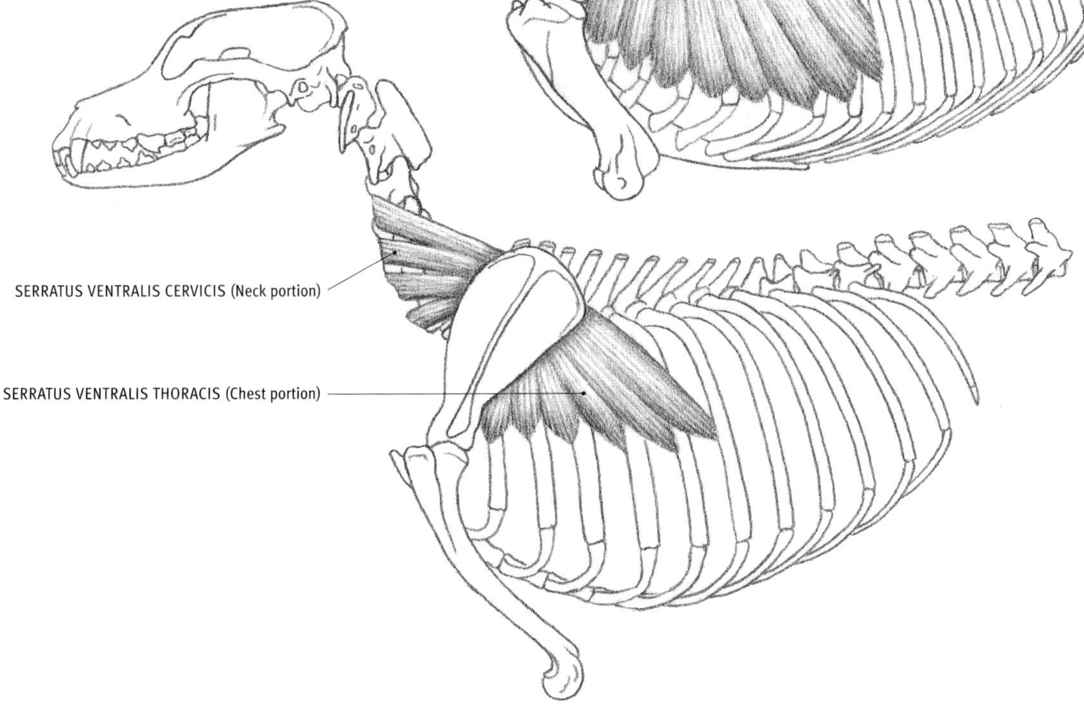

Serratus ventralis (cervicis & thoracis)

HORSE

• Origin: Neck portion: Sides of the third or fourth to the seventh neck vertebrae. Chest portion: Sides of the lower ends of the first eight or nine ribs.

• Insertion: Deep surface of the upper half of the bony shoulder blade, and a narrow strip of the adjacent cartilage.

• Action: Neck portion: Pulls the upper end of the shoulder blade forward; lifts the neck; bends the neck to one side. Chest portion: Pulls the upper end of the shoulder blade backward and downward, which can rotate the shoulder blade, advancing the shoulder joint. The chest portion on both sides of the body forms an interrupted sling, between the upper ends of both shoulder blades, which supports the body. Both sides together raise the chest.

• Structure: The serratus ventralis is divided into distinct neck and chest portions. The **neck portion** (serratus ventralis cervicis), divisible into several converging bundles, comes to the surface on the side of the neck between the trapezius and the brachiocephalicus. It is homologous to the levator scapulae in humans. The **chest portion** (serratus ventralis thoracis, serratus magnus) is a fan-shaped muscle connecting the upper end of the shoulder blade to the side of the rib cage. Its lower rear portion becomes superficial where it emerges from under the latissimus dorsi. The muscular bulk of the chest portion can be seen under the latissimus, to the rear of the triceps muscle. The pointed tips of the last four segments alternate (interdigitate) with the originating ends of the segments of the external abdominal oblique, giving the lower border of the serratus a saw-like "serrated" edge.

OX

• Structure: The neck portion is covered by a layer of muscle. The chest portion projects beyond the lower edge of the latissimus dorsi. The pectoralis ascendens covers the lower ends of the forward segments of the chest portion.

DOG AND FELINE

• Structure: The entire serratus ventralis is covered by other muscles. The chest portion, covered by the latissimus dorsi, adds a muscular fullness on the side of the rib cage to the rear of the shoulder blade. It also conceals the forms of the underlying individual ribs. Those ribs covered only by the latissimus may often be seen on the surface. The attachments are very similar to those of the horse.

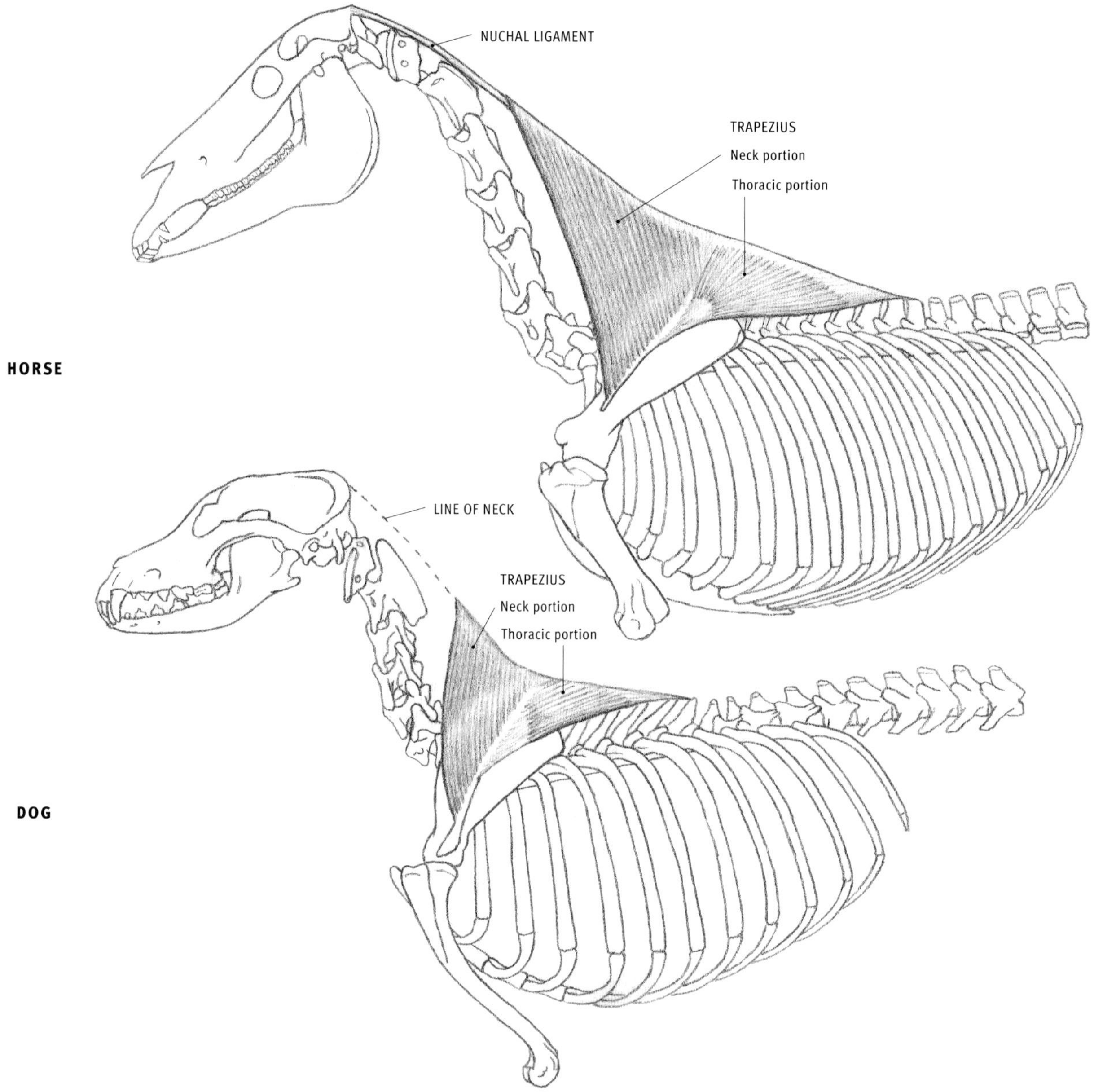

Trapezius

HORSE

• Origin: Single, continuous line of origin on the midline of the back of the neck and chest for the entire muscle. Neck portion: On the nuchal ligament from the level of the second neck vertebra to the top of the shoulder. Thoracic portion: Along the tips of the thoracic vertebrae and intervening ligament from the shoulder to the middle of the chest.
• Insertion: Neck portion: Entire elongated raised ridge (spine) of the shoulder blade. Thoracic portion: Bony expansion one third of the way down the spine of the shoulder blade.
• Action: Entire muscle pulls the shoulder blade upward; it can also hold the shoulder blade against the body. The neck portion pulls it upward and forward; the thoracic portion pulls it upward and rearward.
• Structure: The trapezius is a large, flat, thin, triangular muscle that is further divided into two smaller triangles by an intervening narrow tendinous area. The front triangle defines the **neck portion** and the rear triangle the **thoracic portion**. The entire length of the originating end of the muscle begins as a tendinous band before becoming a muscular sheet. The thoracic portion becomes tendinous again before inserting into the expansion of the spine. The larger neck portion inserts lower down on the spine of the shoulder blade than the thoracic portion. The trapezius is usually not seen defined on the surface, allowing the underlying structures to be seen through its thin layer. The lower edge of the thoracic portion may occasionally be seen directly.

OX

• Structure: The trapezius is thicker in the ox, and begins on the neck closer to the base of the skull than in the horse. The two portions are also less distinct. The upper part of the front edge is in contact with the brachiocephalicus, closing up the interval present in the horse, which allows deeper neck muscles to come to the surface.

DOG AND FELINE

• Origin: Midline of the lower portion of the back of the neck and the front portion of the thorax, from the third neck vertebra to the ninth thoracic vertebra in the dog, and from the second neck vertebra to the twelfth thoracic vertebra in the feline.
• Insertion: Neck portion: Upper three-fourths of the spine of the shoulder blade. Thoracic portion: Dog: Upper one third of the spine; Feline: Bony expansion one third of the way down the spine.
• Structure: The trapezius is thicker in the dog and the feline than in the horse; more so in the feline. The thoracic portion is thicker than the neck portion.

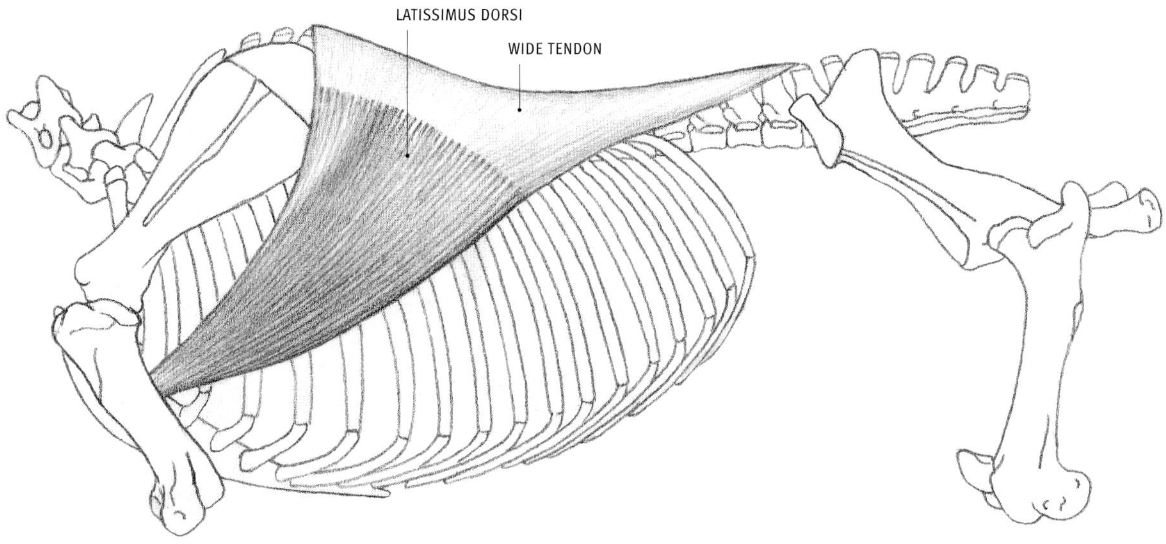

HORSE

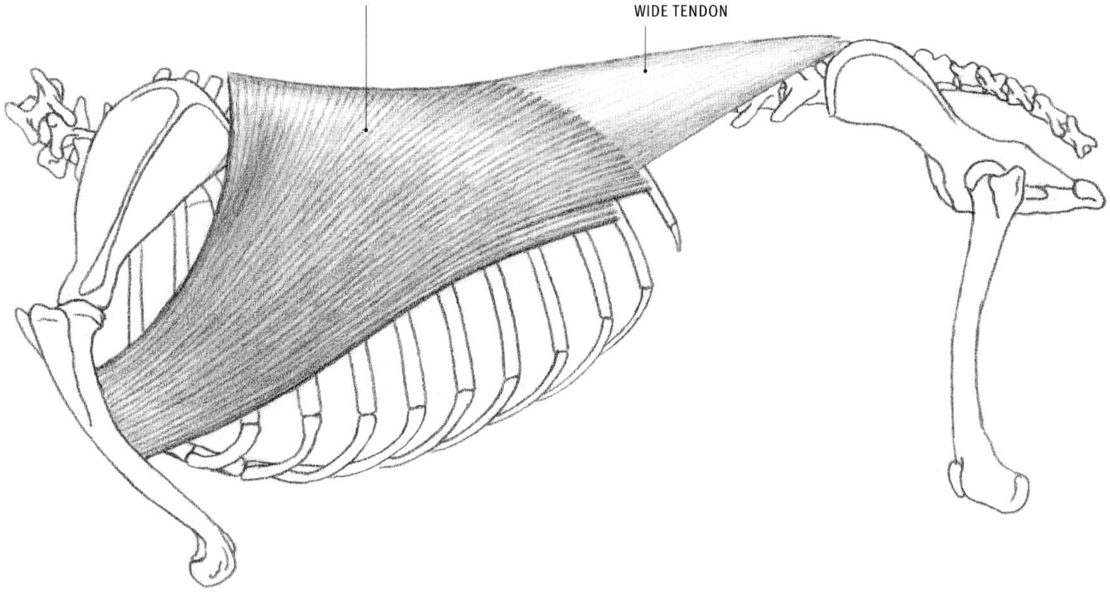

DOG

Latissimus dorsi

HORSE

• Origin: Surface of the spinal muscles from the top of the shoulder through the lumbar region (ultimately from the tips of the vertebrae in this region).

• Insertion: Inner surface of the humerus, slightly less than halfway down the bone, in common with the teres major.

• Action: Flexes the shoulder joint, pulling the humerus upward and back; pulls the body forward when the front limb is advanced and set firmly on the ground.

• Structure: The latissimus dorsi is a large, thin, triangular muscle that lies on the side of the chest. Because it is relatively thin, it allows the mass of the serratus ventralis and the forms of the individual ribs to be seen underneath. The diagonal lower edge of the muscle is often quite conspicuous in life as it passes over the ribs and then over the segments of the serratus ventralis (thoracis). The latissimus begins as a wide tendon fused to the fascia of the spinal muscles. The front free edge of the muscle emerges from under the trapezius and then passes over the upper rear corner of the shoulder blade (and over the infraspinatus). The latissimus narrows and thickens on its way to its insertion, and then disappears as it dives deep to the tensor fasciae antebrachii and triceps.

OX

• Origin: Also from the sides of ribs nine through twelve.

• Structure: The latissimus covers a larger surface area than in the horse.

DOG AND FELINE

• Origin: Dog only: Also from the last two or three ribs.

• Insertion: Inner surface of the humerus, approximately one third of the way down the bone, in common with the teres major. Also, into a tendinous arch that begins at the previous insertion, arches over the biceps, and expands to attach to the inner front corner of the upper half of the humerus. Because the lower extent of this arch ends approximately halfway down the humerus (further down in the feline), the lower edge of the latissimus, which can be visible on the surface, is seen to be directed much lower on the humerus than the bony insertion one third of the way down the humerus.

• Structure: The inserting end (front end) of the muscle is wider than in the horse (it tapers less), which brings the lower edge of the latissimus closer to the bottom of the chest before it passes under the triceps.

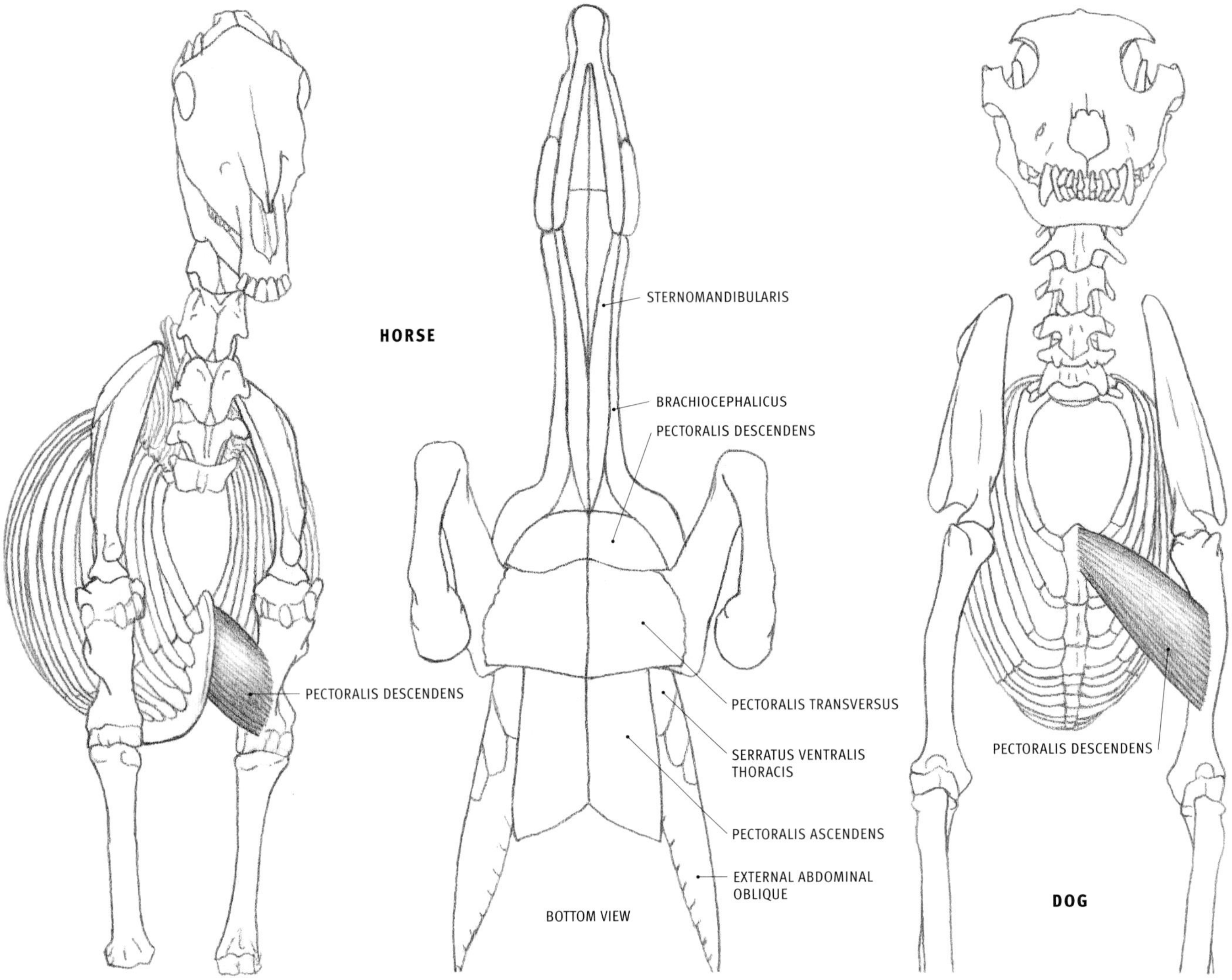

Pectoralis muscle group

The pectoralis muscle group consists basically of two major layers of muscle—the **superficial pectorals** (pectoralis descendens and pectoralis transversus in the horse, the ox, and the dog, plus the pectoantibrachialis in the feline) and the **deep pectorals** (subclavius and pectoralis ascendens in the horse and the ox; pectoralis profundus in the dog, and pectoralis profundus and xiphihumeralis in the feline). The superficial pectorals are homologous to the pectoralis major in humans, whereas the deep pectoral is represented by the human pectoralis minor. In animals, the pectorals are sometimes also called pectoralis major and minor. In the horse and the ox, the superficial and deep layers each have an anterior (front) portion and a posterior (rear) portion.

Pectoralis descendens

HORSE AND OX **(Anterior superficial pectoral)**

• Origin: Line on the front edge of the cartilage at the front end of the sternum (except the front tip), continuing back to the level of the second rib.
• Insertion: Diagonal line, inclined downward and inward, on the front of the lower half of the humerus, and the adjacent outer surface of the muscles of the limb.
• Action: Pulls the front limb toward the centerline of the body; advances the front limb.
• Structure: In the horse, the pectoralis descendens forms a thick, conspicuous, oval form on the front of the chest between the sternum and the lower end of the upper arm. It passes over the biceps to insert between the biceps and the brachialis. The bulging muscles of both sides of the body create a furrow on the midline of the chest at the bottom of which lies the sternum. The rear edge of the muscle overlaps the pectoralis transversus. In the ox, this muscle is thin and closely attached to the pectoralis transversus, which it overlaps.

DOG AND FELINE

• Origin: Front end of the sternum. Feline: Also from a tendinous line on the midline of the base of the neck in front of the tip of the sternum.
• Insertion: Short vertical line on the middle of the front of the humerus.
• Structure: The pectoralis descendens lies diagonally on top of the pectoralis transversus. It passes over the biceps and under the brachiocephalicus to insert on the humerus between the biceps and the brachialis.

In the feline, there is an additional superficial muscle, the **pectoantibrachialis** (see page 61), that lies on top of the two superficial pectorals. This narrow muscle originates on the sternum a short distance back from its tip and eventually tapers into a flat, thin tendon that passes over the forearm flexor muscles (on the inside of the elbow) before inserting into the ulna a short distance below the tip of the elbow. It lies alongside the edge of the brachiocephalicus.

HORSE

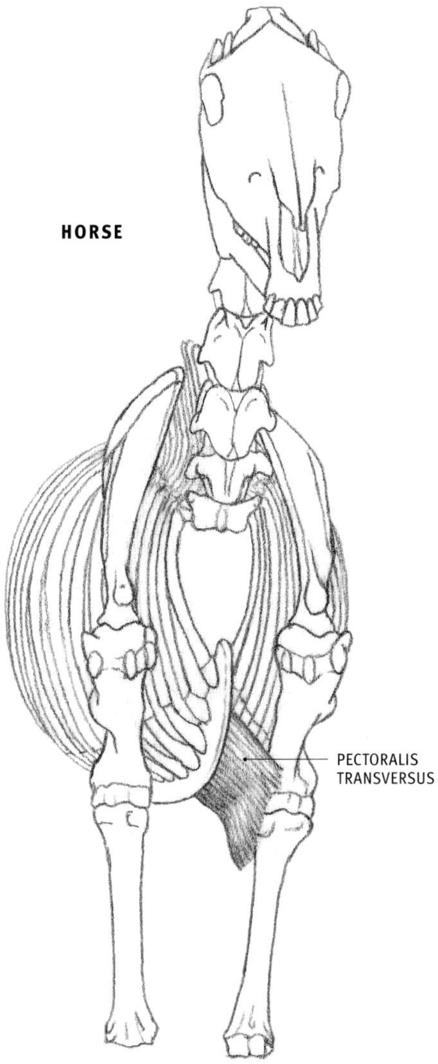

DOG

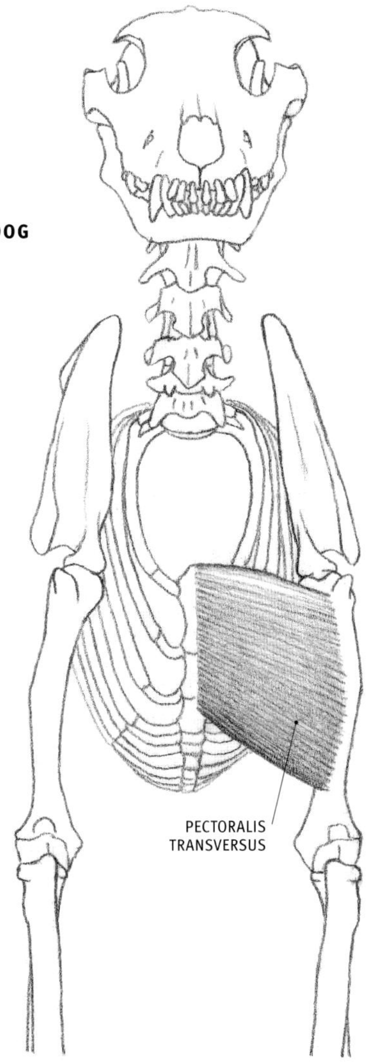

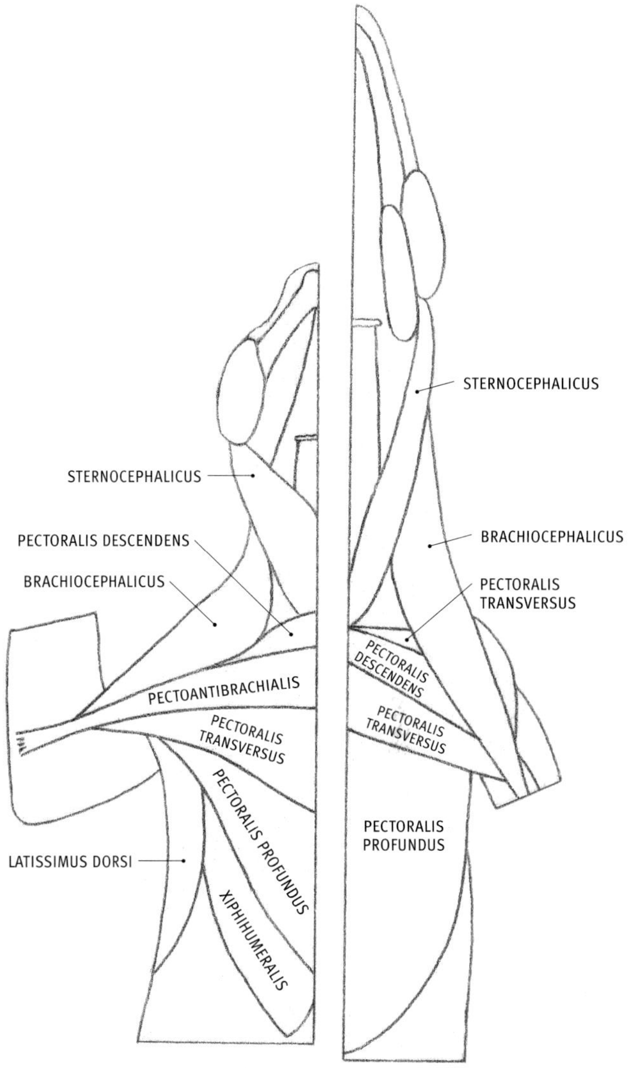

FELINE **DOG**

BOTTOM VIEWS

Pectoralis transversus

HORSE AND OX **(Posterior superficial pectoral)**

• Origin: Lower edge of the sternum, from the second to the sixth rib, and from an overlying fibrous partition on the midline of the chest (from which the muscles of both sides originate).

• Insertion: Primarily into the inner surface of the upper third of the forearm muscles. In the horse, a small portion at the front end of the muscle inserts directly into the front of the lower end of the humerus.

• Action: Pulls the front limb toward the centerline of the body.

• Structure: The pectoralis transversus is a rectangular muscular sheet sitting on the bottom of the chest, passing from the sternum to the inside of the elbow region and the upper end of the forearm. Its front edge is overlapped by the pectoralis descendens. This is a thin muscle in the ox.

DOG AND FELINE

• Origin: Front portion of the sternum, to the level of the fourth rib.

• Insertion: Line running down most of the front of the humerus.

• Structure: The pectoralis transversus is a flat, rectangular muscle that passes from the midline of the chest to the shaft of the humerus. Along with the pectoralis descendens (which lies on top of it in the dog), it passes over the biceps and under the brachiocephalicus to insert on the humerus between the biceps and the brachialis.

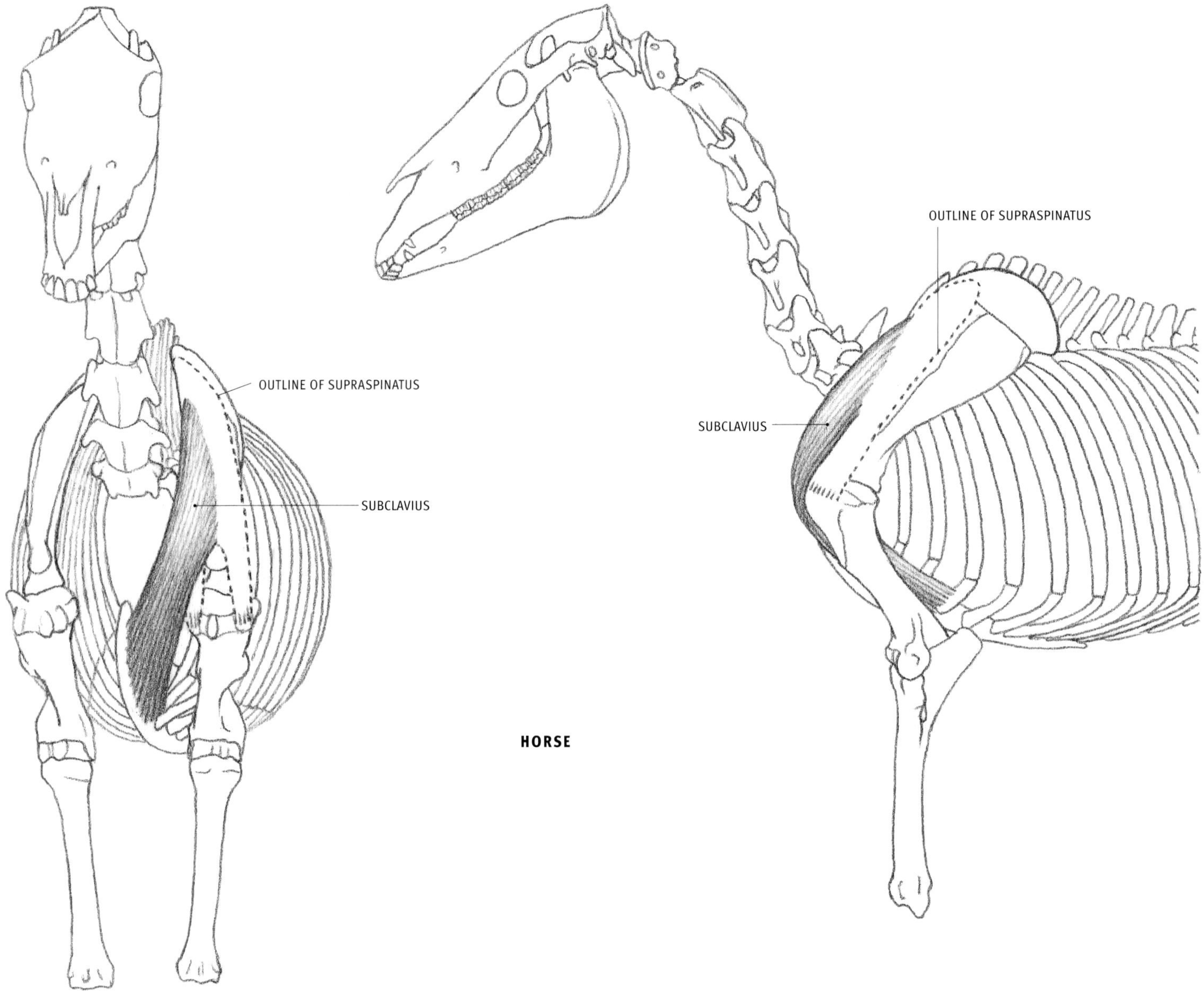

HORSE

Subclavius (Anterior deep pectoral)

HORSE

• Origin: Cartilages of the first four ribs and the adjacent sternum (exclusive of the front edge of the sternum and its front tip).

• Insertion: Upper front surface of the supraspinatus muscle, toward its inner side; there is no bony insertion.

• Action: Pulls the limb toward the centerline of the body; pulls the shoulder blade, and therefore the limb, backward. When the limb is advanced forward and set firmly on the ground, the subclavius pulls the body forward.

• Structure: The subclavius is a thick, powerful muscle that begins on the side of the chest and ends on the front of the shoulder. It passes upward, forward, and outward, then curves backward, ending on the surface of the supraspinatus. The center section of the upper portion is not covered by other muscle. It creates the forwardmost convex form of the shoulder muscles, which can be quite visible on the side of the base of the neck.

OX

• Origin: Cartilage and lower end of the first rib.

• Insertion: Deep surface of the brachiocephalicus, in the region of the front of the upper end of the humerus.

• Structure: The subclavius is a small, deep muscle not seen on the surface. It does not extend onto the surface of the supraspinatus, as in the horse.

The subclavius is not present in the dog or the feline.

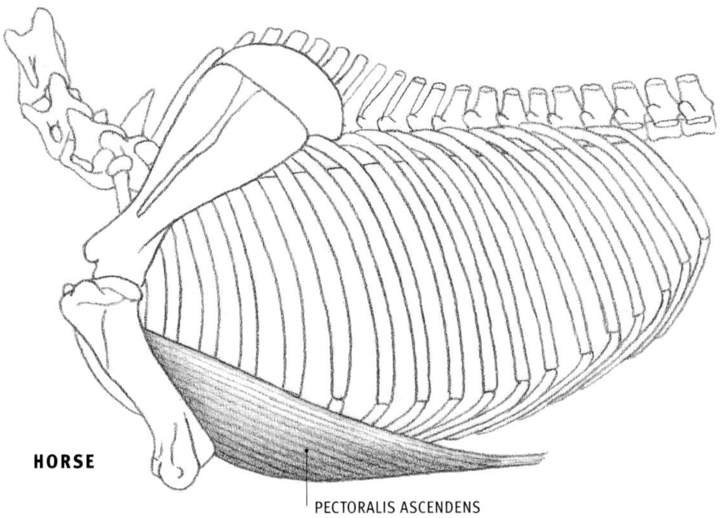

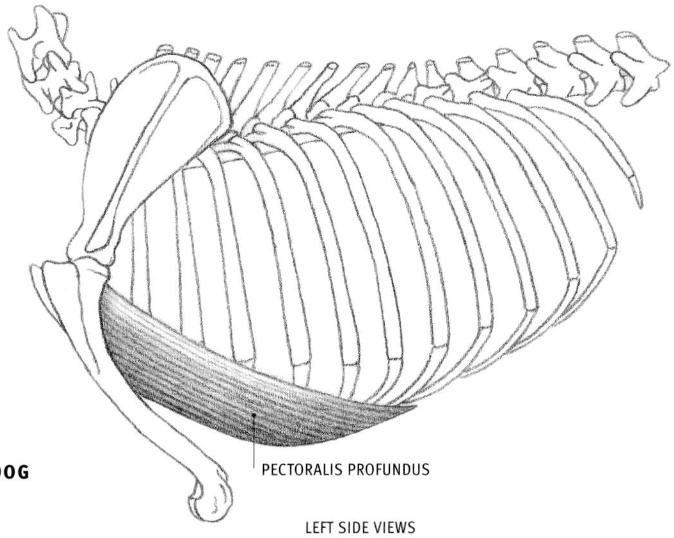

LEFT SIDE VIEWS

◂ FRONT

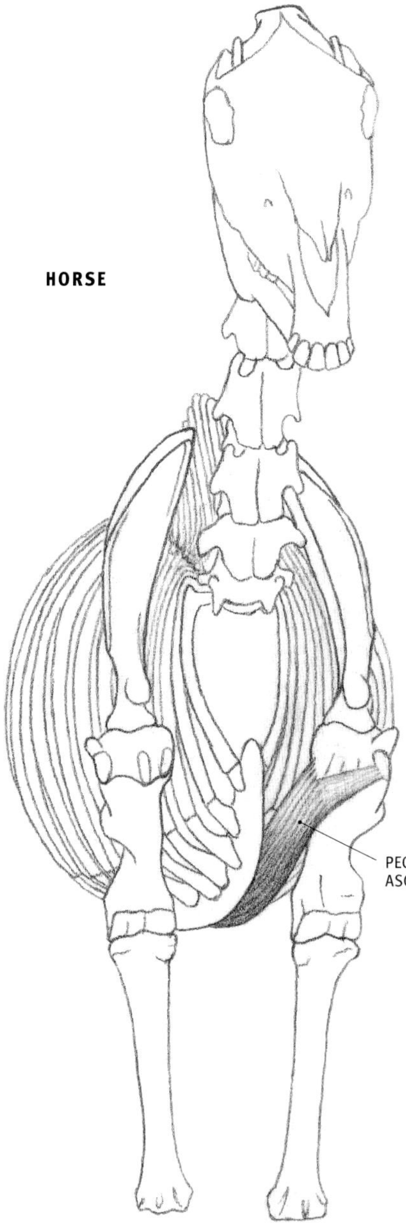

Pectoralis ascendens (Posterior deep pectoral)

HORSE

• Origin: Cartilage of the fourth through the ninth ribs and the adjacent surface of the sternum; the xiphoid cartilage at the rear end of the sternum; the surface of the front end of the abdomen.

• Insertion: Inner and outer front corners of the upper end of the humerus (and the adjacent tendon of origin of the coracobrachialis in the horse).

• Action: Pulls the limb toward the midline of the body; pulls the limb rearward. If the limb is advanced and set firmly on the ground, it pulls the body forward during walking or running.

• Structure: The pectoralis ascendens begins from a large area of attachment on the lower portion of the rib cage and the abdomen and converges on the upper end of the humerus. The muscle inserts primarily onto the inner front corner of the upper end of the humerus. Tendinous fibers continue over the biceps to insert onto the outer front corner. The pectoralis ascendens is roughly triangular, beginning as a thin and wide muscle that lies on the chest, and thickening as it ascends. The muscle is seen on the lower portion of the side of the chest, to the rear of the elbow and lower portion of the triceps. Its upper edge is directed to a point just below the shoulder joint. The front portion is covered by the superficial pectorals.

OX

• Origin: Surface of the sternum, beginning at the level of the second rib; a midline tendinous partition overlying this attachment; the surface of the front end of the abdomen.

Pectoralis profundus (Pectoralis minor)

DOG AND FELINE

• Origin: Most of the sternum (except its front tip) and from the surface of the front end of the abdomen (in the region of the xiphoid process).

• Insertion: Upper inner surface of the humerus, and onto a vertical line on the upper third to upper half of the front of the humerus.

• Structure: The pectoralis profundus is seen on the side of the lower portion of the chest, its upper edge directed toward the shoulder joint. In the feline, the portion at the outer edge of the muscle forms a separate division called the **xiphihumeralis**. Its inserting end passes deep to the remainder of the muscle (see diagram in "Pectoralis transversus," page 61) and ultimately inserts onto the upper portion of the humerus.

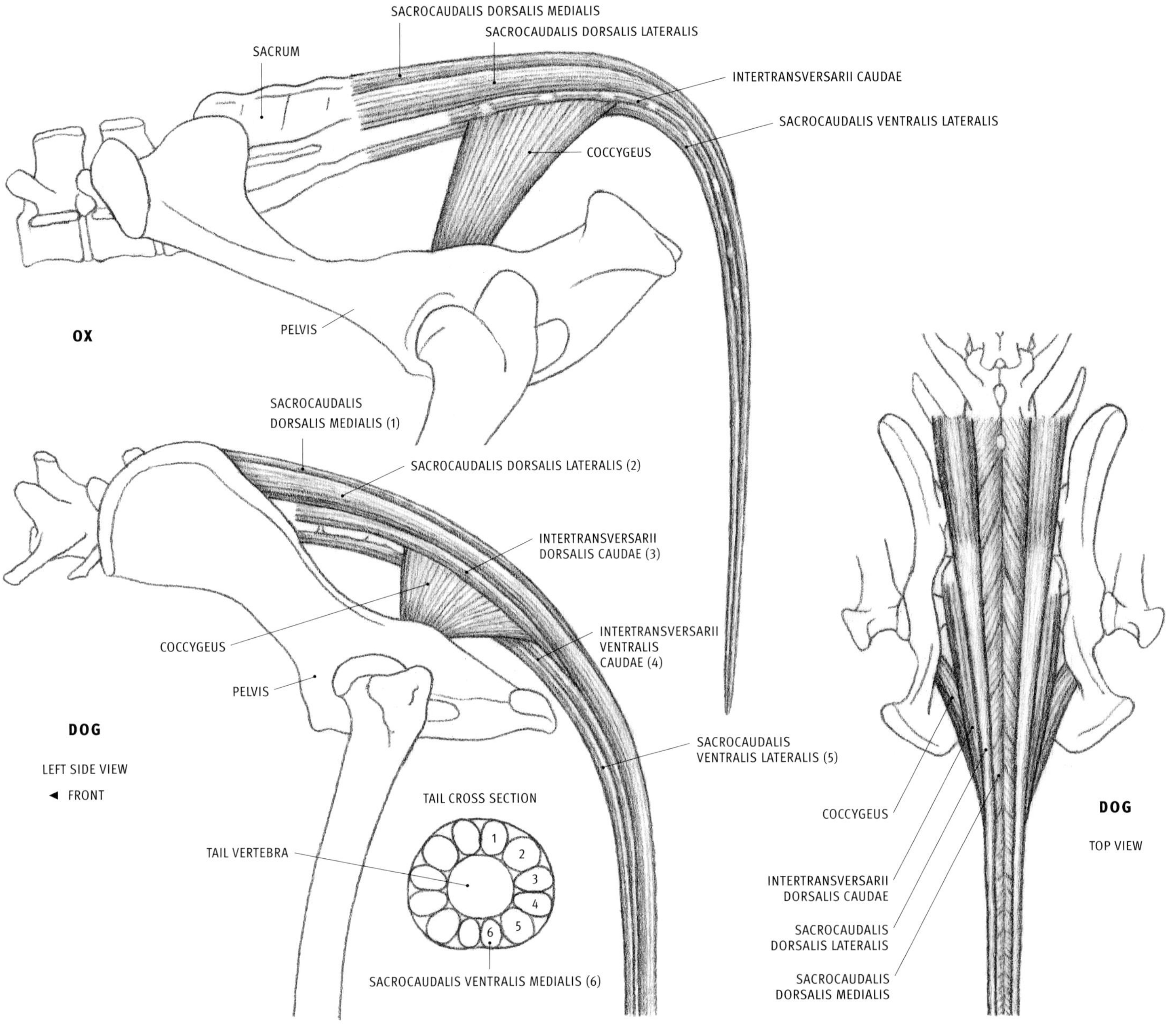

Tail muscles

The entire tail is surrounded by a total of twelve muscles—six per side of the body—that pass longitudinally and get thinner as they pass along its length. On one side of the body, they can be divided into three groups. Each group has a primary function—two elevators above, which extend the tail upward, the **sacrocaudalis dorsalis medialis and lateralis**; two lateral flexors on the side, which bend the tail to the side, the **intertransversarii dorsales and ventrales caudae**, and two depressors below which flex the tail downward, the **sacrocaudalis ventralis medialis and lateralis**. The two upper elevators are a continuation of the spinal muscles of the back. The two lateral flexors, which begin on the sacrum and the tail vertebrae, taper as they pass along the side of the tail. In the dog, the upper lateral flexor (intertransversarii dorsalis caudae) is especially thick where it begins at the sacrum and ends shortly on the side of the tail. In the horse and the ox, the lateral flexors tend to be segmented between the transverse processes of the tail vertebrae. The lateral flexors are incompletely divided into upper and lower bundles in the ox. The two depressors begin on the bottom of the lumbar vertebrae and sacrum. The lateral depressor is larger than the medial one.

Coccygeus (Coccygeus lateralis; Feline: Abductor caudae internus)

- Origin: The inner surface of the midsection of the pelvis (above the level of the hip socket) in the ox, the dog, and the feline; also from the broad sacrotuberal ligament in the ox; only from the broad sacrotuberal ligament in the region of the hip socket in the horse.
- Insertion: Sides of the tail vertebrae at the base of the tail (tail vertebrae 1–4 in the horse, 1–3 in the ox, and 2–5 in the dog and the feline)
- Action: Both sides of the body together: Pull the base of the tail downward. One side only: Pulls the tail to that side.
- Structure: The coccygeus is a small, flat muscle connecting the pelvis to the base of the tail. Basically triangular, it originates narrow at the pelvis and fans out as it approaches the tail. It lies deep to the sacrotuberal ligament. Although inconspicuous, it may create a curved transition between the top of the rear portion of the pelvis and the base of the tail. Its curved rear edge is most likely to be seen directly when the tail is raised.

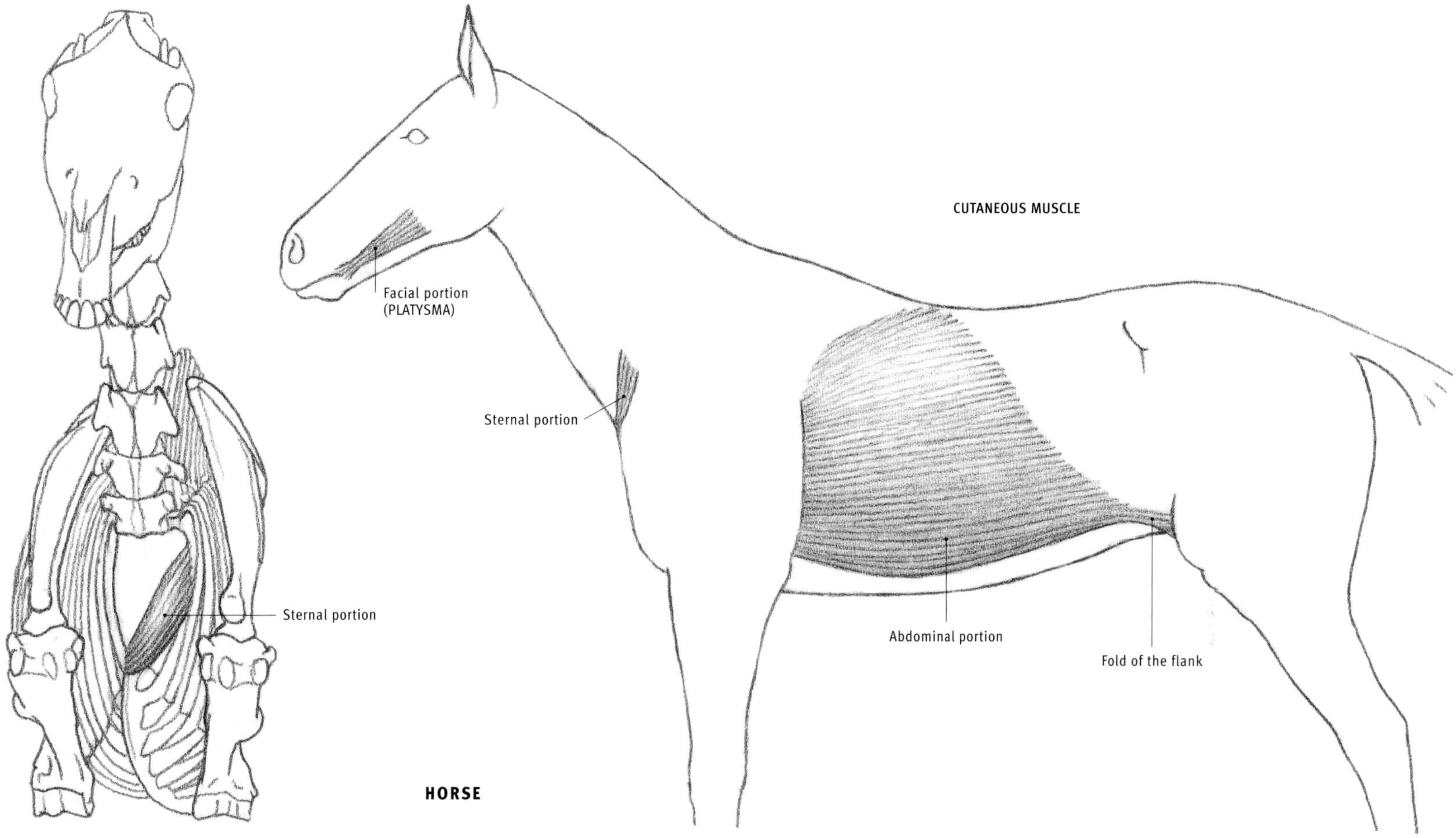

Cutaneous muscle (Panniculus carnosus, Cutaneous maximus)

HORSE

The cutaneous muscle, or **skin muscle**, is a thin, blanketing sheet of muscle that covers a large part, but not all, of the body. It has very little attachment directly to the skeleton, and is divisible into several portions. The cutaneous muscle and the overlying skin soften the definition of the underlying muscles and other structures. One of its functions is to twitch the skin to get rid of flies. Portions that affect surface form are described below.

On the front of the chest, the **sternal portion**, a part of the neck portion, thickens into a muscular band that can be seen on the surface as a distinct ovoid bulge. It attaches directly to the tip of the sternum, where it is thickest, and then thins and widens as it ascends upward and outward. It passes diagonally over the brachiocephalicus.

The large **trunk portion** covers the side of the trunk. As it approaches the upper arm, it gets considerably thicker and can obscure some of the definition of the underlying latissimus dorsi, serratus ventralis, and pectoralis ascendens. It ultimately inserts into the humerus along with the latissimus dorsi and the pectoralis ascendens. In front of the knee region, along with the skin, it creates the triangular **fold of the flank**, or stifle fold. This flap spans from the side of the abdomen to the front of the thigh. The muscular fibers of the trunk portion begin on the side of the chest and abdomen on a line directed variably from the top of the shoulder or the middle of the back to the front of the knee. The lower portion of this line of origin, convex forward, coincides with a distinct line that appears prominently on the surface of the animal in life. This line is seen only in the horse.

A division of the **facial portion** separates into a unit that attaches to the corner of the mouth, called the **platysma**. When it contracts, it retracts the corner of the mouth, altering its shape.

OX

In the ox, the cutaneous muscle is generally reduced and can be seen directly only at the fold of the flank. This fold is larger and descends lower in the ox than in the horse, reaching below the knee to the shin of the lower leg.

DOG AND FELINE

The cutaneous muscle is seen where it forms the fold of the flank. It varies in where it attaches to the leg, ranging from the upper end of the thigh down to the knee, depending on the species and breed.

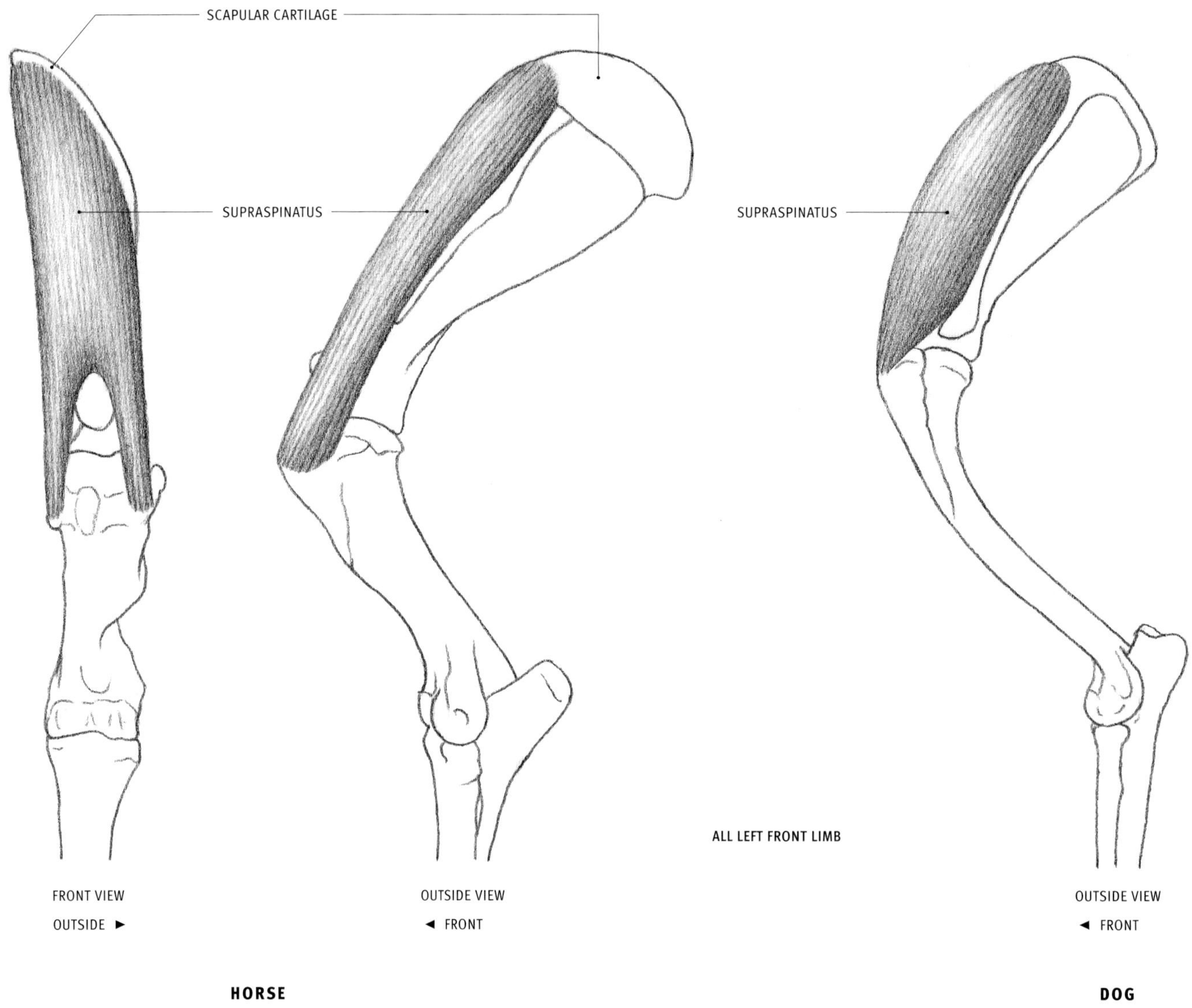

Supraspinatus

HORSE AND OX

• Origin: Outer surface of the front portion of the scapula and the adjacent cartilage.

• Insertion: Inner and outer front corners of the top of the humerus.

• Action: Extends the shoulder joint, advancing the limb.

• Structure: The belly of the supraspinatus is thin where it begins, on the outside of the top of the shoulder blade; it twists to face forward at the front of the shoulder joint, and then splits before inserting into the two areas of insertion on the humerus. In the ox it is completely covered by thin muscles. In the horse a small piece of the middle of the belly comes to the surface, and the subclavius muscle (attached to the front of the supraspinatus) and the supraspinatus together create the rounded front edge of the shoulder form (located at the base of the side of the neck). In the ox, however, the supraspinatus alone creates the front of the shoulder form (the subclavius is deep).

DOG AND FELINE

• Origin: Same as in the horse and the ox, except no scapular cartilage is present.

• Insertion: Single area of insertion on top of the humerus. Belly doesn't twist or split before inserting.

• Structure: Although it is mostly covered by thin muscle, the supraspinatus creates the front form of the shoulder.

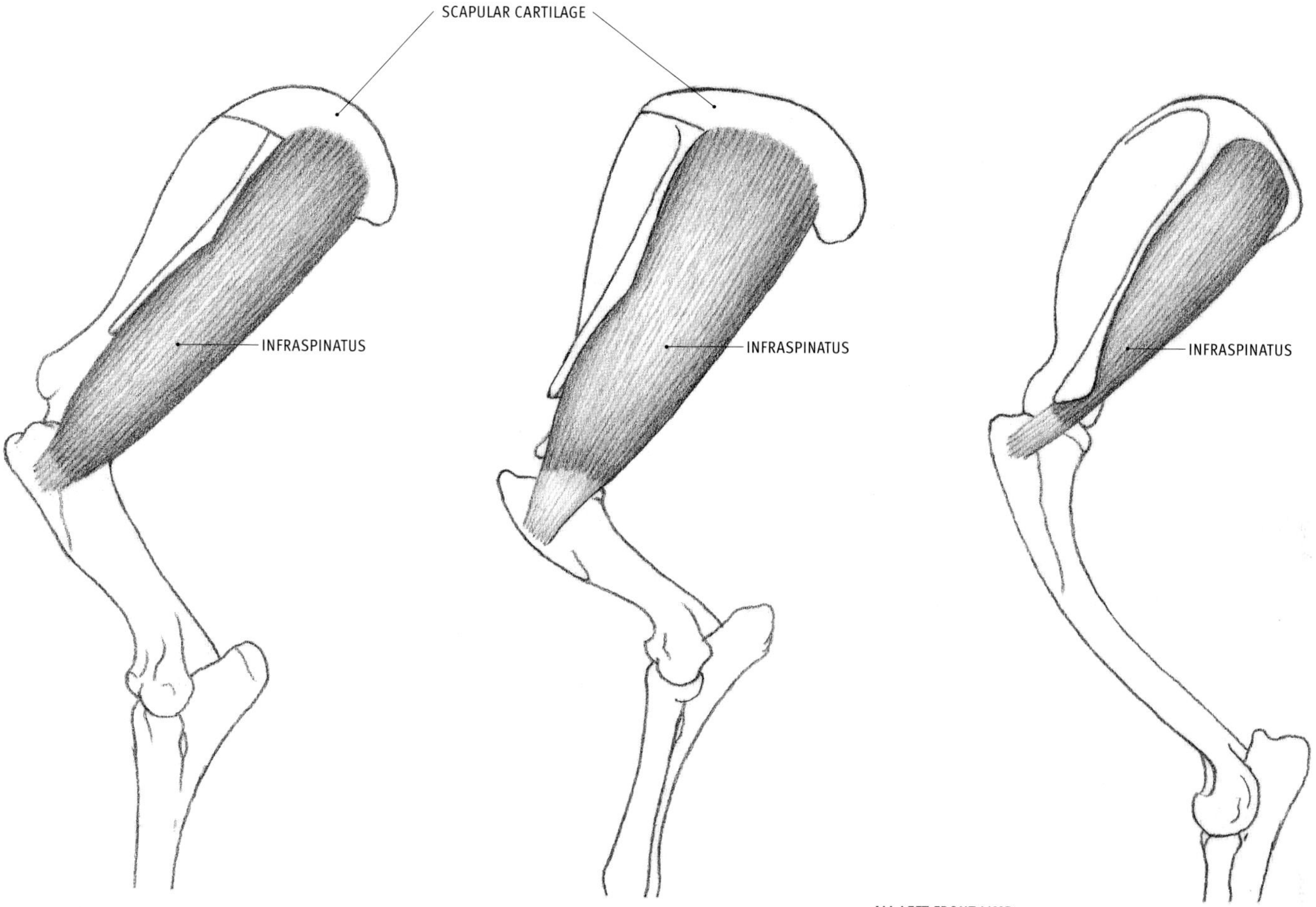

ALL LEFT FRONT LIMB

OUTSIDE VIEW
◂ FRONT

HORSE

OUTSIDE VIEW
◂ FRONT

OX

OUTSIDE VIEW
◂ FRONT

DOG

Infraspinatus

HORSE AND OX

• Origin: Outer surface of the rear portion of the scapula and the adjacent cartilage.

• Insertion: Outer side of the top of the humerus.

• Action: Rotates the arm outward; pulls the limb away from the body.

• Structure: The infraspinatus lies on the outer surface of the rear portion of the shoulder blade. Its flat belly (lying on the flat surface of the scapula) contributes to the planar quality of the shoulder region. The trapezius and latissimus dorsi cover the upper portion of the muscle, and the deltoid belly and its wide tendon cover the lower portion. Only a small part of the infraspinatus reaches the surface, although the portion covered by the wide tendon of the deltoid also directly creates surface form.

DOG AND FELINE

• Origin: Same as in the horse and ox, except there is no scapular cartilage.

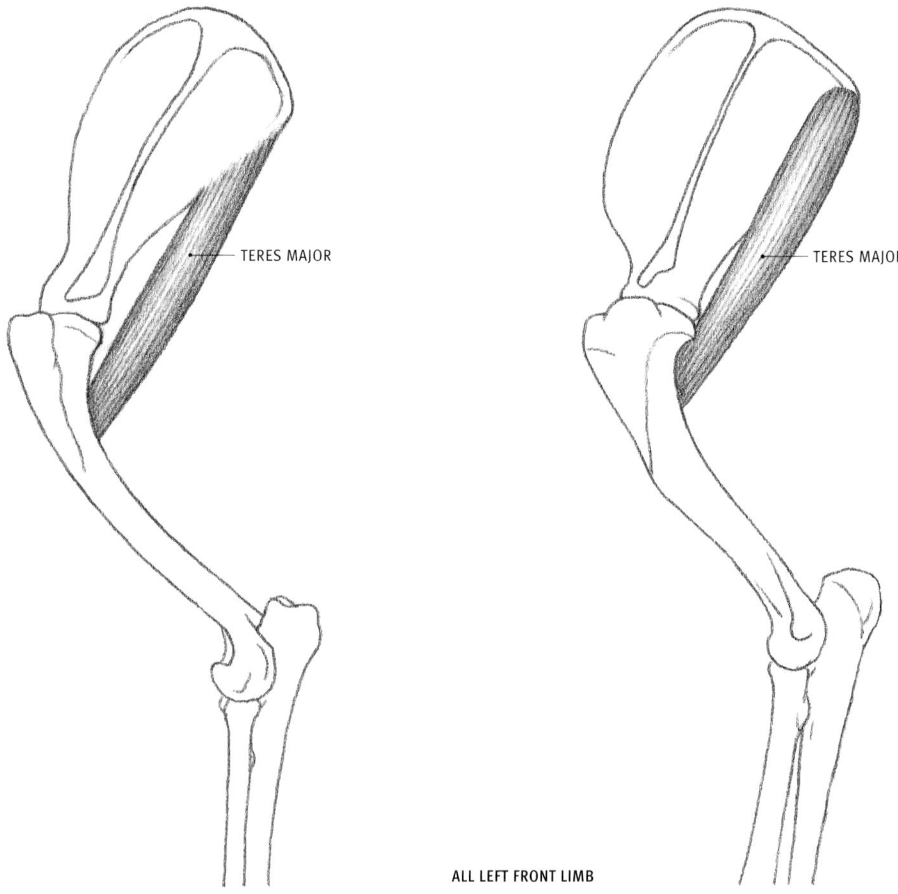

OUTSIDE VIEW
◂ FRONT

DOG

OUTSIDE VIEW
◂ FRONT

LION

Teres major

DOG AND FELINE

• Origin: Upper third of the rear edge of the shoulder blade. Feline: Also the adjacent surface of the infraspinatus muscle.
• Insertion: Short vertical line on the inner surface of the humerus approximately one fourth of the way down the bone. The teres major and latissimus dorsi insert together via a common tendon on the humerus.
• Action: Flexes the shoulder joint.
• Structure: The teres major is a narrow, slightly flattened muscle that comes to the surface only in the feline. In the other species, it is covered by the latissimus dorsi and the triceps. As it descends, it dives under the long head of the triceps. It can be seen directly where it is not covered by muscle, or indirectly through the latissimus dorsi, which is thin enough to reveal its form. The triceps is too thick to let the teres major show through. In the dog, the elongated form of the teres major may be evident on the surface under cover of the latissimus dorsi when it is strongly contracted while pulling the arm backward. Because the thick triceps muscle begins high on the scapula in the horse and the ox, the teres major remains hidden from view (the triceps originates lower down, on the rear edge of the scapula in the dog and the feline).

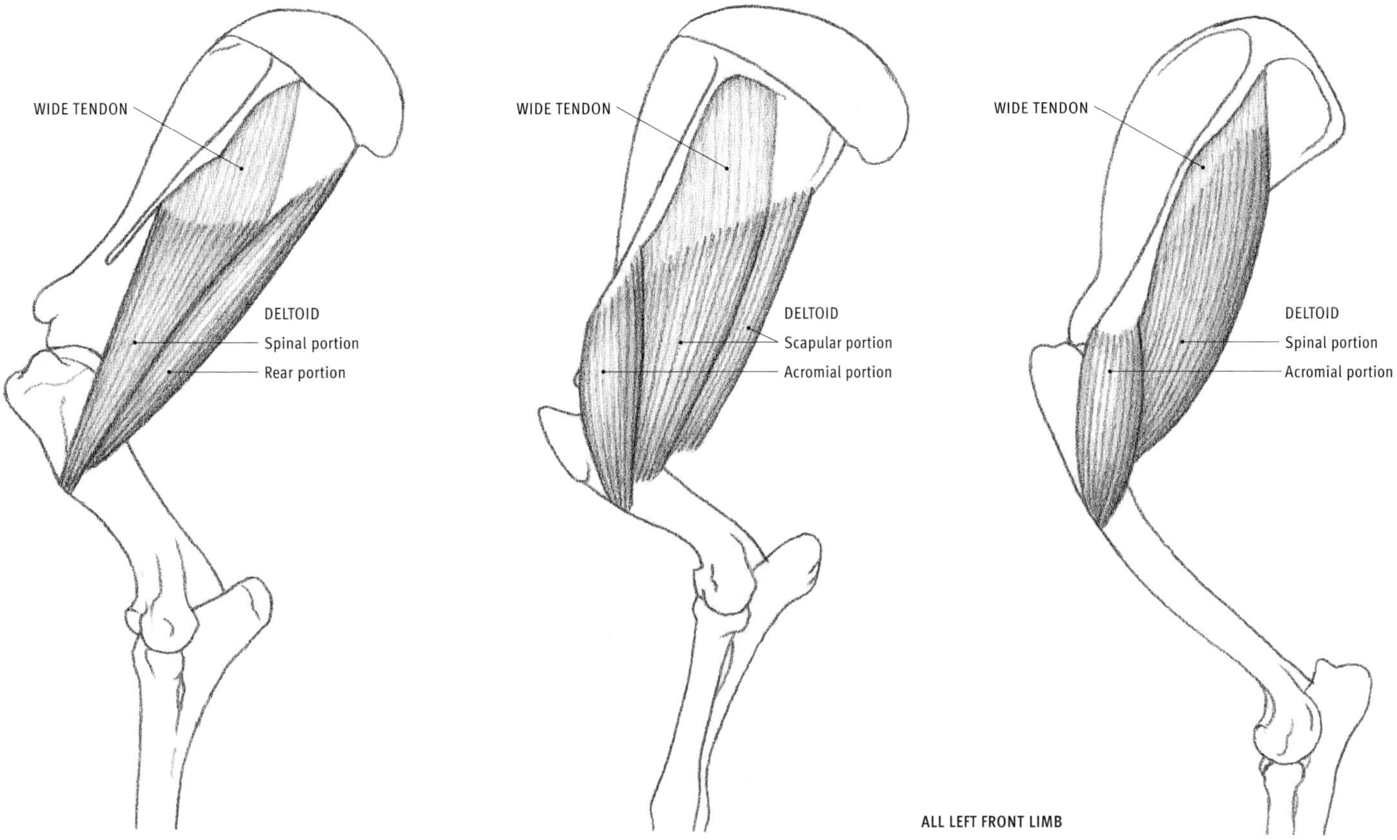

OUTSIDE VIEW
◄ FRONT

HORSE

OUTSIDE VIEW
◄ FRONT

OX

OUTSIDE VIEW
◄ FRONT

DOG

Deltoid

HORSE

• Origin: Spinal portion: Spine of the scapula and surface of the underlying infraspinatus muscle via a wide tendon. Rear portion: Upper back corner of the bony scapula

• Insertion: Into the outside of the humerus, one third of the way down the bone.

• Action: Flexes the shoulder joint and pulls the forelimb away from the body.

• Structure: The deltoid consists of two portions. The wider spinal (front) portion arises from the spine of the scapula and the surface of the infraspinatus as a wide, flat tendon before becoming fleshy. The more prominent rear portion is entirely fleshy, and it tapers at both ends.

OX

• Origin: Acromial portion: Acromion at the lower end of the spine of the scapula and along the spine for a short distance. Scapular portion: Spine of the scapula via a wide tendon, and partly into the rear edge of the bony scapula one fourth of the way down the bone.

• Insertion: One third of the way down on the outside of the humerus. The scapular portion also inserts onto the surface of the lateral head of the triceps.

• Structure: The acromial portion originates from the acromion, as well as from the lower end of the spine. The scapular portion is quite flat and is made up of a wide front portion, which originates via a wide tendon, and a narrower rear portion, which originates directly from the rear edge of the scapula by fleshy fibers. Because the scapular portion inserts, in part, onto the surface of the triceps, the lower end of the deltoid is wider than in the other species where it tapers almost to a point.

DOG AND FELINE

• Origin: Acromial portion: Acromion at the lower end of the spine of the scapula. Spinal portion: Spine of the scapula. In the feline, the spinal portion originates from the lower two thirds of the spine.

• Insertion: One third of the way down, on the outside of the humerus.

• Structure: The larger spinal portion dives under the acromial portion toward the point of their common insertion. The spinal portion may begin as a fleshy belly directly at the scapular spine or as a wide flat tendon of varying size.

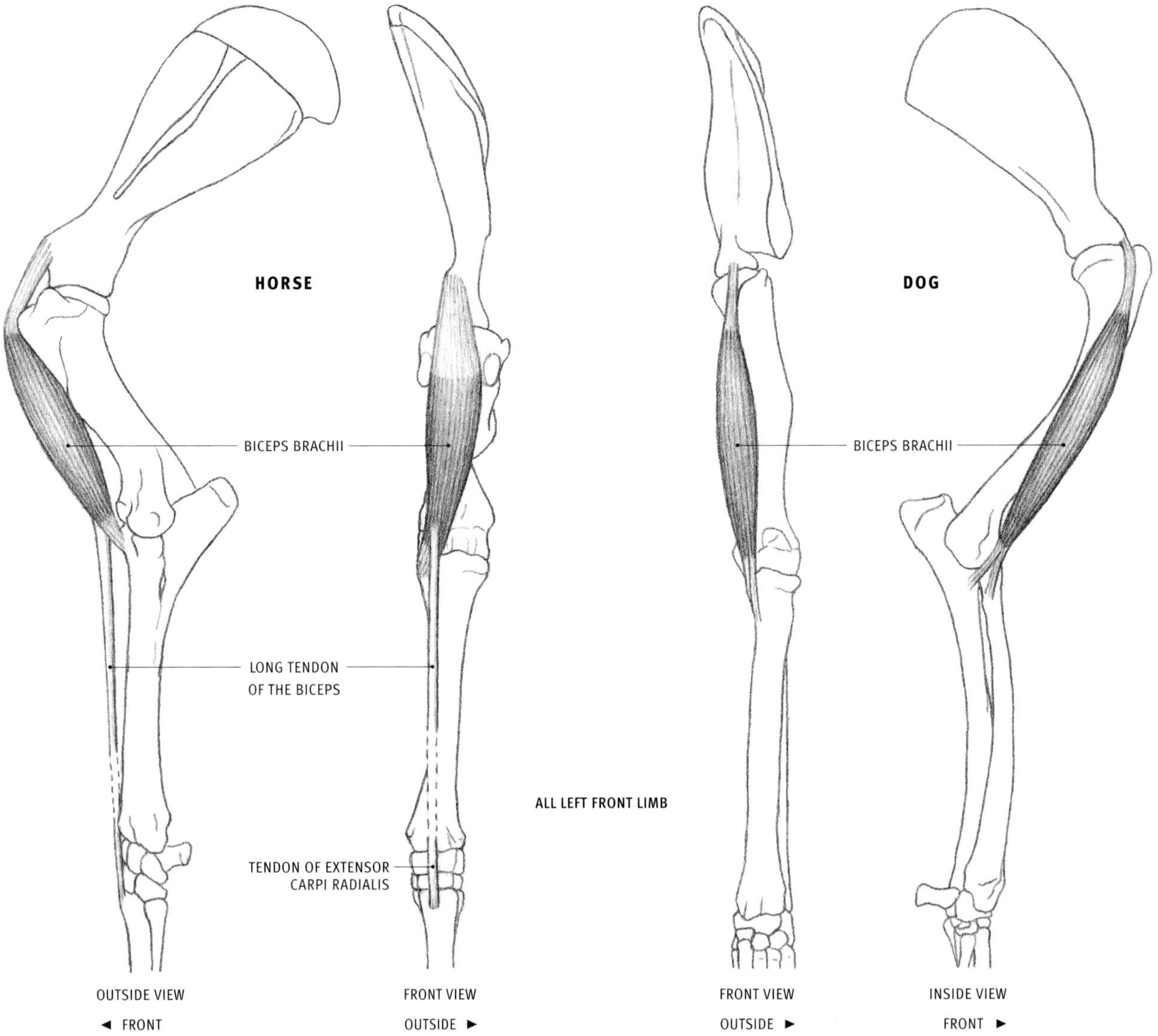

Biceps brachii

HORSE

• Origin: Bony prominence on the front of the lower end of the scapula.

• Insertion: 1. Inner front corner of the top of the radius. 2. Ligament on the inside of the elbow. 3. By a special long tendinous extension, into the tendon of the extensor carpi radialis muscle (and therefore indirectly into the front of the metacarpal bone).

• Action: Flexes the elbow joint; extends the shoulder joint (and locks the shoulder in place when the animal is in the standing position).

• Structure: The biceps brachii begins as a very strong, flattened tendon at its origin. After passing through a bony groove at the top of the humerus, it develops into a thick, fleshy belly, tapered at both ends. The lower end splits and inserts into the radius and the inner elbow ligament. Strong tendinous fibers running through the entire length of the belly, beginning at the tendon of origin above, emerge at the bottom of the muscle and form the **long tendon of the biceps** (**lacerta fibrosus**). The long tendon passes down the surface of the extensor carpi radialis muscle and soon joins its tendon, thereby gaining insertion into the metacarpal bone. This strong "cable," stretching from the shoulder blade to the wrist, prevents the shoulder from flexing when the animal is standing, reducing the muscular energy necessary to maintain that position. The muscular mass of the biceps brachii does not come to the surface in the horse, but rather adds muscle mass onto the front of the humerus.

OX

• Structure: Similar to that in the horse, but the long tendon is less developed.

DOG

• Insertion: The lower end of the muscle splits into two tendons that insert into adjacent areas on the inside of the radius and ulna, just below the elbow joint.

• Structure: The biceps is slender, and the long tendon is not present. The lower end of the belly comes to the surface on the inside front of the elbow region.

FELINE

• Insertion: Into the radius only, just below the elbow joint. When the forearm is pronated, with the palm facing backward, the insertion area is on the rear side of the bone. As the forearm is supinated (with the palm rotating forward), the radius rotates, bringing the insertion area around toward the front.

• Action: Flexes the elbow joint; supinates the forearm, rotating the palm forward (or upward, depending on the position of the forearm).

In four-legged animals, only one head of the biceps is present.
In primates, a second head is present, descending from the coracoid process of the scapula and inserting into the inside of the humerus.

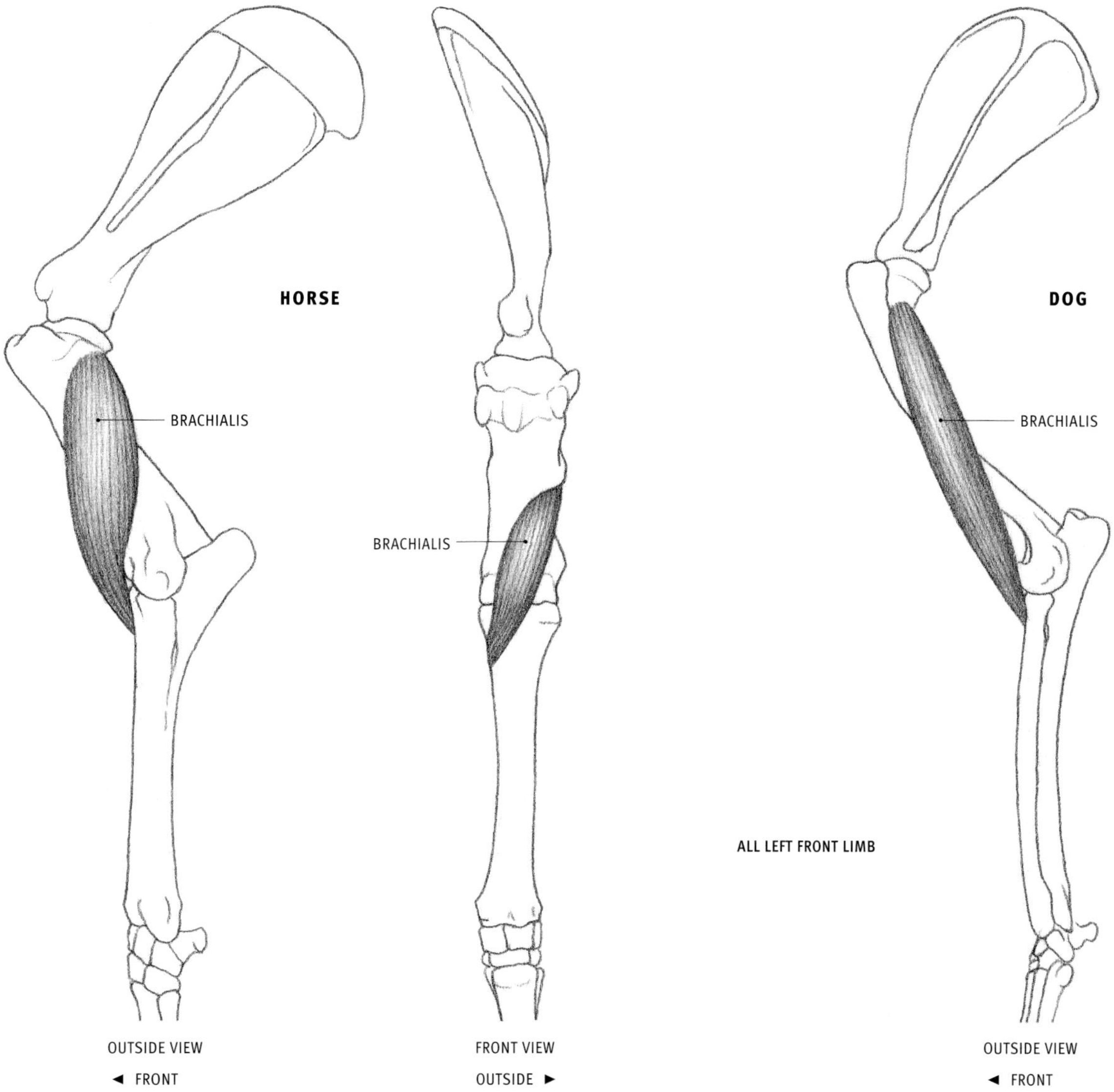

Brachialis

HORSE

• Origin: Upper *third* of the rear surface of the humerus.

• Insertion: Inner side of the radius near its top, slightly below and to the inside of the insertion of the biceps muscle.

• Action: Flexes the elbow joint.

• Structure: Beginning on the back of the humerus, the belly curves around the outside of the bone, passes in front of the elbow joint, and ends on the inside of the elbow region. Only a small piece of the outer side of the brachialis comes to the surface in front of the elbow joint.

OX

• Insertion: Same as in the horse. In some small ruminants, the lower end of the brachialis splits and also inserts into an adjacent area on the ulna.

DOG

• Origin: Upper *half* of the back of the humerus.

• Insertion: Inner side of the ulna, just below the elbow joint. Some fibers attach to the inserting end of the biceps tendon, thereby inserting indirectly into the radius.

FELINE

• Origin: From *most* of the length of the back of the humerus.

• Insertion: Inner side of the ulna, just below the elbow joint (not into the radius at all).

The brachialis is exclusively a flexor of the forearm. In animals that rotate the forearm (pronation and supination), like felines and primates, the brachialis inserts only into the ulna, and not into the radius (in these animals, supination is produced by the biceps brachii pulling on the radius). Animals that do not rotate the forearm, such as the horse and the ox, have a reduced ulna, and the brachialis inserts into the radius, producing only flexion at the elbow joint.

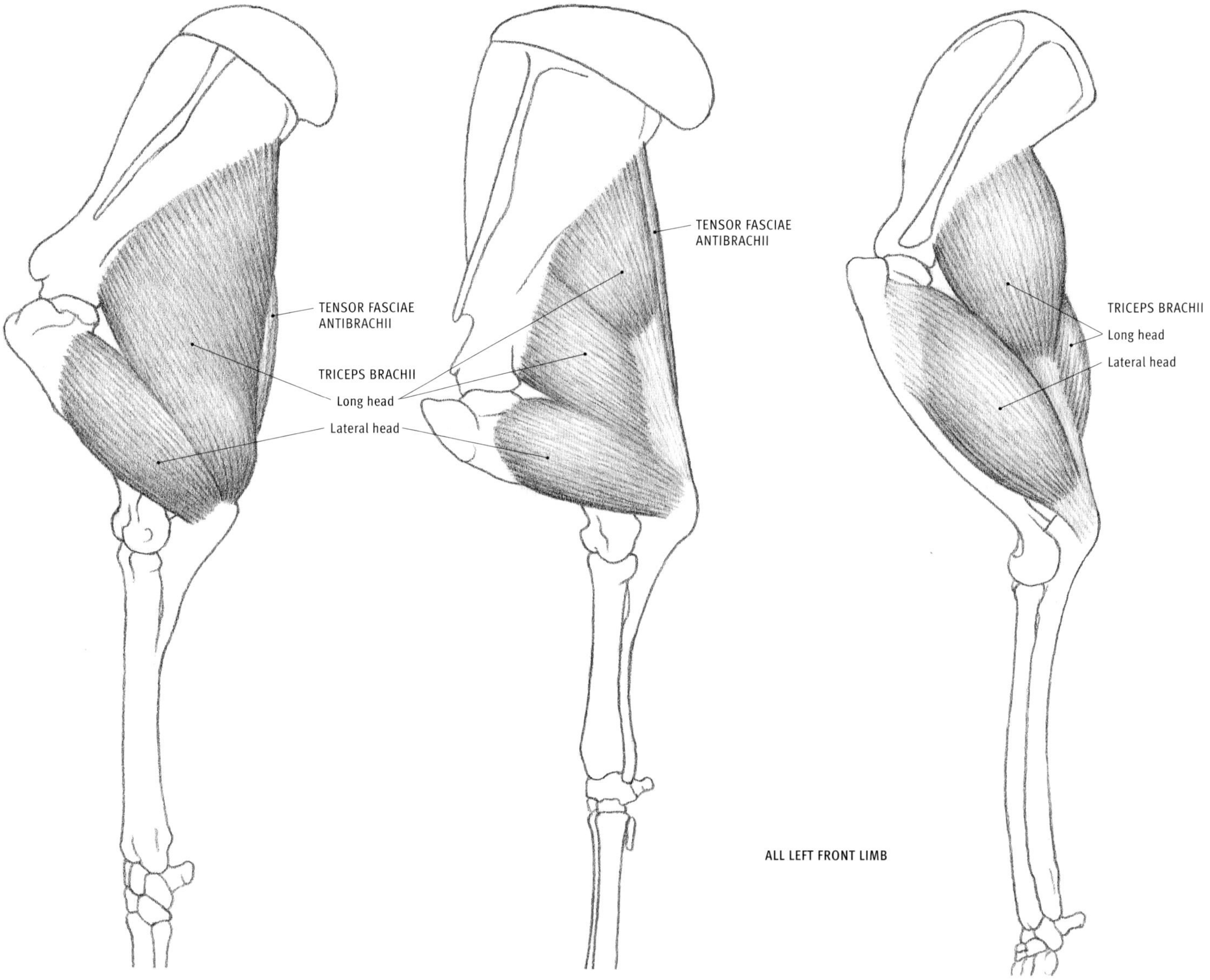

OUTSIDE VIEW ◄ FRONT **HORSE** | OUTSIDE VIEW ◄ FRONT **OX** | OUTSIDE VIEW ◄ FRONT **DOG**

Triceps brachii

HORSE AND OX

• Origin: Long head: Most or all of the rear border of the scapula. Lateral head: Curved ridge on upper outer surface of the humerus.

• Insertion: Side and top of the olecranon of the humerus (point of the elbow).

• Action: Long head: Both extends the elbow joint and flexes the shoulder joint. Lateral head: Extends the elbow joint only.

• Structure: Large fleshy muscle consisting of three or more heads. Only the long and lateral heads are visible; the medial head lies deep to the lateral head. The lateral head has a flattened, somewhat rectangular form. The long head is triangular. When the muscle is tensed, the rear edge straightens. When relaxed, the soft muscle mass drops down and produces a bulging form above (and separate from) the olecranon.

DOG AND FELINE

• Origin: Long head: Dog: Lower half to two thirds of the rear edge of the scapula. Feline: Lower one third to one half of the rear edge of the scapula.

• Structure: The long head separates into two forms—a higher, more forward part, and a lower, more posterior part. The two parts are separated by a furrow. In the dog, when the arm is stretched forward the medial head of the triceps, which originates from the inside of the shaft of the humerus, may be seen on the inside of the elbow region, directed toward its insertion on the olecranon.

The **tensor fasciae antebrachii (dorso-epitrochlearis, scapulo-ulnaris)** is a wide, flat, thin muscle that lies deep to the triceps. It *originates* from the tendon of insertion of the latissimus dorsi muscle, and often from the upper end of the rear border of the bony scapula as well. It *inserts* into the inner side of the olecranon. Its *action* is to assist in extending the elbow joint. Only a narrow strip of the muscle may be visible past the rear edge of the long head of the triceps, usually most evident in the ox.

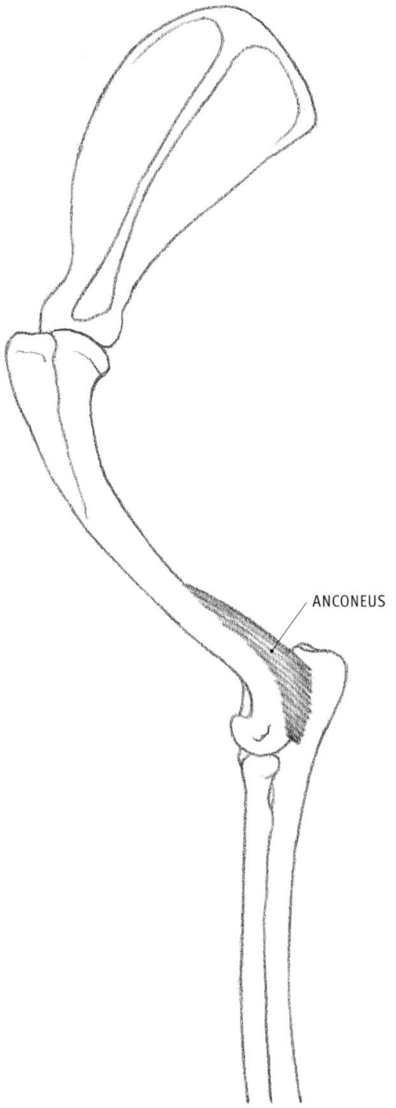

DOG

Anconeus

DOG AND FELINE

• Origin: A line on the rear surface and outer back edge of the lower third of the humerus.
• Insertion: A line on the outer surface of the upper end of the ulna.
• Action: Extends the elbow joint.
• Structure: The anconeus is a short, strong, triangular muscle. The upper portion is covered by the lateral head of the triceps. The lower, exposed portion creates a small, simple, flat plane between the humerus and the ulna, below the bulging lateral head of the triceps.

In the horse and the ox, this muscle is completely covered by the lateral head of the triceps.

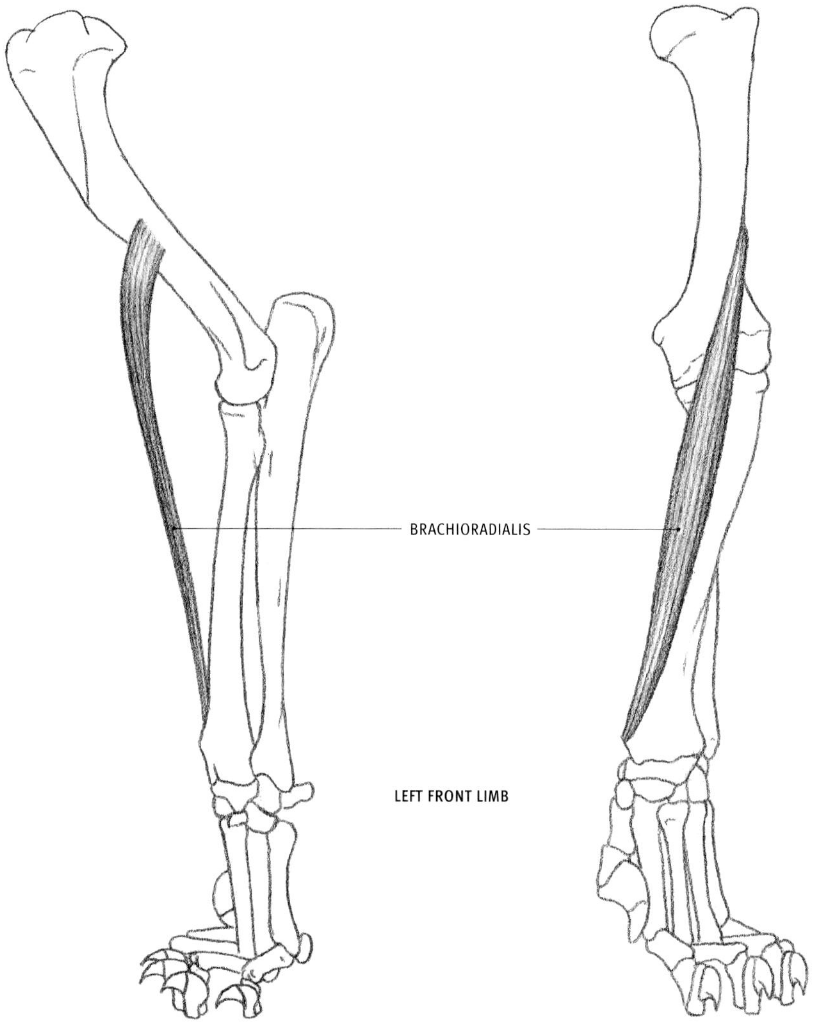

LION

Brachioradialis (Supinator longus)

DOG AND FELINE

• Origin: A short line on the outer surface of the humerus, below the halfway point.

• Insertion: In the dog, three fourths of the way down the radius, on its inner front edge. In the feline, it inserts further down, into the top of the bony prominence on the inside of the lower end of the radius.

• Action: Flexes the elbow joint; supinates the forearm in the feline, rotating the palm inward then forward (the dog forearm does not supinate).

• Structure: This long, thin, flat muscle is developed in felines (and primates), reduced or absent in dogs, and absent in the horse and the ox. It begins on the outside of the humerus and descends downward and slightly inward on the front of the forearm, to end on the inner surface of the radius, above the wrist. Its upper end is covered by the lateral head of the triceps. In the domestic cat, there is a gap between the upper ends of the brachioradialis and the extensor carpi radialis.

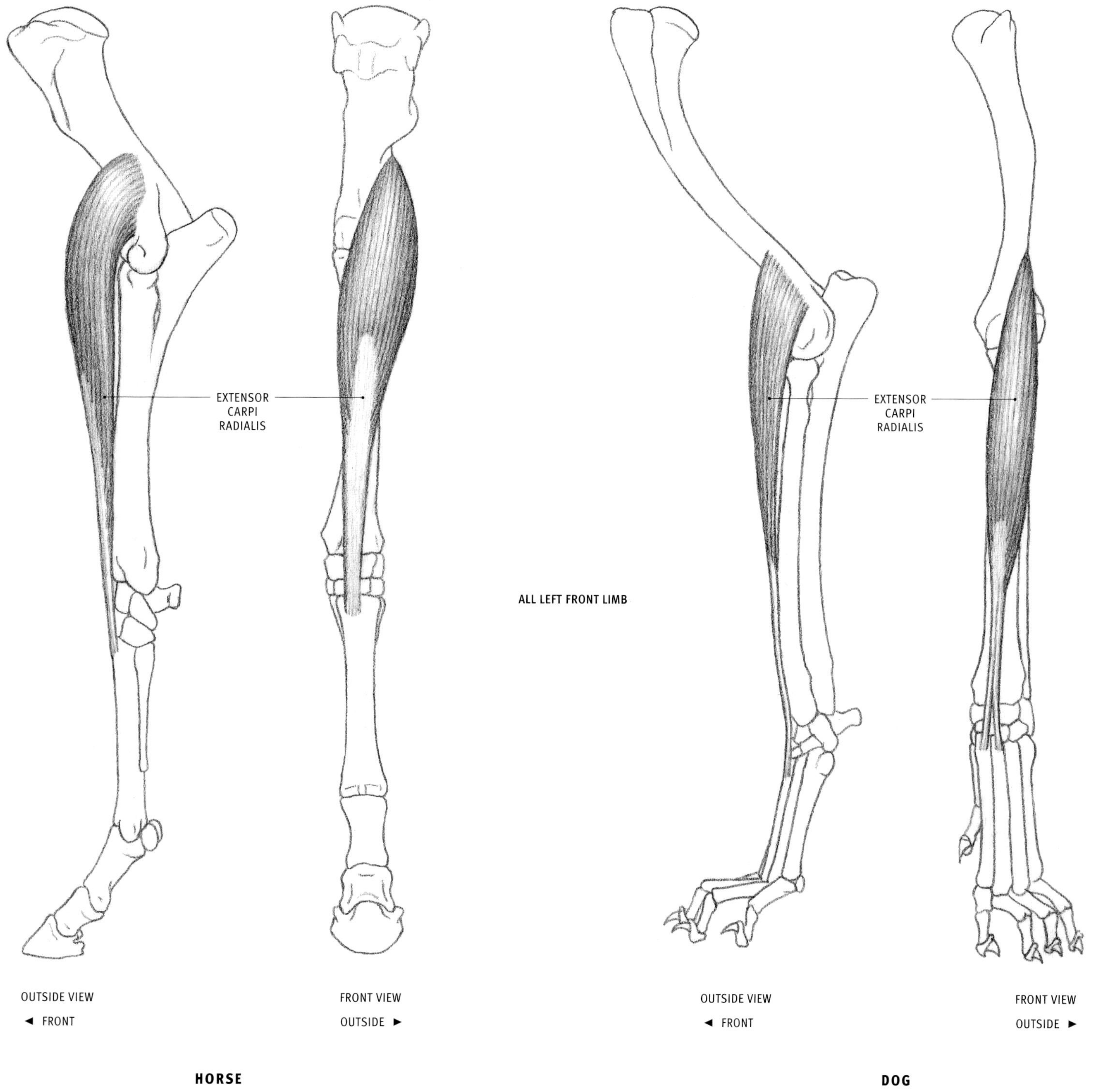

Extensor carpi radialis (Extensor metacarpi magnus)

HORSE AND OX

- Origin: Bony ridge on the outside lower third of the humerus.
- Insertion: Top of the front surface of the metacarpal bone (cannon bone of the horse).
- Action: Extends and locks the wrist joint; flexes the elbow joint.
- Structure: The extensor carpi radialis is the largest of the extensor muscles on the forearm. This powerful muscle lies on the front of the radius. Its fleshy belly begins flattened and faces outward at its origin, then shifts to the front of the limb, becoming oval in cross section. Two thirds of the way down the radius it develops into a wide flat tendon, which is joined by the long tendon of the biceps brachii from the front of the upper arm. The upper end of the muscle is covered by the lateral head of the triceps.

DOG AND FELINE

- Insertion: Upper ends of the front of the second and third metacarpal bones.
- Structure: In the dog and feline, the extensor carpi radialis is more slender than in the horse and the ox. In the dog, the lower end separates into two tendons, corresponding to the extensor carpi radialis longus and brevis. In the feline, the entire muscle is divisible into separate longus and brevis muscles.

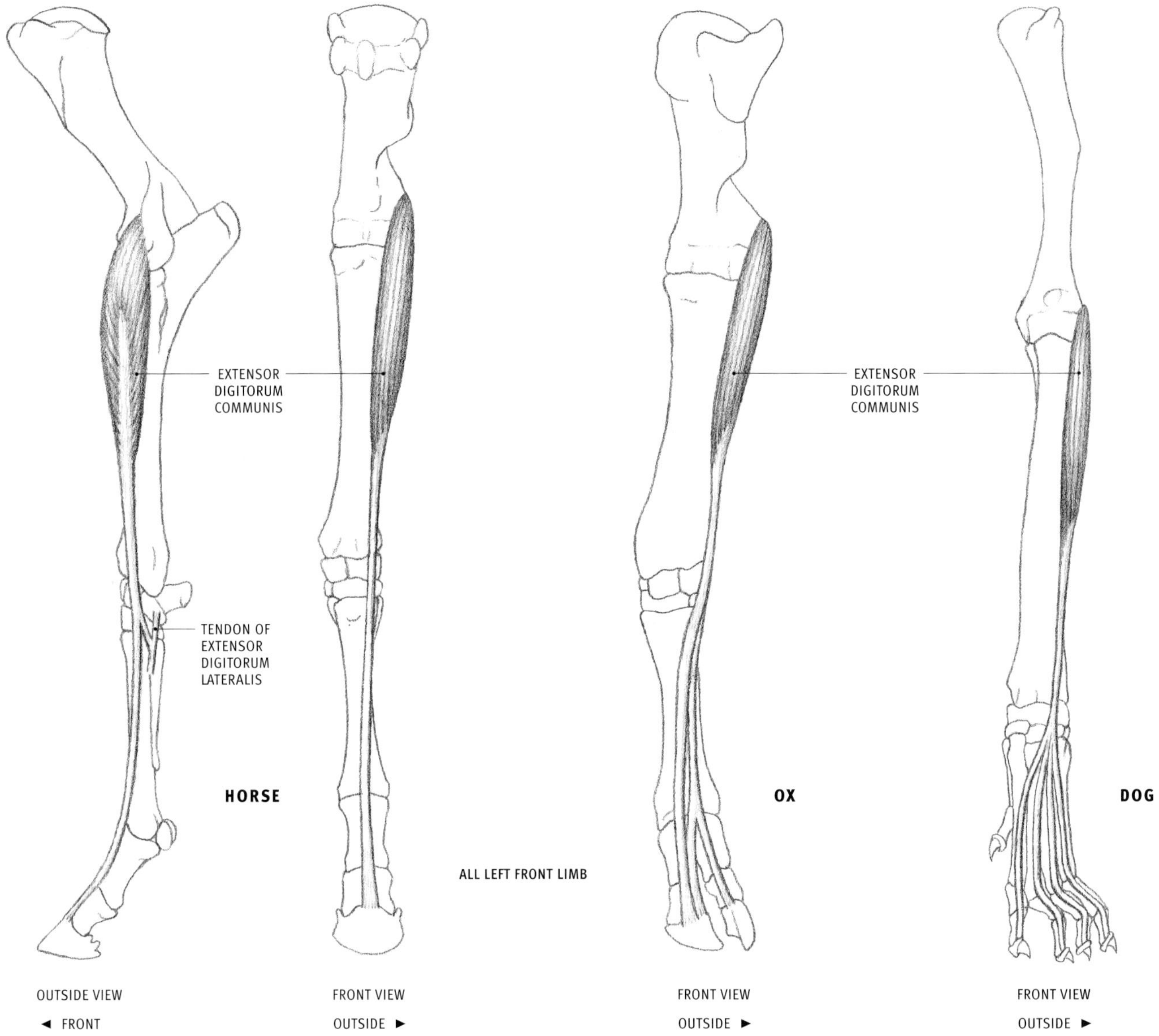

Extensor digitorum communis (Extensor pedis)

HORSE

• Origin: Extensive area from the outer front portion and outer ridge at the lower end of the humerus, the vertical ligament connecting the outer side of the humerus to the ulna (at the elbow), and the outer edge of the upper third of the radius.

• Insertion: Upper edge of the front of all three toe bones, primarily into the last one.

• Action: Extends the wrist joint and all three toe joints.

• Structure: The extensor digitorum communis travels from the elbow to the toe. Its muscle belly, tapered at both ends, often shows a groove down its length. It becomes tendinous two thirds of the way down the radius. A small tendon that branches off this tendon at the level of the bottom of the radius passes downward and outward to join the tendon of the extensor digitorum lateralis (shown here in side view). A deep head originates from an area on the outside of the ulna and adjacent radius; it is not visible on the surface.

OX

• Insertion: Ultimately into the upper edge of the front of the last toe bone on both toes.

• Structure: The muscle consists of two distinct, parallel narrow bellies. The more forward belly sends a single tendon to the inner toe. The tendon of the other belly splits at its lower end and inserts into both toes.

DOG AND FELINE

• Origin: Outer side of the lower end of the humerus. In the feline, the origin continues upward for a short distance on the outer bony ridge of the humerus.

• Insertion: Last toe bone of the four outer toes.

• Structure: The single belly becomes tendinous two thirds of the way down the radius. In front of the wrist, the tendons diverge toward their insertions. The first and second digits have their own extensor muscle, the **extensor digiti I & II,** separate from the extensor digitorum communis (the second digit therefore receives two tendons). The belly of the extensor digiti I & II is located deep in the forearm under other muscles, but its very thin tendons come to the surface (see page 134). This muscle is typically found in species where first and second digits are present.

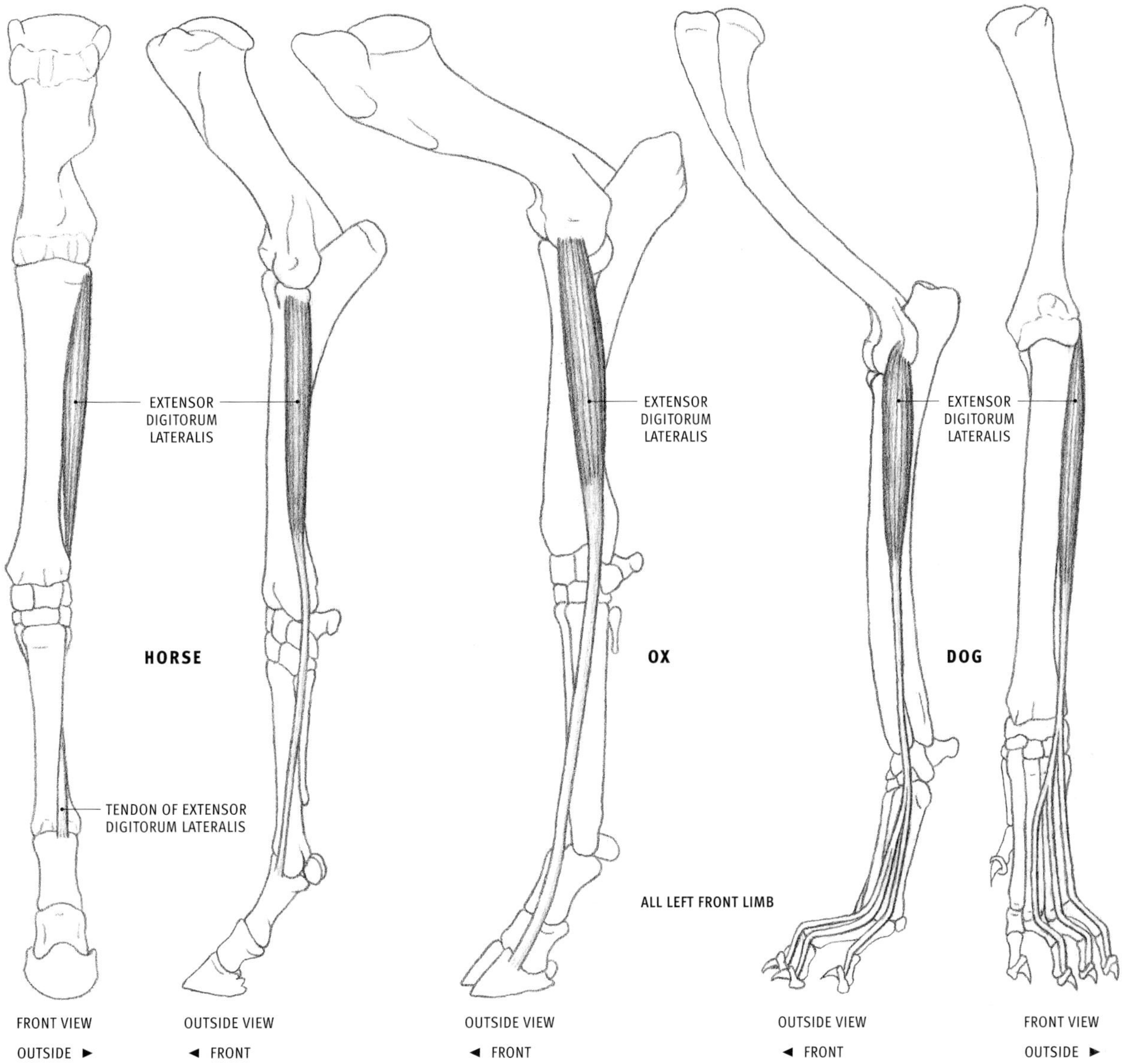

Extensor digitorum lateralis (Extensor suffraginis)

HORSE

• Origin: Upper fourth of the outer surface of the radius, part of the elbow ligament above, and an adjacent area on the ulna.
• Insertion: Upper edge on the front of the upper toe bone.
• Action: Extends the first toe joint.
• Structure: This is a narrow muscle lying on the outside of the forearm. Its belly becomes tendinous two thirds of the way down the forelimb. After passing over the *outside* of the wrist, the tendon descends diagonally toward the front of the limb, not quite reaching the midline. Below the wrist it receives a small tendon from the extensor digitorum communis. The lower portion of the belly is more visible on the surface than the upper part.

OX

• Origin: Similar to the horse, but additionally from the lower end of the humerus, and less so from the shaft of the radius.
• Insertion: Upper edge of the front of the two lower toe bones of the outer digit.
• Action: Extends all the outer toe joints; flexes the elbow joint.
• Structure: The muscle belly is wider than in the horse, and it is visible throughout its length.

DOG

• Origin: Front edge of the vertical ligament on the outside of the elbow joint, and the upper end of the outer surface of the radius.
• Insertion: The three tendons of the extensor digitorum lateralis unite with the tendons of the extensor digitorum communis to ultimately insert into the last toe bone of the *three* outer digits (toes 3, 4, and 5).
• Action: Extends all the joints of the three outer toes; extends the wrist joint.
• Structure: The elongated belly becomes tendinous two thirds of the way down the forearm, and then passes over the *front* of the wrist, toward the outside. It splits into two tendons; then the inner tendon splits again, forming three tendons in total.

FELINE

• Origin: The lower end of the bony ridge on the outside of the humerus (no attachment to the radius).
• Insertion: Same as in the dog, but into the outer *four* digits (toes 2–4).
• Structure: Lower end of the muscle belly separates into four tendons.

In the anatomy literature, among the different animal species, the extensor digitorum lateralis is described as inserting in various combinations into the top edges of the upper, middle, and terminal toe bones, as well as fusing into the sides of the tendons of the extensor digitorum communis of the outer toes.

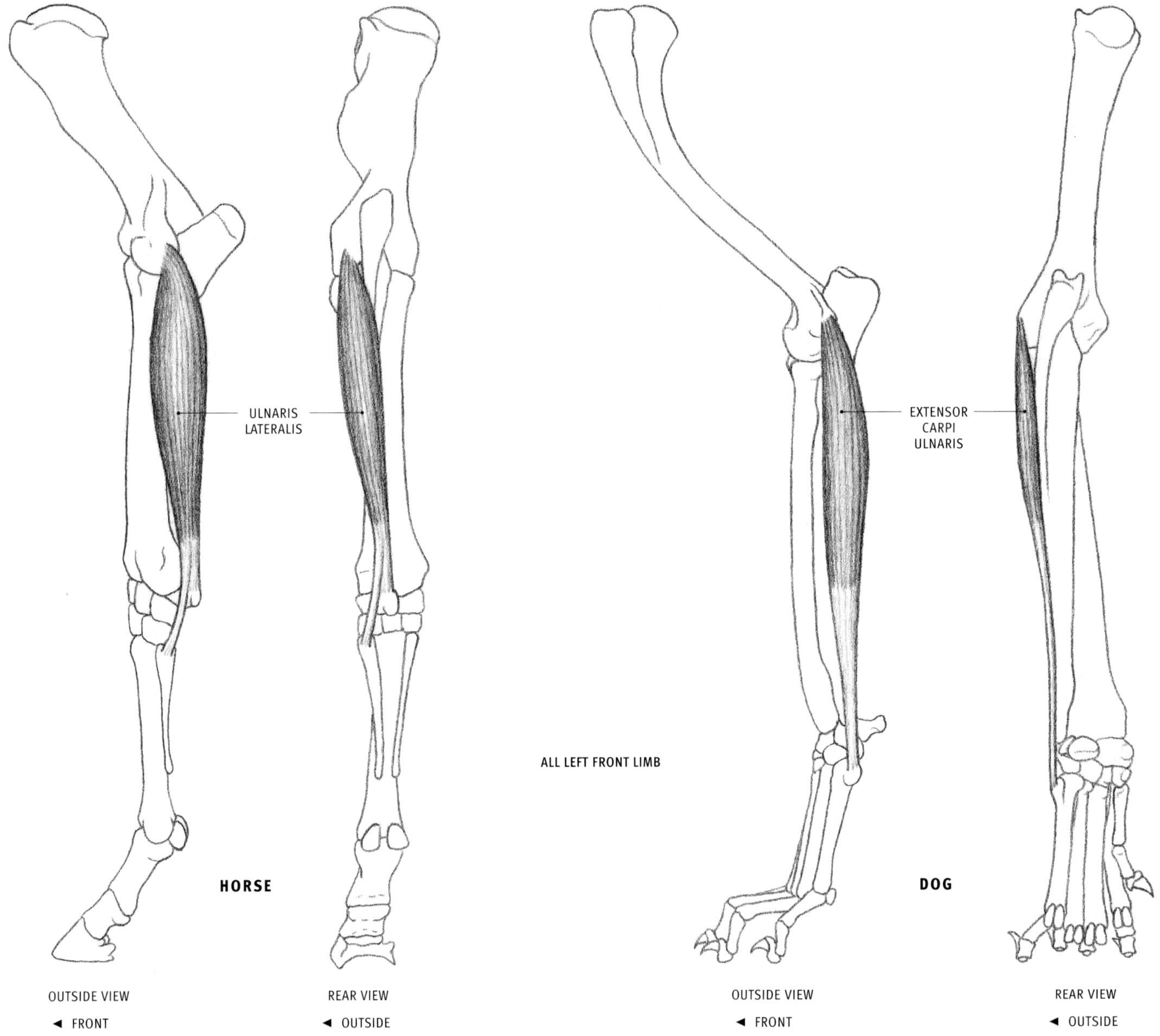

Ulnaris lateralis (Flexor metacarpi externus)

HORSE

• Origin: Outer surface of the lower end of the humerus, behind the elbow joint ligament.

• Insertion: Top and outer surface of the accessory carpal (pisiform) bone of the wrist; upper end of the outer splint bone.

• Action: *Flexes* the wrist joint; extends the elbow joint. Although technically a part of the extensor group of the forearm, this muscle is functionally a flexor of the wrist joint because its main tendon inserts behind the wrist joint. It is therefore called the ulnaris lateralis rather than the extensor carpi ulnaris.

• Structure: Elongated, flattened muscle that lies on the outside of the forearm toward the rear. It begins on the outside of the elbow and, as it descends, inclines toward the midline on the back of the wrist. The muscle belly partially overlaps the extensor digitorum lateralis in front of it. Below, it separates into two tendons—a short, broad tendon to the accessory carpal bone, and a longer, thinner, rounded tendon to the splint bone. On the back of the wrist, its tendon to the accessory carpal bone is fused to the tendon of the flexor carpi ulnaris.

OX

• Insertion: Also into the top of the outer surface of the single metacarpal bone.

• Structure: Wider than in the horse, and less tapered at its ends. The lower portion of the muscle belly fuses with the belly of the flexor carpi ulnaris on the back of the forearm. They insert together as a single tendon into the accessory carpal bone.

Extensor carpi ulnaris

DOG AND FELINE

• Insertion: Top of the outer surface of the fifth, or outer, metacarpal bone. There is no insertion into the accessory carpal bone.

• Action: *Extends* the wrist joint.

• Structure: Elongated muscle, followed by a strong, broad tendon, which passes down the outside of the forearm and ends on the outside of the wrist.

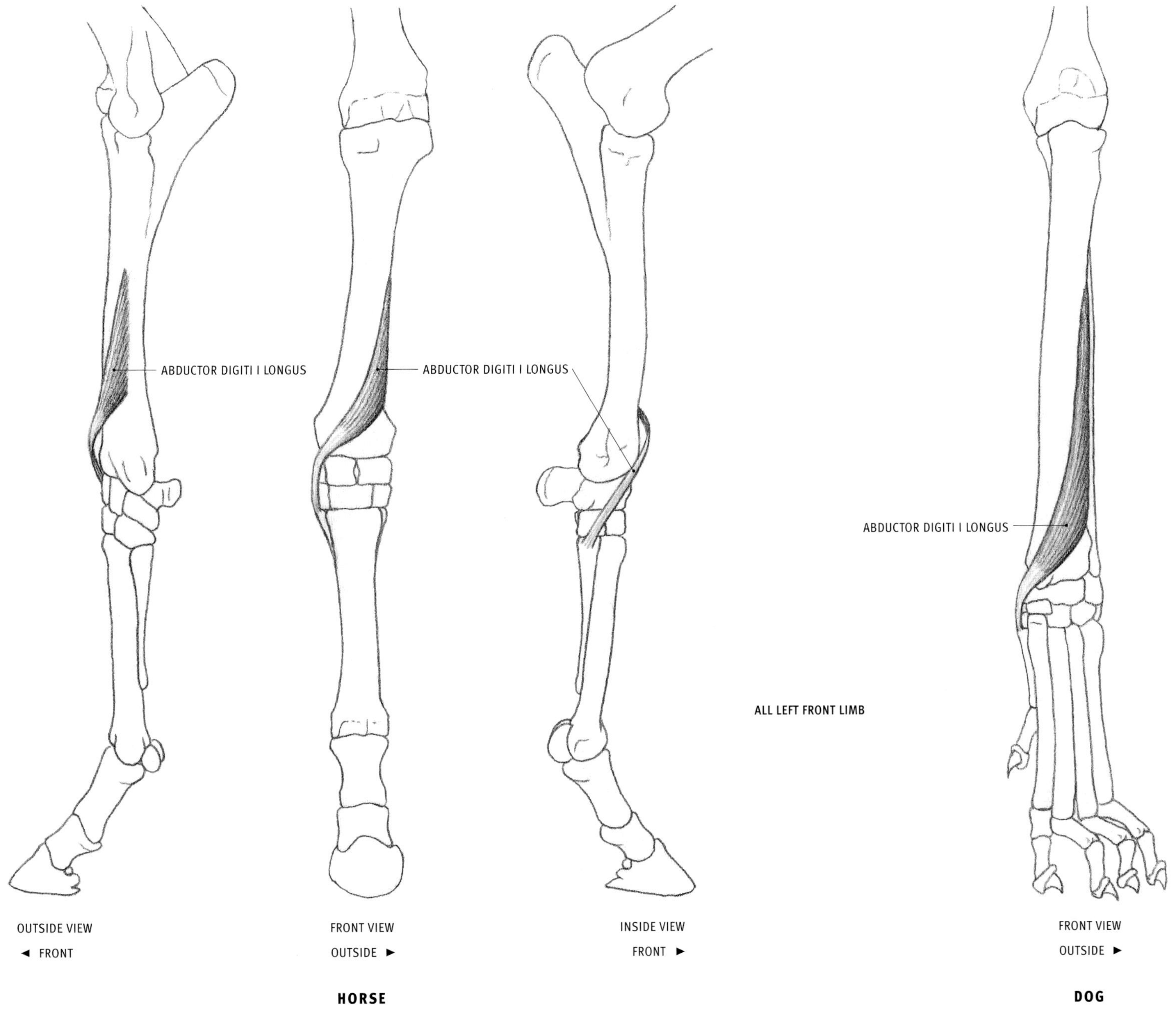

Abductor digiti I (pollicis) longus (Extensor carpi obliquus)

HORSE

- Origin: Middle section of the outer surface of the radius.
- Insertion: Head of the inner splint bone.
- Action: Extends the carpal joint.
- Structure: The flat, triangular muscle belly begins on the outside of the forearm, then curves down, around, and to the inside of the wrist, ending as a tendon. It emerges from under the extensor digitorum communis and then passes over the tendon of the extensor carpi radialis. It may produce a very subtle effect on the surface.

OX

- Origin: Lower half of the outer surface of the radius and an adjacent area on the ulna.
- Insertion: Inner side of the upper end of the metacarpal bone.

DOG AND FELINE

- Origin: Outer surface of the middle portion of the radius and the ulna.
- Insertion: Inner surface of the upper end of the first (inner) metacarpal bone.
- Action: Pulls the first digit away from the paw and extends it.
- Structure: More developed deep in the forearm in the feline than in the dog. Surface exposure is about the same in both.

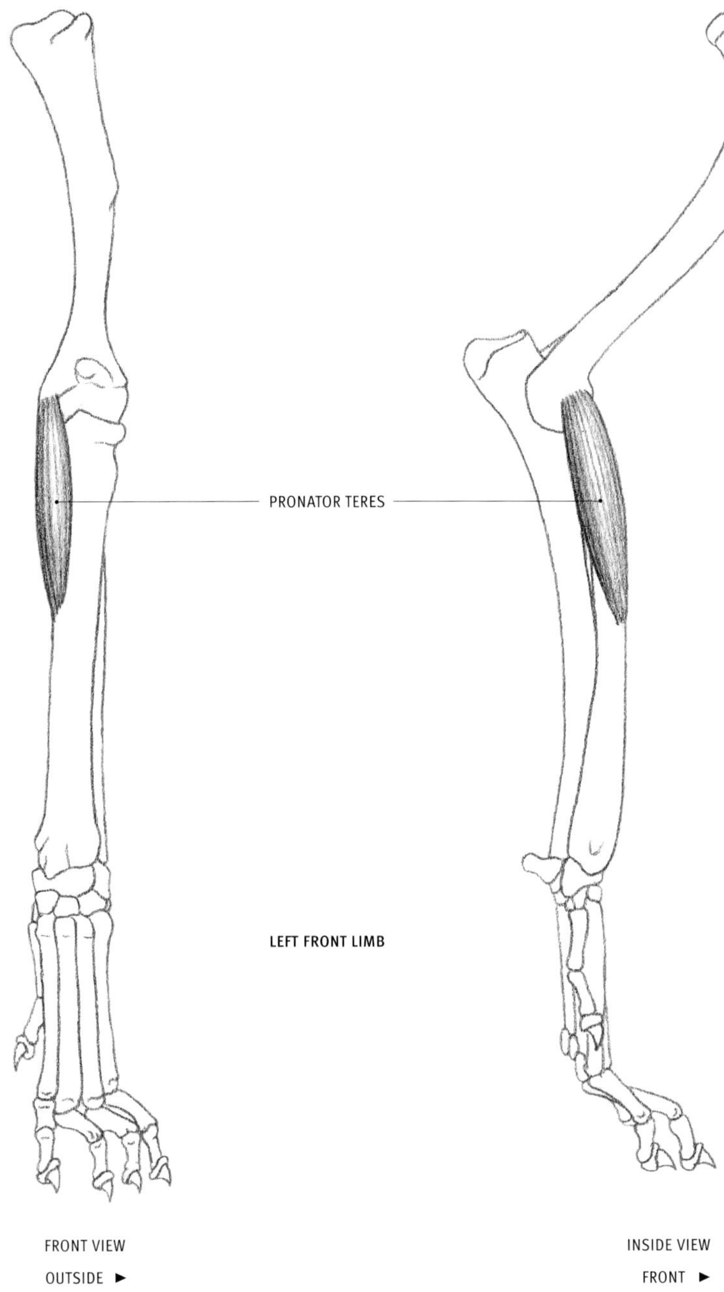

DOG

Pronator teres

DOG AND FELINE

• Origin: Inner surface of the lower end of the humerus. It is the forward-most attachment of all the flexor muscles.
• Insertion: Inner front edge of the radius, approximately a third to halfway down the bone.
• Action: Pronates the forearm, rotating it so the palm is directed backward. It also flexes the elbow joint. Pronation is minor in the dog, because there is very little movement of the radius rotating around the ulna. In the feline, however, movement is fairly extensive because there is full pronation and supination of the forearm, and the muscle is therefore more developed.
• Structure: The pronator teres is the first muscle of the flexor muscles. Its cylindrical belly, passing downward and forward, lies on the upper third of the inside of the forearm.

The pronator teres is not present in the horse. In the ox, it is a weak, fibrous band, occasionally containing a few muscular fibers. It does not create surface form.

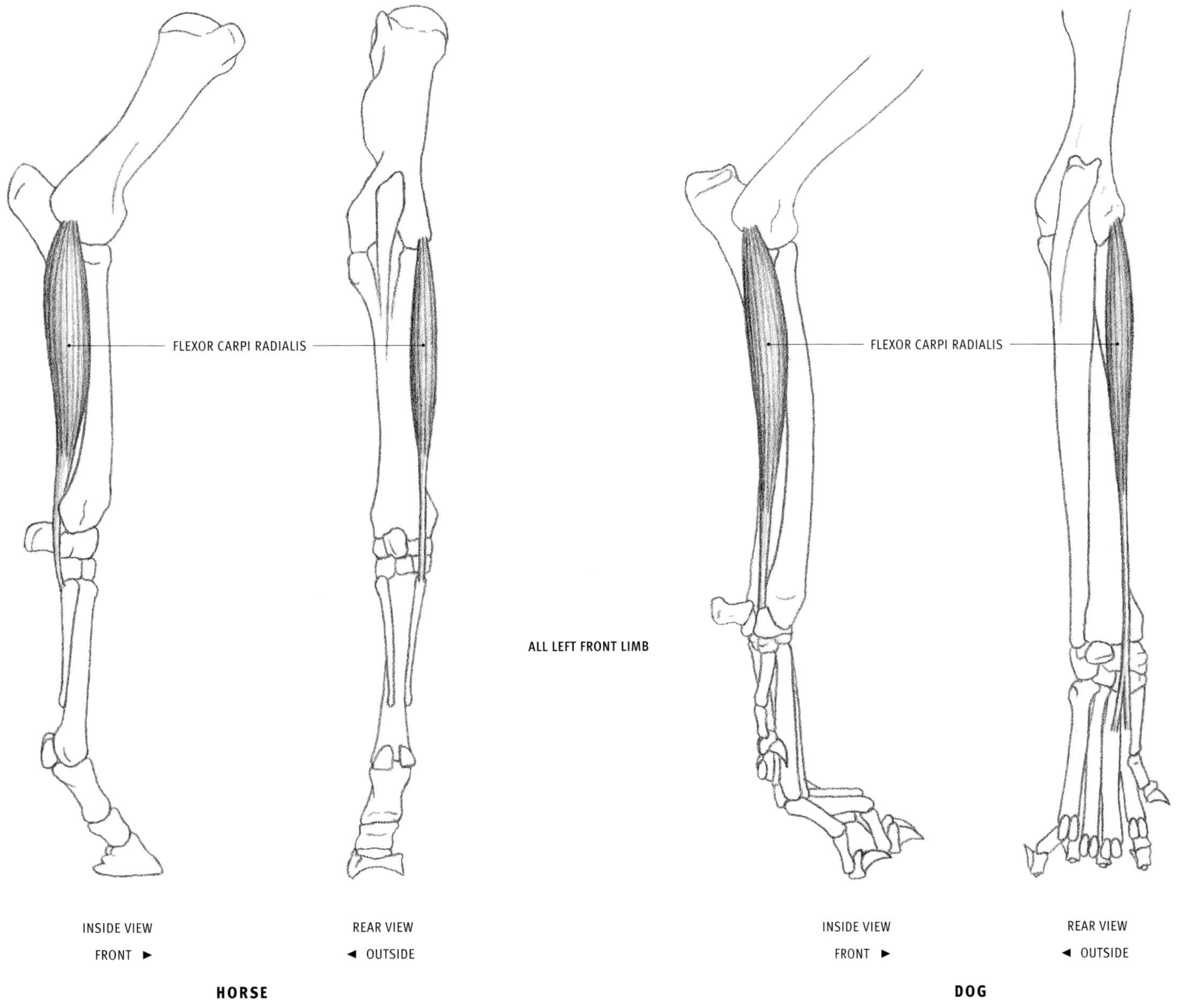

Flexor carpi radialis (Flexor metacarpi internus)

HORSE

- Origin: Lower end of the inner surface of the humerus.
- Insertion: Upper end of the rear surface of the inner splint bone.
- Action: Flexes the wrist joint; extends the elbow joint.
- Structure: Long, slightly flattened muscle belly becomes tendinous three fourths of the way down the forearm. The entire front edge lies up against the exposed radius.

OX

- Insertion: Upper inner corner of the metacarpal bone.

DOG AND FELINE

- Insertion: Upper end of the rear surface of the second and third metacarpals.
- Structure: The short, thick belly becomes tendinous halfway down the forearm; its tendon splits at the back of the wrist. The flexor carpi radialis is quite narrow in the feline.

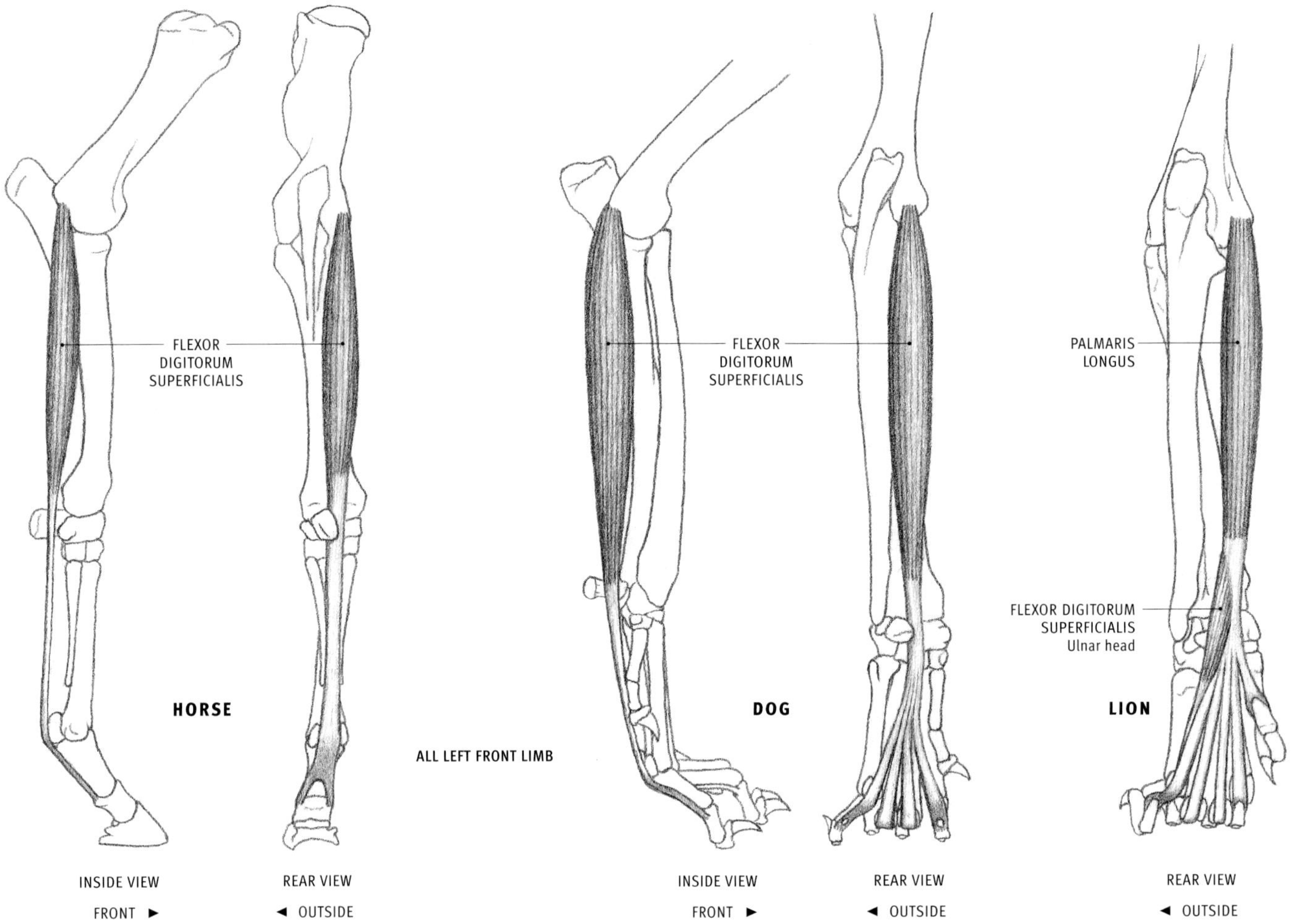

Flexor digitorum superficialis (Flexor digitorum sublimis, Flexor perforatus)

HORSE

- Origin: Lower end of the inner surface of the humerus.
- Insertion: Inner and outer corners, on the rear surface of the lower end of the upper toe bone and the upper end of the middle toe bone.
- Action: Flexes the wrist joint and the upper two toe joints; extends the elbow joint.
- Structure: The muscle belly lies deep to the other muscles of the forearm. Its strong, flat tendon emerges at the back of the wrist, descends as the most superficial tendon on the back of the lower part of the limb, widens behind the metacarpophalangeal joint, and then splits before inserting. The tendon of the flexor digitorum profundus emerges through this split. A deep radial head, consisting of a fibrous band, is not visible. The tendons of the superficial and deep digital flexors appear as a single powerful cable on the back of the metacarpal.

OX

- Insertion: Upper rear surface of the middle toe bone of both toes.
- Structure: A small portion of the fleshy belly is visible on the surface, on the inner side of the limb, above the wrist. The long tendon splits on the back of the metacarpal bone for each toe. Just before it inserts, the tendon is perforated with a single hole to allow passage of the tendon of the flexor digitorum profundus.

DOG

- Insertion: Upper end of the rear surface of the middle toe bone of the four outer digits.
- Structure: The entire muscle belly is visible on the surface, in marked contrast to the horse and the ox. It becomes tendinous just above the wrist, then splits into four tendons. The inserting ends are perforated with a single hole to allow passage of the tendon of the flexor digitorum profundus.

FELINE

- Origin: Outer portion of the rear surface of the tendon of the palmaris longus, just above the back of the wrist.
- Insertion: Upper rear surface of the middle toe bone of the two outer digits (4 & 5).
- Action: Flexes the upper two toe joints of the outer two toes (4 & 5).
- Structure: In the feline, the flexor digitorum superficialis is a small, minor muscle that lies on the back of the wrist. Only the ulnar head comes to the surface (the radial head is deep). It has a small, flat belly and two tendons that pass deep to the outer tendons of the palmaris longus.

Palmaris longus

FELINE

- Origin: Lower end of the inner surface of the humerus.
- Insertion: Upper end of the rear surface of the upper toe bone of all the toes; also into the skin and carpal pad.
- Action: Flexes the wrist joint and the upper toe joint; extends the elbow joint.
- Structure: In felines, the superficial flexor of the digits that begins on the humerus and lies in the forearm is called the "palmaris longus."

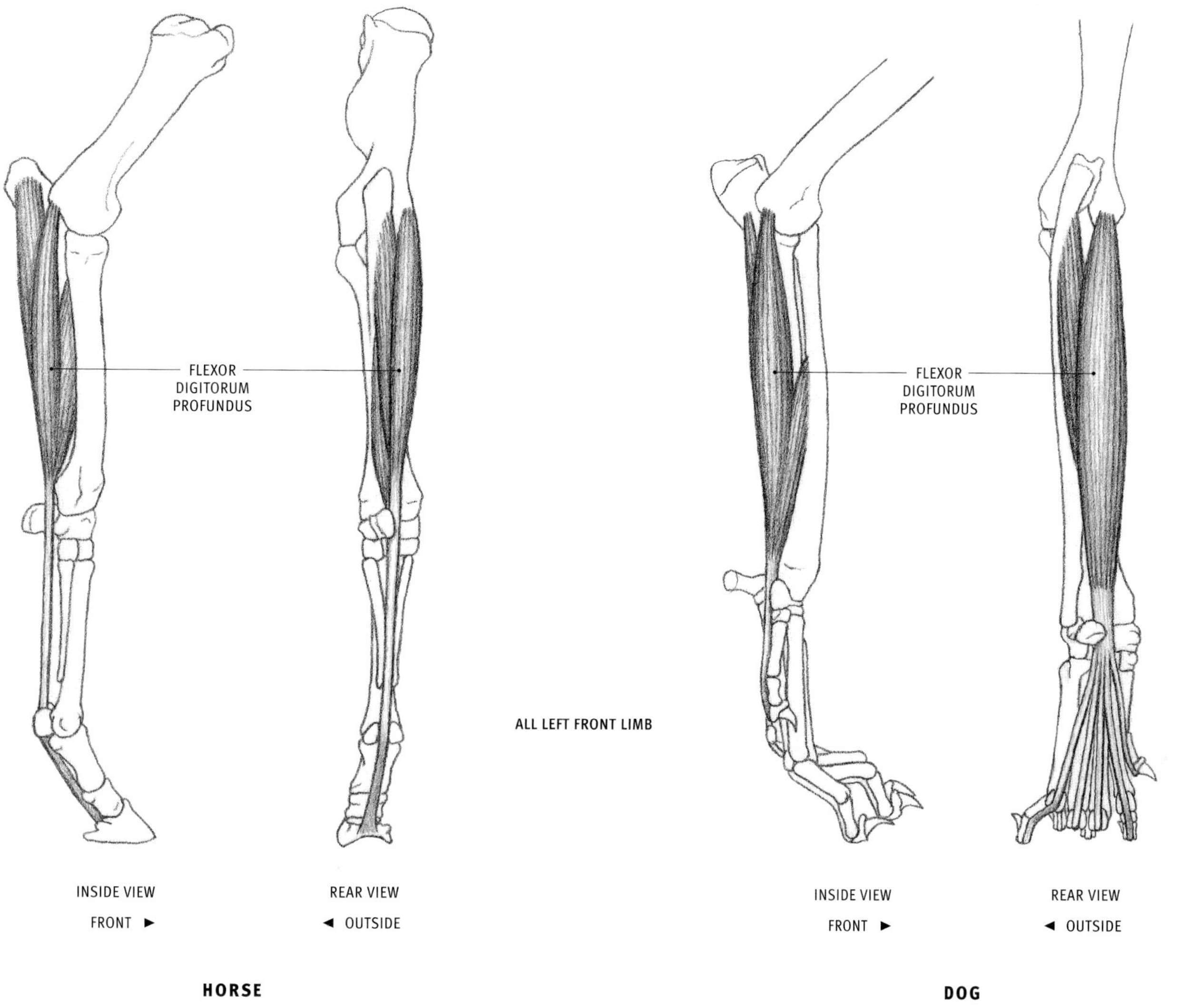

Flexor digitorum profundus (Flexor perforans)

HORSE

• Origin: Lower end of the inner surface of the humerus; inner surface of the olecranon of the ulna; rear surface of the radius.

• Insertion: Rear edge of the last toe bone.

• Action: Flexes the wrist joint and all the toe joints; extends the elbow joint.

• Structure: Located behind the radius, the flexor digitorum profundus is the largest of the flexor muscles and consists of three major heads that contribute substantially to the mass of the forearm. Its belly lies mostly deep to the other forearm muscles. Only a small portion comes to the surface between the ulnaris lateralis and the flexor carpi ulnaris on the back of the forearm below the elbow, and between the ulnaris lateralis and the extensor digitorum lateralis on the outside of the forearm just above the wrist. Below the wrist, its tendon lies deep to, and is in contact with, the tendon of the flexor digitorum superficialis; both tendons form a single powerful cable on the back of the metacarpal.

OX

• Origin: Also from the rear and outer surface of the olecranon of the ulna.

• Insertion: Rear surface of the last toe bone of both toes.

• Structure: The lower end of the tendon separates into two tendons, one for each digit. The muscle belly comes to the surface for a short distance just below the elbow.

DOG AND FELINE

• Origin: Ulnar origin is from the rear edge of the ulna.

• Insertion: Bottom of the last toe bone of all five digits.

• Structure: A small portion of the belly comes to the surface on the inside of the forearm, between the radius and the flexor digitorum superficialis (palmaris longus in the feline). The tendon of the flexor carpi radialis lies on top of it in this interval. In the feline, the ulnar portion of the muscle can be seen on the outer back corner of the forearm between the extensor carpi ulnaris and the flexor carpi ulnaris, running from the elbow down to the wrist. The remainder of the muscle and its five tendons are not visible on the surface.

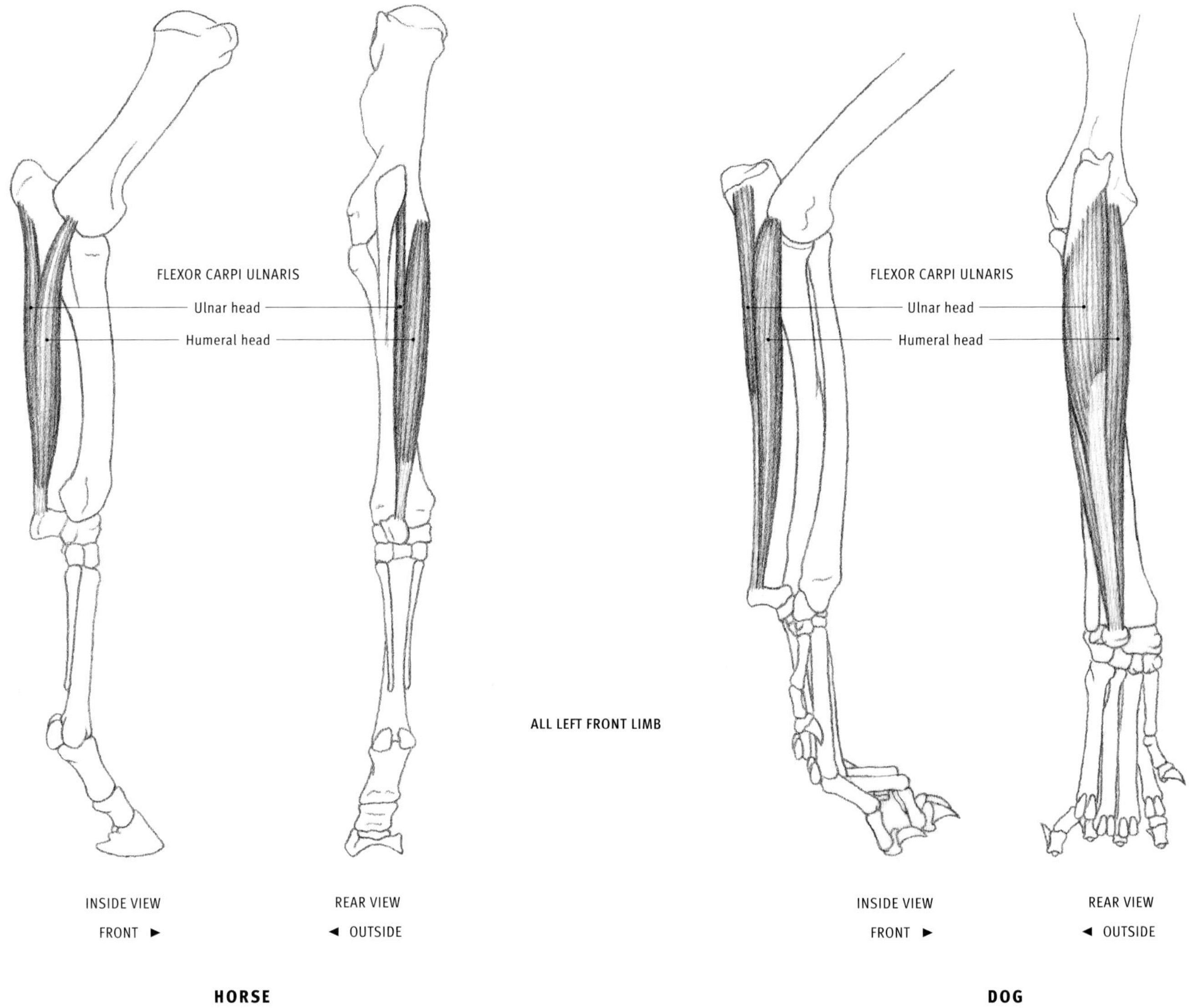

Flexor carpi ulnaris (Flexor metacarpi medius)

HORSE

• Origin: Lower end of the inside surface of the humerus; inner surface, toward the rear, of the upper end of the ulna.

• Insertion: Upper edge of the accessory carpal bone of the wrist.

• Action: Flexes the wrist joint; extends the elbow joint.

• Structure: Begins on the inside of the elbow region and ends on the back of the wrist. The muscle consists of two heads—a larger, flattened, curved humeral head and a thinner ulnar head. They join above the midpoint of the forearm, and the fused heads insert into the top of the accessory carpal bone via a strong, short tendon. The upper ends of both heads are covered by the pectoralis.

OX

• Structure: More flattened and wider than in the horse.

DOG AND FELINE

• Structure: The humeral and ulnar heads descend in contact with each other, yet remain distinct throughout. The humeral head is massive, and the ulnar head is very thin and lies on top of it. In the dog, the upper portion of the humeral head lies completely deep to both the ulnar head and the flexor digitorum superficialis; only its lower *outer* edge comes to the surface. The upper end of the ulnar head is slightly covered by the medial head of the triceps. In the feline, only a narrow strip of the humeral head comes to the surface between the ulnar head and the palmaris longus.

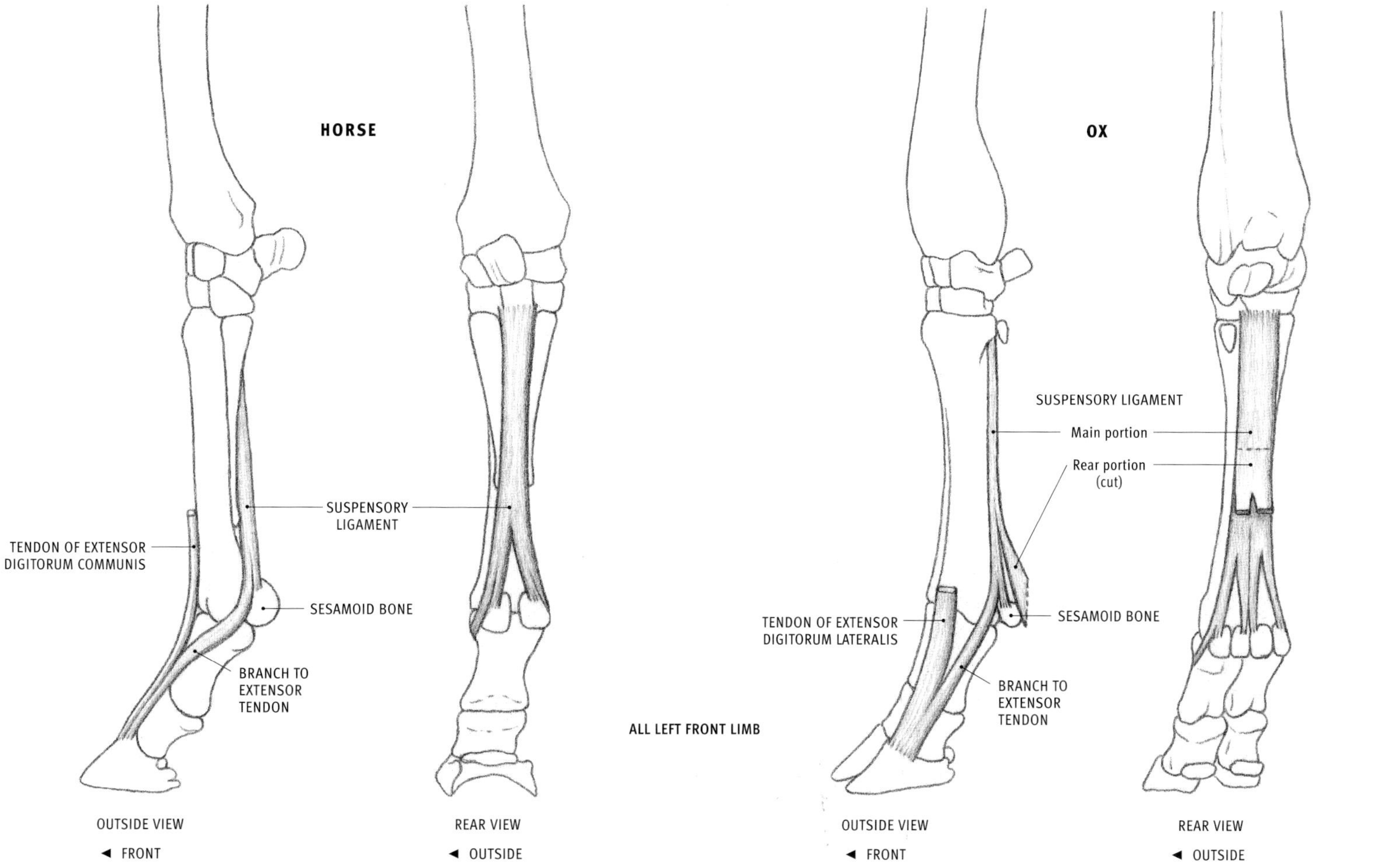

Suspensory ligament (Interosseous medius)

HORSE

• Origin: Upper end of the rear surface of the large metacarpal bone and the back of the lower row of carpal bones.

• Insertion: Upper outer surface of each sesamoid bone on the back of the metacarpophalangeal joint; ultimately into the front top edge of the last (distal) toe bone by its connection to the tendon of the extensor digitorum communis.

• Action: Supports the metacarpophalangeal (fetlock) joint, holding the joint passively in position while the animal is standing. However, because it is elastic, it allows the fetlock joint to be extended to almost ninety degrees while the animal is running, and then springs the limb back to the normal position as the weight of the body is removed.

• Structure: The suspensory ligament is a wide, thick, flat band lying on the back of the large metacarpal, deep to the flexor tendons of the toe. It contains only a few muscle fibers, recalling its relationship to the interossei muscle of other species. Three fourths of the way down the metacarpal, it splits. These parts then split into two branches. The short, inner branches insert into the sesamoids; the long outer branches continue downward and forward around both sides of the upper toe bone, reaching and then fusing with the tendon of the extensor digitorum communis. The edges of the suspensory ligament can be seen prominently behind the large metacarpal bone, in front of the flexor tendons. The long branches wrapping around the sides of the toe bone may also be seen on the surface.

OX

• Insertion: Main portion: Top surface of both sesamoid bones of each toe; ultimately into the front top edge of the last toe bone of both toes by its connection to the tendons of the extensor digitorum lateralis on the outer toe and the extensor digitorum communis on the inner toe. Rear portion: Into the tendon of the flexor digitorum superficialis.

• Structure: Because the suspensory ligament in the ox involves two toes, is becomes quite complex in its numerous branchings, with more than ten areas of insertion. This description is restricted to its superficial structures. As in the horse, it begins as a wide band on the back of the carpus, then, two thirds of the way down, splits for each toe. It then splits again to send a short branch to each of the sesamoid bones of each toe and a long branch around the outsides of the toes to fuse with the extensor tendons—the extensor digitorum lateralis on the outside of the foot and the extensor digitorum communis on the inside.

At about the middle of the metacarpal bone, a separate wide tendinous band comes off the back surface of the suspensory ligament and goes on to split into two branches. It then descends to the back of the metacarpophalangeal joint and attaches to the tendon of the flexor digitorum superficialis, wrapping around the tendon of the deeper flexor digitorum profundus. It softens the details of this region. The suspensory ligament of the ox contains more muscle fiber than that of the horse.

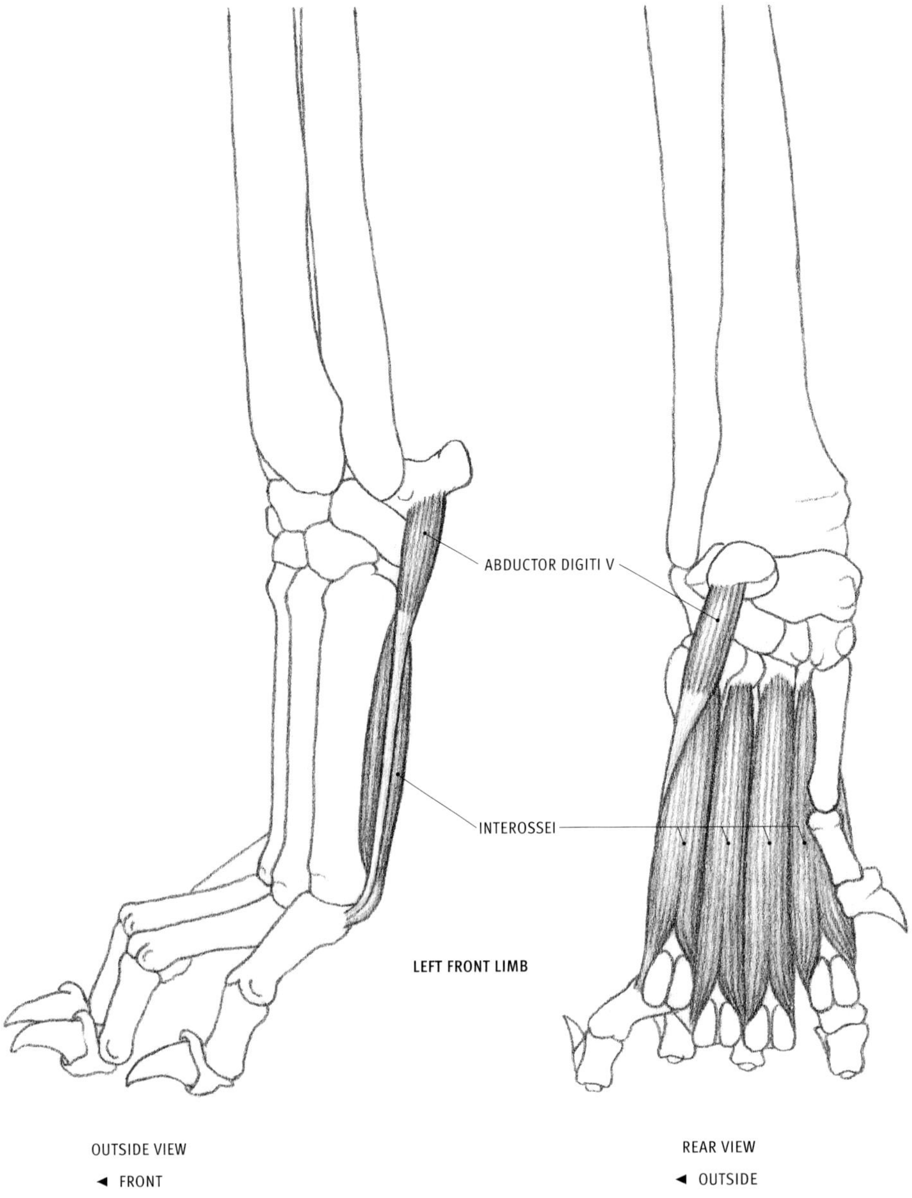

DOG

Interossei

DOG AND FELINE

• Origin: Upper end of the rear surface of each of the four major metacarpal bones (digits 2 through 5) of the front paw.

• Insertion: By tendon into both sesamoid bones at the lower end of each of the four major metacarpal bones, and further down onto the adjacent upper end of the upper toe bone. A branch of each tendon continues around each side of each toe bone to the front of the paw, where it inserts into the tendon of the extensor digitorum communis (similar to the suspensory ligament of the horse and the ox).

• Action: Flexes the metacarpophalangeal joints.

• Structure: The interossei consist of four elongated muscle bellies lying on the rear surface of the four major metacarpals. Their lower ends split and then develop short tendons. The outermost interosseous adds a slight muscular fullness on the outer edge of the rear of the paw.

Abductor digiti V

DOG AND FELINE

• Origin: Bottom of the accessory carpal bone.

• Insertion: Outer sesamoid bone of the outer metacarpal and the adjacent upper end of the upper toe bone.

• Action: Pulls the outer toe away from the paw.

• Structure: The abductor digiti V lies on the outermost interosseous muscle, and with it adds fullness to the outer back edge of the paw. It has a short muscle belly and a long tendon. The belly lies higher up on the paw than the outer interosseous.

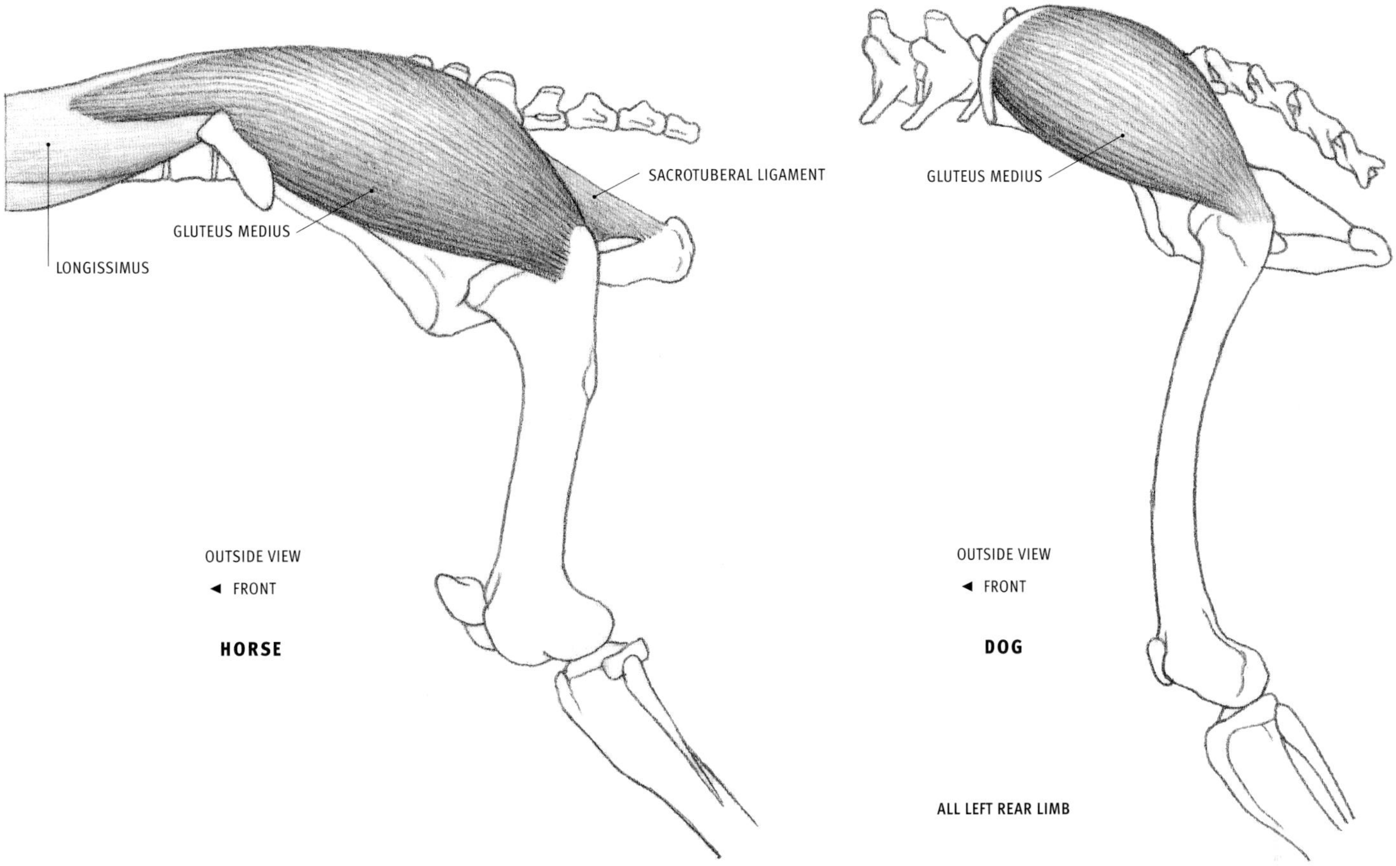

Gluteus medius

HORSE

• Origin: Surface of the depression in the top of the longissimus muscle; upper surface of the ilium of the pelvis; from wide ligaments connecting the sacrum to the ilium and the sacrum to the ischiatic tuberosity (sacrotuberal ligament).

• Insertion: Top and back of the upper end of the femur.

• Action: Extends the hip joint (important muscle for rearing, jumping, kicking, and forward propulsion); pulls the limb away from the body.

• Structure: Beginning thin in front, on top of the longissimus, the gluteus medius becomes a thick, massive muscle that gives the buttocks its rounded form. Its rear edge is covered by the gluteus superficialis and the biceps femoris.

OX

• Structure: Similar to, but much less developed than in the horse. The front end is narrower and does not extend as far forward as it does in the horse. Although it has a convex form, the gluteus medius often lies recessed in relation to the surrounding bony prominences. Its rear edge is covered by the gluteobiceps.

DOG AND FELINE

• Origin: Dog: Outer surface of the front end of the ilium of the pelvis, and from the ligament connecting the sacrum to the ilium. Feline: Upper half of the outer surface of the ilium, and from the transverse processes (side projections) of the last sacral vertebra and the first tail vertebra.

• Insertion: Upper end of the femur.

• Structure: The thick, fleshy belly ends in a short wide tendon before inserting on the femur. Its rear edge is covered by the gluteus superficialis.

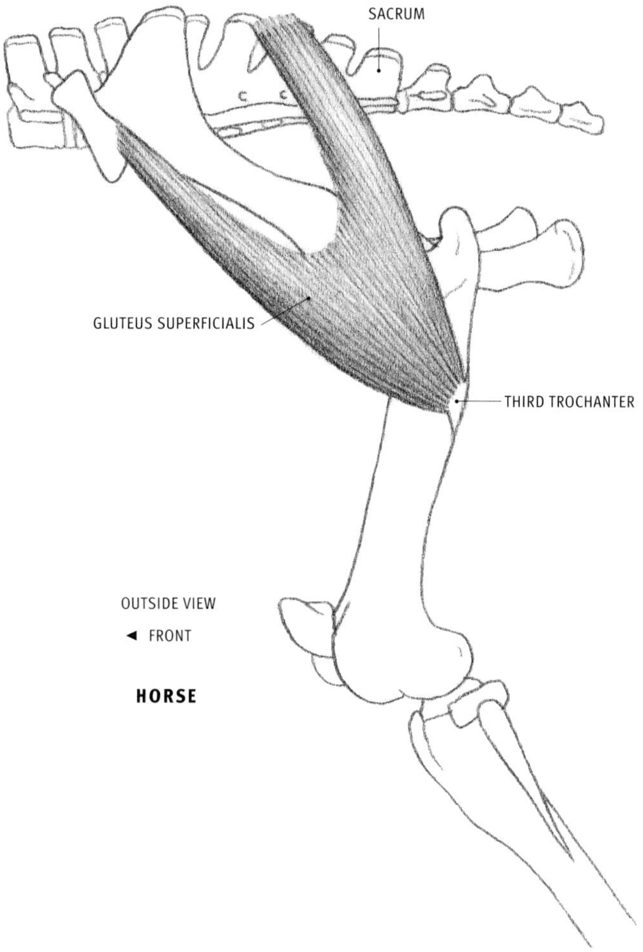

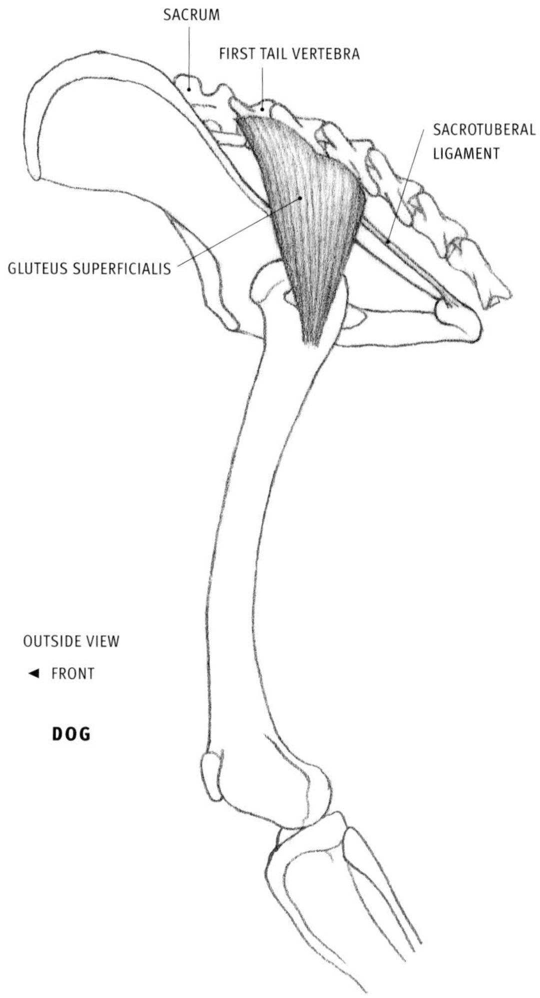

ALL LEFT REAR LIMB

Gluteus superficialis

HORSE

- Origin: Point of the hip (coxal tuberosity) and an adjacent area on the outer edge of the ilium of the pelvis; from fascia covering the gluteus medius (in part ultimately originating from the ligament connecting the sacrum to the ilium).
- Insertion: Third trochanter of the femur, one third of the way down the outside of the bone.
- Action: Flexes the hip joint; pulls the limb away from the body.
- Structure: The gluteus superficialis is a thin, V-shaped muscle that converges on the femur. The front portion is partly covered by, and firmly attached to, the tensor fasciae latae muscle. The rear portion sits on top of the gluteus medius; its rear edge is covered by the biceps femoris.

DOG AND FELINE

- Origin: The sacrum, the first tail vertebra, the front half of the ligament connecting the sacrum to the ischiatic tuberosity (sacrotuberal ligament), and the fascia covering the gluteus medius.
- Insertion: Outer surface of the femur, about one-eighth of the way down the bone.
- Structure: The gluteus superficialis is a small, flat muscle appearing somewhat rectangular on the surface. It is smaller than the gluteus medius.

The gluteus superficialis is not present in the ox. The upper front portion of the gluteobiceps muscle of the ox is believed to be the rear portion of the gluteus superficialis, and the rear portion of the tensor fasciae latae may be the front portion of the gluteus medius.

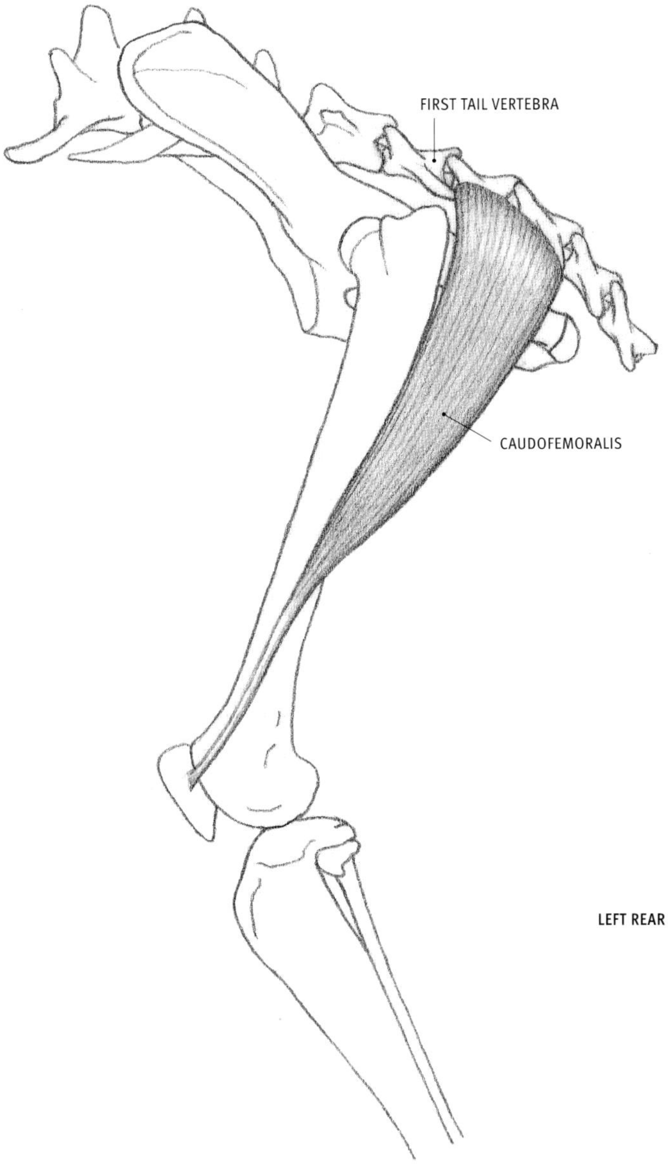

Caudofemoralis (Gluteofemoralis)

FELINE

- Origin: Side projections of the first, second, and third tail vertebrae.
- Insertion: The fascia of the leg in front of the biceps femoris muscle, and the middle of the outside edge of the patella.
- Action: Extends the hip joint; pulls the limb away from the body.
- Structure: The caudofemoralis muscle, exclusive to the felines, is an elongated triangular muscle located behind the gluteus superficialis. Approximately one third of the way down the thigh, it disappears under the biceps femoris. About two thirds of the way down, it develops a long, very thin tendon. The visible superficial portion of the muscle belly is approximately the same size as the gluteus superficialis.

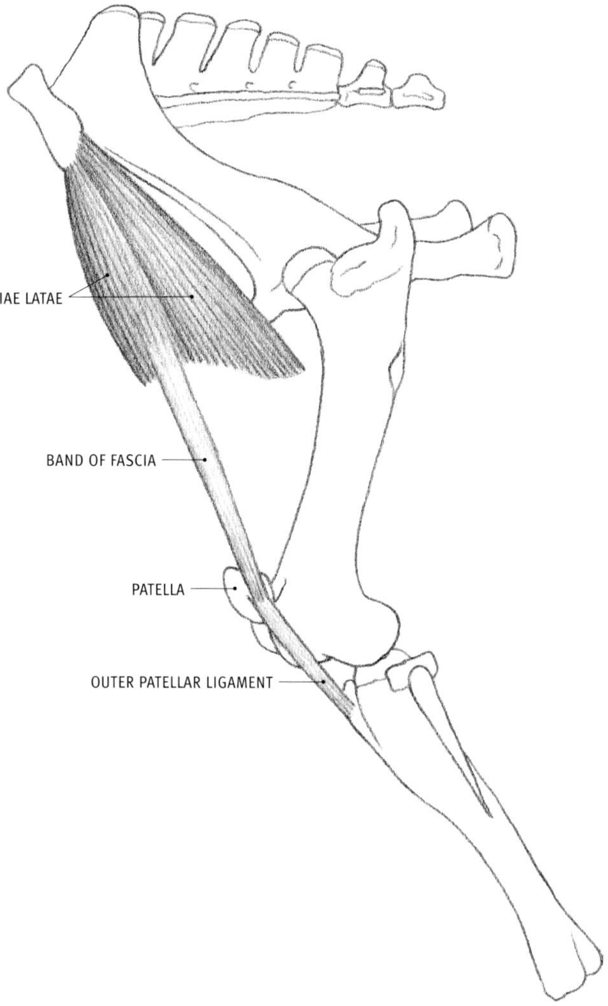

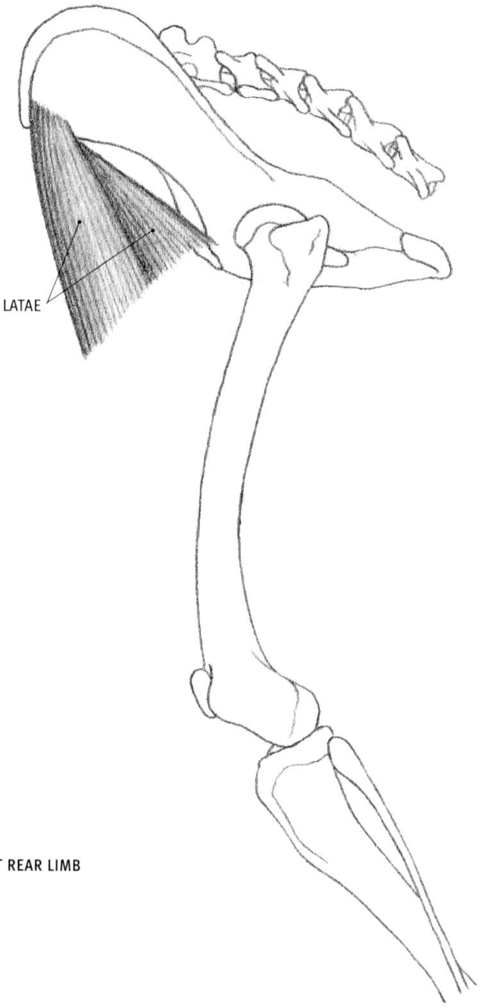

Tensor fasciae latae

HORSE

• Origin: Point of the hip (outer front corner of the ilium of the pelvis).

• Insertion: Into the fascia of the leg that surrounds the vastus lateralis and the rectus femoris, therefore indirectly into the patella, the outer patellar ligament, and the front edge of the tibia.

• Action: Flexes the hip joint and, by its ultimate attachment to the patella and the tibia, extends the knee joint.

• Structure: The tensor fasciae latae is a triangular muscle that forms the front edge of the upper end of the thigh. Its belly begins on the point of the hip and ends midway between the point of the hip and the patella. Its rear edge tightly adheres to the gluteus superficialis. The muscle belly may separate into two forms upon contraction.

A thickened, narrow **band of fascia** coming off the belly passes over the thigh muscles and attaches to the patellar ligament. When the tensor fasciae latae is tensed, the fascial band tightens and compresses the underlying vastus lateralis muscle. This can create a narrow form, directed from the point of the hip to the patella.

OX

• Structure: The lower end of the belly ends in a wide inverted "V." The front edge of the belly ends a short distance above the patella.

DOG AND FELINE

• Origin: Lower edge of the front end of the pelvis; the surface of the gluteus medius.

• Insertion: Into the fascia covering the thigh muscles.

• Structure: The triangular muscle separates into two forms on the surface. The muscle belly ends high on the thigh; its lower edge is directed downward and forward from the upper end of the femur. The sartorius, not the tensor fasciae latae, is the leading muscle on the front of the thigh.

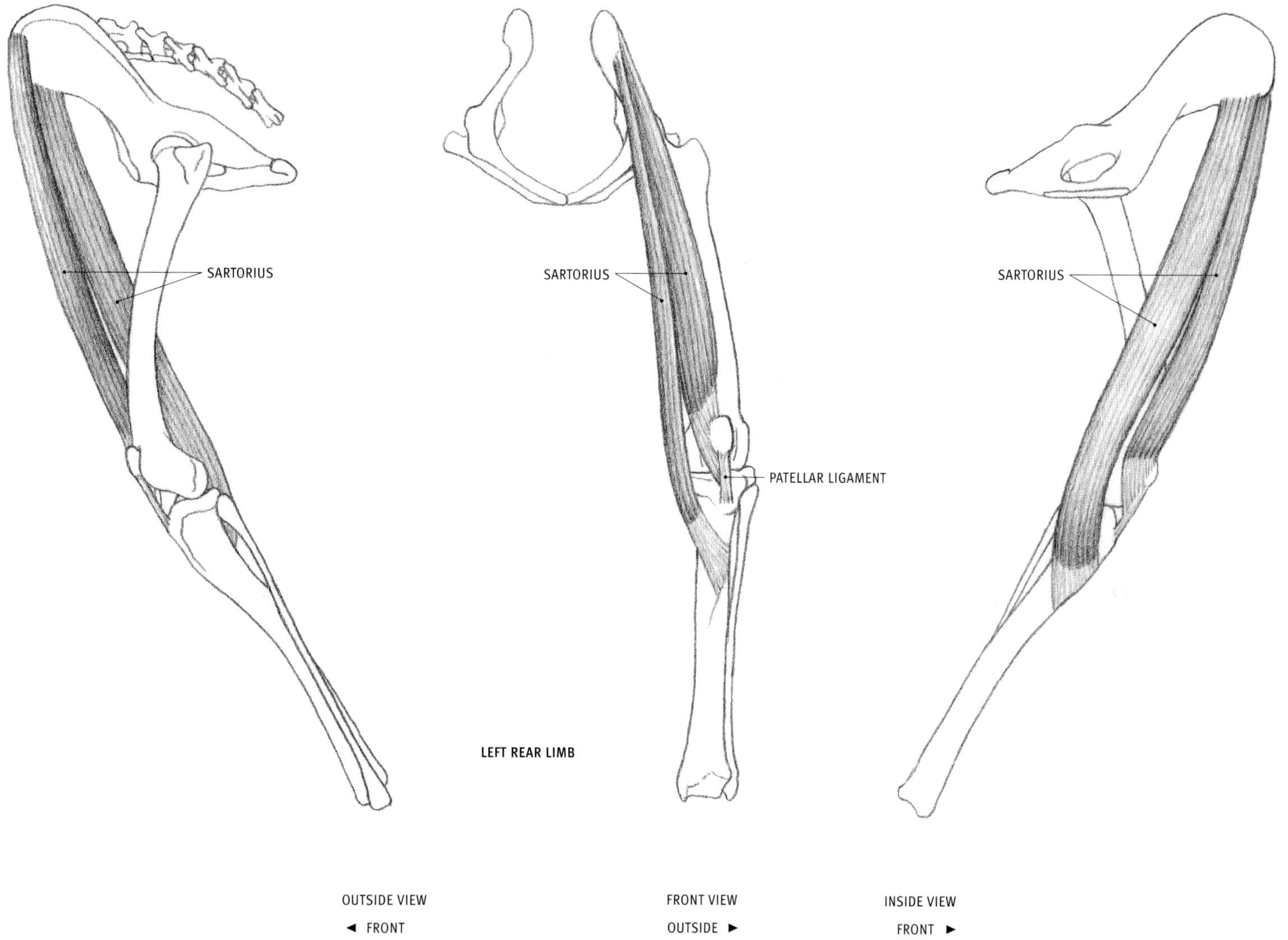

DOG

Sartorius

HORSE AND OX

The sartorius is a minor muscle and is rarely visible on the surface. It is a small, narrow muscle that lies on the inside of the thigh, just in front of the gracilis. Originating deep on the fascia and tendon in the region where the upper inner end of the thigh meets the rear of the abdomen, it becomes tendinous above the knee. Its tendon ultimately inserts into the medial patellar ligament and the tibia.

DOG AND FELINE

• Origin: Front portion: Line on the front edge of the pelvis. Rear portion: Line on the lower edge of the front end of the pelvis.

• Insertion: Dog: Front portion: With the vastus medialis and the rectus femoris into the patella and the fascia of the knee. Rear portion: Front edge of the tibia. Feline: Continuous insertion from the patella to the upper end of the tibia.

• Action: Flexes the hip joint; pulls the limb toward the centerline of the body.

• Structure: The sartorius begins on the front end of pelvis and ends on the inside of the knee. It passes down the front and inside of the thigh, veering to the inside of the knee and becoming a wide tendon before inserting. In the side view of the body, the front edge of the sartorius can be seen passing down most of the front of the thigh and disappearing as it shifts to the inside. The lower half of the muscle passes over the lower end of the rectus femoris and the vastus medialis, adding muscular thickness on the lower end of the inside of the thigh. The muscle can also be seen in the front and inside views of the leg.

The sartorius consists of two elongated parallel muscular bands—a front and a rear portion—in the dog, but a single, wider muscle in the feline.

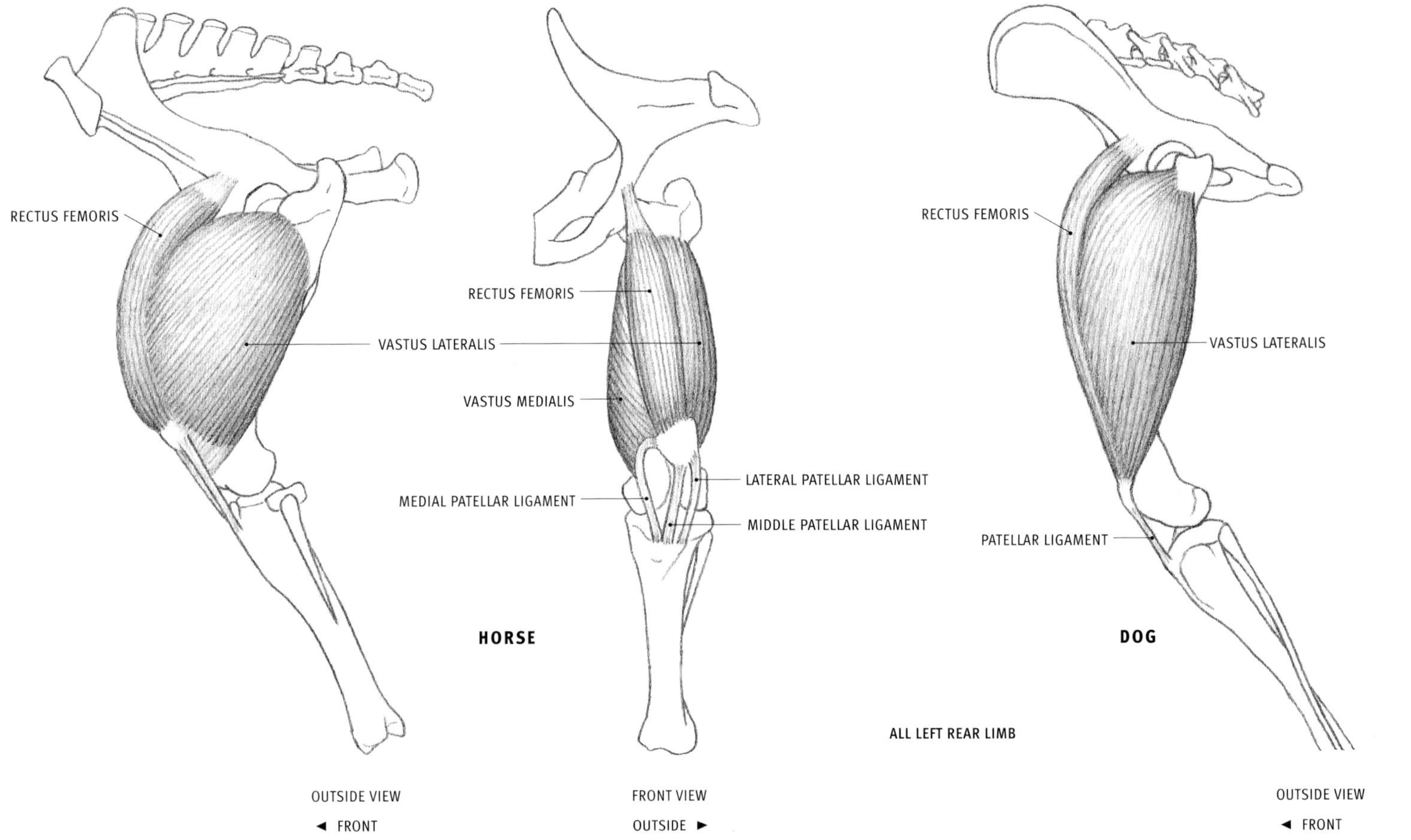

Quadriceps femoris: Vastus lateralis, medialis, and intermedius, Rectus femoris

HORSE

• Origin: Vastus lateralis: *Outer* surface of the femur, from a level just below the hip socket to two thirds of the way down the bone. Vastus medialis: *Inner* surface of the femur, from a level just below the hip socket to two thirds of the way down the bone. Rectus femoris: Two small adjacent areas on the body of the pelvis just in front of the hip socket.

• Insertion: All parts: The entire front surface and upper edge of the patella, and because of the attachment of the three patellar ligaments to the tibia, ultimately into the front of the upper end of the tibia (the tibial tuberosity). The vastus lateralis and medialis also insert into the sides of the rectus femoris, attaching to the fascia covering its surface. In addition, the vastus medialis inserts into the upper half of the medial patellar ligament.

• Action: All parts extend the knee joint; the rectus femoris also flexes the hip joint.

• Structure: The quadriceps muscle consists of the vastus lateralis, the vastus medialis, the deep vastus intermedius, and the rectus femoris. The three vastus muscles all begin on the femur, and the rectus femoris originates on the pelvis. These four components form a large, wide (front-to-back) but flattened (side-to-side) muscle mass. It embraces the inside, outside, and front of the femur, but it lies for the most part in front of it. The vastus lateralis lies on the outside of the thigh and is somewhat oval in outline. Its rear edge is straighter than the front edge, and its rear portion is covered by the biceps femoris. The vastus medialis is similar in shape, and lies on the inside of the thigh. There is a wide groove running down the front of the mass of the three vastus muscles in which the rectus femoris sits. The rectus femoris is an elongated muscle, tapered at both ends.

The **patellar ligaments,** although termed “ligaments” because they connect bone to bone (the patella to the tibia), are actually a continuation of the quadriceps muscle and are its tendons of insertion. In the horse and the ox, three patellar ligaments—inner, middle, and outer—converge on the tibial tuberosity.

OX

• Insertion: Vastus lateralis: Also into the lateral patellar ligament.

DOG AND FELINE

• Origin: Small areas on the inside (vastus medialis) and outside (vastus lateralis) of the femur near its upper end. The rectus femoris originates from a single area on the pelvis.

• Insertion: All parts into the patella, therefore ultimately into the tibia. The vastus muscles insert into their respective sides of the rectus femoris.

• Structure: The quadriceps femoris in the dog and feline does not bulge forward as much as in the horse, but the vastus lateralis bulges out to the side quite a bit, especially at its upper end. Although it is partially covered by the biceps femoris, the tensor fasciae latae, and the sartorius, the quadriceps femoris produces the bulk of the form on the front of the thigh.

There is a single **patellar ligament** between the patella and the tibia.

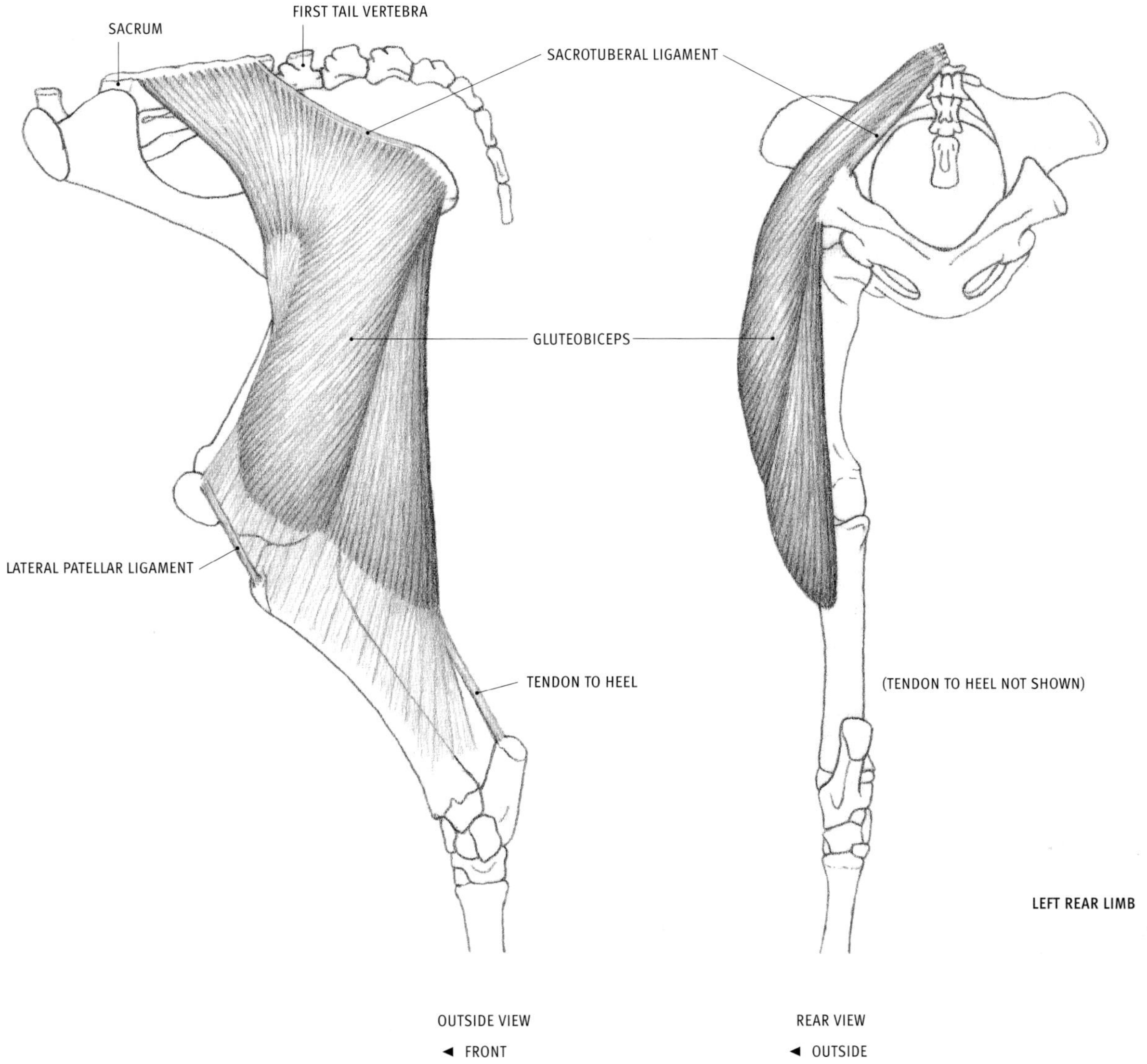

OX

Gluteobiceps

OX

• Origin: Spines of the sacrum, the sacrotuberal ligament, the ischiatic tuberosity at the rear end of the pelvis, and the fascia covering the gluteus medius and the tail.

• Insertion: Into the fascia of the leg, ultimately into the patella, the lateral patellar ligament, the front edge of the tibia, and the heel bone.

• Action: Extends the hip joint; extends the ankle joint; pulls the limb away from the body. With different portions, it both flexes and extends the knee joint.

• Structure: The gluteobiceps is a very large, roughly rectangular muscle, wide above and below, and narrower in the middle. Its front edge is thin, and its rear edge is thick. It is divisible into two portions—a large front portion passing from the hip region to the knee, and a long triangular rear portion beginning at the rear end of the pelvis. The division between these two portions is more visible near the pelvis, and it diminishes lower down, where the muscle fibers attach to the leg fascia. A long, narrow, tendinous band passes from the lower end of the muscle to the heel.

The gluteobiceps consists of the biceps femoris fused to the rear portion of the gluteus superficialis. It is not present in the horse, dog, or feline, where there are separate gluteus superficialis and biceps femoris muscles.

Biceps femoris

HORSE

• Origin: Long head: From the ligament connecting the sacrum to the ilium of the pelvis, in the vicinity of the third and fourth sacral spines, and from the surface of the gluteal muscles and the tail. Short head: Lower edge of the rear end of the pelvis.

• Insertion: All portions fuse deeply and then first insert into the back of the femur, about one third of the way down the bone. The lower ends of the muscle develop into a wide aponeurotic (tendinous) sheet that fuses into the fascia of the leg at and below the knee. The two heads ultimately insert as follows: Long head—into the patella and lateral patellar ligament. Short head/front portion—into the lateral patellar ligament and the front edge of the tibia. Short head/rear portion—into the leg fascia, and the end of the heel bone (calcaneus).

• Action: Entire muscle extends the hip joint (forward propulsion, kicking, rearing), and pulls the limb away from the body. The long head *extends* the knee joint, the short head/front portion *flexes* the knee joint, and the short head/rear portion flexes the knee joint and extends the ankle joint (extends the foot).

• Structure: The biceps femoris is a massive muscle that consists of a long head **(long vastus)** and a short head that separates into two portions, producing a total of three forms. The long head is crescent-shaped—widest at its center (where it covers the greater trochanter of the femur) and tapered at its ends. It begins at the top of the sacrum and ends at the level of the bottom of the patella. Its front edge is thin, whereas its rear edge is thicker and more clearly defined on the surface. The short head is a triangular volume that separates into two forms. Its front portion flattens and lies on the outside of the knee. The rear portion, which is thicker and rounder, ends distinctly on the surface of the outer side of the gastrocnemius muscle. A long, narrow tendon passes from the lower end of the biceps femoris muscle to the heel.

The semitendinosus muscle covers the rear edge of the upper half of the long head and the upper end of the short head. A strong vertical groove on the back of the thigh separates the biceps femoris from the semitendinosus.

DOG

• Origin: Superficial head: Outer corner of the ischiatic tuberosity at the rear end of the pelvis, and the rear third of the sacrotuberal ligament. Deep head: Bottom of the outer corner of ischiatic tuberosity, deep to the origin of the superficial portion.

• Insertion: Into the fascia of the leg, ultimately into the patella, the patellar ligament, the front edge of the upper end of the tibia, and the end of the heel bone (calcaneus).

• Action: The entire muscle extends the hip joint. The upper front fibers extend the knee joint, and the lower rear fibers extend the ankle joint and may also flex the knee joint.

• Structure: Large, wide muscle that begins narrow at the pelvis and then fans out to cover the rear portion of the outside of the thigh. Because its muscle fibers insert into a wide sheet of fascia that ultimately inserts further on, contracting muscle fibers pull on the fascia and may create raised ridges in line with the direction of those muscle fibers. This pulling can distort the volumes of the underlying muscles. The line where the muscle fibers attach to the fascia can occasionally be seen on the surface, which can also confuse the volumes of the muscles of the leg.

Along the rear edge of the muscle, new fibers begin deeply, wrap around to the outside, and then pass downward and forward on the surface. This structure may divide the overall muscle into several subtle forms.

A long, narrow tendon develops on the deep surface of the biceps femoris, emerges at its lower end, and descends along the surface of the gastrocnemius muscle. It eventually fuses with the Achilles tendon, which attaches to the heel bone (calcaneus).

FELINE

• Origin: Only from the ischial tuberosity, not from the sacrotuberal ligament.

• Structure: Because of its small point of origin, the biceps femoris assumes a more fan-shaped belly, and its fiber arrangement is simpler, than it is in the dog. It is divisible into a large front portion and a smaller rear portion.

The ox has no biceps femoris, but rather a gluteobiceps, which is an extensive, complex, single-bellied muscle consisting of the combined biceps femoris and gluteus superficialis.

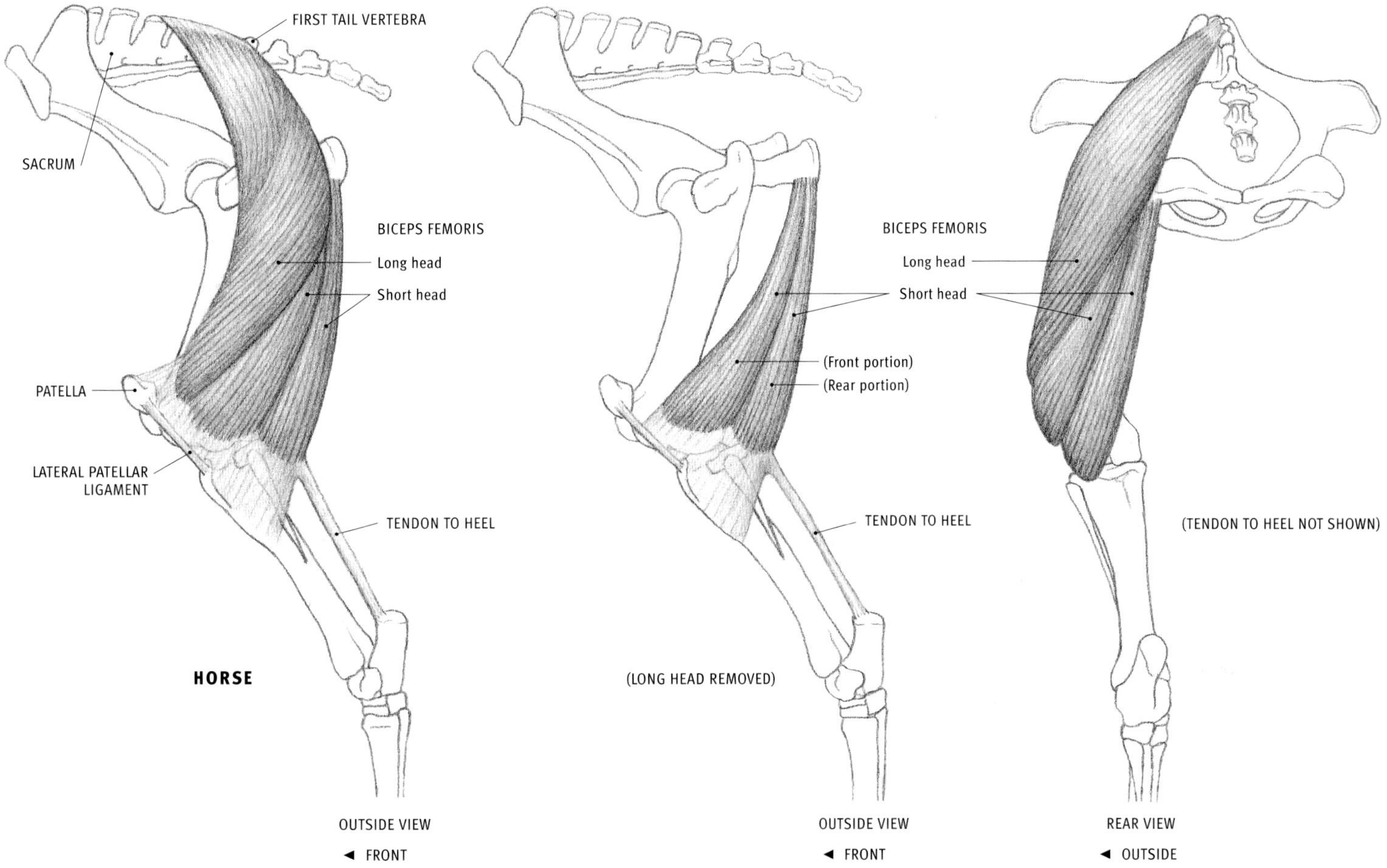

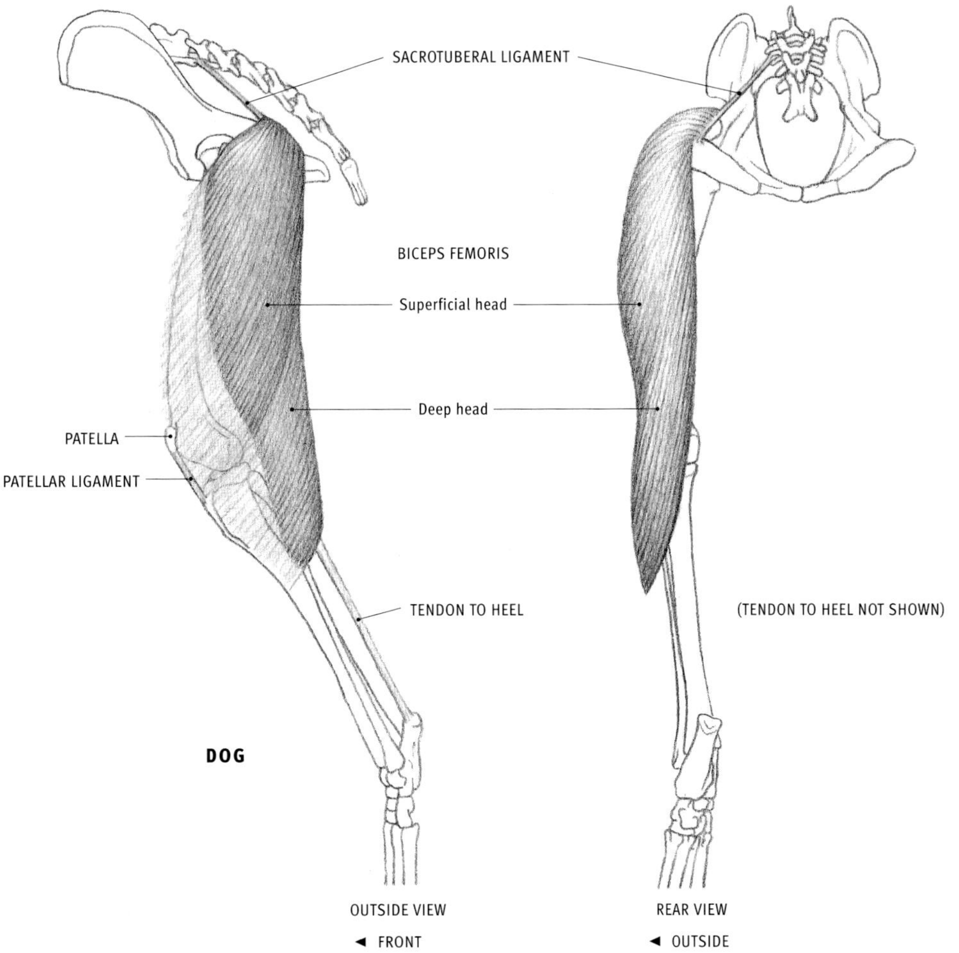

ALL LEFT REAR LIMB

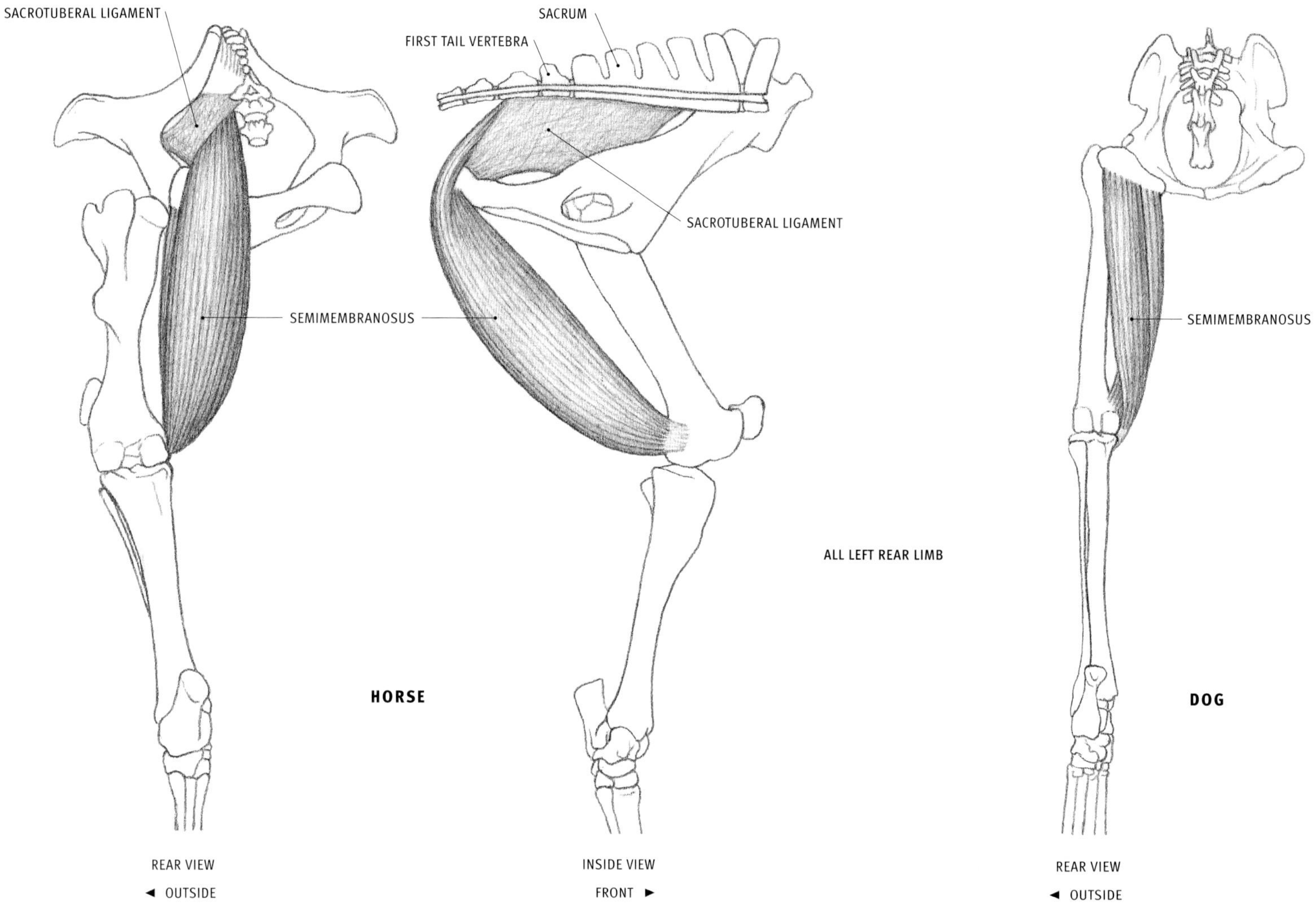

Semimembranosus

HORSE

• Origin: Rear free edge of the sacrotuberal ligament (passing from the second tail vertebra to the top of the rear end of the pelvis) and the lower edge of the rear end of the pelvis.

• Insertion: Inner surface of the lower end of the femur.

• Action: Extends the hip joint; pulls the limb toward the centerline of the body.

• Structure: The semimembranosus is a large, thick muscle located on the rear portion of the inside of the thigh, where most of it comes to the surface. It runs alongside the semitendinosus and is partly covered by the gracilis, mostly at its lower end. The muscle begins at the base of the tail and ends on the inside of the knee. Pointed on its upper end, the descending muscle belly is joined by a deep head that originates from the rear end of the pelvis. The upper end of the muscle, between the tail and the pelvis, is unique to the horse. The semimembranosus is not seen in the side view of the thigh (it does not form part of the rear profile).

OX

• Origin: From the lower edge of the rear end of the pelvis only, but from a more extensive area than in the horse.

• Insertion: Inner surface of the lower end of the femur, and the inner surface of the uppermost end of the tibia.

• Structure: The semimembranosus in the ox more closely resembles this muscle of the dog than the horse. The lower end splits and sends a major portion to the femur and a smaller portion to the tibia. This separation and insertion is deep and not visible on the surface.

The upper end of the belly slightly projects past the semitendinosus to form the upper portion of the rear profile of the thigh.

DOG AND FELINE

• Origin: A line on the lower edge of the rear end of the pelvis.

• Insertion: A vertical line on the inner back corner of the lower end of the femur, ending a short distance from the bottom of the bone, and a small area on the inner side of the uppermost end of the tibia.

• Structure: This is a thick fleshy muscle consisting of two heads. One head inserts into the femur, while the other crosses the knee joint and inserts into the tibia. The belly comes to the surface on the upper, inner rear corner of the thigh, between the semitendinosus and the gracilis. The upper portion of the muscle projects past the semitendinosus to form the upper portion of the rear profile of the thigh.

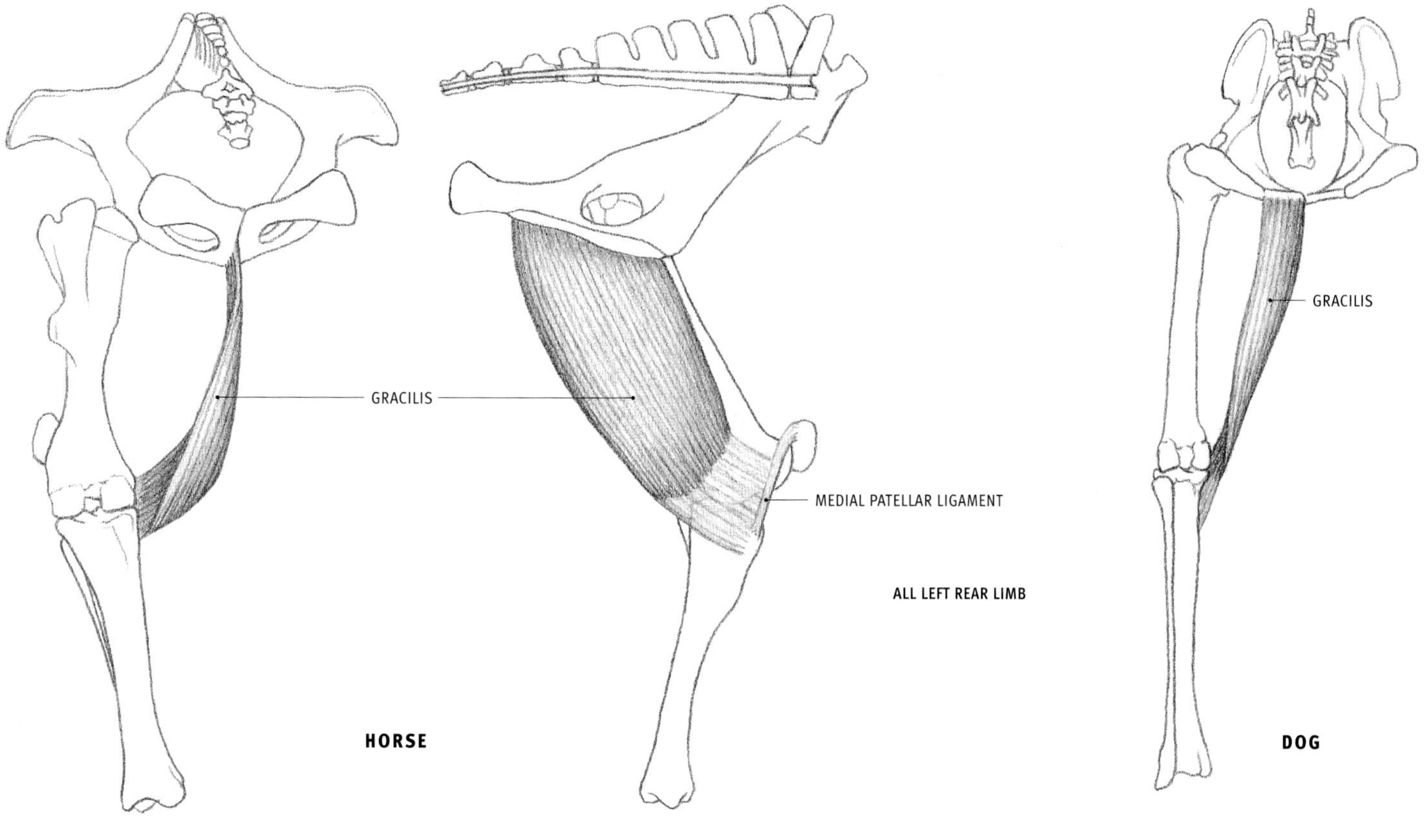

REAR VIEW
◄ OUTSIDE

INSIDE VIEW
FRONT ►

REAR VIEW
◄ OUTSIDE

Gracilis

HORSE

• Origin: Front two thirds of the line of fusion of the two halves of the pelvis, on the midline on the bottom of the pelvis (variously from bone, ligament, and tendon).

• Insertion: Medial patellar ligament, inner surface of the tibia, and the fascia of the leg.

• Action: Primarily pulls the limb toward the centerline of the body; extends the hip joint.

• Structure: The gracilis is a wide, thin, somewhat rectangular muscle lying on the rear portion of the inner side of the thigh. This flat muscle thins toward its rear edge. It shares its origin with the same muscle of the other leg; the upper ends of the two muscles are in contact with each other when the animals is in the standing position. The muscle belly ends below, developing a wide tendon that fuses with the fascia of the leg.

OX

• Insertion: Also to the heel bone.

• Action: Also extends the ankle joint.

• Structure: The lower end of the muscle belly also sends a tendinous band to the heel bone.

DOG AND FELINE

• Origin: Line on the midline on the bottom of the pelvis that veers outward as the rear projections of the pelvis diverge.

• Insertion: Ultimately into the front edge of the tibia and into the heel bone.

• Action: Also flexes the knee joint and extends the ankle joint.

• Structure: The muscle thickens toward its rear edge, opposite to that of the horse. The muscle belly is also narrower than in the horse. In addition to the tendon to the front of the tibia, the lower end of the belly sends a tendinous band back to the heel bone, along with the semi-tendinosus.

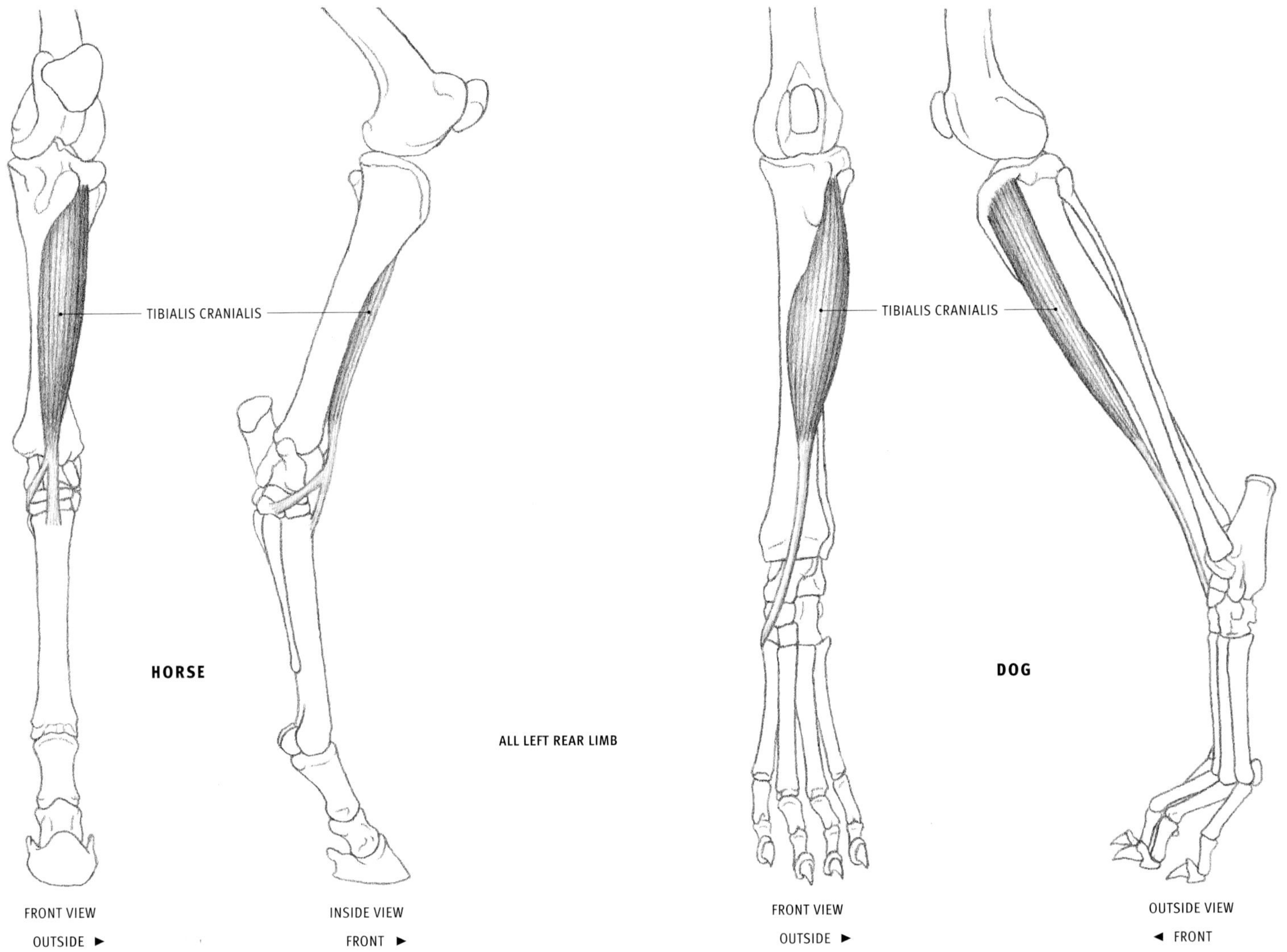

Tibialis cranialis (Tibialis anterior in humans)

HORSE

• Origin: Upper end of the outer side of the tibia, including the concavity and adjacent bony prominences, and the fascia of the leg.

• Insertion: Front of the upper end of the large metatarsal bone, and the inside back corner of the ankle (into the rear bone on the lower tarsal row).

• Action: Flexes the ankle joint.

• Structure: The tibialis cranialis is a flattened muscle lying on the front of the tibia. Its flat face is directed forward and outward; the extensor digitorum longus and the peroneus tertius lie on this surface. The muscle begins fleshy above and becomes tendinous below. In front of the ankle, its tendon emerges through the perforated tendon of the overlying peroneus tertius, and then splits, sending one branch straight down and the other around to the inside of the ankle.

Only the inner edge of the muscle belly is visible on the surface between the tibia and the extensor digitorum longus. The inner branch of the tendon can be seen when the ankle is flexed.

OX

• Structure: The tibialis cranialis is a thinner and more concealed muscle than in the horse. Only the upper end of the belly, between the tibia and the peroneus tertius, and the tendon, is superficial. The tendon remains single and veers to the inside of the ankle to attach into adjacent areas on the lower row of tarsal bones and the upper end of the large metatarsal. It pierces the tendon of the peroneus tertius, as in the horse.

DOG AND FELINE

• Origin: Vertical line on outer side of tibia, just to the outside of the front edge, continuing up into the concavity at the top of the outside of the bone. Feline: Also into the upper end of the fibula.

• Insertion: Dog: Inner edge of the foot, into the lower tarsal bone and the adjacent upper end of the inner metatarsal. Feline: Into the metatarsal only.

• Action: Flexes the ankle joint; rotates the foot slightly outward.

• Structure: This elongated muscle is wider at its upper end. In the dog, it develops a flat tendon two thirds of the way down the bone. In the feline, the lower end of the muscle belly becomes tendinous closer to the ankle than in the dog, covering more of the belly of the extensor digitorum longus. The tendon descends and then veers inward, crossing the front of the foot, and then ends on the inner edge of the foot. The slightly flattened belly sits on the outer front edge of the lower leg and wraps (side-to-side) around the underlying muscles. The tibialis cranialis is not covered by the extensor digitorum longus and the peroneus tertius, as it is in the horse and the ox.

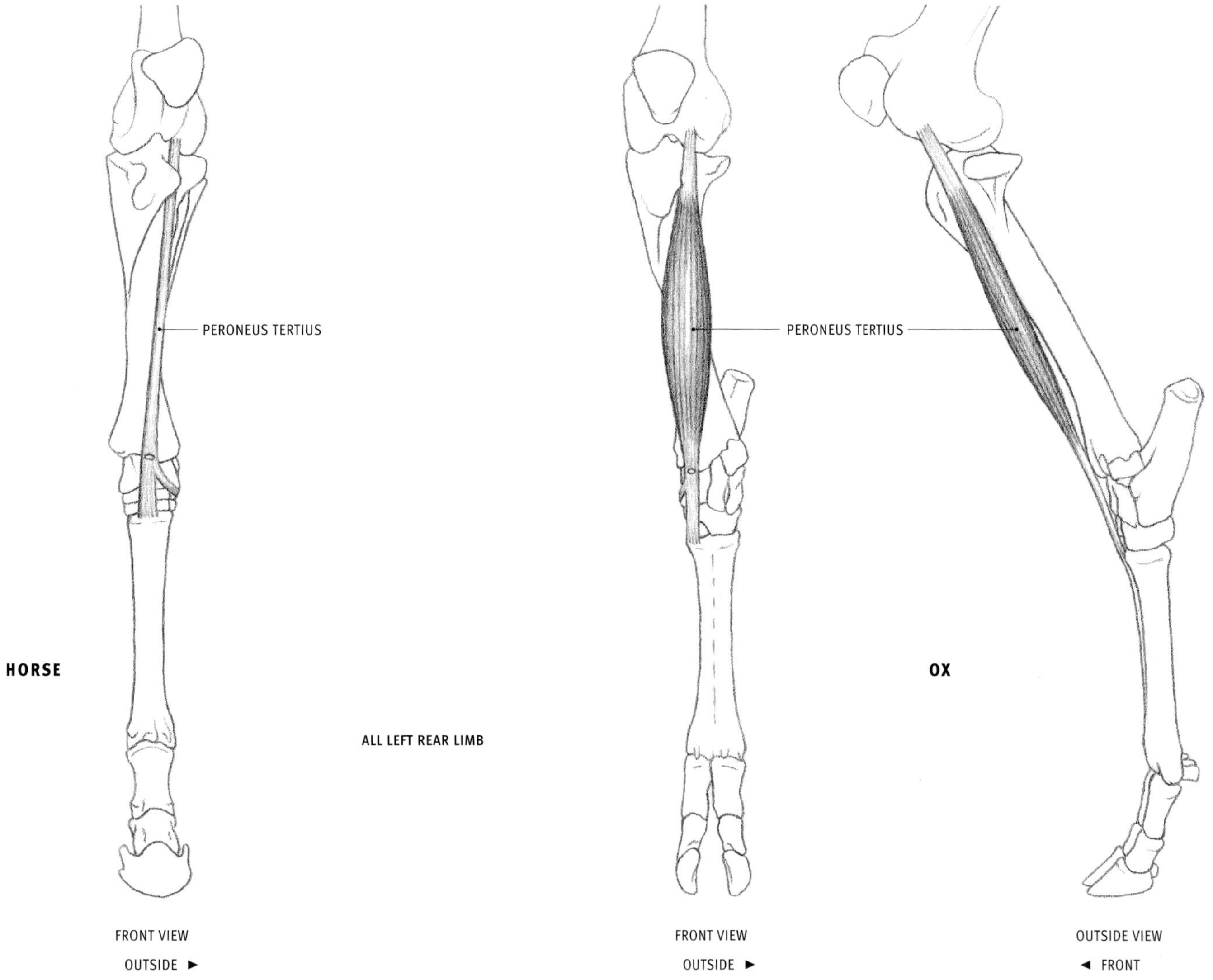

Peroneus tertius (Fibularis tertius)

HORSE

• Origin: From a depression on the outer surface of the very bottom of the femur.

• Insertion: Upper front end of the large metatarsal bone and the front of the tarsal bone above it; the outside of the ankle, into the base of the heel bone and the adjacent tarsal bone just below it.

• Action: Rigid cable that forces the ankle joint to flex when the knee joint is flexed.

• Structure: The peroneus tertius is a strong tendon, devoid of any muscle fibers, which begins on the femur and ends on the ankle. Sandwiched between the bellies of the tibialis cranialis and the extensor digitorum longus on the front of the lower leg, it emerges from between them approximately two thirds of the way down the leg. At the level of the bottom of the tibia, the peroneus tertius is perforated, and the tendon of the underlying tibialis cranialis emerges through this hole. The peroneus tertius then continues straight down to the metatarsal bone. Below the level of the perforation, it sends off a small tendinous branch that passes around to the *outside* of the ankle, splits, and then attaches to the outside of the ankle.

The peroneus tertius has virtually no effect on the surface, but is presented here because its lower end is superficial, and for comparison with the same muscle of the ox.

OX

• Insertion: Inner front corner of the upper end of the large (fused) metatarsal; inner rear corner of the ankle, into several adjacent bones, including the upper end of the large metatarsal bone.

• Action: Flexes the ankle joint.

• Structure: The muscle has a fleshy, slightly flattened belly, rather than just a tendon, as in the horse. It lies superficially on the front of the lower leg. Passing from the knee to the ankle, it begins and ends with tendons; its muscle belly is pointed at both ends. At the level of the lower end of the tibia, the tendon is perforated, allowing the tendon of the underlying tibialis cranialis to emerge, as in the horse. Below the perforation, it sends a tendinous branch to the *inside* of the ankle (opposite that of the horse). The peroneus tertius covers most of the extensor digitorum longus and is closely adherent to it.

The peroneus tertius is not present in the dog or the feline; the extensor digitorum lateralis has in the past been called the peroneus tertius.

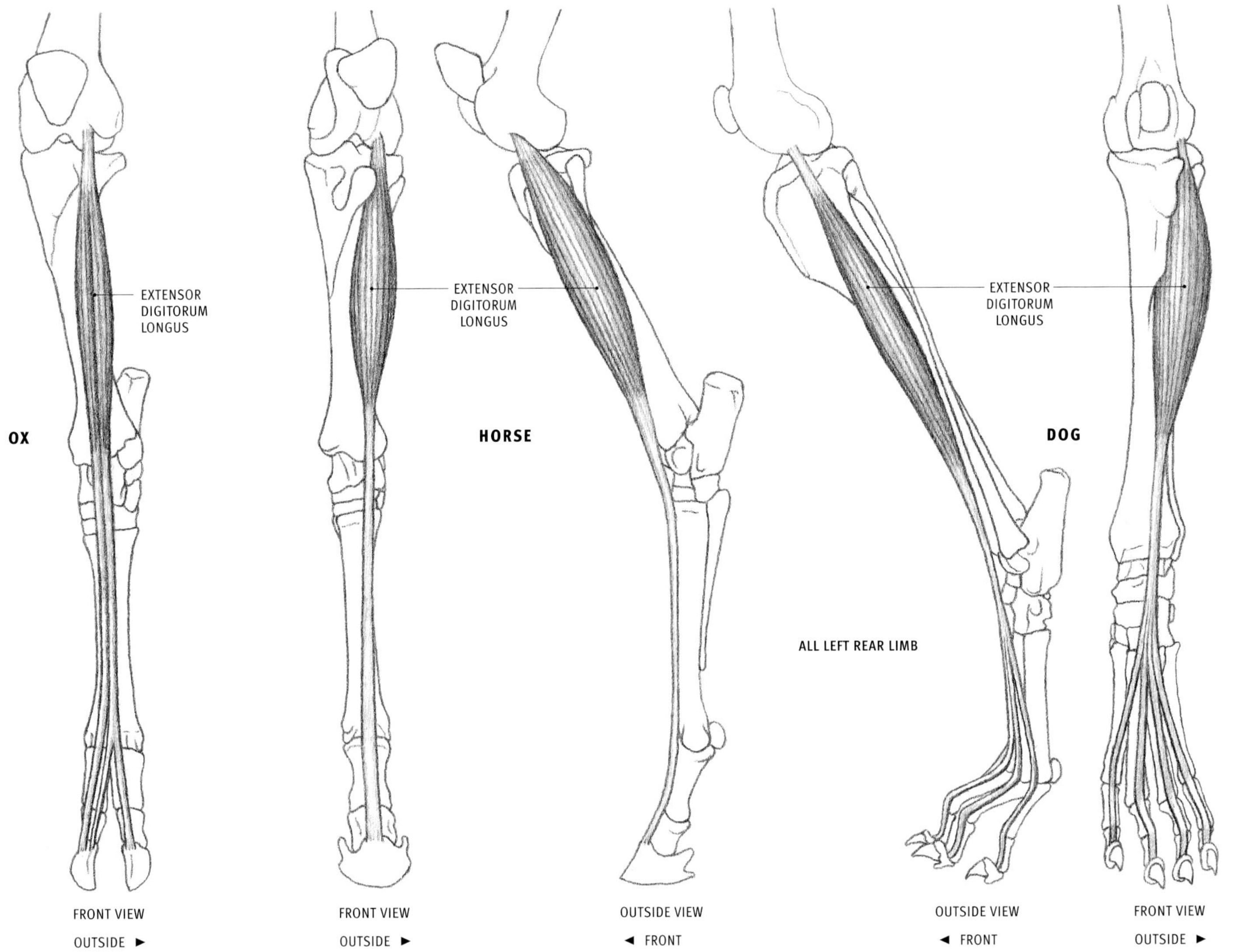

Extensor digitorum longus (Extensor pedis)

HORSE

• Origin: From a depression on the outer surface of the very bottom of the femur, in common with the tendon of the peroneus tertius.
• Insertion: Upper edge of the front surface of all three toe bones, primarily into the last.
• Action: Extends all three toe joints; flexes the ankle joint.
• Structure: The extensor digitorum longus is a long muscle with a very long tendon that passes from the femur to the last toe. The slightly flattened muscle belly, tapered at both ends, lies on the outer front corner of the lower leg. It becomes tendinous above the level of the ankle joint. The long tendon lies on the front of the leg bones and disappears under the hoof. Halfway down the metatarsal bone, the tendon is joined by the tendon of the extensor digitorum lateralis. Lower down, on the upper toe bone, both edges of the tendon receive branches from the suspensory ligament.

OX

• Insertion: Upper edge of the front surface of the last toe bone of both toes, and the upper edge of the middle toe bone of the inner toe.
• Structure: The muscle is much thinner than in the horse, and also more concealed, as its inner portion is covered by, and closely adheres to, the peroneus tertius. The muscle, overall, is pointed at both ends and consists of two bellies, each of which develops a long tendon at the level of the ankle joint. The inner tendon inserts into the inner toe. The outer tendon splits at its lower end and inserts into both toes.

DOG AND FELINE

• Insertion: Last toe bone of all four digits.
• Structure: The upper end of the belly of the extensor digitorum longus is covered by the tibialis cranialis and the peroneus longus. The extensor digitorum longus then emerges from between them, one third of the way down the tibia. It becomes tendinous before reaching the ankle joint, and then travels alongside the tendon of the tibialis cranialis for a short distance. The tendon of the tibialis cranialis soon moves away, veering to the inside of the ankle. The tendon of the extensor digitorum longus then separates into four tendons, one for each toe.

In the feline, the belly of the tibialis cranialis is wider and descends lower than in the dog, thereby covering more of the extensor digitorum longus, which closely adheres to it. This leaves the outer part of the lower portion of the extensor digitorum longus visible on the surface. The muscle fibers of the belly continue down to the level of the ankle joint before it becomes tendinous.

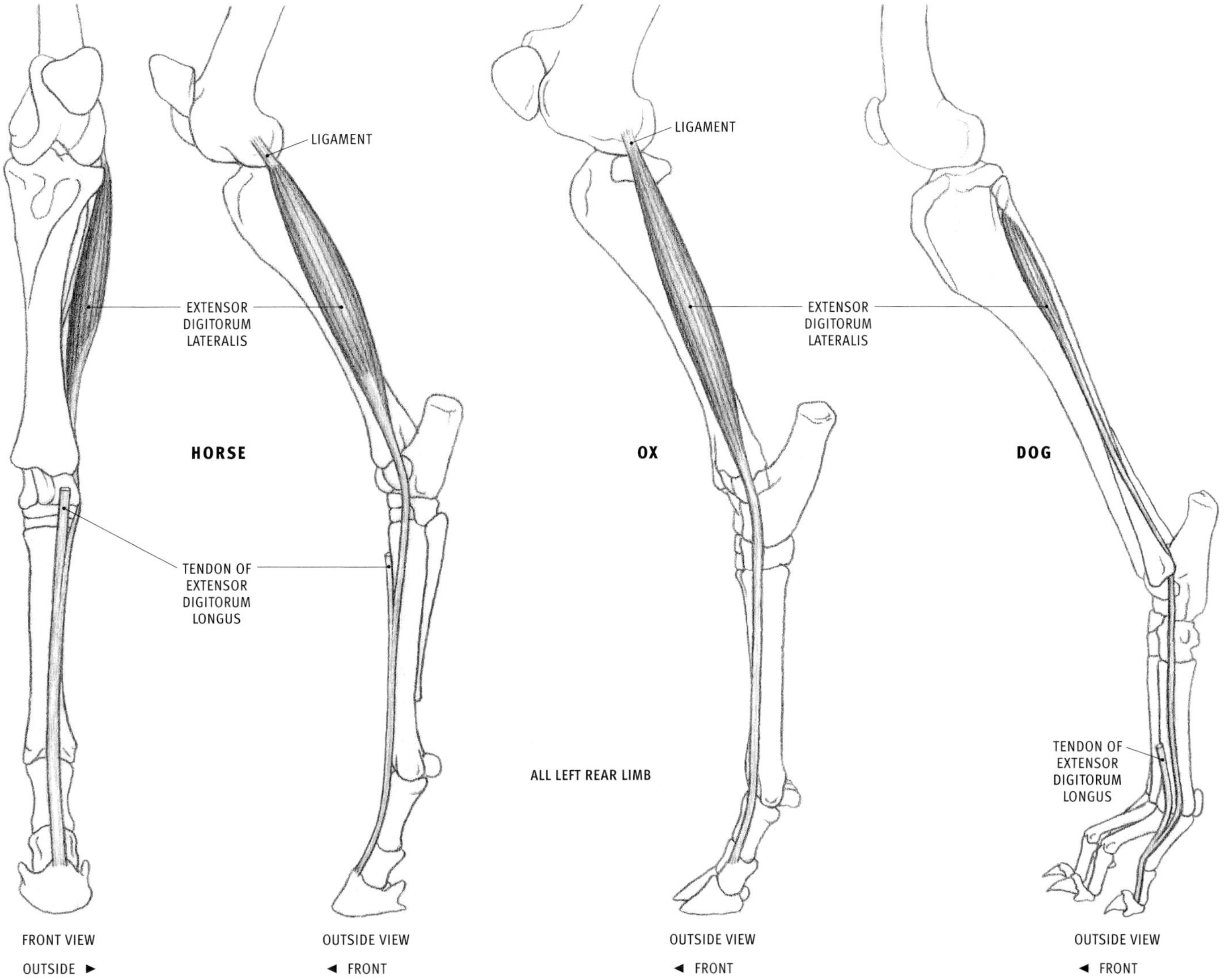

Extensor digitorum lateralis

HORSE **(Peroneus)**

• Origin: Outer surface of the upper end of the tibia, outer surface of the fibula, wide ligament between the tibia and the fibula, and the ligament on the outside of the knee joint between the femur and the fibula.

• Insertion: Into the tendon of the extensor digitorum longus, one third of the way down the metatarsal, therefore ultimately into the three toe bones.

• Action: Assists the extensor digitorum longus in extending the toe bones.

• Structure: The extensor digitorum lateralis has an elongated, flattened belly located on the outside of the lower leg. The belly begins at the level of the knee joint and becomes tendinous at the lower end of the tibia. The tendon passes through a shallow groove on the *outside* of the lower end of the tibia, passes over the spool of the adjacent tarsal bone, and *then* angles forward. It veers inwardly in its descent and then merges with the tendon of the extensor digitorum longus.

OX

• Origin: Outer surfaces of the upper end of the tibia and the vestigial head of the fibula, and the ligament on the outside of the knee between the femur and the tibia.

• Insertion: Upper front end of the middle toe bone of the outer toe.

• Action: Extends the upper two toe joints of the outer toe.

• Structure: Similar to that in the horse, but the tendon continues independently all the way down to the toe.

DOG AND FELINE

• Origin: Dog: Front surface of the upper third of the shaft of the fibula. Feline: Outer surface of the upper half of the shaft of the fibula.

• Insertion: Into the tendon of the extensor digitorum longus to the outermost toe, therefore ultimately into the last toe bone.

• Action: Extends the toe bones of the outermost toe; pulls the outermost toe away from the foot.

• Structure: The extensor digitorum lateralis is a small muscle lying deep in the lower leg. In the dog, only its tendon comes to the surface on the lower half of the outer side of the lower leg, where it lies between the tendons of the peroneus longus in front and the peroneus brevis behind. In the feline, some of the lower part of the muscular belly can be seen on the surface. The tendon hooks *behind* the lower end of the fibula, along with, but in front of, the tendon of the peroneus brevis. It passes under the tendon of the peroneus longus, and then descends along the outer edge of the front surface of the foot. It merges into the tendon of the extensor digitorum longus on top of the upper toe bone.

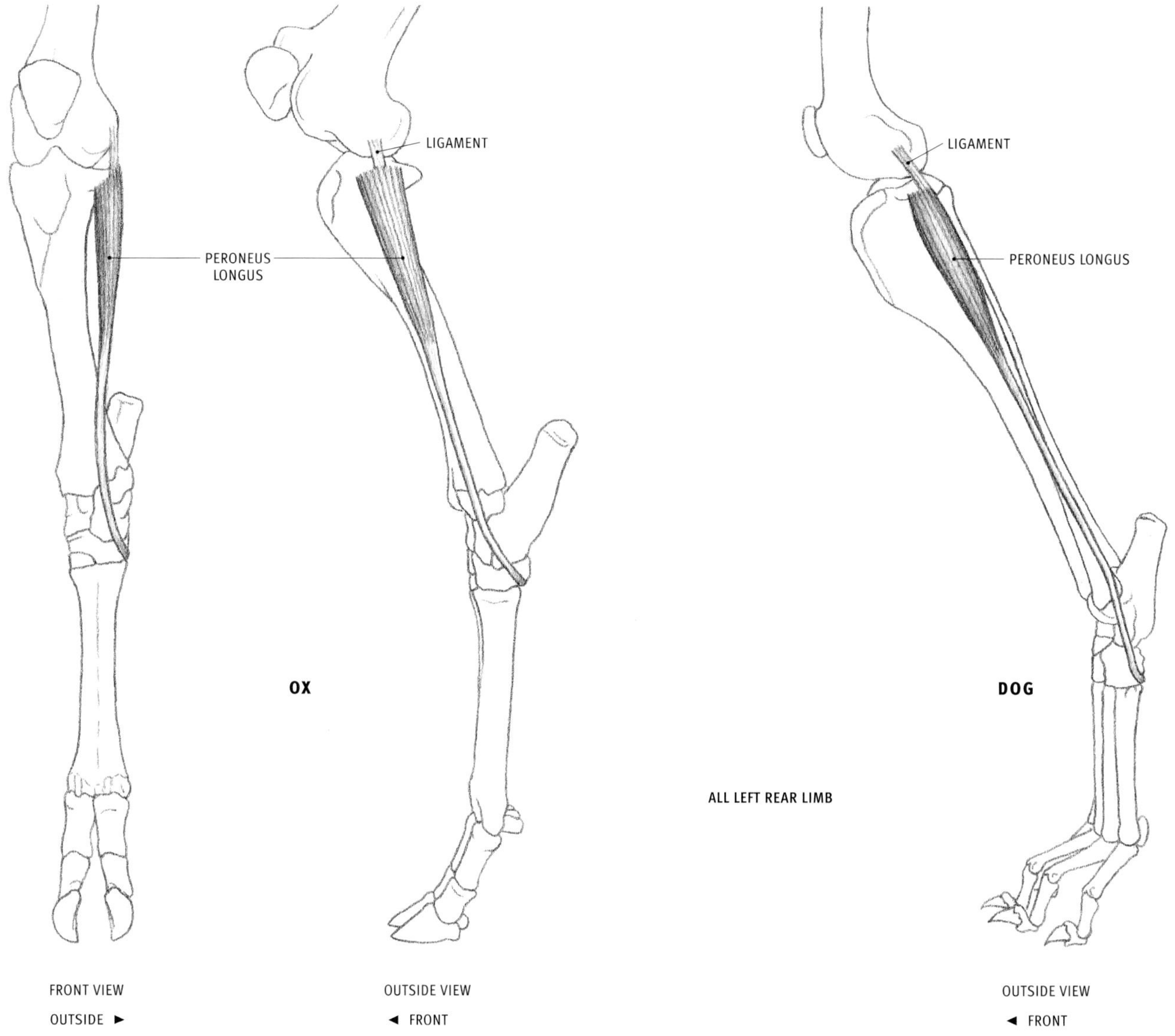

Peroneus longus (Fibularis longus)

OX

- Origin: Outer surface of the upper end of the tibia, and the ligament connecting the femur to the tibia.
- Insertion: Upper end of the inner rear corner of the large metatarsal bone and the adjacent tarsal bone above it.
- Action: Flexes the ankle joint; rotates the foot inwardly.
- Structure: The muscle belly forms a narrow, elongated, inverted triangle that lies on the upper half of the outside of the lower leg. The belly begins wide at its origin, and it then tapers before becoming tendinous halfway down the tibia. The tendon passes over the outside of the ankle and then curves around the back of the foot to insert on its inner rear corner.

DOG AND FELINE

- Origin: Outer surface of the upper end of the tibia, upper end of the fibula, and the ligament connecting the femur to the fibula.
- Insertion: Upper ends of the first (vestigial), second, and fifth metatarsals, on the back of the foot.
- Action: Rotates the foot, directing the rear surface outward.
- Structure: The peroneus longus consists of a short belly lying on the upper half of the outside of the lower leg and a long tendon that reaches the foot. The upper end of the belly, along with the tibialis cranialis which it touches, covers the upper portion of the extensor digitorum longus. Its long tendon passes over the outside of the fibula, in its own groove, angles forward slightly, descends to the level of the upper end of the metatarsals, and then sharply curves around to the back of the foot to insert in a horizontal line across the tops of the metatarsals.

In the feline, the peroneus longus becomes tendinous two thirds of the way down the fibula.

In the horse, the muscle formerly called the peroneus is not a true peroneus muscle, but is correctly called the extensor digitorum lateralis. The horse does not have a peroneus longus or a peroneus brevis. The ox has only a peroneus longus, and the dog and the feline have both.

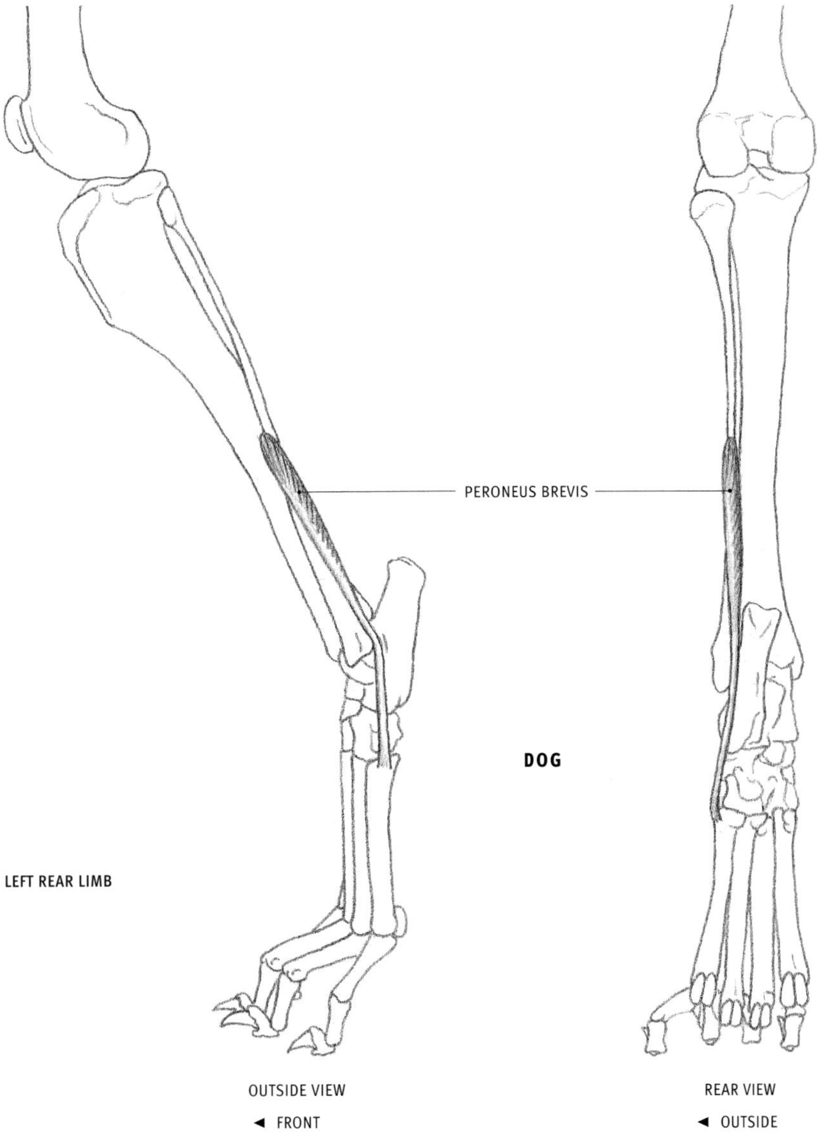

Peroneus brevis (Fibularis brevis)

DOG AND FELINE

- Origin: Outer surface of the lower two thirds of the fibula (except for the lower expansion), and a small area on the middle of the outside of the tibia.
- Insertion: Upper end of the outer surface of the outermost metatarsal.
- Action: Extends the ankle joint.
- Structure: The peroneus brevis is a small, elongated muscle lying partly buried on the lower half of the outside of the lower leg. Its tendon begins on the surface of the muscle belly and passes downward in close contact with the tendon of the extensor digitorum lateralis in front of it. Both tendons hook behind the lower end of the fibula, pass under the tendon of the peroneus longus, and then diverge slightly. The tendon of the peroneus brevis finally inserts into the outside of the foot.

The horse and the ox do not have a peroneus brevis.

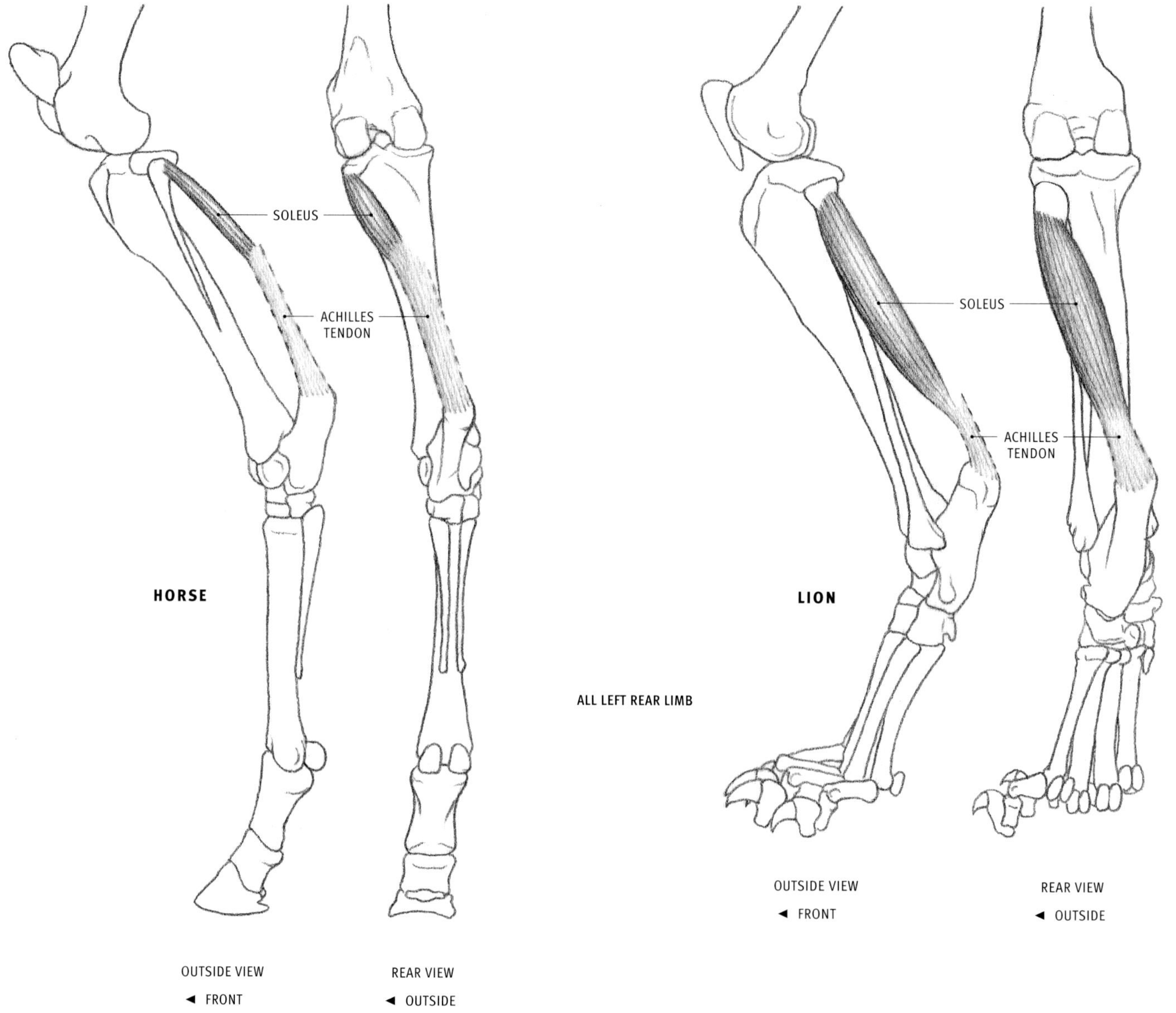

Soleus

HORSE AND OX

- Origin: Outer surface of the upper end (head) of the fibula.
- Insertion: Into the tendon of the gastrocnemius, ultimately into the top of the heel bone (calcaneus).
- Action: Assists the gastrocnemius in extending the ankle joint.
- Structure: The soleus is a small, thin, flattened muscle passing from the outside of the knee region toward the heel. Its belly runs along the outer head of the gastrocnemius. It is not part of the volume created by the gastrocnemius, but rather lies on the flexor digitorum profundus and adds slightly to that form.

FELINE

- Origin: Also from the upper third of the fibula.
- Insertion: Here the soleus is fairly well developed. The muscle fibers descend further toward the heel than in the horse.

The soleus is not present in the dog.

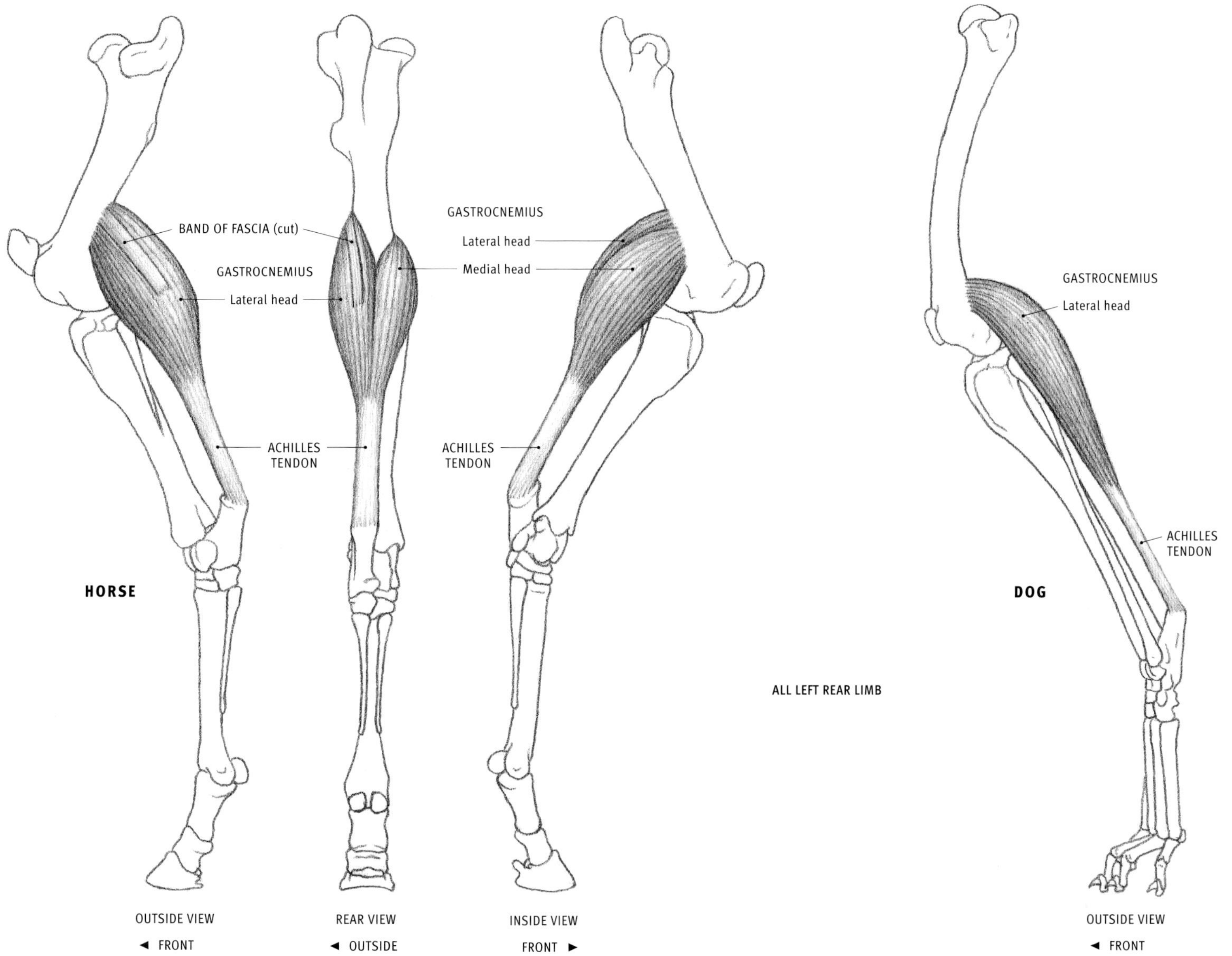

Gastrocnemius

HORSE

• Origin: Outer head: Vertical line on the outer rear edge of the femur, three fourths of the way down the bone. Inner head: Area on the inner rear corner of the femur, at a level lower than the origin of the outer head.

• Insertion: Top of the heel bone (calcaneus).

• Action: Flexes the knee joint; powerfully extends the ankle joint, propelling the animal forward.

• Structure: The gastrocnemius is a very thick, club-shaped muscle that forms the bulge of the calf. It begins on the back of the lower end of the femur and ends on the summit of the heel bone. The belly consists of two heads, an outer (lateral) head and an inner (medial) head, which come together soon after originating from either side of the femur. This thick, ovoid muscle mass is flattened on its deep surface, which is also grooved to receive the belly of the flexor digitorum superficialis. A good portion of the belly is covered by the lower ends of the biceps femoris on the outside and the semitendinosus and gracilis on the inside.

Approximately halfway down the lower leg, the gastrocnemius tapers into a very strong, thick tendon, which descends in contact with the tendon of the flexor digitorum superficialis; the two tendons twist around each other as they approach the heel. The flexor tendon begins deep to (anterior to) the gastrocnemius tendon, curves around its inner edge to lie on top of it (posterior to it), and then passes over and beyond the top of the heel bone.

A strong, narrow band of fascia begins at the origin of the outer head of the gastrocnemius and passes down the surface of the muscle, forming a grooved depression in the muscle belly. This fascial band eventually joins the tendinous bands from the biceps femoris and the semitendinosus to insert into the top of the heel, along with the thick tendons of the gastrocnemius and flexor digitorum superficialis. All the above-mentioned tendons and the fascial band, which insert into the heel, are collectively called the **common calcaneal tendon**.

The term **triceps surae** refers to the gastrocnemius and the soleus muscles together. Their common tendon (without the other tendinous and fascial contributions) is called the **Achilles tendon**.

OX, DOG, AND FELINE

• Structure: In the ox, the dog, and the feline, there is no fascial band coming off the origin of the outer head of the gastrocnemius. In the dog and the feline, the gracilis muscle sends an additional tendinous band to the common calcaneal tendon.

In the feline, the muscle fibers of the gastrocnemius descend further on the lower leg, toward the heel, before becoming tendinous.

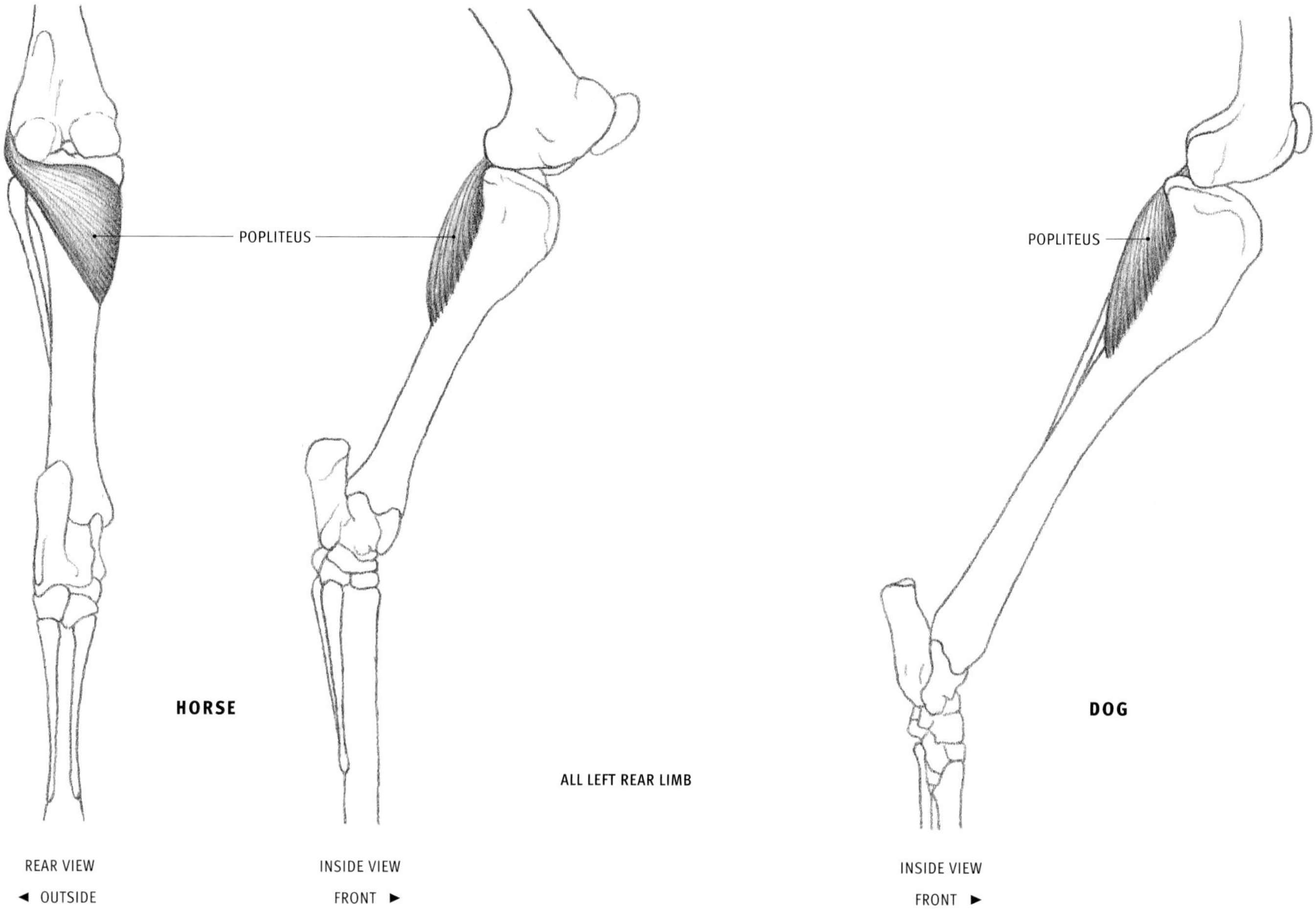

Popliteus

HORSE, OX, DOG, AND FELINE

• Origin: Lower end of the outside of the femur, toward the rear, close to the lower edge of the bone.

• Insertion: Area on the inner half of the rear surface of the upper end of the tibia, continuing around to the inner surface of the bone for a short distance.

• Action: Flexes the knee joint; rotates the tibia inward (turns the heel out, pointing the toe[s] inward).

• Structure: The popliteus is a thick, triangular muscle lying on the back of the tibia, just below the knee joint. It begins deep on the outside of the knee as a narrow tendon, widens and wraps around the back of the knee, and ends on the inside. A small vertical portion of its inner edge, passing approximately one third of the way down the tibia, becomes superficial on the inside of the leg, toward the rear of the tibia. Because this portion of the popliteus is covered by the wide, tough tendons of the gracilis and the semitendinosus, its influence on the surface is quite subdued.

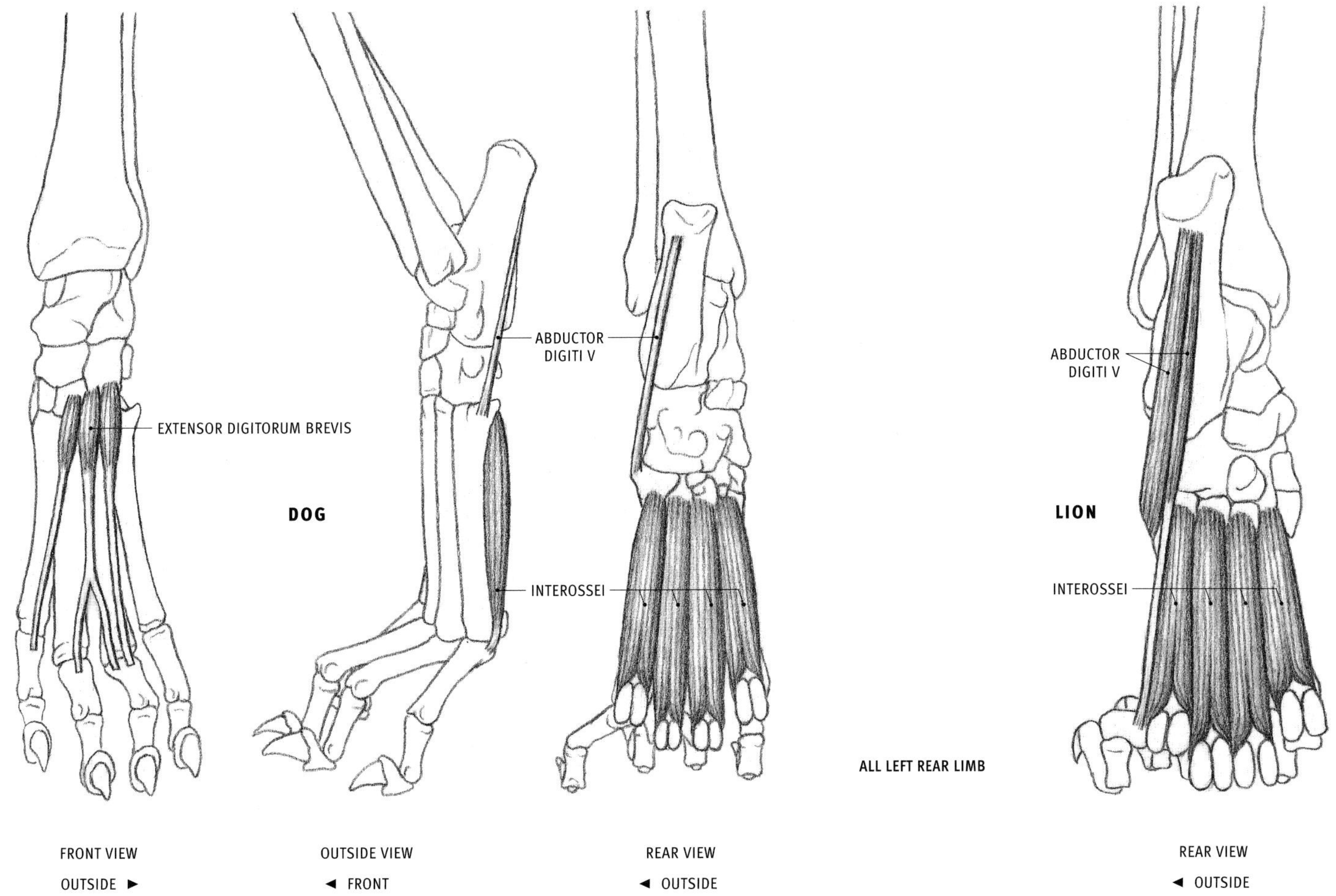

Extensor digitorum brevis

DOG AND FELINE
• Origin: Front of the tarsal bones at the ankle.
• Insertion: Into various tendons on the top of the bones of the three inner toes.
• Action: Extends all the toe joints of the three inner toes
• Structure: This is a minor, flat muscle located on the front of the foot. It is covered by the tendons of the extensor digitorum longus and has virtually no effect on the surface.

Interossei

DOG AND FELINE
• Origin: Upper end of the rear surface the four metatarsal bones.
• Insertion: By tendon into both sesamoid bones at the lower end of each metatarsal bone, and further down onto the adjacent upper end of the upper toe bone. A branch of each tendon continues around each side of a toe bone to the front of the paw, where it inserts into the tendon of the extensor digitorum longus.
• Action: Flexes the metatarsophalangeal joints.
• Structure: The interossei consist of four separate, elongated muscle bellies lying on the rear surface of the foot. Their lower ends split and then develop short tendons. They add a slight muscular fullness on the inner and outer edges of the back of the foot.

Abductor digiti V (Abductor digiti quinti)

FELINE
• Origin: Rear surface (bottom) of the heel bone.
• Insertion: Upper end of the outer metatarsal bone; outer surface of the base of the first toe bone of the outer digit.
• Action: Stabilizes the bottom of the foot; pulls the outer toe away from the foot.
• Structure: The abductor digiti V adds a very slight fullness to the outer back edge of the upper half of the foot. It consists of two bellies with different insertions, one with a long tendon.

The extensor digitorum brevis is very small in the horse and has no influence on the surface. It is minor or absent in the ox. The interosseous (medius) in the horse and the ox is also called the **suspensory ligament**. Its structure in the hind limb is the same as in the front limb, and is described and illustrated with that limb (see page 85). The abductor digiti V is not present in the horse or the ox. In the dog, it is a small, mostly tendinous band connecting the heel bone to the outer metatarsal, and has no effect on the surface.

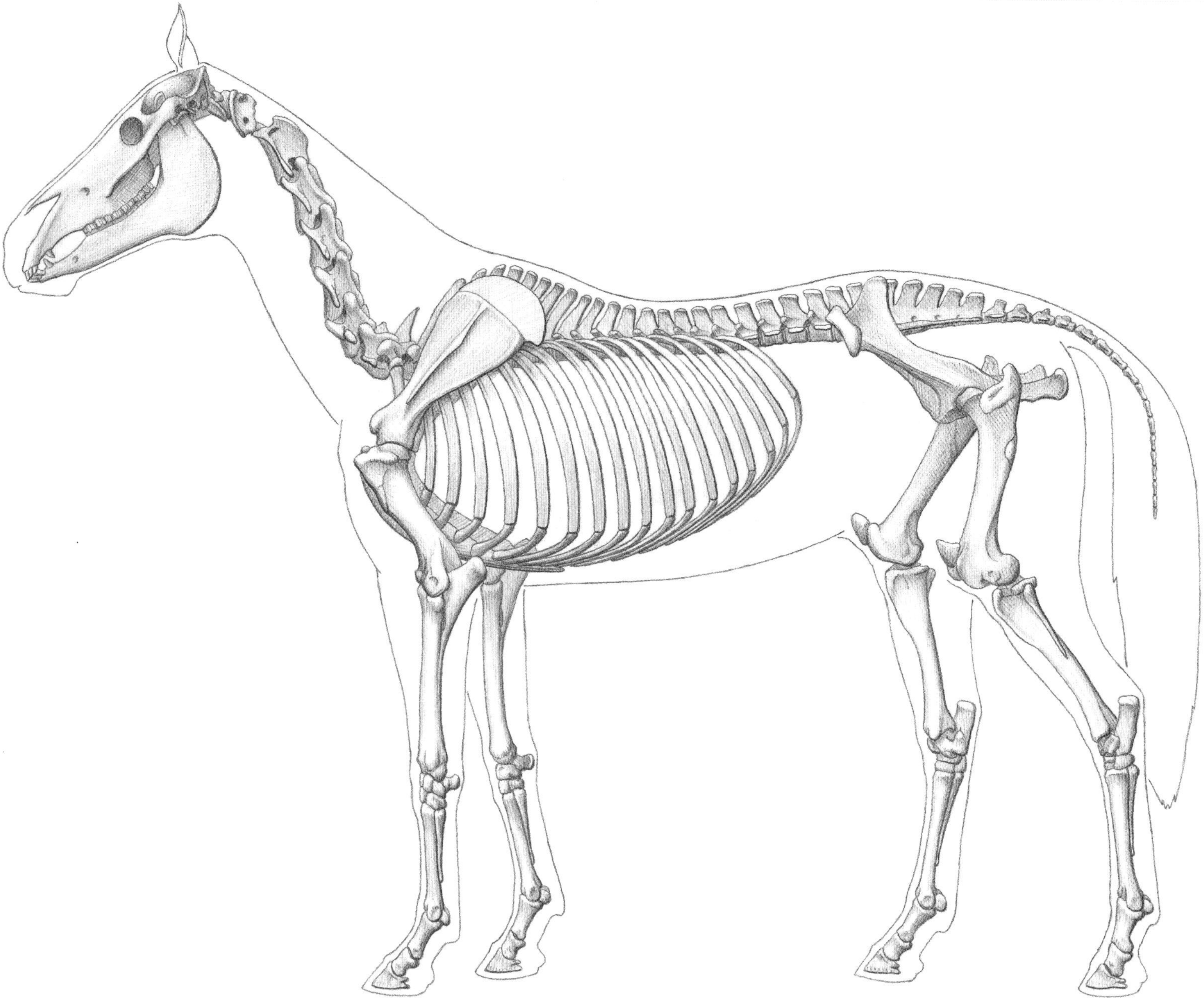

(ANATOMICAL DRAWINGS AFTER ELLENBERGER; ASHDOWN; FROM DISSECTIONS)

Horse (equid) characteristics: One digit per foot ending in symmetrical, horny hoof. Walks on very tip of toe. Elongated skull; large lower jaw. Large upper and lower incisors. In side view, neck widens as it approaches shoulder (elongated triangular shape). Mane present, upright on wild species. Tuft of hair often present on forehead ("forelock"). Rear profile of neck straight or arched. Pointed, upright ears. Long, slender limbs. Humerus and femur short; lower portion of limb long, especially forefoot and hind foot (adaptation for speed by shifting weight of muscles mass upward, close to the body). Ulna and fibula reduced and fused to adjacent, weight-supporting bones. Femur has projecting third trochanter on outer side of shaft for attachment of the gluteus superficialis muscle. Barrel-like trunk. Long hair on tail. In same group as tapirs and rhinoceroses.

AbD1L *Abductor digiti I longus;* **Adduc** *Adductor;* **AT** *Achilles' tendon;* **Bicep** *Biceps brachii;* **BiFemLH** *Biceps femoris, long head;* **BiFemSH** *Biceps femoris, short head;* **Brach** *Brachialis;* **Brcph** *Brachiocephalicus;* **Bucc** *Buccinator;* **Canin** *Caninus;* **Coccy** *Coccygeus;* **DelRe** *Deltoid, rear portion;* **DelSp** *Deltoid, spinal portion;* **Digas** *Digastric;* **DLaMn** *Depressor labii mandibularis;* **ECR** *Extensor carpi radialis;* **EDC** *Extensor digitorum communis;* **EDLat** *Extensor digitorum lateralis;* **EDLon** *Extensor digitorum longus;* **ExAbO** *External abdominal oblique;* **FCR** *Flexor carpi radialis;* **FCU** *Flexor carpi ulnaris;* **FDP** *Flexor digitorum profundus;* **FDS** *Flexor digitorum superficialis;* **GasLa** *Gastrocnemius, lateral head;* **GluMe** Gluteus medius; **GluSu** *Gluteus superficialis;* **Grac** *Gracilis;* **Iliac** *Iliacus;* **Ilioc** *Iliocostalis;* **InAbO** *Internal abdominal oblique;* **Infra** *Infraspinatus;* **LAOM** *Levator anguli oculi medialis;* **LatDo** *Latissimus dorsi;* **LatNa** *Lateralis nasi;* **LeNas** *Levator nasolabialis;* **LLaMx** *Levator labii maxillaris;* **LngCa** *Longus capitis;* **LonAt** *Longissimus atlantis;* **LonCa** *Longissimus capitis;* **Longi** *Longissimus;* **Malar** *Malaris;* **Mass** *Masseter;* **NuLig** *Nuchal ligament;* **Omohy** *Omohyoid;* **Omotr** *Omotransversarius;* **OCCau** *Obliquus capitis caudalis;* **OCCra** *Obliquus capitis cranialis;* **OrOc** *Orbicularis oculi;* **OrOr** *Orbicularis oris;* **PecAs** *Pectoralis ascendens;* **PecDe** *Pectoralis descendens;* **PecTr** *Pectoralis transversus;* **PerTe** *Peroneus tertius;* **Pop** *Popliteus;* **RecAb** *Rectus abdominis;* **RecFe** *Rectus femoris;* **Rhom** *Rhomboid;* **SacLi** *Sacrotuberal ligament;* **SemCa** *Semispinalis capitis;* **SerDC** *Serratus dorsalis caudalis;* **SerVC** *Serratus ventralis cervicis;* **SerVT** *Serratus ventralis thoracis;* **Smemb** *Semimembranosus;* **Sol** *Soleus;* **Spin & Semsp** *Spinalis & semispinalis;* **Splen** *Splenius;* **Stend** *Semitendinosus;* **Sthy** *Sternohyoid;* **Stman** *Sternomandibularis;* **Stthh** *Sternothyrohyoid;* **Stthy** *Sternothyroid;* **Subcl** *Subclavius;* **Supra** *Supraspinatus;* **SusLi** *Suspensory ligament;* **TeMin** *Teres minor;* **Temp** *Temporalis;* **TenFA** *Tensor fasciae antibrachii;* **TenFL** *Tensor fasciae latae;* **TibCr** *Tibialis cranialis;* **Trach** *Trachea;* **Trap** *Trapezius;* **TriLa** *Triceps brachii, lateral head;* **TriLo** *Triceps brachii, long head;* **TrnAb** *Transversus abdominis;* **Troc3** *Third trochanter;* **UlLat** *Ulnaris lateralis;* **VasLa** *Vastus lateralis;* **Zyg** *Zygomaticus.*

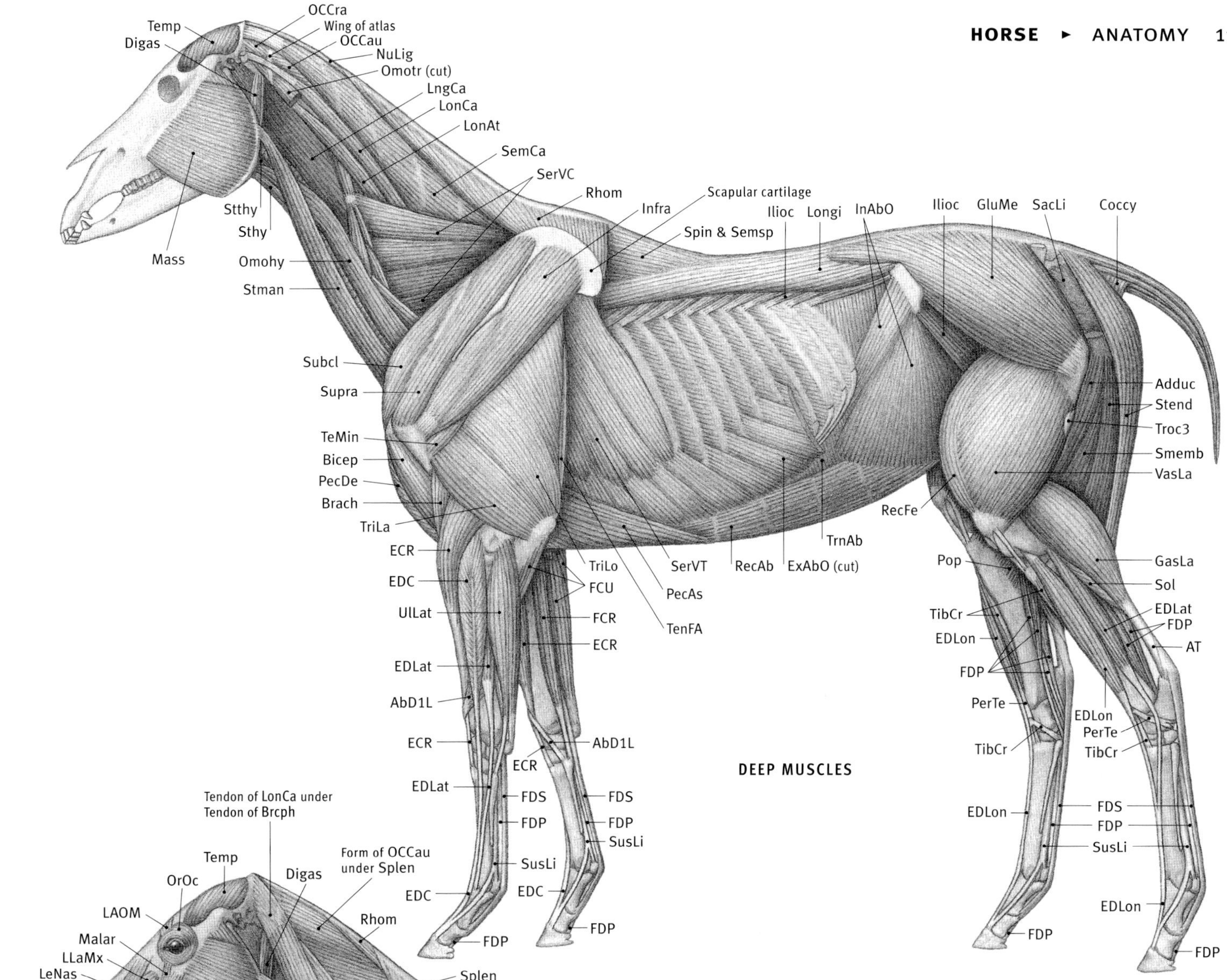

DEEP MUSCLES

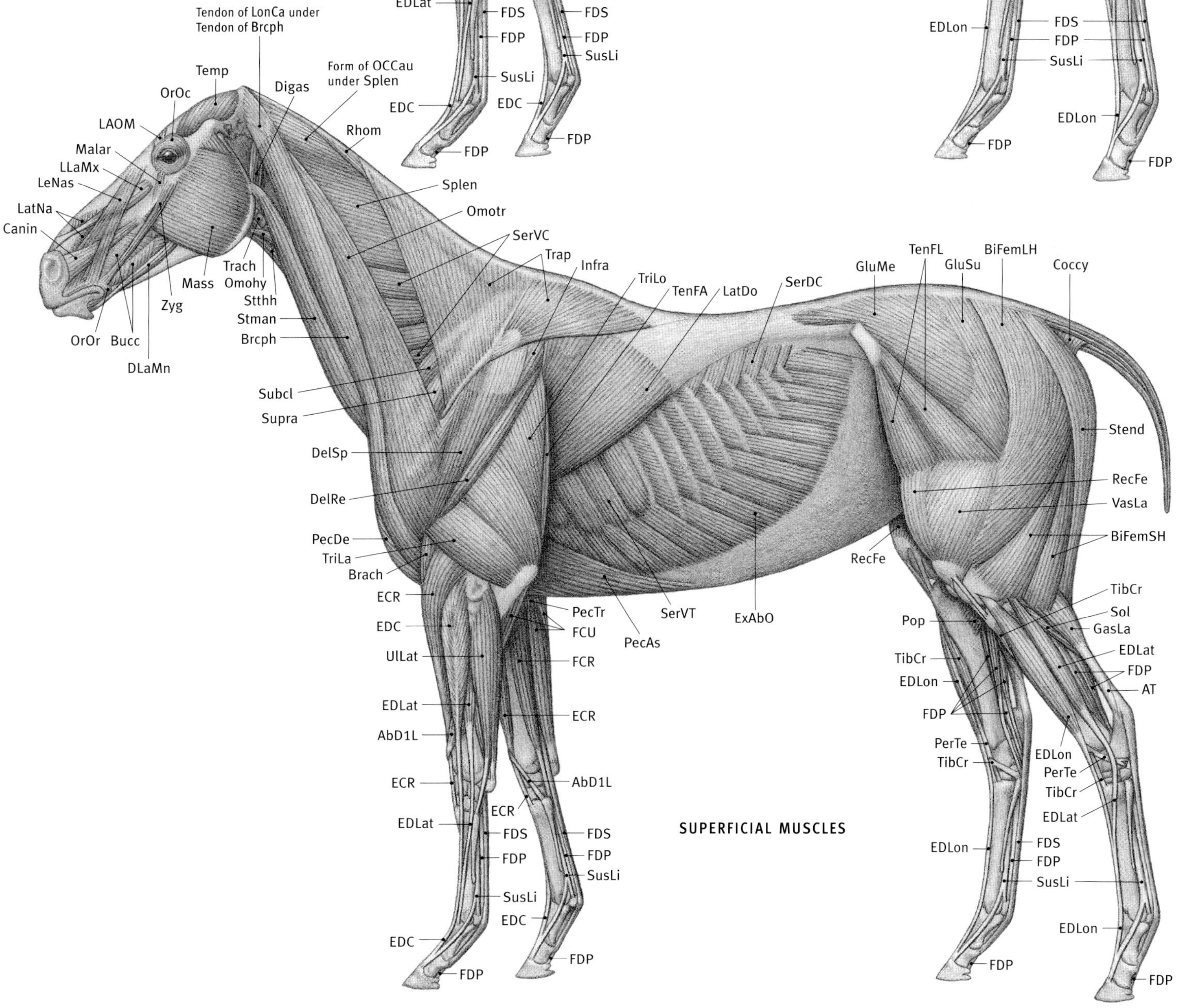

SUPERFICIAL MUSCLES

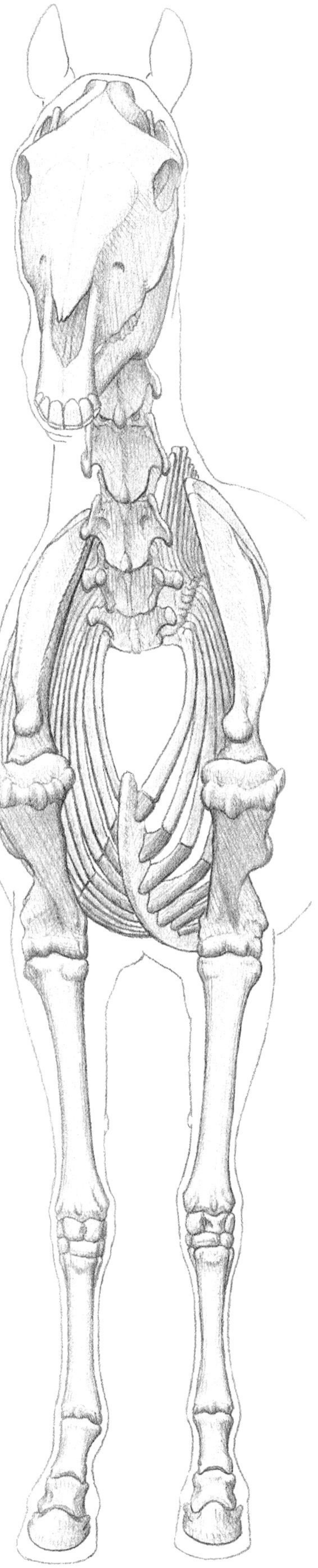

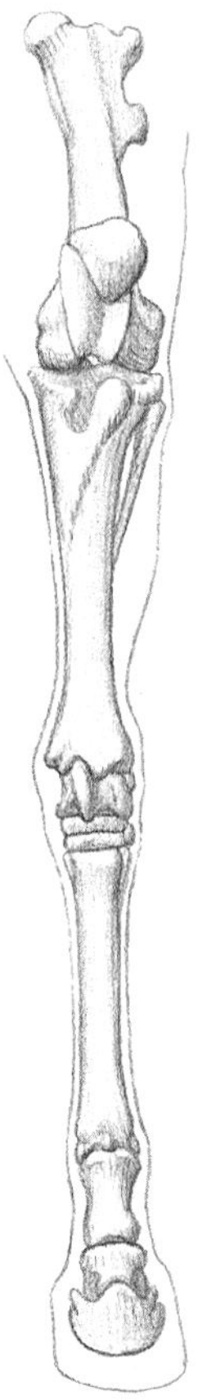

LEFT REAR LIMB
FRONT VIEW

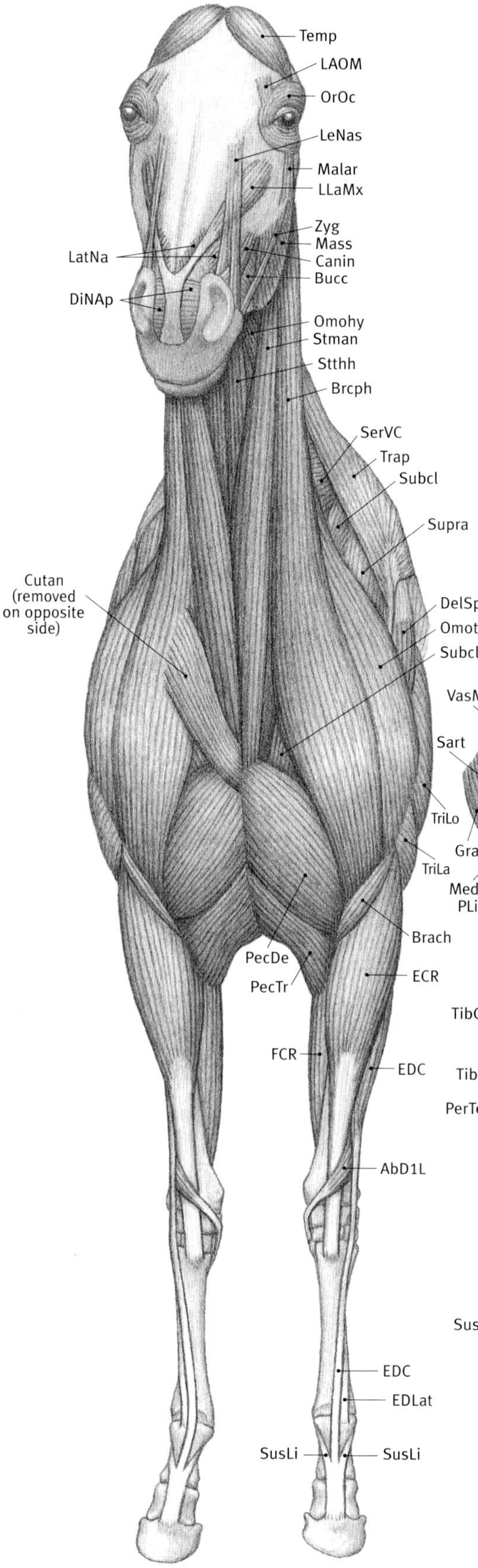

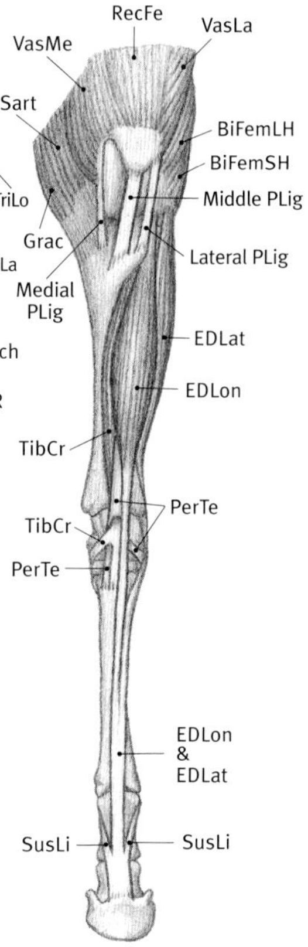

LEFT REAR LIMB
FRONT VIEW

AbD1L *Abductor digiti I longus;* **BiFemLH** *Biceps femoris, long head;* **BiFemSH** *Biceps femoris, short head;* **Brach** *Brachialis;* **Brcph** *Brachiocephalicus;* **Bucc** *Buccinator;* **Canin** *Caninus;* **Cutan** *Cutaneous muscle;* **DelSp** *Deltoid, spinal portion;* **DiNAp** *Dilator naris apicalis;* **ECR** *Extensor carpi radialis;* **EDC** *Extensor digitorum communis;* **EDLat** *Extensor digitorum lateralis;* **EDLon** *Extensor digitorum longus;* **FCR** *Flexor carpi radialis;* **Grac** *Gracilis;* **LAOM** *Levator anguli oculi medialis;* **LatNa** *Lateralis nasi;* **LeNas** *Levator nasolabialis;* **LLaMx** *Levator labii maxillaris;* **Malar** *Malaris;* **Mass** *Masseter;* **Omohy** *Omohyoid;* **Omotr** *Omotransversarius;* **OrOc** *Orbicularis oculi;* **PecDe** *Pectoralis descendens;* **PecTr** *Pectoralis transversus;* **PerTe** *Peroneus tertius;* **PLig** *Patellar ligament;* **RecFe** *Rectus femoris*; **Sart** *Sartorius;* **SerVC** *Serratus ventralis cervicis;* **Stman** *Sternomandibularis;* **Stthh** *Sternothyrohyoid;* **Subcl** *Subclavius;* **Supra** *Supraspinatus;* **SusLi** *Suspensory ligament;* **Temp** *Temporalis;* **TibCr** *Tibialis cranialis;* **Trap** *Trapezius;* **TriLa** *Triceps brachii, lateral head;* **TriLo** *Triceps brachii, long head;* **VasLa** *Vastus lateralis;* **VasMe** *Vastus medialis;* **Zyg** *Zygomaticus.*

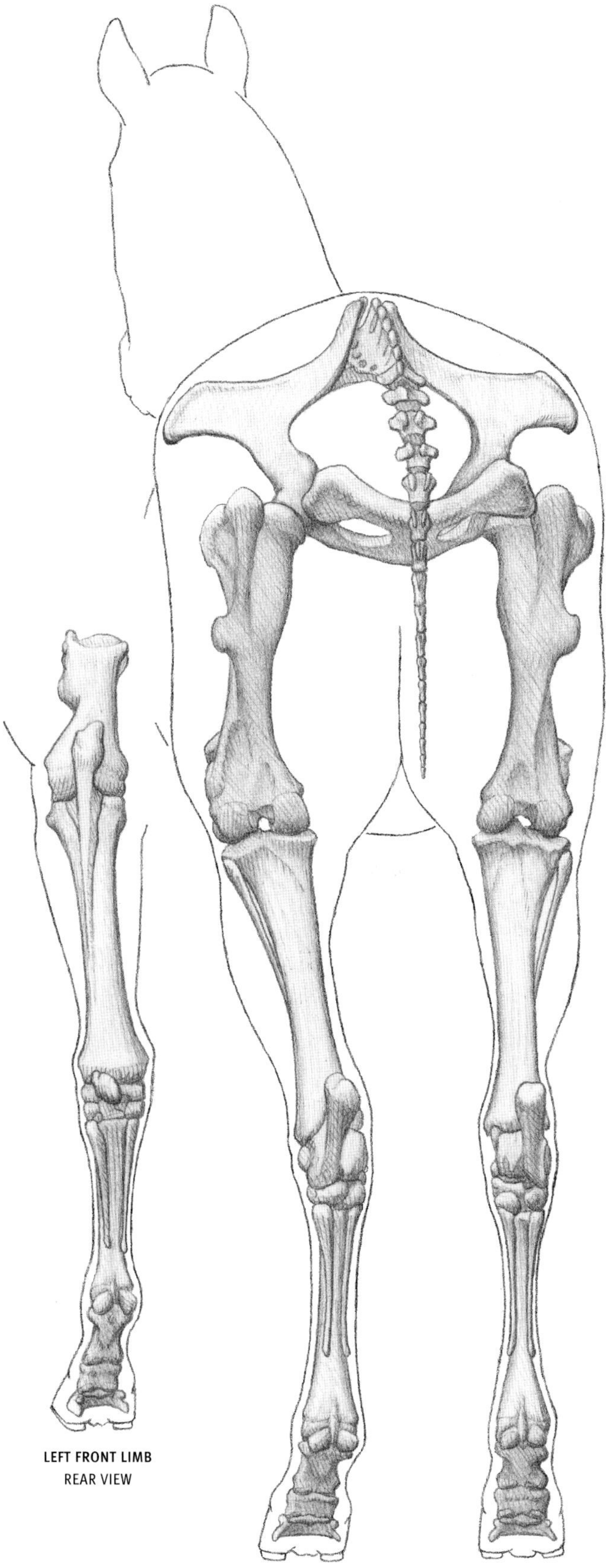

LEFT FRONT LIMB
REAR VIEW

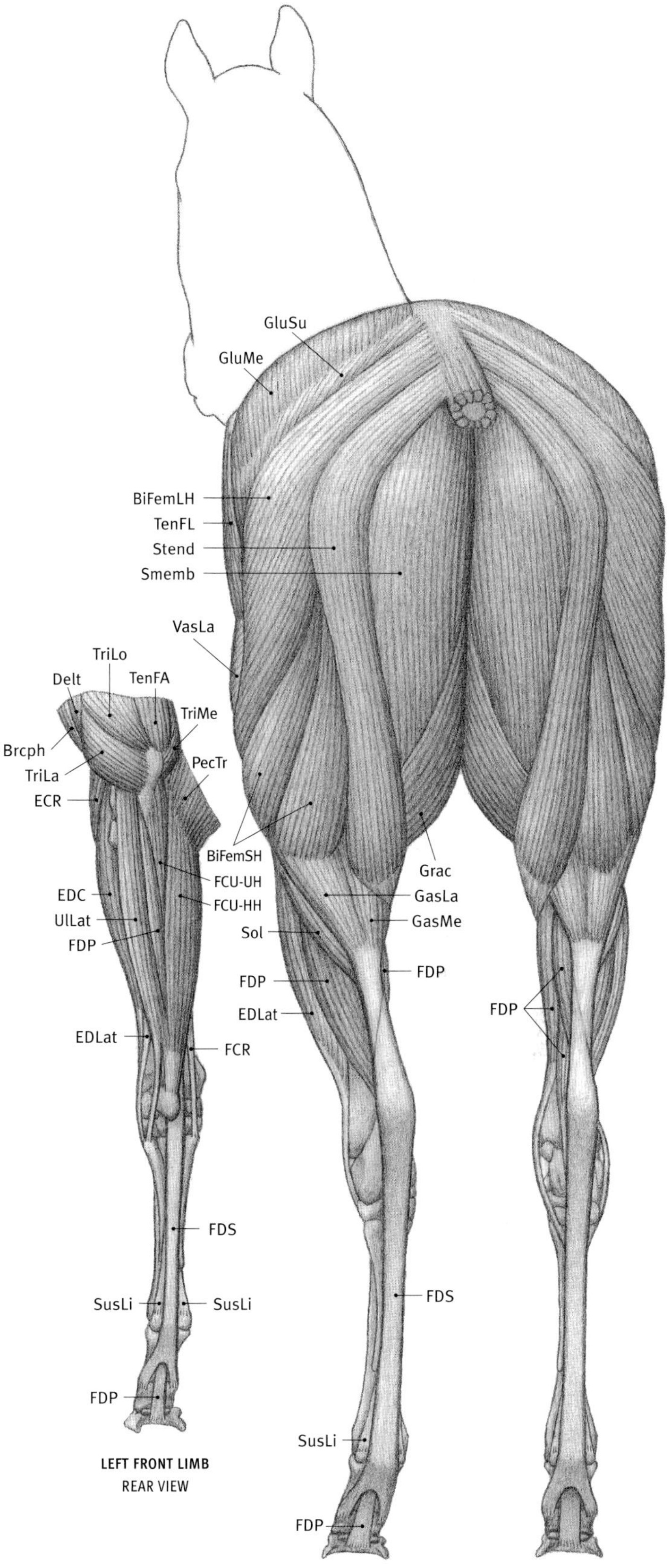

LEFT FRONT LIMB
REAR VIEW

BiFemLH *Biceps femoris, long head;* **BiFemSH** *Biceps femoris, short head;* **Brcph** *Brachiocephalicus;* **Delt** *Deltoid;* **ECR** *Extensor carpi radialis;* **EDC** *Extensor digitorum communis;* **EDLat** *Extensor digitorum lateralis;* **FCR** *Flexor carpi radialis;* **FCU-HH** *Flexor carpi ulnaris, humeral head;* **FCU-UH** *Flexor carpi ulnaris, ulnar head;* **FDP** *Flexor digitorum profundus;* **FDS** *Flexor digitorum superficialis;* **GasLa** *Gastrocnemius, lateral head;* **GasMe** *Gastronecmius, medial head;* **GluMe** *Gluteus medius;* **GluSu** *Gluteus superficialis;* **Grac** *Gracilis;* **PecTr** *Pectoralis transversus;* **Smemb** *Semimembranosus;* **Sol** *Soleus;* **Stend** *Semitendinosus;* **SusLi** *Suspensory ligament;* **TenFA** *Tensor fasciae antibrachii;* **TenFL** *Tensor fasciae latae;* **TriLa** *Triceps brachii, lateral head;* **TriLo** *Triceps brachii, long head;* **TriMe** *Triceps brachii, medial head;* **UlLat** *Ulnaris lateralis;* **VasLa** *Vastus lateralis.*

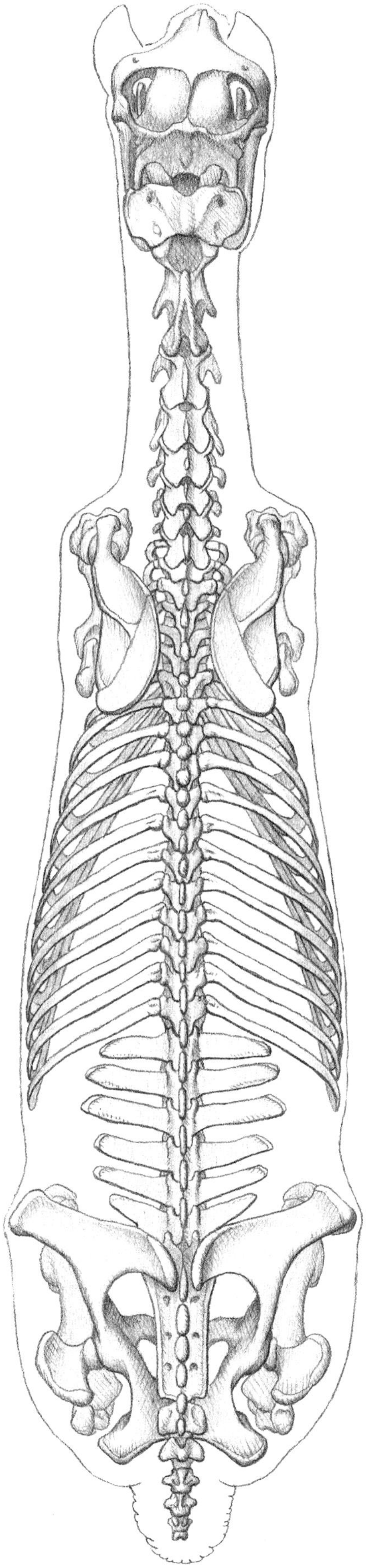

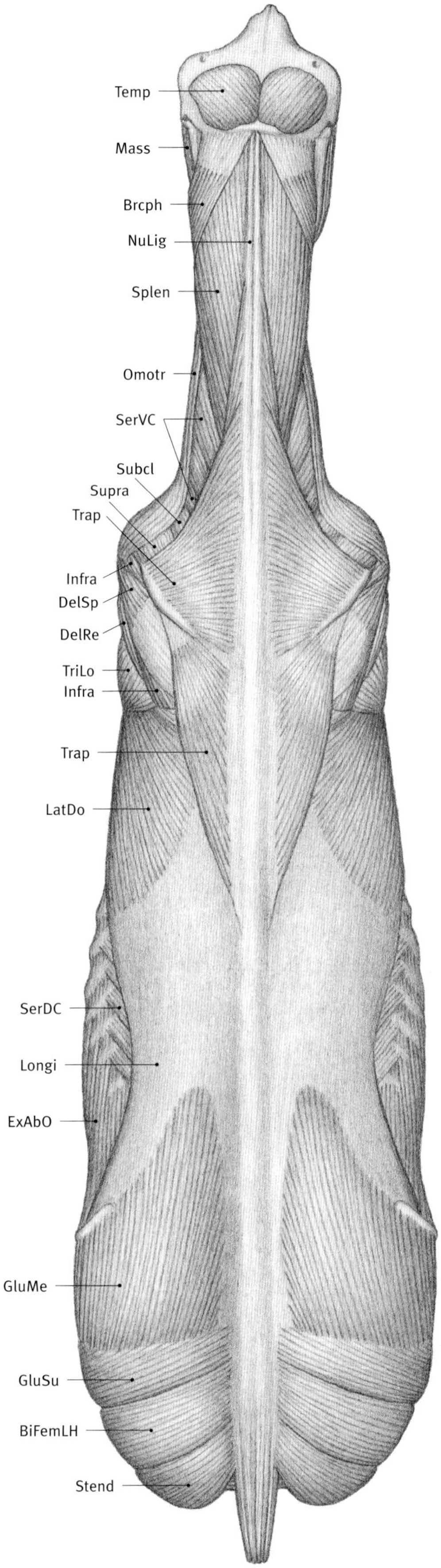

BiFemLH *Biceps femoris, long head;* **Brcph** *Brachiocephalicus;* **DelRe** *Deltoid, rear portion;* **DelSp** *Deltoid, spinal portion;* **ExAbO** *External abdominal oblique;* **GluMe** *Gluteus medius;* **GluSu** *Gluteus superficialis;* **Infra** *Infraspinatus;* **LatDo** *Latissimus dorsi;* **Longi** *Longissimus;* **Mass** *Masseter;* **NuLig** *Nuchal ligament;* **Omotr** *Omotransversarius;* **SerDC** *Serratus dorsalis caudalis;* **SerVC** *Serratus ventralis cervicis;* **Splen** *Splenius;* **Stend** *Semitendinosus;* **Subcl** *Subclavius;* **Supra** *Supraspinatus;* **Temp** *Temporalis;* **Trap** *Trapezius;* **TriLo** *Triceps brachii, long head.*

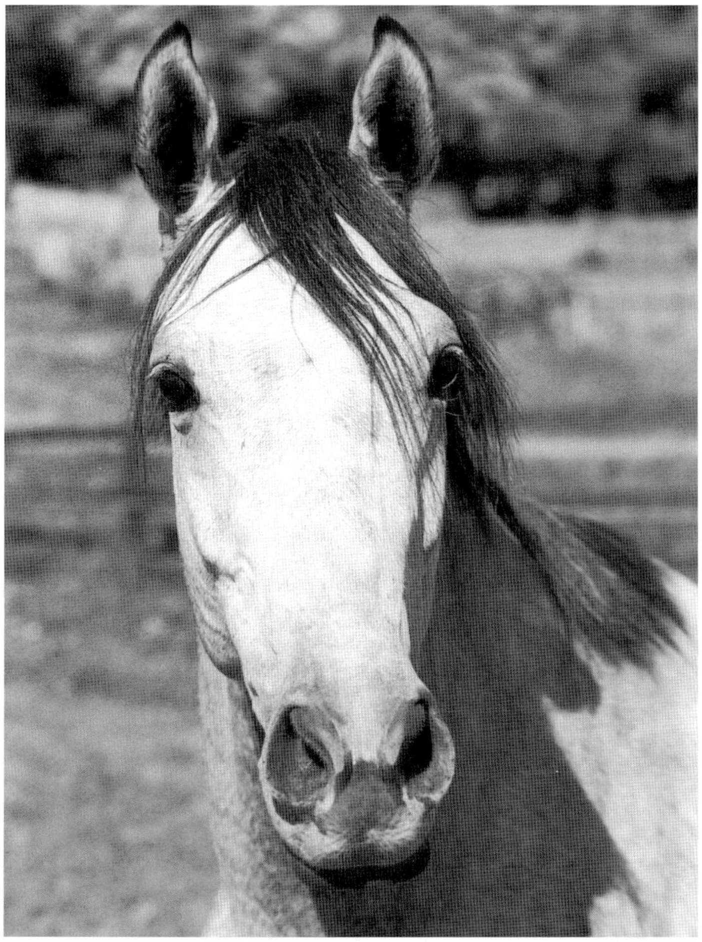

THOROUGHBRED; 5 YEARS OLD (MALE)

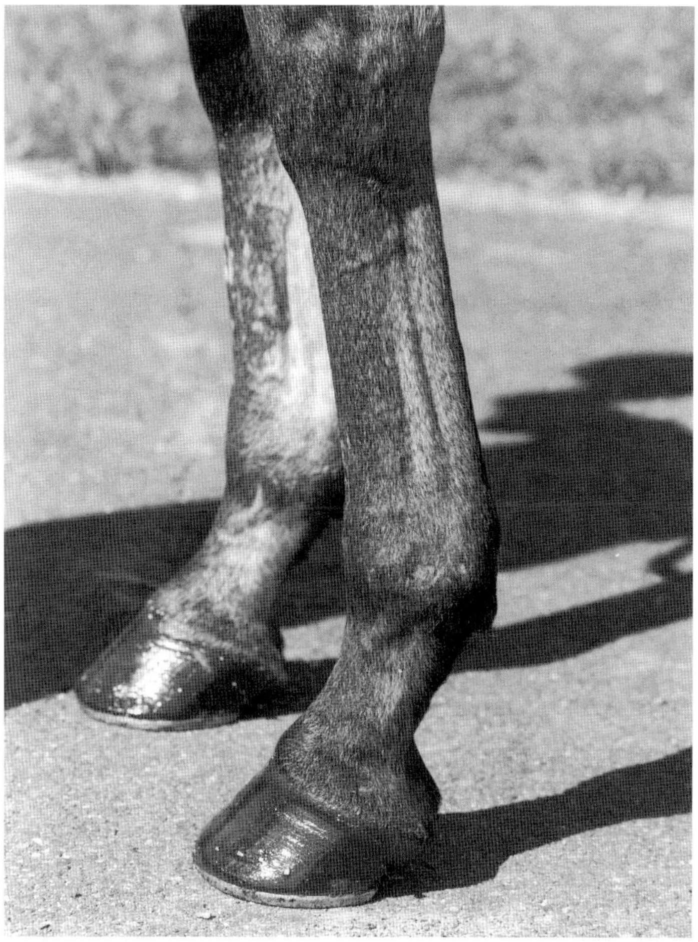

THOROUGHBRED; 5 YEARS OLD (MALE)

FRONT LIMBS

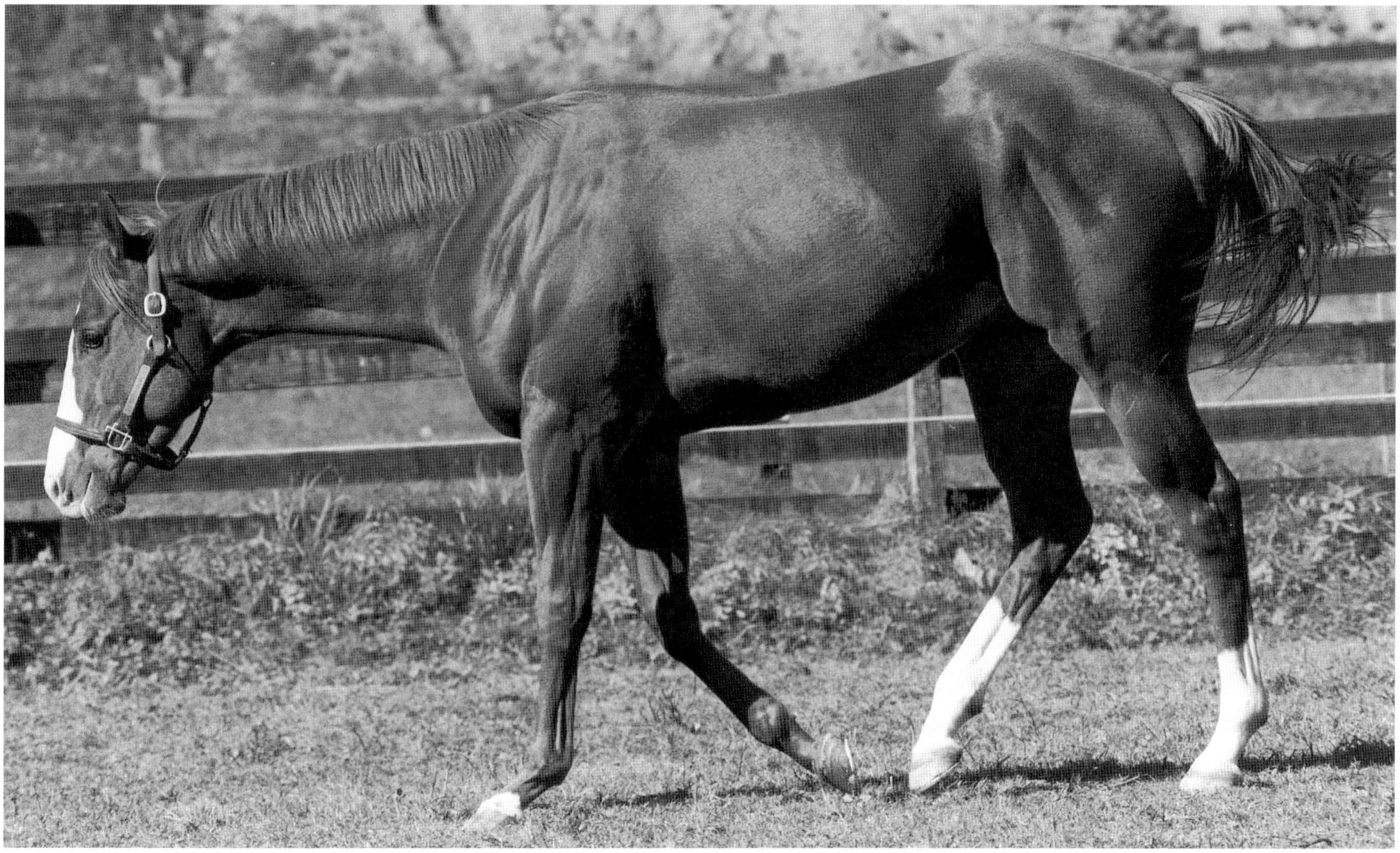

THOROUGHBRED; 2 YEARS OLD (MALE)

Equus caballus

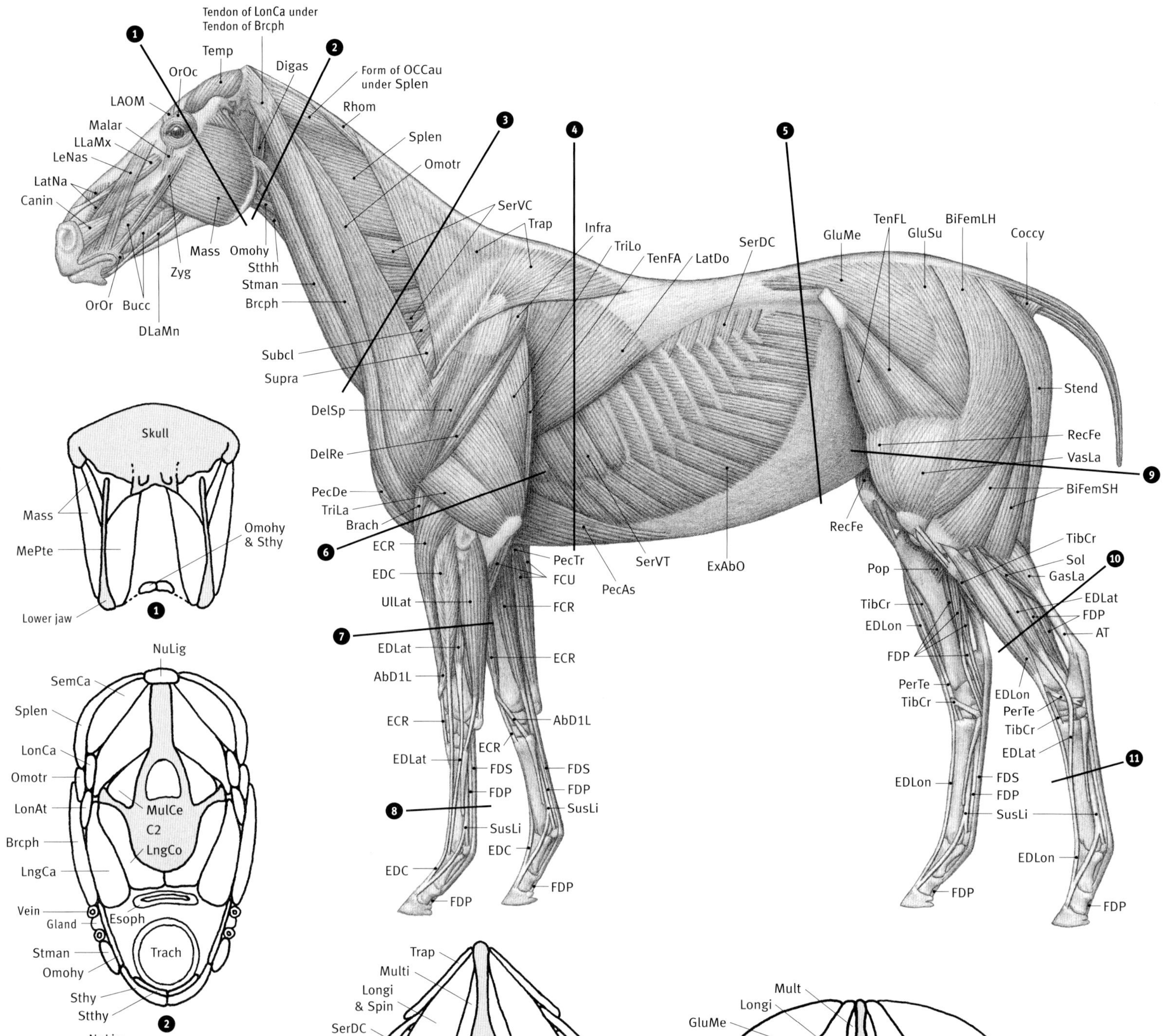

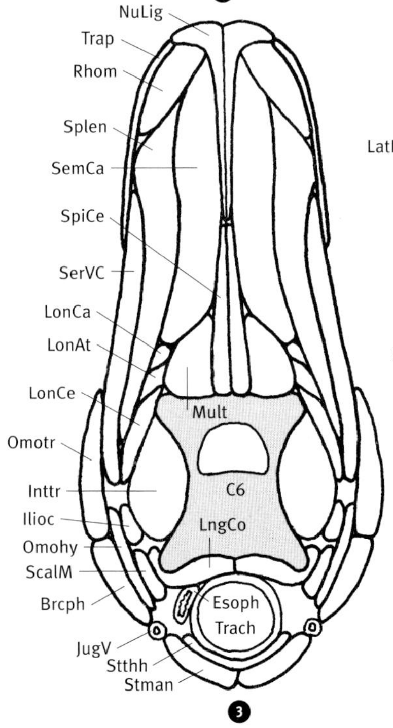

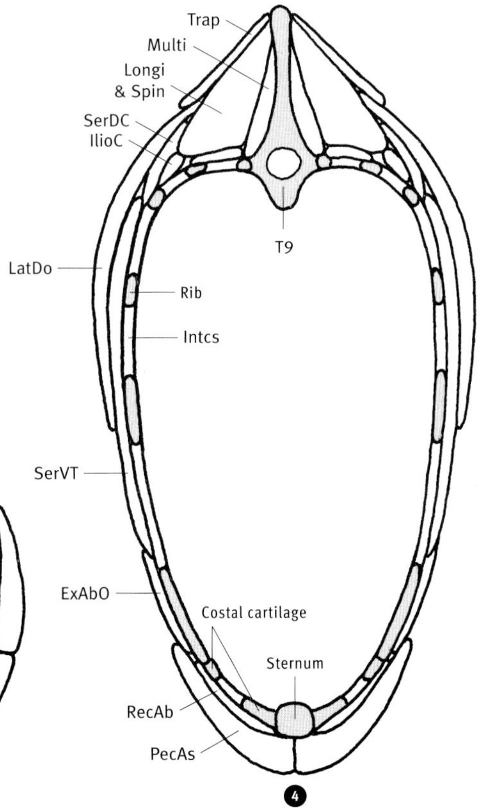

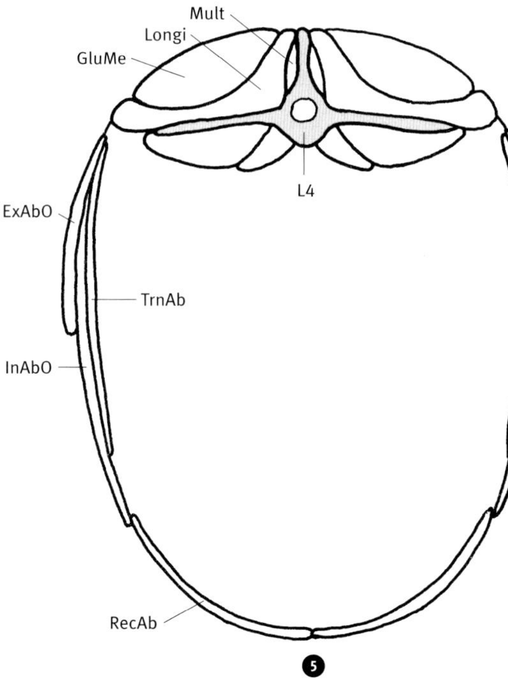

DRAWINGS NOT TO SCALE

(CROSS SECTIONS AFTER ELLENBERGER; SCHMALTZ; POPESCO)

FORELIMB

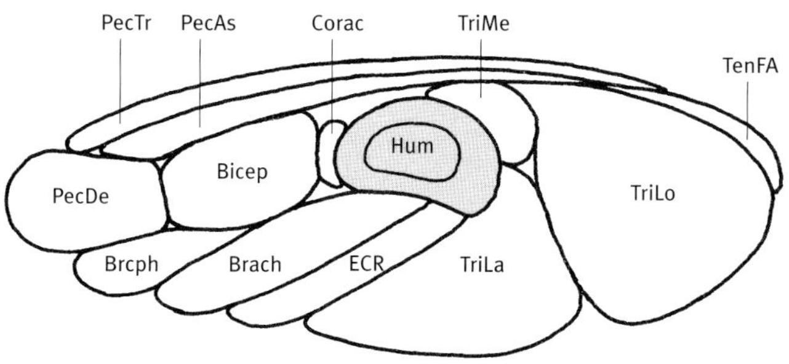

6

UPPER ARM

HIND LIMB

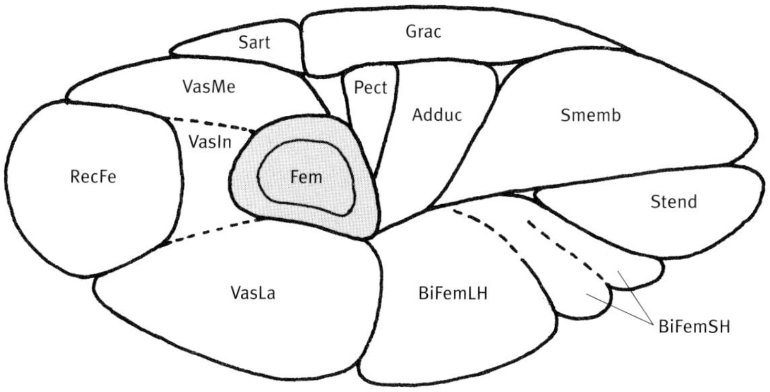

9

THIGH

▲
INSIDE
◀ FRONT REAR ▶
OUTSIDE
▼

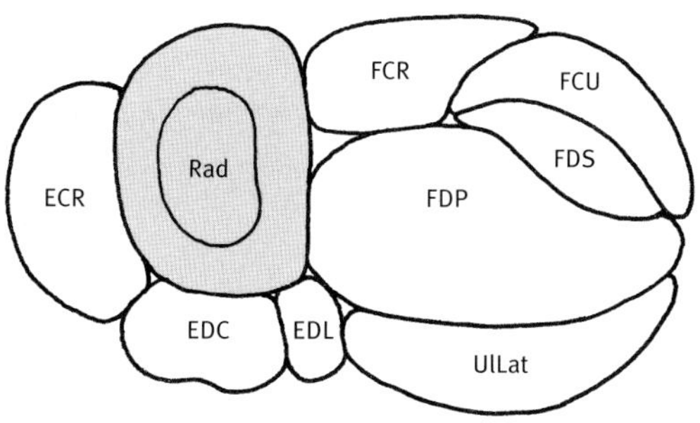

7

FOREARM

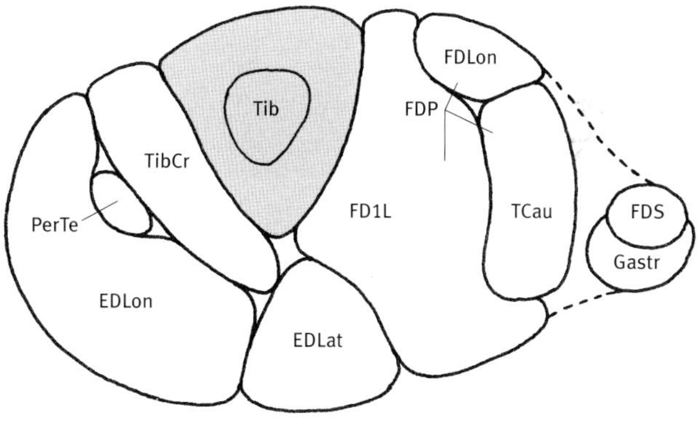

10

LOWER LEG

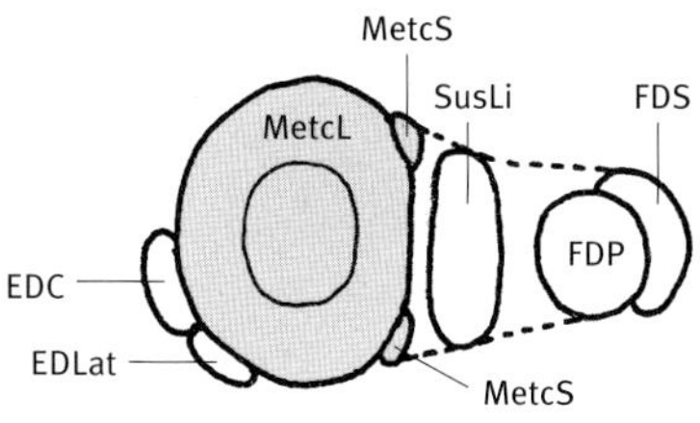

8

FOREFOOT

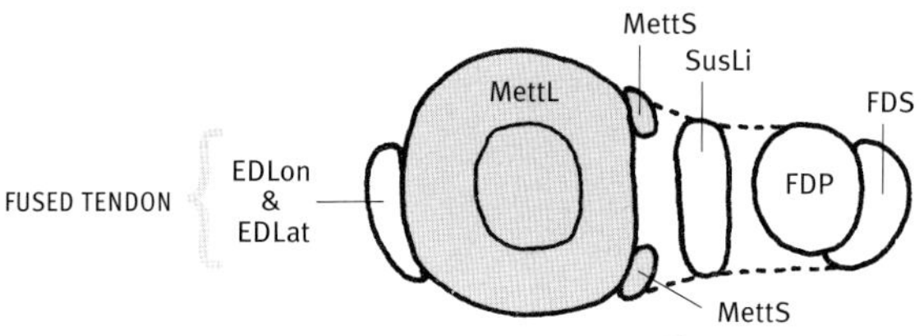

11

HIND FOOT

Adduc *Adductor;* **Bicep** *Biceps brachii;* **BiFemLH** *Biceps femoris, long head;* **BiFemSH** *Biceps femoris, short head;* **Brach** *Brachialis;* **Brcph** *Brachiocephalicus;* **C2** *Second cervical vertebra;* **C6** *Sixth cervical vertebra;* **Corac** *Coracobrachialis;* **ECR** *Extensor carpi radialis;* **EDC** *Extensor digitorum communis;* **EDLat** *Extensor digitorum lateralis;* **EDLon** *Extensor digitorum longus;* **Esoph** *Esophagus;* **ExAbO** *External abdominal oblique;* **FCR** *Flexor carpi radialis;* **FCU** *Flexor carpi ulnaris;* **FD1L** *Flexor digiti I longus;* **FDLon** *Flexor digitorum longus;* **FDP** *Flexor digitorum profundus;* **FDS** *Flexor digitorum superficialis;* **Fem** *Femur;* **Gastr** *Gastrocnemius;* **GluMe** *Gluteus medius;* **Grac** *Gracilis;* **Hum** *Humerus;* **IlioC** *Iliocostalis cervicis;* **Ilioc** *Iliocostalis;* **InAbO** *Internal abdominal oblique;* **Intcs** *Intercostals;* **Inttr** *Intertransversarii;* **JugV** *Jugular vein;* **L4** *Fourth lumbar vertebra;* **LatDo** *Latissimus dorsi;* **LngCa** *Longus capitis;* **LngCo** *Longus colli;* **LonAt** *Longissimus atlantis;* **LonCa** *Longissimus capitis;* **LonCe** *Longissimus cervicis;* **Longi** *Longissimus;* **Mass** *Masseter;* **MePte** *Medial pterygoid;* **MetcL** *Large metacarpal;* **MetcS** *Small metacarpal;* **MettL** *Large metatarsal;* **MettS** *Small metatarsal;* **MulCe** *Multifidus cervicis;* **Mult** *Multifidus;* **NuLig** *Nuchal ligament;* **Omohy** *Omohyoid;* **Omotr** *Omotransversarius;* **OCCau** *Obliquus capitis caudalis;* **PecAs** *Pectoralis ascendens;* **PecDe** *Pectoralis descendens;* **Pect** *Pectineus;* **PecTr** *Pectoralis transversus;* **PerTe** *Peroneus tertius;* **Rad** *Radius;* **RecAb** *Rectus abdominis;* **RecFe** *Rectus femoris;* **Rhom** *Rhomboid;* **Sart** *Sartorius;* **ScalM** *Scalenus medius;* **SemCa** *Semispinalis capitis;* **SerDC** *Serratus dorsalis caudalis;* **SerVC** *Serratus ventralis cervicis;* **SerVT** *Serratus ventralis thoracis;* **Smemb** *Semimembranosus;* **SpiCe** *Spinalis cervicis;* **Spin** *Spinalis;* **Splen** *Splenius;* **Stend** *Semitendinosus;* **Sthy** *Sternohyoid;* **Stman** *Sternomandibularis;* **Stthh** *Sternothyrohyoid;* **Stthy** *Sternothyroid;* **SusLi** *Suspensory ligament;* **T9** *Ninth thoracic vertebra;* **TenFA** *Tensor fasciae antibrachii;* **Tib** *Tibia;* **TibCa** *Tibialis caudalis;* **TibCr** *Tibialis cranialis;* **Trach** *Trachea;* **Trap** *Trapezius;* **TriLa** *Triceps brachii, lateral head;* **TriLo** *Triceps brachii, long head;* **TriMe** *Triceps brachii, medial head;* **TrnAb** *Transversus abdominis;* **UlLat** *Ulnaris lateralis;* **VasIn** *Vastus intermedius;* **VasLa** *Vastus lateralis;* **VasMe** *Vastus medialis.*

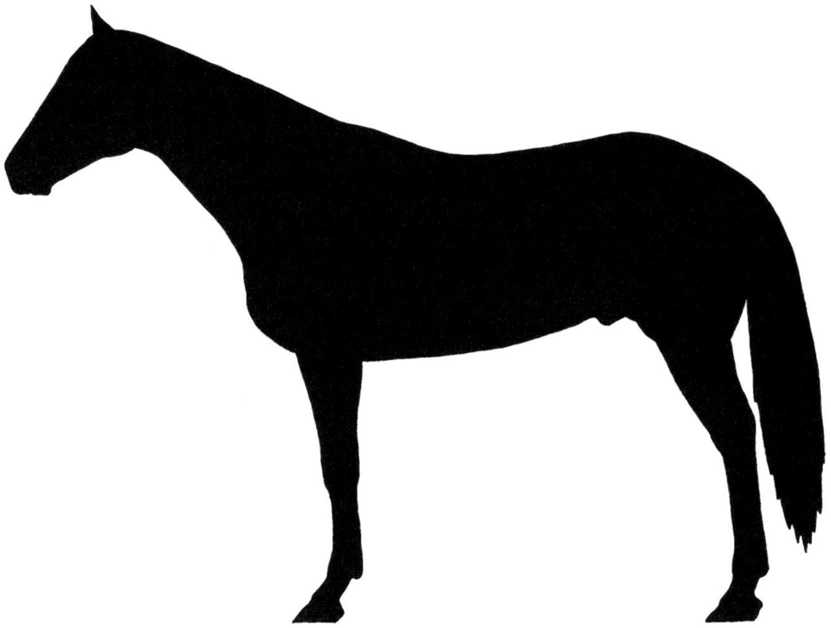

THOROUGHBRED

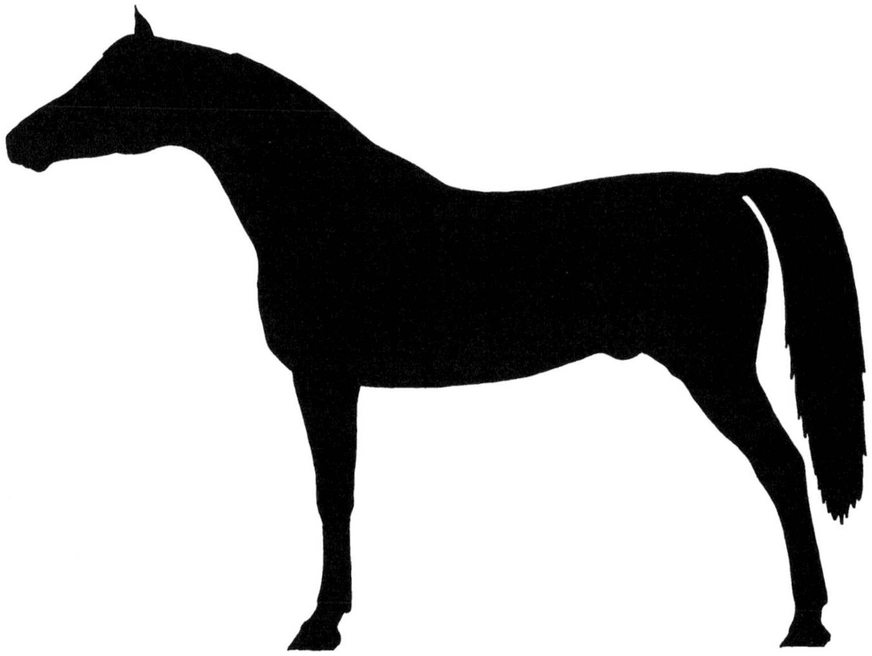

ARABIAN

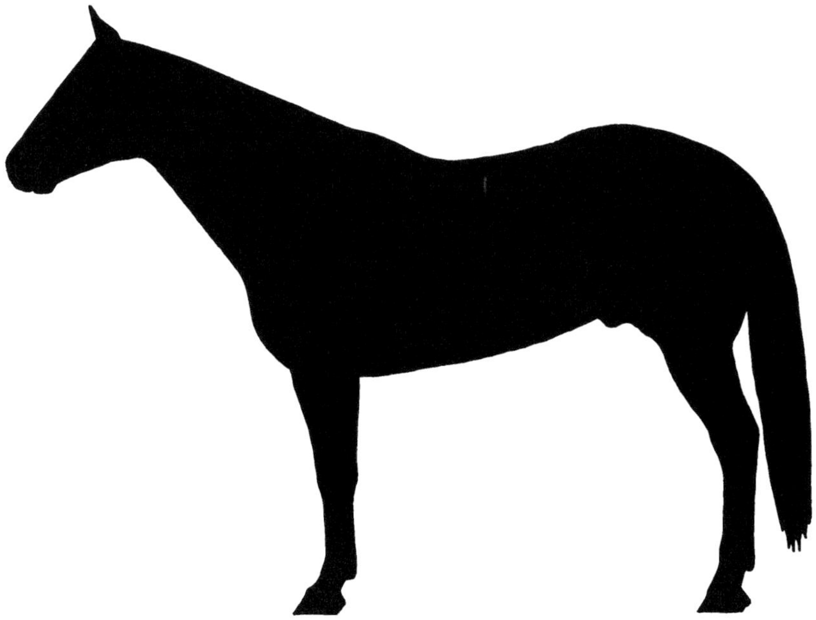

QUARTER HORSE

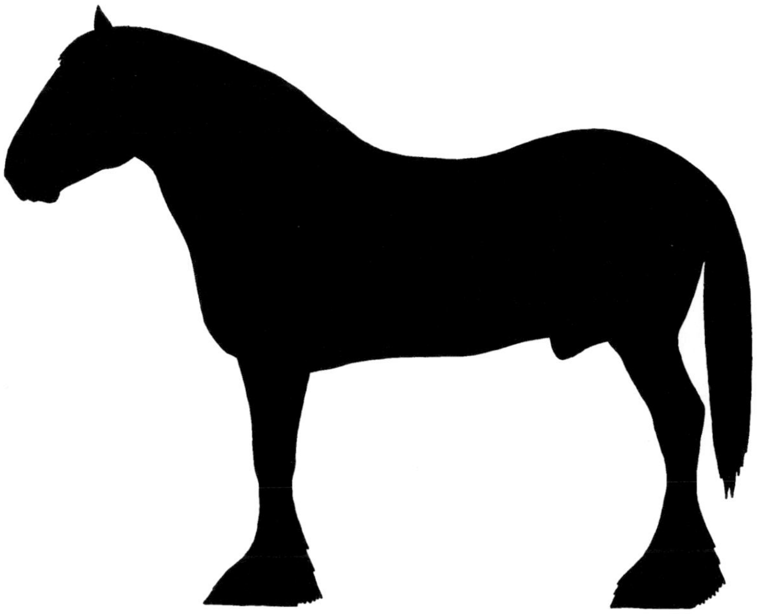

CLYDESDALE

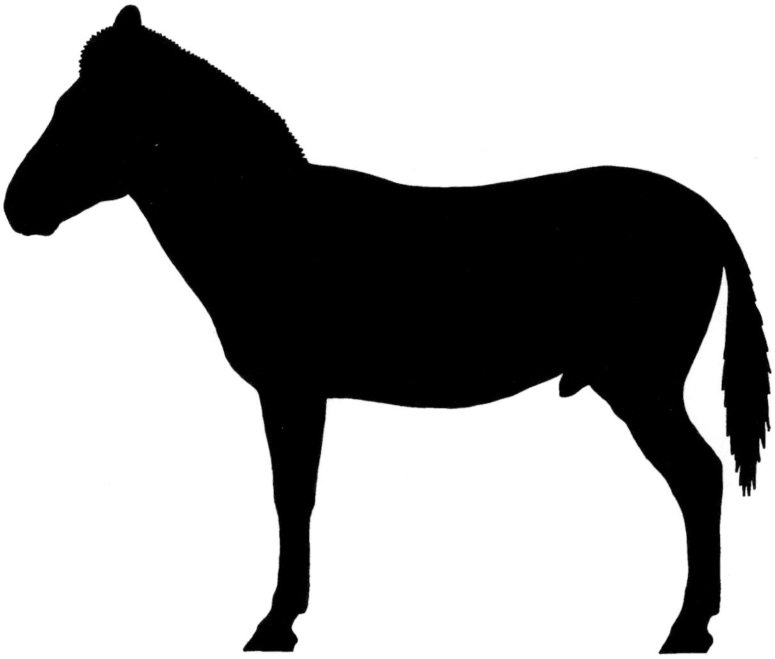

ZEBRA

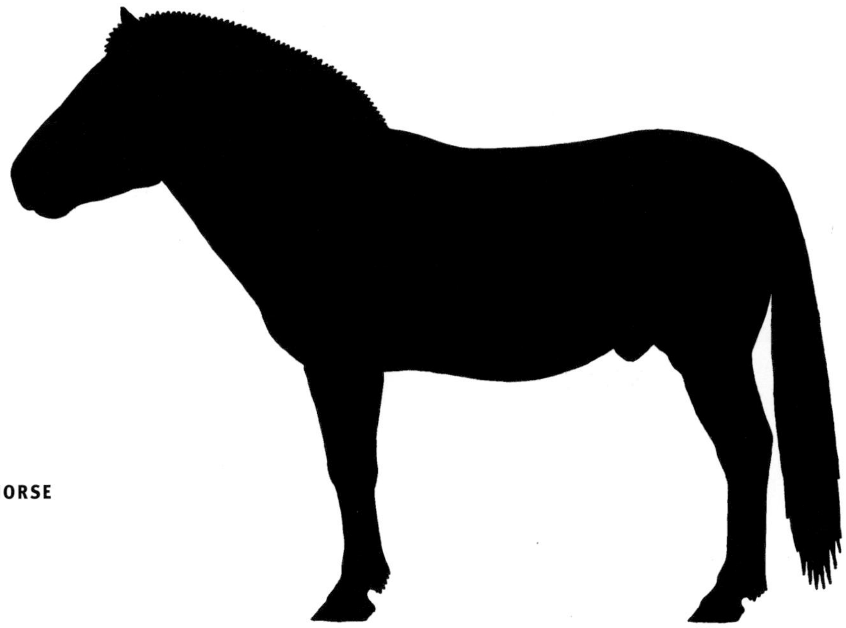

MONGOLIAN WILD HORSE

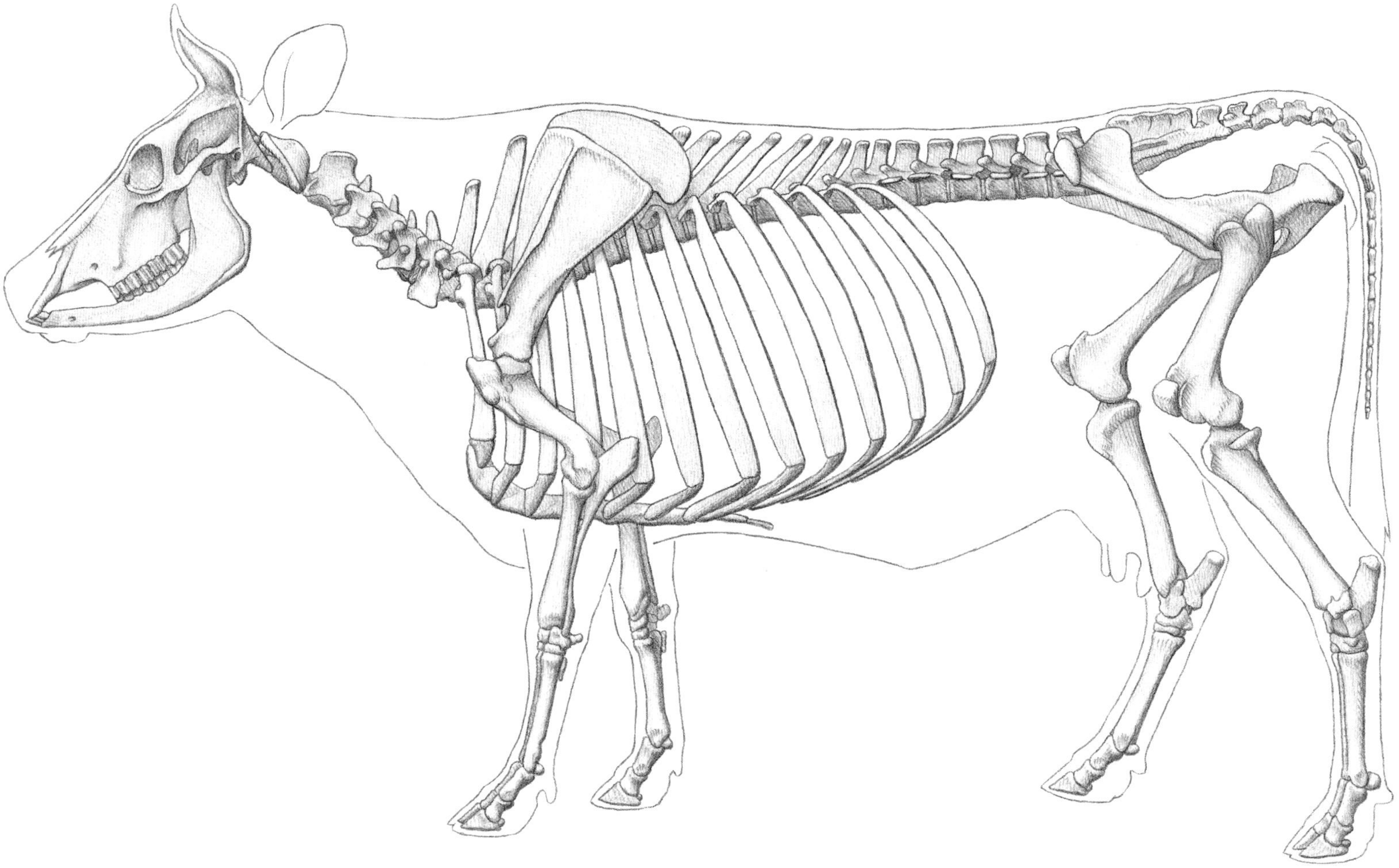

(ANATOMICAL DRAWINGS AFTER ELLENBERGER; POPESCO; ASHDOWN)

Ox (domestic cattle) characteristics: Unbranched, permanent horn has bony core covered with hard sheath, present usually in both male and female. Horns often cut off by owner ("polled"). No front teeth (incisors) in upper jaw; lower incisors press against toughened skin of palate. Ulna complete, but thin and fused to thicker radius. Only the upper and lower ends of the fibula are present, connected by a fibrous cord that replaces the shaft. The lower end is attached to the underside of the outer portion of the tibia. Four digits with hoofs per limb. Two central toes are large and weight bearing; vestigial inner and outer toes, with hoofs, are very small and located higher on side of foot and to the rear (they do not articulate with the skeleton and do not touch the ground). Walks on toes. Long, horizontal back line. Males tend to be bulky and muscular, whereas females are more angular, muscles less developed, with numerous prominent bony landmarks showing.

AbD1L *Abductor digiti I longus;* **Adduc** *Adductor;* **AT** *Achilles' tendon;* **Bicep** *Biceps brachii;* **Brach** *Brachialis;* **Brcph** *Brachiocephalicus;* **Bucc** *Buccinator;* **Canin** *Caninus;* **Clmas** *Cleidomastoid;* **ClOcc** *Cleido-occipitalis;* **Coccy** *Coccygeus;* **DelAc** *Deltoid, acromial portion;* **DelSc** *Deltoid, scapular portion;* **DLaMn** *Depressor labii mandibularis;* **DLaMx** *Depressor labii maxillaris;* **ECR** *Extensor carpi radialis;* **EDBr** *Extensor digitorum brevis;* **EDC** *Extensor digitorum communis;* **EDLat** *Extensor digitorum lateralis;* **EDLon** *Extensor digitorum longus;* **ExAbO** *External abdominal oblique;* **FCR** *Flexor carpi radialis;* **FCU** *Flexor carpi ulnaris;* **FDP** *Flexor digitorum profundus;* **FDS** *Flexor digitorum superficialis;* **Front** *Frontalis;* **GasLa** *Gastrocnemius, lateral head;* **GasMe** *Gastrocnemius, medial head;* **Glubi** *Gluteobiceps;* **GluMe** *Gluteus medius;* **Iliac** *Iliacus;* **Ilioc** *Iliocostalis;* **InAbO** *Internal abdominal oblique;* **Infra** *Infraspinatus;* **LatDo** *Latissimus dorsi;* **LatNa** *Lateralis nasi;* **LeNas** *Levator nasolabialis;* **LLaMx** *Levator labii maxillaris;* **LonAt** *Longissimus atlantis;* **LonCa** *Longissimus capitis;* **Longi** *Longissimus;* **Malar** *Malaris;* **Mass** *Masseter;* **Myloh** *Mylohyoid;* **OCCra** *Obliquus capitis cranialis;* **Omotr** *Omotransversarius;* **OrOc** *Orbicularis oculi;* **OrOr** *Orbicularis oris;* **PecAs** *Pectoralis ascendens;* **PecDe** *Pectoralis descendens;* **PecTr** *Pectoralis transversus;* **PerLo** *Peroneus longus;* **PerTe** *Peroneus tertius;* **Pop** *Popliteus;* **PrTer** *Pronator teres;* **RecAb** *Rectus abdominis;* **RecFe** *Rectus femoris;* **Rhom** *Rhomboid;* **SacLi** *Sacrotuberal ligament;* **Sart** *Sartorius;* **SerDC** *Serratus dorsalis caudalis;* **SerVC** *Serratus ventralis cervicis;* **SerVT** *Serratus ventralis thoracis;* **Smemb** *Semimembranosus;* **Sol** *Soleus;* **Splen** *Splenius;* **Stend** *Semitendinosus;* **Sthy** *Sternohyoid;* **Stman** *Sternomandibularis;* **Stmas** *Sternomastoid;* **Stthh** *Sternothyrohyoid;* **Stthy** *Sternothyroid;* **Supra** *Supraspinatus;* **SusLi** *Suspensory ligament;* **TeMaj** *Teres major;* **TeMin** *Teres minor;* **Temp** *Temporalis;* **TenFA** *Tensor fasciae antibrachii;* **TenFL** *Tensor fasciae latae;* **TibCr** *Tibialis cranialis;* **Trap** *Trapezius;* **TriLa** *Triceps brachii, lateral head;* **TriLo** *Triceps brachii, long head;* **UlLat** *Ulnaris lateralis;* **VasLa** *Vastus lateralis;* **Zyg** *Zygomaticus.*

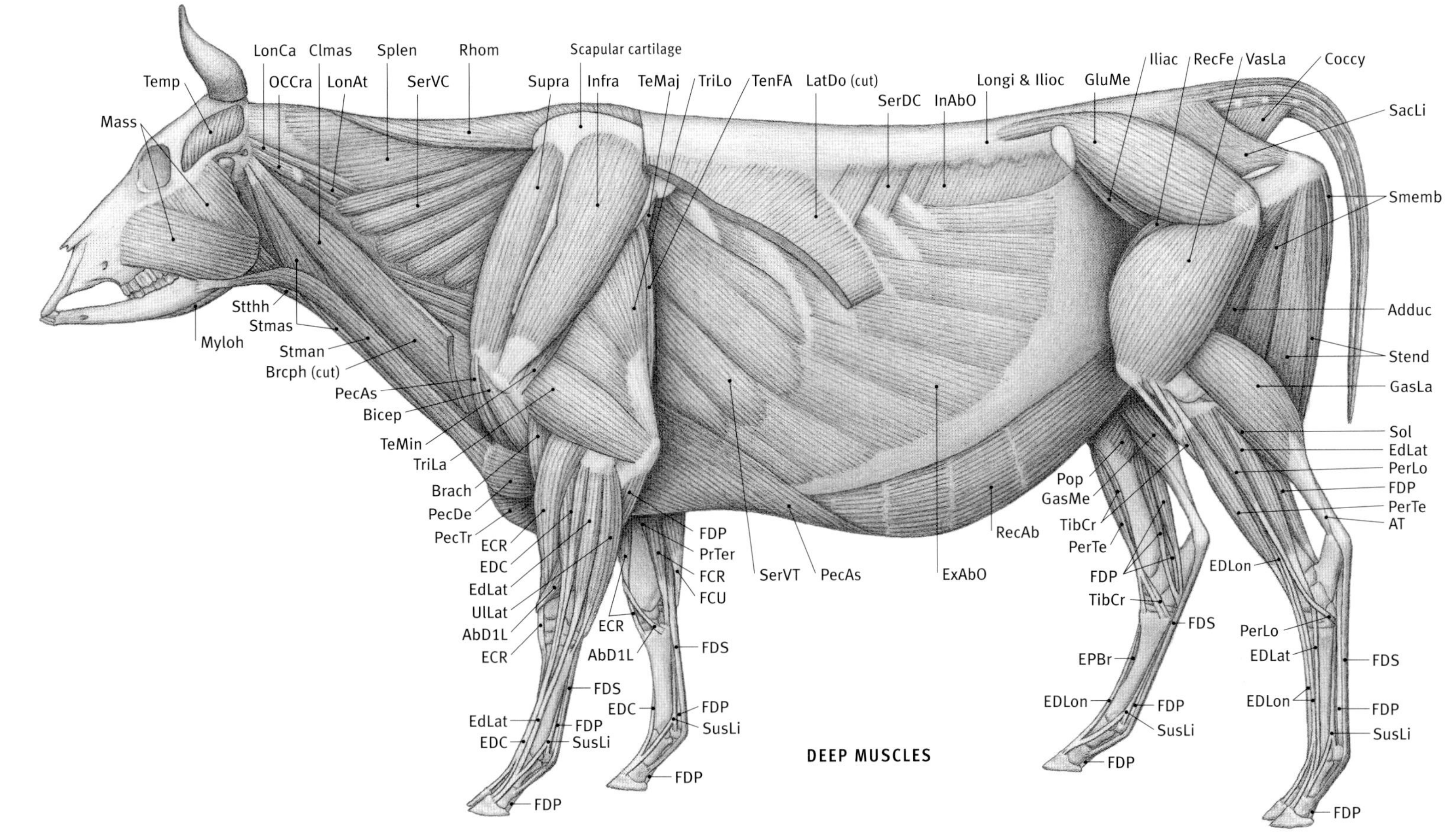

DEEP MUSCLES

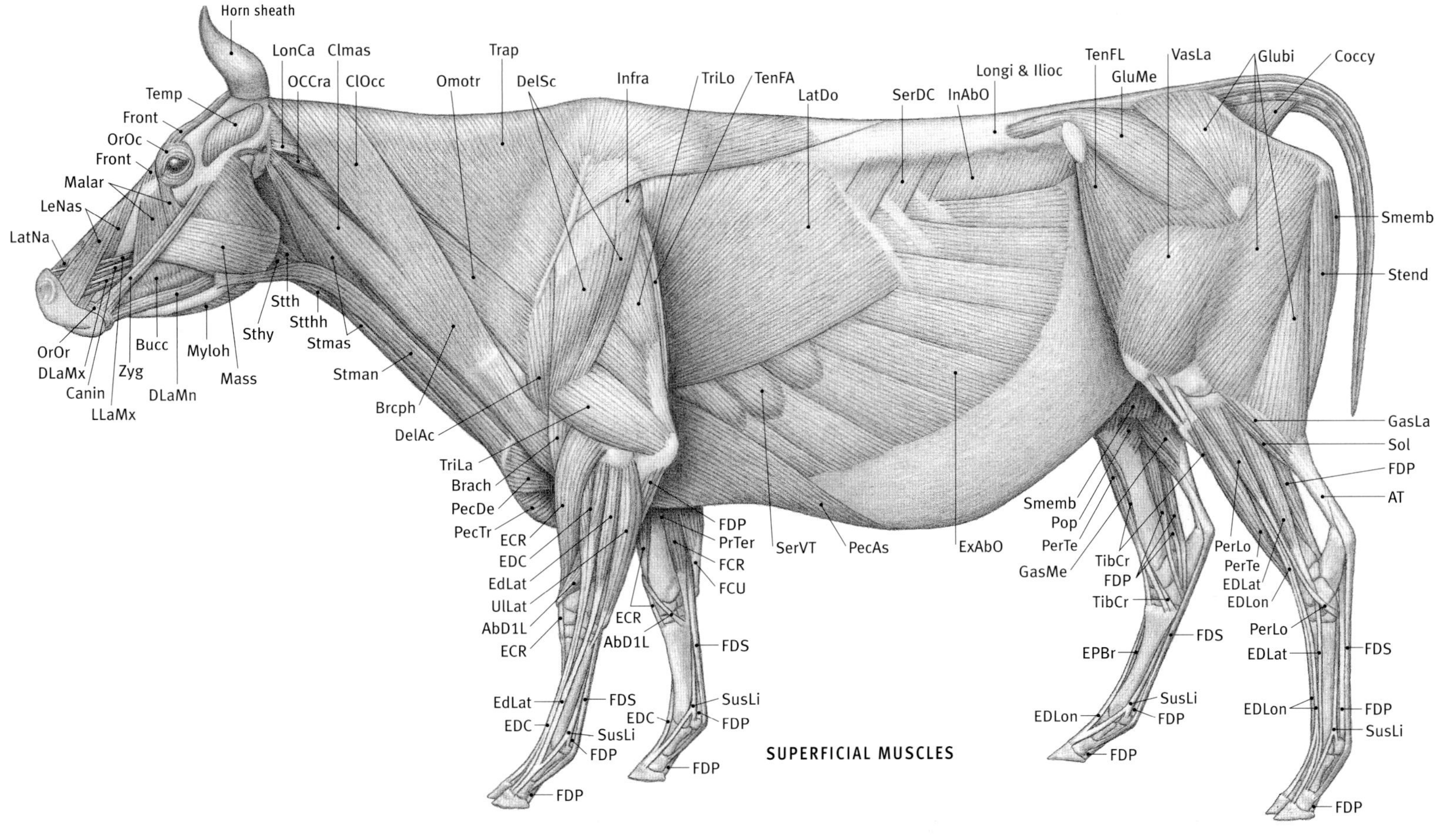

SUPERFICIAL MUSCLES

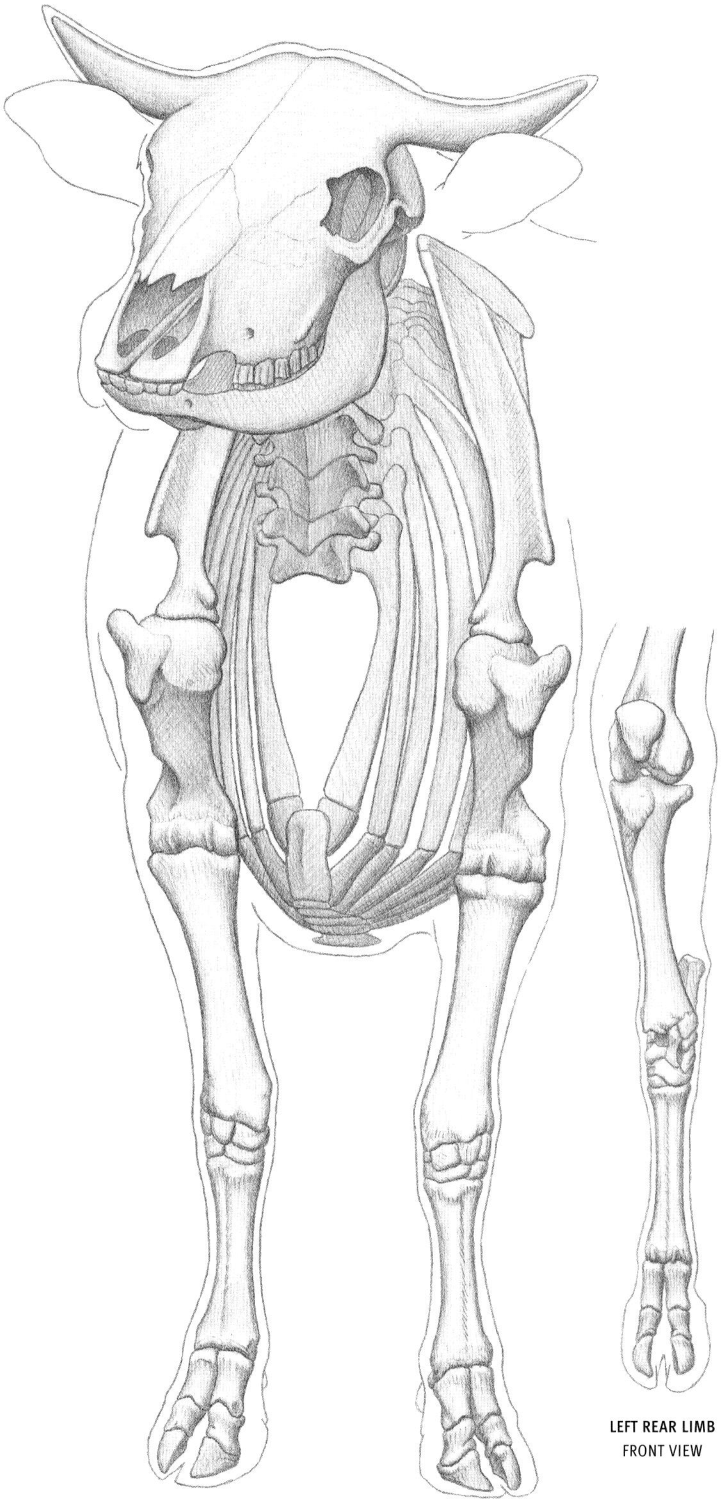

LEFT REAR LIMB
FRONT VIEW

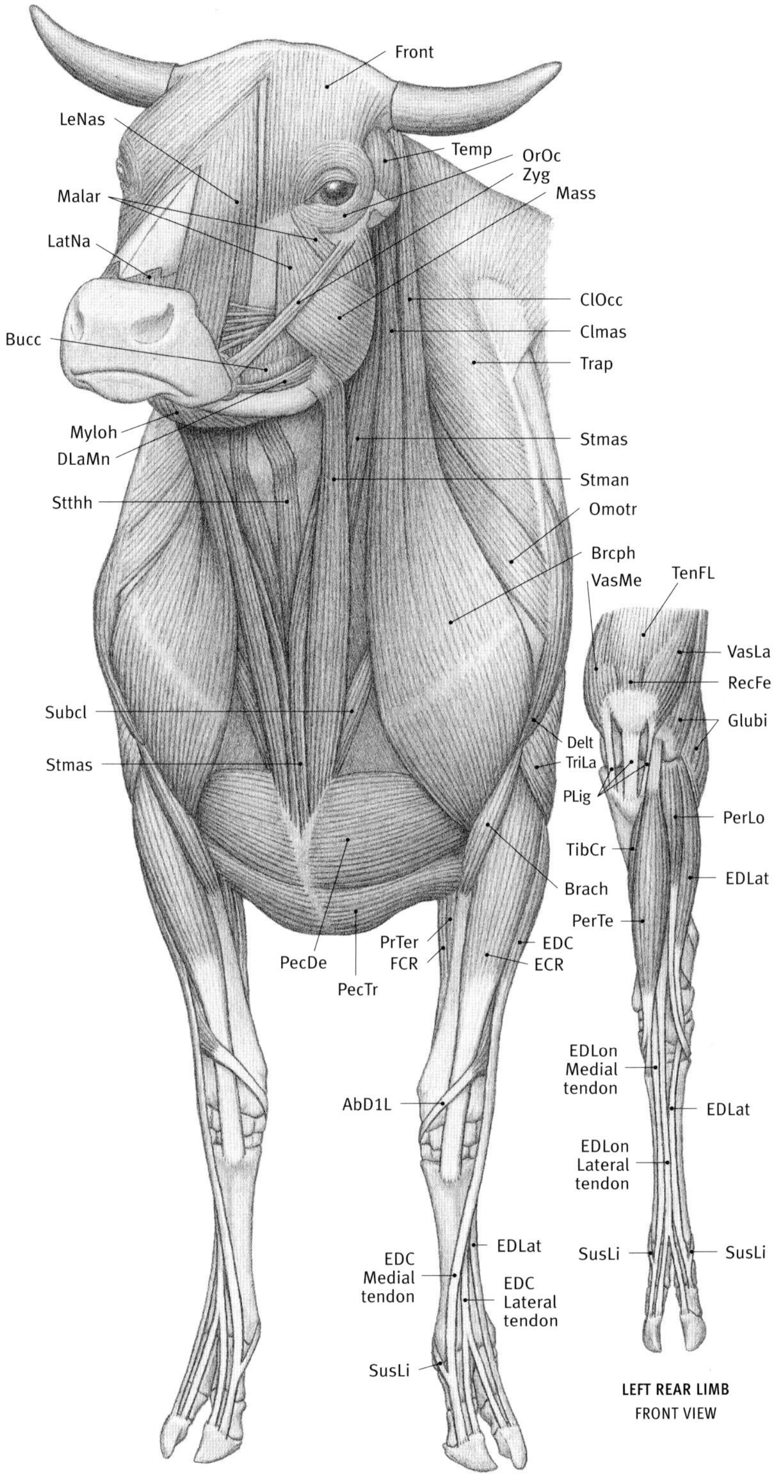

LEFT REAR LIMB
FRONT VIEW

AbD1L *Abductor digiti I longus;* **Brach** *Brachialis;* **Brcph** *Brachiocephalicus;* **Bucc** *Buccinator;* **Clmas** *Cleidomastoid;* **ClOcc** *Cleido-occipitalis;* **Delt** *Deltoid;* **DLaMn** *Depressor labii mandibularis;* **ECR** *Extensor carpi radialis;* **EDC** *Extensor digitorum communis;* **EDLat** *Extensor digitorum lateralis;* **EDLon** *Extensor digitorum longus;* **FCR** *Flexor carpi radialis;* **Front** *Frontalis;* **Glubi** *Gluteobiceps;* **LatNa** *Lateralis nasi;* **LeNas** *Levator nasolabialis;* **Malar** *Malaris;* **Mass** *Masseter;* **Myloh** *Mylohyoid;* **Omotr** *Omotransversarius;* **OrOc** *Orbicularis oculi;* **PecDe** *Pectoralis descendens;* **PecTr** *Pectoralis transversus;* **PerLo** *Peroneus longus;* **PerTe** *Peroneus tertius;* **PLig** *Patellar ligaments;* **PrTer** *Pronator teres;* **RecFe** *Rectus femoris;* **Stman** *Sternomandibularis;* **Stmas** *Sternomastoid;* **Stthh** *Sternothyrohyoid;* **Subcl** *Subclavius;* **SusLi** *Suspensory ligament;* **Temp** *Temporalis;* **TenFL** *Tensor fasciae latae;* **TibCr** *Tibialis cranialis;* **Trap** *Trapezius;* **TriLa** *Triceps brachii, lateral head;* **VasLa** *Vastus lateralis;* **VasMe** *Vastus medialis;* **Zyg** *Zygomaticus.*

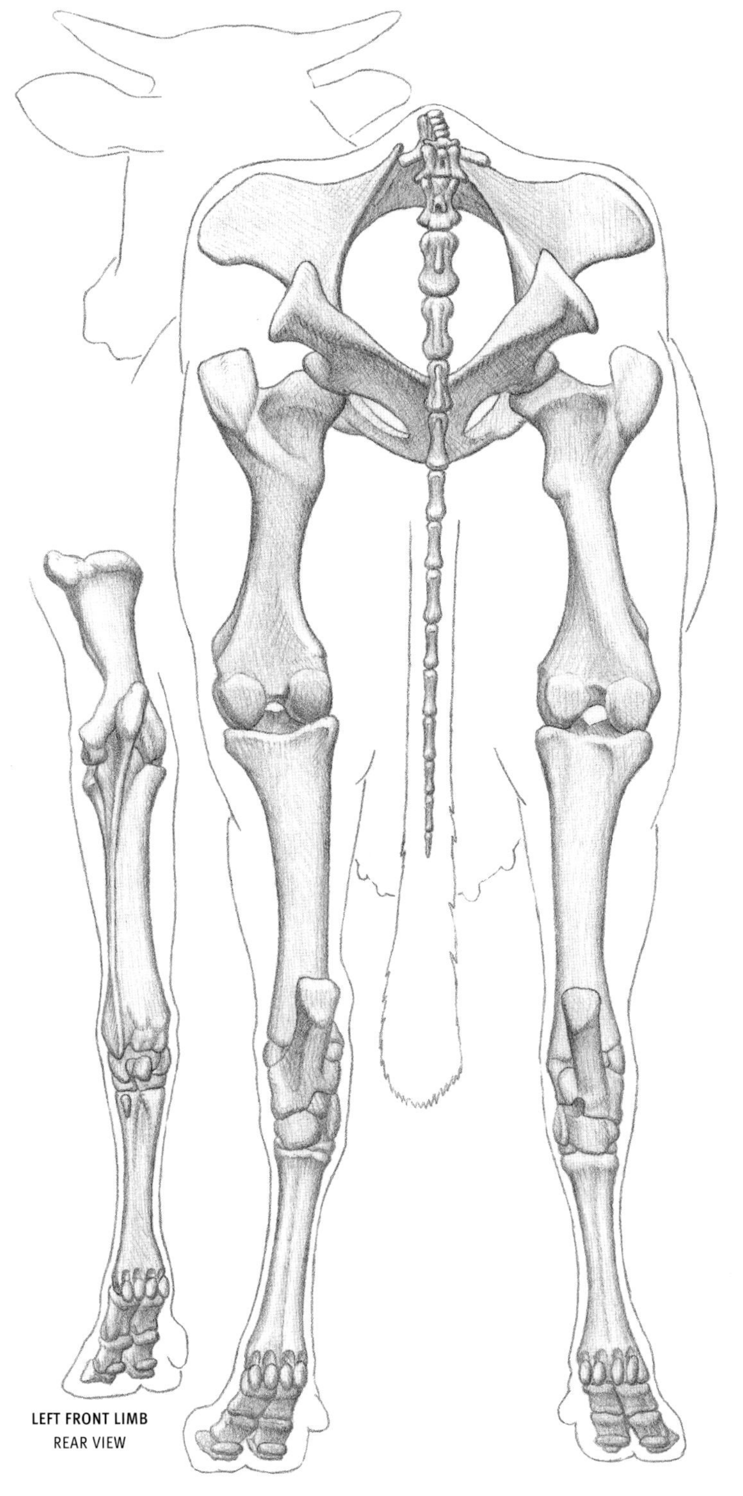

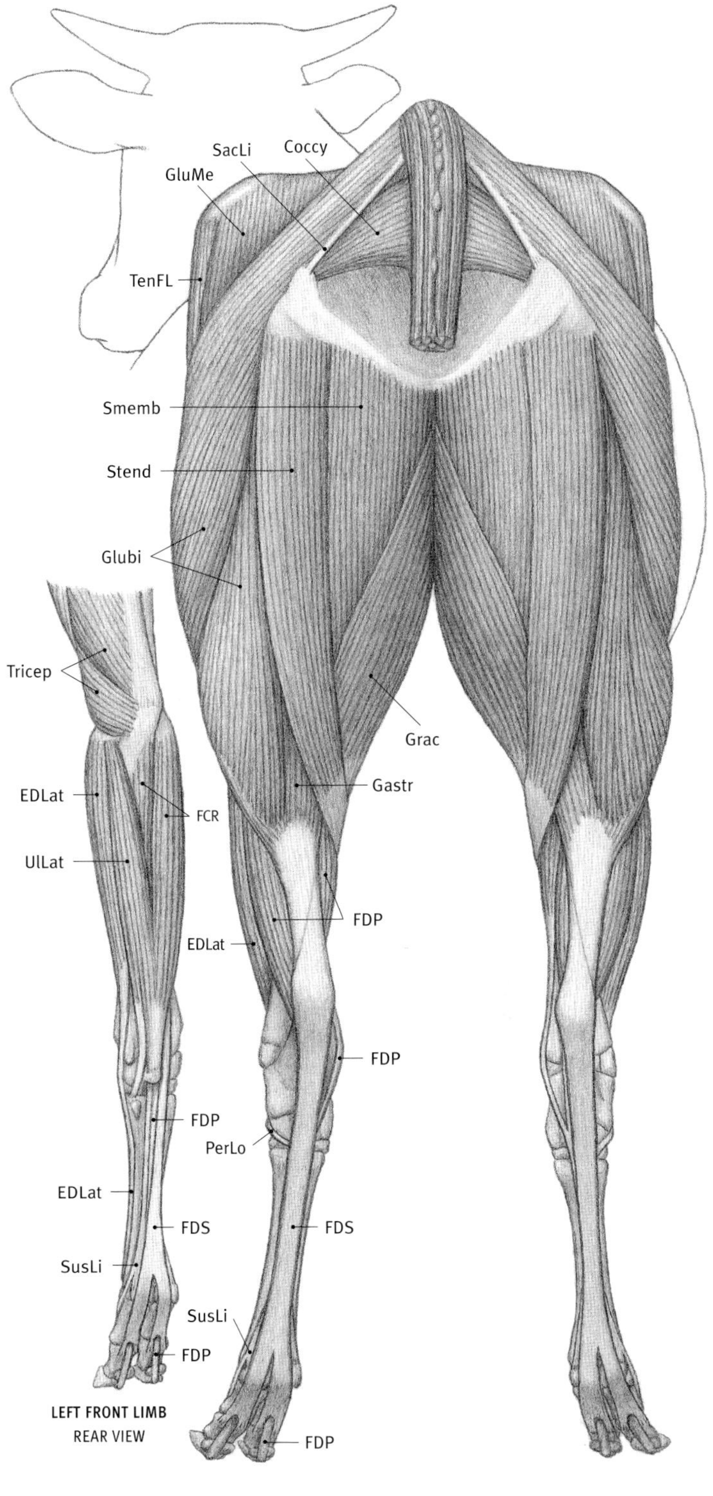

Coccy *Coccygeus;* **EDLat** *Extensor digitorum lateralis;* **FCR** *Flexor carpi radialis;* **FDP** *Flexor digitorum profundus;* **FDS** *Flexor digitorum superficialis;* **Gastr** *Gastrocnemius;* **Glubi** *Gluteobiceps;* **GluMe** *Gluteus medius;* **Grac** *Gracilis;* **PerLo** *Peroneus longus;* **SacLi** *Sacrotuberal ligament;* **Smemb** *Semimembranosus;* **Stend** *Semitendinosus;* **SusLi** *Suspensory ligament;* **TenFL** *Tensor fasciae latae;* **Tricp** *Triceps brachii;* **UlLat** *Ulnaris lateralis.*

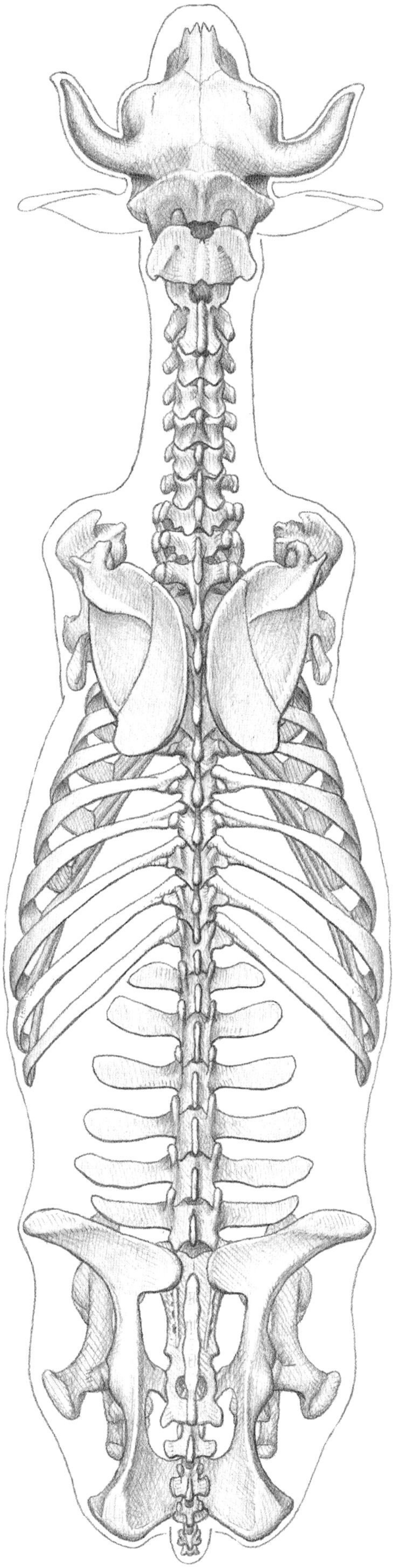

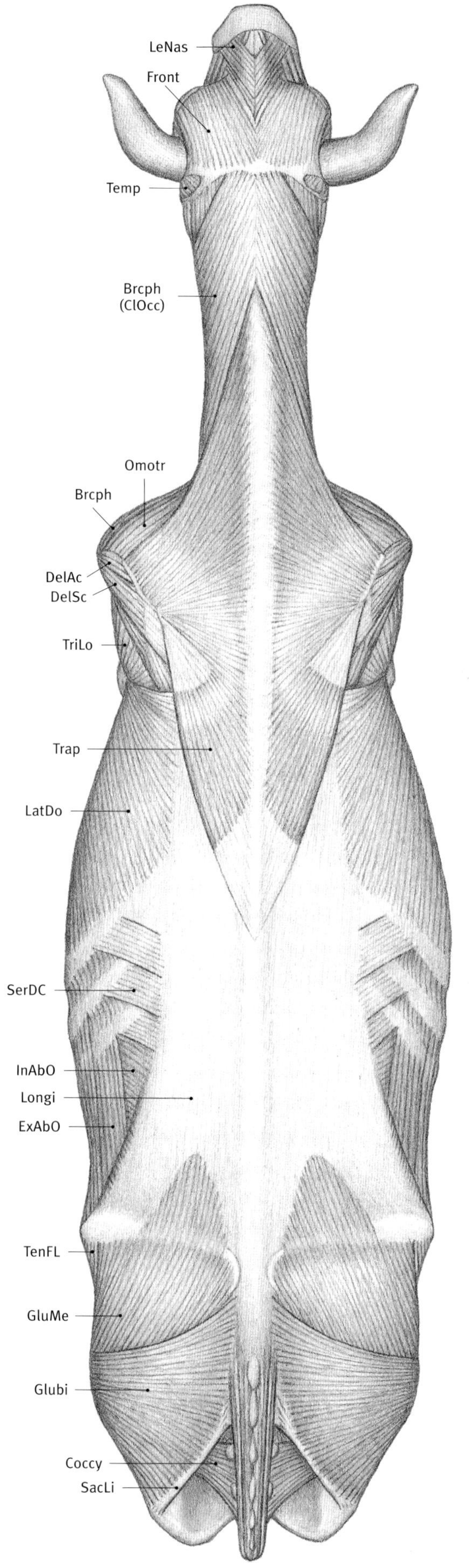

Brcph *Brachiocephalicus;* **ClOcc** *Cleido-occipitalis;* **Coccy** *Coccygeus;* **DelAc** *Deltoid, acromial portion;* **DelSc** *Deltoid, scapular portion;* **ExAbO** *External abdominal oblique;* **Front** *Frontalis;* **Glubi** *Gluteobiceps;* **GluMe** *Gluteus medius;* **InAbO** *Internal abdominal oblique;* **LatDo** *Latissimus dorsi;* **LeNas** *Levator nasolabialis;* **Longi** *Longissimus;* **Omotr** *Omotransversarius;* **SacLi** *Sacrotuberal ligament;* **SerDC** *Serratus dorsalis caudalis;* **Temp** *Temporalis;* **TenFL** *Tensor fasciae latae;* **Trap** *Trapezius;* **TriLo** *Triceps brachii, long head.*

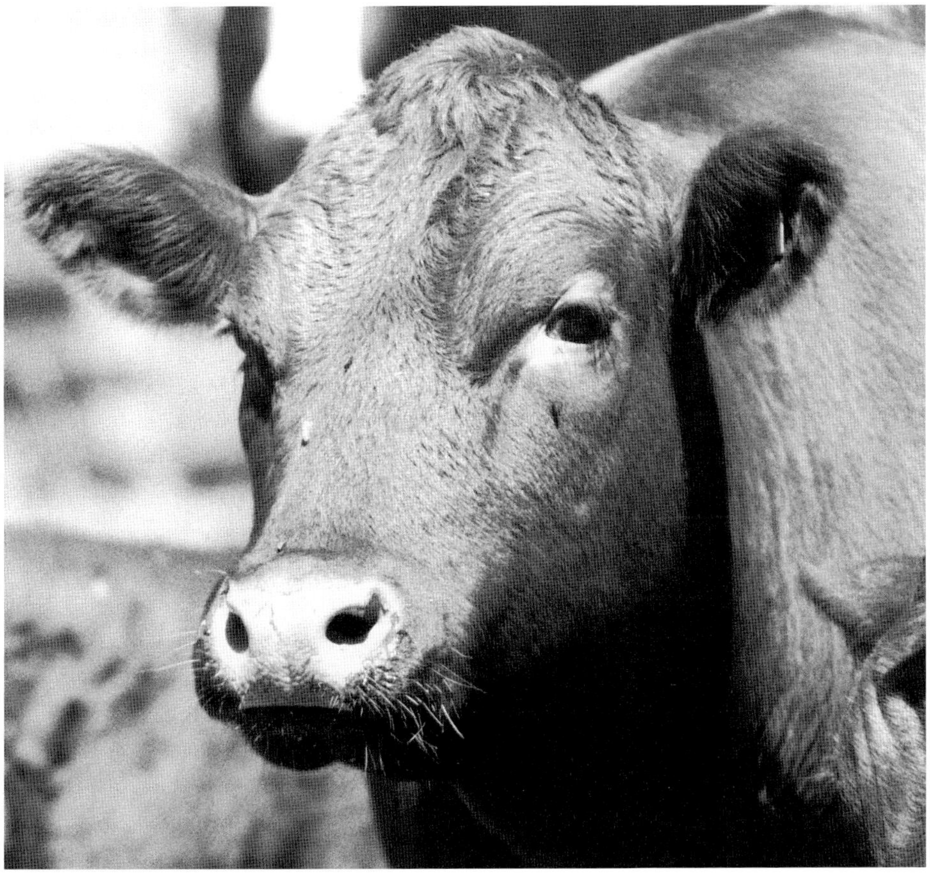

DEVON (FEMALE)

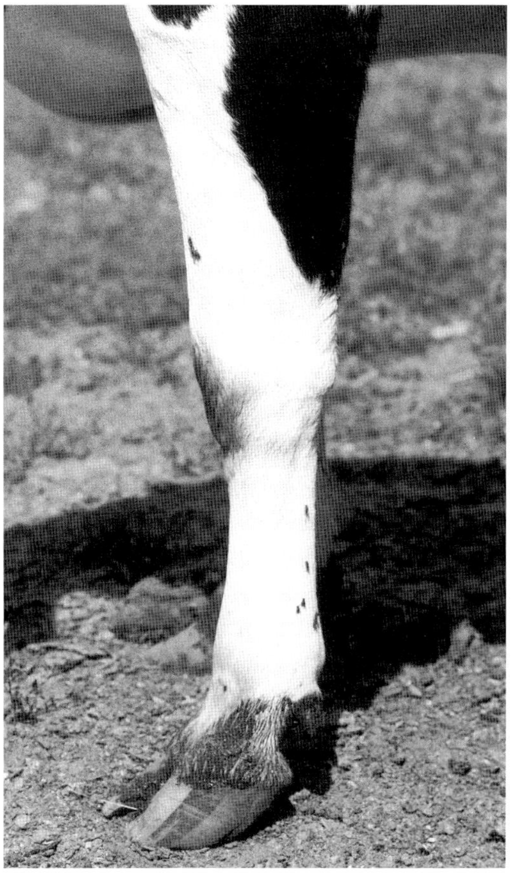

HOLSTEIN (FEMALE)

LEFT FRONT LIMB
OUTSIDE VIEW

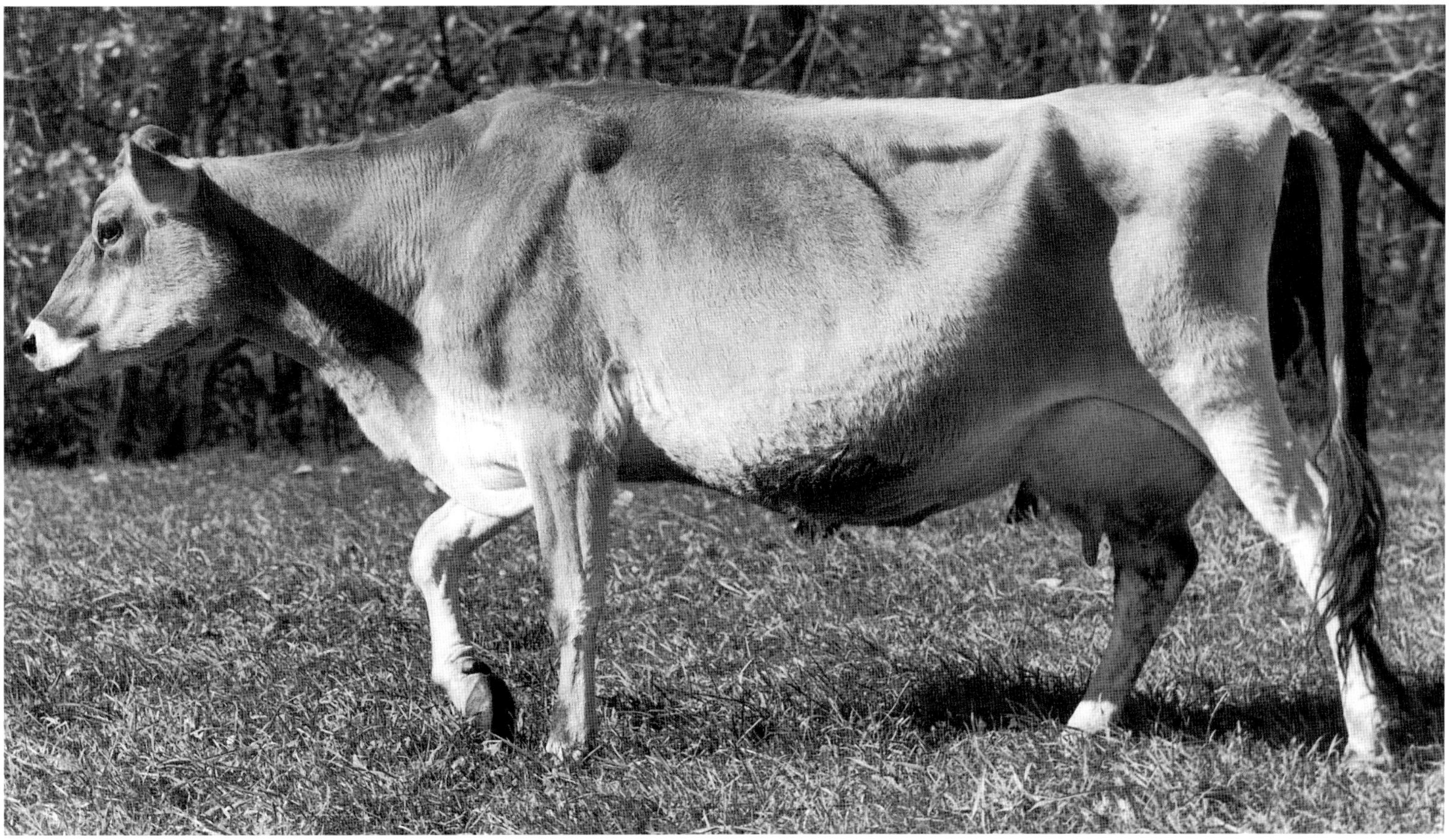

BROWN SWISS (FEMALE)

Bos taurus

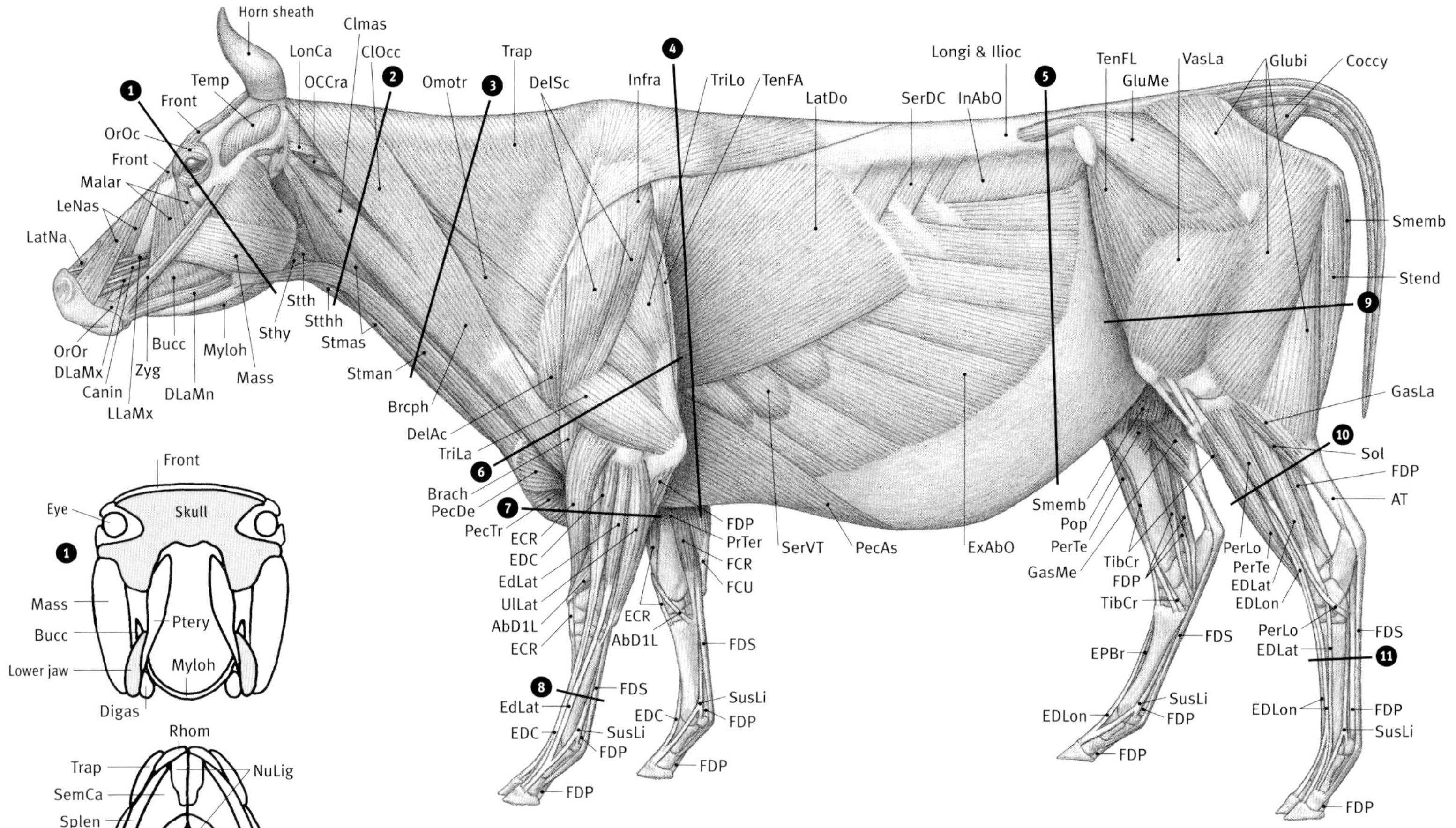

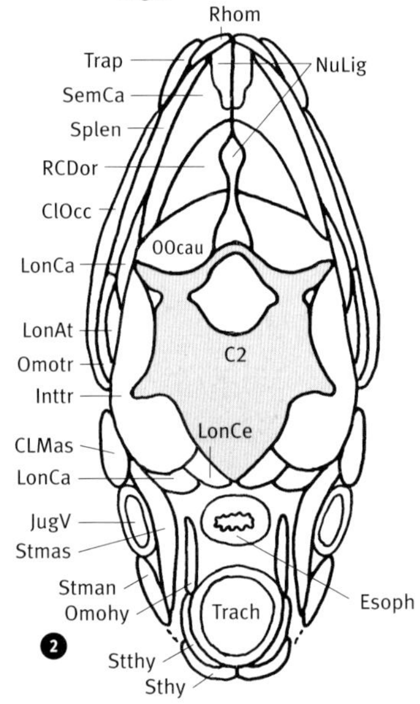

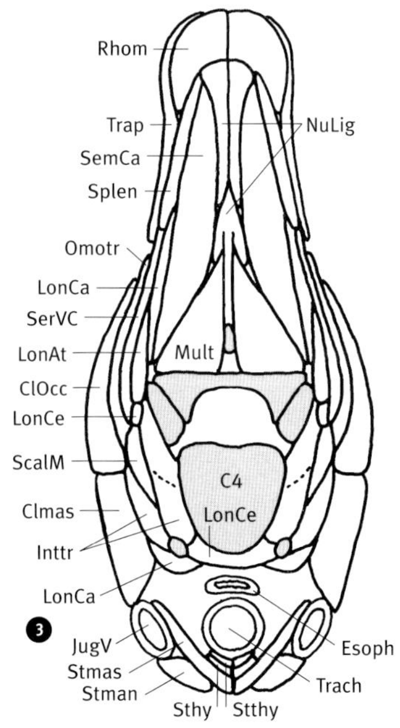

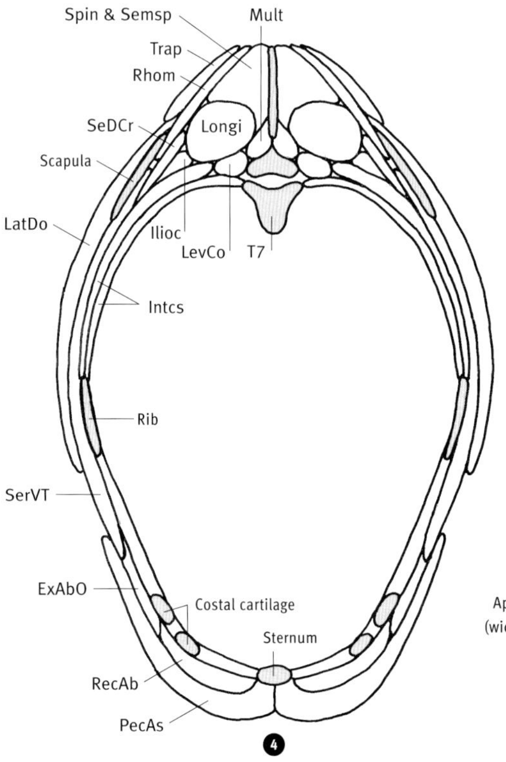

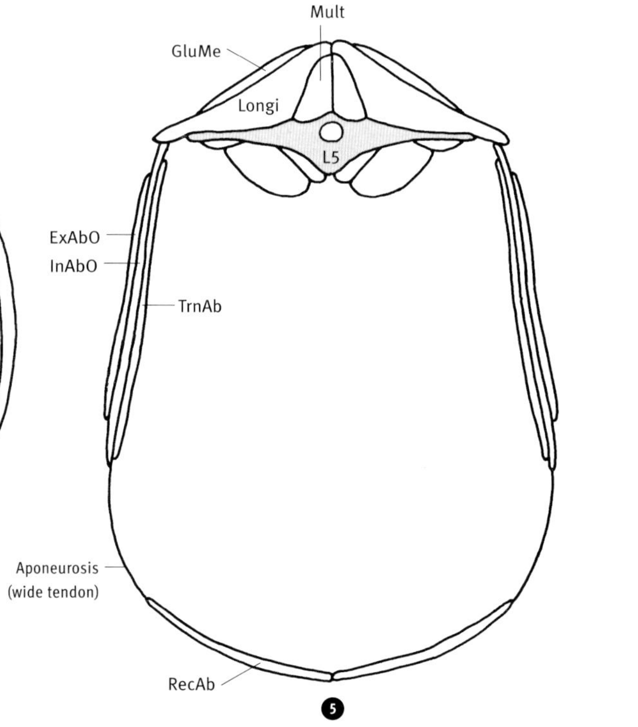

DRAWINGS NOT TO SCALE

(CROSS SECTIONS AFTER POPESCO; ELLENBERGER)

FORELIMB

HIND LIMB

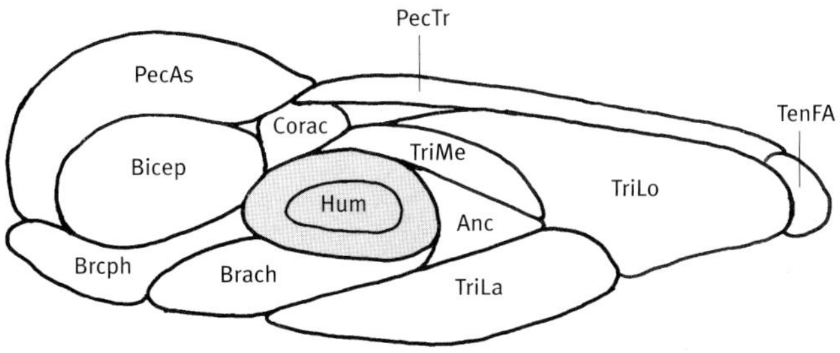

6

UPPER ARM

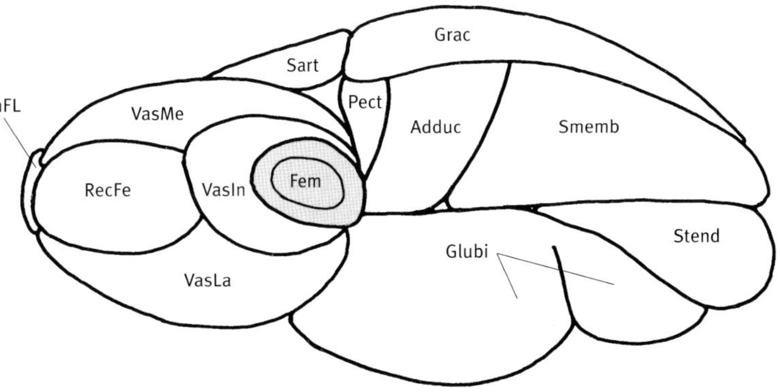

9

THIGH

▲ INSIDE
◀ FRONT REAR ▶
OUTSIDE ▼

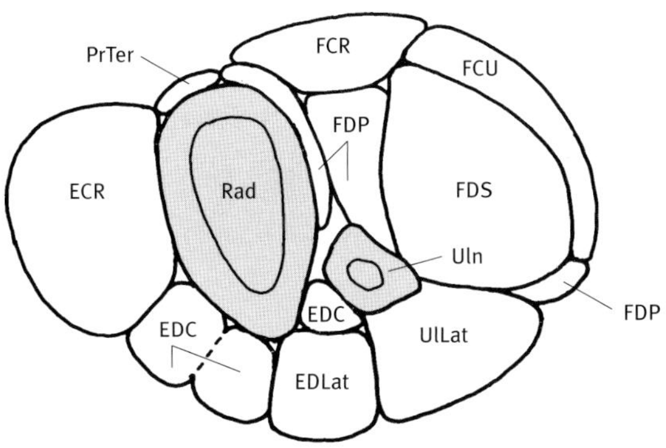

7

FOREARM

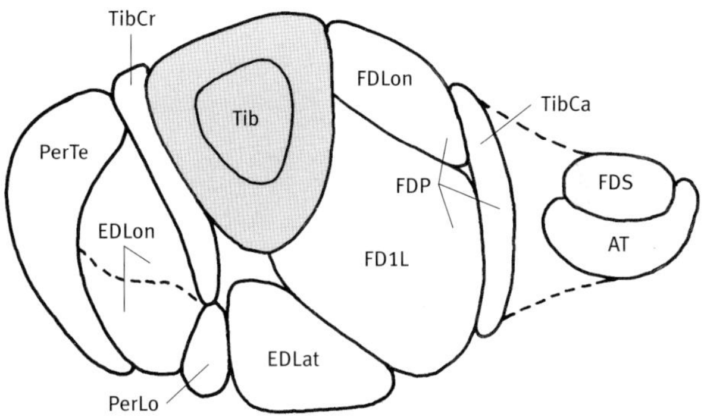

10

LOWER LEG

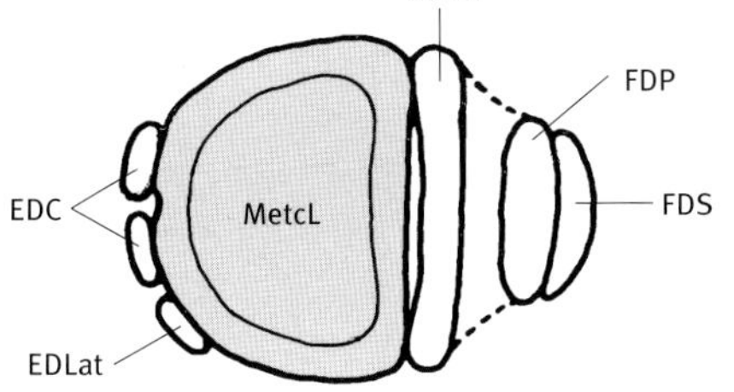

8

FOREFOOT

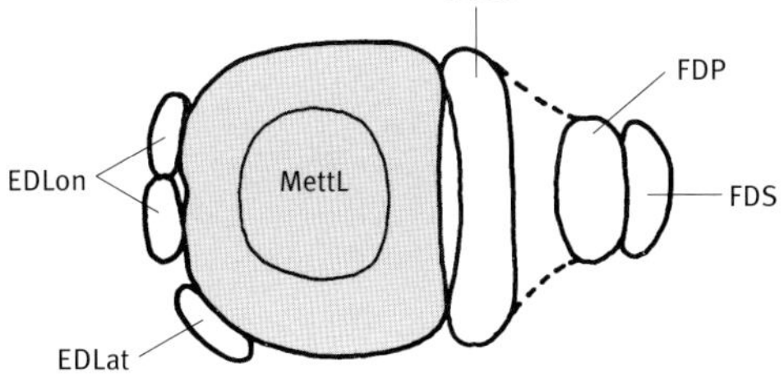

11

HIND FOOT

Adduc *Adductor;* **Anc** *Anconeus;* **AT** *Achilles' tendon;* **Bicep** *Biceps brachii;* **Brach** *Brachialis;* **Brcph** *Brachiocephalicus;* **Bucc** *Buccinator;* **C2** *Second cervical vertebra;* **C4** *Fourth cervical vertebra;* **Clmas** *Cleidomastoid;* **ClOcc** *Cleido-occipitalis;* **Corac** *Coracobrachialis;* **Digas** *Digastric;* **ECR** *Extensor carpi radialis;* **EDC** *Extensor digitorum communis;* **EDLat** *Extensor digitorum lateralis;* **EDLon** *Extensor digitorum longus;* **Esoph** *Esophagus;* **ExAbO** *External abdominal oblique;* **FFCR** *Flexor carpi radialis;* **FCU** *Flexor carpi ulnaris;* **FD1L** *Flexor digiti I longus;* **FDLon** *Flexor digitorum longus;* **FDP** *Flexor digitorum profundus;* **FDS** *Flexor digitorum superficialis;* **Fem** *Femur;* **Front** *Frontalis;* **Glubi** *Gluteobiceps*; **GluMe** *Gluteus medius;* **Grac** *Gracilis;* **Hum** *Humerus;* **Ilioc** *Iliocostalis;* **InAbO** *Internal abdominal oblique;* **Intcs** *Intercostals;* **Inttr** *Intertransversarii;* **JugV** *Jugular vein;* **L5** *Fifth lumbar vertebra;* **LatDo** *Latissimus dorsi;* **LevCo** *Levator costae;* **LngCa** *Longus capitis;* **LngCo** *Longus colli;* **LonAt** *Longissimus atlantis;* **LonCa** *Longissimus capitis;* **LonCe** *Longissimus cervicis;* **Longi** *Longissimus;* **Mass** *Masseter;* **MetcL** *Large metacarpal;* **MettL** *Large metatarsal;* **Mult** *Multifidus;* **Myloh** *Mylohyoid;* **NuLig** *Nuchal ligament;* **OCCau** *Obliquus capitis caudalis;* **Omohy** *Omohyoid;* **Omotr** *Omotransversarius;* **PecAs** *Pectoralis ascendens;* **Pect** *Pectineus;* **PecTr** *Pectoralis transversus;* **PerLo** *Peroneus longus;* **PerTe** *Peroneus tertius;* **PrTer** *Pronator teres;* **Ptery** *Pterygoid;* **Rad** *Radius;* **RCDor** *Rectus capitis dorsalis;* **RecAb** *Rectus abdominis;* **RecFe** *Rectus femoris;* **Rhom** *Rhomboid;* **Sart** *Sartorius;* **ScalM** *Scalenus medius;* **SeDCr** *Serratus dorsalis cranialis;* **SemCa** *Semispinalis capitis;* **SerVC** *Serratus ventralis cervicis;* **SerVT** *Serratus ventralis thoracis;* **Smemb** *Semimembranosus;* **Spin & Semsp** *Spinalis & semispinalis;* **Splen** *Splenius;* **Stend** *Semitendinosus;* **Sthy** *Sternohyoid;* **Stman** *Sternomandibularis;* **Stmas** *Sternomastoid;* **Stthy** *Sternothyroid;* **SusLi** *Suspensory ligament;* **T8** *Seventh thoracic vertebra;* **TenFA** *Tensor fasciae antibrachii;* **TenFL** *Tensor fasciae latae;* **Tib** *Tibia;* **TibCa** *Tibialis caudalis;* **TibCr** *Tibialis cranialis;* **Trach** *Trachea;* **Trap** *Trapezius;* **TriLa** *Triceps brachii, lateral head;* **TriLo** *Triceps brachii, long head;* **TriMe** *Triceps brachii, medial head;* **TrnAb** *Transversus abdominis*; **UlLat** *Ulnaris lateralis;* **Uln** *Ulna;* **VasIn** *Vastus intermedius;* **VasLa** *Vastus lateralis;* **VasMe** *Vastus medialis.*

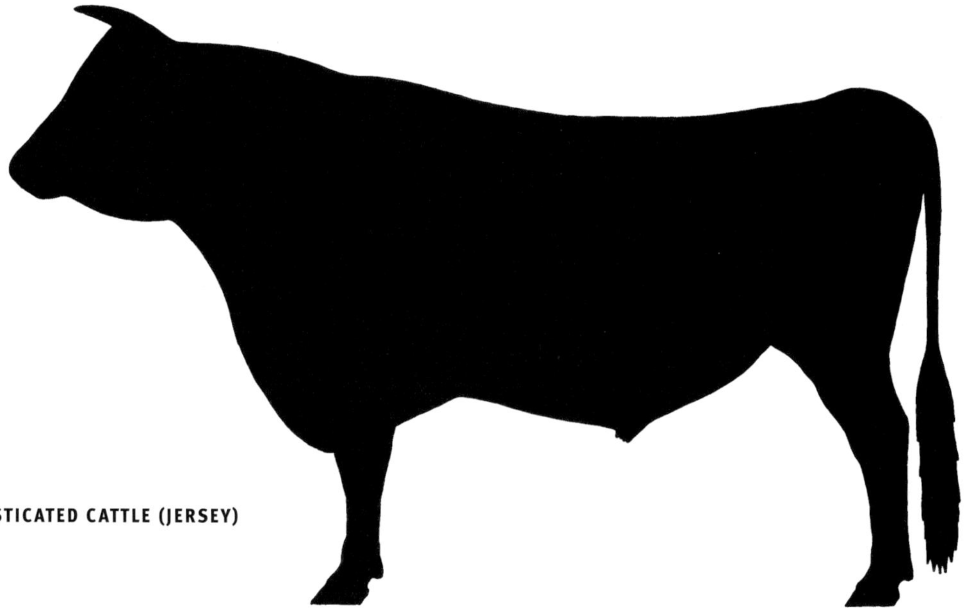

OX/DOMESTICATED CATTLE (JERSEY)

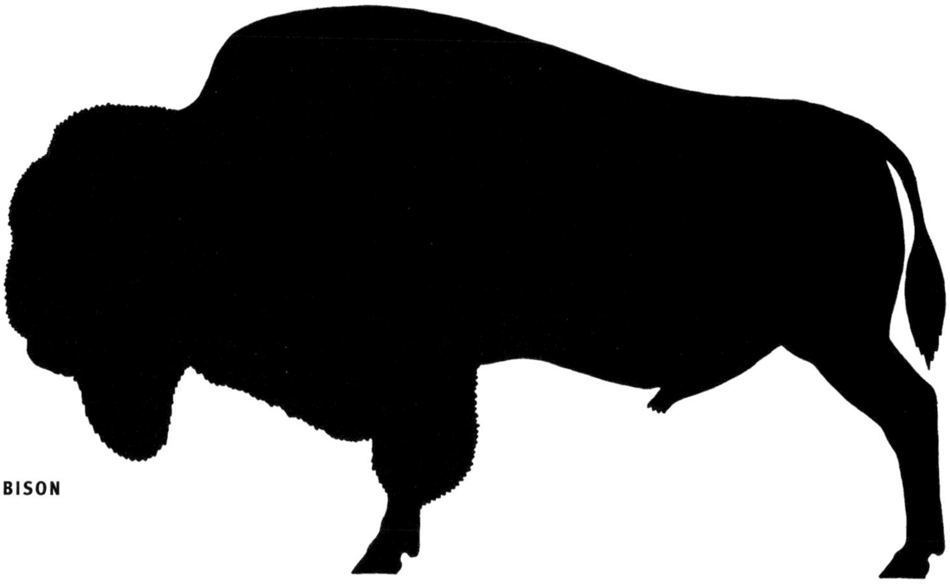

AMERICAN BISON

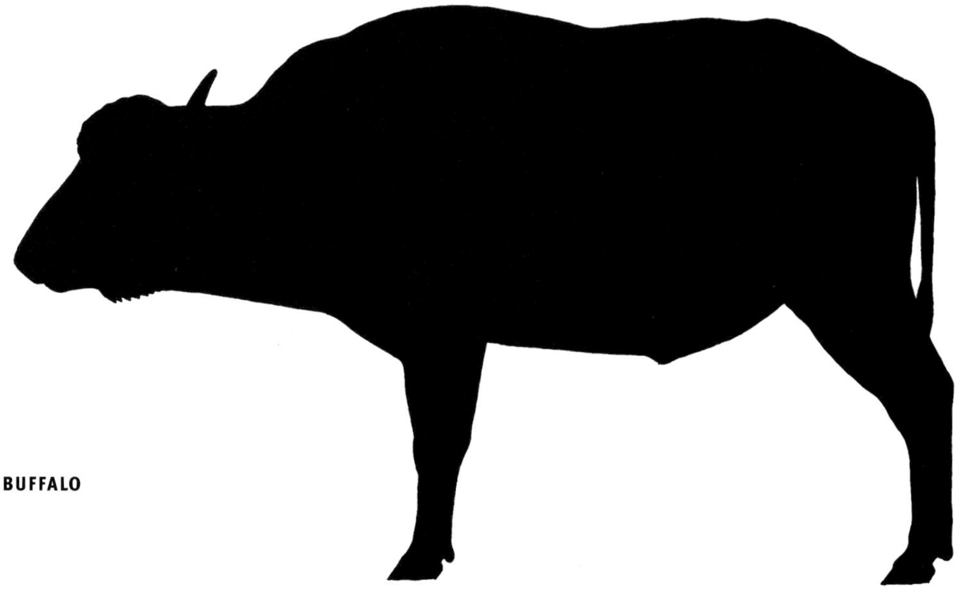

AFRICAN BUFFALO

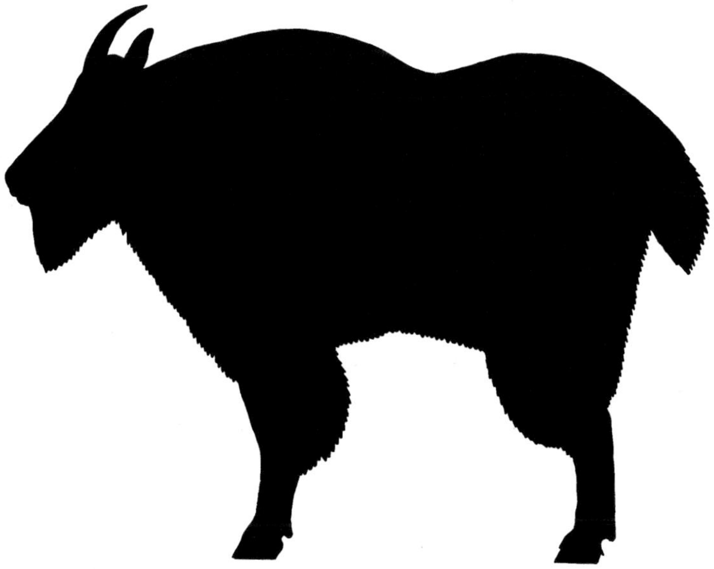

MOUNTAIN GOAT

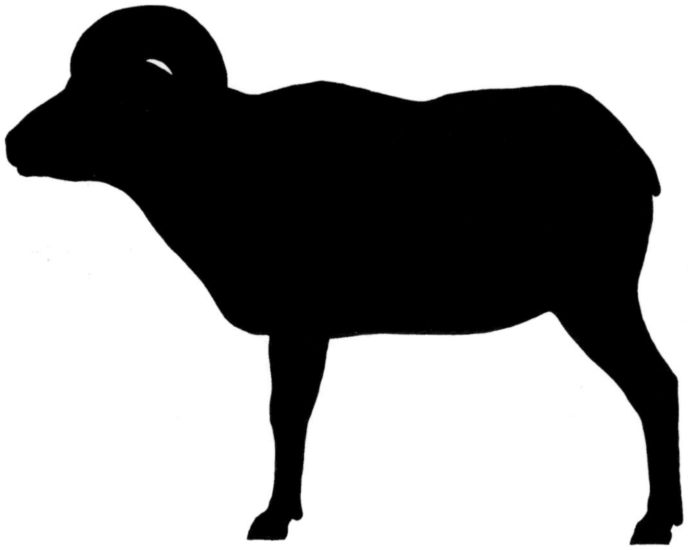

BIGHORN SHEEP

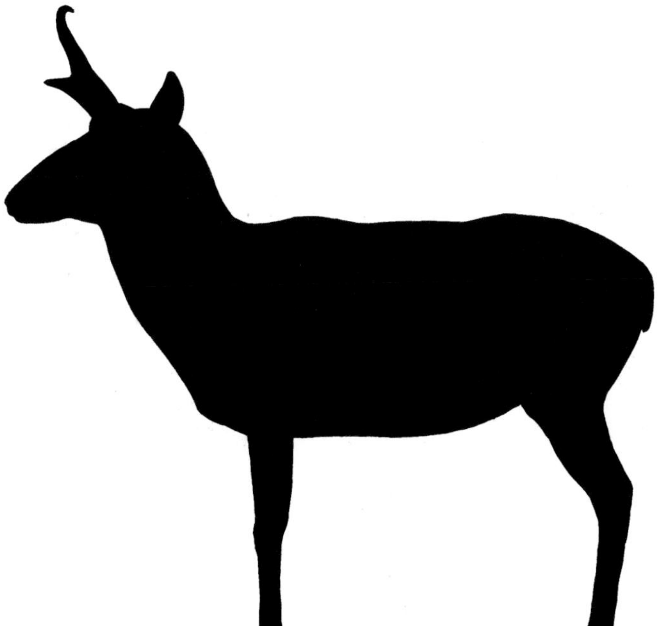

PRONGHORN ANTELOPE

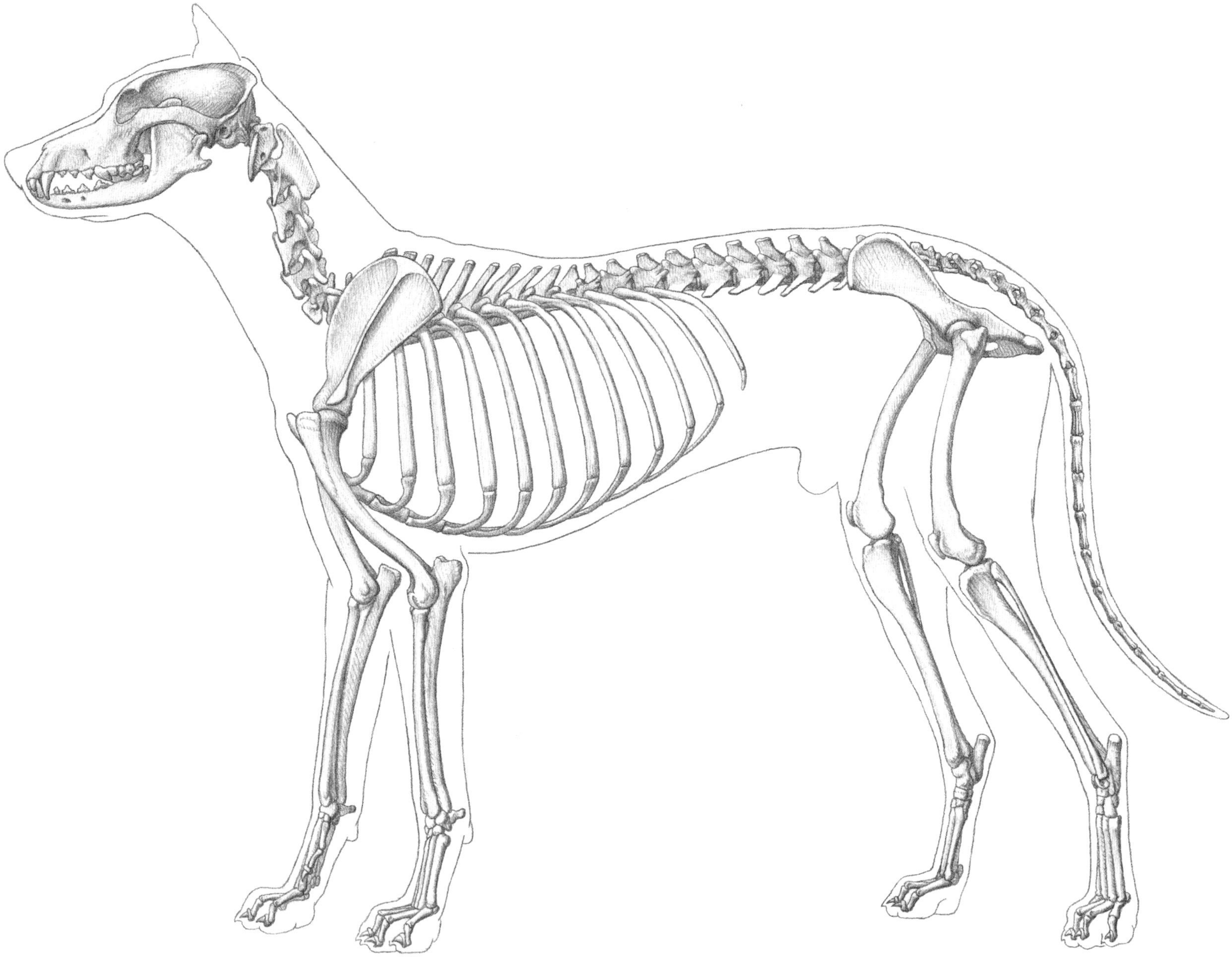

(ANATOMICAL DRAWINGS AFTER ELLENBERGER; DONE; FROM DISSECTIONS)

Dog (canid) characteristics: Anatomy is the same in various domestic breeds and wild species—major difference is size and proportion (Dachshund to Great Dane). Typically with elongated skull—snout long and narrow (some domestic breeds have short muzzles). Large canines. Cheek teeth with sharp edges for shearing. Large, pointed ears—upright in all wild species and in many domestic breeds; hanging in some breeds. Deep chest (top to bottom); long, thin limbs. Five digits on front limb (thumb reduced), four on hind limb (big toe absent). Blunt, nonretractile claws. Walks on toes. Forearm does not rotate (pronate/supinate). Long, bushy tail usually in wild species. Lives from the arctic to the tropics.

AbD1L *Abductor digiti I longus;* **AbDi5** *Abductor digiti V;* **Adduc** *Adductor;* **Anc** *Anconeus;* **AT** *Achilles' tendon;* **Bicep** *Biceps brachii;* **BiFemDp** *Biceps femoris, deep head;* **BiFemSu** *Biceps femoris, superficial head;* **Brach** *Brachialis;* **Brcph** *Brachiocephalicus;* **Brrad** *Brachioradialis;* **Bucc** *Buccinator*; **Canin** *Caninus;* **Clbra** *Cleidobrachialis;* **Clcer** *Cleidocervicalis;* **Coccy** *Coccygeus;* **DelAc** *Deltoid, acromial portion;* **DelSp** *Deltoid, spinal portion;* **Digas** *Digastric;* **ECR** *Extensor carpi radialis;* **ECU** *Extensor carpi ulnaris;* **EDBr** *Extensor digitorum brevis;* **EDC** *Extensor digitorum communis;* **EDLat** *Extensor digitorum lateralis;* **EDLon** *Extensor digitorum longus;* **ExAbO** *External abdominal oblique;* **FCR** *Flexor carpi radialis;* **FCU** *Flexor carpi ulnaris;* **FCU-HH** *Flexor carpi ulnaris, humeral head;* **FCU-UH** *Flexor carpi ulnaris, ulnar head;* **FDP** *Flexor digitorum profundus;* **FDS** *Flexor digitorum superficialis;* **GasLa** *Gastrocnemius, lateral head;* **GasMe** *Gastrocnemius, medial head;* **GluMe** *Gluteus medius;* **GluSu** *Gluteus superficialis;* **Grac** *Gracilis;* **Ilioc** *Iliocostalis;* **InAbO** *Internal abdominal oblique;* **Infra** *Infraspinatus;* **IntDC** *Intertransversarii dorsales caudae;* **Inter** *Interossei;* **IntVC** *Intertransversarii ventralis caudae;* **LAOM** *Levator anguli oculi medialis;* **LatDo** *Latissimus dorsi;* **LeNas** *Levator nasolabialis;* **LLaMx** *Levator labii maxillaris;* **Longi** *Longissimus;* **Malar** *Malaris;* **Mass** *Masseter;* **Myloh** *Mylohyoid;* **Omotr** *Omotransversarius;* **OrLig** *Orbital ligament;* **OrOc** *Orbicularis oculi;* **OrOr** *Orbicularis oris;* **PecDe** *Pectoralis descendens;* **PecPr** *Pectoralis profundus;* **PecTr** *Pectoralis transversus;* **PerBr** *Peroneus brevis;* **PerLo** *Peroneus longus;* **Pop** *Popliteus;* **PrTer** *Pronator teres;* **RAOL** *Retractor anguli oculi lateralis;* **RecAb** *Rectus abdominis;* **RecFe** *Rectus femoris;* **Rhom** *Rhomboid;* **SacDL** *Sacrocaudalis dorsalis lateralis;* **SacLi** *Sacrotuberal ligament;* **SacVL** *Sacrocaudalis ventralis lateralis;* **Sart** *Sartorius;* **ScalM** *Scalenus medius;* **SerDC** *Serratus dorsalis caudalis;* **SerVC** *Serratus ventralis cervicis;* **SerVT** *Serratus ventralis thoracis;* **Smemb** *Semimembranosus;* **Spin & Semsp** *Spinalis & semispinalis;* **Splen** *Splenius;* **Stcph** *Sternocephalicus;* **Stend** *Semitendinosus;* **Sthy** *Sternohyoid;* **Stmas** *Sternomastoid;* **StOcc** *Sterno-occipitalis;* **Stthy** *Sternothyroid;* **Supra** *Supraspinatus;* **TeMaj** *Teres major;* **TeMin** *Teres minor;* **Temp** *Temporalis;* **TenFL** *Tensor fasciae latae;* **TibCr** *Tibialis cranialis;* **Trap** *Trapezius;* **TriLa** *Triceps brachii, lateral head;* **TriLo** *Triceps brachii, long head;* **TriMe** *Triceps brachii, medial head;* **VasLa** *Vastus lateralis;* **Zyg** *Zygomaticus.*

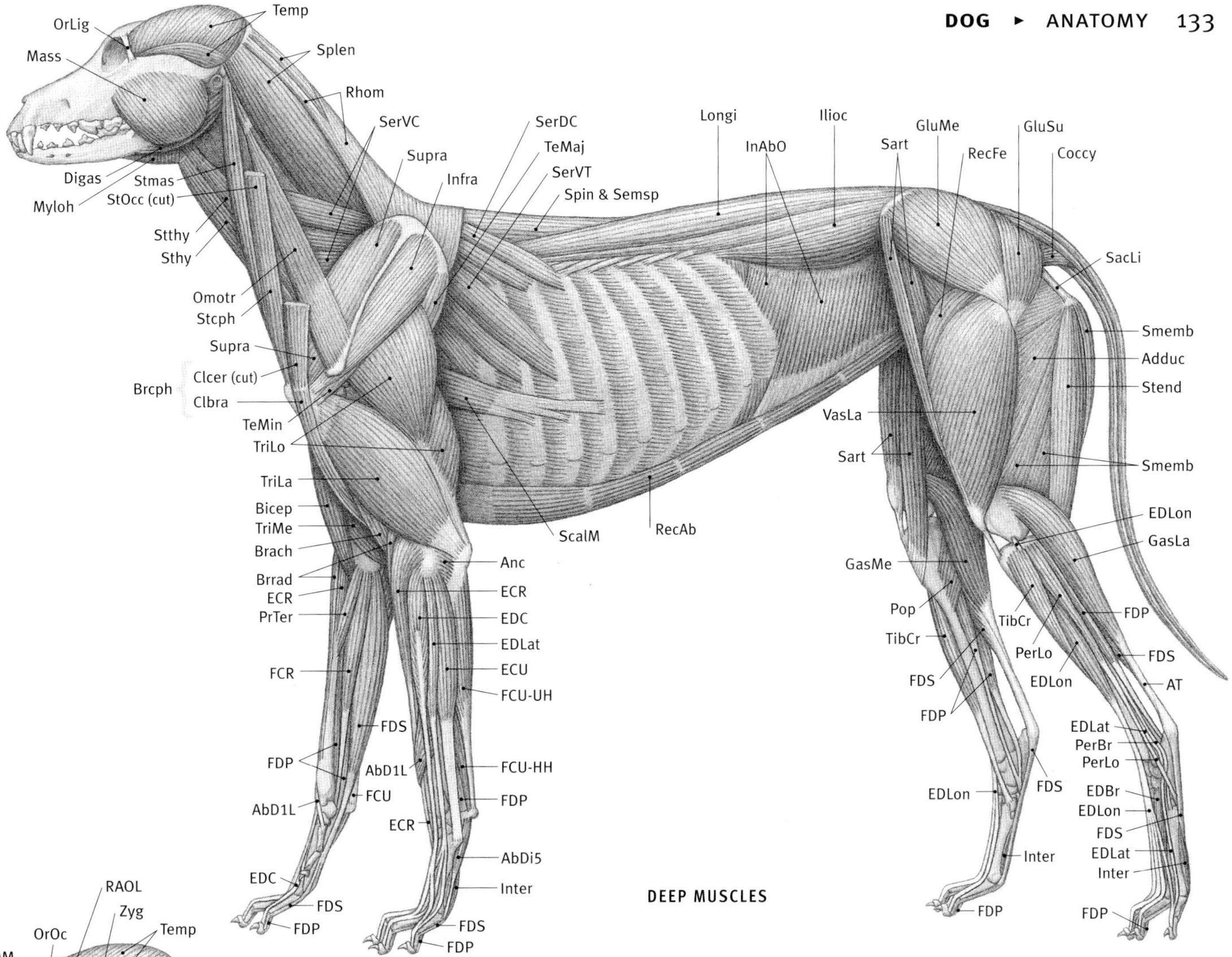

DEEP MUSCLES

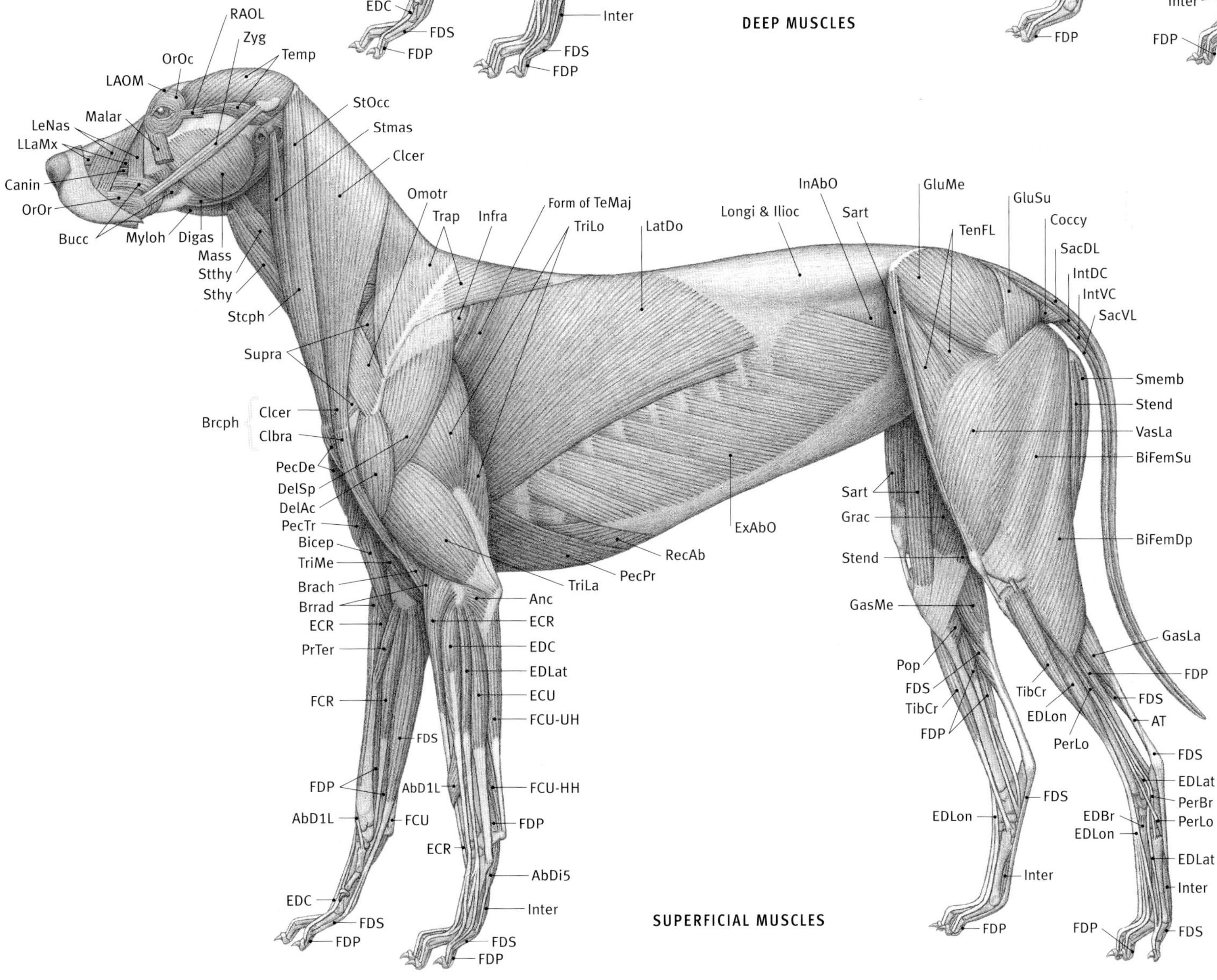

SUPERFICIAL MUSCLES

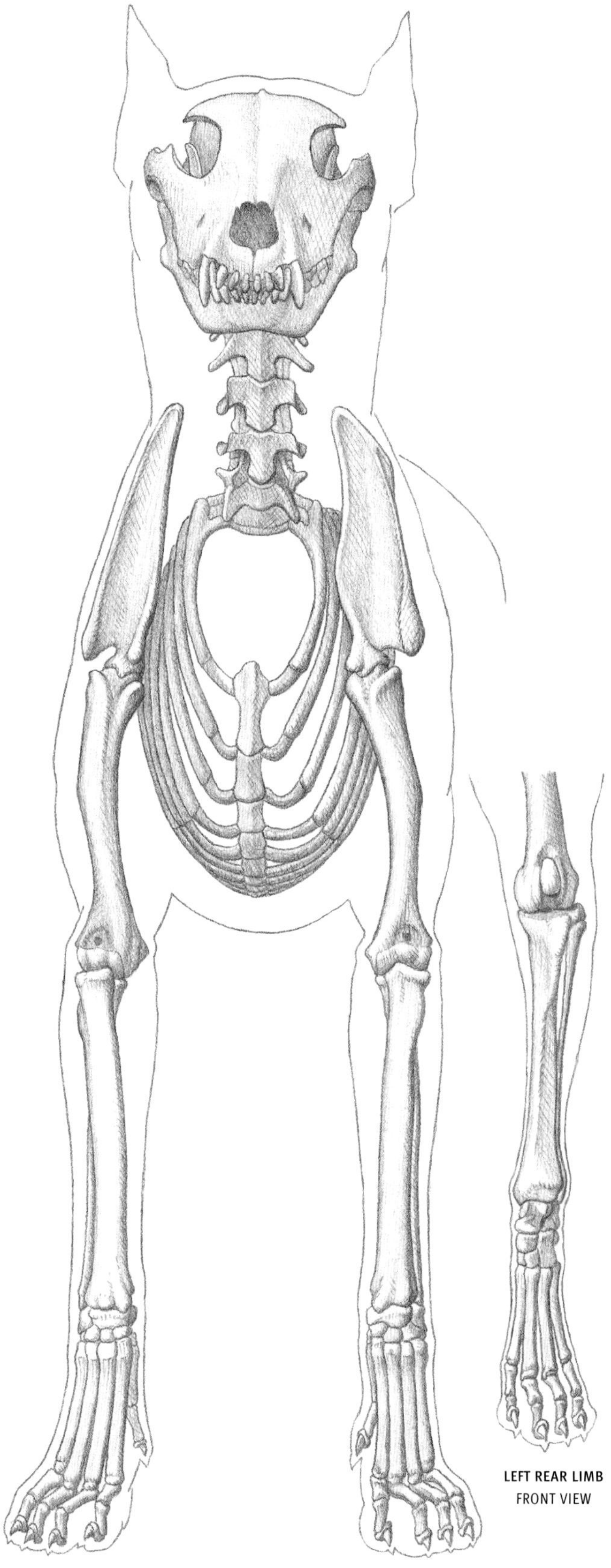

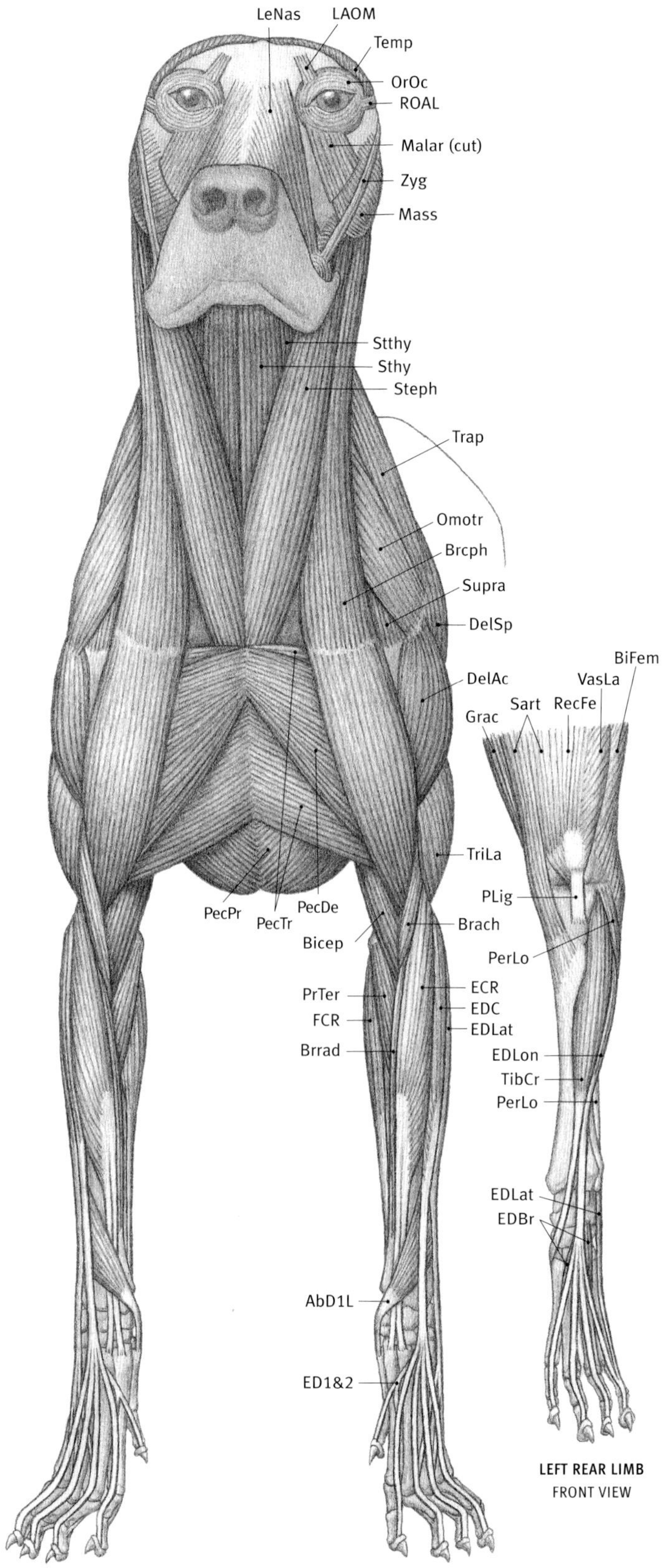

AbD1L *Abductor digiti I longus;* **Bicep** *Biceps brachii;* **BiFem** *Biceps femoris;* **Brach** *Brachialis;* **Brcph** *Brachiocephalicus;* **Brrad** *Brachioradialis;* **DelAc** *Deltoid, acromial portion;* **DelSp** *Deltoid, spinal portion;* **ECR** *Extensor carpi radialis;* **ED1&2** *Extensor digiti I & II;* **EDBr** *Extensor digitorum brevis;* **EDC** *Extensor digitorum communis;* **EDLat** *Extensor digitorum lateralis;* **EDLon** *Extensor digitorum longus;* **FCR** *Flexor carpi radialis;* **Grac** *Gracilis;* **LAOM** *Levator anguli oculi medialis;* **LeNas** *Levator nasolabialis;* **Malar** *Malaris;* **Mass** *Masseter;* **Omotr** *Omotransversarius;* **OrOc** *Orbicularis oculi;* **PecDe** *Pectoralis descendens;* **PecPr** *Pectoralis profundus;* **PecTr** *Pectoralis transversus;* **PerLo** *Peroneus longus;* **PLig** *Patellar ligament;* **PrTer** *Pronator teres;* **RAOL** *Retractor anguli oculi lateralis;* **RecFe** *Rectus femoris;* **Sart** *Sartorius;* **Stcph** *Sternocephalicus;* **Sthy** *Sternohyoid;* **Stthy** *Sternothyroid;* **Supra** *Supraspinatus;* **Temp** *Temporalis;* **TibCr** *Tibialis cranialis;* **Trap** *Trapezius;* **TriLa** *Triceps brachii, lateral head;* **VasLa** *Vastus lateralis;* **Zyg** *Zygomaticus.*

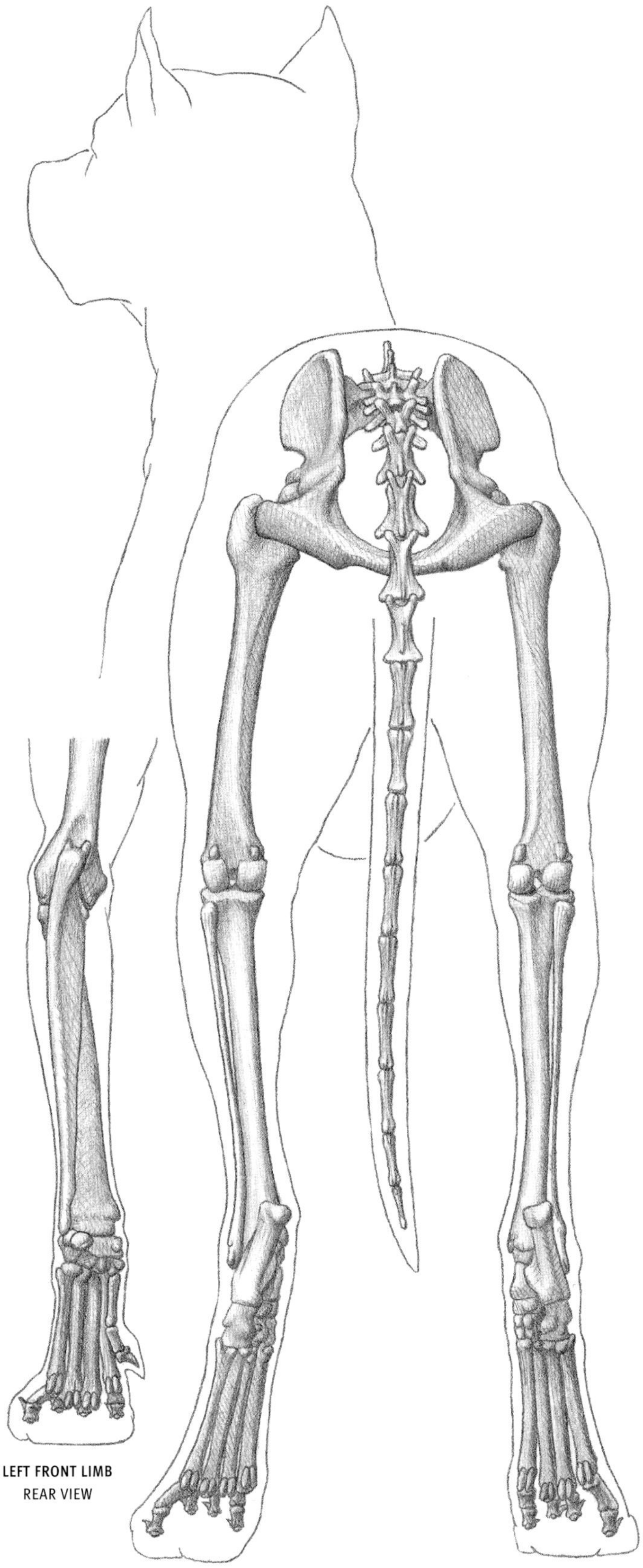

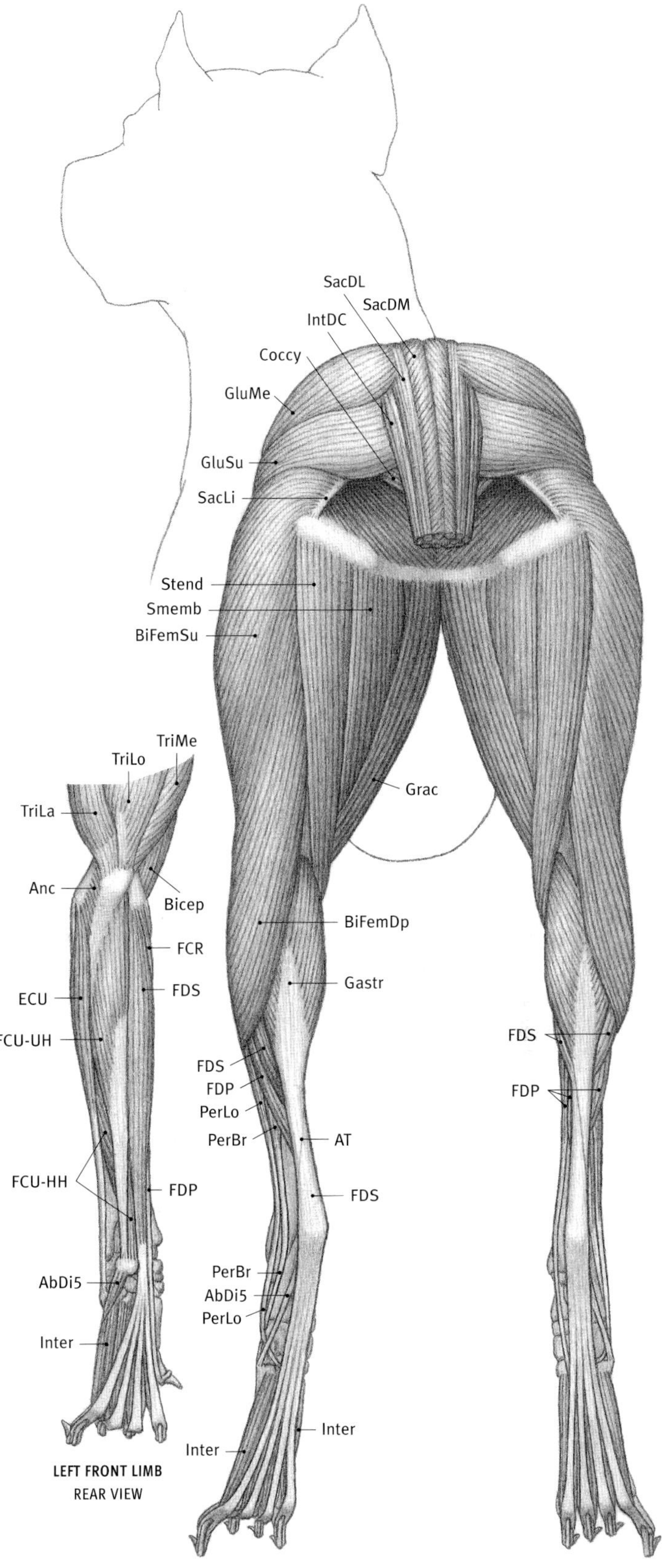

AbDi5 *Abductor digiti V;* **Anc** *Anconeus;* **AT** *Achilles' tendon;* **Bicep** *Biceps brachii;* **BiFemDp** *Biceps femoris, deep head;* **BiFemSu** *Biceps femoris, superficial head;* **Coccy** *Coccygeus;* **ECU** *Extensor carpi ulnaris;* **FCR** *Flexor carpi radialis;* **FCU—HH** *Flexor carpi ulnaris, humeral head;* **FCU—UH** *Flexor carpi ulnaris, ulnar head;* **FDP** *Flexor digitorum profundus;* **FDS** *Flexor digitorum superficialis;* **Gastr** *Gastrocnemius;* **GluMe** *Gluteus medius;* **GluSu** *Gluteus superficialis;* **Grac** *Gracilis;* **IntDC** *Intertransversarii dorsales caudae;* **Inter** *Interossei;* **PerBr** *Peroneus brevis;* **PerLo** *Peroneus longus;* **SacDL** *Sacrocaudalis dorsalis lateralis;* **SacDM** *Sacrocaudalis dorsalis medialis;* **SacLi** *Sacrotuberal ligament;* **Smemb** *Semimembranosus;* **Stend** *Semitendinosus;* **TriLa** *Triceps brachii, lateral head;* **TriLo** *Triceps brachii, long head;* **TriMe** *Triceps brachii, medial head.*

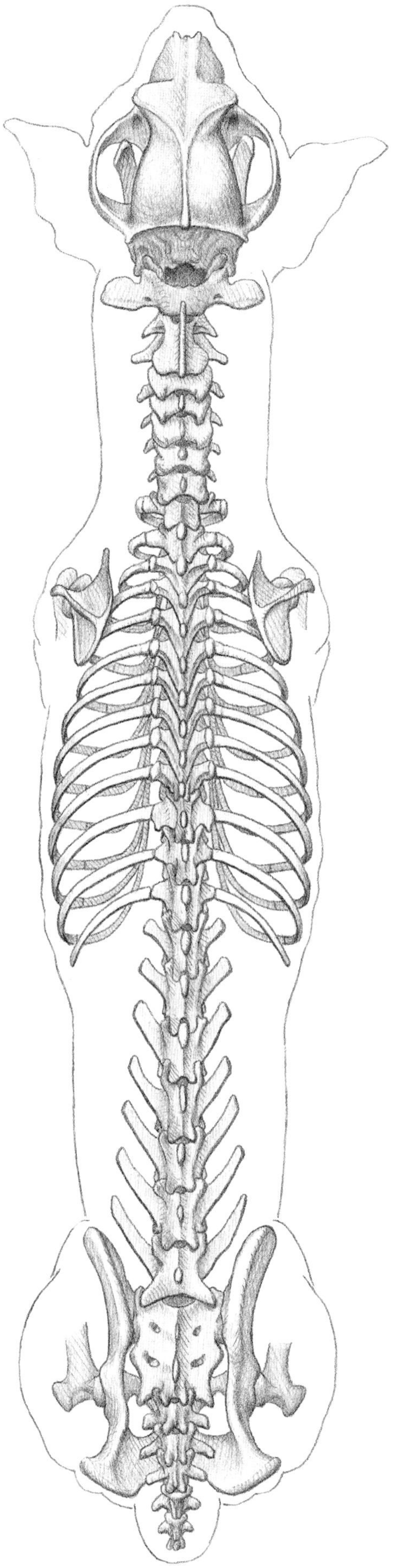

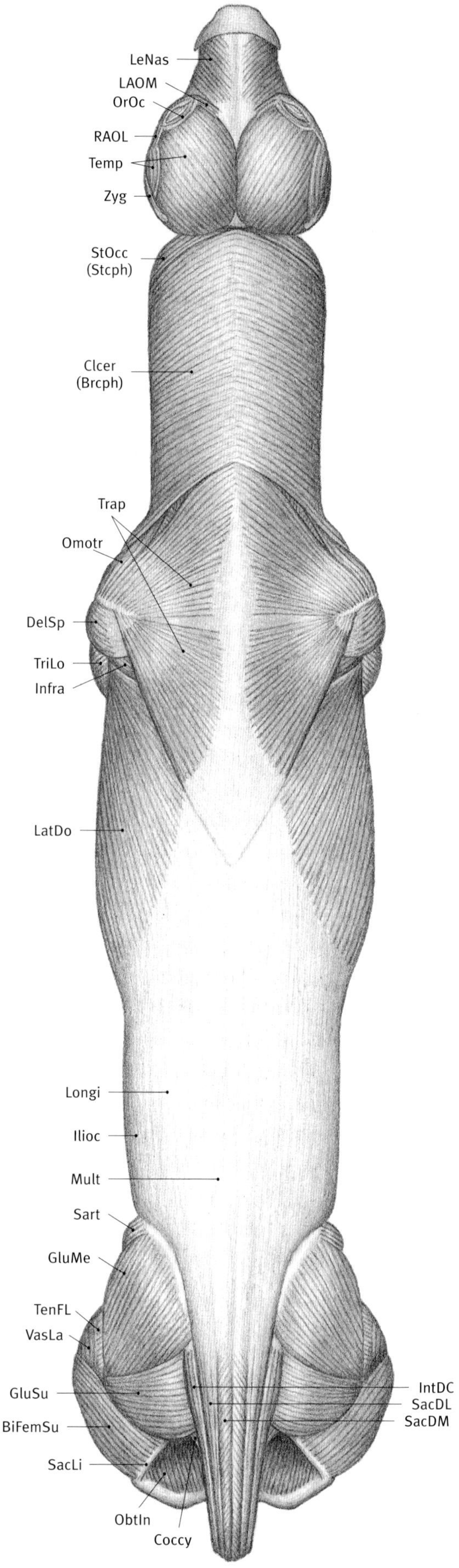

BiFemSu *Biceps femoris, superficial head;* **Brcph** *Brachiocephalicus;* **Clcer** *Cleidocervicalis;* **Coccy** *Coccygeus;* **DelSp** *Deltoid, spinal portion;* **GluMe** *Gluteus medius;* **GluSu** *Gluteus superficialis;* **Ilioc** *Iliocostalis;* **Infra** *Infraspinatus;* **IntDC** *Intertransversarii dorsales caudae;* **LAOM** *Levator anguli oculi medialis;* **LatDo** *Latissimus dorsi;* **LeNas** *Levator nasolabialis;* **Longi** *Longissimus;* **Mult** *Multifidus;* **ObtIn** *Obturator internus;* **Omotr** *Omotransversarius;* **OrOc** *Orbicularis oculi;* **RAOL** *Retractor anguli oculi lateralis;* **SacDL** *Sacrocaudalis dorsalis lateralis;* **SacDM** *Sacrocaudalis dorsalis medialis;* **SacLi** *Sacrotuberal ligament;* **Sart** *Sartorius;* **Stcph** *Sternocephalicus;* **StOcc** *Sterno-occipitalis;* **Temp** *Temporalis;* **TenFL** *Tensor fasciae latae;* **Trap** *Trapezius;* **TriLo** *Triceps brachii, long head;* **VasLa** *Vastus lateralis;* **Zyg** *Zygomaticus.*

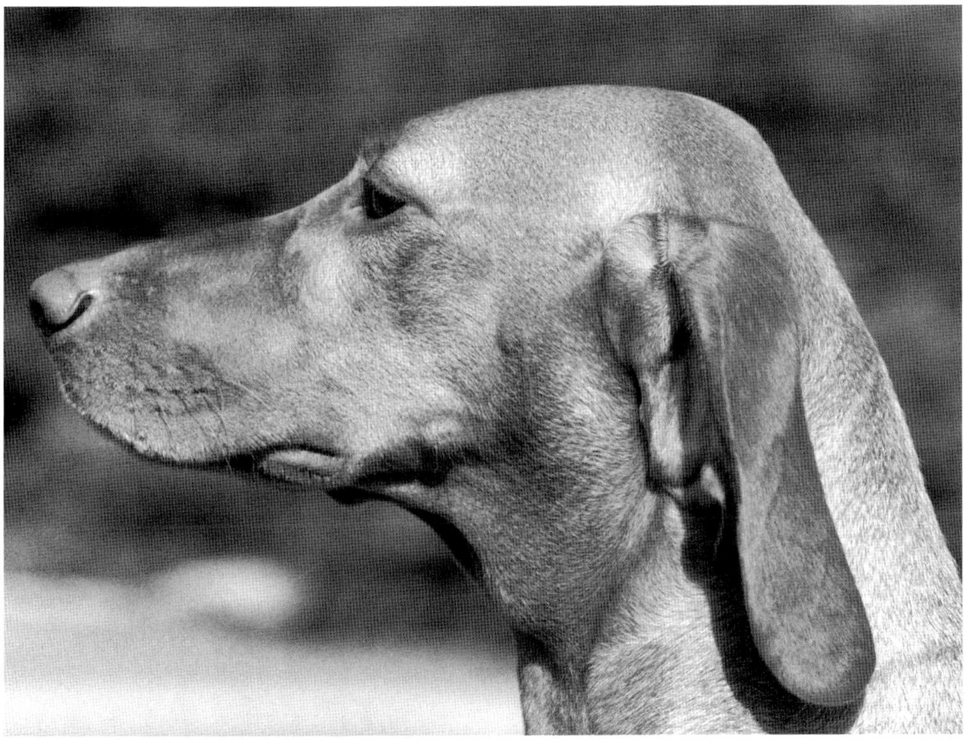

VISLA (FEMALE)

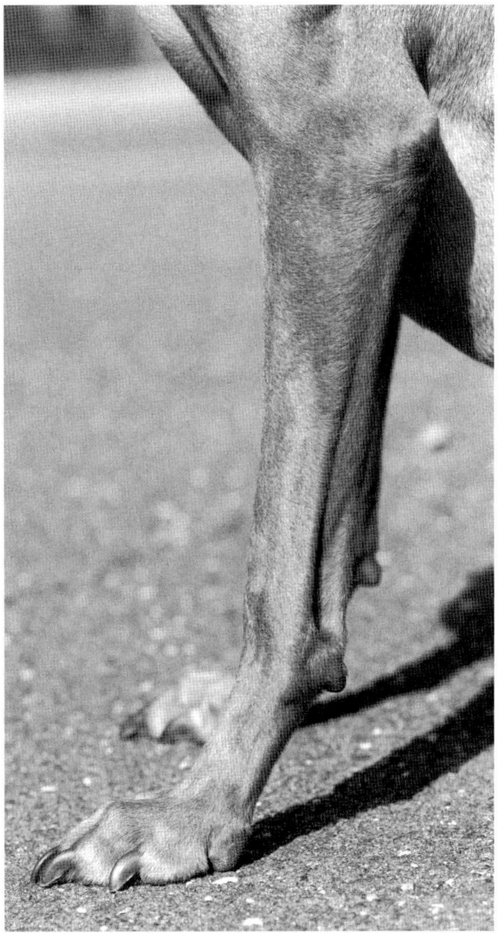

VISLA (FEMALE)
FRONT LIMBS

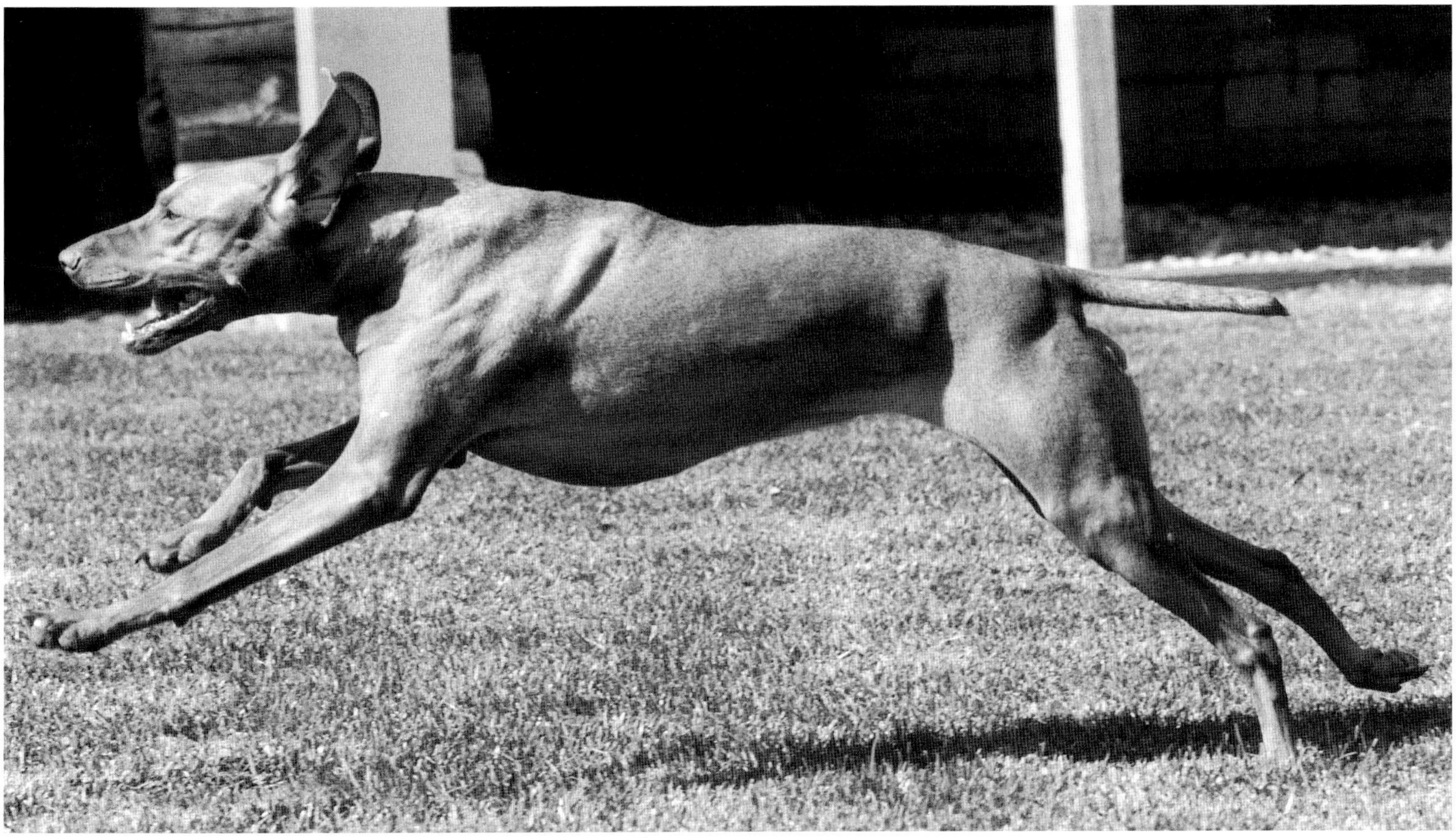

VISLA (FEMALE)
Canis familiaris

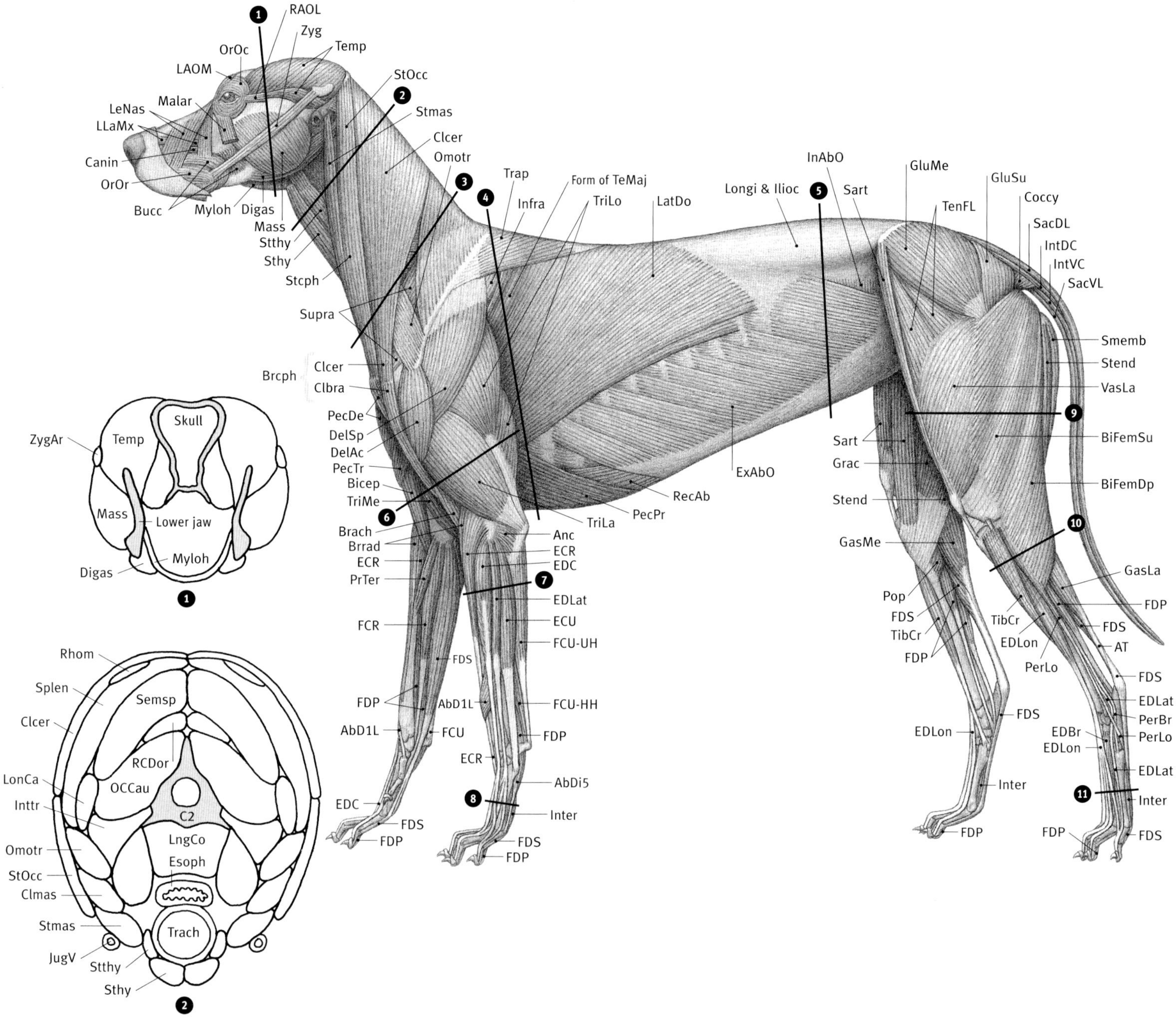

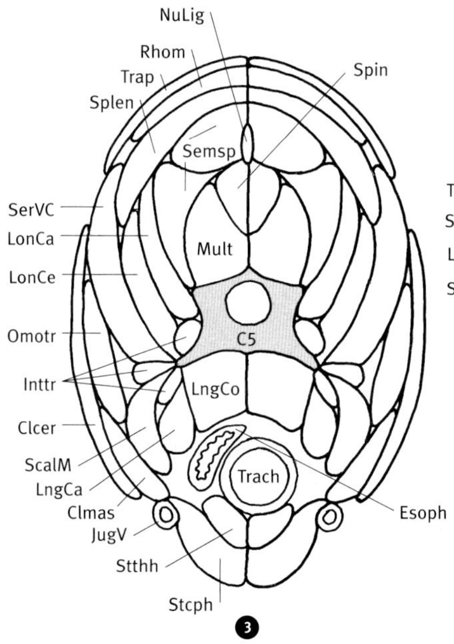

3

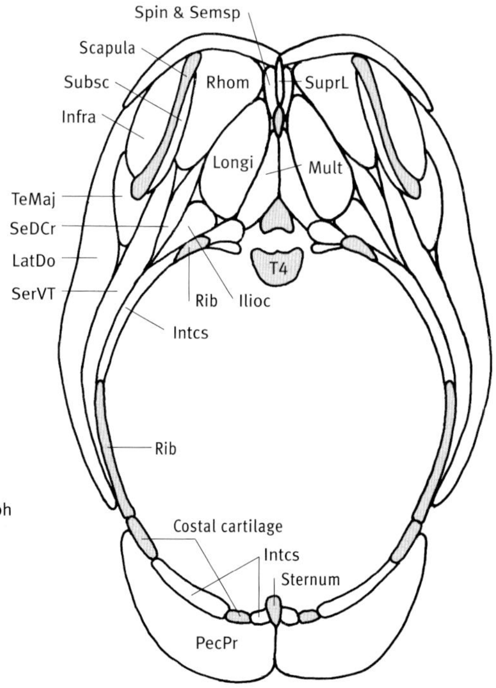

4

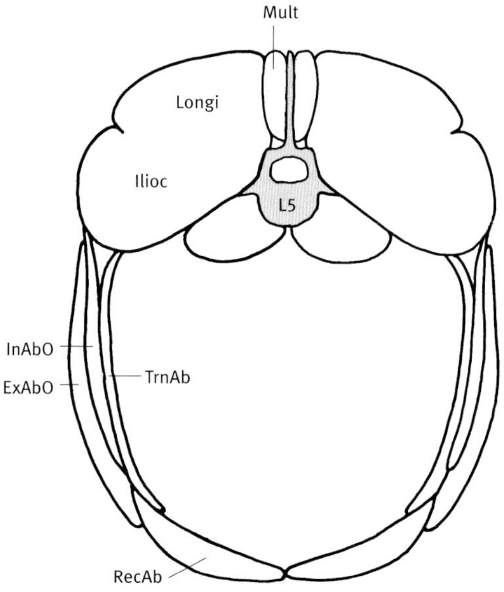

5

DRAWINGS NOT TO SCALE

(CROSS SECTIONS AFTER DONE; MILLER; POPESCO)

FORELIMB

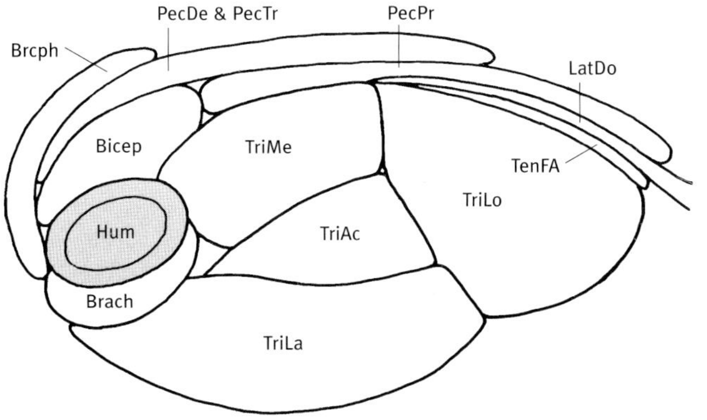

6
UPPER ARM

HIND LIMB

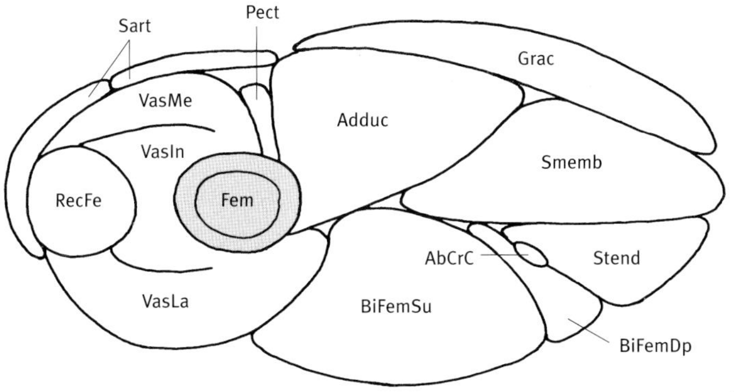

9
THIGH

▲
INSIDE
◄ FRONT REAR ►
OUTSIDE
▼

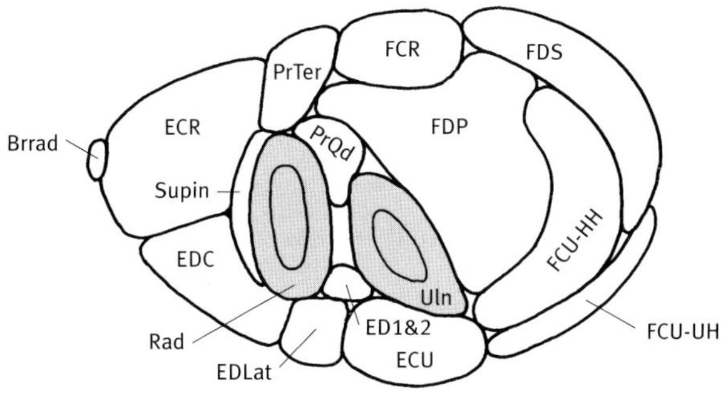

7
FOREARM

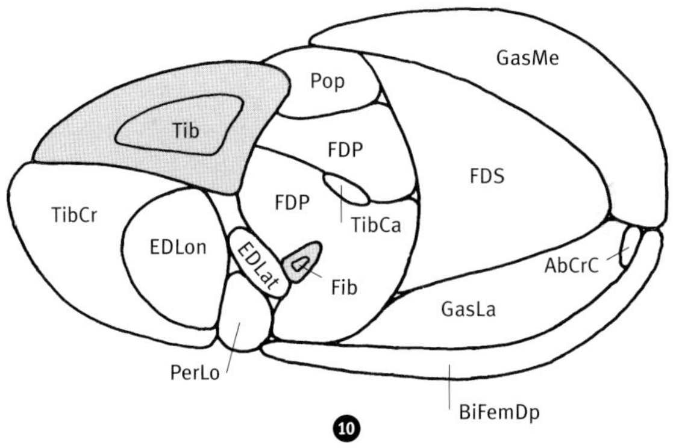

10
LOWER LEG

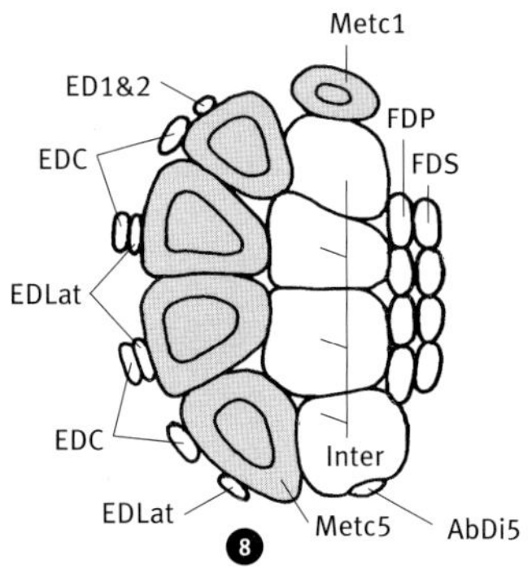

8
FOREPAW

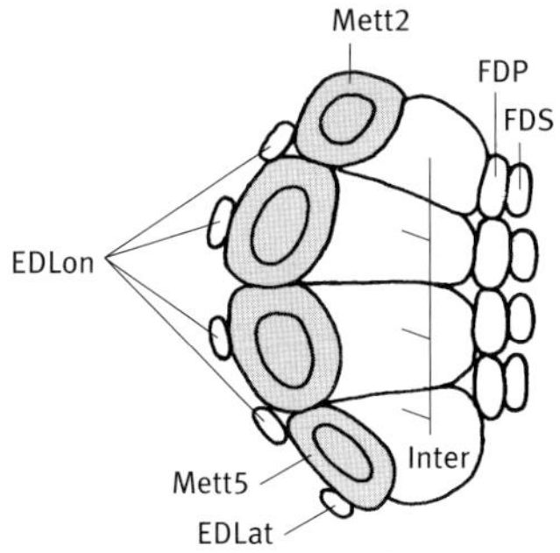

11
HIND PAW

AbCrC *Abductor cruris caudalis;* **AbDi5** *Abductor digiti V;* **Adduc** *Adductor;* **Bicep** *Biceps brachii;* **BiFemDp** *Biceps femoris, deep head;* **BiFemSu** *Biceps femoris, superficial head;* **Brach** *Brachialis;* **Brcph** *Brachiocephalicus;* **Brrad** *Brachioradialis;* **C2** *Second cervical vertebra;* **C5** *Fifth cervical vertebra;* **Clcer** *Cleidocervicalis;* **Clmas** *Cleidomastoid;* **Digas** *Digastric;* **ECR** *Extensor carpi radialis;* **ECU** *Extensor carpi ulnaris;* **ED1&2** *Extensor digiti I & II;* **EDC** *Extensor digitorum communis;* **EDLat** *Extensor digitorum lateralis;* **EDLon** *Extensor digitorum longus;* **Esoph** *Esophagus;* **ExAbO** *External abdominal oblique;* **FCR** *Flexor carpi radialis;* **FCU-HH** *Flexor carpi ulnaris, humeral head;* **FCU-UH** *Flexor carpi ulnaris, ulnar head;* **FDP** *Flexor digitorum profundus;* **FDS** *Flexor digitorum superficialis;* **Fem** *Femur;* **Fib** *Fibula;* **GasLa** *Gastrocnemius, lateral head;* **GasMe** *Gastrocnemius, medial head;* **Grac** *Gracilis;* **Hum** *Humerus;* **Ilioc** *Iliocostalis;* **InAbO** *Internal abdominal oblique;* **Infra** *Infraspinatus;* **Intcs** *Intercostals;* **Inter** *Interossei;* **Inttr** *Intertransversarii;* **JugV** *Jugular vein;* **L5** *Fifth lumbar vertebra;* **LatDo** *Latissimus dorsi;* **LngCa** *Longus capitis;* **LngCo** *Longus colli;* **LonAt** *Longissimus atlantis;* **LonCa** *Longissimus capitis;* **LonCe** *Longissimus cervicis;* **Longi** *Longissimus;* **Mass** *Masseter;* **Metc1** *First metacarpal;* **Metc5** *Fifth metacarpal;* **Mett2** *Second metatarsal;* **Mett5** *Fifth metatarsal;* **Mult** *Multifidus;* **Myloh** *Mylohyoid;* **NuLig** *Nuchal ligament;* **OCCau** *Obliquus capitis caudalis;* **Omotr** *Omotransversarius;* **PecDe** *Pectoralis descendens;* **PecPr** *Pectoralis profundus;* **Pect** *Pectineus;* **PecTr** *Pectoralis transversus;* **PerLo** *Peroneus longus;* **Pop** *Popliteus;* **PrQd** *Pronator quadratus;* **PrTer** *Pronator teres;* **Rad** *Radius;* **RCDor** *Rectus capitis dorsalis;* **RecAb** *Rectus abdominis;* **RecFe** *Rectus femoris;* **Rhom** *Rhomboid;* **Sart** *Sartorius;* **ScalM** *Scalenus medius;* **SeDCr** *Serratus dorsalis cranialis;* **Semsp** *Semispinalis;* **SerVC** *Serratus ventralis cervicis;* **SerVT** *Serratus ventralis thoracis;* **Smemb** *Semimembranosus;* **Spin & Semsp** *Spinalis & semispinalis;* **Spin** *Spinalis;* **Splen** *Splenius;* **Stcph** *Sternocephalicus;* **Stend** *Semitendinosus;* **Sthy** *Sternohyoid;* **Stmas** *Sternomastoid;* **StOcc** *Sterno-occipitalis;* **Stthh** *Sternothyrohyoid;* **Stthy** *Sternothyroid;* **Subsc** *Subscapularis;* **Supin** *Supinator;* **SuprL** *Supraspinal ligament;* **T4** *Fourth thoracic vertebra;* **TeMaj** *Teres major;* **Temp** *Temporalis;* **TenFA** *Tensor fasciae antibrachii;* **Tib** *Tibia;* **TibCa** *Tibialis caudalis;* **TibCr** *Tibialis cranialis;* **Trach** *Trachea;* **Trap** *Trapezius;* **TriAc** *Triceps brachii, accessory head;* **TriLa** *Triceps brachii, lateral head;* **TriLo** *Triceps brachii, long head;* **TriMe** *Triceps brachii, medial head;* **TrnAb** *Transversus abdominis;* **Uln** *Ulna;* **VasIn** *Vastus intermedius;* **VasLa** *Vastus lateralis;* **VasMe** *Vastus medialis;* **ZygAr** *Zygomatic arch.*

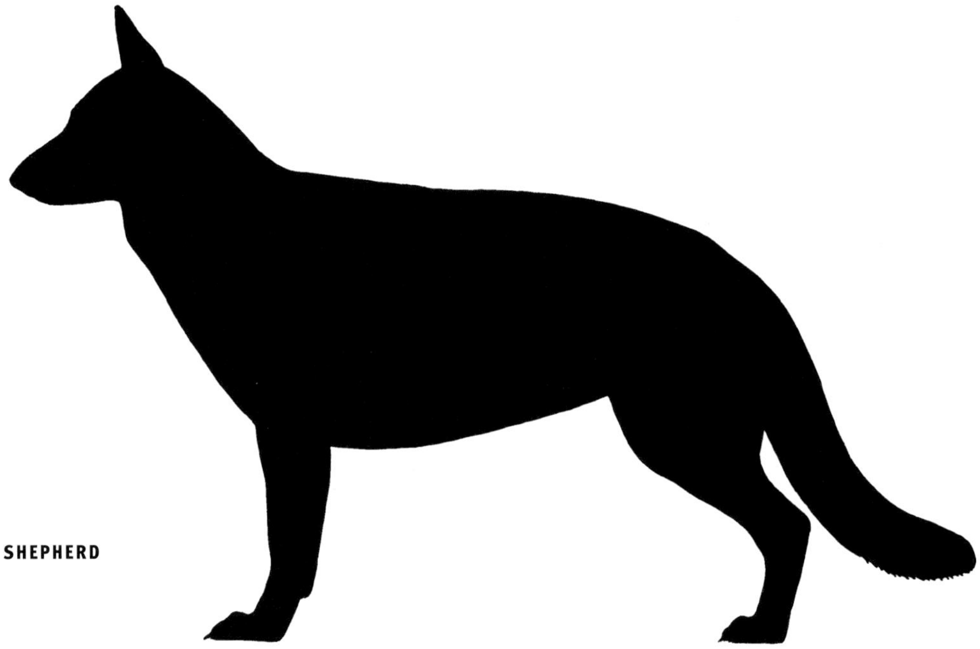

GERMAN SHEPHERD

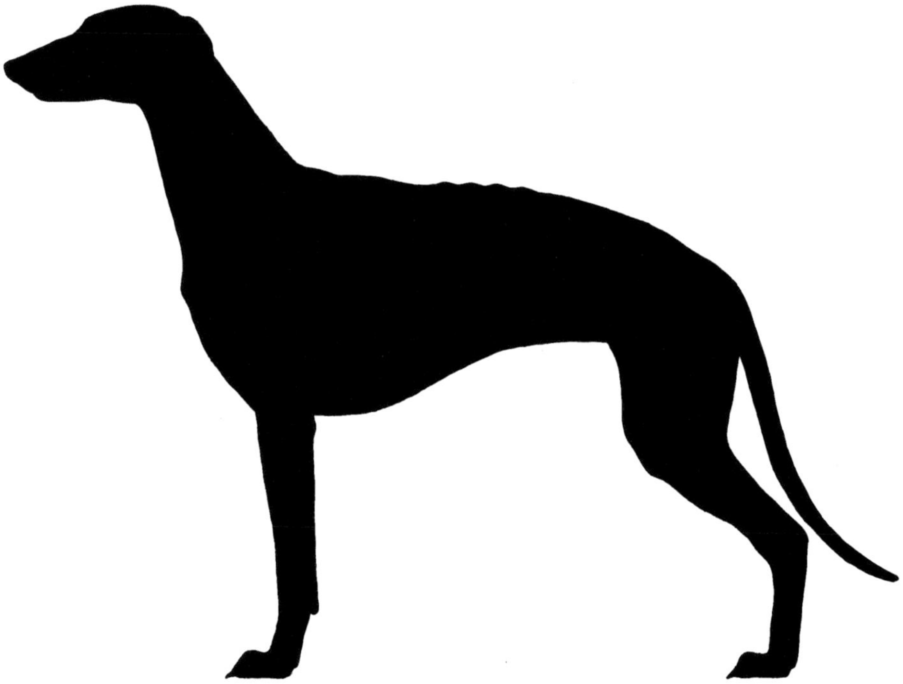

GREYHOUND

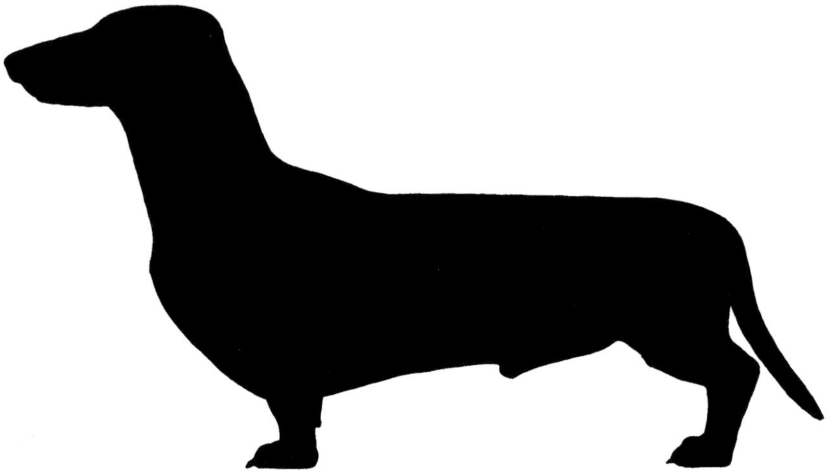

DACHSHUND

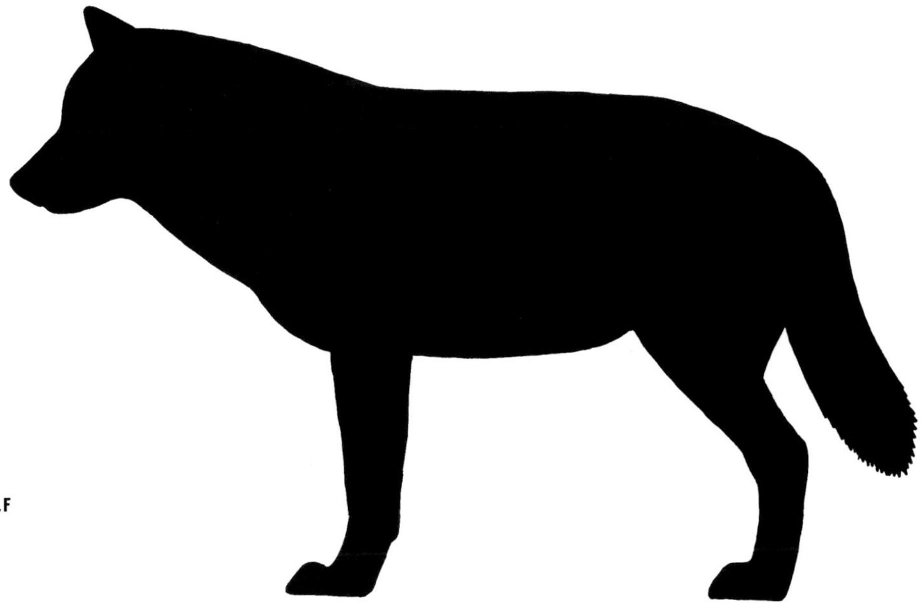

GRAY WOLF

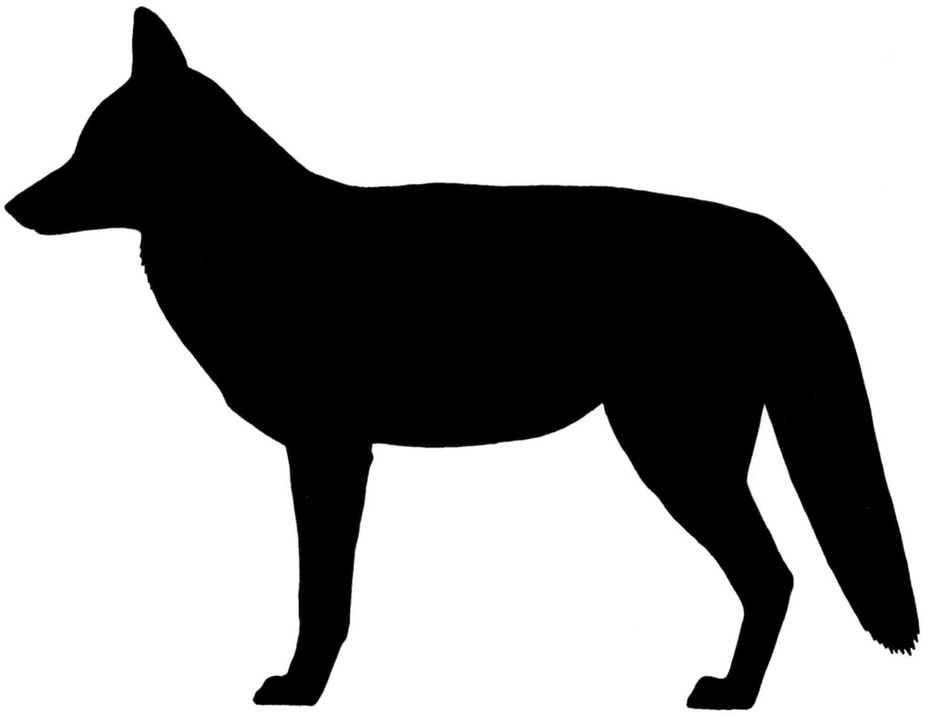

COYOTE

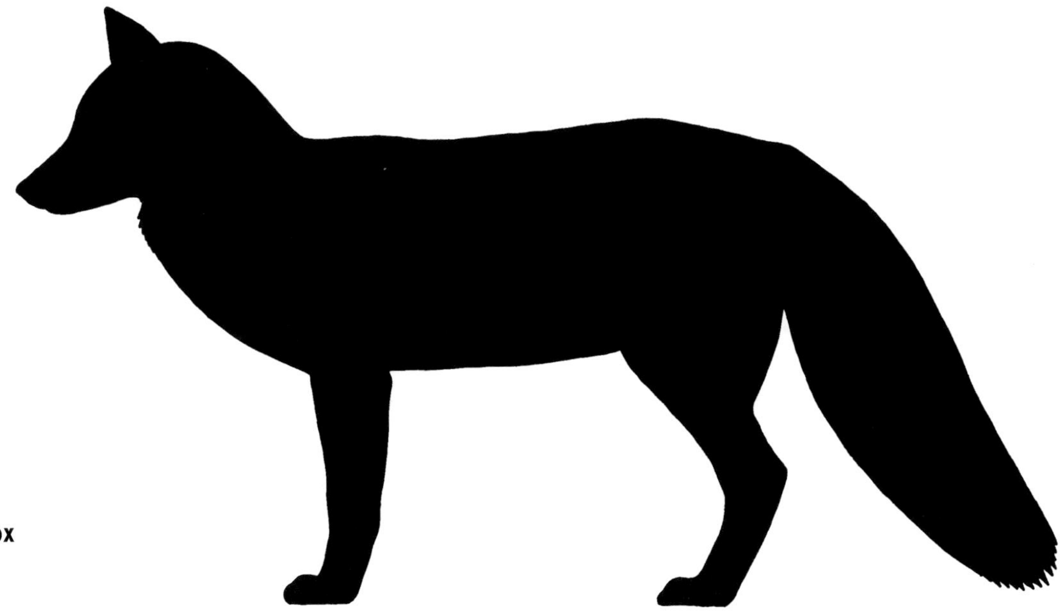

RED FOX

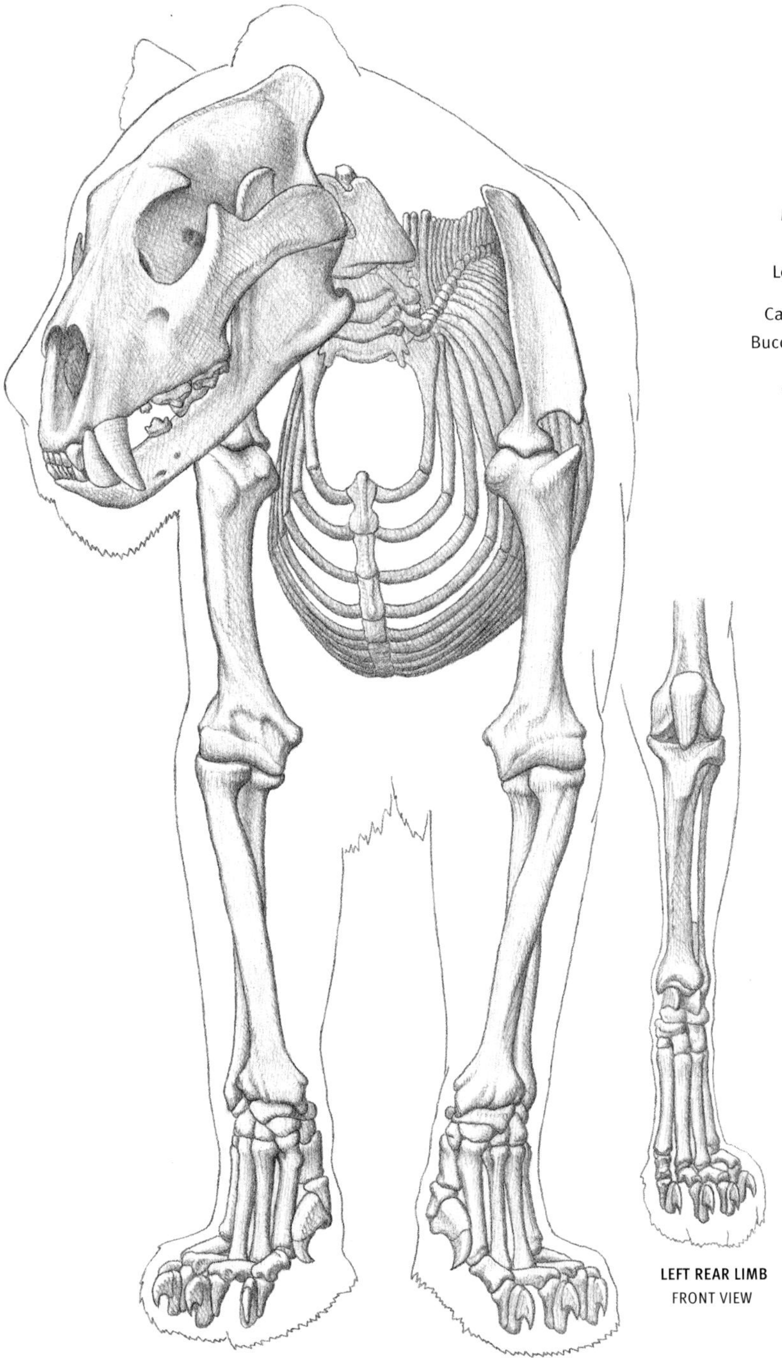

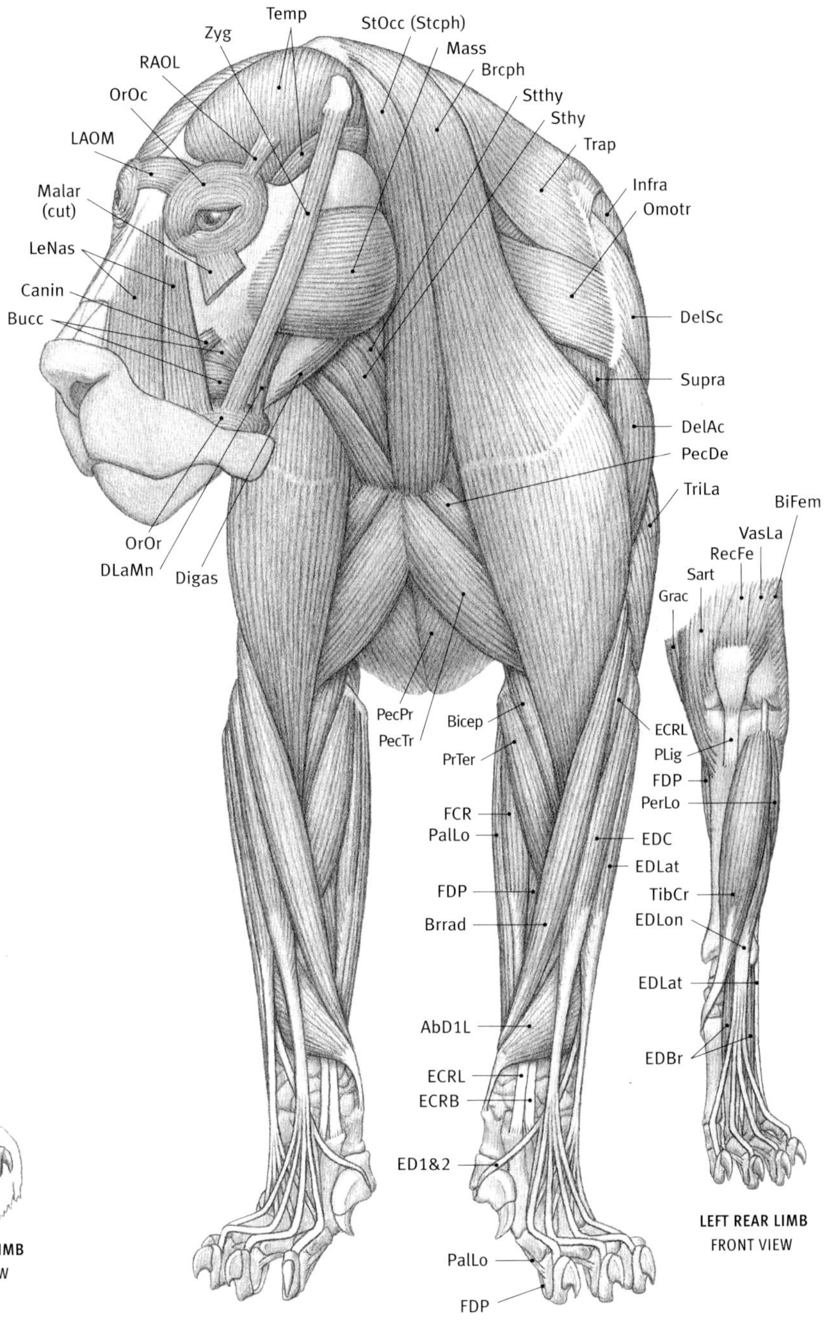

AbD1L *Abductor digiti I longus;* **Bicep** *Biceps brachii;* **BiFem** *Biceps femoris;* **Brcph** *Brachiocephalicus;* **Brrad** *Brachioradialis;* **Bucc** *Buccinator;* **Canin** *Caninus;* **DelAc** *Deltoid, acromial portion;* **DelSp** *Deltoid, spinal portion;* **Digas** *Digastric;* **DLaMn** *Depressor labii mandibularis;* **ECRB** *Extensor carpi radialis brevis;* **ECRL** *Extensor carpi radialis longus;* **ED1&2** *Extensor digiti I & II;* **EDBr** *Extensor digitorum brevis;* **EDC** *Extensor digitorum communis;* **EDLat** *Extensor digitorum lateralis;* **EDLon** *Extensor digitorum longus;* **FCR** *Flexor carpi radialis;* **FDP** *Flexor digitorum profundus;* **Grac** *Gracilis;* **Infra** *Infraspinatus;* **LAOM** *Levator anguli oculi medialis;* **LeNas** *Levator nasolabialis;* **Malar** *Malaris;* **Mass** *Masseter;* **Omotr** *Omotransversarius;* **OrOc** *Orbicularis oculi;* **OrOr** *Orbicularis oris;* **PalLo** *Palmaris longus;* **PecDe** *Pectoralis descendens;* **PecPr** *Pectoralis profundus;* **PecTr** *Pectoralis transversus;* **PerLo** *Peroneus longus;* **PLig** *Patellar ligament;* **PrTer** *Pronator teres;* **RAOL** *Retractor anguli oculi lateralis;* **RecFe** *Rectus femoris;* **Sart** *Sartorius;* **Stcph** *Sternocephalicus;* **Sthy** *Sternohyoid;* **StOcc** *Sterno-occipitalis;* **Stthy** *Sternothyroid;* **Supra** *Supraspinatus;* **Temp** *Temporalis;* **TibCr** *Tibialis cranialis;* **Trap** *Trapezius;* **TriLa** *Triceps brachii, lateral head;* **VasLa** *Vastus lateralis;* **Zyg** *Zygomaticus.*

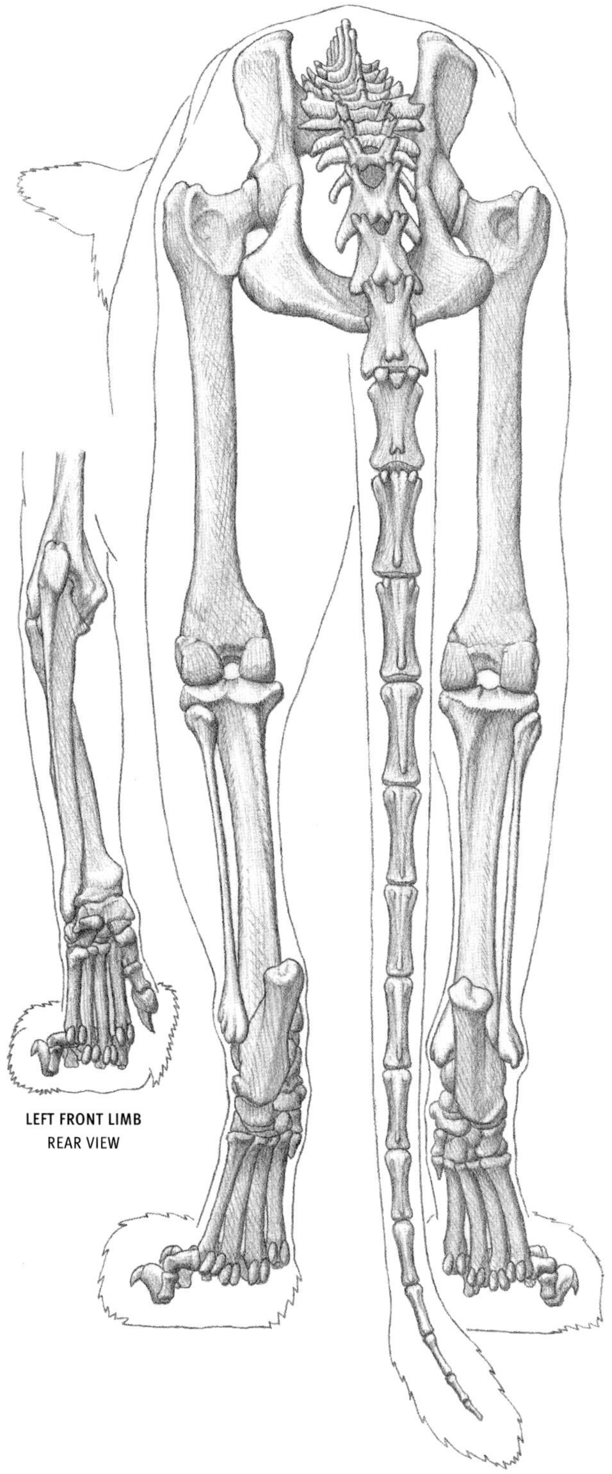

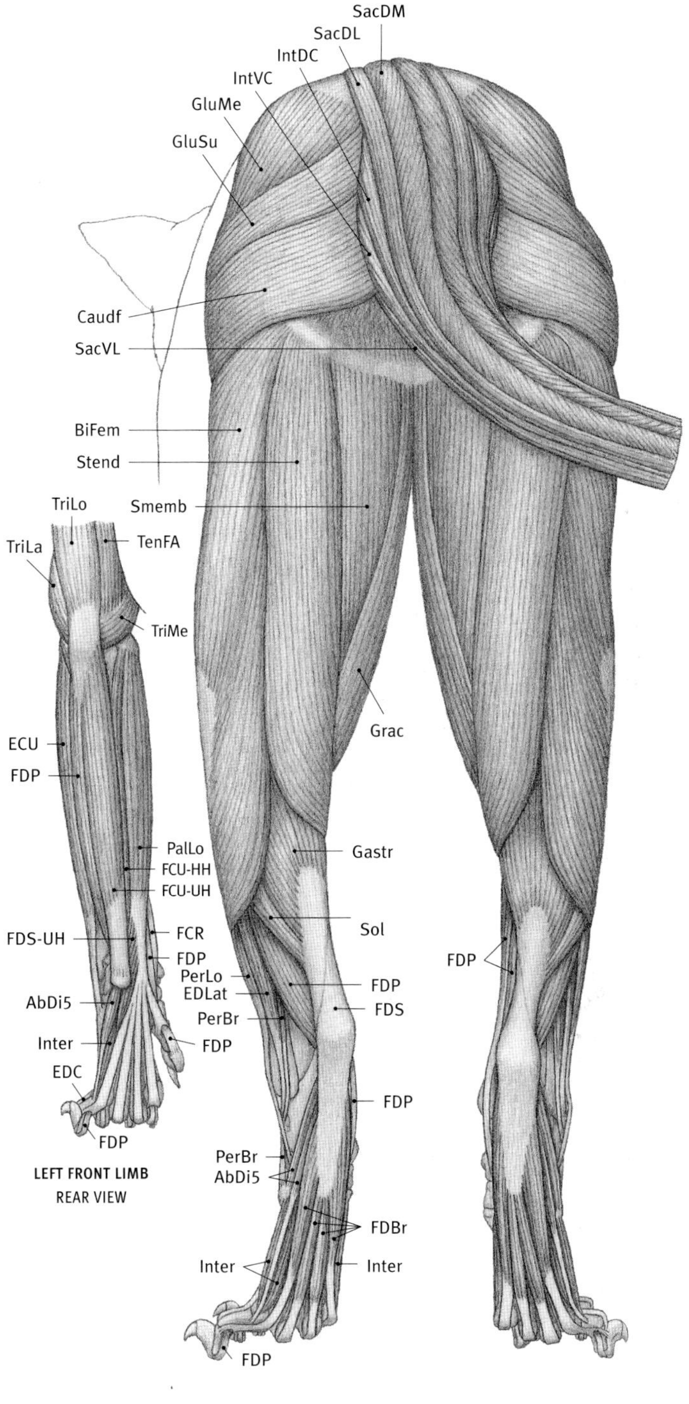

AbDi5 *Abductor digiti V;* **BiFem** *Biceps femoris;* **Caudf** *Caudofemoralis;* **ECU** *Extensor carpi ulnaris;* **EDC** *Extensor digitorum communis;* **EDLat** *Extensor digitorum lateralis;* **FCR** *Flexor carpi radialis;* **FCU-HH** *Flexor carpi ulnaris, humeral head;* **FCU-UH** *Flexor carpi ulnaris, ulnar head;* **FDBr** *Flexor digitorum brevis;* **FDP** *Flexor digitorum profundus;* **FDS** *Flexor digitorum superficialis;* **FDS-UH** *Flexor digitorum superficialis, ulnar head;* **Gastr** *Gastrocnemius;* **GluMe** *Gluteus medius;* **GluSu** *Gluteus superficialis;* **Grac** *Gracilis;* **IntDC** *Intertransversarii dorsales caudae;* **Inter** *Interossei;* **IntVC** *Intertransversarii ventralis caudae;* **PalLo** *Palmaris longus;* **PerBr** *Peroneus brevis;* **PerLo** *Peroneus longus;* **SacDL** *Sacrocaudalis dorsalis lateralis;* **SacDM** *Sacrocaudalis dorsalis medialis;* **SacVL** *Sacrocaudalis ventralis lateralis;* **Smemb** *Semimembranosus;* **Sol** *Soleus;* **Stend** *Semitendinosus;* **TenFA** *Tensor fasciae antibrachii;* **TriLa** *Triceps brachii, lateral head;* **TriLo** *Triceps brachii, long head;* **TriMe** *Triceps brachii, medial head.*

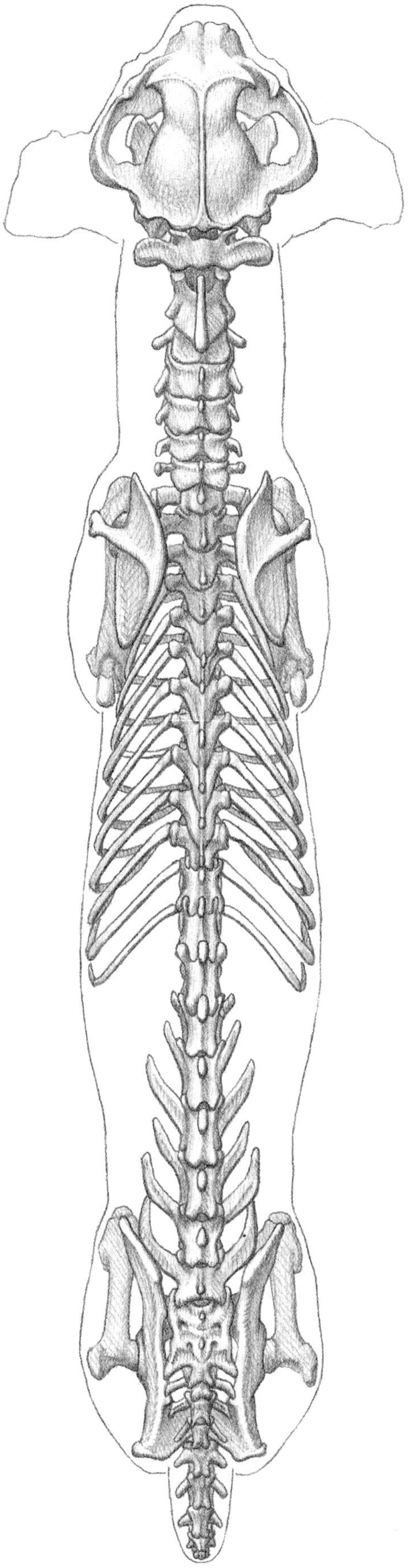

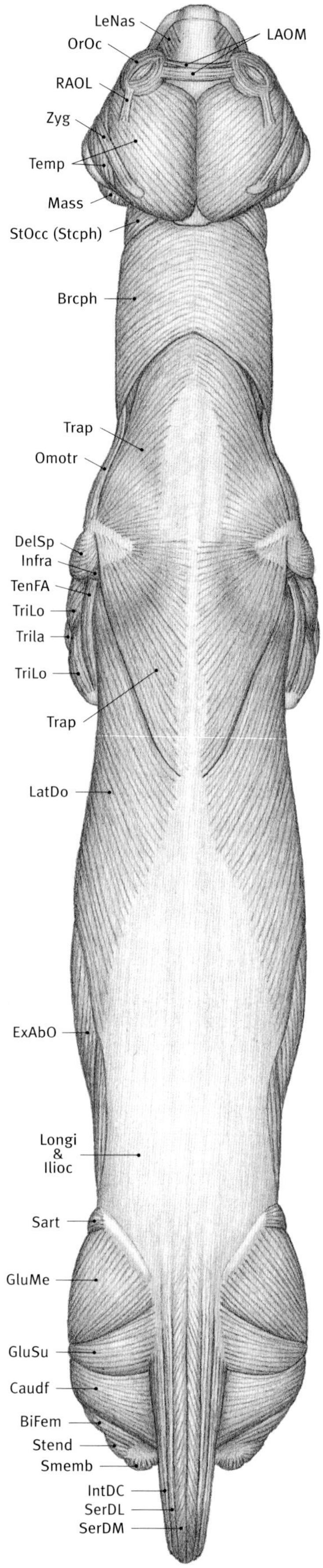

BiFem *Biceps femoris;* **Brcph** *Brachiocephalicus;* **Caudf** *Caudofemoralis;* **DelSp** *Deltoid, spinal portion;* **ExAbO** *External abdominal oblique;* **GluMe** *Gluteus medius;* **GluSu** *Gluteus superficialis;* **Ilioc** *Iliocostalis;* **Infra** *Infraspinatus;* **IntDC** *Intertransversarii dorsales caudae*; **LAOM** *Levator anguli oculi medialis;* **LatDo** *Latissimus dorsi;* **LeNas** *Levator nasolabialis;* **Longi** *Longissimus;* **Mass** *Masseter;* **Omotr** *Omotransversarius;* **OrOc** *Orbicularis oculi;* **RAOL** *Retractor anguli oculi lateralis;* **SacDL** *Sacrocaudalis dorsalis lateralis;* **SacDM** *Sacrocaudalis dorsalis medialis;* **Sart** *Sartorius;* **Smemb** *Semimembranosus;* **Stcph** *Sternocephalicus;* **Stend** *Semitendinosus;* **StOcc** *Sterno-occipitalis;* **Temp** *Temporalis;* **TenFA** *Tensor fasciae antibrachii;* **Trap** *Trapezius;* **TriLa** *Triceps brachii, lateral head;* **TriLo** *Triceps brachii, long head;* **Zyg** *Zygomaticus.*

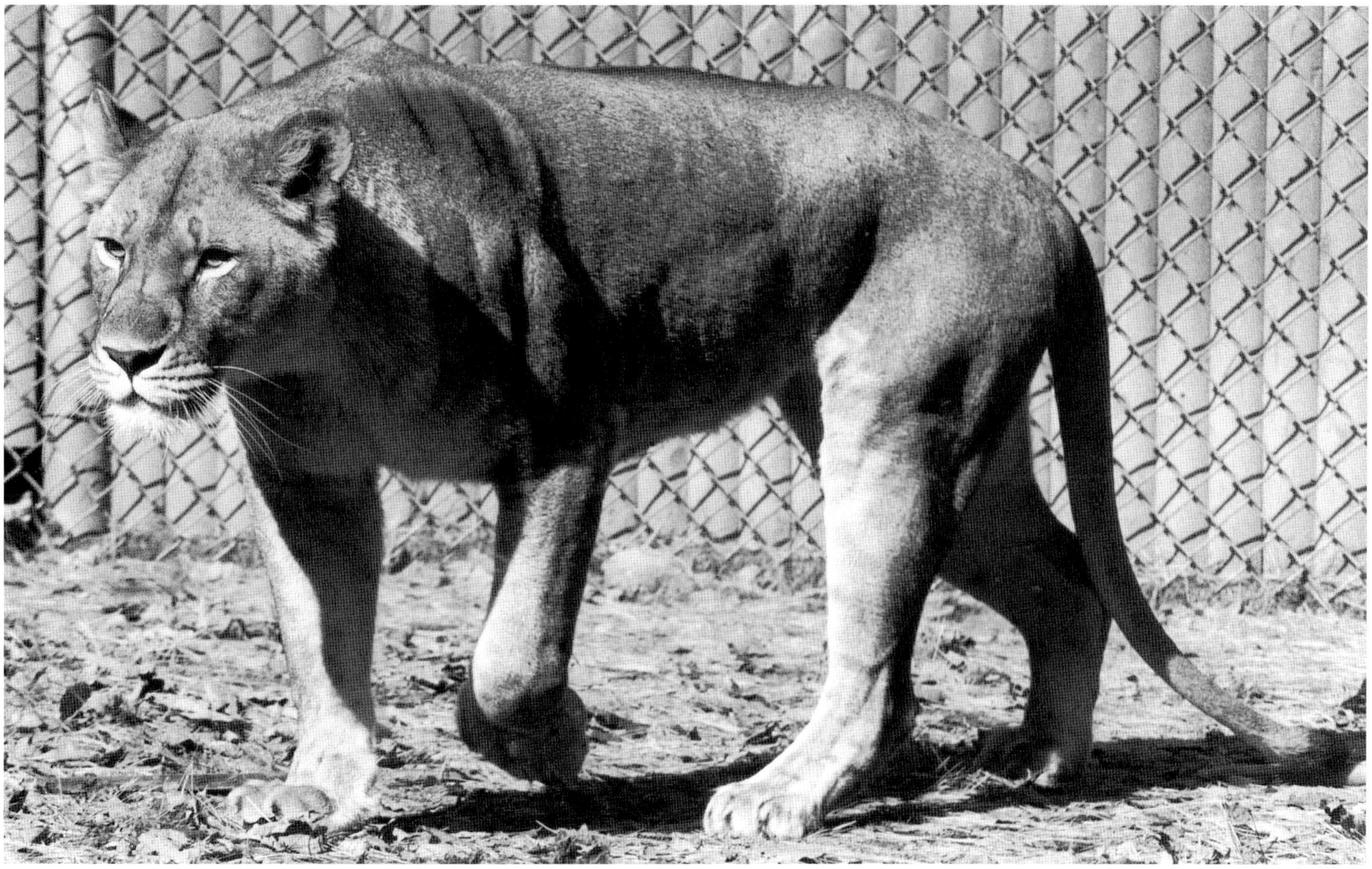

LIONESS

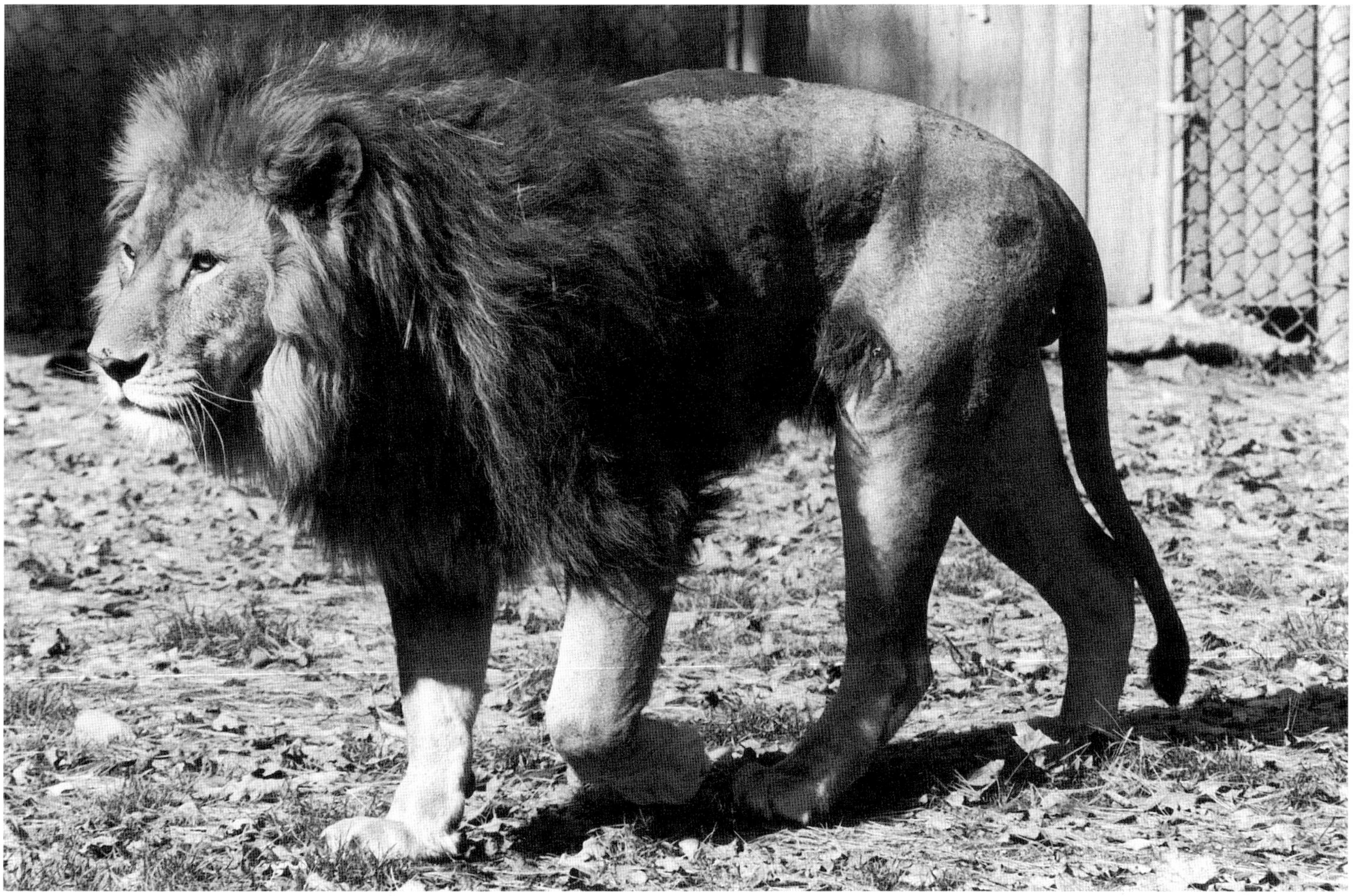

LION
Panthera leo

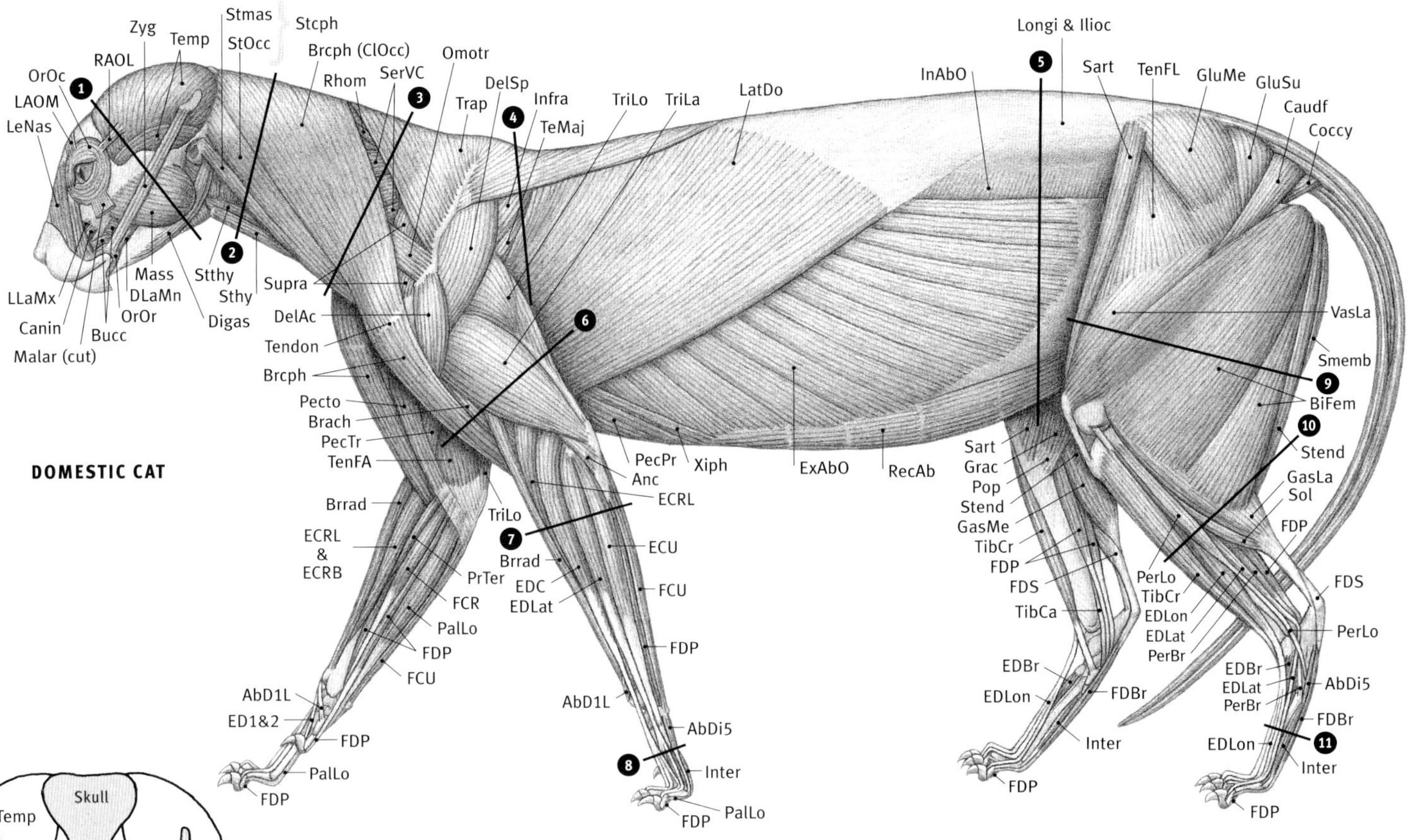

DOMESTIC CAT

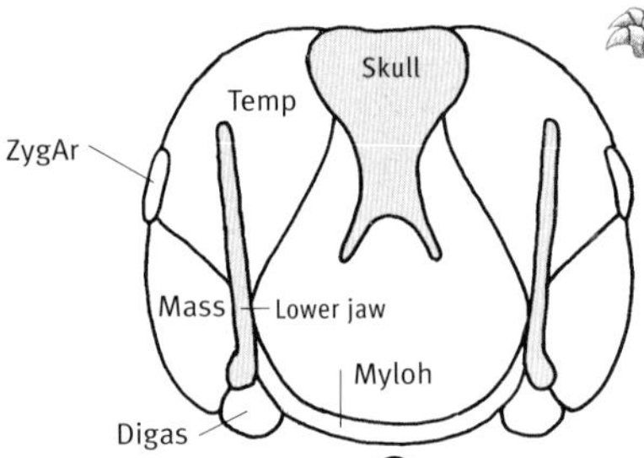

1

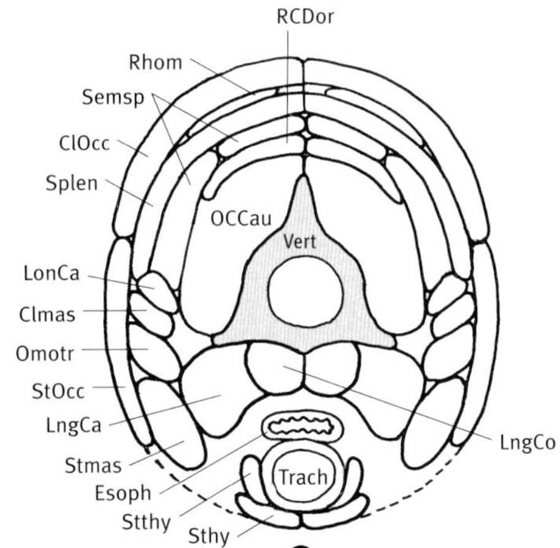

2

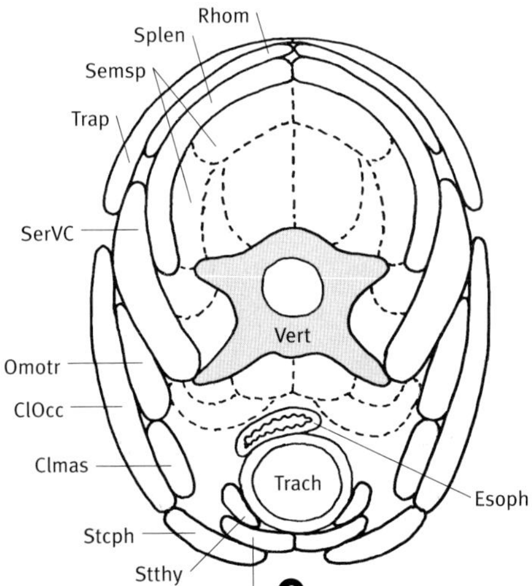

3

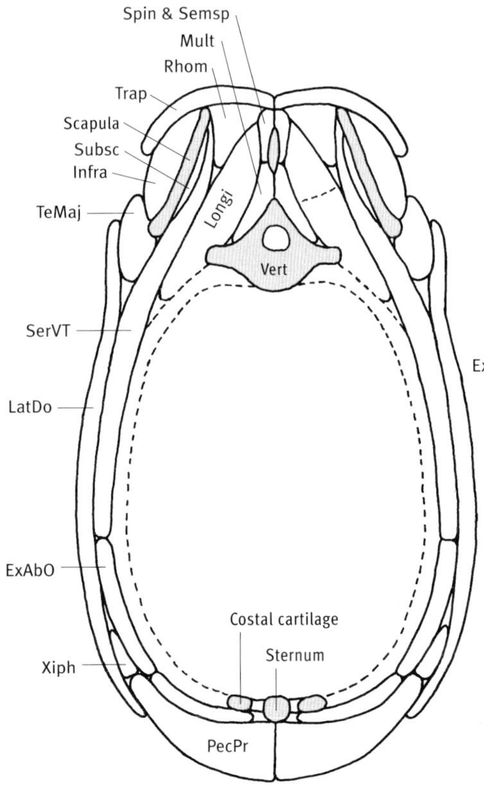

4

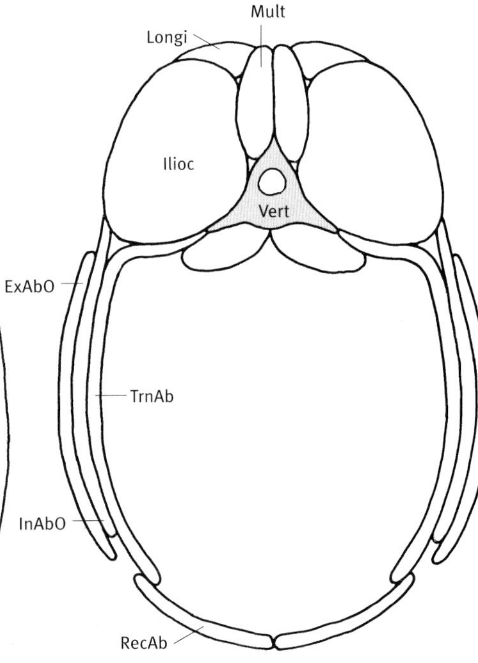

5

DRAWINGS NOT TO SCALE
(CROSS SECTIONS FROM SECTIONED PRESERVED SPECIMENS)

FORELIMB

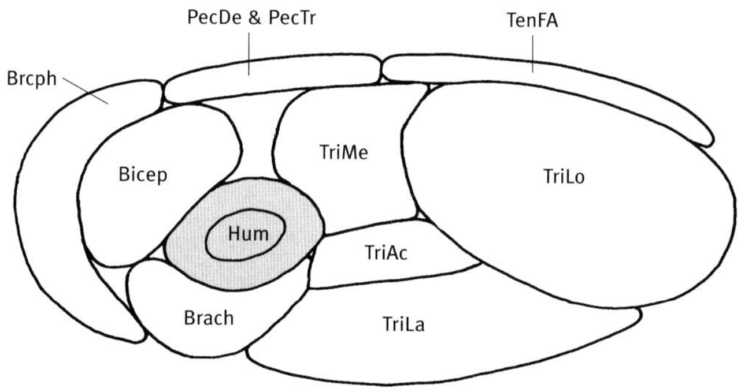

❻ **UPPER ARM**

HIND LIMB

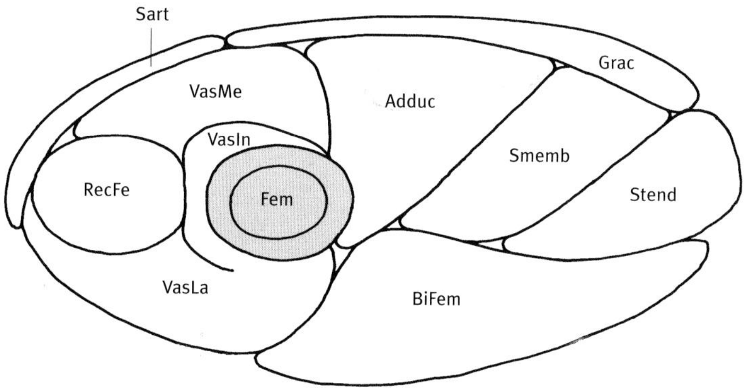

❾ **THIGH**

▲
INSIDE
◄ FRONT REAR ►
OUTSIDE
▼

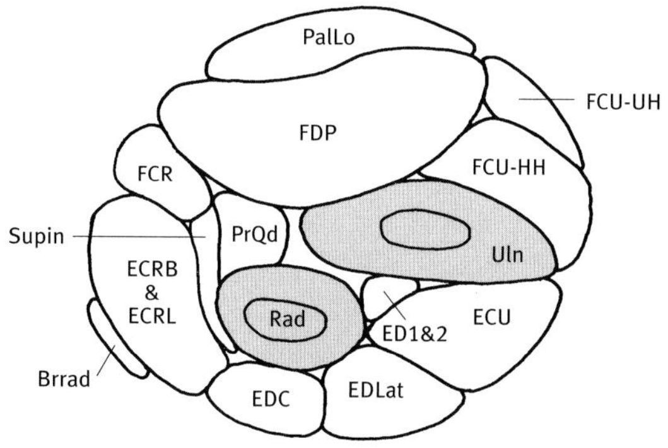

❼ **FOREARM**

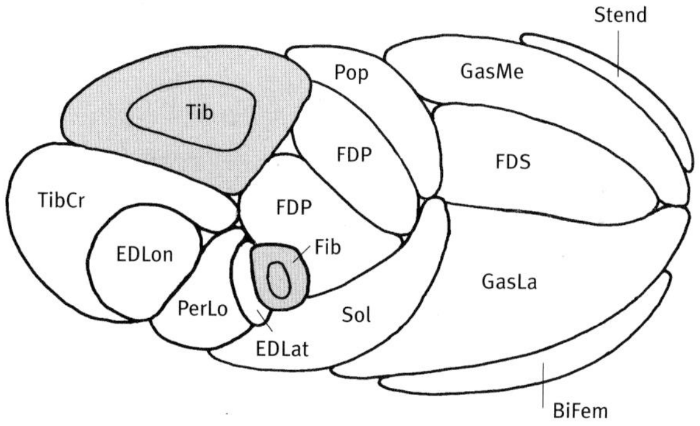

❿ **LOWER LEG**

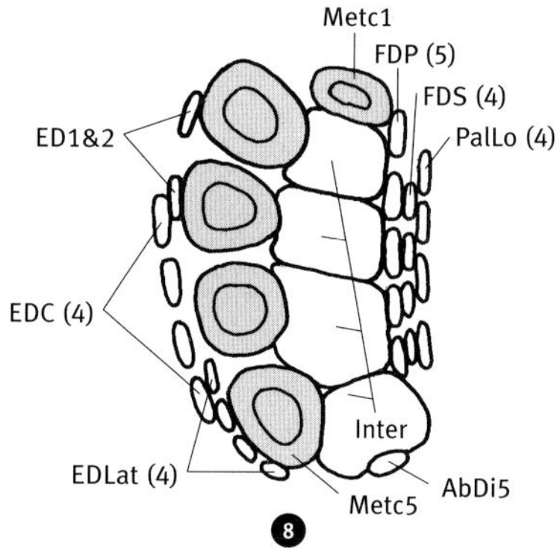

❽ **FOREPAW**

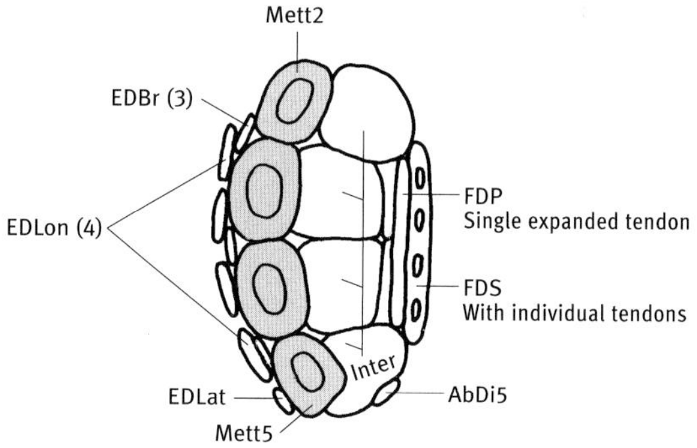

⓫ **HIND PAW**

AbDi5 *Abductor digiti V;* **Adduc** *Adductor;* **Bicep** *Biceps brachii;* **BiFem** *Biceps femoris;* **Brach** *Brachialis;* **Brcph** *Brachiocephalicus;* **Brrad** *Brachioradialis;* **Clmas** *Cleidomastoid;* **ClOcc** *Cleido-occipitalis;* **Digas** *Digastric;* **ECRB** *Extensor carpi radialis brevis;* **ECRL** *Extensor carpi radialis longus;* **ECU** *Extensor carpi ulnaris;* **ED1&2** *Extensor digiti I & II;* **EDBr** *Extensor digitorum brevis;* **EDC** *Extensor digitorum communis;* **EDLat** *Extensor digitorum lateralis;* **EDLon** *Extensor digitorum longus;* **Esoph** *Esophagus;* **ExAbO** *External abdominal oblique;* **FCR** *Flexor carpi radialis;* **FCU—HH** *Flexor carpi ulnaris, humeral head;* **FCU—UH** *Flexor carpi ulnaris, ulnar head;* **FDP** *Flexor digitorum profundus;* **FDS** *Flexor digitorum superficialis;* **Fem** *Femur;* **Fib** *Fibula;* **GasLa** *Gastrocnemius, lateral head;* **GasMe** *Gastrocnemius, medial head;* **Grac** *Gracilis;* **Hum** *Humerus;* **Ilioc** *Iliocostalis;* **InAbO** *Internal abdominal oblique;* **Infra** *Infraspinatus;* **Inter** *Interossei;* **LatDo** *Latissimus dorsi;* **LngCa** *Longus capitis;* **LngCo** *Longus colli;* **LonCa** *Longissimus capitis;* **Longi** *Longissimus;* **Mass** *Masseter;* **Metc1** *First metacarpal;* **Metc5** *Fifth metacarpal;* **Mett2** *Second metatarsal;* **Mett5** *Fifth metatarsal;* **Mult** *Multifidus;* **Myloh** *Mylohyoid;* **OCCau** *Obliquus capitis caudalis;* **Omotr** *Omotransversarius;* **PalLo** *Palmaris longus;* **PecDe** *Pectoralis descendens;* **PecPr** *Pectoralis profundus;* **PecTr** *Pectoralis transversus;* **PerLo** *Peroneus longus;* **Pop** *Popliteus;* **PrQd** *Pronator quadratus;* **Rad** *Radius;* **RCDor** *Rectus capitis dorsalis;* **RecAb** *Rectus abdominis;* **RecFe** *Rectus femoris;* **Rhom** *Rhomboid;* **Sart** *Sartorius;* **Semsp** *Semispinalis;* **SerVC** *Serratus ventralis cervicis;* **SerVT** *Serratus ventralis thoracis;* **Smemb** *Semimembranosus;* **Sol** *Soleus;* **Spin & Semsp** *Spinalis & semispinalis;* **Splen** *Splenius;* **Stcph** *Sternocephalicus;* **Stend** *Semitendinosus;* **Sthy** *Sternohyoid;* **Stmas** *Sternomastoid;* **StOcc** *Sterno-occipitalis;* **Stthy** *Sternothyroid;* **Subsc** *Subscapularis;* **Supin** *Supinator;* **TeMaj** *Teres major;* **Temp** *Temporalis;* **TenFA** *Tensor fasciae antibrachii;* **Tib** *Tibia;* **TibCr** *Tibialis cranialis;* **Trach** *Trachea;* **Trap** *Trapezius;* **TriAc** *Triceps brachii, accessory head;* **TriLa** *Triceps brachii, lateral head;* **TriLo** *Triceps brachii, long head;* **TriMe** *Triceps brachii, medial head;* **TrnAb** *Transversus abdominis;* **Uln** *Ulna;* **VasIn** *Vastus intermedius;* **VasLa** *Vastus lateralis;* **VasMe** *Vastus medialis;* **Vert** *Vertebra;* **Xiph** *Xiphihumeralis;* **ZygAr** *Zygomatic arch.*

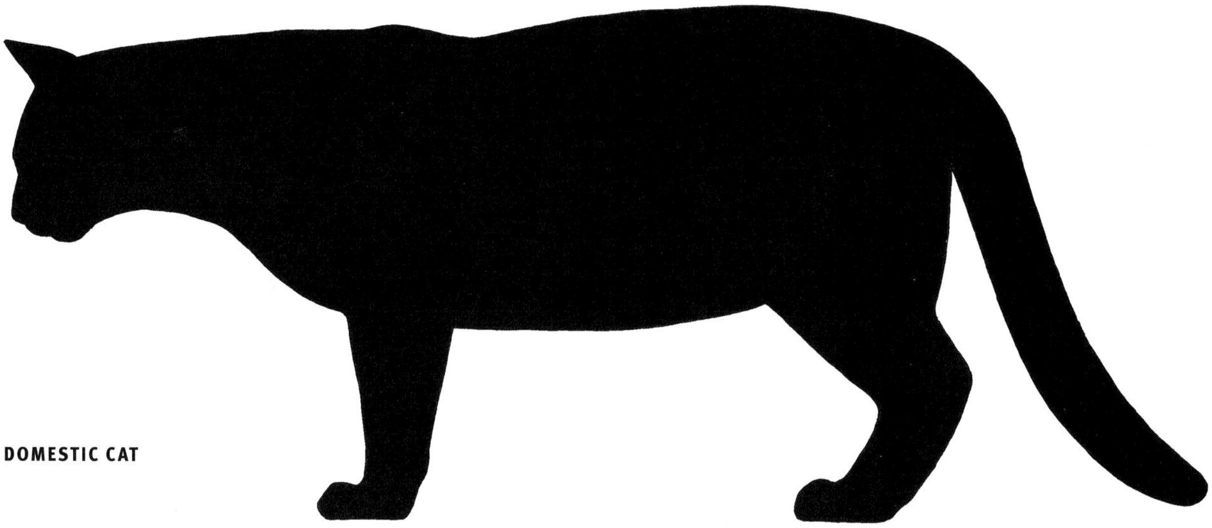

DOMESTIC CAT

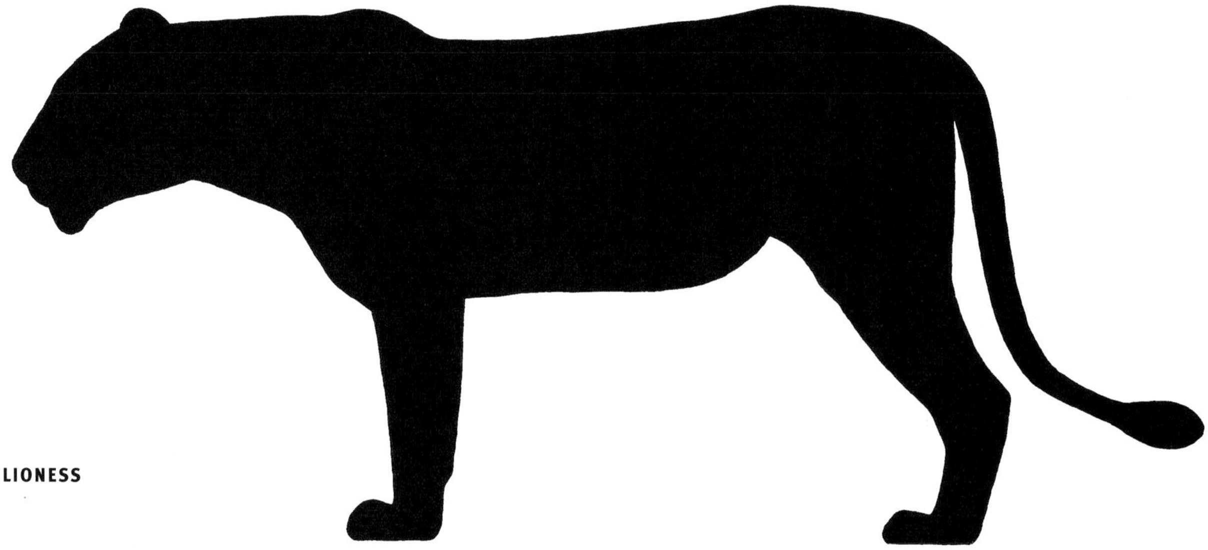

LIONESS

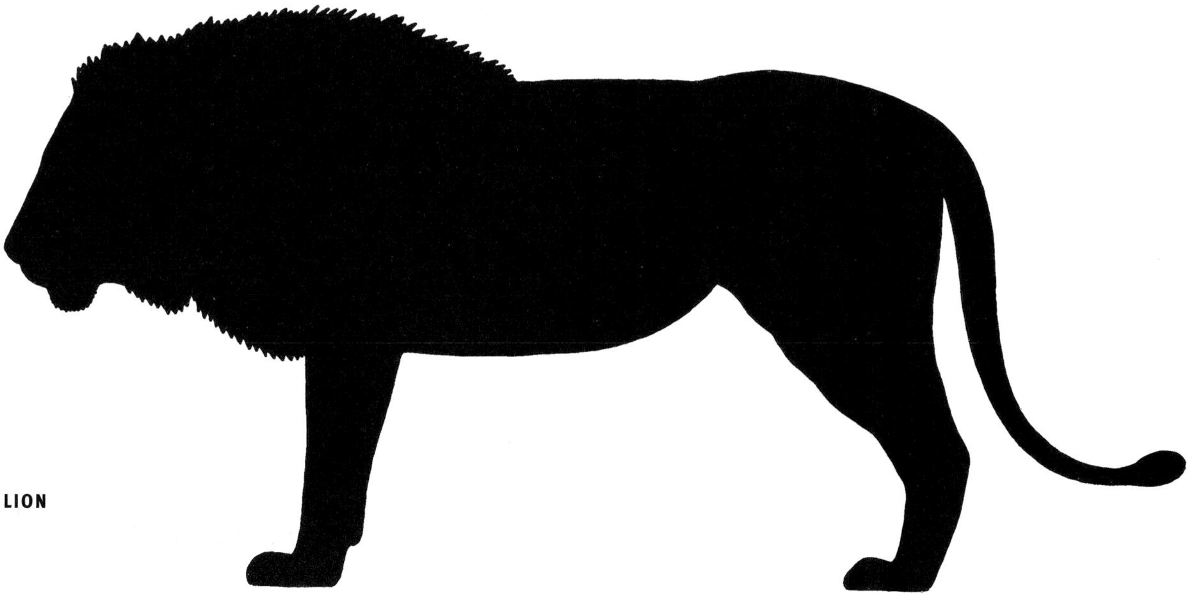

LION

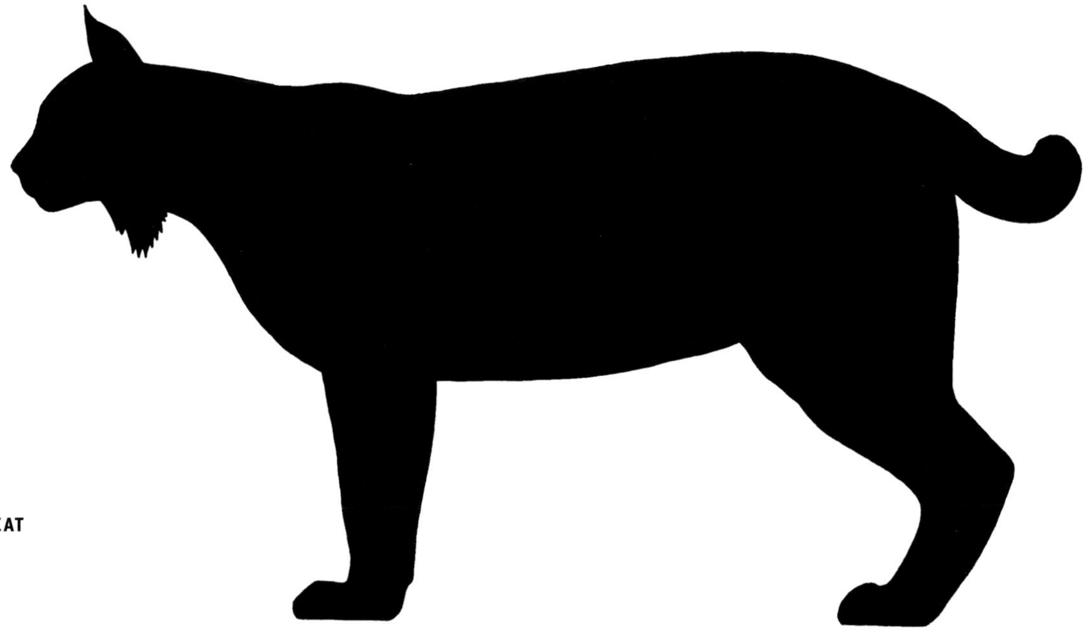

BOBCAT

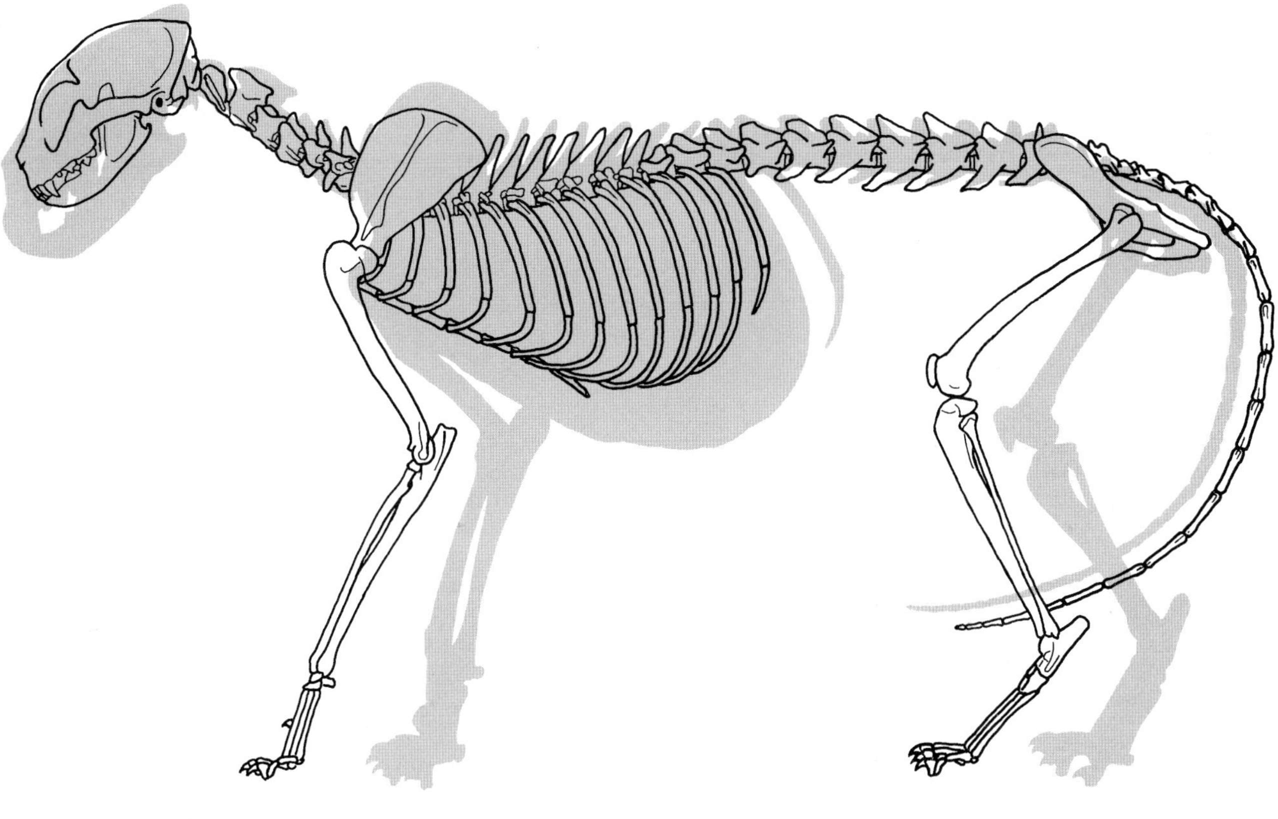

SKELETON COMPARISON

DOMESTIC CAT — BLACK OUTLINE
LIONESS — GRAY

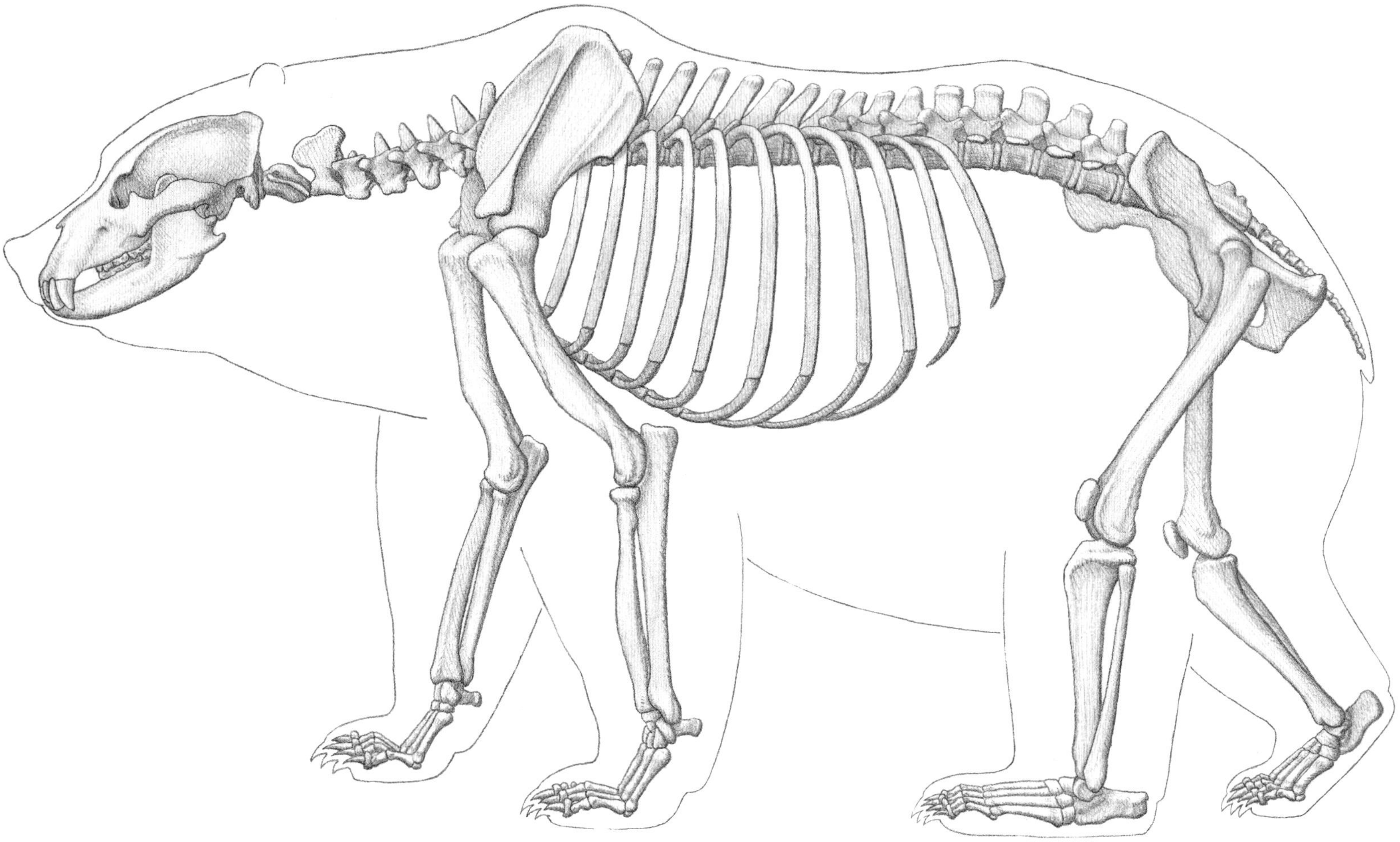

BROWN BEAR
Ursus arctos

(FROM SPECIMEN PHOTO; SKULL FROM SPECIMEN; AFTER BLAINVILLE)

Bear characteristics: Large, powerful body; powerful limbs appear relatively short. Rear feet wide. Walks on sole and heel of rear foot and usually on digits of front foot. Five digits per limb with long, curved, nonretractile claws. Front claws longer than rear claws. Large head, small eyes. Small, round, erect, furry ears. Large canines; flat, grinding molars. Short tail. Arched back, high shoulder. Grizzly has most prominent shoulder hump and dished, slightly concave face (in profile). Can have very thick layer of fur. Grizzly and brown bear belong to the same species, but differ in geographical range and size. The giant panda is now considered to be a member of the bear family, not the raccoon family.

AbD1L *Abductor digiti I longus;* **AbDi5** *Abductor digiti V;* **Bicep** *Biceps brachii;* **BiFem** *Biceps femoris;* **Brach** *Brachialis;* **Brcph** *Brachiocephalicus;* **Brrad** *Brachioradialis;* **Bucc** *Buccinator;* **Canin** *Caninus;* **Corac** *Coracobrachialis;* **DelAc** *Deltoid, acromial portion;* **DelSp** *Deltoid, spinal portion;* **Digas** *Digastric;* **ECRB** *Extensor carpi radialis brevis;* **ECRL** *Extensor carpi radialis longus;* **ECU** *Extensor carpi ulnaris;* **ED1&2** *Extensor digiti I & II;* **ED1L** *Extensor digiti I longus;* **EDBr** *Extensor digitorum brevis;* **EDC** *Extensor digitorum communis;* **EDLat** *Extensor digitorum lateralis;* **EDLon** *Extensor digitorum longus;* **ExAbO** *External abdominal oblique;* **FCR** *Flexor carpi radialis;* **FCU** *Flexor carpi ulnaris;* **FDBr** *Flexor digitorum brevis;* **FDP** *Flexor digitorum profundus;* **FDS** *Flexor digitorum superficialis;* **GasLa** *Gastrocnemius, lateral head;* **GasMe** *Gastrocnemius, medial head;* **GluMe** *Gluteus medius;* **GluSu** *Gluteus superficialis;* **Grac** *Gracilis;* **Ilioc** *Iliocostalis;* **LatDo** *Latissimus dorsi;* **LeNas** *Levator nasolabialis;* **LLaMx** *Levator labii maxillaris;* **Longi** *Longissimus;* **Malar** *Malaris;* **Mass** *Masseter;* **Myloh** *Mylohyoid;* **Omohy** *Omohyoid;* **Omotr** *Omotransversarius;* **OrOc** *Orbicularis oculi;* **OrOr** *Orbicularis oris;* **PecDe** *Pectoralis descendens;* **PecPr** *Pectoralis profundus;* **PecTr** *Pectoralis transversus;* **PerBr** *Peroneus brevis;* **PerLo** *Peroneus longus;* **Plant** *Plantaris;* **PrTer** *Pronator teres;* **RecAb** *Rectus abdominis;* **Sart** *Sartorius;* **SerDC** *Serratus dorsalis caudalis;* **SerVT** *Serratus ventralis thoracis;* **Sol** *Soleus;* **Stcph** *Sternocephalicus;* **Stend** *Semitendinosus;* **Sthy** *Sternohyoid;* **Supra** *Supraspinatus;* **Temp** *Temporalis;* **TenFL** *Tensor fasciae latae;* **TibCa** *Tibialis caudalis;* **TibCr** *Tibialis cranialis;* **Trach** *Trachea;* **TriLa** *Triceps brachii, lateral head;* **TriLo** *Triceps brachii, long head;* **TriMe** *Triceps brachii, medial head;* **VasLa** *Vastus lateralis;* **Zyg** *Zygomaticus.*

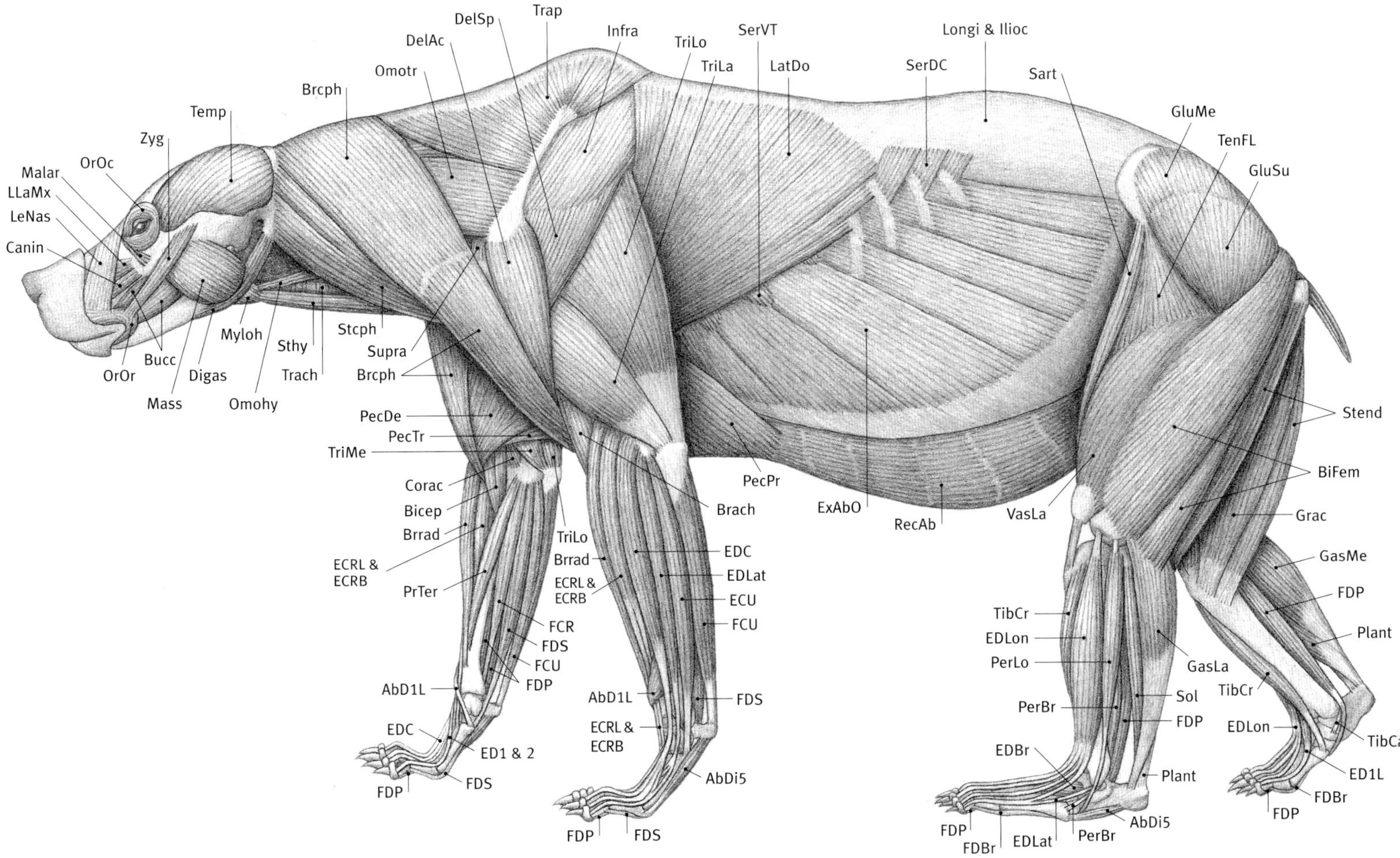

(AFTER CUVIER)

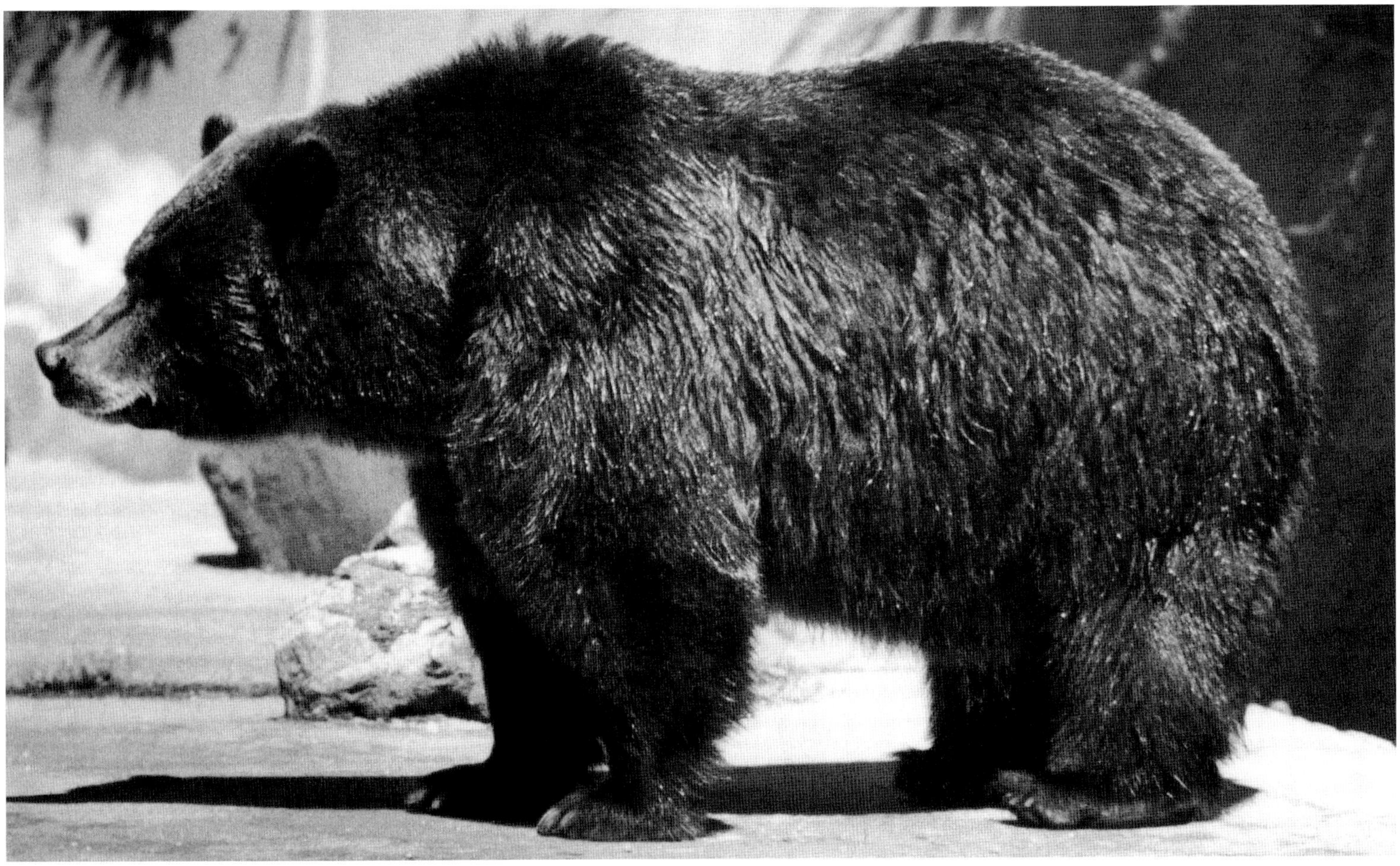

GRIZZLY BEAR

Ursus arctos

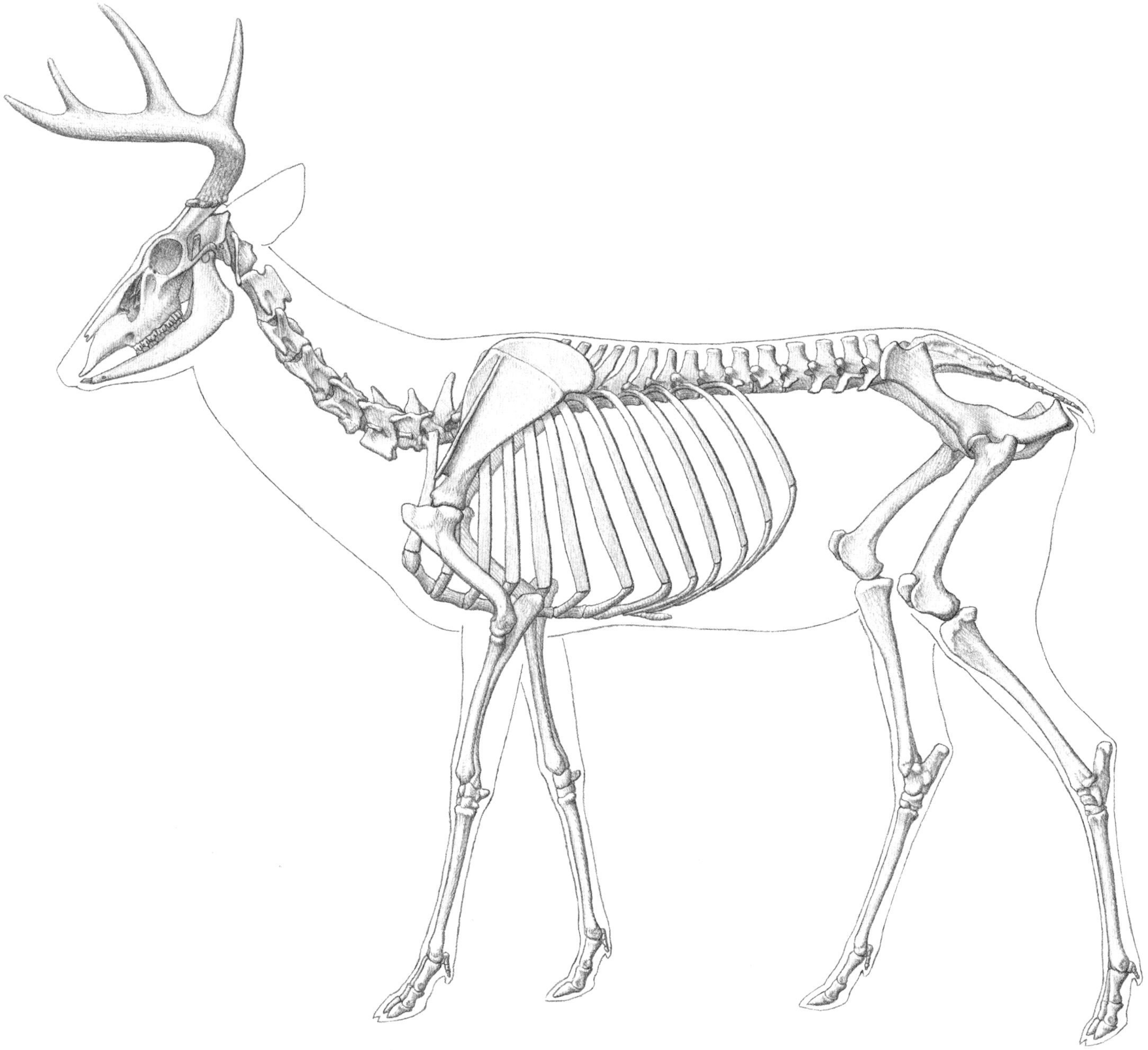

(AFTER ELLENBERGER; SKULL FROM SPECIMEN)

Deer (cervid) characteristics: Male has branching, bony antlers, which are shed and regrown every year; maximum size is reached before mating begins. Antlers shed after mating season. Both male and female caribou and reindeer have antlers. No upper teeth in front. Generally graceful, delicate, and light; elk and moose are heavier species in deer family. Straight, horizontal back line usually in the lighter species. Neck of female thinner and more delicate than male. Thin limbs. Four digits per limb, only middle two are functional; outer and inner digits very reduced. Hoofs on toes. Walks on toes. Short tail.

AbD1L *Abductor digiti I longus;* **Brach** *Brachialis;* **Brcph** *Brachiocephalicus;* **Bucc** *Buccinator;* **Canin** *Caninus;* **Clmas** *Cleidomastoid;* **ClOcc** *Cleido-occipitalis;* **DelAc** *Deltoid, acromial portion;* **DelSc** *Deltoid, scapular portion;* **DLaMn** *Depressor labii mandibularis;* **ECR** *Extensor carpi radialis;* **EDC** *Extensor digitorum communis;* **EDLat** *Extensor digitorum lateralis;* **EDLon** *Extensor digitorum longus;* **ExAbO** *External abdominal oblique;* **FCR** *Flexor carpi radialis;* **FCU** *Flexor carpi ulnaris;* **FDP** *Flexor digitorum profundus;* **FDS** *Flexor digitorum superficialis;* **GasLa** *Gastrocnemius, lateral head;* **GasMe** *Gastrocnemius, medial head;* **Glubi** *Gluteobiceps;* **GluMe** *Gluteus medius;* **Ilioc** *Iliocostalis;* **InAbO** *Internal abdominal oblique;* **Infra** *Infraspinatus;* **LatDo** *Latissimus dorsi;* **LeNas** *Levator nasolabialis;* **LLaMx** *Levator labii maxillaris;* **Longi** *Longissimus;* **Malar** *Malaris;* **Mass** *Masseter;* **Myloh** *Mylohyoid;* **Omotr** *Omotransversarius;* **OrOc** *Orbicularis oculi;* **OrOr** *Orbicularis oris;* **PecAs** *Pectoralis ascendens;* **PecDe** *Pectoralis descendens;* **PecTr** *Pectoralis transversus;* **PerLo** *Peroneus longus;* **PerTe** *Peroneus tertius;* **RecAb** *Rectus abdominis;* **SerDC** *Serratus dorsalis caudalis;* **SerVT** *Serratus ventralis thoracis;* **Smemb** *Semimembranosus;* **Sol** *Soleus;* **Stend** *Semitendinosus;* **Stman** *Sternomandibularis;* **Stmas** *Sternomastoid;* **Stthh** *Sternothyrohyoid;* **SusLi** *Suspensory ligament;* **Temp** *Temporalis;* **TenFA** *Tensor fasciae antibrachii;* **TenFL** *Tensor fasciae latae;* **TibCr** *Tibialis cranialis;* **Trap** *Trapezius;* **TriLa** *Triceps brachii, lateral head;* **TriLo** *Triceps brachii, long head;* **UlLat** *Ulnaris lateralis;* **VasLa** *Vastus lateralis;* **Zyg** *Zygomaticus.*

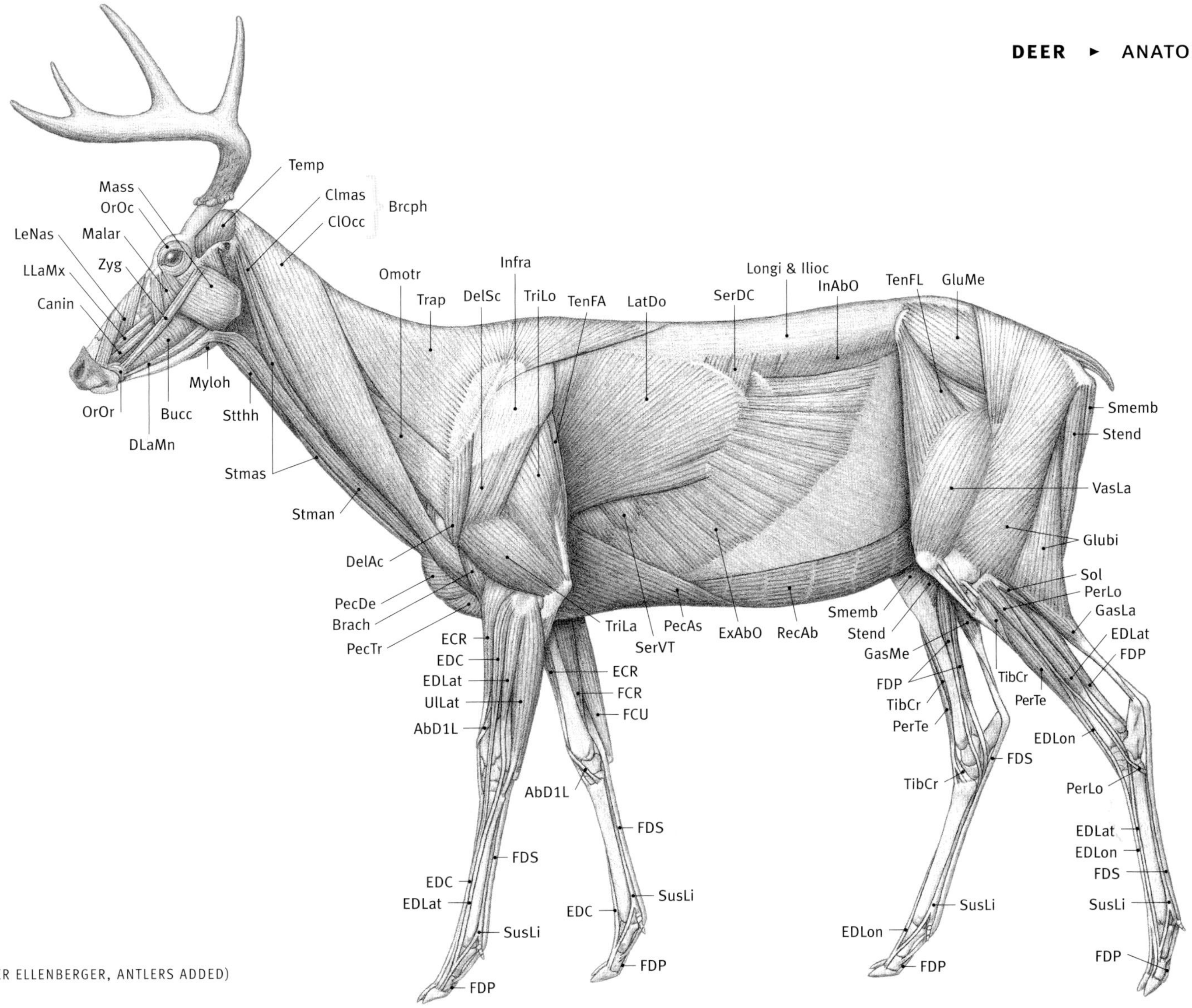

(AFTER ELLENBERGER, ANTLERS ADDED)

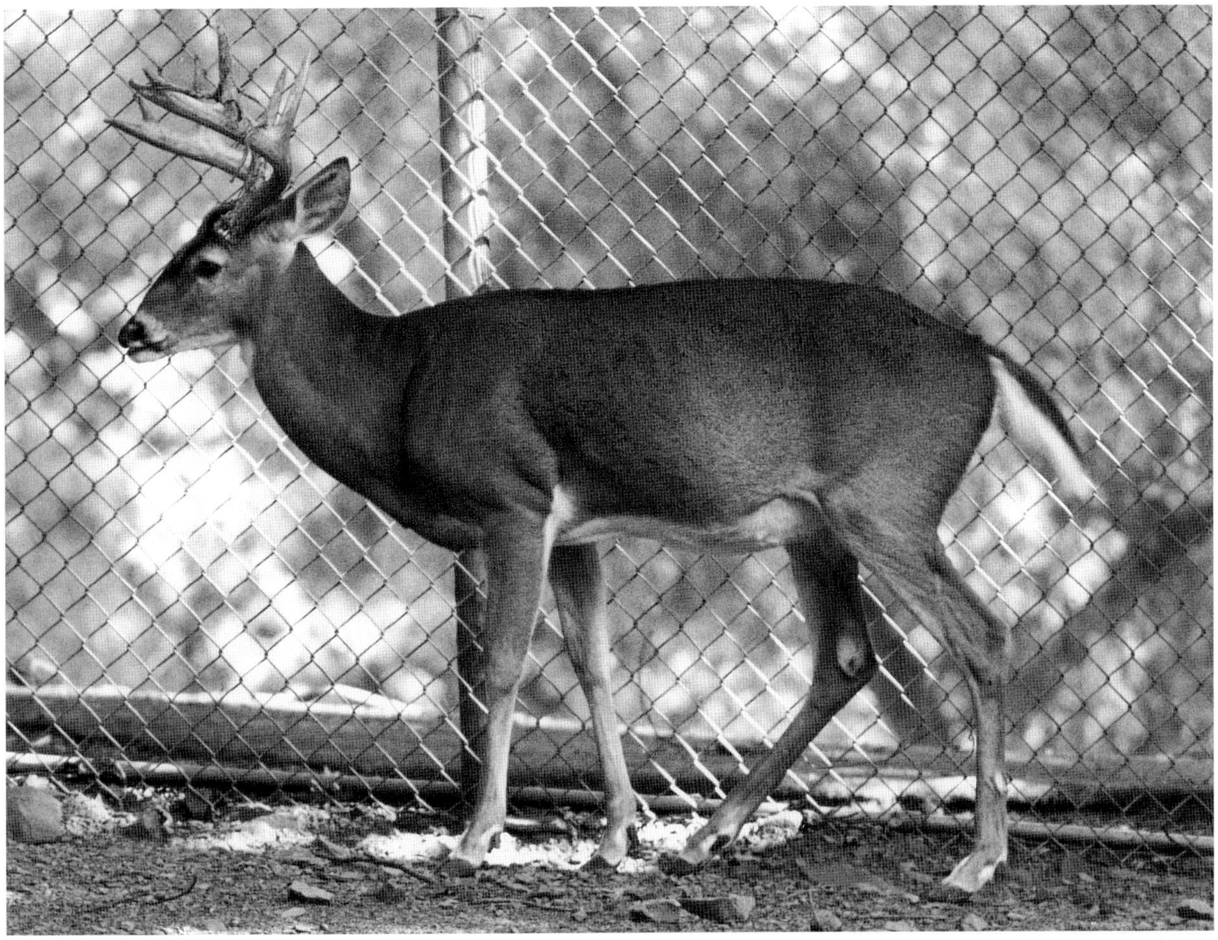

WHITE-TAILED DEER (MALE)

Odocoileus virginianus

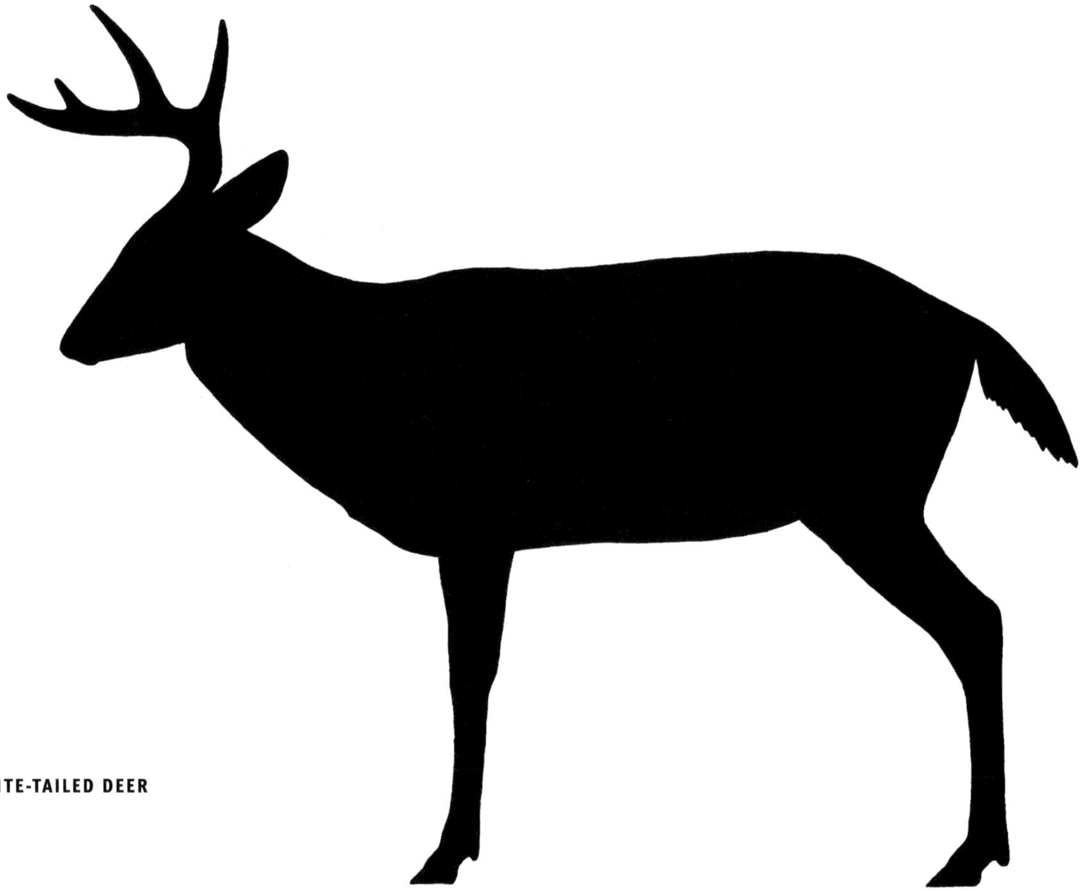

WHITE-TAILED DEER

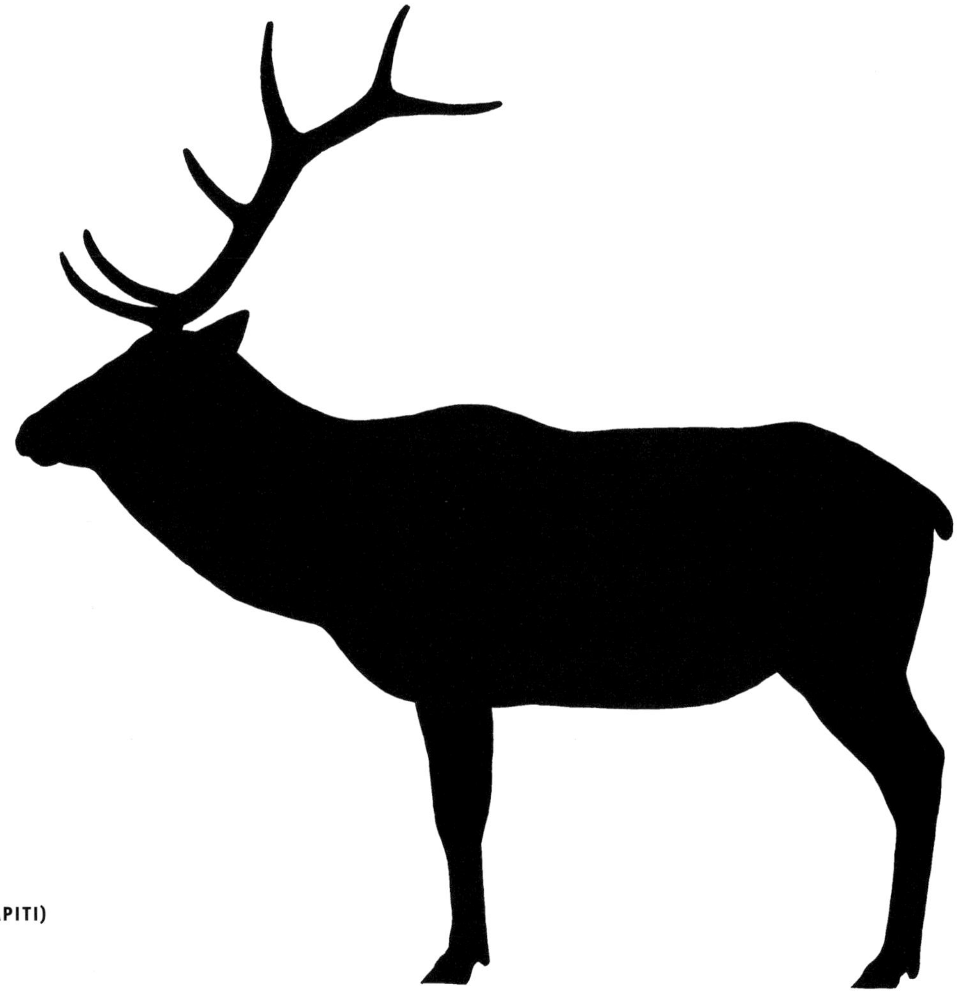

ELK (WAPITI)

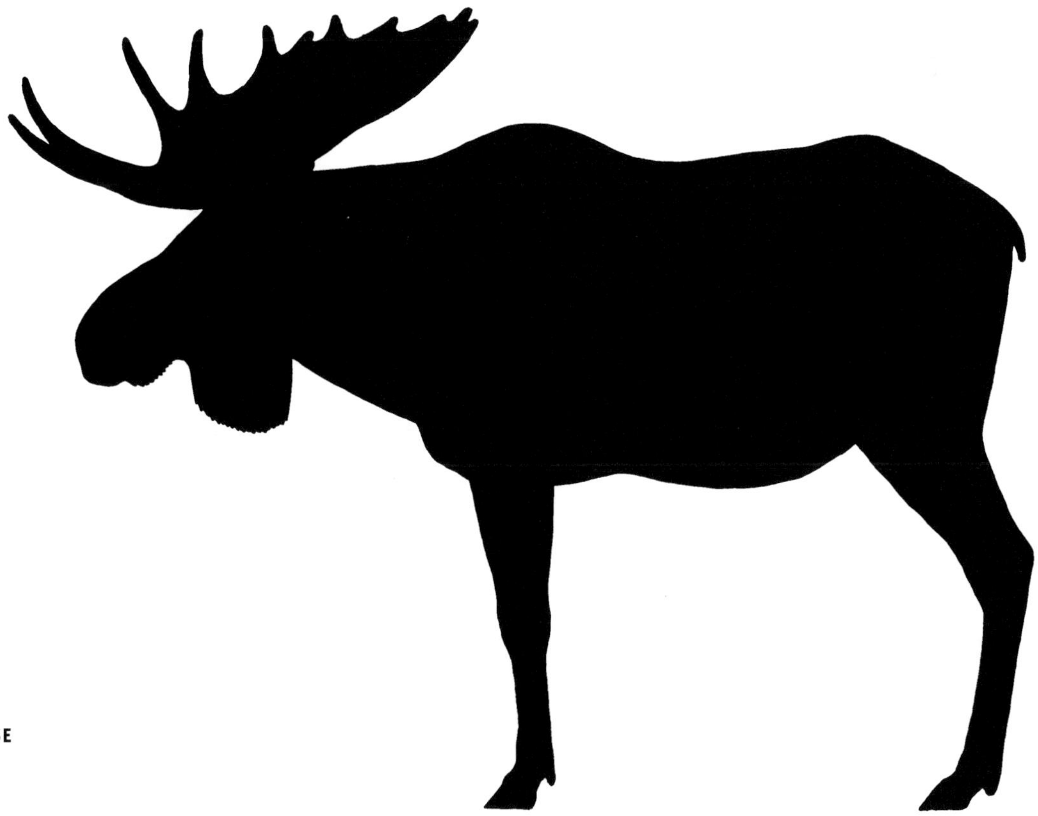

MOOSE

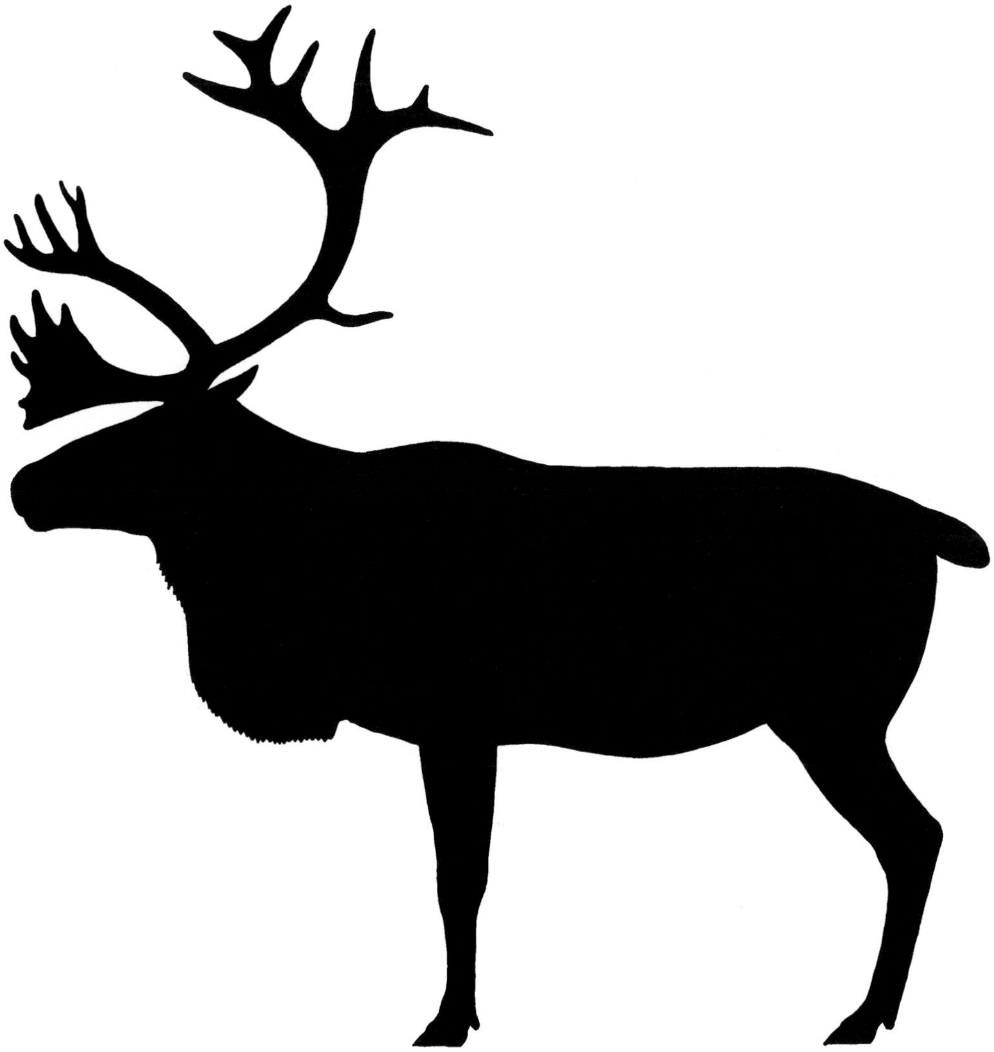

CARIBOU

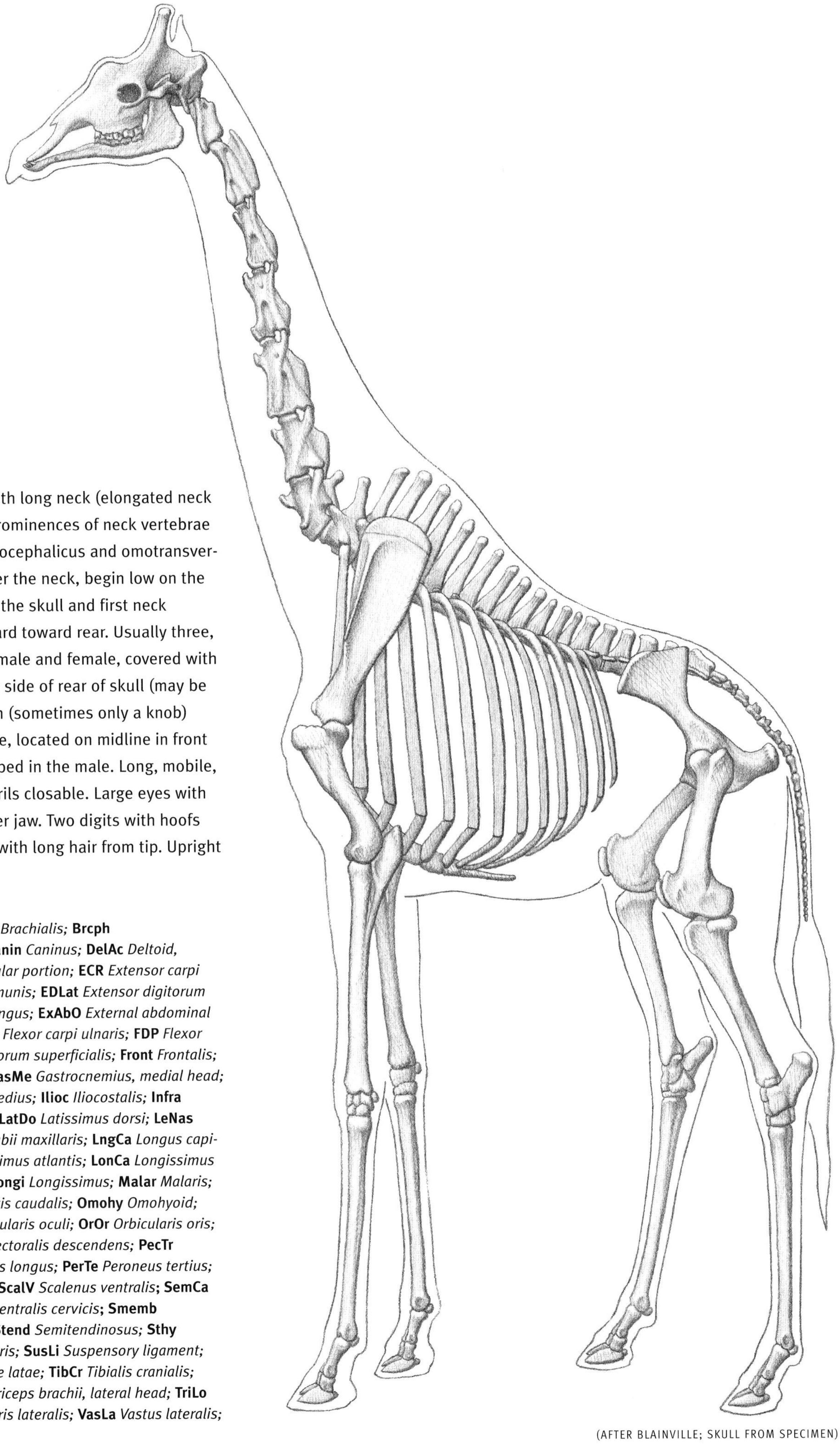

(AFTER BLAINVILLE; SKULL FROM SPECIMEN)

Giraffe characteristics: Very tall with long neck (elongated neck vertebrae) and long limbs. Bony prominences of neck vertebrae can be seen on the surface; brachiocephalicus and omotransversarius muscles, which usually cover the neck, begin low on the side of the neck, rather than up at the skull and first neck vertebra. Back line slopes downward toward rear. Usually three, permanent, bony "horns" in both male and female, covered with skin and fur. Two located on either side of rear of skull (may be topped with hairy tufts); third horn (sometimes only a knob) wider, stubbier, and of variable size, located on midline in front of the other horns, is more developed in the male. Long, mobile, prehensile lips; long tongue. Nostrils closable. Large eyes with long lashes. No front teeth in upper jaw. Two digits with hoofs per limb. Walks on toes. Long tail with long hair from tip. Upright mane on midline of neck.

AbD1L *Abductor digiti I longus;* **Brach** *Brachialis;* **Brcph** *Brachiocephalicus* **Bucc** *Buccinator;* **Canin** *Caninus;* **DelAc** *Deltoid, acromial portion;* **DelSc** *Deltoid, scapular portion;* **ECR** *Extensor carpi radialis;* **EDC** *Extensor digitorum communis;* **EDLat** *Extensor digitorum lateralis;* **EDLon** *Extensor digitorum longus;* **ExAbO** *External abdominal oblique;* **FCR** *Flexor carpi radialis;* **FCU** *Flexor carpi ulnaris;* **FDP** *Flexor digitorum profundus;* **FDS** *Flexor digitorum superficialis;* **Front** *Frontalis;* **GasLa** *Gastrocnemius, lateral head;* **GasMe** *Gastrocnemius, medial head;* **Glubi** *Gluteobiceps;* **GluMe** *Gluteus medius;* **Ilioc** *Iliocostalis;* **Infra** *Infraspinatus;* **Inttr** *Intertransversarii;* **LatDo** *Latissimus dorsi;* **LeNas** *Levator nasolabialis;* **LLaMx** *Levator labii maxillaris;* **LngCa** *Longus capitis;* **LngCo** *Longus colli;* **LonAt** *Longissimus atlantis;* **LonCa** *Longissimus capitis;* **LonCe** *Longissimus cervicis;* **Longi** *Longissimus;* **Malar** *Malaris;* **Mass** *Masseter;* **OCCau** *Obliquus capitis caudalis;* **Omohy** *Omohyoid;* **Omotr** *Omotransversarius;* **OrOc** *Orbicularis oculi;* **OrOr** *Orbicularis oris;* **PecAs** *Pectoralis ascendens;* **PecDe** *Pectoralis descendens;* **PecTr** *Pectoralis transversus;* **PerLo** *Peroneus longus;* **PerTe** *Peroneus tertius;* **Pop** *Popliteus;* **RecFe** *Rectus femoris;* **ScalV** *Scalenus ventralis;* **SemCa** *Semispinalis capitis;* **SerVC** *Serratus ventralis cervicis;* **Smemb** *Semimembranosus;* **Splen** *Splenius;* **Stend** *Semitendinosus;* **Sthy** *Sternohyoid;* **Stman** *Sternomandibularis;* **SusLi** *Suspensory ligament;* **Temp** *Temporalis;* **TenFL** *Tensor fasciae latae;* **TibCr** *Tibialis cranialis;* **Trach** *Trachea;* **Trap** *Trapezius;* **TriLa** *Triceps brachii, lateral head;* **TriLo** *Triceps brachii, long head;* **UlLat** *Ulnaris lateralis;* **VasLa** *Vastus lateralis;* **Zyg** *Zygomaticus.*

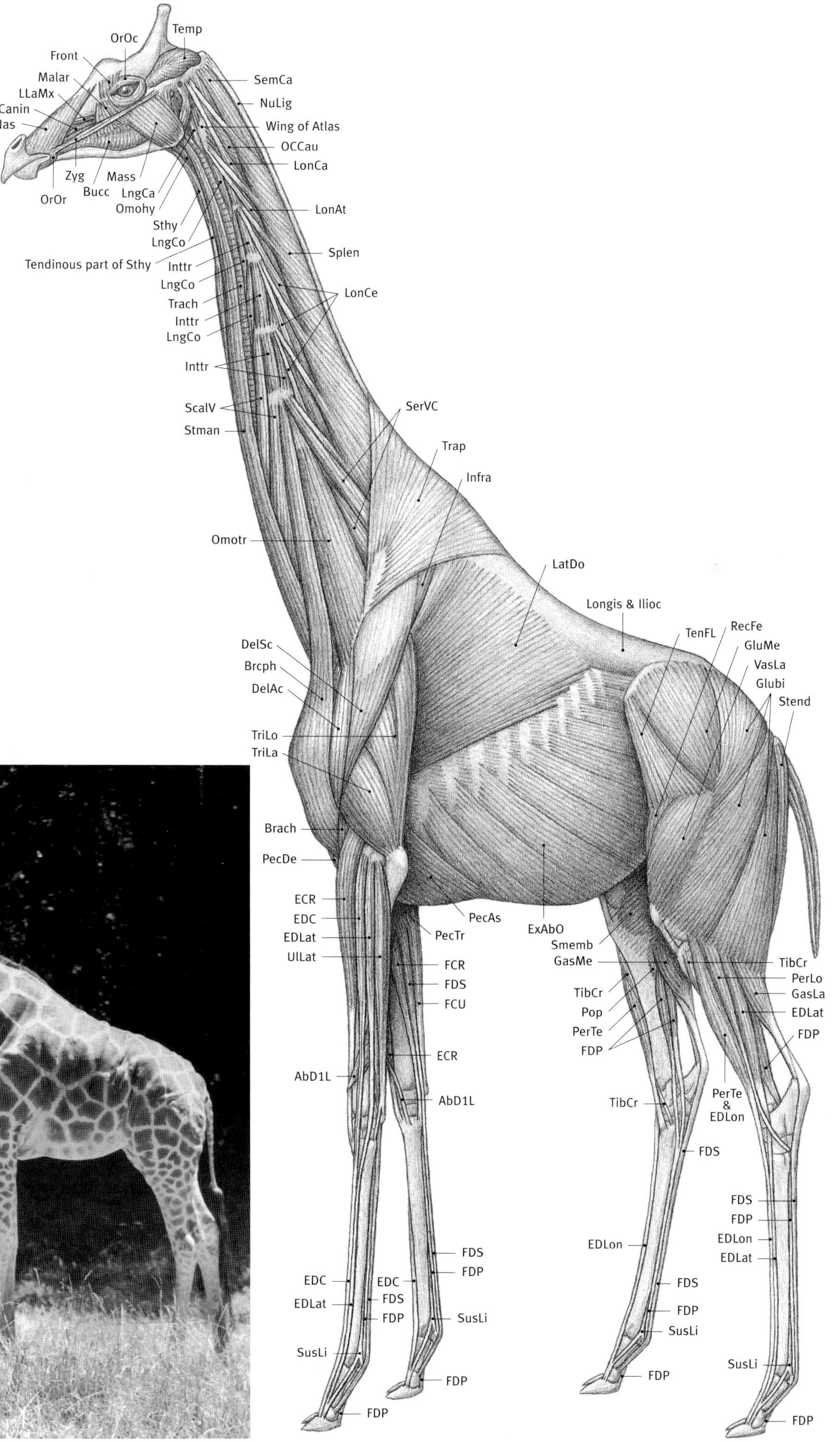

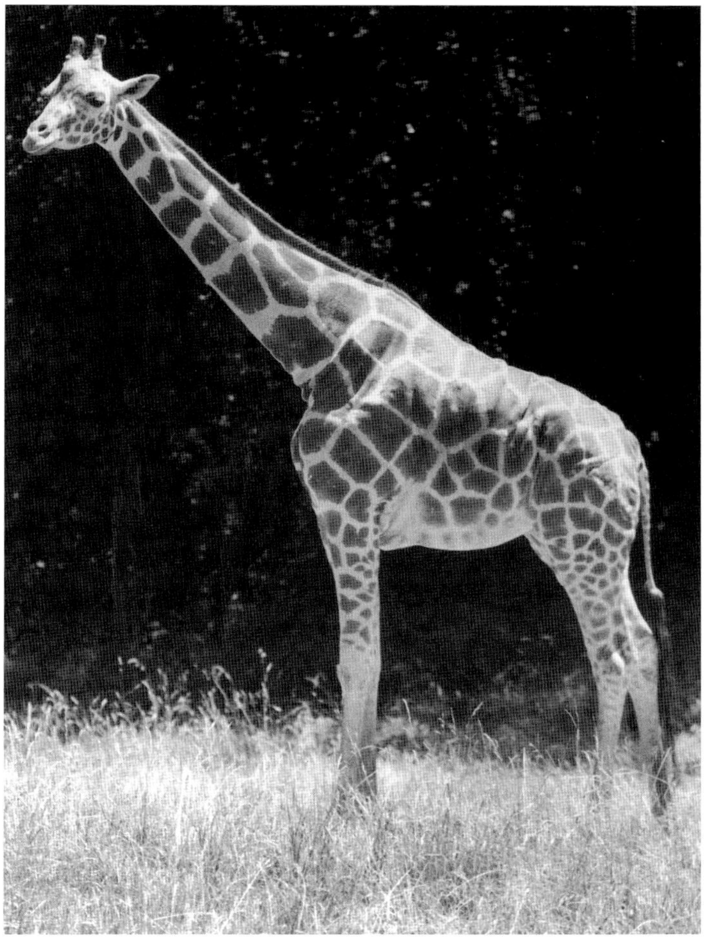

BARINGO GIRAFFE (FEMALE)
Giraffa camelopardalis

(AFTER MURIE; SOLUONIAS; REAR LIMB FROM DISSECTION)

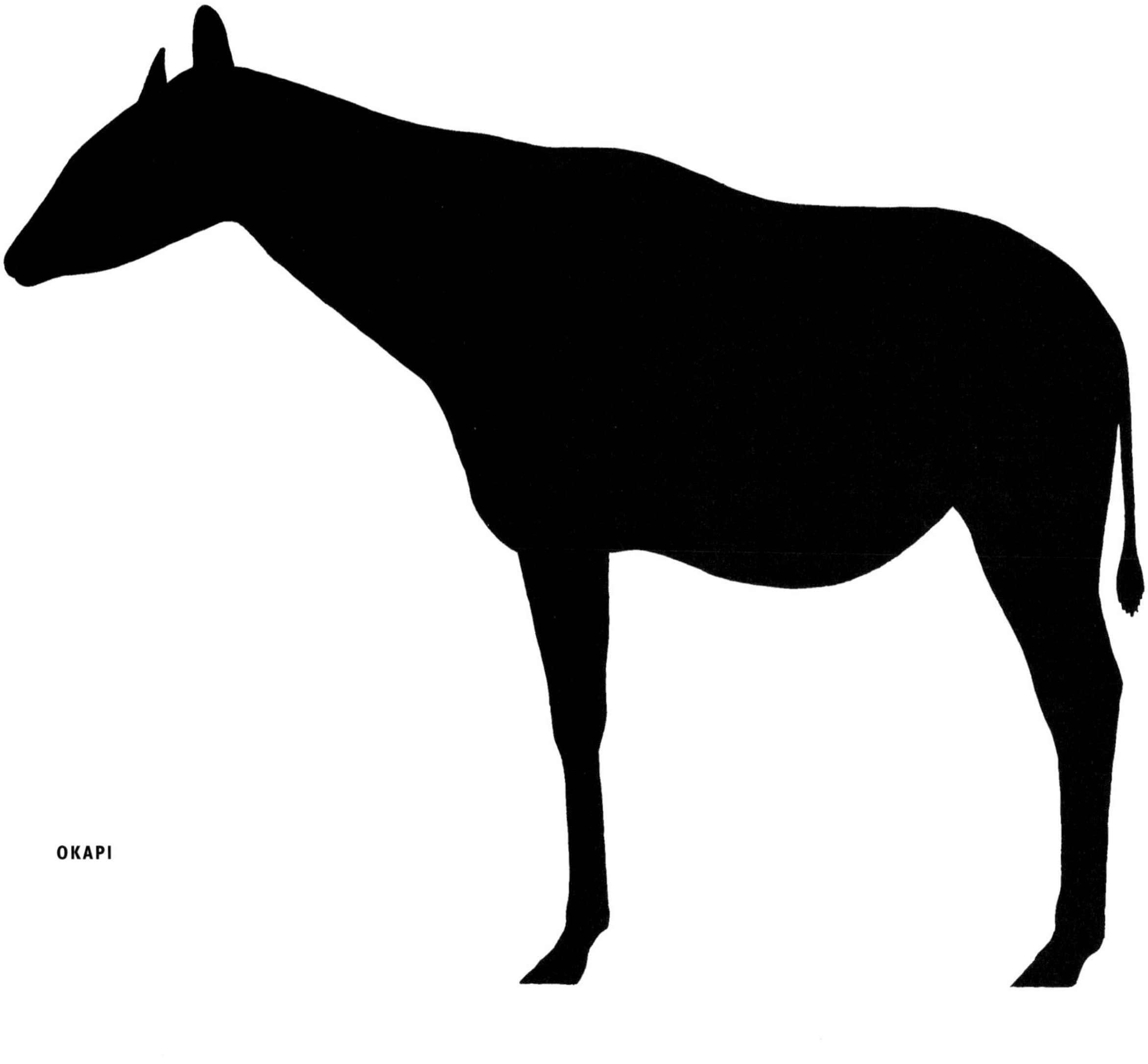

OKAPI

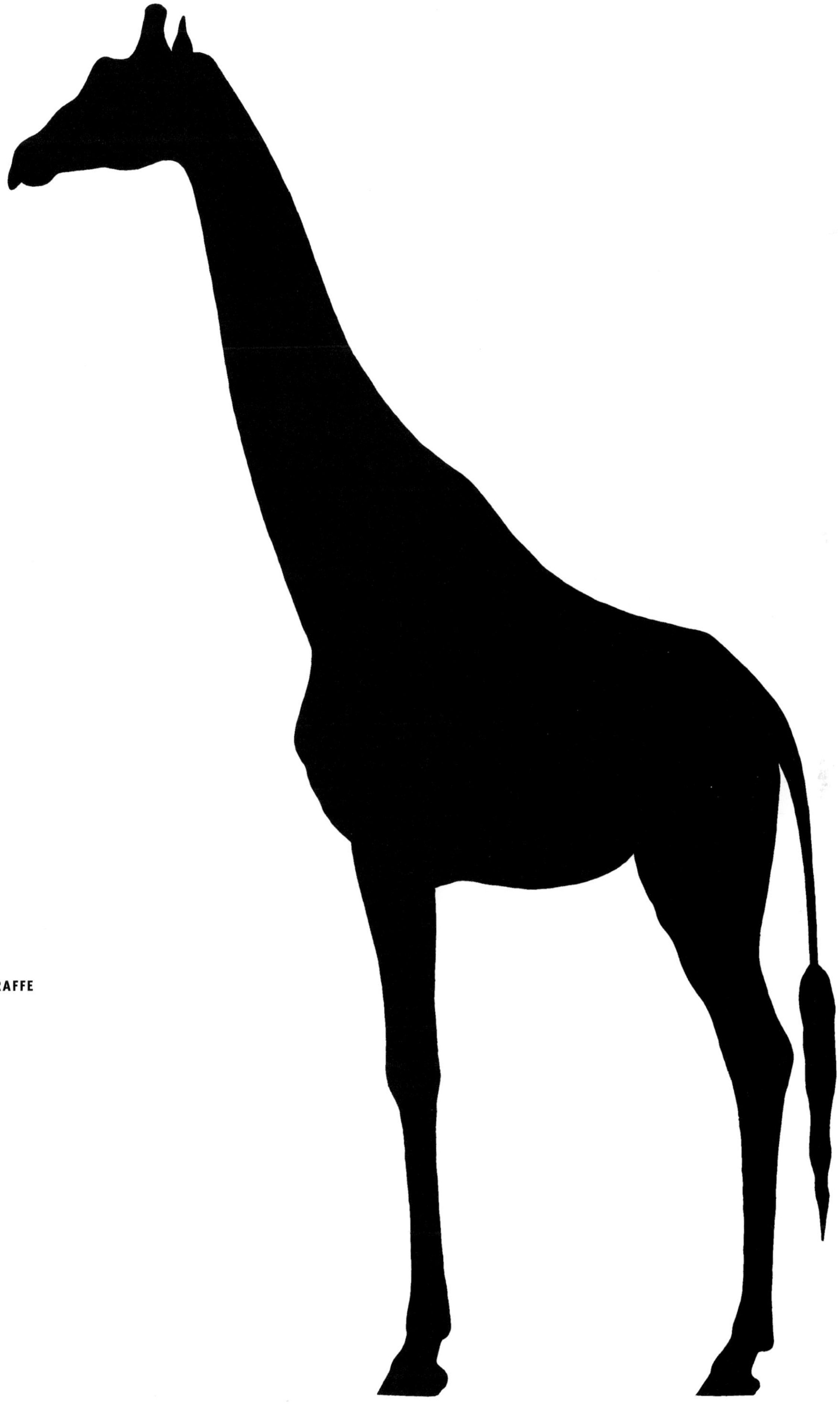

GIRAFFE

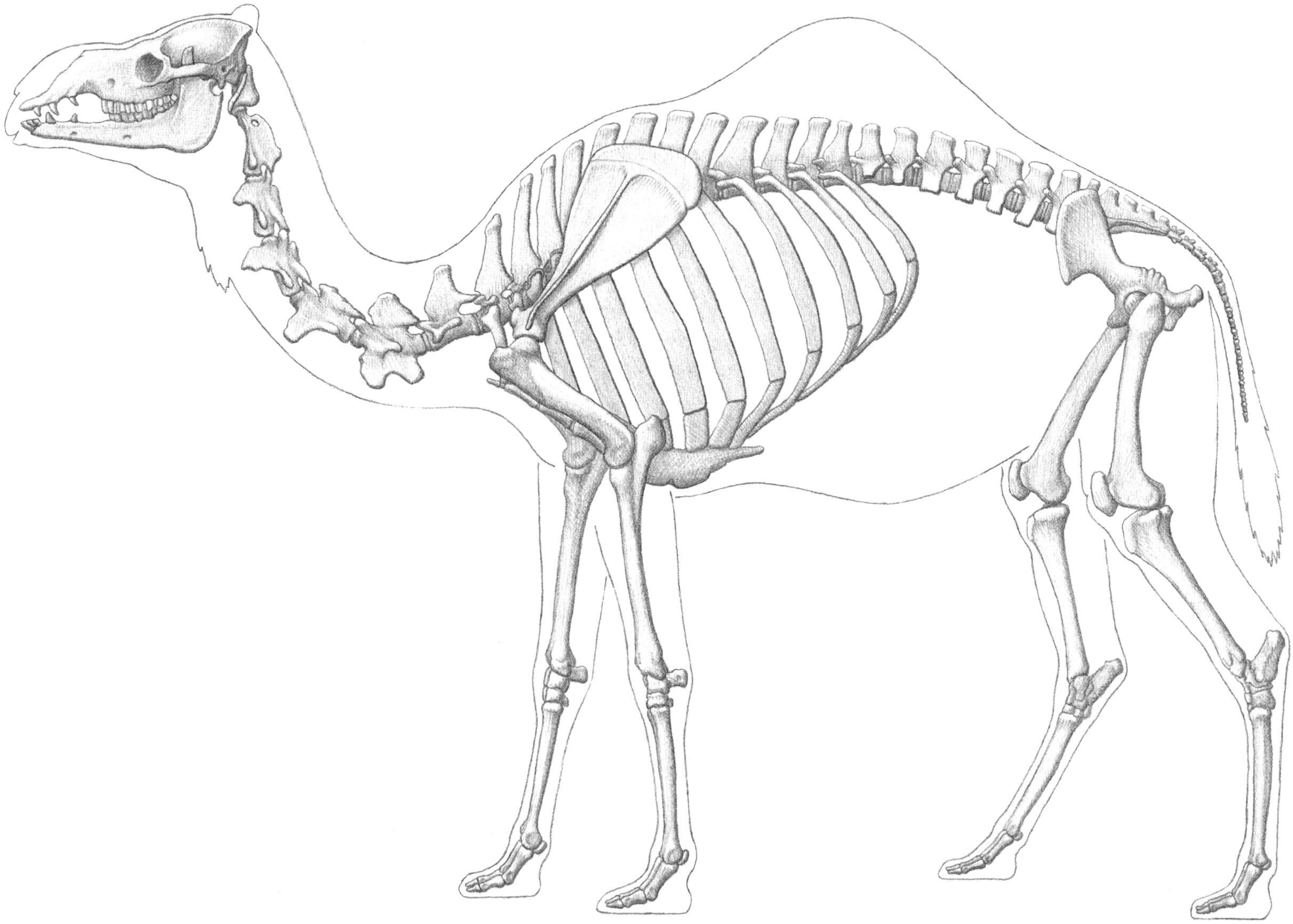

DROMEDARY CAMEL

(AFTER SMUTS; BLAINVILLE)

Camel characteristics: Dromedary with one hump; Bactrian, with two. Same family as the wild guanaco and vicuna, as well as the domesticated llama and alpaca (both derived from the guanaco). Cleft upper lip, slit-like nostrils, which can be closed. Long, thin, upcurved neck, flattened side-to-side. Thin legs (Bactrian with shorter legs). Ulna and fibula reduced. Long, vertical femur and low knee joint keeps thigh away from abdomen and makes leg appear very long. Two digits per limb, splayed outward to widen foot. Last two toe bones almost horizontal. Undivided sole of foot expanded into broad pad. Nail, not hoof, on toe. Single cannon (metacarpal/metatarsal) bone divided at lower end for attachment of two toes. When lying on belly, knee touches ground (femur angled downward); sole and heel of foot rest on ground. Heavy skin calluses on front of wrist (carpus), knee, and bottom of rear end of sternum (on enlarged portion of bony sternum) for kneeling and resting on ground. Brachiocephalicus muscle reduced—does not cover neck. Hump made of soft, fatty tissue—largest when well fed.

AbD1L *Abductor digiti I longus;* **Bicep** *Biceps brachii;* **Brach** *Brachialis;* **Brcph** *Brachiocephalicus;* **Bucc** *Buccinator;* **Canin** *Caninus*; **Coccy** *Coccygeus;* **DelAc** *Deltoid, acromial portion;* **DelSc** *Deltoid, scapular portion;* **DiNAp** *Dilator naris apicalis;* **DLaMx** *Depressor labii maxillaris;* **ECR** *Extensor carpi radialis;* **ECU** *Extensor carpi ulnaris;* **EDC** *Extensor digitorum communis;* **EDLat** *Extensor digitorum lateralis;* **EDLon** *Extensor digitorum longus;* **ExAbO** *External abdominal oblique;* **FCR** *Flexor carpi radialis;* **FCU** *Flexor carpi ulnaris;* **FDP** *Flexor digitorum profundus;* **FDS** *Flexor digitorum superficialis;* **Front** *Frontalis;* **GasLa** *Gastrocnemius, lateral head;* **GasMe** *Gastrocnemius, medial head;* **Glubi** *Gluteobiceps;* **GluMe** *Gluteus medius;* **Grac** *Gracilis;* **Ilioc** *Iliocostalis;* **Infra** *Infraspinatus;* **InDCe** *Intertransversarii dorsalis cervicis;* **InVCe** *Intertransversarii ventralis cervicis;* **LatDo** *Latissimus dorsi;* **LeNas** *Levator nasolabialis;* **LLaMx** *Levator labii maxillaris*; **LonAt** *Longissimus atlantis;* **LonCa** *Longissimus capitis;* **LonCe** *Longissimus cervicis;* **Longi** *Longissimus*; **Mass** *Masseter;* **Ment** *Mentalis;* **Myloh** *Mylohyoid;* **NuLig** *Nuchal ligament;* **OCCau** *Obliquus capitis caudalis;* **OCCra** *Obliquus capitis cranialis;* **Omohy** *Omohyoid;* **OrOc** *Orbicularis oculi*; **OrOr** *Orbicularis oris;* **PecAs** *Pectoralis ascendens;* **PecDe** *Pectoralis descendens;* **PecTr** *Pectoralis transversus;* **PerLo** *Peroneus longus;* **PerTe** *Peroneus tertius;* **Pop** *Popliteus;* **RecAb** *Rectus abdominis;* **RecFe** *Rectus femoris;* **ScalV** *Scalenus ventralis;* **SemCa** *Semispinalis capitis;* **SerDC** *Serratus dorsalis caudalis;* **SerVC** *Serratus ventralis cervicis;* **SerVT** *Serratus ventralis thoracis;* **Stcph** *Sternocephalicus;* **Stend** *Semitendinosus;* **Sthy** *Sternohyoid;* **Supra** *Supraspinatus;* **SusLi** *Suspensory ligament;* **Temp** *Temporalis;* **TenFL** *Tensor fasciae latae;* **TibCr** *Tibialis cranialis;* **Trap** *Trapezius;* **TriLa** *Triceps brachii, lateral head;* **TriLo** *Triceps brachii, long head;* **UlLat** *Ulnaris lateralis;* **VasLa** *Vastus lateralis;* **VasMe** *Vastus medialis;* **Zyg** *Zygomaticus.*

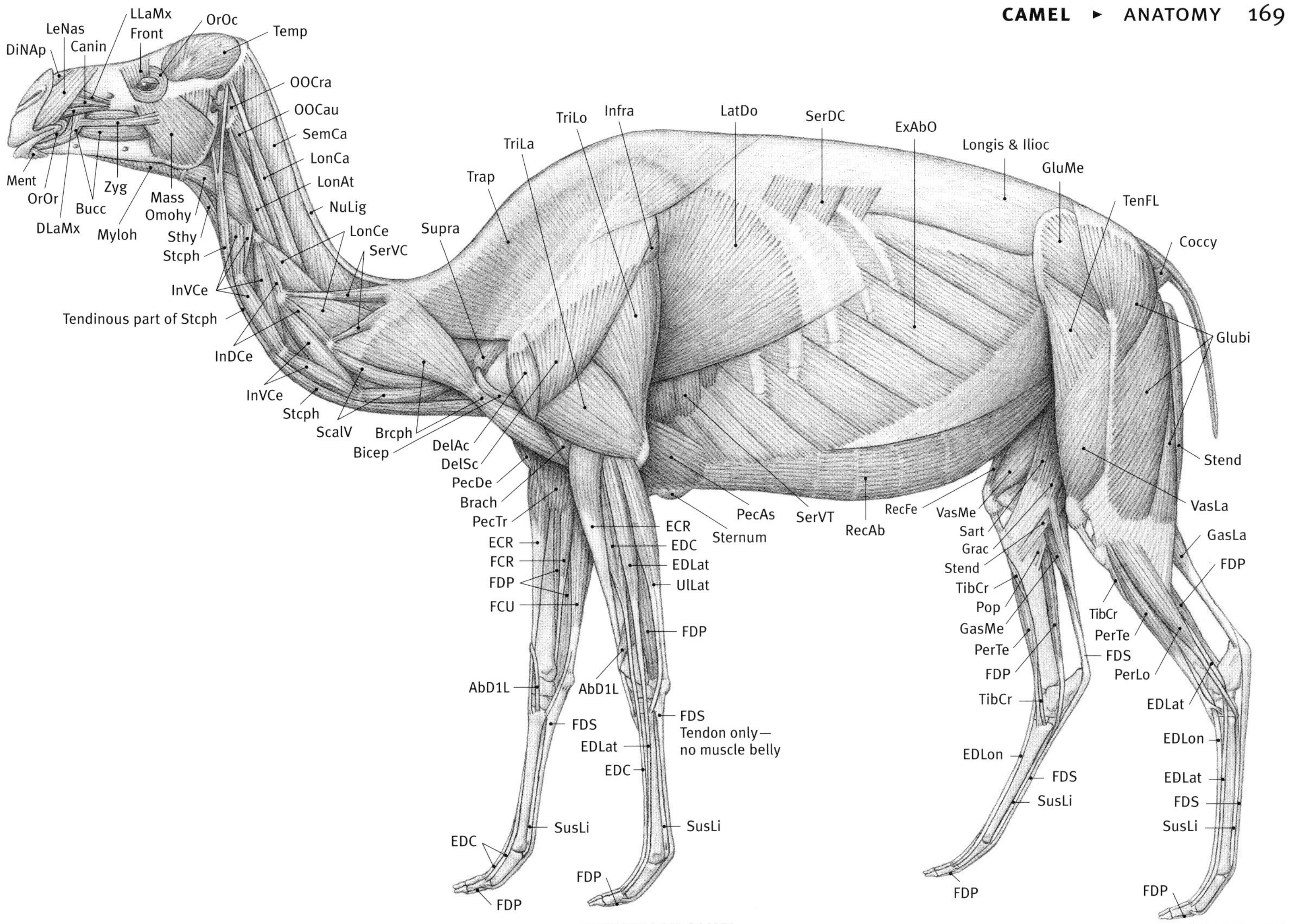

DROMEDARY CAMEL

(AFTER SMUTS)

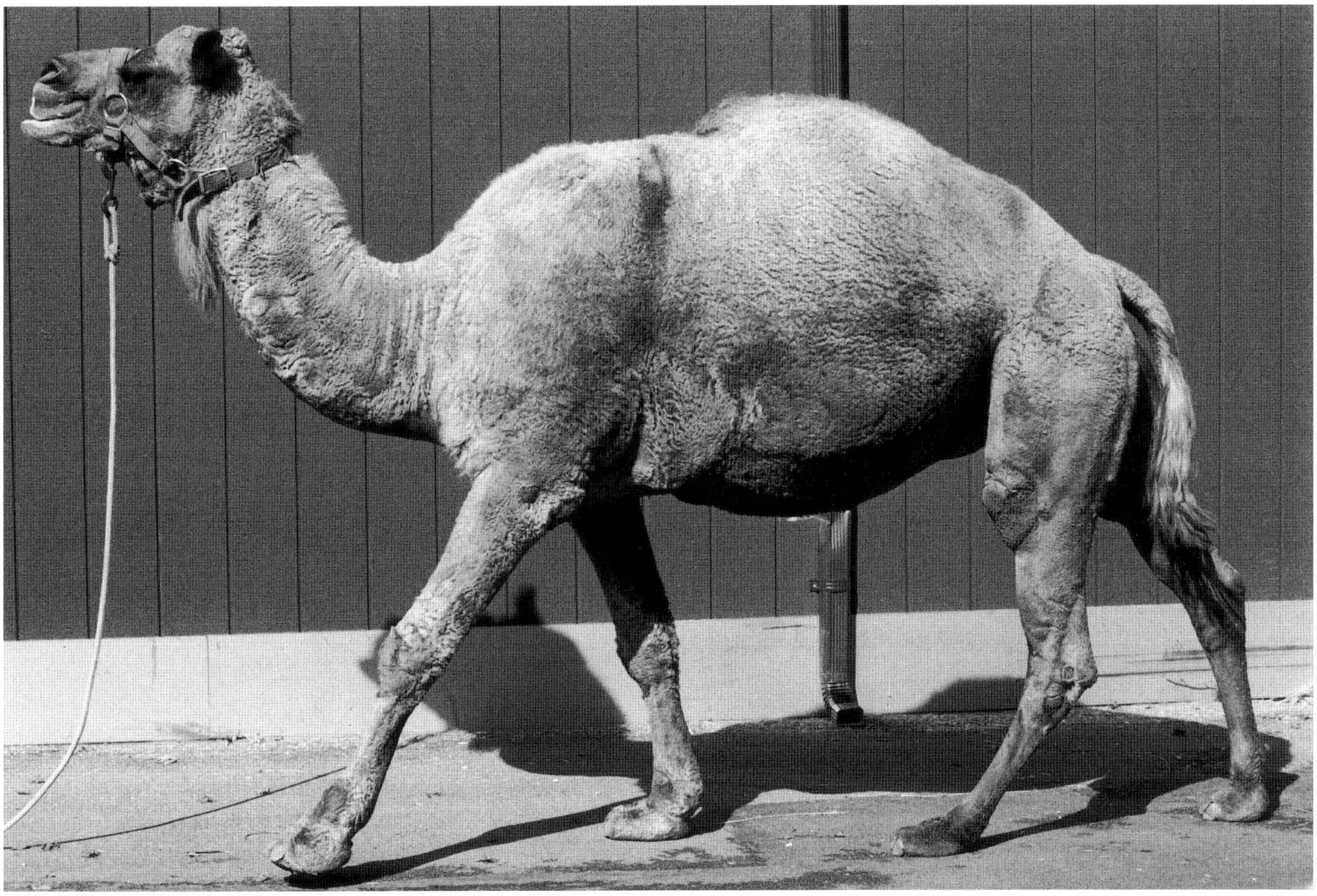

DROMEDARY CAMEL (FEMALE)

Camelus dromedarius

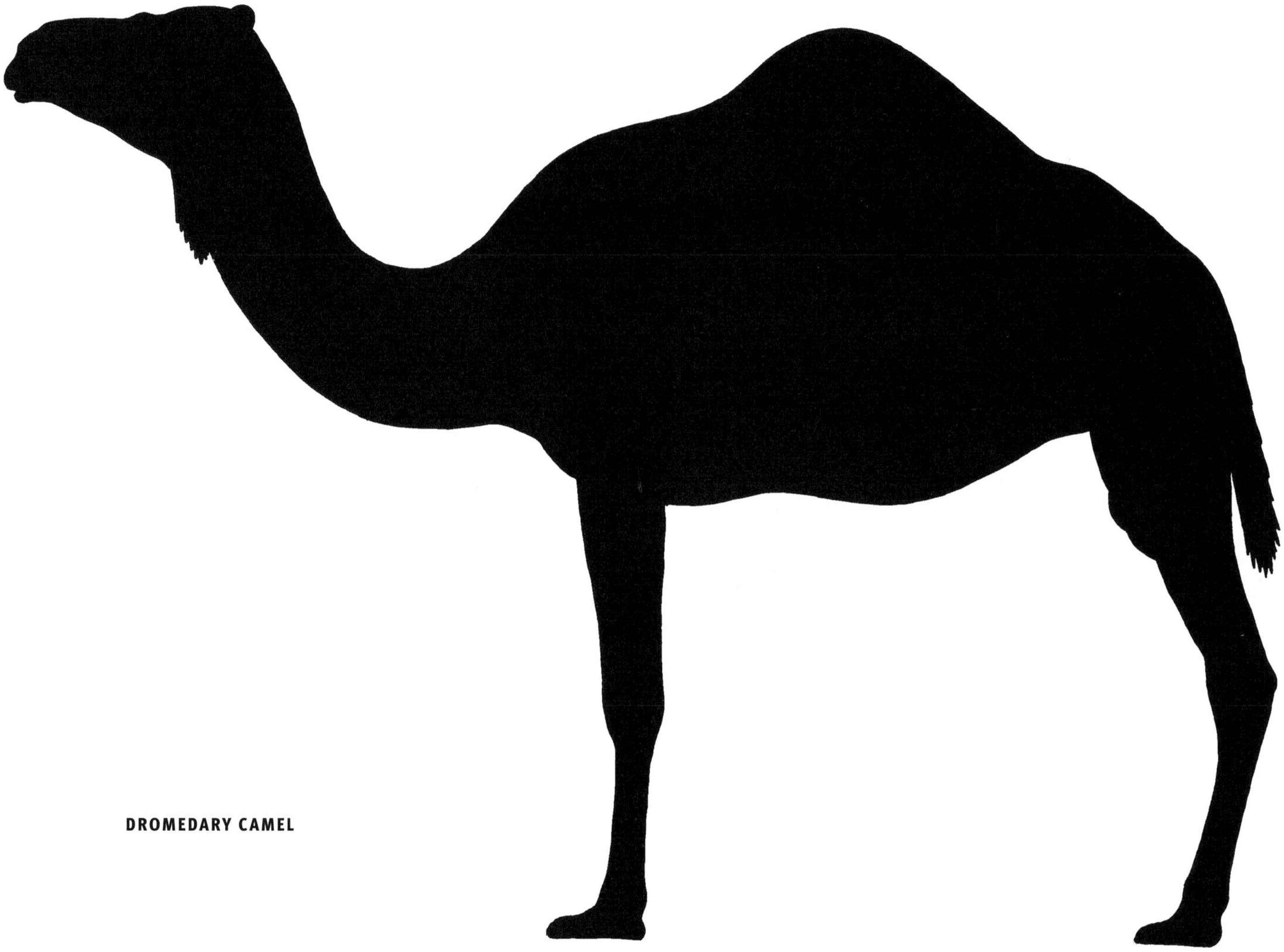

DROMEDARY CAMEL

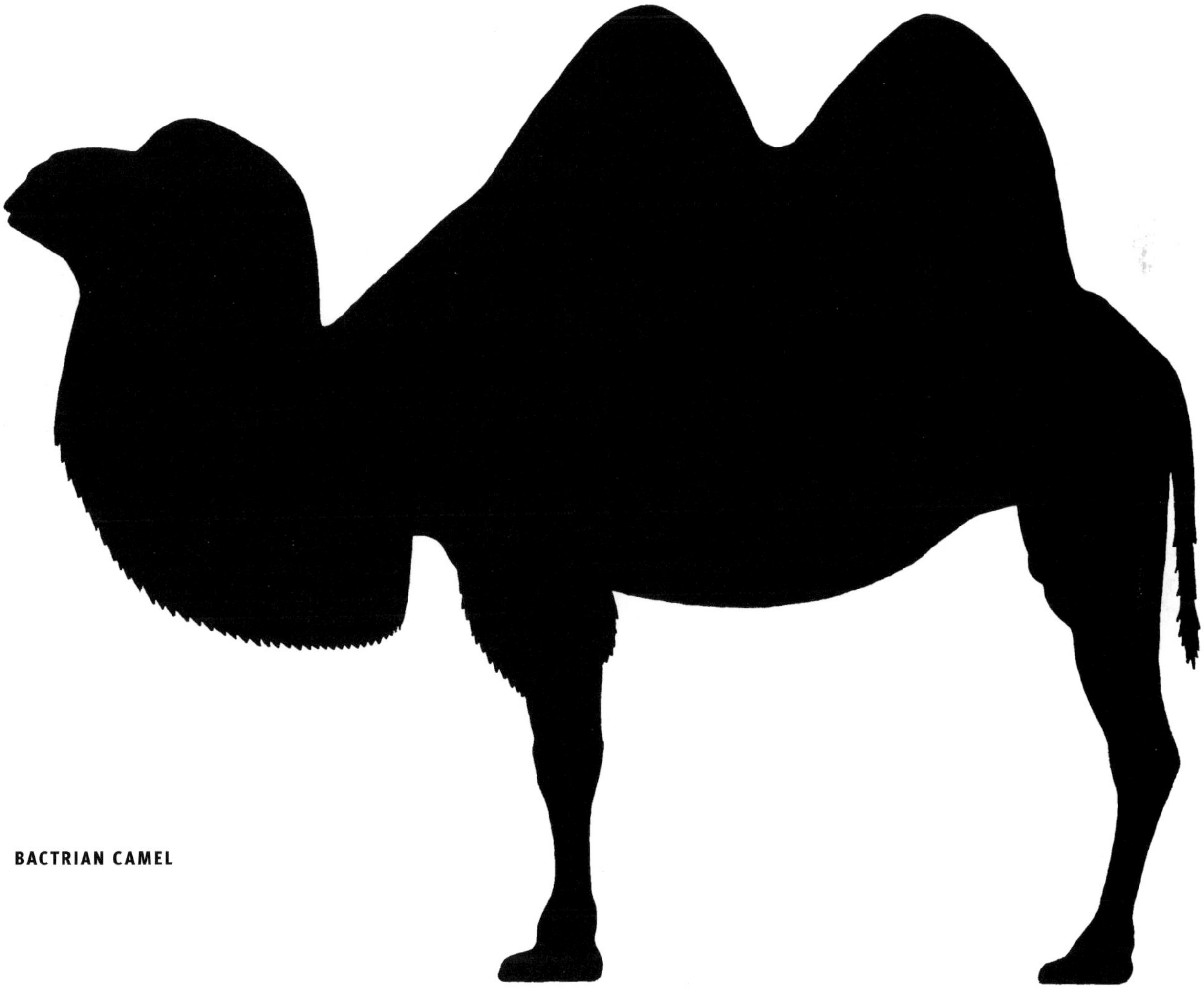

BACTRIAN CAMEL

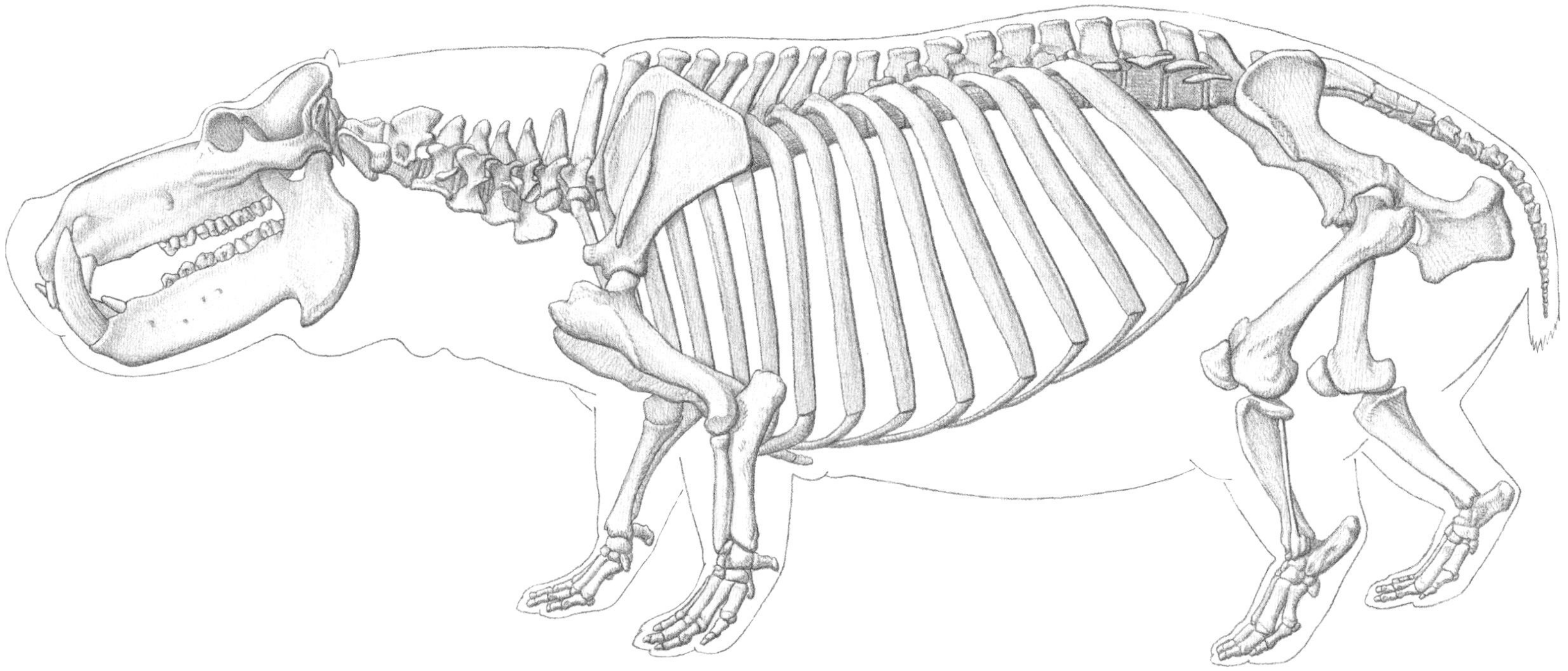

(AFTER BLAINVILLE; SKULL FROM SPECIMEN)

Hippopotamus characteristics: Large tusk-like incisors and canines, especially inner pair of lower incisors. Lower canines much larger than upper canines. Wide snout; nostrils on top of snout. Nostrils and ears can be closed under water. Huge mouth opens very wide to display tusks. Rear of lower jaw projects downward. Four digits per limb; all support weight. Nail-like hoofs on toes. Massive, barrel-shaped body; short, stocky legs. Belly close to ground. Hairless. Thick layer of body fat. Skin glands produce oily reddish-pink secretions ("blood sweat"). Short tail. Good swimmer and diver.

AbD1L *Abductor digiti I longus;* **AbDi5** *Abductor digiti V;* **Anc** *Anconeus;* **Bicep** *Biceps brachii;* **Brach** *Brachialis;* **Brcph** *Brachiocephalicus;* **Bucc** *Buccinator;* **Canin** *Caninus;* **Clmas** *Cleidomastoid;* **ClOcc** *Cleido-occipitalis;* **DelAc** *Deltoid, acromial portion*; **DelSc** *Deltoid, scapular portion;* **Digas** *Digastric;* **DLaMn** *Depressor labii mandibularis;* **ECR** *Extensor carpi radialis;* **EDBr** *Extensor digitorum brevis;* **EDC** *Extensor digitorum communis;* **EDLat** *Extensor digitorum lateralis;* **EDLon** *Extensor digitorum longus;* **ExAbO** *External abdominal oblique;* **FCR** *Flexor carpi radialis;* **FCU** *Flexor carpi ulnaris;* **FDP** *Flexor digitorum profundus;* **FDS** *Flexor digitorum superficialis;* **GasLa** *Gastrocnemius, lateral head;* **GasMe** *Gastrocnemius, medial head;* **Glubi** *Gluteobiceps;* **GluMe** *Gluteus medius;* **Ilioc** *Iliocostalis;* **Infra** *Infraspinatus;* **LatDo** *Latissimus dorsi;* **LeNas** *Levator nasolabialis;* **LLaMx** *Levator labii maxillaris;* **Longi** *Longissimus;* **Mass** *Masseter;* **Omotr** *Omotransversarius;* **OrOc** *Orbicularis oculi;* **OrOr** *Orbicularis oris;* **PecAs** *Pectoralis ascendens;* **PecSu** *Pectoralis superficialis;* **PerLo** *Peroneus longus;* **PerTe** *Peroneus tertius;* **Pop** *Popliteus;* **RAOL** *Retractor anguli oculi lateralis;* **RecAb** *Rectus abdominis;* **RecFe** *Rectus femoris;* **SerDC** *Serratus dorsalis caudalis;* **SerVT** *Serratus ventralis thoracis;* **Smemb** *Semimembranosus;* **Stend** *Semitendinosus;* **Stmas** *Sternomastoid;* **Stthh** *Sternothyrohyoid;* **Subcl** *Subclavius;* **Supra** *Supraspinatus;* **Temp** *Temporalis;* **TenFL** *Tensor fasciae latae;* **TibCr** *Tibialis cranialis;* **Trap** *Trapezius;* **TriLa** *Triceps brachii, lateral head;* **TriLo** *Triceps brachii, long head;* **UlLat** *Ulnaris lateralis;* **VasLa** *Vastus lateralis;* **Zyg** *Zygomaticus.*

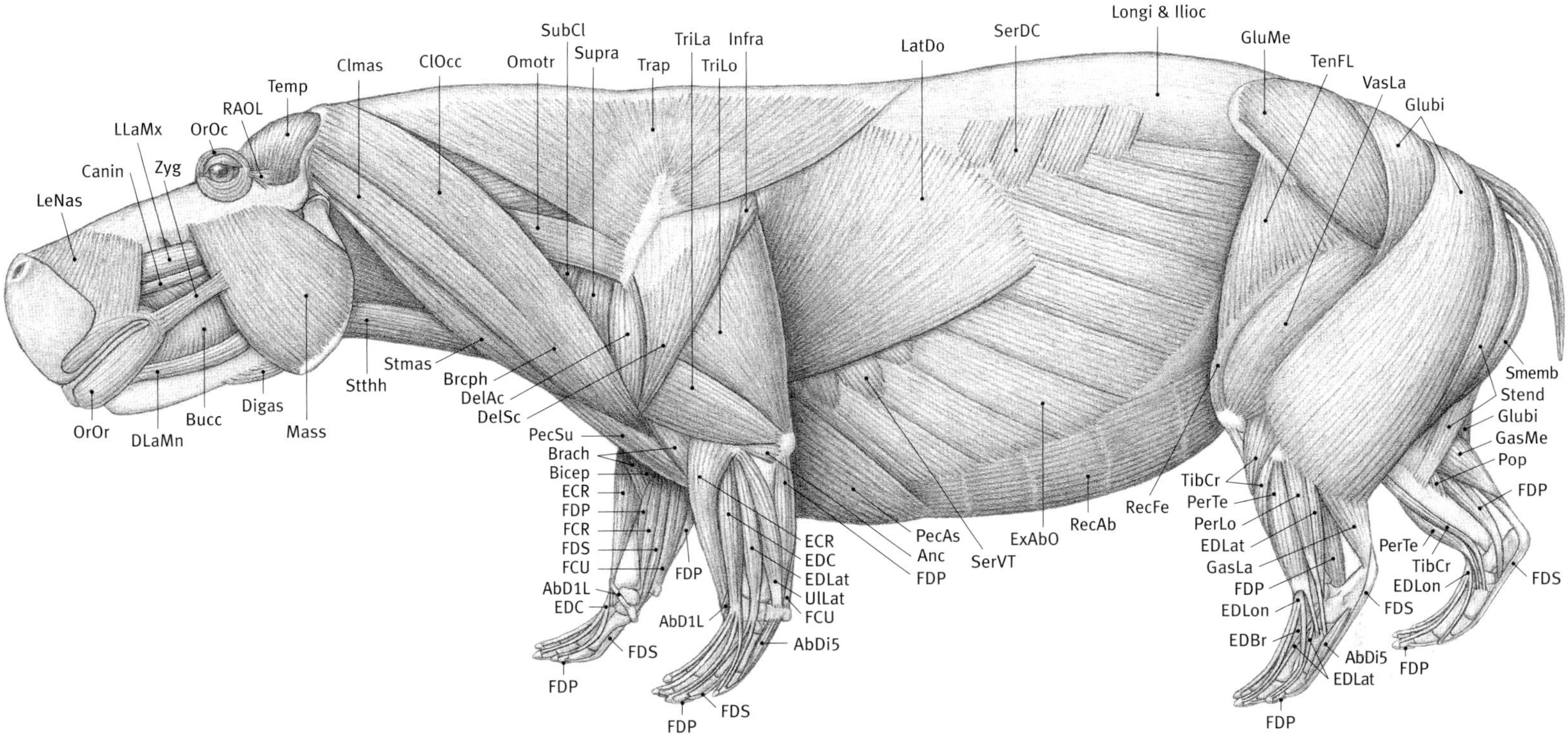

(AFTER CUVIER)

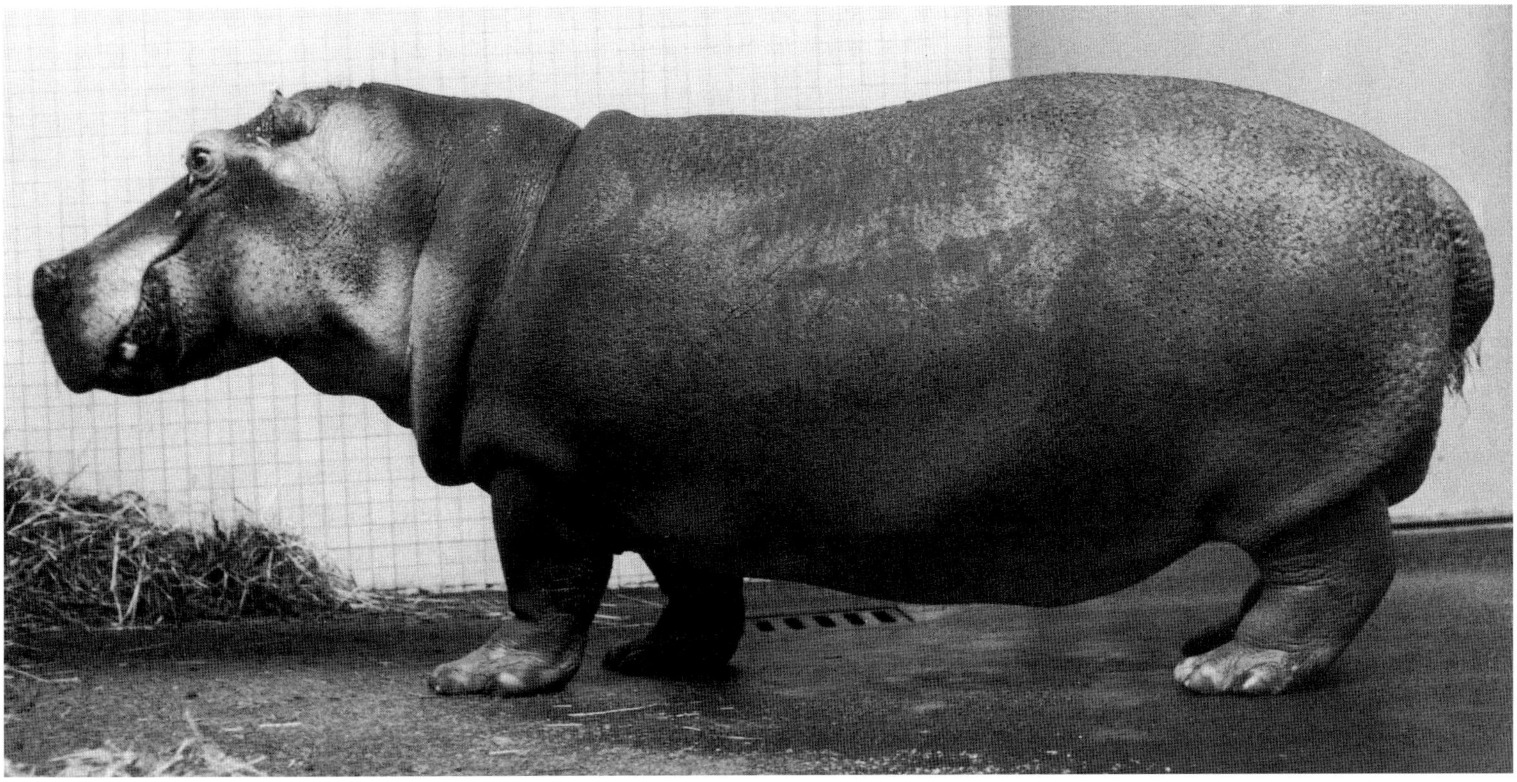

Hippopotamus amphibius

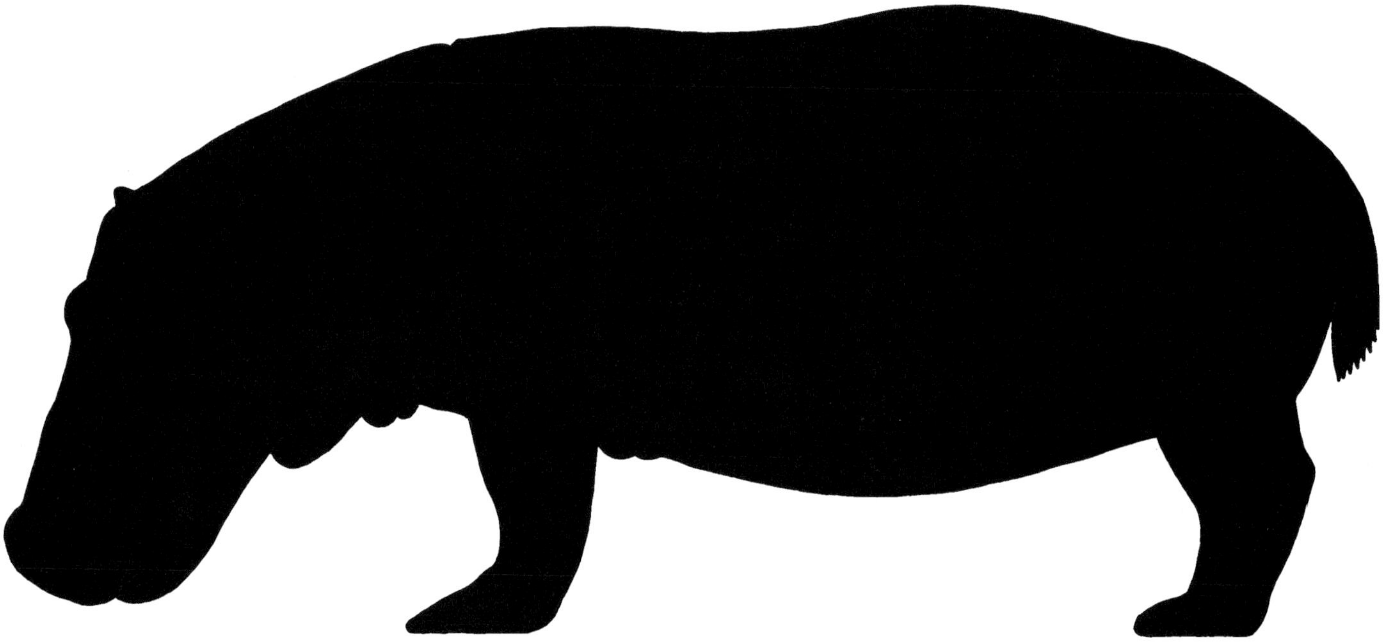

HIPPOPOTAMUS

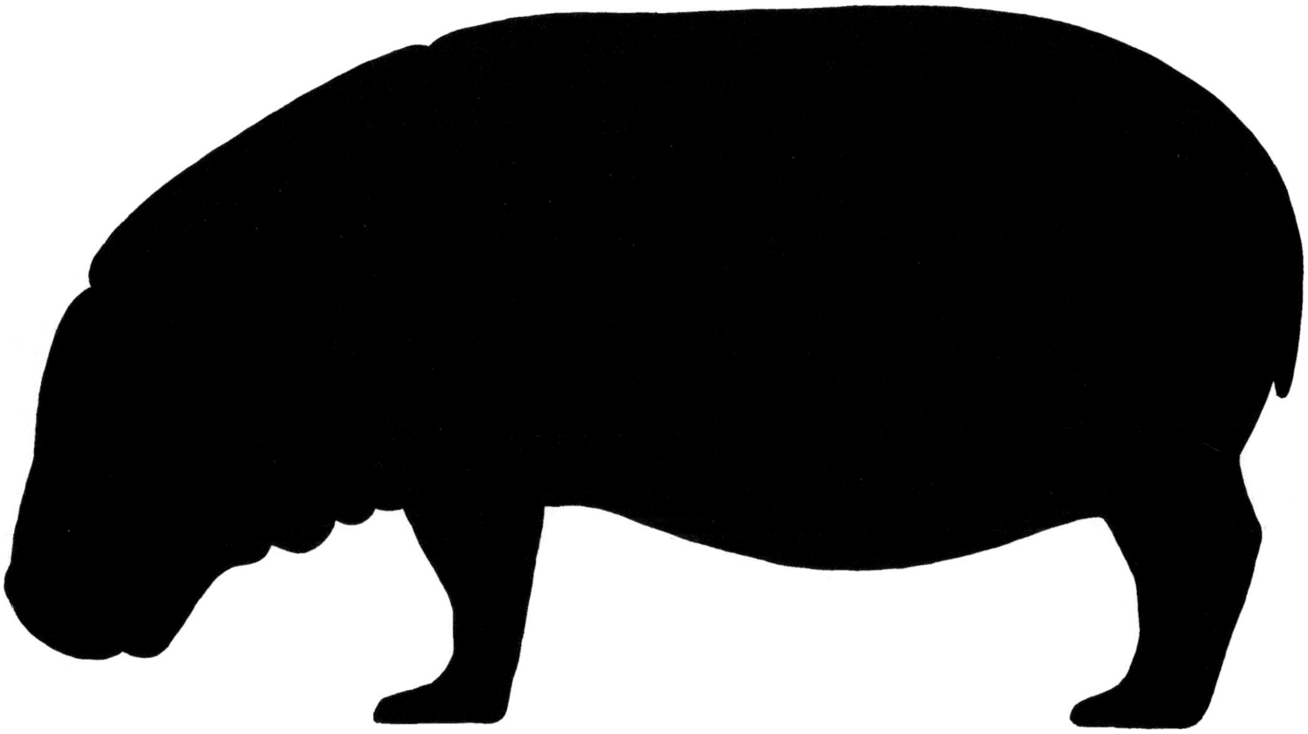

PYGMY HIPPOPOTAMUS

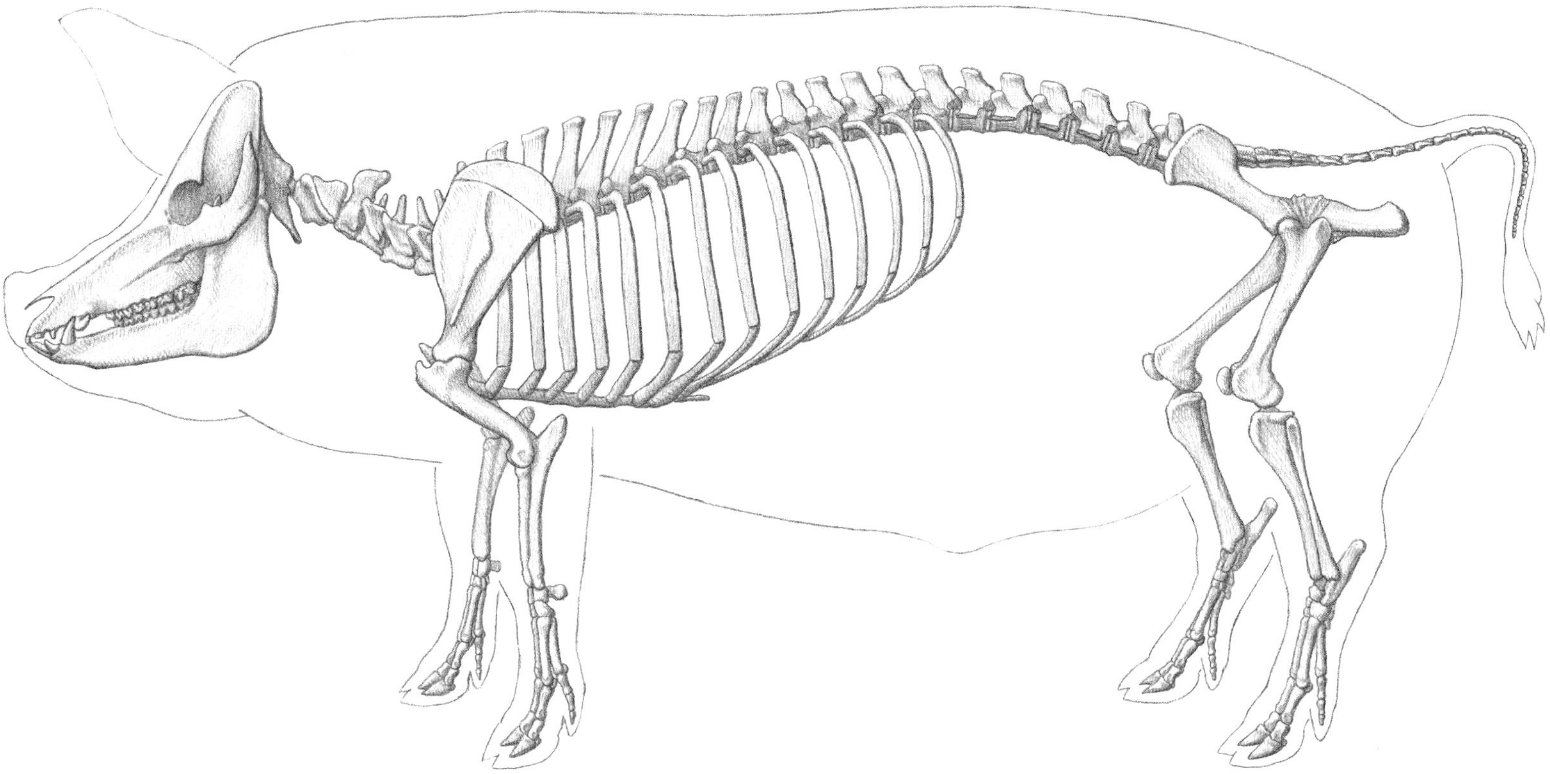

(AFTER ELLENBERGER; POPESCO)

Domestic pig characteristics: Domestic pig derived from European wild boar. Snout movable—specialized for digging roots and tubers from soil. Nostrils located at end of flattened nose. Tusk-like upper canines (larger in males) grow upward and outward. Lower canines grow upward and backward to fit against larger upper canines. Upper and lower canines rub against each other, usually producing sharp edges. Elongated skull has sloping profile. Long, pointed head, small eyes, long ears; short neck. Four digits per limb, only two middle digits functional; walks on toes. Hoofs on toes (reduced side toes have small hoofs). Domestic pig has stocky body with thick fat layer and curly tail; often sparsely haired. Wild species have full fur coat, less fat, and straight tail.

AbD1L *Abductor digiti I longus;* **AbDi5** *Abductor digiti V;* **Brach** *Brachialis;* **Brcph** *Brachiocephalicus;* **Bucc** *Buccinator;* **Canin** *Caninus;* **Clmas** *Cleidomastoid;* **ClOcc** *Cleido-occipitalis;* **Coccy** *Coccygeus;* **Delt** *Deltoid;* **DLaMn** *Depressor labii mandibularis;* **DLaMx** *Depressor labii maxillaris;* **ECR** *Extensor carpi radialis;* **ED1L** *Extensor digiti I longus;* **EDBr** *Extensor digitorum brevis;* **EDC** *Extensor digitorum communis;* **EDLat** *Extensor digitorum lateralis;* **EDLon** *Extensor digitorum longus;* **ExAbO** *External abdominal oblique;* **FDP** *Flexor digitorum profundus;* **FDS** *Flexor digitorum superficialis;* **GasLa** *Gastrocnemius, lateral head;* **GasMe** *Gastrocnemius, medial head;* **Glubi** *Gluteobiceps;* **GluMe** *Gluteus medius;* **Ilioc** *Iliocostalis;* **Infra** *Infraspinatus;* **LAOM** *Levator anguli oculi medialis;* **LatDo** *Latissimus dorsi;* **LeNas** *Levator nasolabialis;* **LLaMx** *Levator labii maxillaris;* **Longi** *Longissimus;* **Malar** *Malaris;* **Mass** *Masseter;* **Ment** *Mentalis;* **Omohy** *Omohyoid;* **Omotr** *Omotransversarius;* **OrOc** *Orbicularis oculi;* **OrOr** *Orbicularis oris;* **PecAs** *Pectoralis ascendens;* **PerLo** *Peroneus longus;* **PerTe** *Peroneus tertius;* **RecAb** *Rectus abdominis;* **RecFe** *Rectus femoris;* **SerDC** *Serratus dorsalis caudalis;* **SerVT** *Serratus ventralis thoracis;* **Smemb** *Semimembranosus;* **Sol** *Soleus;* **Stcph** *Sternocephalicus;* **Stend** *Semitendinosus;* **Sthy** *Sternohyoid;* **Subcl** *Subclavius;* **Supra** *Supraspinatus;* **Temp** *Temporalis;* **TenFA** *Tensor fasciae antibrachii;* **TenFL** *Tensor fasciae latae; Tibialis cranialis; Trapezius; Triceps brachii, lateral head;* **TriLo** *Triceps brachii, long head;* **UlLat** *Ulnaris lateralis;* **VasLa** *Vastus lateralis;* **Zyg** *Zygomaticus.*

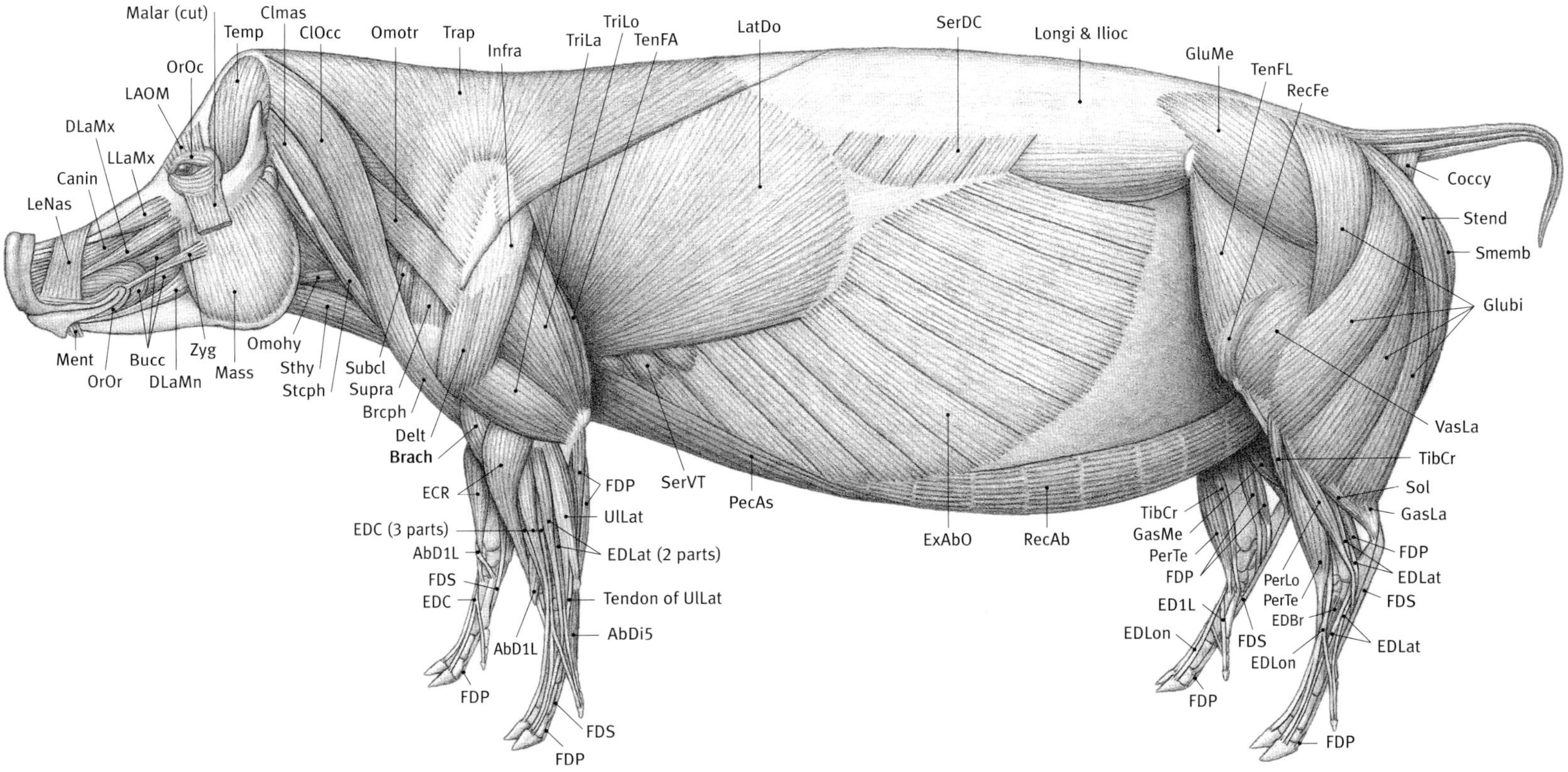

(AFTER ELLENBERGER; POPESCO)

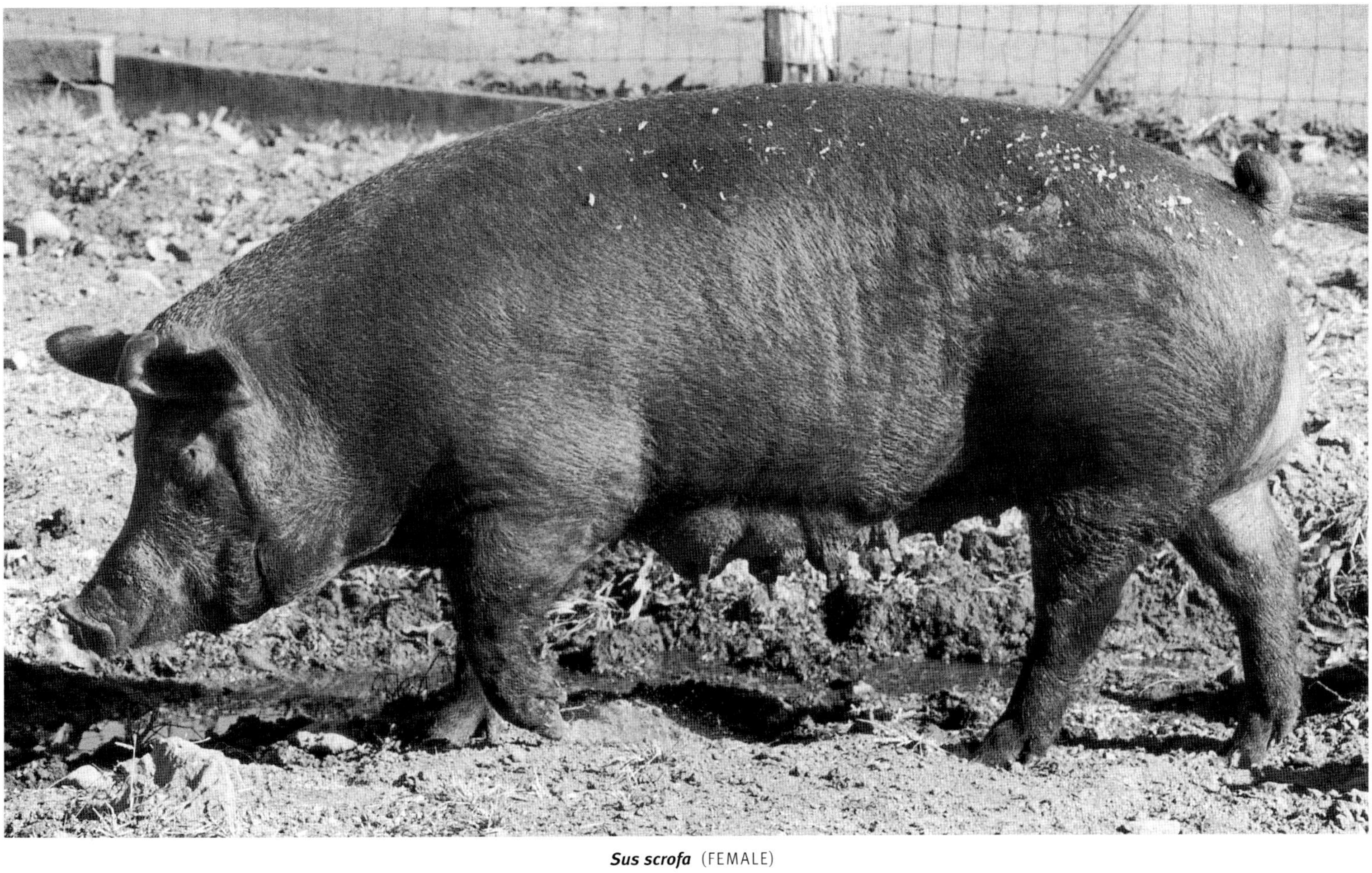

Sus scrofa (FEMALE)

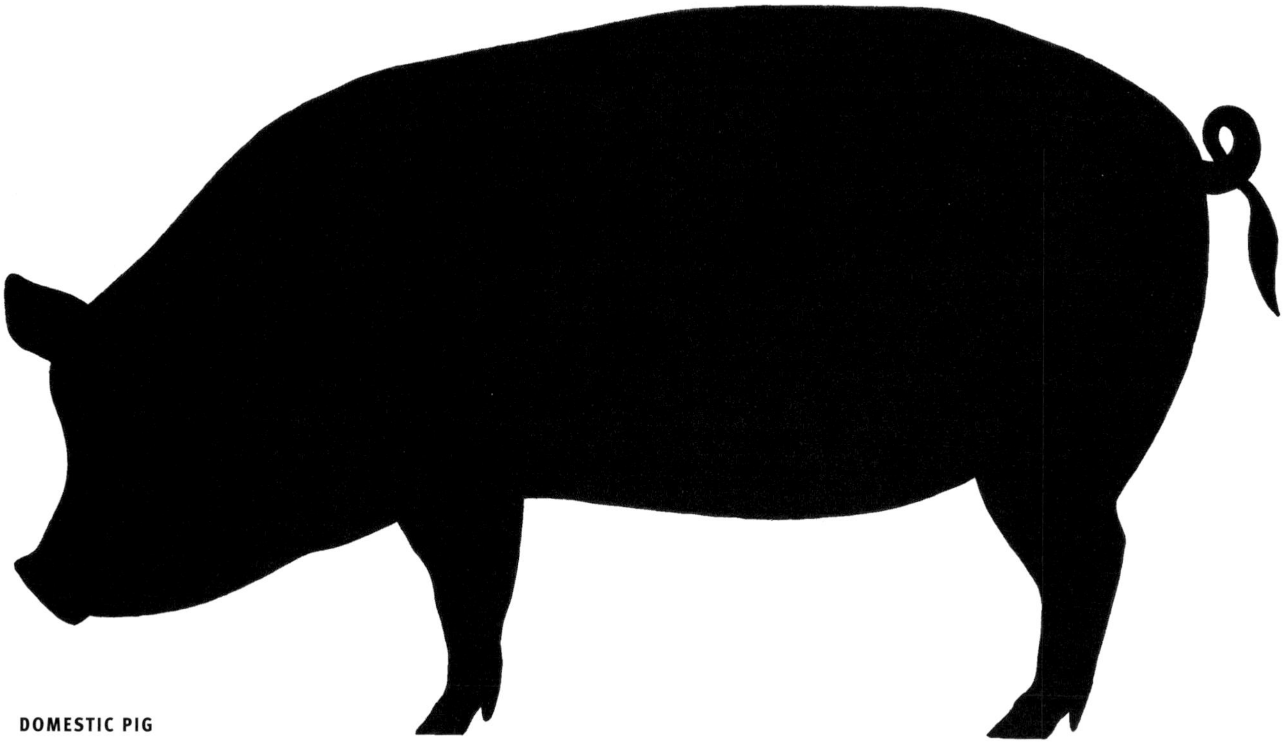

DOMESTIC PIG

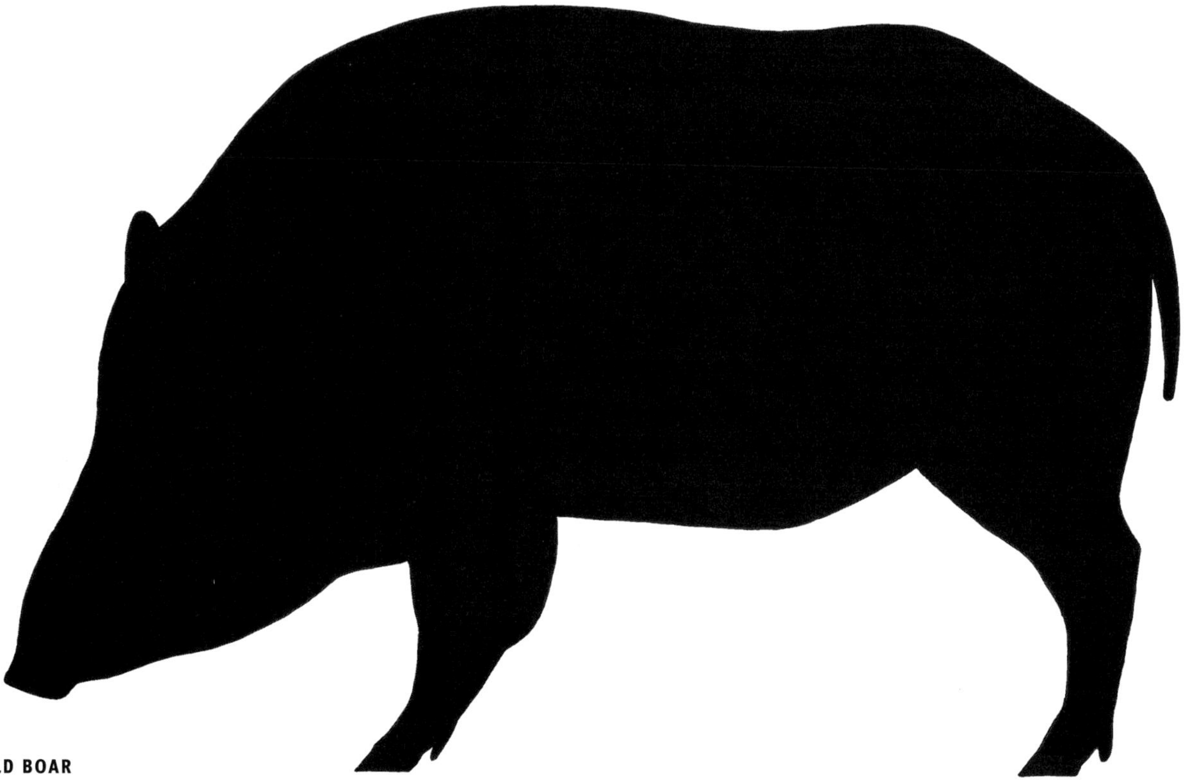

WILD BOAR

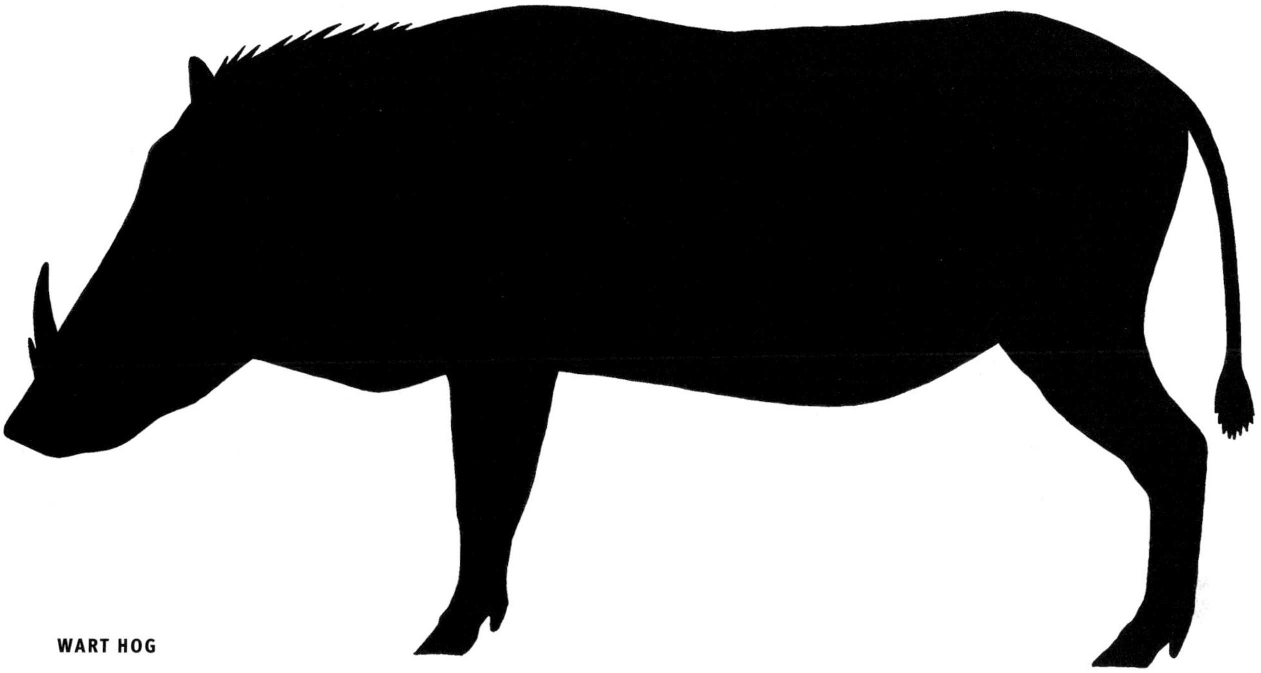

WART HOG

PECCARY

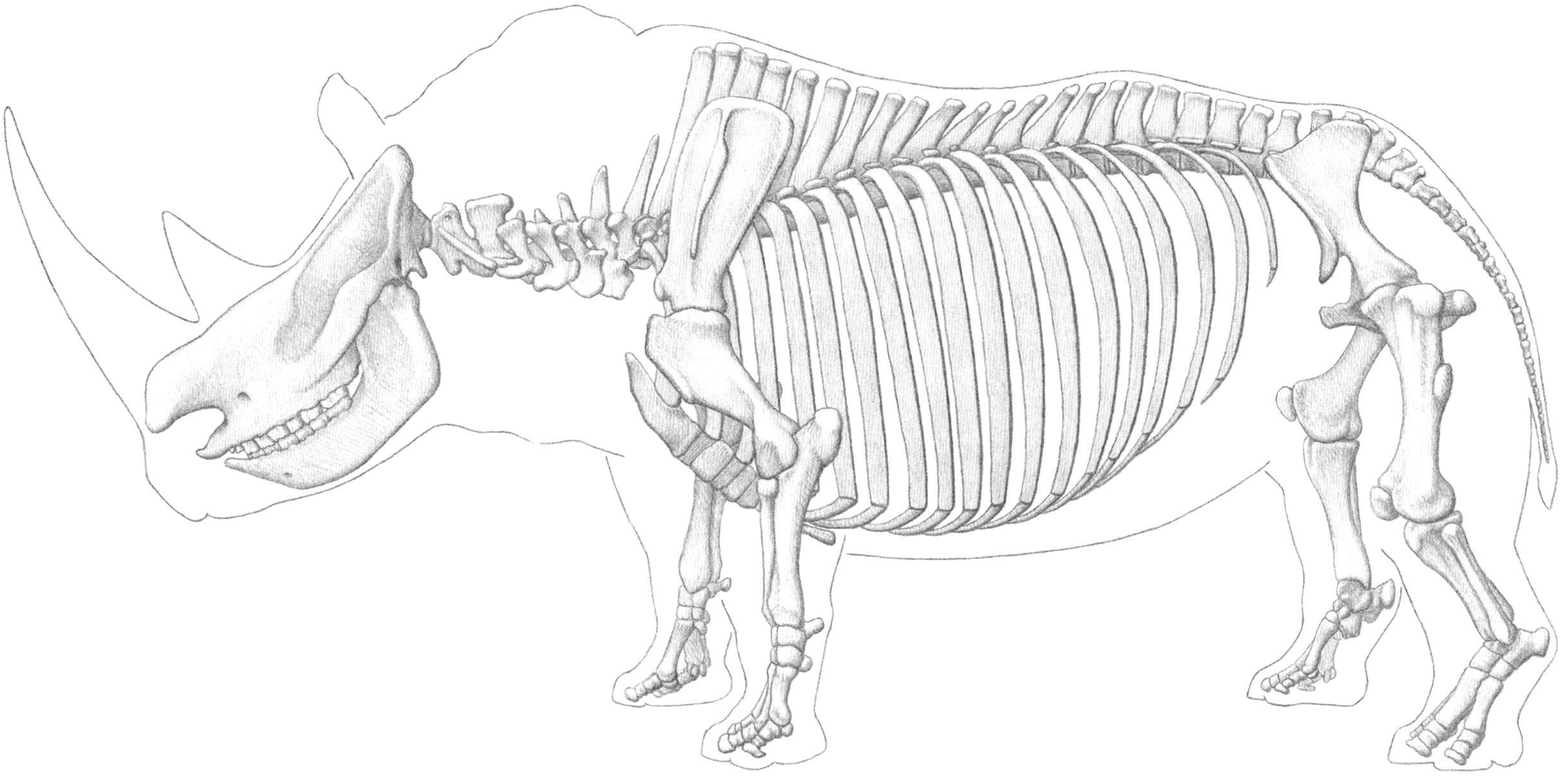

WHITE RHINOCEROS
Ceratotherium simum

(FROM SPECIMEN PHOTO)

Rhinoceros characteristics: One or two conical, tapering "horns" made up of cemented hair-like fibers (with no bony core) present on snout. Nasal bones project past front of mouth bones; nasal bones are thickened to support horn. Forehead concave (rear end of skull rises up). Large temporal area on skull (behind orbit). Well-developed occipital crest at rear end of skull. Small eyes, erect ears. Upper lip prehensile in black and Indian rhinos—squared and broad in white rhino. Short neck; massive body with broad chest. Short, stocky, pillar-like limbs to support heavy body. Three digits per limb, hoofs on toes. Walks on toes. Femur has projecting third trochanter on outer side of shaft for attachment of the gluteus superficialis muscle. Tufted tail. Thick skin may develop prominent folds; in Indian rhino, folds always present and specific in location. White rhino has prominent shoulder hump. In same group as horses and tapirs.

AbD1L *Abductor digiti I longus;* **BiFemLH** *Biceps femoris, long head;* **BiFemSH** *Biceps femoris, short head;* **Brach** *Brachialis;* **Brcph** *Brachiocephalicus;* **Brrad** *Brachioradialis;* **Bucc** *Buccinator;* **Canin** *Caninus;* **Cutan** *Cutaneous muscle;* **Delt** *Deltoid;* **ECR** *Extensor carpi radialis;* **EDBr** *Extensor digitorum brevis;* **EDC** *Extensor digitorum communis;* **EDLat** *Extensor digitorum lateralis;* **EDLon** *Extensor digitorum longus;* **ExAbO** *External abdominal oblique;* **FCR** *Flexor carpi radialis;* **FCU** *Flexor carpi ulnaris;* **FDP** *Flexor digitorum profundus;* **FDS** *Flexor digitorum superficialis;* **GasLa** *Gastrocnemius, lateral head;* **GasMe** *Gastrocnemius, medial head;* **GluMe** *Gluteus medius;* **GluSu** *Gluteus superficialis;* **Ilioc** *Iliocostalis;* **Infra** *Infraspinatus;* **Inter** *Interossei;* **LAOM** *Levator anguli oculi medialis;* **LatDo** *Latissimus dorsi;* **LeNas** *Levator nasolabialis;* **LLaMx** *Levator labii maxillaris;* **Longi** *Longissimus;* **Malar** *Malaris;* **Mass** *Masseter;* **Omotr** *Omotransversarius;* **OrOc** *Orbicularis oculi;* **OrOr** *Orbicularis oris;* **PecAs** *Pectoralis ascendens;* **PecSu** *Pectoralis superficialis;* **PerLo** *Peroneus longus;* **PerTe** *Peroneus tertius;* **Pop** *Popliteus;* **SerVC** *Serratus ventralis cervicis;* **SerVT** *Serratus ventralis thoracis;* **Smemb** *Semimembranosus;* **Splen** *Splenius;* **Stend** *Semitendinosus;* **Sthy** *Sternohyoid;* **Stman** *Sternomandibularis;* **Temp** *Temporalis;* **TenFL** *Tensor fasciae latae;* **TibCr** *Tibialis cranialis;* **Trap** *Trapezius;* **TriLa** *Triceps brachii, lateral head;* **TriLo** *Triceps brachii, long head;* **UlLat** *Ulnaris lateralis;* **VasLa** *Vastus lateralis;* **Zyg** *Zygomaticus.*

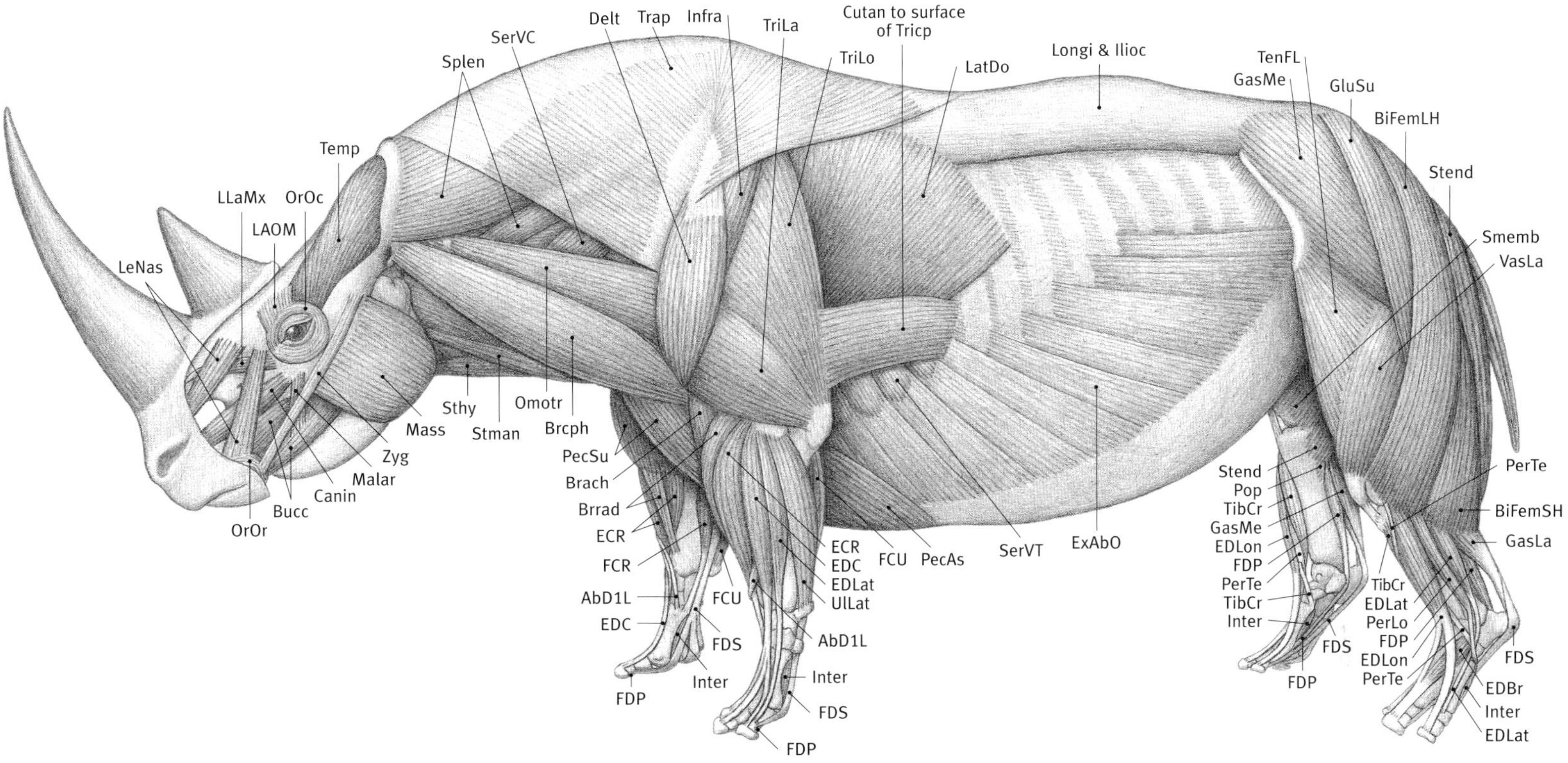

(AFTER BEDDARD; KINGDON)

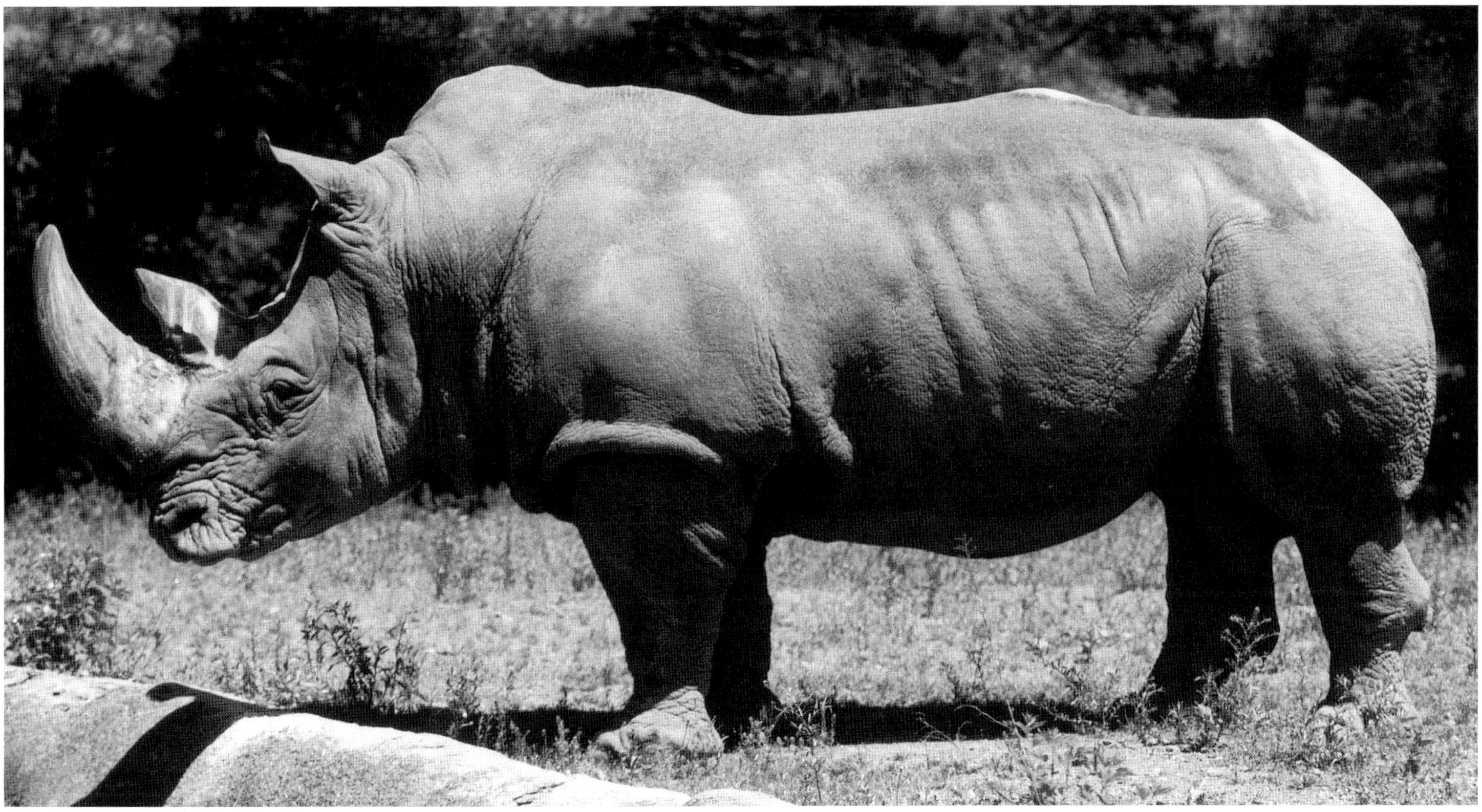

WHITE RHINOCEROS (MALE)

Ceratotherium simum

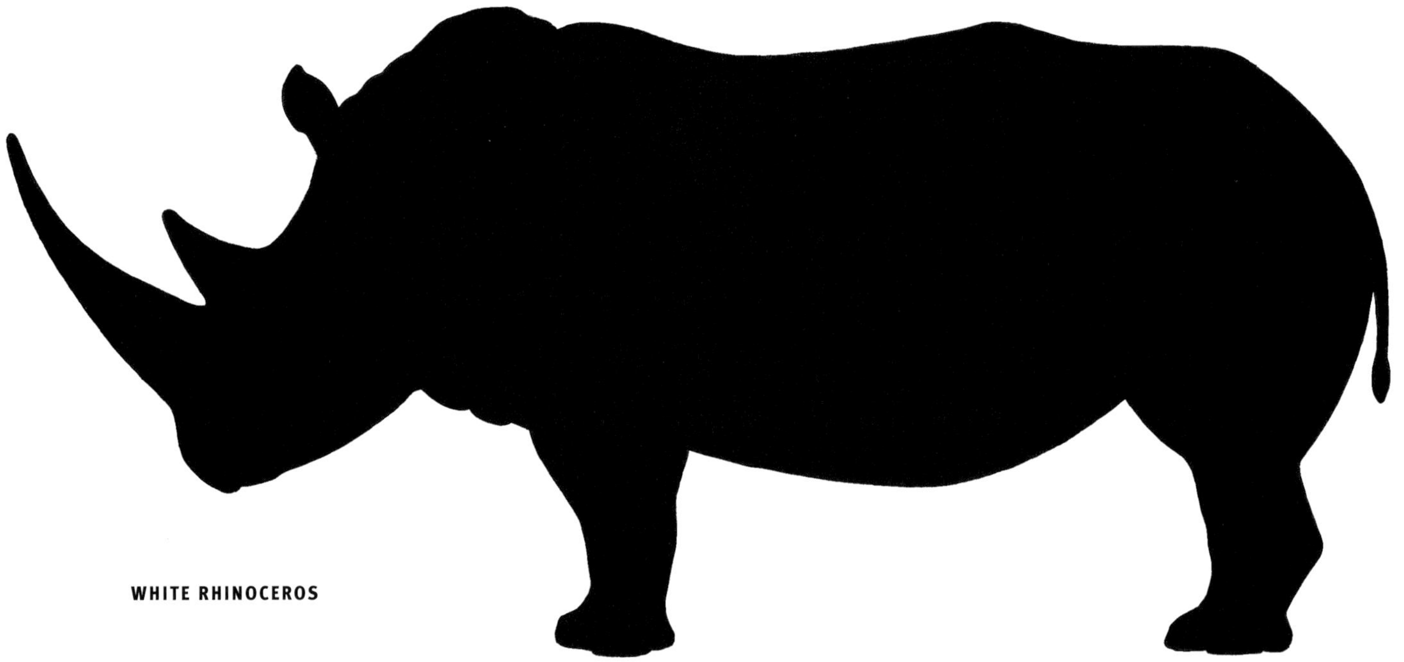

WHITE RHINOCEROS

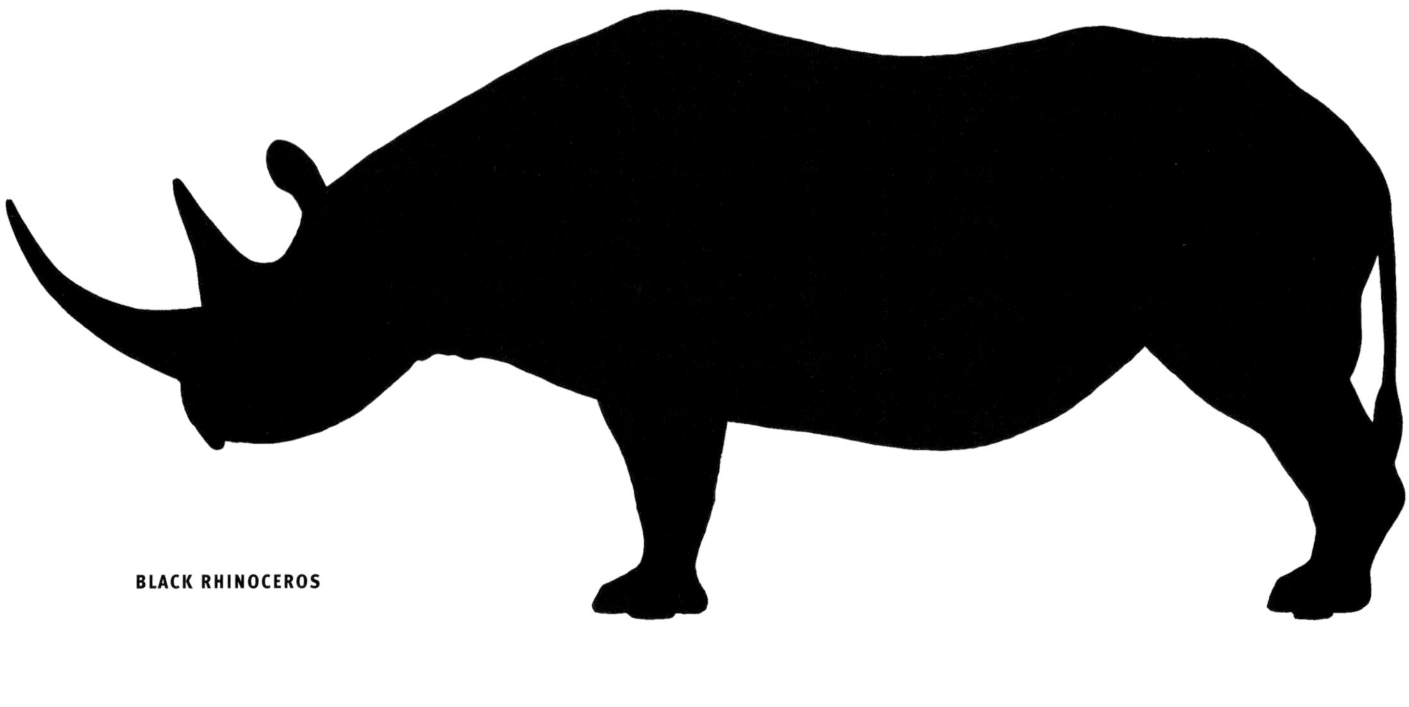

BLACK RHINOCEROS

INDIAN RHINOCEROS

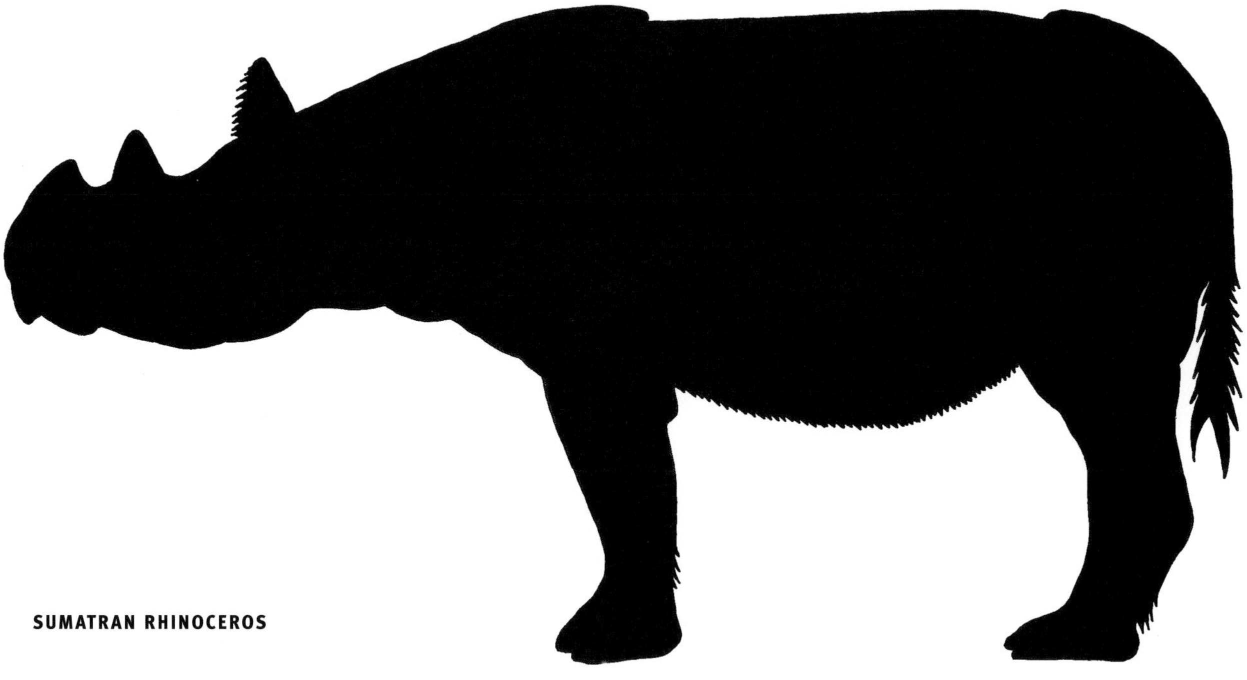

SUMATRAN RHINOCEROS

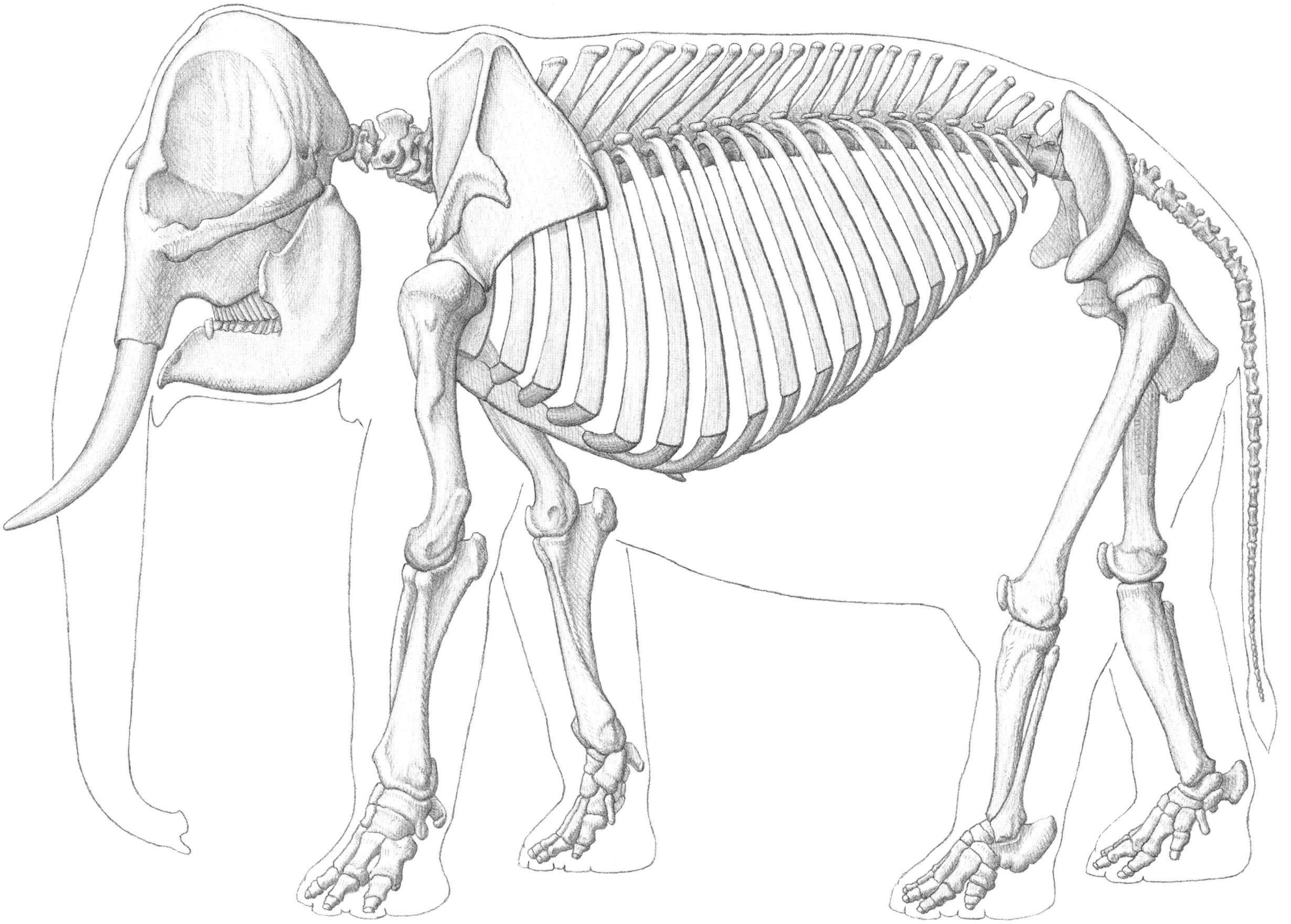

(AFTER BLAINVILLE)

Indian elephant characteristics: Largest land animal. Middle of back profile convex/high (concave/low in African). Nose extends into long, flexible, muscular trunk with nostrils and two prehensile finger-like projections at tip (one projection in African). Large skull; short nasal bones located high on skull (for attachment of trunk). Brain surrounded by thick, airy bone. Two rounded prominences on top of head (single prominence in African). Upper incisors elongated into continuously growing tusks, usually lacking in female (present in African male and female). Very large ears (considerably larger in African). Short neck—cervical vertebrae compressed front to back. Rib cage extends to pelvis. Thick, pillar-like columnar limbs (bones in almost vertical straight line) and shoulder and hip sockets face downward, all to support massive body weight. Short feet. All feet have five digits—some inner and outer toes may be reduced and without hoofs. Both front and rear feet have an extra small, elongated bone (prepollex in front and prehallux in rear) just to the inside of the first digit. Five hoofs on front foot (four or five in African). Four or five hoofs on hind foot (three, four, or five in African). Thick elastic pad on sole of foot. Foot in life somewhat cylindrical or conical. When lying on belly, knee touches ground (femur directed downward); lower leg continues straight back. Long tail has wispy tuft of coarse hair.

AbD1L *Abductor digiti I longus;* **AbDi5** *Abductor digiti V;* **Anc** *Anconeus;* **Bicep** *Biceps brachii;* **BiFem** *Biceps femoris;* **Brach** *Brachialis;* **Brcph** *Brachiocephalicus;* **Brrad** *Brachioradialis;* **Bucc** *Buccinator;* **BuccPR** *Buccinator, pars rimana (depressor proboscidis);* **BuccPS** *Buccinator, pars supra-labialis;* **Corac** *Coracobrachialis;* **DelAc** *Deltoid, acromial portion;* **DelSc** *Deltoid, scapular portion;* **Digas** *Digastric;* **DLaMn** *Depressor labii mandibularis;* **ECR** *Extensor carpi radialis;* **ECU** *Extensor carpi ulnaris;* **ED1&2** *Extensor digiti I & II;* **EDBr** *Extensor digitorum brevis;* **EDC** *Extensor digitorum communis;* **EDLat** *Extensor digitorum lateralis;* **EDLon** *Extensor digitorum longus;* **ExAbO** *External abdominal oblique;* **FCR** *Flexor carpi radialis;* **FCU** *Flexor carpi ulnaris;* **FDP** *Flexor digitorum profundus;* **GasLa** *Gastrocnemius, lateral head;* **GasMe** *Gastrocnemius, medial head;* **Glubi** *Gluteobiceps;* **GluSu** *Gluteus superficialis;* **Grac** *Gracilis;* **Ilioc** *Iliocostalis;* **Infra** *Infraspinatus;* **LatDo** *Latissimus dorsi;* **LeNas** *Levator nasolabialis;* **LLaMx** *Levator labii maxillaris (levator proboscidis);* **Longi** *Longissimus;* **Mass** *Masseter;* **Nasal** *Nasalis;* **OccFr** *Occipito-frontalis;* **Omotr** *Omotransversarius;* **OrOc** *Orbicularis oculi;* **OrOr** *Orbicularis oris;* **PalLo** *Palmaris longus;* **PecAs** *Pectoralis ascendens;* **PerBr** *Peroneus brevis;* **PerLo** *Peroneus longus;* **Plant** *Plantaris;* **PosOr** *Post-orbicularis;* **PrOrD** *Pre-orbicularis dorsalis;* **PrOrV** *Pre-orbicularis ventralis;* **PrTer** *Pronator teres;* **RecAb** *Rectus abdominis;* **RecFe** *Rectus femoris;* **Rhom** *Rhomboid;* **Sol** *Soleus;* **Splen** *Splenius;* **Stend** *Semitendinosus;* **Sthy** *Sternohyoid;* **Stman** *Sternomandibularis;* **Stmas** *Sternomastoid;* **Subcl** *Subclavius;* **SupOr** *Supra-orbicularis;* **Supra** *Supraspinatus;* **Temp** *Temporalis;* **TenFA** *Tensor fasciae antibrachii;* **TenFL** *Tensor fasciae latae;* **TibCa** *Tibialis caudalis;* **TibCr** *Tibialis cranialis;* **Trap** *Trapezius;* **TriLa** *Triceps brachii, lateral head;* **TriLo** *Triceps brachii, long head;* **TriMe** *Triceps brachii, medial head;* **VasLa** *Vastus lateralis.*

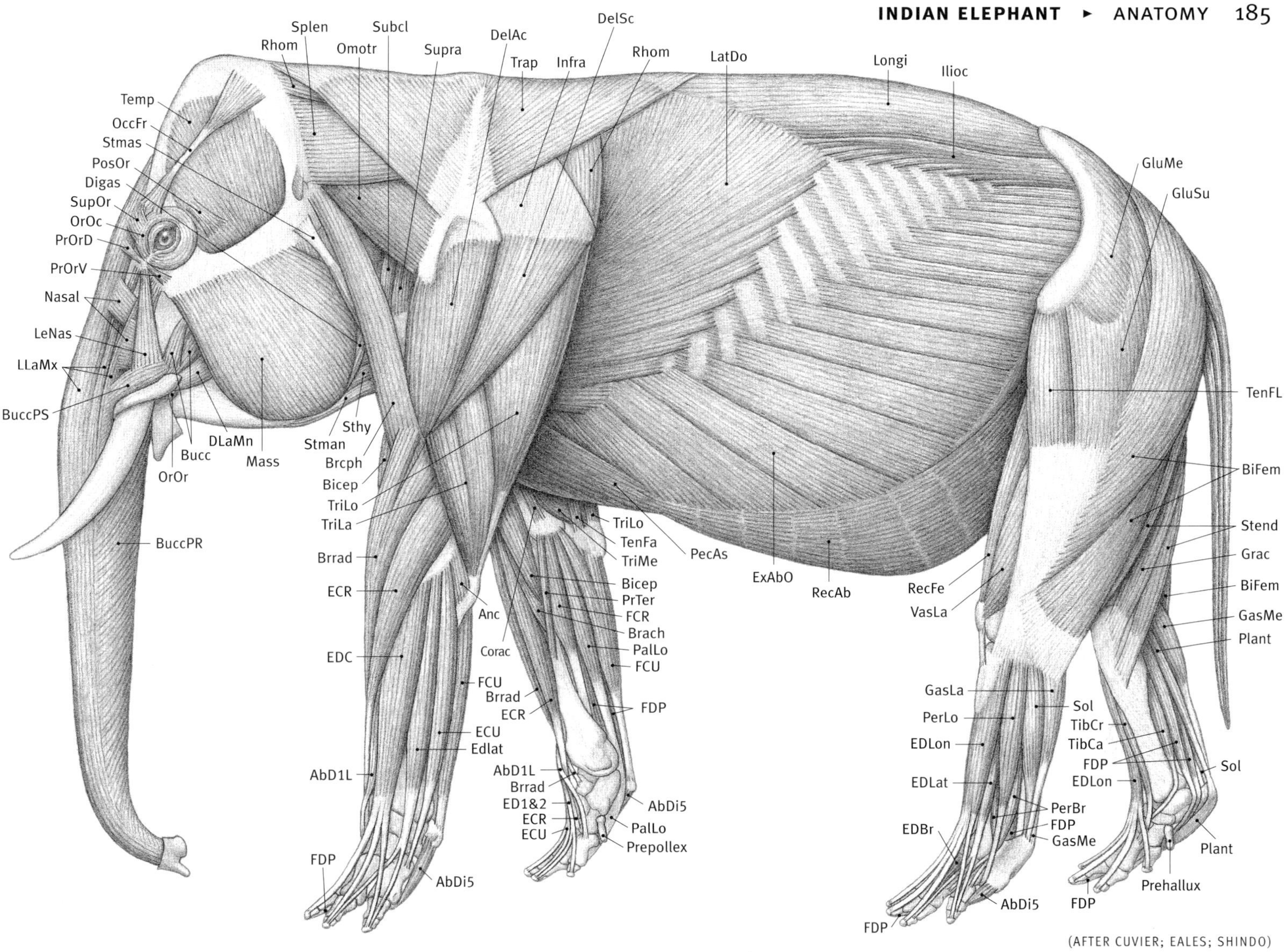

(AFTER CUVIER; EALES; SHINDO)

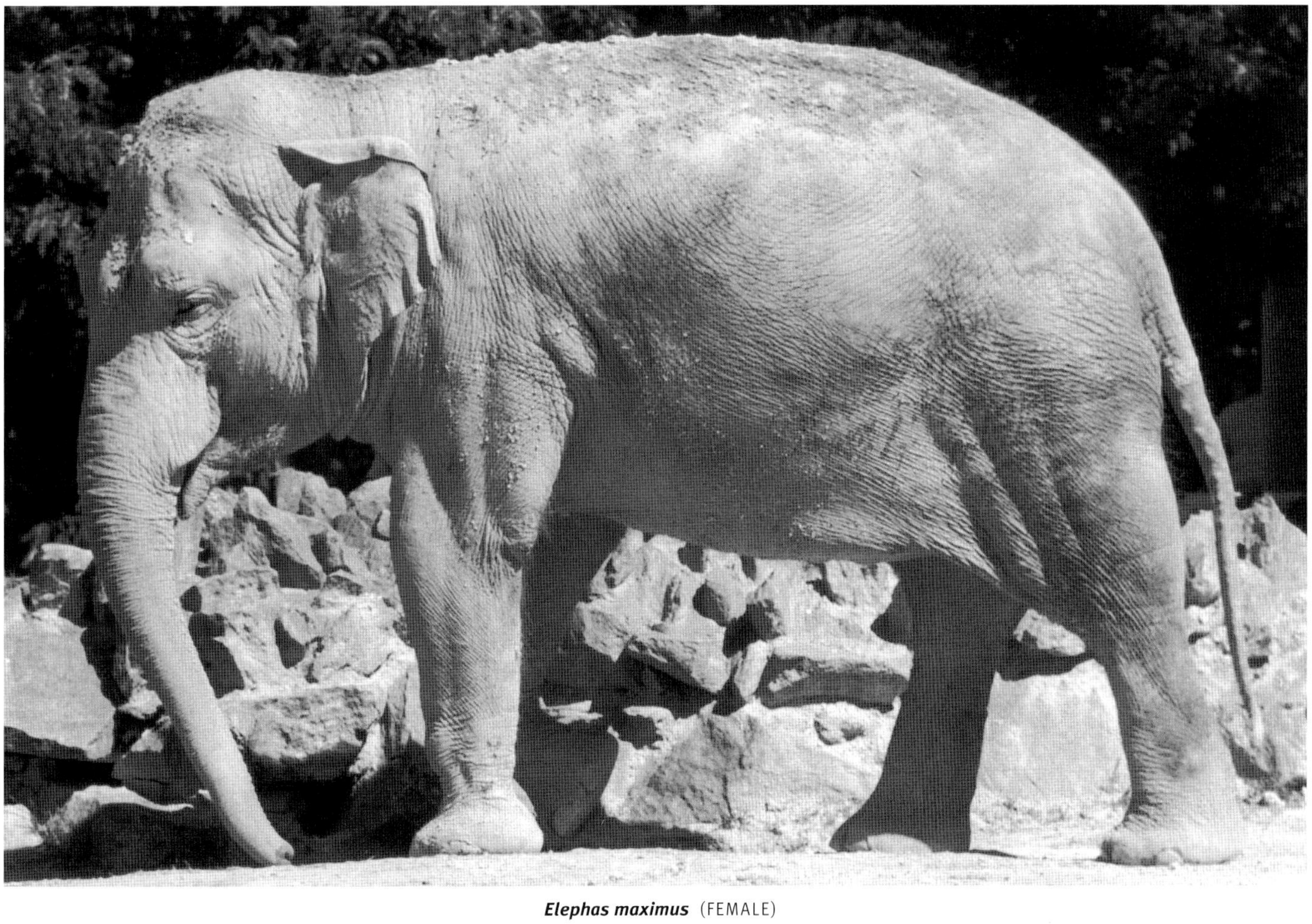

Elephas maximus (FEMALE)

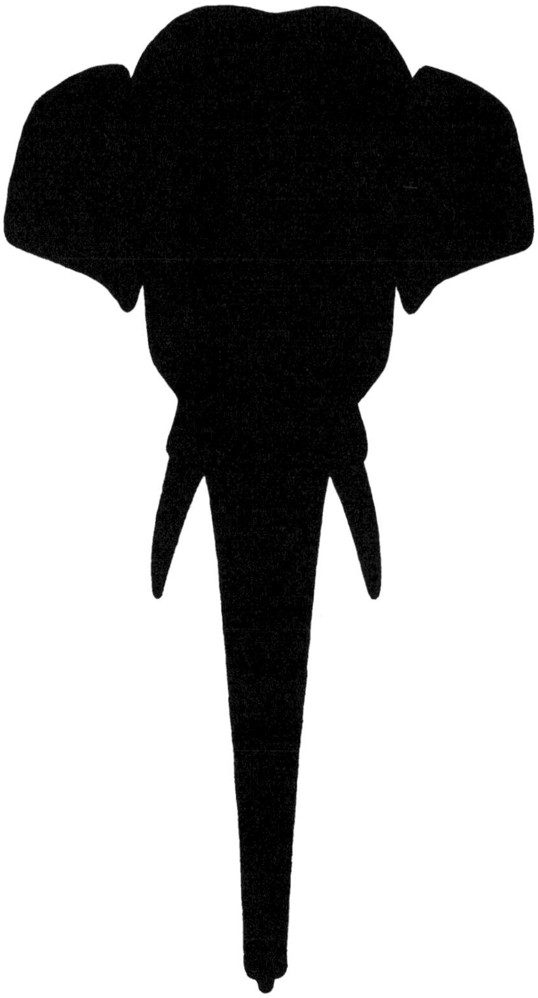

INDIAN ELEPHANT

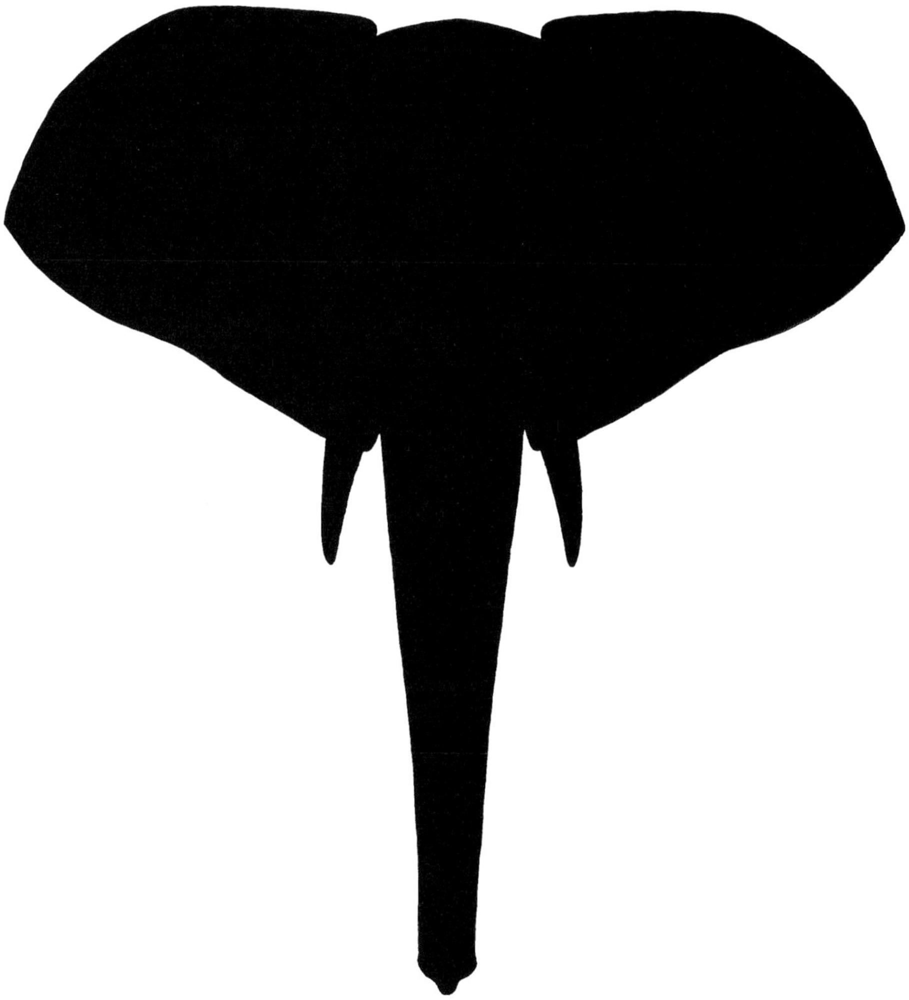

AFRICAN ELEPHANT

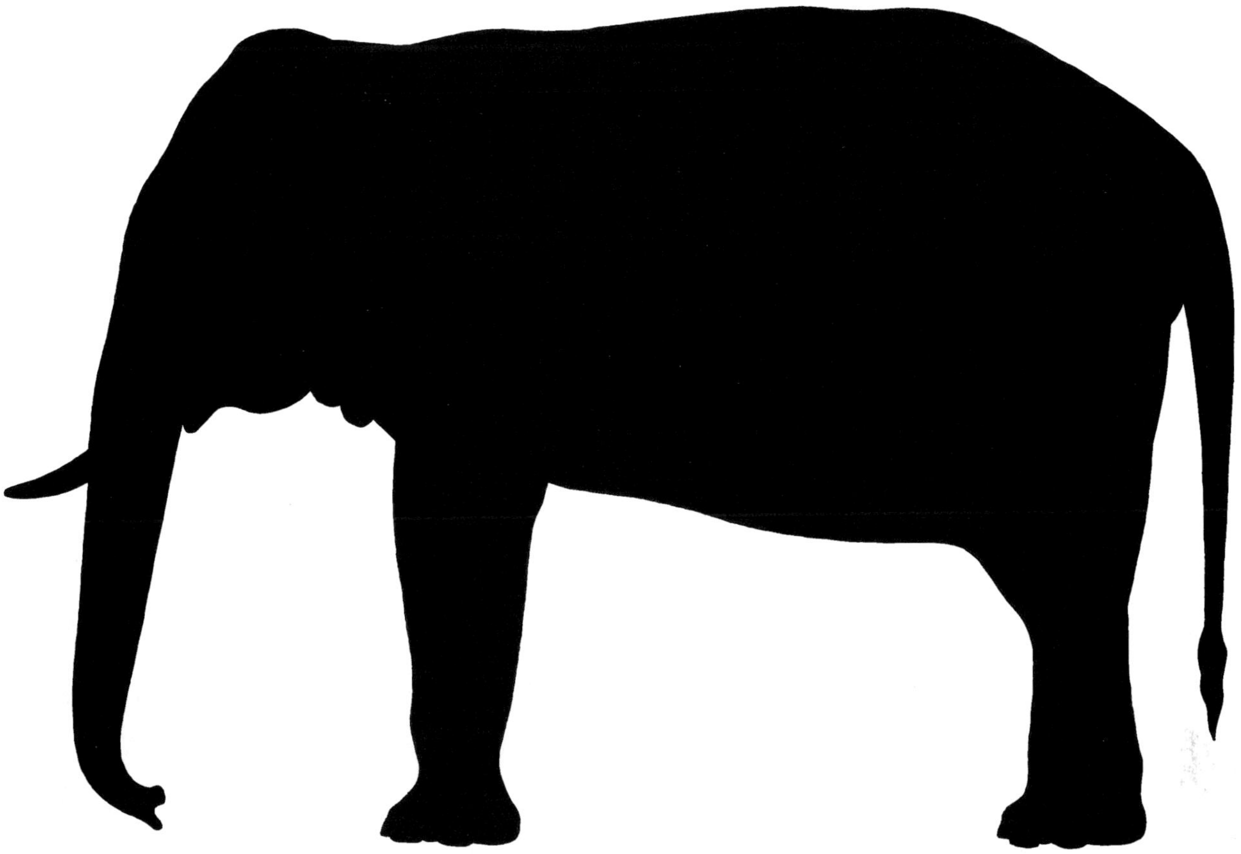

INDIAN ELEPHANT

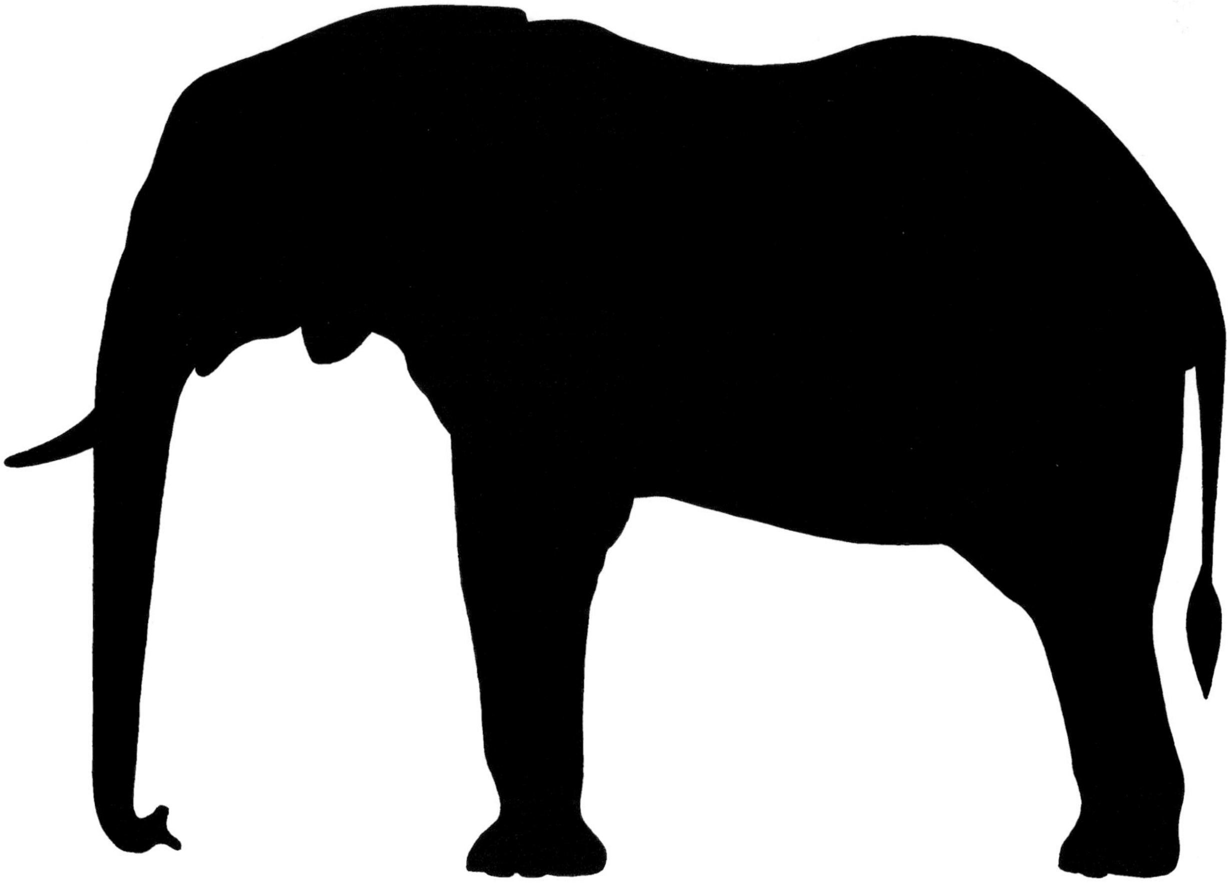

AFRICAN ELEPHANT

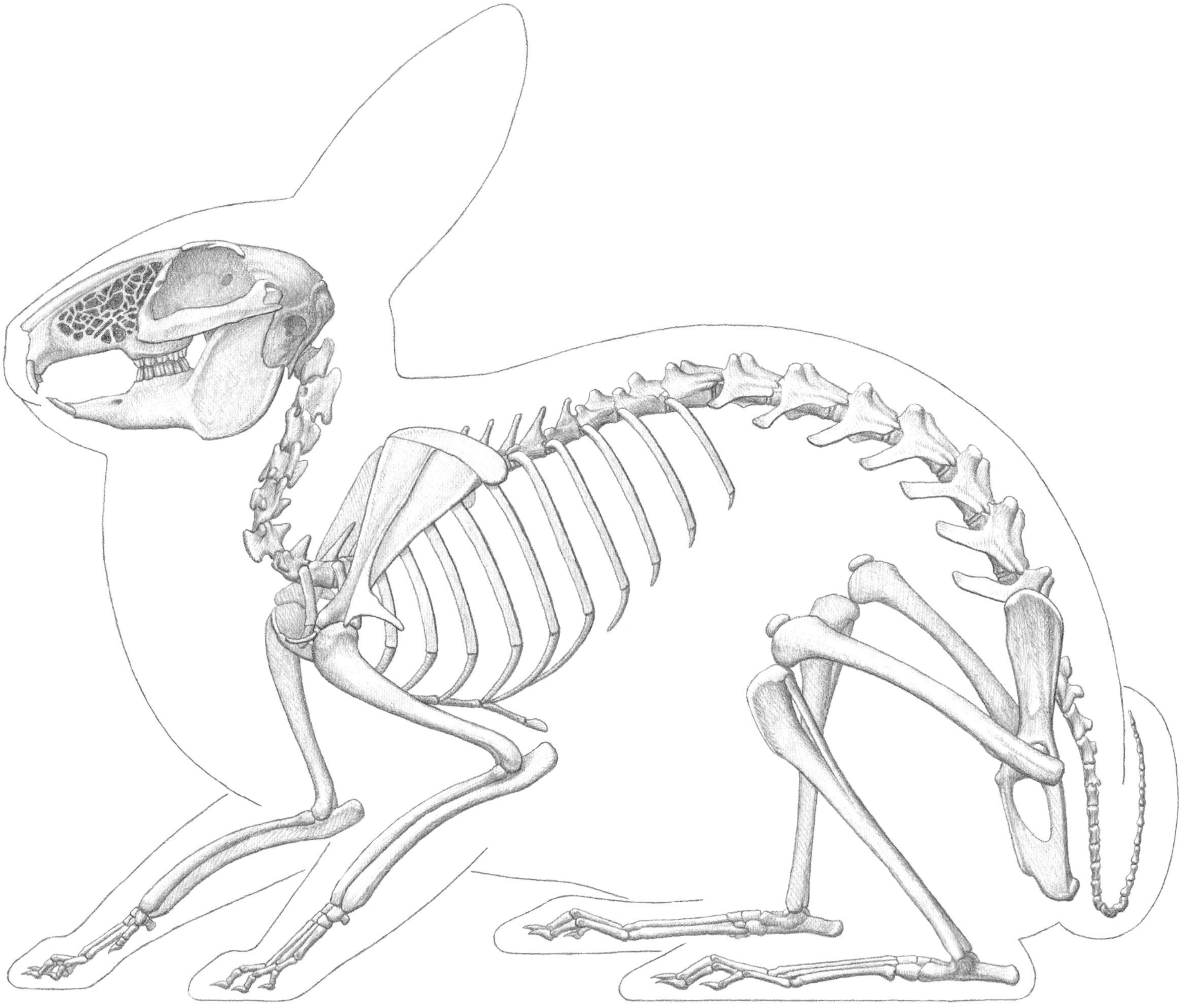

DOMESTIC RABBIT
Oryctolagus cuniculus

(FROM SPECIMEN)

Rabbit characteristics: Two pairs of upper incisors; second pair small and peg-like, located just behind the front pair. Perforated lace-like texture of bone on side of skull in front of eye socket. (Both features not found in rodents). Long and pointed large ears. Arched upper profile of skull. Strong extension of spine where neck vertebrae meet thoracic vertebrae. Strong extension of middle tail vertebrae, raising tufted tail. Relatively thin, delicate bones. Rear-projecting "metacromion" from lower end of shoulder blade (for insertion of trapezius and omotransversarius muscles). Long hind limbs with large feet. Sits on sole and heel of foot at rest; pushes off with toes. Front limb walks on toes. Five digits on front limb; four on rear limb. Females larger than males. Moves by hopping. Covered with thick fur. Bottom of feet covered with fur. Claws on digits. Hares generally larger, more upright, slender, with longer ears than rabbit, but true difference is in development of young at birth.

AbD1L *Abductor digiti I longus;* **AbDi5** *Abductor digiti V;* **Bascl** *Basioclavicularis;* **Bicep** *Biceps brachii;* **BiFem** *Biceps femoris;* **Brac** *Brachialis;* **Bucc** *Buccinator;* **Canin** *Caninus;* **Cldel** *Clavodeltoid;* **Clmas** *Cleidomastoid;* **DelAc** *Deltoid, acromial portion;* **DelSc** *Deltoid, scapular portion;* **DLaMn** *Depressor labii mandibularis;* **ECR** *Extensor carpi radialis;* **ECU** *Extensor carpi ulnaris;* **ED1&2** *Extensor digiti I & II;* **ED1L** *Extensor digiti I longus;* **EDC** *Extensor digitorum communis;* **EDLat** *Extensor digitorum lateralis;* **EDLon** *Extensor digitorum longus;* **ExAbO** *External abdominal oblique;* **FCR** *Flexor carpi radialis;* **FCU** *Flexor carpi ulnaris;* **FDP** *Flexor digitorum profundus;* **FDS** *Flexor digitorum superficialis;* **GasLa** *Gastrocnemius, lateral head;* **Gastr** *Gastrocnemius;* **GluMe** *Gluteus medius;* **GluSu** *Gluteus superficialis;* **Ilioc** *Iliocostalis;* **Infra** *Infraspinatus;* **LatDo** *Latissimus dorsi;* **LeNas** *Levator nasolabialis;* **LLaMx** *Levator labii maxillaris;* **Longi** *Longissimus;* **Malar** *Malaris;* **Mass** *Masseter;* **Omotr** *Omotransversarius;* **OrOc** *Orbicularis oculi;* **OrOr** *Orbicularis oris;* **PecSu** *Pectoralis superficialis;* **PerBr** *Peroneus brevis;* **PerLo** *Peroneus longus;* **PrTer** *Pronator teres;* **RecAb** *Rectus abdominis;* **RecFe** *Rectus femoris;* **Rhom** *Rhomboid;* **SerVT** *Serratus ventralis thoracis;* **Smemb** *Semimembranosus;* **Sol** *Soleus;* **Splen** *Splenius;* **Stend** *Semitendinosus;* **Sthy** *Sternohyoid;* **Stmas** *Sternomastoid;* **Supra** *Supraspinatus;* **TeMaj** *Teres major;* **Temp** *Temporalis;* **TenFL** *Tensor fasciae latae;* **TibCr** *Tibialis cranialis;* **Trap** *Trapezius;* **TriAc** *Triceps brachii, accessory head;* **TriLa** *Triceps brachii, lateral head;* **TriLo** *Triceps brachii, long head;* **TriMe** *Triceps brachii, medial head;* **VasLa** *Vastus lateralis;* **Zyg** *Zygomaticus.*

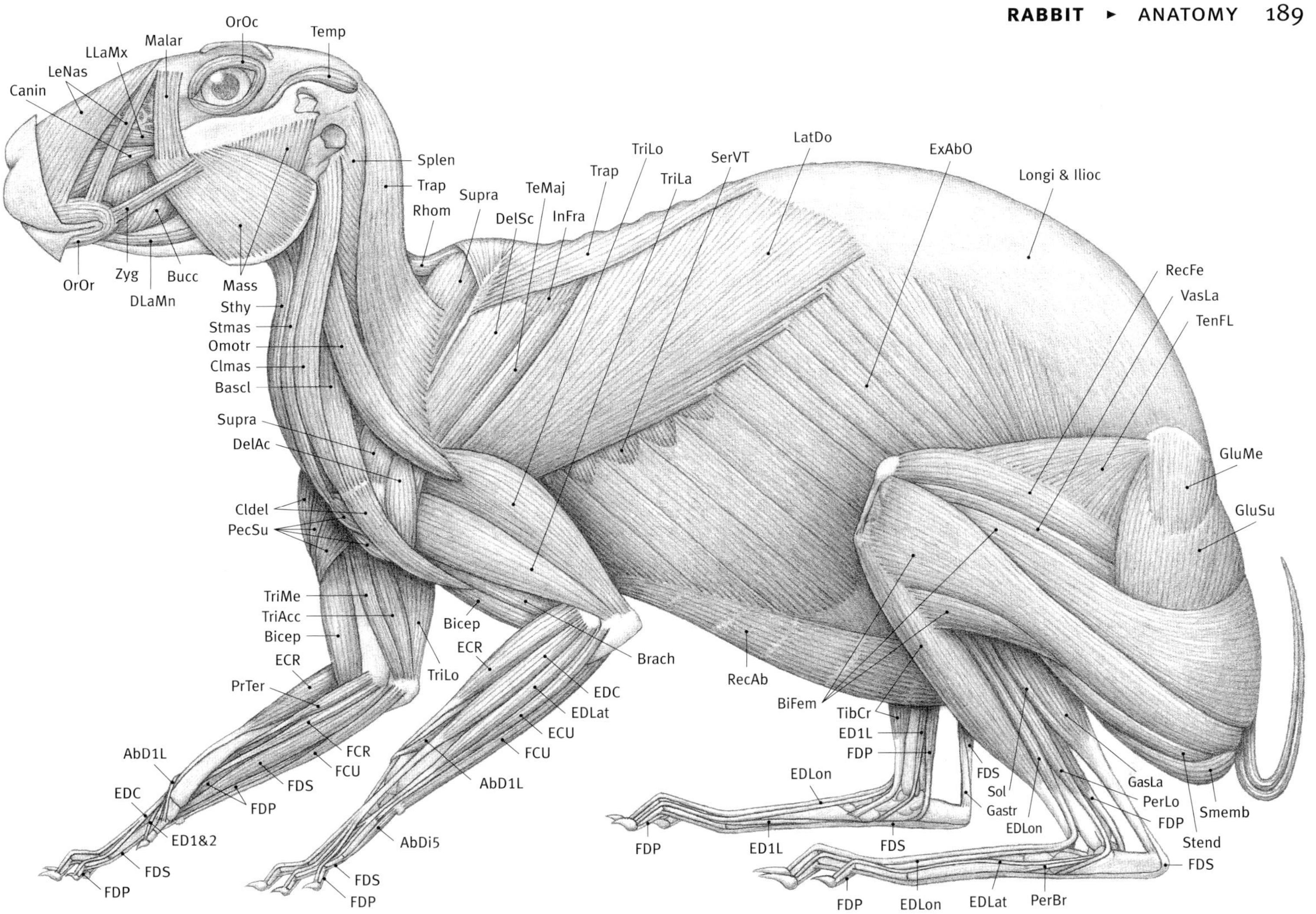

DOMESTIC RABBIT

(FROM DISSECTIONS)

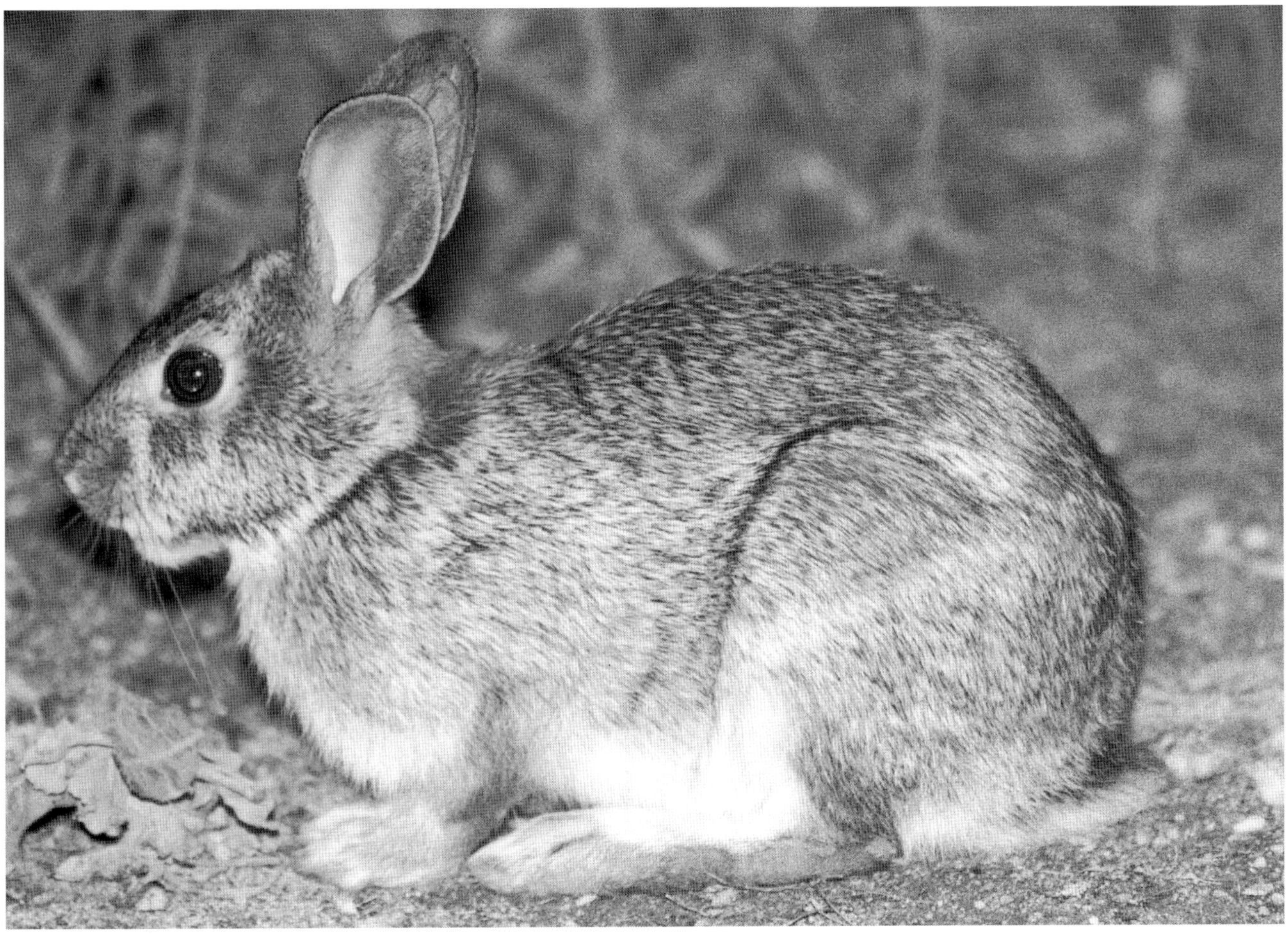

EASTERN COTTONTAIL

Sylvilagus floridanus

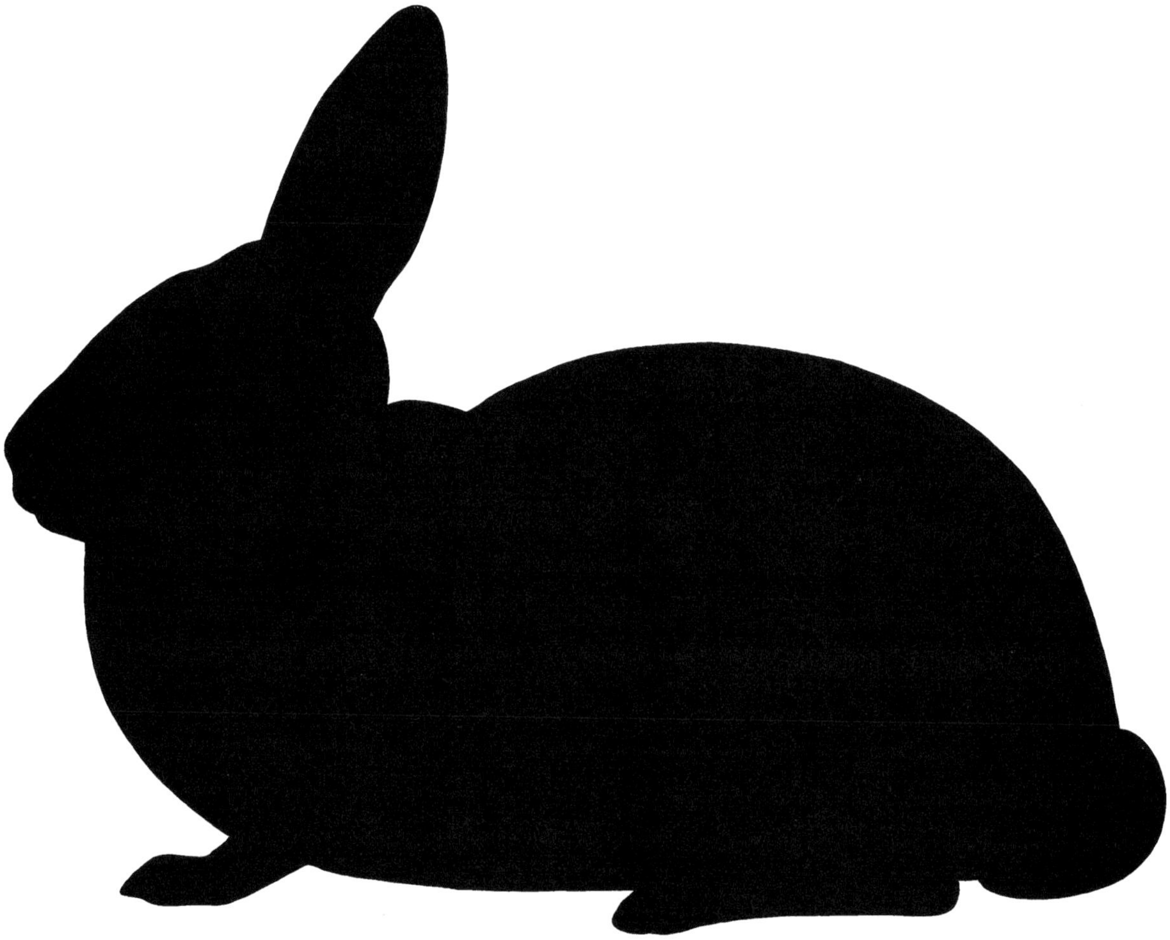

RABBIT (COTTONTAIL)

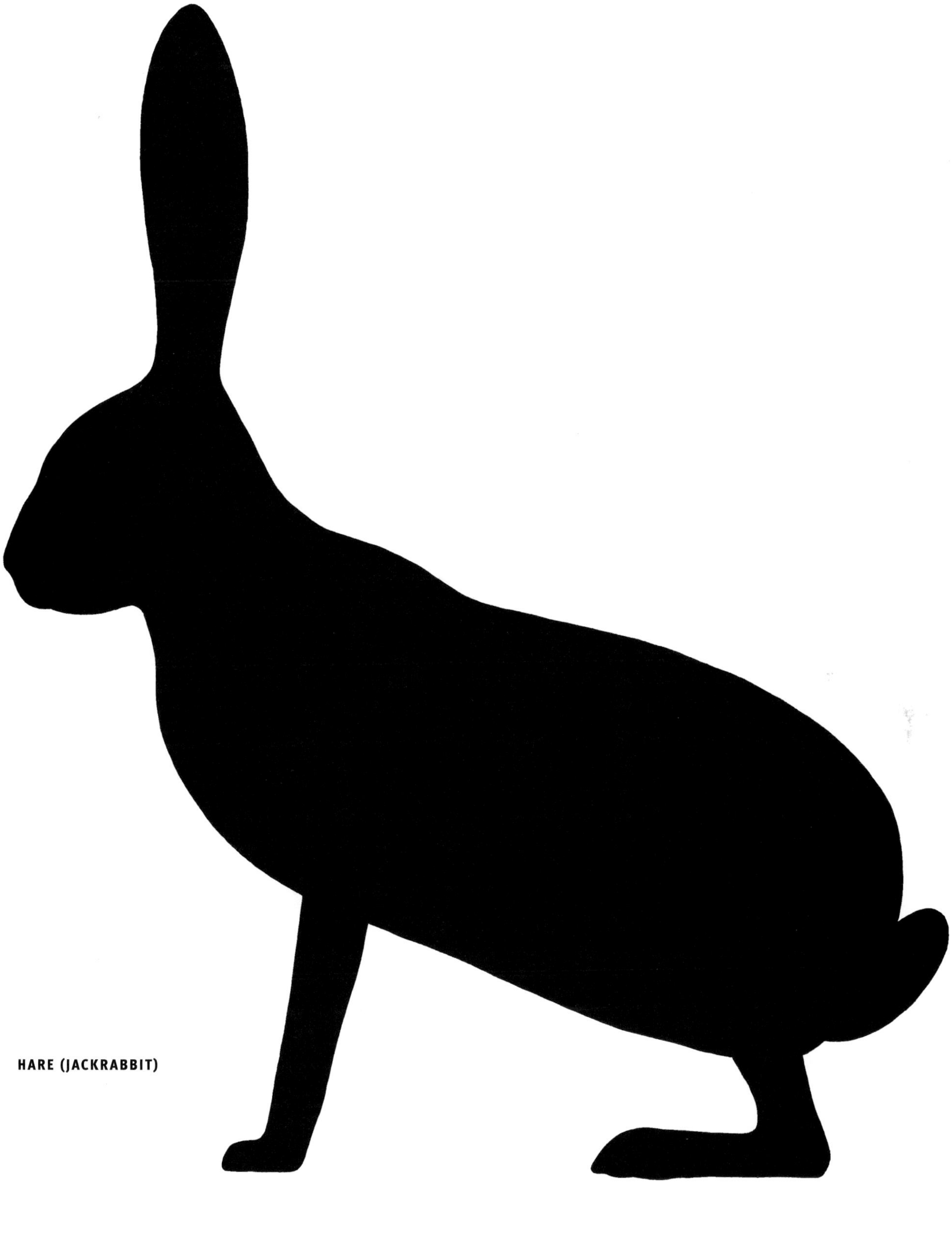

HARE (JACKRABBIT)

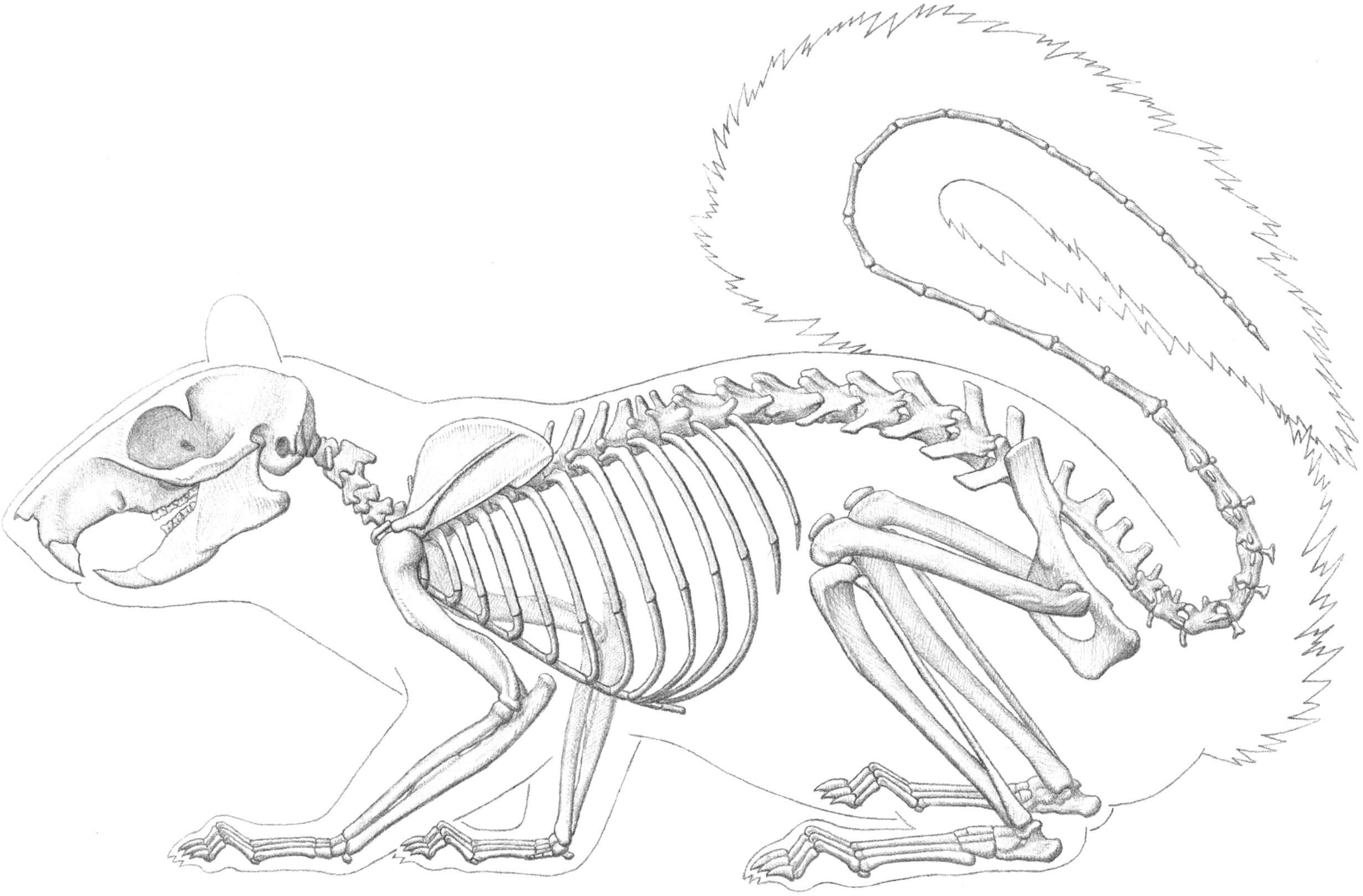

EASTERN GRAY SQUIRREL (FROM SPECIMENS)
Sciurus carolinensis

Squirrel characteristics: Strong extension of tail vertebrae at base of tail (to bend tail onto back). Walks on palm of hand (not on digits like dog). Good rotation of joints of rear limb so sole of foot can face down (or backward) when leg is extended. This enables squirrel to climb down trees with its rear leg extended and the sole of its foot in contact with the tree. Five digits on front limb (with very reduced but visible first digit); five digits on rear limb.

Rodent characteristics: Highly variable. Body very small (mouse) to dog-size (capybara). Single pair of incisors in upper and lower jaws grow continuously and wear against each other, keeping their front edges sharp and chisel-like. No canines—gap present between incisors and cheek teeth. Often has arched upper profile of skull. Receding lower jaw ("weak jaw"). Forearm rotates (pronates/supinates). Walks on palm and wrist of front limb and sole and heel of rear foot. Four or five digits on front limb (often with reduced first digit), three to five on hind limb. Digits may be webbed in semiaquatic species. Claws on digits. Usually medium to long tails: naked and scaly (rat), lightly haired (mouse), or very bushy (squirrel). Tail horizontally flattened and wide in beaver; vertically flattened in muskrat (both swimmers). Prehensile tails in some species. Hair modified into long, stiff quills in porcupine. Habits: running, gliding, climbing, swimming, burrowing, and jumping (hopping).

AbCaE *Abductor caudae externus;* **AbD1L** *Abductor digiti I longus;* **AbDi5** *Abductor digiti V;* **Anc** *Anconeus;* **Bicep** *Biceps brachii;* **BiFem** *Biceps femoris;* **Brach** *Brachialis;* **Brrad** *Brachioradialis;* **Bucc** *Buccinator;* **Cldel** *Clavodeltoid;* **ClOcc** *Cleido-occipitalis;* **DAnOr** *Depressor anguli oris;* **DelAc** *Deltoid, acromial portion;* **DelSp** *Deltoid, spinal portion;* **Digas** *Digastric;* **DLaMn** *Depressor labii mandibularis;* **ECRB** *Extensor carpi radialis brevis;* **ECRL** *Extensor carpi radialis longus;* **ECU** *Extensor carpi ulnaris;* **EDC** *Extensor digitorum communis;* **EDLat** *Extensor digitorum lateralis;* **EDLon** *Extensor digitorum longus;* **ExAbO** *External abdominal oblique;* **FCR** *Flexor carpi radialis;* **FCU** *Flexor carpi ulnaris;* **FDP** *Flexor digitorum profundus;* **FDS** *Flexor digitorum superficialis;* **GasLa** *Gastrocnemius, lateral head;* **GasMe** *Gastrocnemius, medial head;* **GluSu** *Gluteus superficialis;* **Ilioc** *Iliocostalis;* **Inter** *Interossei;* **LatDo** *Latissimus dorsi;* **LeNas** *Levator nasolabialis;* **LLaMx** *Levator labii maxillaris;* **Longi** *Longissimus;* **Mass** *Masseter;* **Omohy** *Omohyoid;* **Omotr** *Omotransversarius;* **OrOc** *Orbicularis oculi;* **OrOr** *Orbicularis oris;* **PalLo** *Palmaris longus;* **PecAb** *Pectoralis abdominis;* **PecSP** *Pectoralis superficialis posterior;* **PerBr** *Peroneus brevis;* **PerLo** *Peroneus longus;* **PrTer** *Pronator teres;* **RecFe** *Rectus femoris;* **Stend** *Semitendinosus;* **Sthy** *Sternohyoid;* **Stmas** *Sternomastoid;* **Supra** *Supraspinatus;* **TeMaj** *Teres major;* **Temp** *Temporalis;* **TenFA** *Tensor fasciae antibrachii;* **TenFL** *Tensor fasciae latae;* **TibCa** *Tibialis caudalis;* **TibCr** *Tibialis cranialis;* **Trap** *Trapezius;* **TriLa** *Triceps brachii, lateral head;* **TriLo** *Triceps brachii, long head;* **VasLa** *Vastus lateralis.*

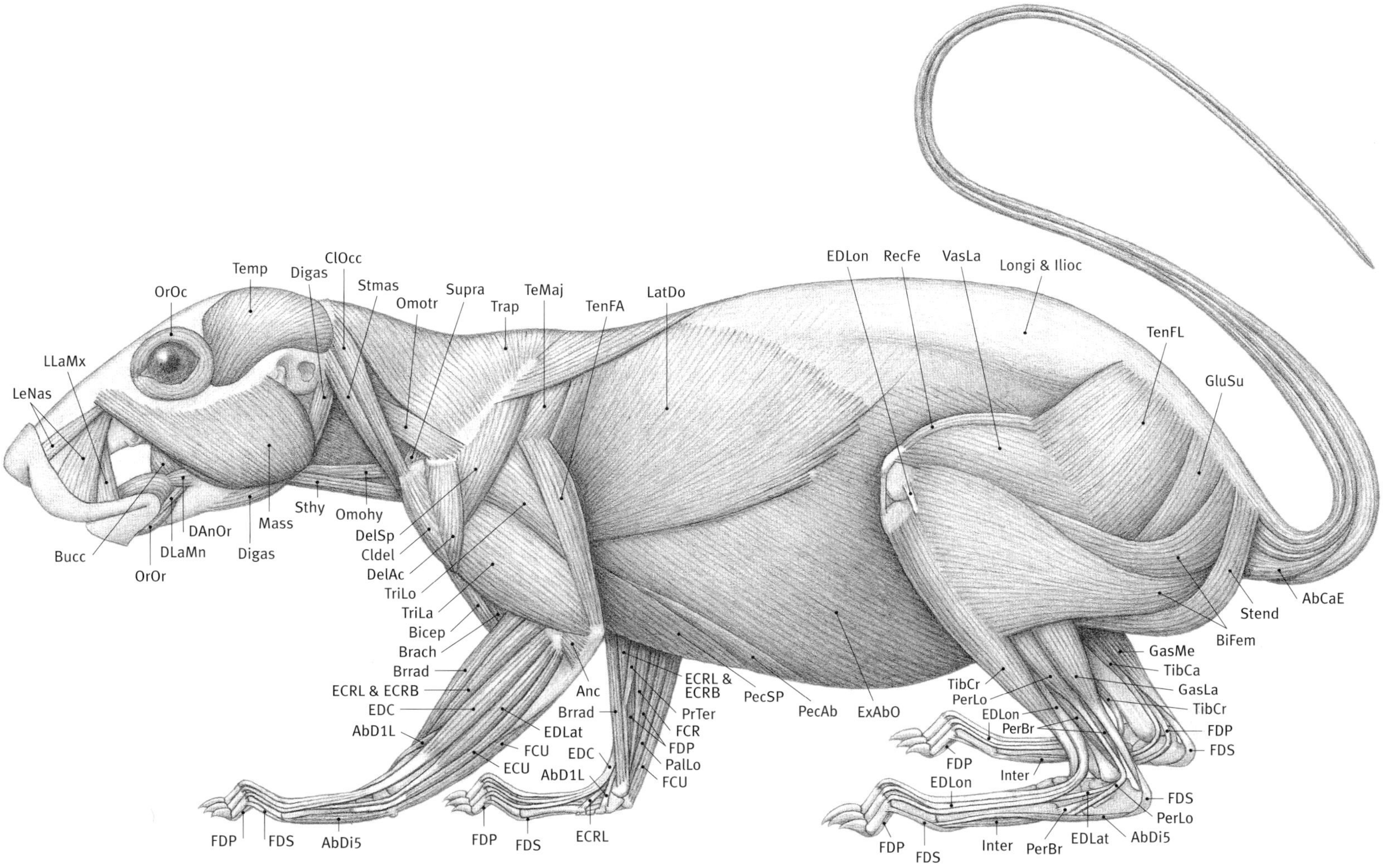

(FROM DISSECTION; AFTER CUVIER; ORWOLL)

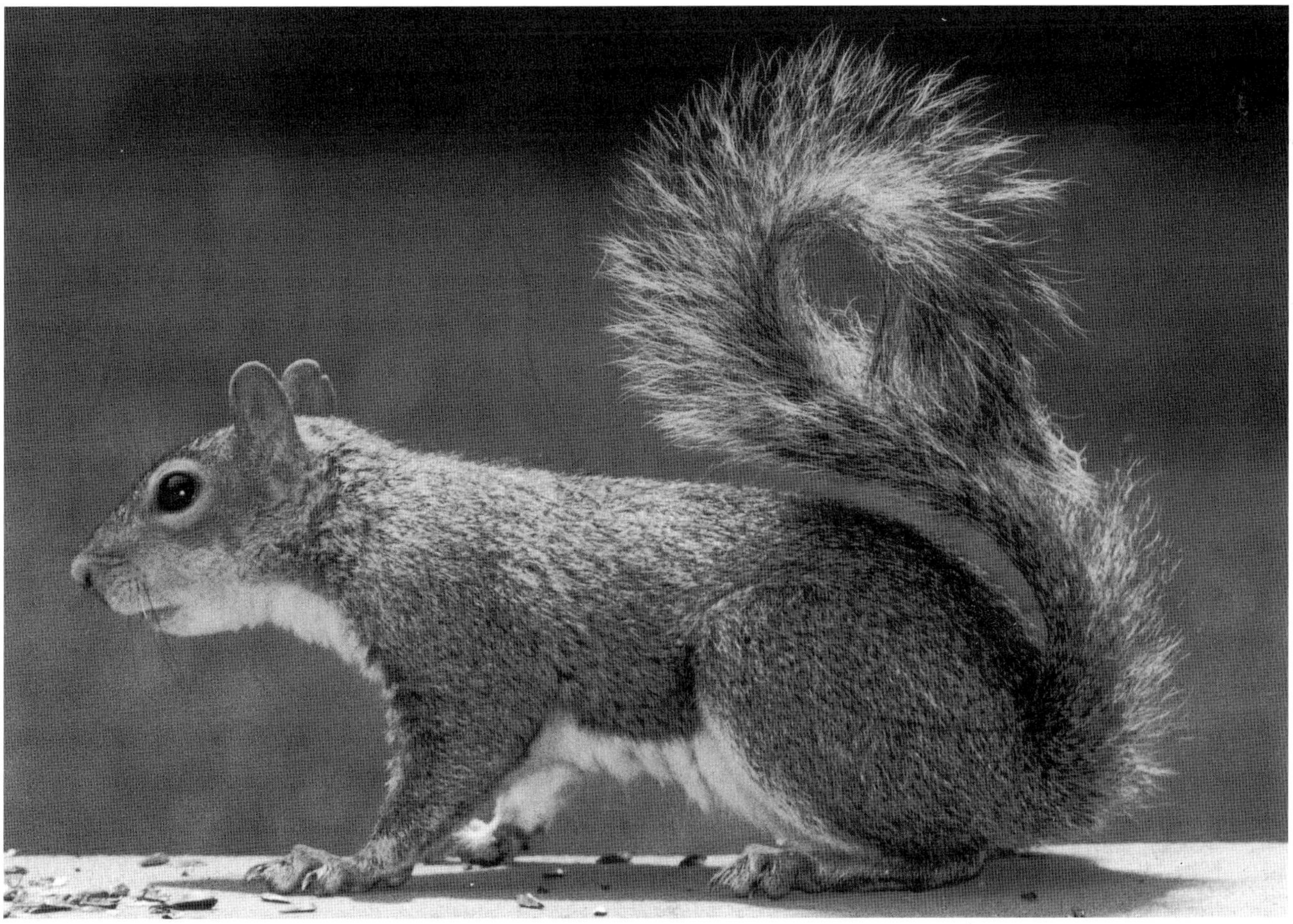

EASTERN GRAY SQUIRREL

Sciurus carolinensis

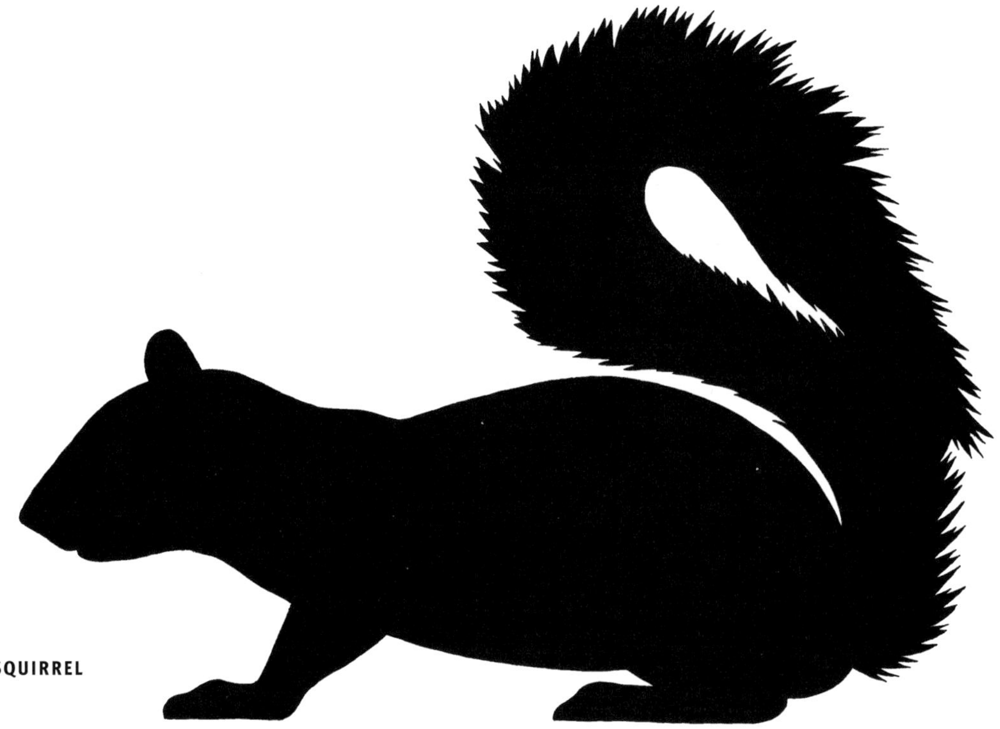

SQUIRREL

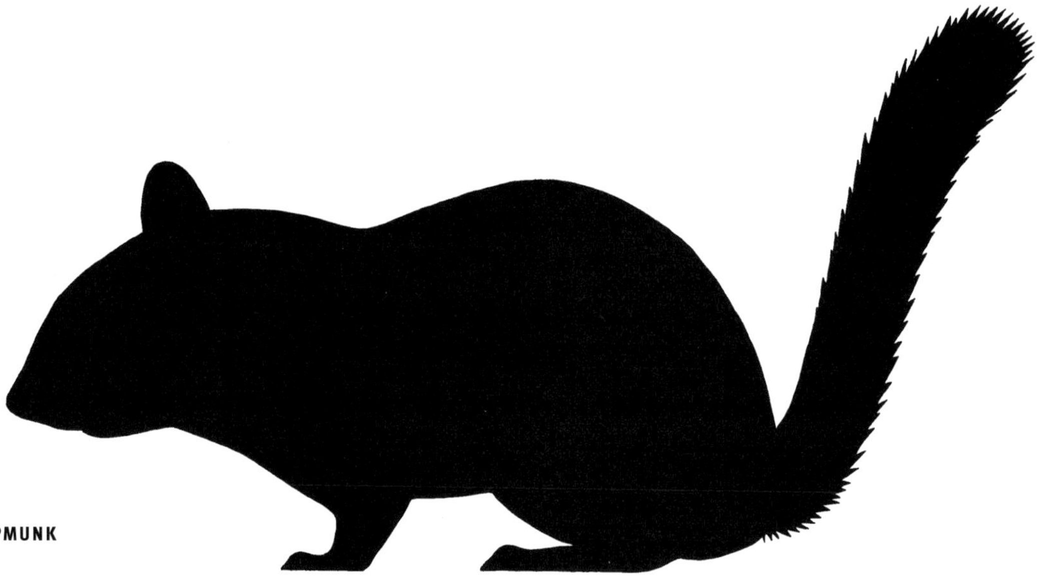

CHIPMUNK

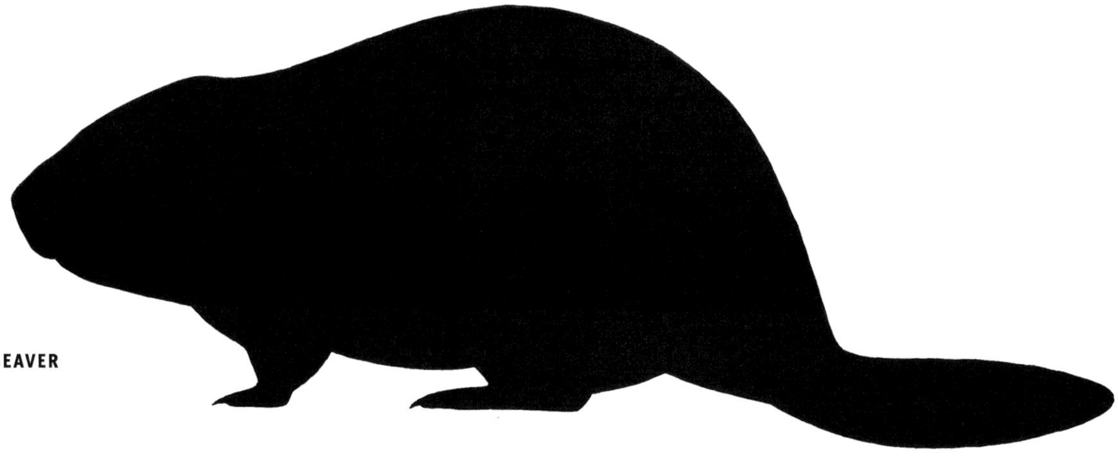

BEAVER

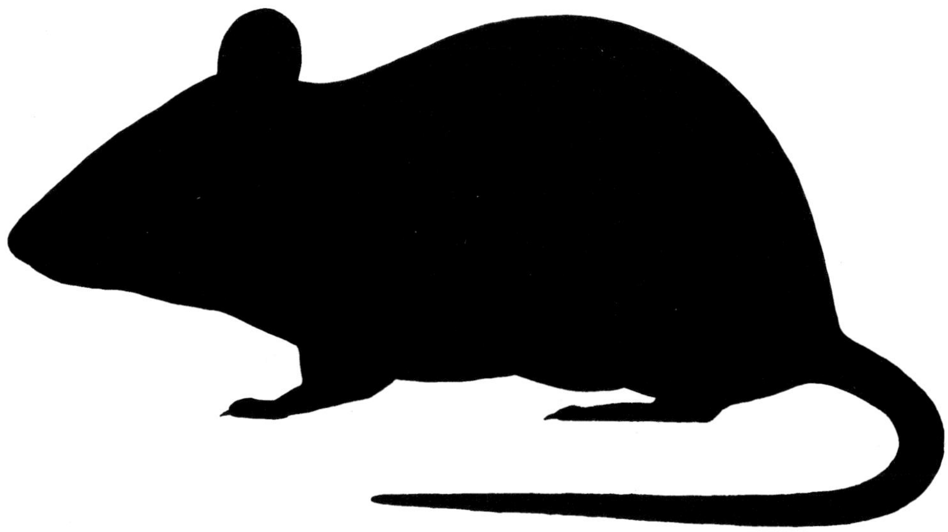

HOUSE MOUSE

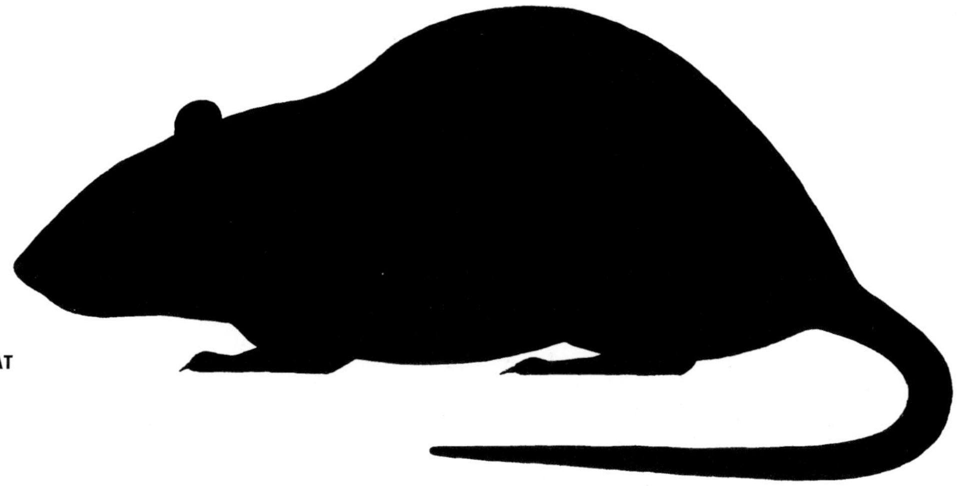

NORWAY (BROWN) RAT

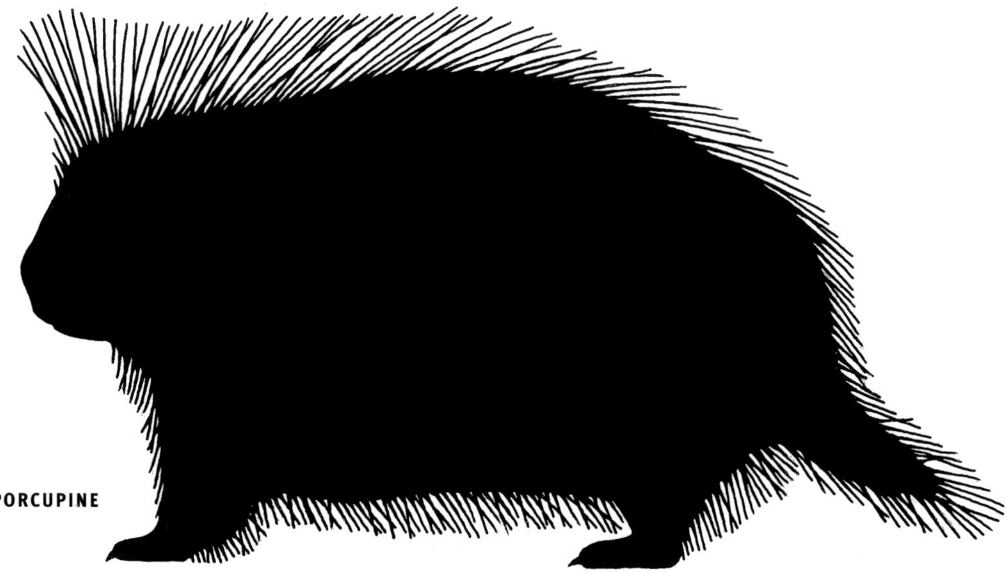

NORTH AMERICAN PORCUPINE

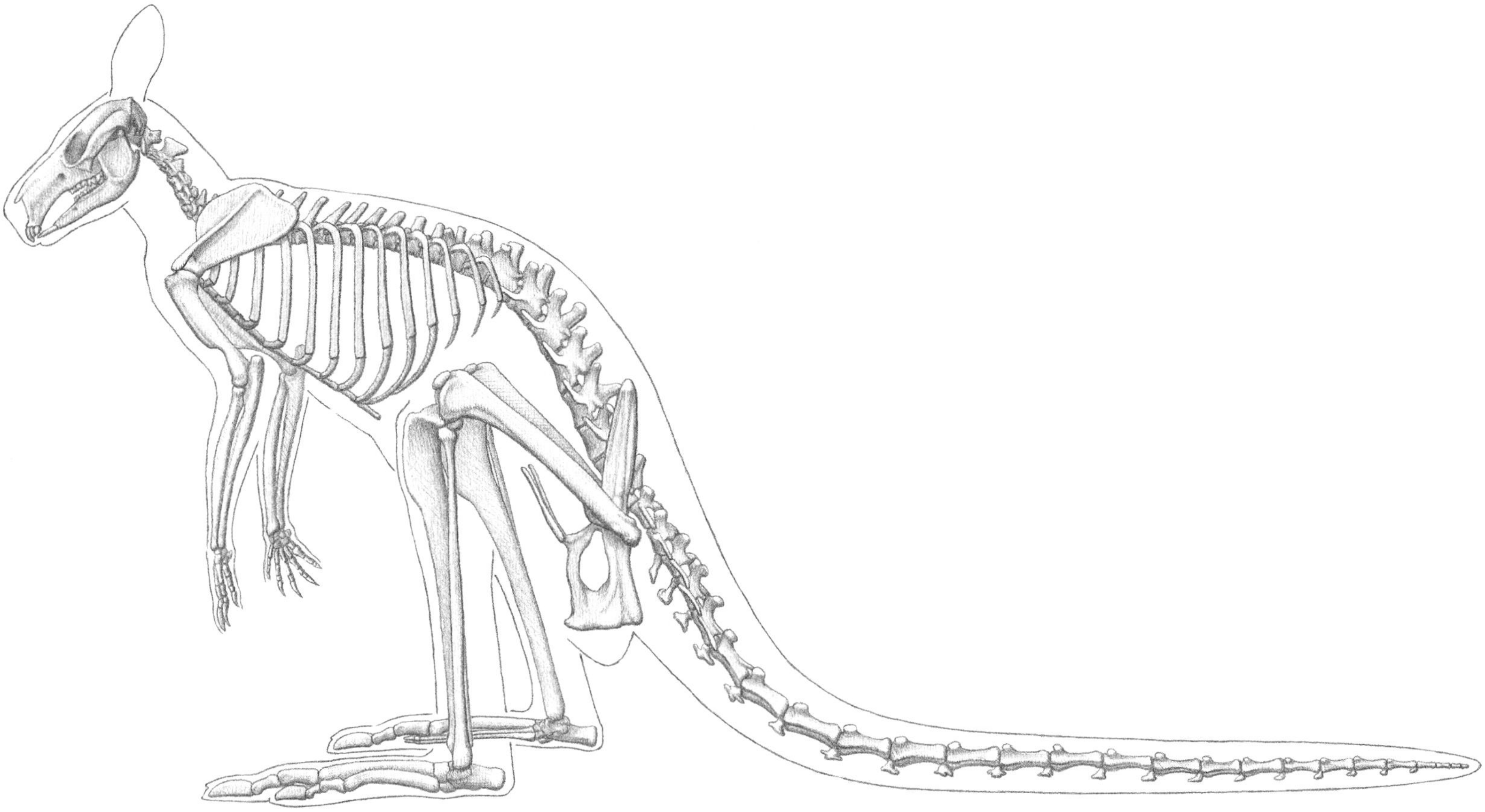

RED KANGAROO (FEMALE) (FROM SPECIMEN)
Macropus rufus

Kangaroo characteristics: Forelimb small; has five digits with strong claws. Large, powerful hind limb with long, strong, narrow foot. Muscular thigh; muscle mass of lower leg positioned on upper half, toward knee. In foot, large fourth and smaller fifth digits transmit force during locomotion; first digit missing, small digits two and three bound together by skin. Long tail, thick at base, used for body support at rest and balance during hopping. Fast locomotion is by leaping with hind limbs only. Walking: Hind limbs, forelimbs, and tail in contact with ground at various times. Sitting: Body rests on entire foot and tail; arms hang loosely. Pouch in female opens forward, supported by two long, thin bones.

AbD1B *Abductor digiti I brevis;* **AbD1L** *Abductor digiti I longus;* **AbDi5** *Abductor digiti V;* **Anc** *Anconeus;* **AT** *Achilles tendon;* **Bicep** *Biceps brachii;* **BiFem** *Biceps femoris;* **Brach** *Brachialis;* **Brrad** *Brachioradialis;* **Bucc** *Buccinator;* **Canin** *Caninus;* **Clmas** *Cleidomastoid;* **Coccy** *Coccygeus;* **Delt** *Deltoid;* **Digas** *Digastric;* **ECRB** *Extensor carpi radialis brevis;* **ECRL** *Extensor carpi radialis longus;* **ECU** *Extensor carpi ulnaris;* **EDC** *Extensor digitorum communis;* **EDLat** *Extensor digitorum lateralis;* **EDLon** *Extensor digitorum longus;* **ED1L** *Extensor hallucis longus;* **ExAbO** *External abdominal oblique;* **FCR** *Flexor carpi radialis;* **FCU** *Flexor carpi ulnaris;* **FDP** *Flexor digitorum profundus;* **FDS** *Flexor digitorum superficialis;* **GasLa** *Gastrocnemius, lateral head;* **GluMe** *Gluteus medius;* **GluSA** *Gluteus superficialis anterior;* **GluSP** *Gluteus superficialis posterior;* **Ilioc** *Iliocostalis;* **InAbO** *Internal abdominal oblique;* **LatDo** *Latissimus dorsi;* **LeNas** *Levator nasolabialis;* **LLaMx** *Levator labii maxillaris;* **Longi** *Longissimus;* **Mass** *Masseter;* **OrOc** *Orbicularis oculi;* **OrOr** *Orbicularis oris;* **PalLo** *Palmaris longus;* **Pec** *Pectoralis;* **PerLo** *Peroneus longus;* **PrTer** *Pronator teres;* **RecAb** *Rectus abdominis;* **Sart** *Sartorius;* **SerVT** *Serratus ventralis thoracis;* **Smemb** *Semimembranosus;* **Sol** *Soleus;* **Stend** *Semitendinosus;* **Sthy** *Sternohyoid;* **Stmas** *Sternomastoid;* **Stthy** *Sternothyroid;* **TeMaj** *Teres major;* **Temp** *Temporalis;* **TenFL** *Tensor fasciae latae;* **TibCa** *Tibialis caudalis;* **TibCr** *Tibialis cranialis;* **Trap** *Trapezius;* **TriLa** *Triceps brachii, lateral head;* **TriLo** *Triceps brachii, long head;* **VasLa** *Vastus lateralis.*

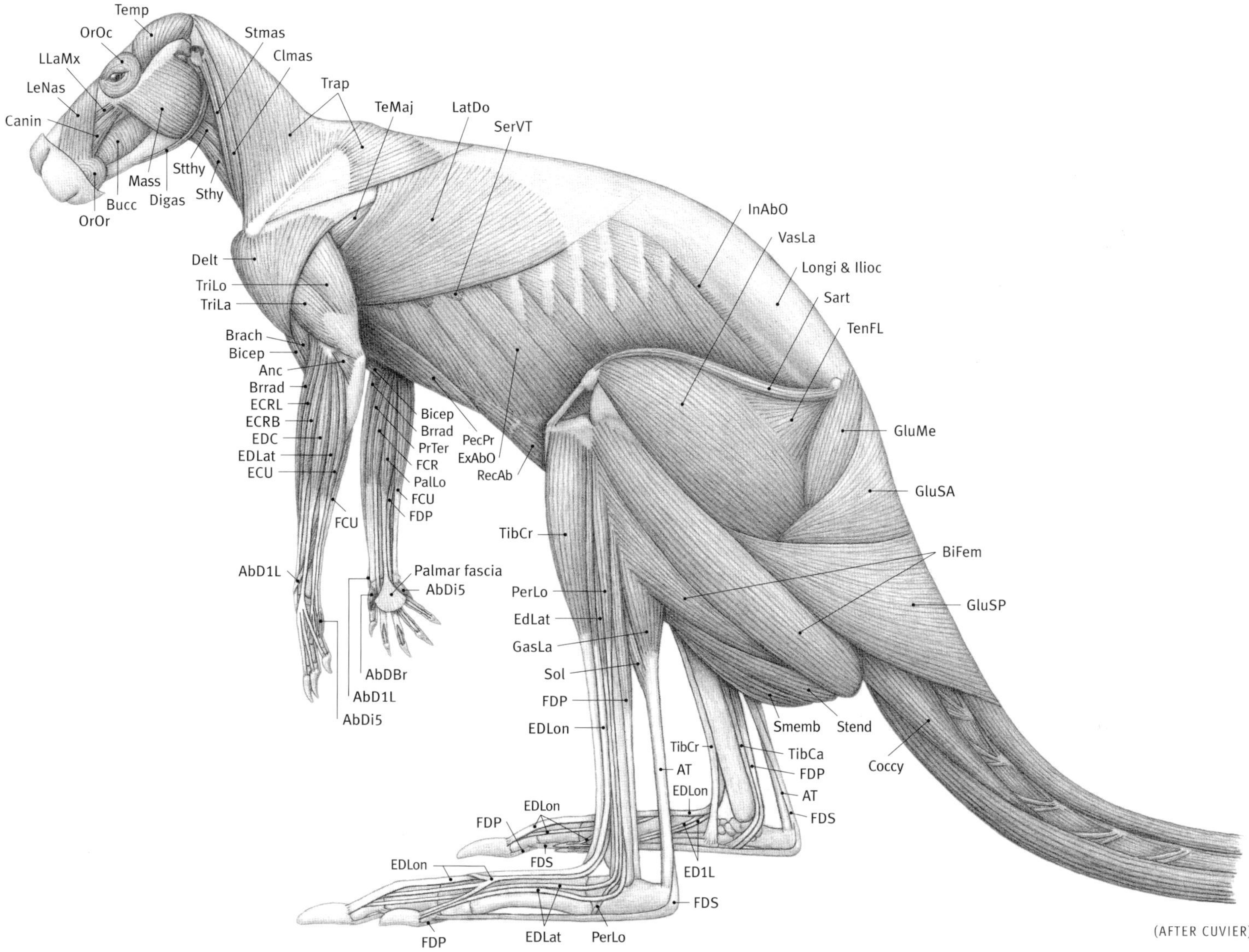

(AFTER CUVIER)

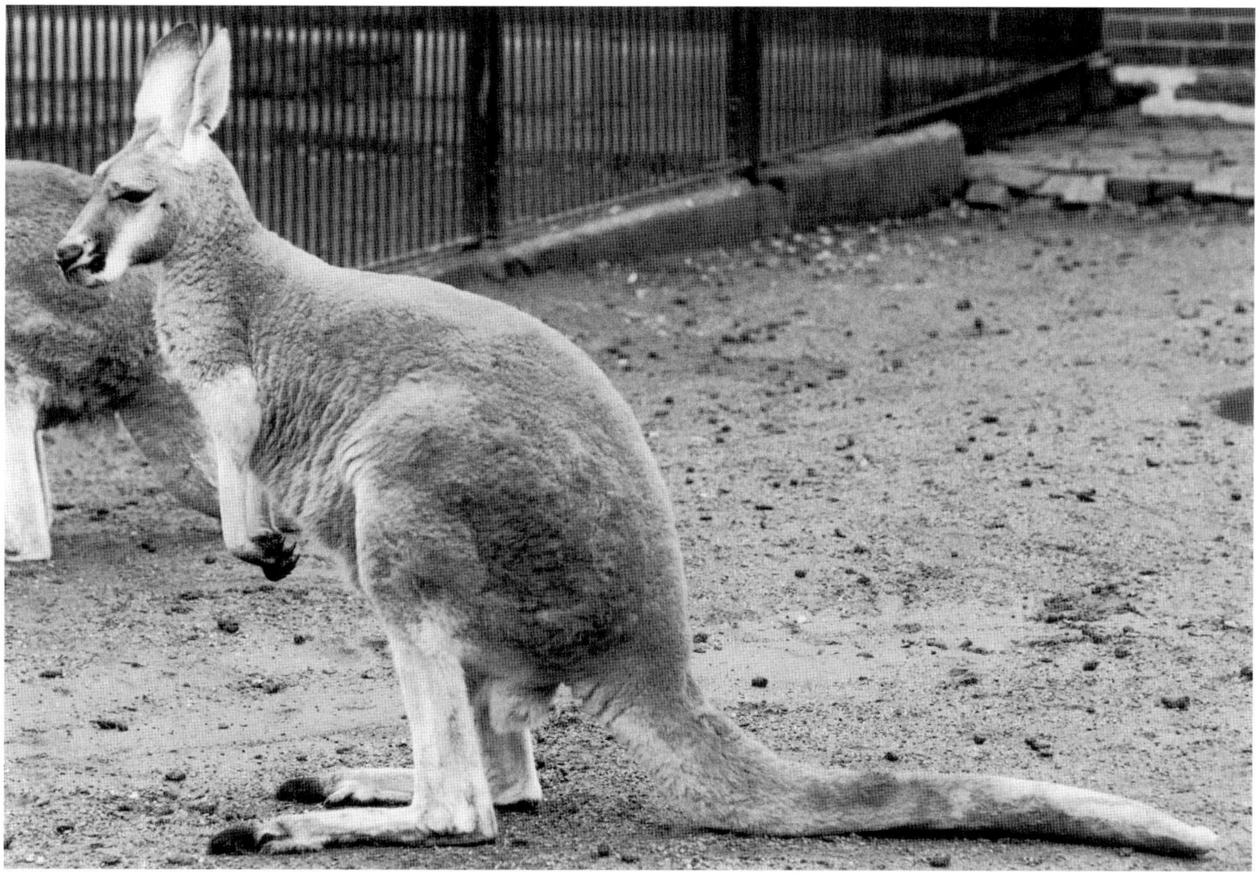

RED KANGAROO (FEMALE)

Macropus rufus

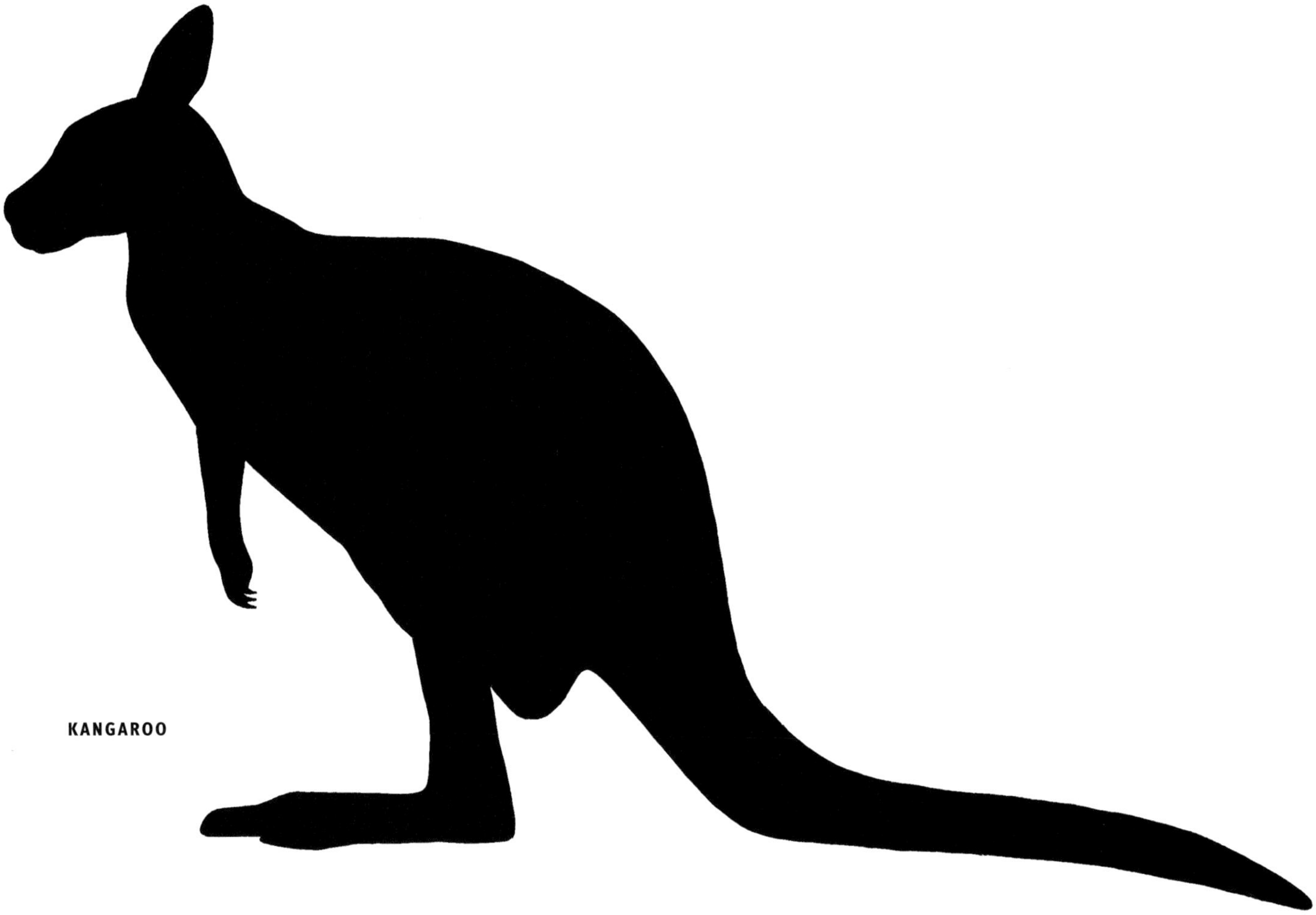

KANGAROO

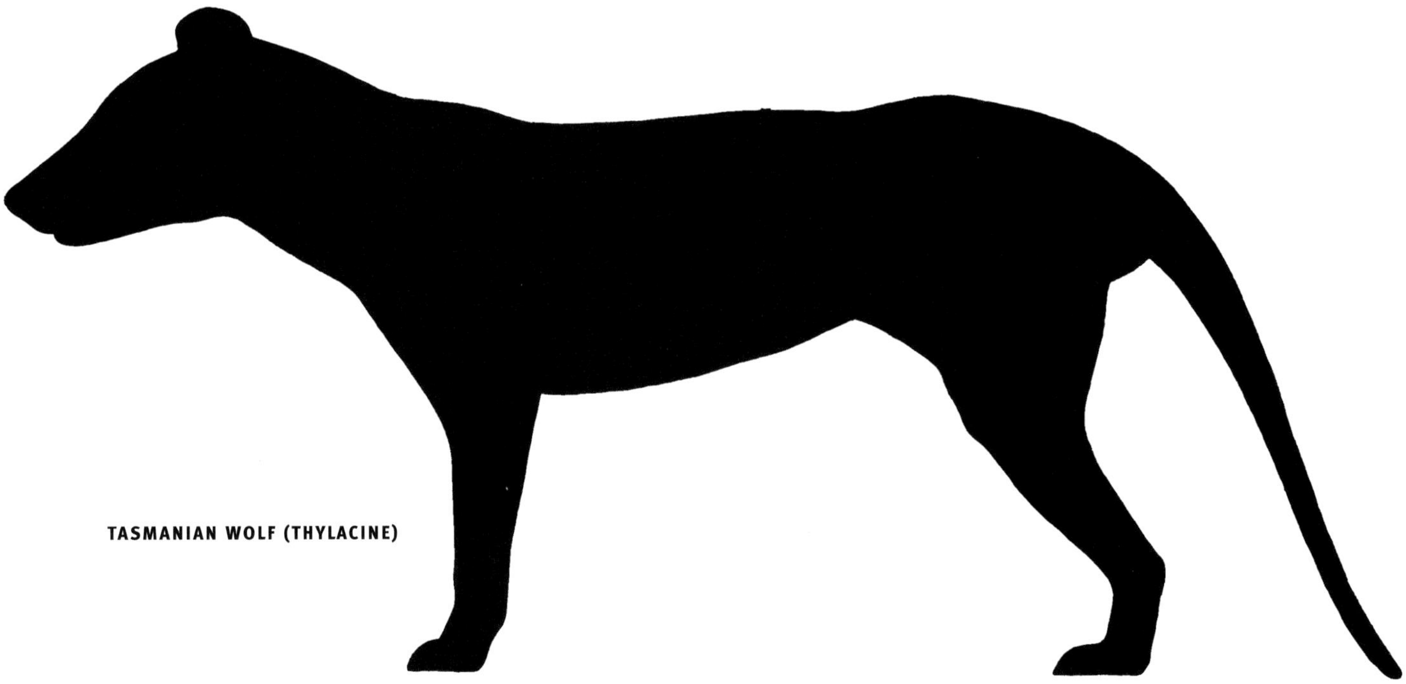

TASMANIAN WOLF (THYLACINE)

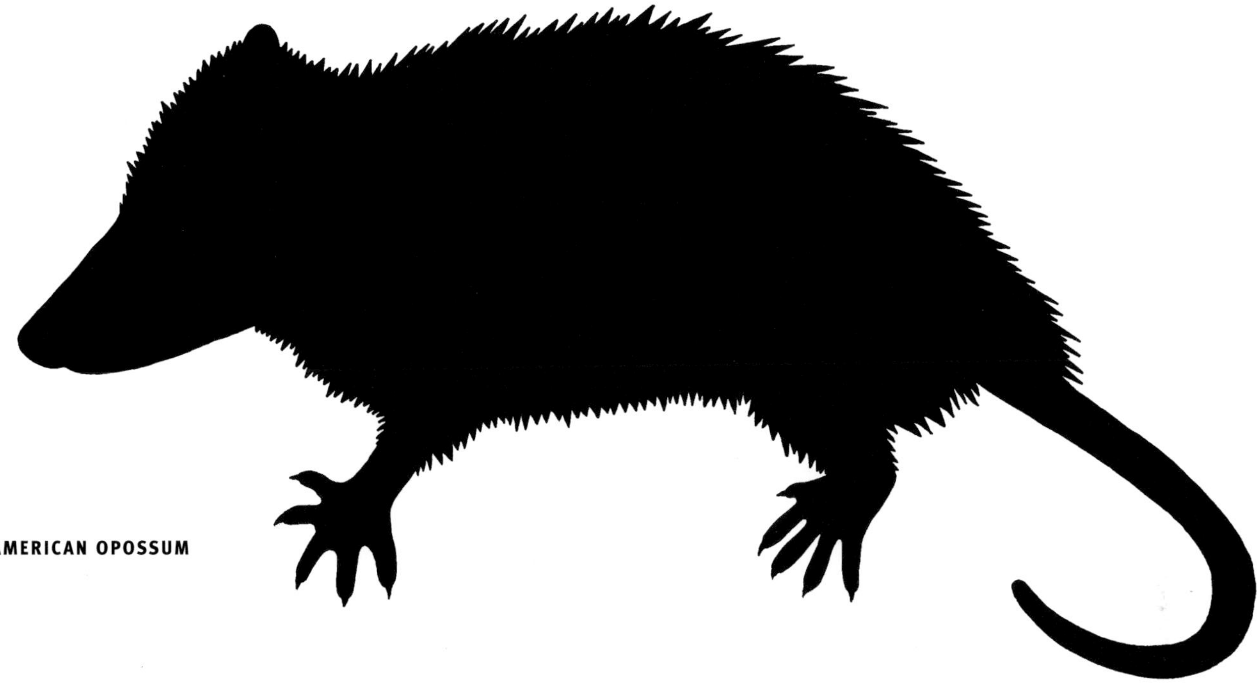

NORTH AMERICAN OPOSSUM

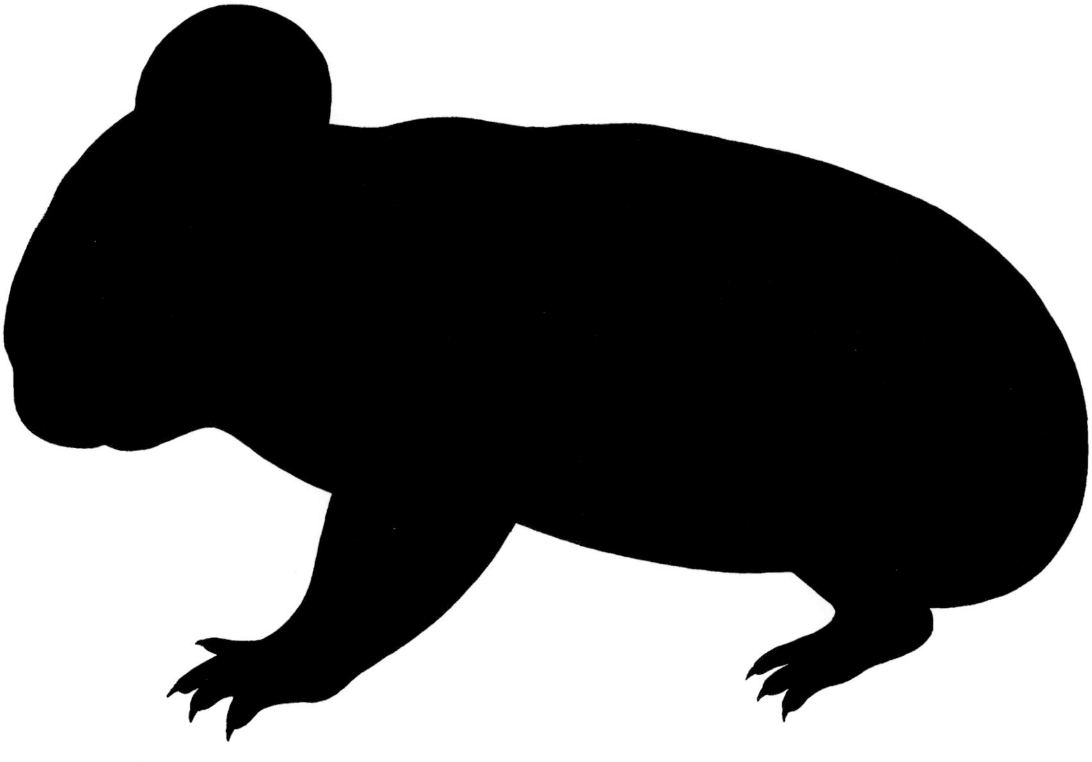

KOALA

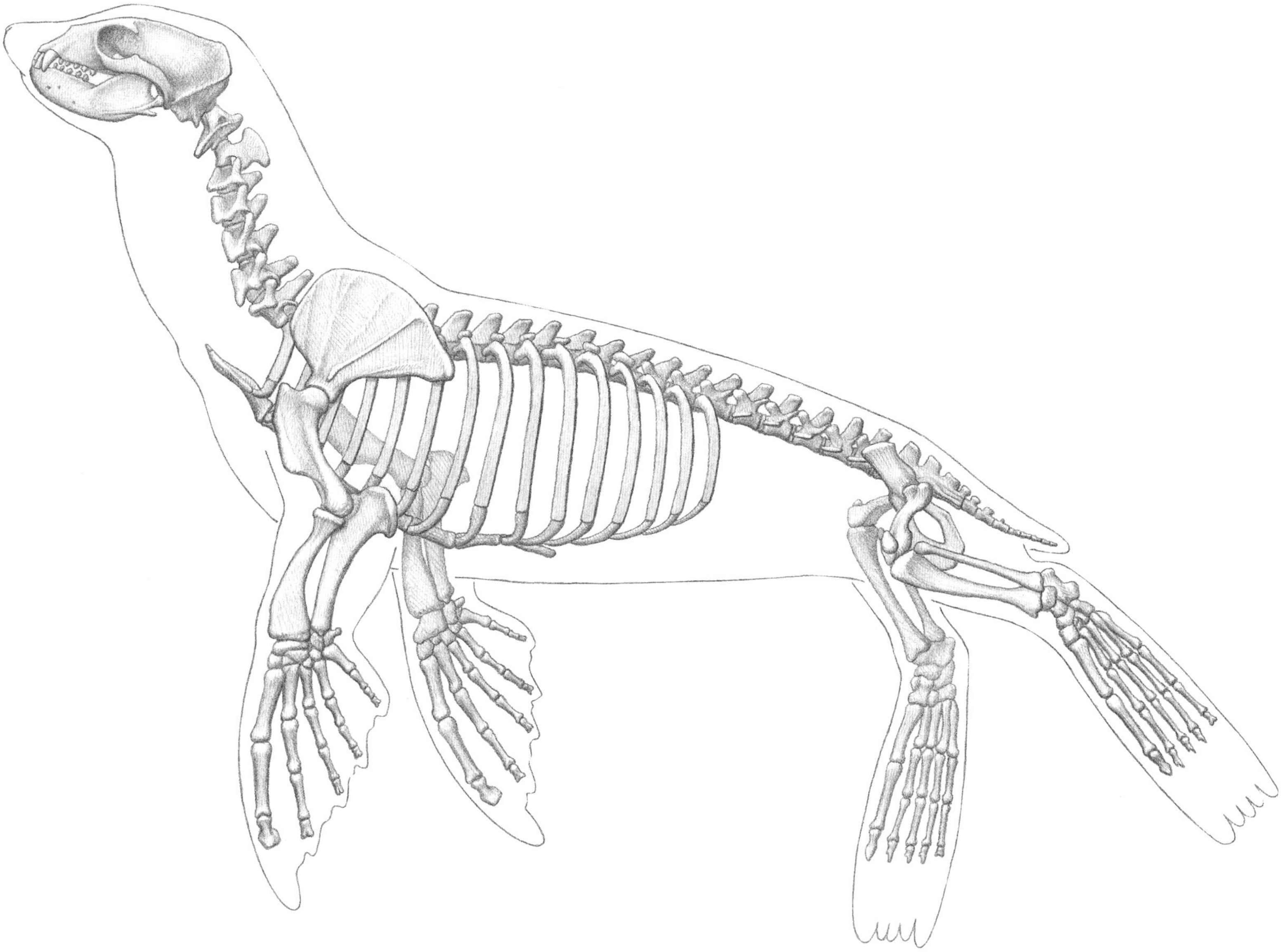

(FROM SPECIMEN; AFTER BLAINVILLE)

Sea lion characteristics: Webbed flipper-like forefoot and hind foot. Front flipper thicker on front edge. Skin of flipper extends past tips of toe bones, supported by individual cartilages attached to ends of toe bones. Noticeable claws on three middle toes of hind foot; other claws tiny and inconspicuous. Front flipper triangular; hind flipper rectangular. Hind limb can be advanced forward—can walk, but thigh and lower leg encased in skin of abdomen (seals can't walk—their hind limbs permanently extended backward). Elbow also enclosed in body skin, but forearms are free. Body streamlined (torpedo-shaped) for swimming. Thick insulating blubber layer between skin and muscles. Thick, flexible, muscular neck. Pelvis and femur small. Sternum has forward projection. Small external ears present (absent in seals). Ears and slit-like nostrils can be closed under water. Short, stubby tail. Very short hair; fur much darker when wet. Body uniform in color (no spots). Males larger than females. Closely related to terrestrial carnivores. Pinniped is not scientific classification, but means "fin footed."

AbD1L *Abductor digiti I longus;* **BiFem** *Biceps femoris;* **Brcph** *Brachiocephalicus;* **Brrad** *Brachioradialis;* **Bucc** *Buccinator;* **Delt** *Deltoid;* **Digas** *Digastric;* **ECRB** *Extensor carpi radialis brevis;* **ECRL** *Extensor carpi radialis longus;* **ECU** *Extensor carpi ulnaris;* **ED1** *Extensor digiti I;* **ED1L** *Extensor digiti I longus;* **EDBr** *Extensor digitorum brevis;* **EDC** *Extensor digitorum communis;* **EDLat** *Extensor digitorum lateralis;* **EDLon** *Extensor digitorum longus;* **ExAbO** *External abdominal oblique;* **FCR** *Flexor carpi radialis;* **FCU** *Flexor carpi ulnaris;* **FD1L** *Flexor digiti I longus;* **FDP** *Flexor digitorum profundus;* **FDS** *Flexor digitorum superficialis;* **Gastr** *Gastrocnemius;* **GluMe** *Gluteus medius;* **GluSu** *Gluteus superficialis;* **Grac** *Gracilis;* **Ilioc** *Iliocostalis;* **LatDo** *Latissimus dorsi;* **LeNas** *Levator nasolabialis;* **LLaMx** *Levator labii maxillaris;* **Longi** *Longissimus;* **Mass** *Masseter;* **Myloh** *Mylohyoid;* **Omohy** *Omohyoid;* **OrOc** *Orbicularis oculi;* **OrOr** *Orbicularis oris;* **PalLo** *Palmaris longus;* **PecPr** *Pectoralis profundus;* **PecSu** *Pectoralis superficialis;* **PerBr** *Peroneus brevis;* **PerLo** *Peroneus longus;* **Plant** *Plantaris;* **PrTer** *Pronator teres;* **RecAb** *Rectus abdominis;* **SerVT** *Serratus ventralis thoracis;* **Smemb** *Semimembranosus;* **Splen** *Splenius;* **Stmas** *Sternomastoid;* **Stthh** *Sternothyrohyoid;* **Temp** *Temporalis;* **TenFA** *Tensor fasciae antibrachii;* **TenFL** *Tensor fasciae latae;* **TibCr** *Tibialis cranialis;* **Trap** *Trapezius;* **TriLa** *Triceps brachii, lateral head;* **TriLo** *Triceps brachii, long head;* **VasLa** *Vastus lateralis.*

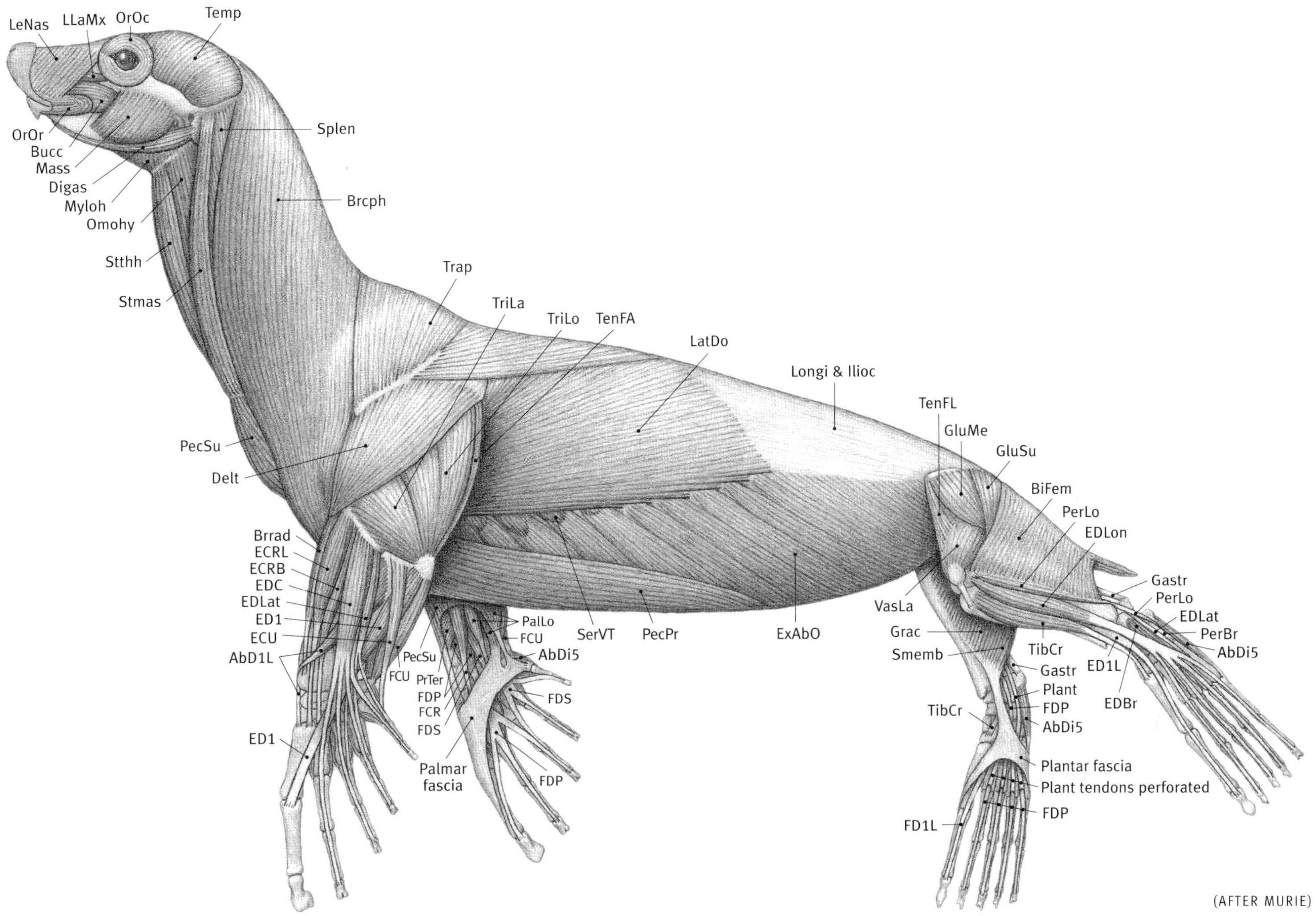

(AFTER MURIE)

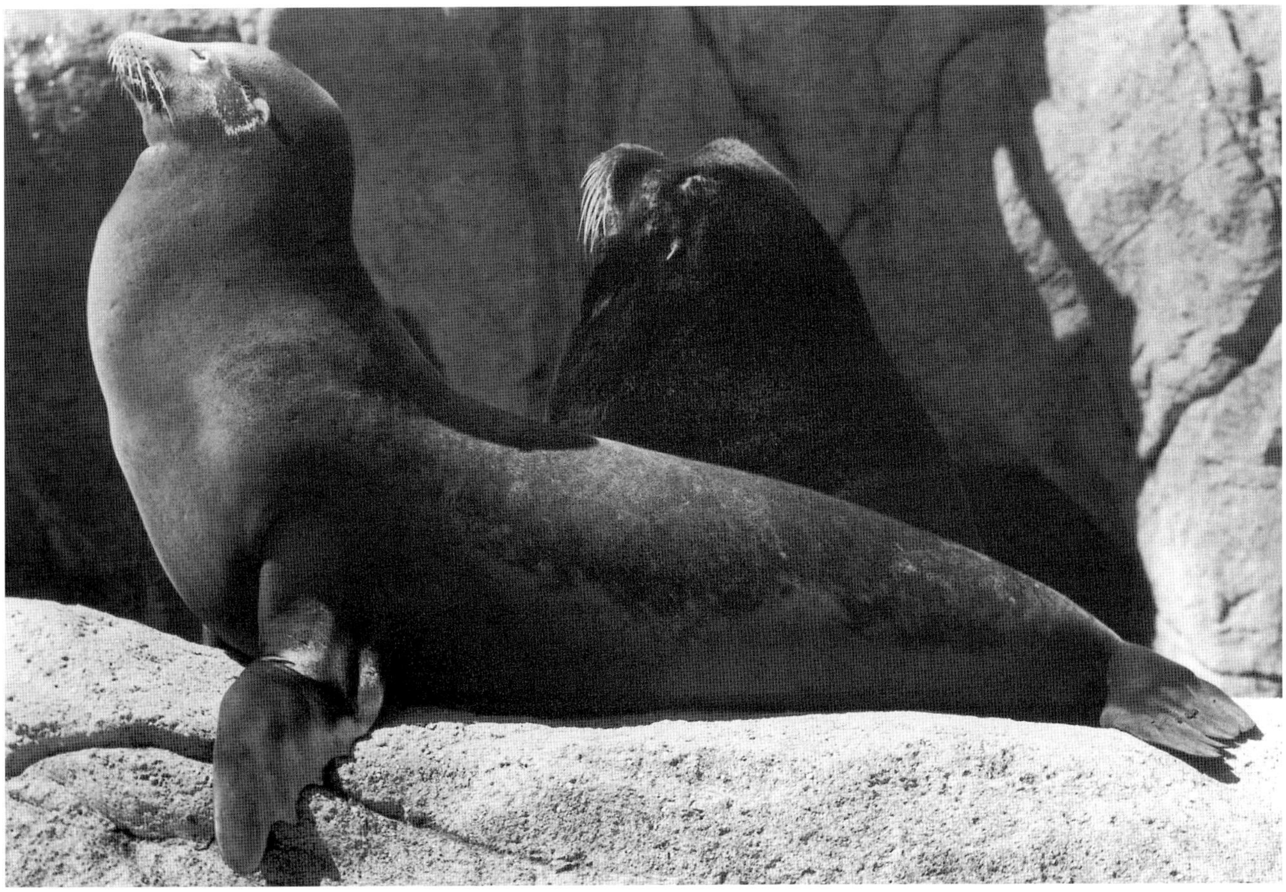

CALIFORNIA SEA LION (FEMALE)

Zalophus californianus

MALE IN BACKGROUND

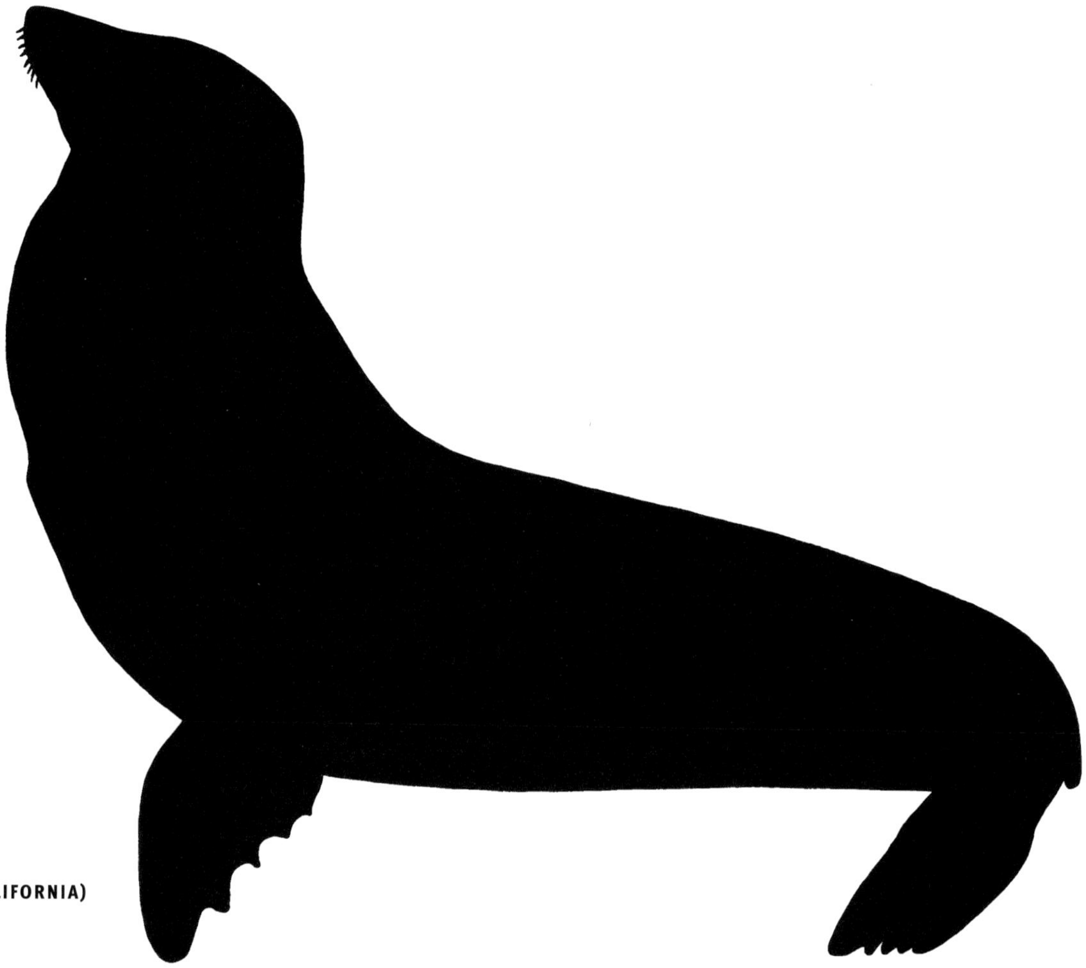

SEA LION (CALIFORNIA)

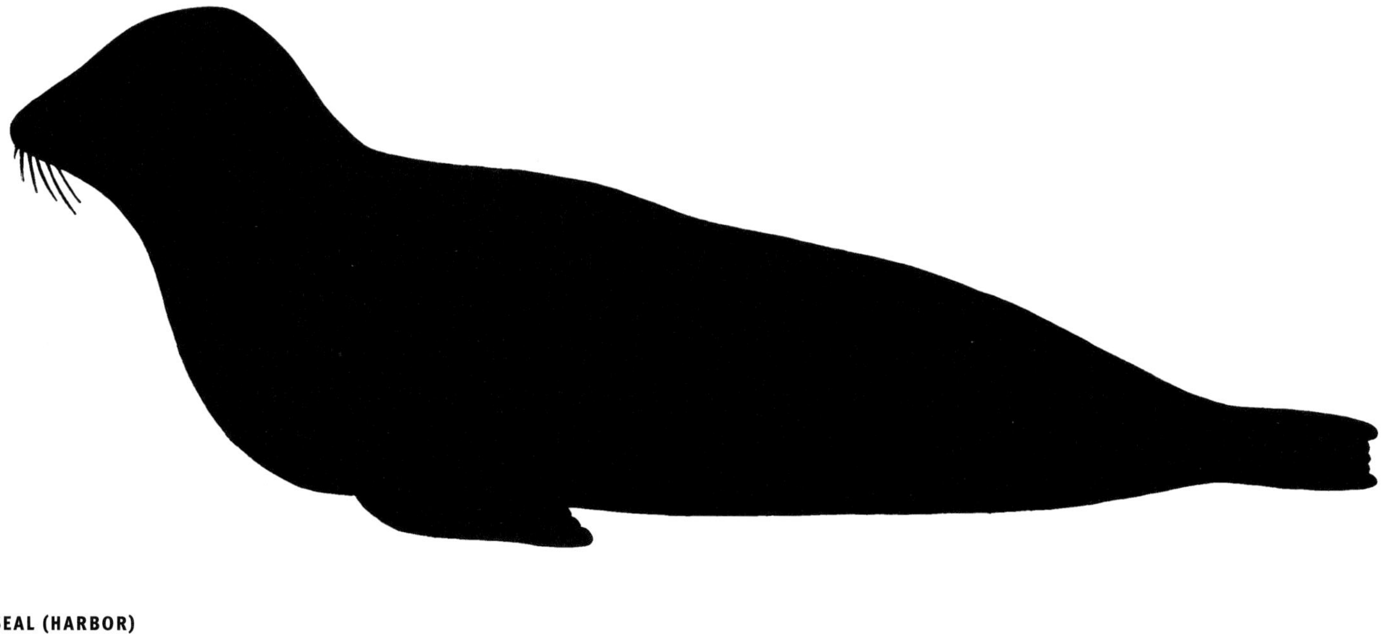

SEAL (HARBOR)

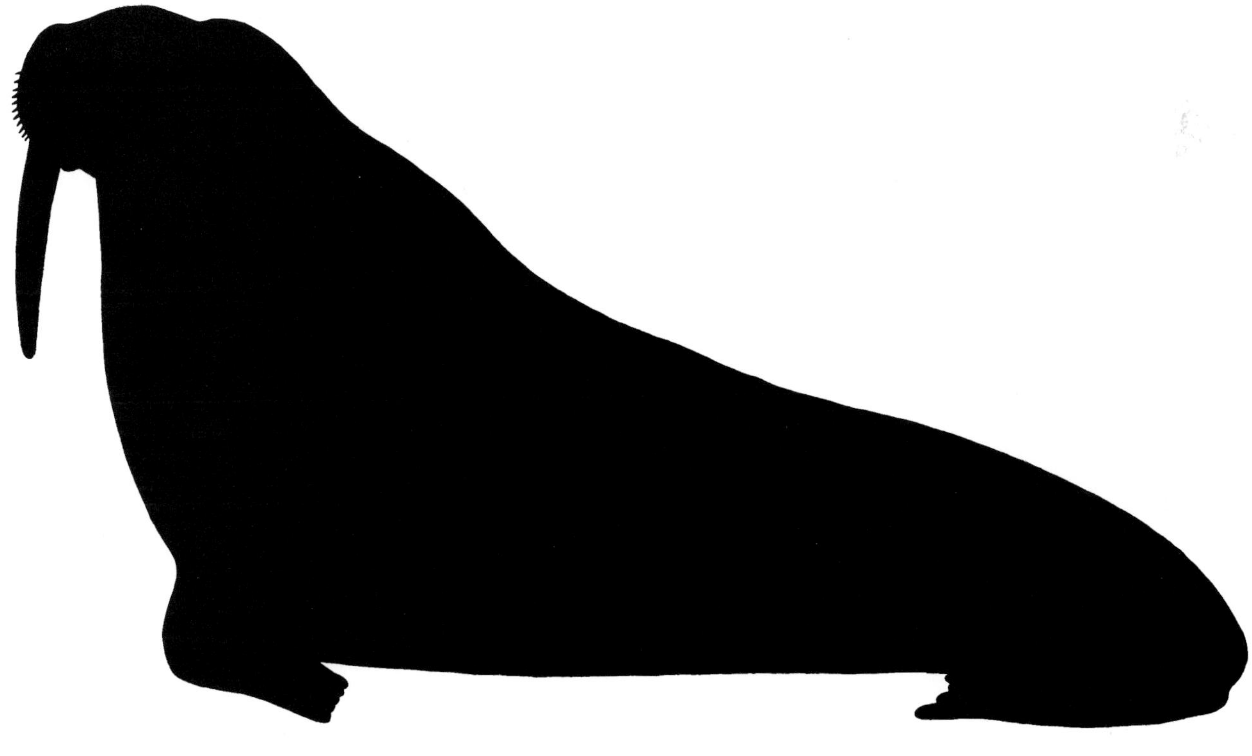

WALRUS

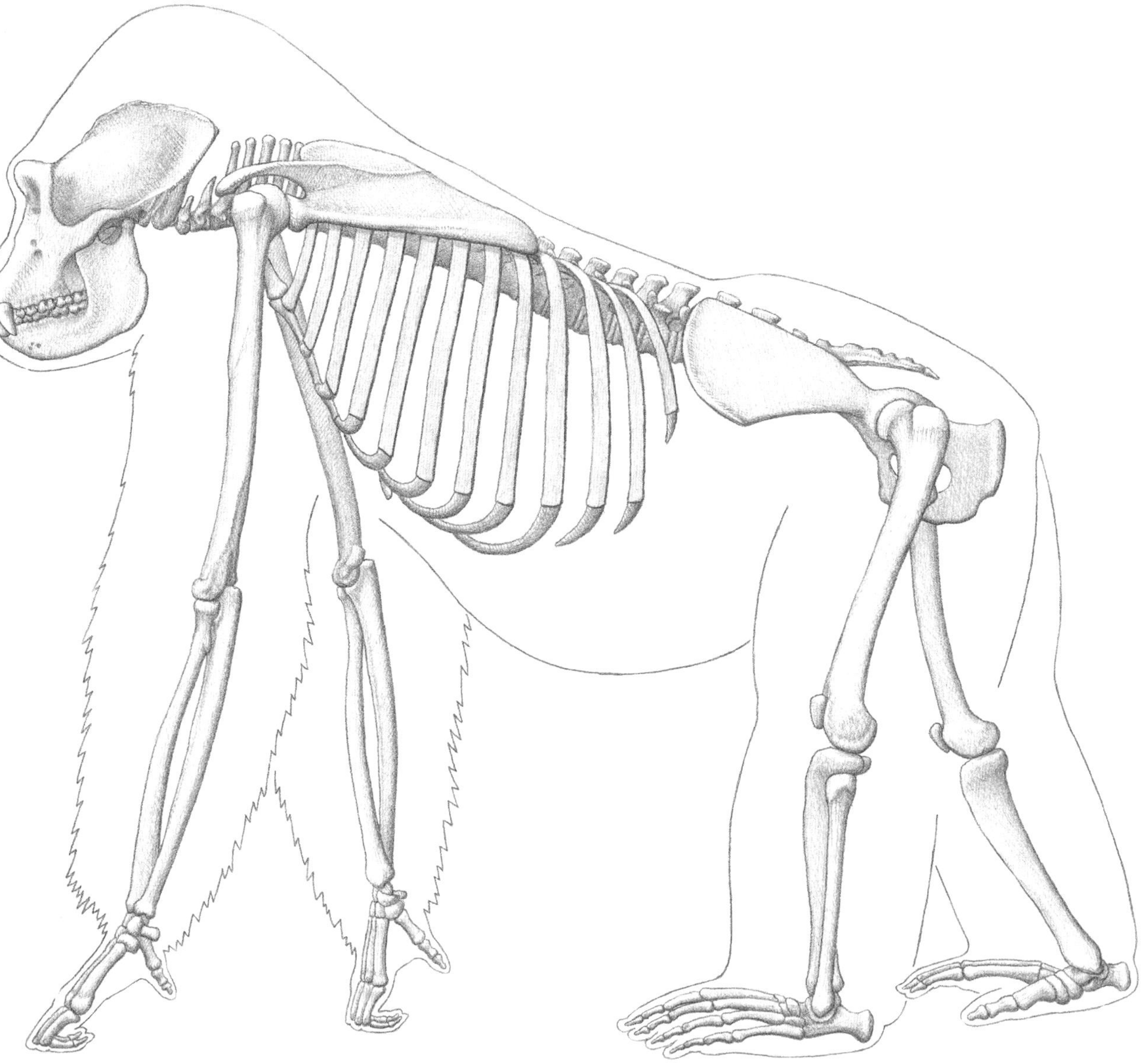

LOWLAND GORILLA (MALE) (FROM SPECIMENS)

Gorilla gorilla

Gorilla characteristics: Walks on ends of uppermost phalanges of hand; middle phalanges rest on ground. Short thumb does not touch the ground. Walks on sole and heel of foot. Thumb and big toe opposable; large big toe angles out, away from foot. Nails on digits. Well-developed clavicle attached to scapula and sternum. Forearm rotates (pronates/supinates). Arms longer than legs. Upper arm longer than forearm (about equal in chimps). Five digits on each limb. Shoulders thrust forward. Thigh longer than lower leg. Stocky body, large abdomen. Sloping forehead, large brow ridges, rounded muzzle. Large bony crest on top of skull in male. Thick crown pad of skin layers and hair on top of the head, especially in male. Large nostrils. Small, deep-set eyes face forward for binocular vision. Small ears (chimps have large ears). Large canine teeth. Foramen magnum (hole for spinal cord) located near bottom of cranium. No tail. Face, ears, bottoms of hands and feet naked. Longest hair on arms, ends at wrist. Thick fur layer on top of gluteal muscles.

AbDi5 *Abductor digiti V;* **AbDM** *Abductor digiti minimi;* **AbHal** *Abductor hallucis;* **AbMD5** *Abductor metatarsi digiti V;* **AbPB** *Abductor pollicis brevis;* **AbPL** *Abductor pollicis longus;* **AdHal** *Adductor hallucis;* **AdPol** *Adductor pollicis;* **Anc** *Anconeus;* **BicLH** *Biceps brachii, long head;* **BicSH** *Biceps brachii, short head;* **BiFemLH** *Biceps femoris, long head;* **BiFemSH** *Biceps femoris, short head;* **Brach** *Brachialis;* **Brrad** *Brachioradialis;* **Bucc** *Buccinator;* **DAnOr** *Depressor anguli oris;* **DelAc** *Deltoid, acromial portion;* **DelSp** *Deltoid, spinal portion;* **Digas** *Digastric;* **DLI** *Depressor labii inferioris (mandibularis);* **ECRB** *Extensor carpi radialis brevis;* **ECRL** *Extensor carpi radialis longus;* **ECU** *Extensor carpi ulnaris;* **ED5** *Extensor digiti V (Extensor digitorum lateralis);* **EDBr** *Extensor digitorum brevis;* **EDC** *Extensor digitorum communis;* **EDLon** *Extensor digitorum longus;* **EHB** *Extensor hallucis brevis;* **EHL** *Extensor hallucis longus;* **EPBr** *Extensor pollicis brevis;* **EPL** *Extensor pollicis longus;* **ExAbO** *External abdominal oblique;* **FCR** *Flexor carpi radialis;* **FCU** *Flexor carpi ulnaris;* **FDBr** *Flexor digitorum brevis;* **FDLon** *Flexor digitorum longus;* **FDP** *Flexor digitorum profundus;* **FDS** *Flexor digitorum superficialis;* **FPB** *Flexor pollicis brevis;* **FPL** *Flexor pollicis longus;* **Front** *Frontalis;* **GasLa** *Gastrocnemius, lateral head;* **GasMe** *Gastrocnemius, medial head;* **GluMe** *Gluteus medius;* **GluMx** *Gluteus maximus (superficialis);* **Grac** *Gracilis;* **Ilioc** *Iliocostalis;* **Infra** *Infraspinatus;* **Inter** *Interossei;* **LatDo** *Latissimus dorsi;* **LLSAN** *Levator labii superioris alaeque nasi (levator nasolabialis);* **LLSup** *Levator labii superioris (maxillaris);* **Longi** *Longissimus;* **Mass** *Masseter;* **Omohy** *Omohyoid;* **OrOc** *Orbicularis oculi;* **OrOr** *Orbicularis oris;* **PalLo** *Palmaris longus;* **PecMa** *Pectoralis major;* **PecQu** *Pectoralis quartus;* **PerBr** *Peroneus brevis;* **PerLo** *Peroneus longus;* **PrTer** *Pronator teres;* **RecAb** *Rectus abdominis;* **RecFe** *Rectus femoris;* **Risor** *Risorius;* **Sart** *Sartorius;* **SerAn** *Serratus anterior (serratus ventralis thoracis);* **Sol** *Soleus;* **Splen** *Splenius;* **Stend** *Semitendinosus;* **Sthy** *Sternohyoid;* **Stman** *Sternomandibularis;* **Stthy** *Sternothyroid;* **TeMaj** *Teres major;* **TeMin** *Teres minor;* **Temp** *Temporalis;* **TenFA** *Tensor fasciae antibrachii;* **TenFL** *Tensor fasciae latae;* **TibAn** *Tibialis anterior (cranialis);* **TibPo** *Tibialis posterior (caudalis);* **Trap** *Trapezius;* **TriLa** *Triceps brachii, lateral head;* **TriLo** *Triceps brachii, long head;* **VasLa** *Vastus lateralis;* **VasMe** *Vastus medialis;* **ZygMa** *Zygomaticus major(zygomaticus);* **ZygMi** *Zygomaticus minor.*

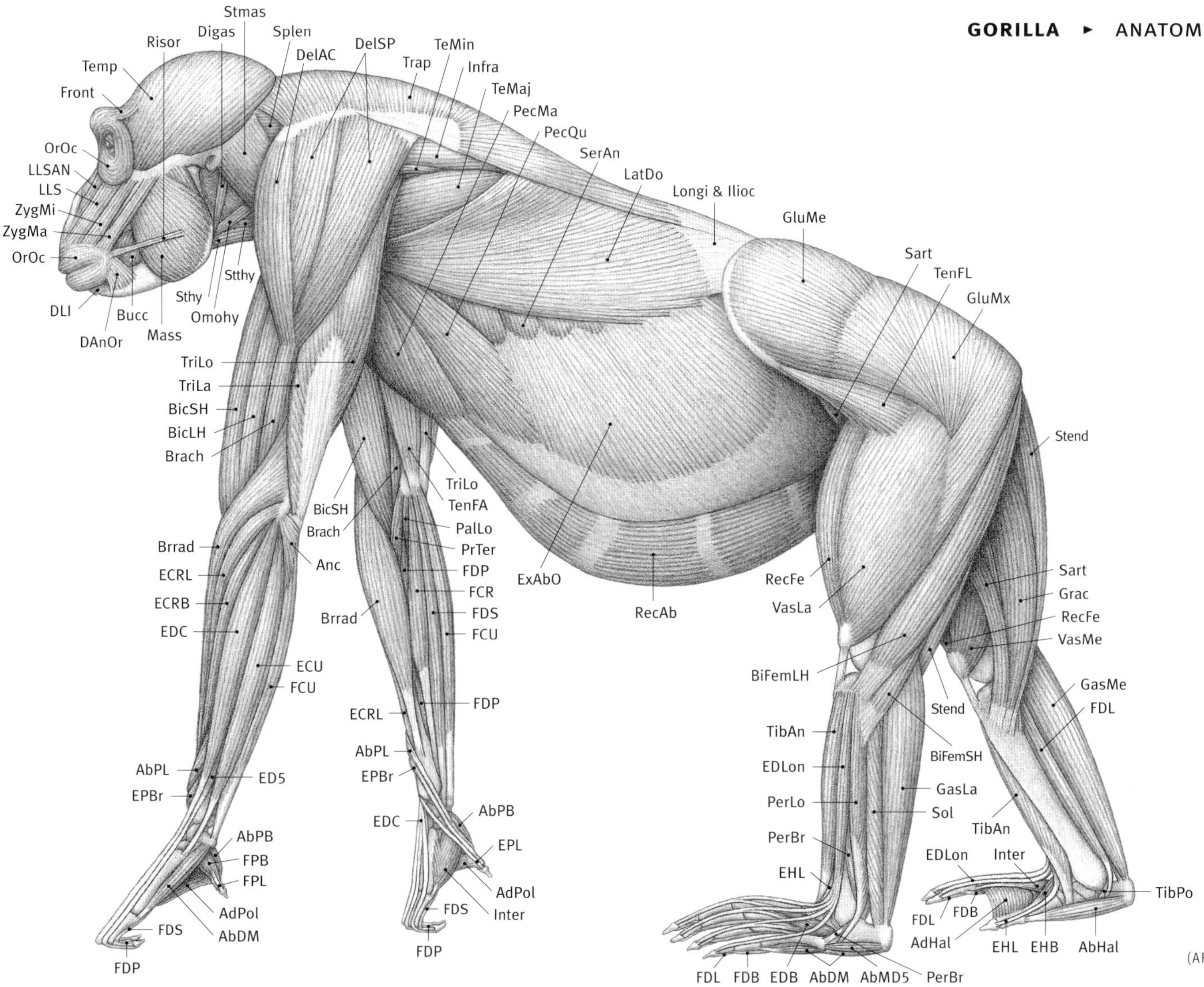

(AFTER RAVEN)

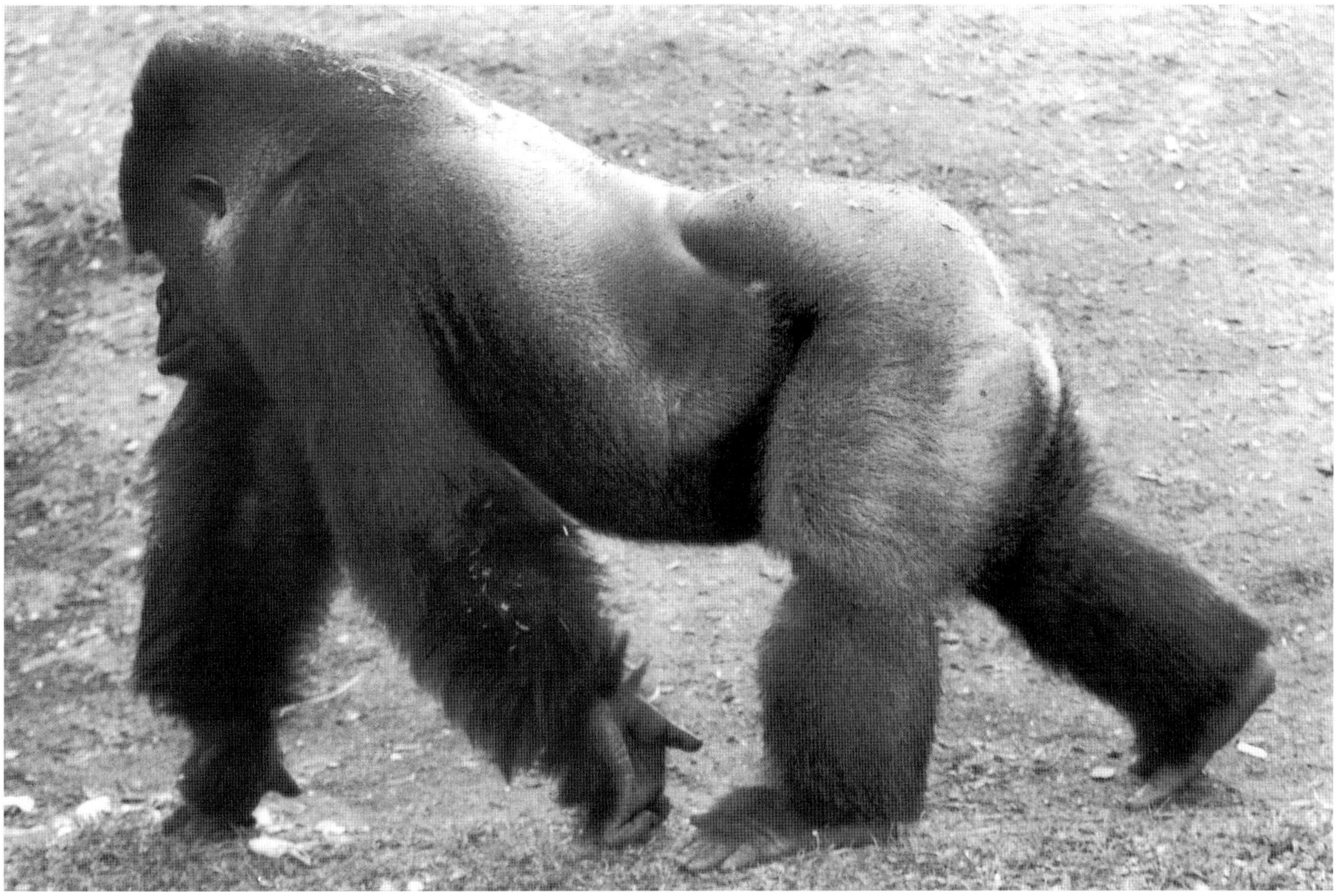

LOWLAND GORILLA (MALE)

Gorilla gorilla

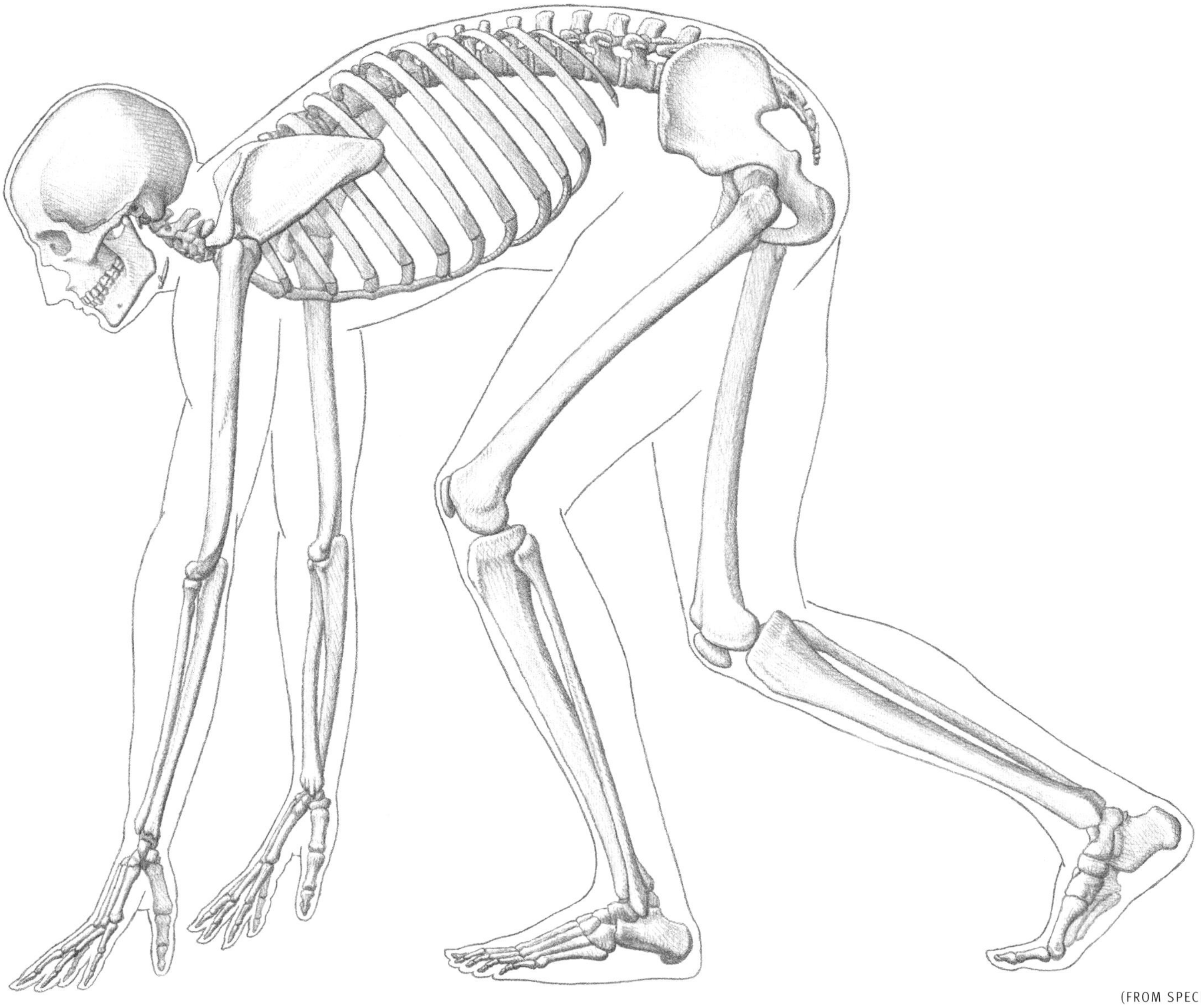

(FROM SPECIMENS)

Human characteristics: Enormous braincase, flat face. Upright forehead (small brow ridges in male). Eyes face forward for binocular vision. Small canine teeth same size as adjacent teeth. Highest development of facial muscle control to broadcast facial expressions. Foramen magnum on bottom of cranium—skull balanced on top of vertical spine when standing. Upright spine has four curves—neck and lumbar portions curve forward; thoracic and sacral portions curve backward. Well-developed clavicle attached to scapula and sternum. Scapula on back surface of rib cage (on side in four-legged animals); rib cage compressed front to back (side to side in four-legged animals). Thumb opposable; big toe is not. Flat nails on digits. Five digits on each limb. Walks upright on two legs, on sole and heel of foot. Legs longer than arms. Upper arm longer than forearm. Thigh longer than lower leg. Forearm rotates (pronates/supinates). No tail.

AbDM *Abductor digiti minimi;* **AbHal** *Abductor hallucis;* **AbPB** *Abductor pollicis brevis;* **AbPL** *Abductor pollicis longus;* **AddMg** *Adductor magnus;* **AdPol** *Adductor pollicis;* **Anc** *Anconeus;* **Bicep** *Biceps brachii;* **BiFemLH** *Biceps femoris, long head;* **BiFemSH** *Biceps femoris, short head;* **Brach** *Brachialis;* **Brrad** *Brachioradialis;* **Bucc** *Buccinator;* **DAnOr** *Depressor anguli oris;* **DelAc** *Deltoid, acromial portion;* **DelSp** *Deltoid, spinal portion;* **DepSu** *Depressor supercilii;* **DLI** *Depressor labii inferioris (mandibularis);* **ECRB** *Extensor carpi radialis brevis;* **ECRL** *Extensor carpi radialis longus;* **ECU** *Extensor carpi ulnaris;* **EDBr** *Extensor digitorum brevis;* **EDC** *Extensor digitorum communis;* **EDLon** *Extensor digitorum longus;* **EHL** *Extensor hallucis longus;* **EPBr** *Extensor pollicis brevis;* **EPL** *Extensor pollicis longus;* **ExAbO** *External abdominal oblique;* **FCR** *Flexor carpi radialis;* **FCU** *Flexor carpi ulnaris;* **FDLon** *Flexor digitorum longus;* **FDS** *Flexor digitorum superficialis;* **FHL** *Flexor hallucis longus;* **FPB** *Flexor pollicis brevis;* **FPL** *Flexor pollicis longus;* **Front** *Frontalis;* **GasLa** *Gastrocnemius, lateral head;* **GasMe** *Gastrocnemius, medial head;* **GluMe** *Gluteus medius;* **GluMx** *Gluteus maximus (superficialis);* **Grac** *Gracilis;* **Ilioc** *Iliocostalis;* **Infra** *Infraspinatus;* **Inter** *Interossei;* **LatDo** *Latissimus dorsi;* **LevSc** *Levator scapulae (serratus ventralis cervicis);* **LLSAN** *Levator labii superioris alaeque nasi (levator nasolabialis);* **LLSup** *Levator labii superioris (maxillaris);* **Longi** *Longissimus;* **Malar** *Malaris;* **Mass** *Masseter;* **Ment** *Mentalis;* **Nasal** *Nasalis;* **Occip** *Occipitalis;* **Omohy** *Omohyoid;* **OrOc** *Orbicularis oculi;* **OrOr** *Orbicularis oris;* **PalLo** *Palmaris longus;* **PecMa** *Pectoralis major;* **PerBr** *Peroneus brevis;* **PerLo** *Peroneus longus;* **PerTe** *Peroneus tertius;* **Proc** *Proceros;* **PrTer** *Pronator teres;* **RecAb** *Rectus abdominis;* **RecFe** *Rectus femoris;* **Rhom** *Rhomboid;* **Risor** *Risorius;* **Sart** *Sartorius;* **SerAn** *Serratus anterior (serratus ventralis thoracis);* **Smemb** *Semimembranosus;* **Sol** *Soleus;* **Splen** *Splenius;* **Stend** *Semitendinosus;* **Sthy** *Sternohyoid;* **Stmas** *Sternomastoid;* **TeMaj** *Teres major;* **TeMin** *Teres minor;* **Temp** *Temporalis;* **TenFL** *Tensor fasciae latae;* **TibAn** *Tibialis anterior (cranialis);* **TibPo** *Tibialis posterior (caudalis);* **Trap** *Trapezius;* **TriLa** *Triceps brachii, lateral head;* **TriLo** *Triceps brachii, long head;* **TriMe** *Triceps brachii, medial head;* **VasLa** *Vastus lateralis;* **VasMe** *Vastus medialis;* **ZygMa** *Zygomaticus major (zygomaticus).*

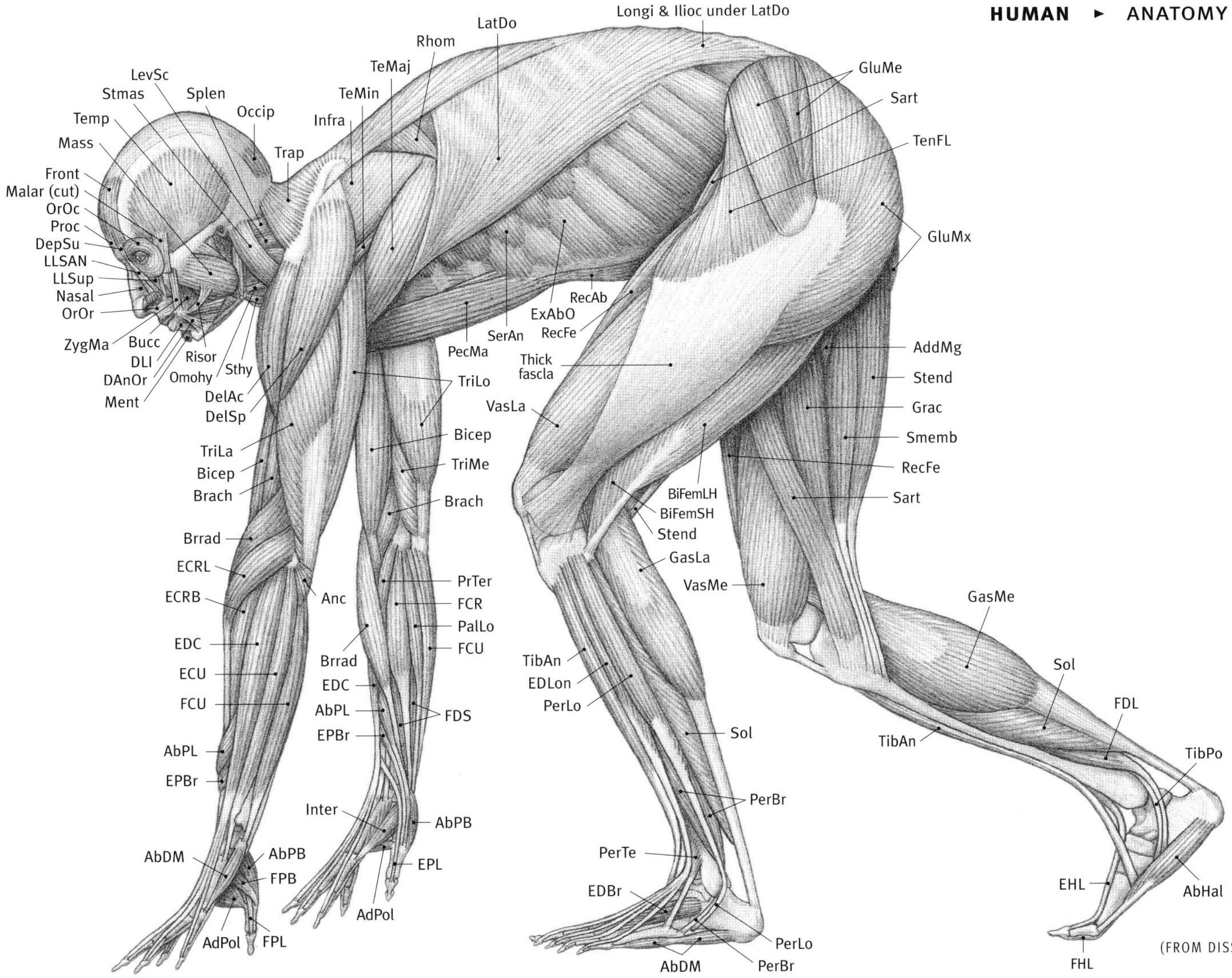

(FROM DISSECTIONS)

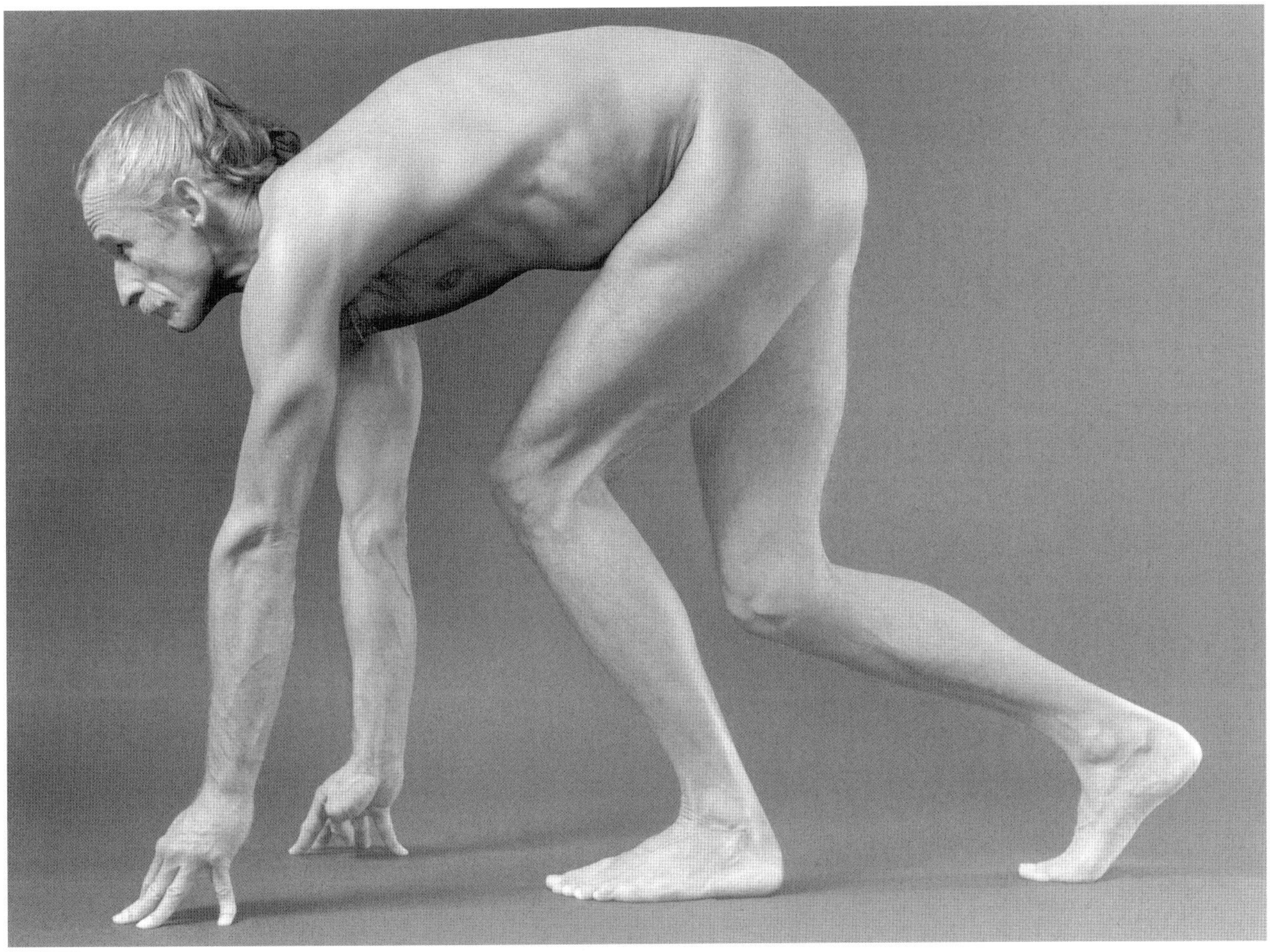

Homo sapiens

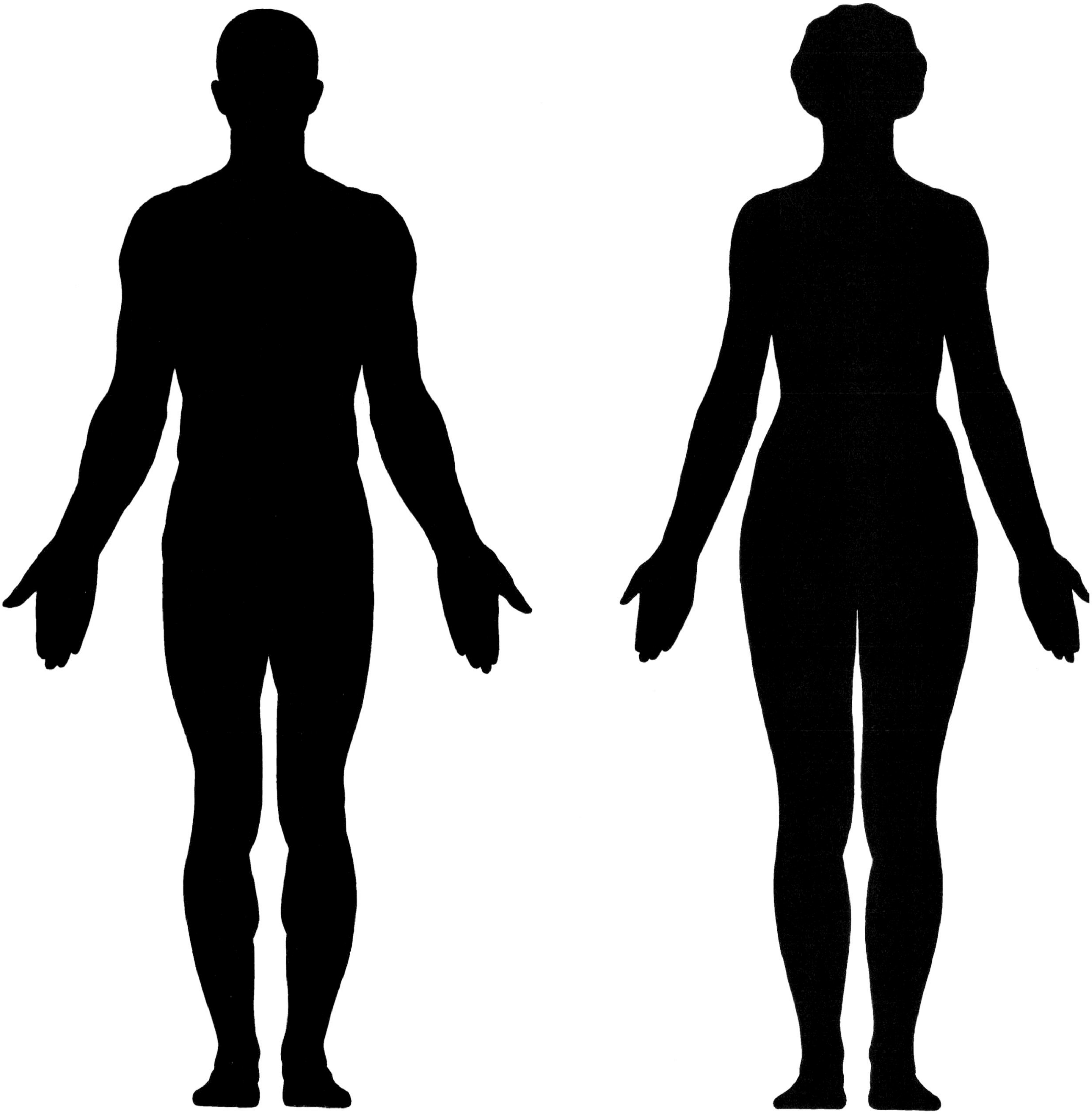

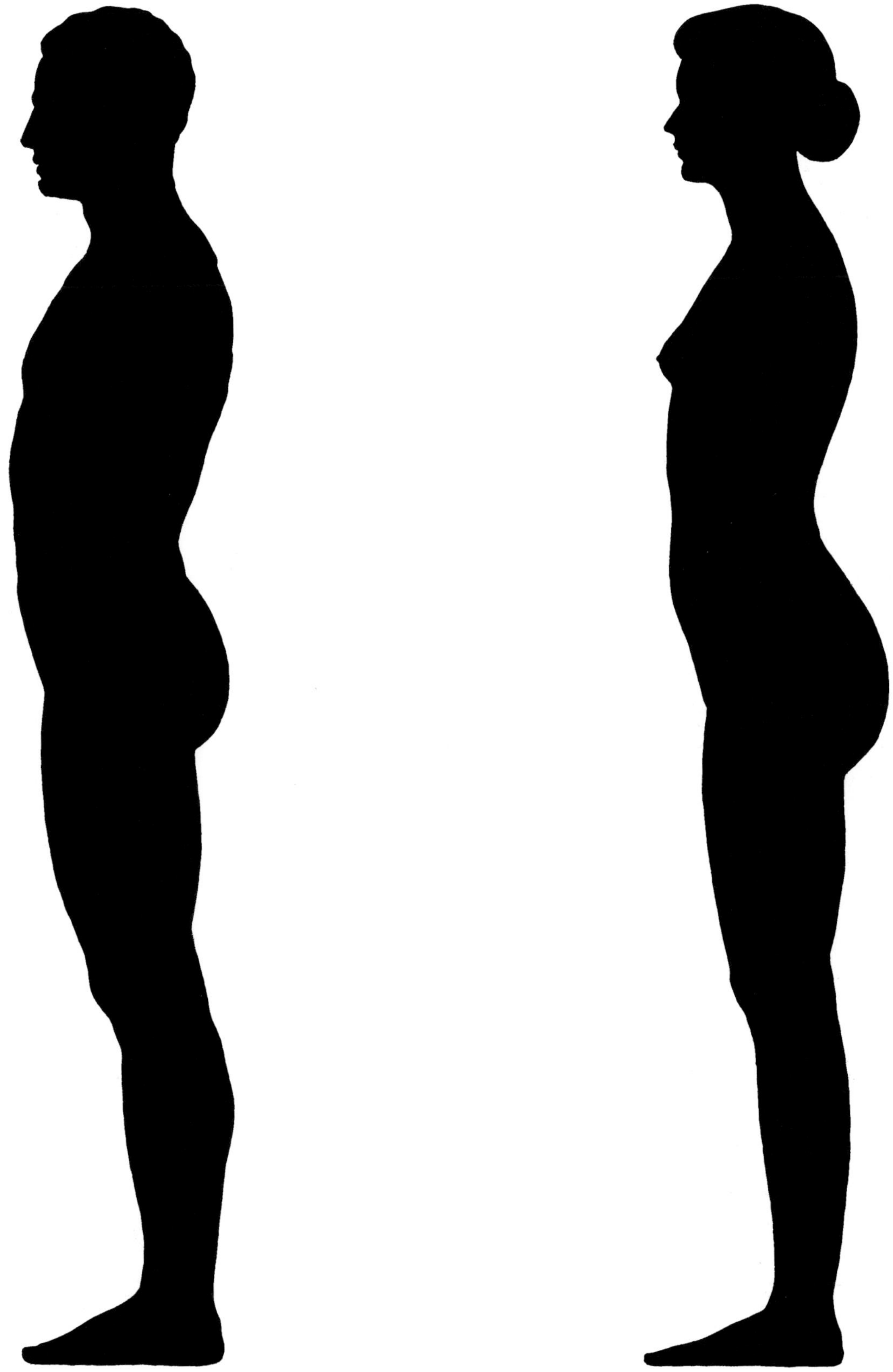

(ALL AFTER RICHER)

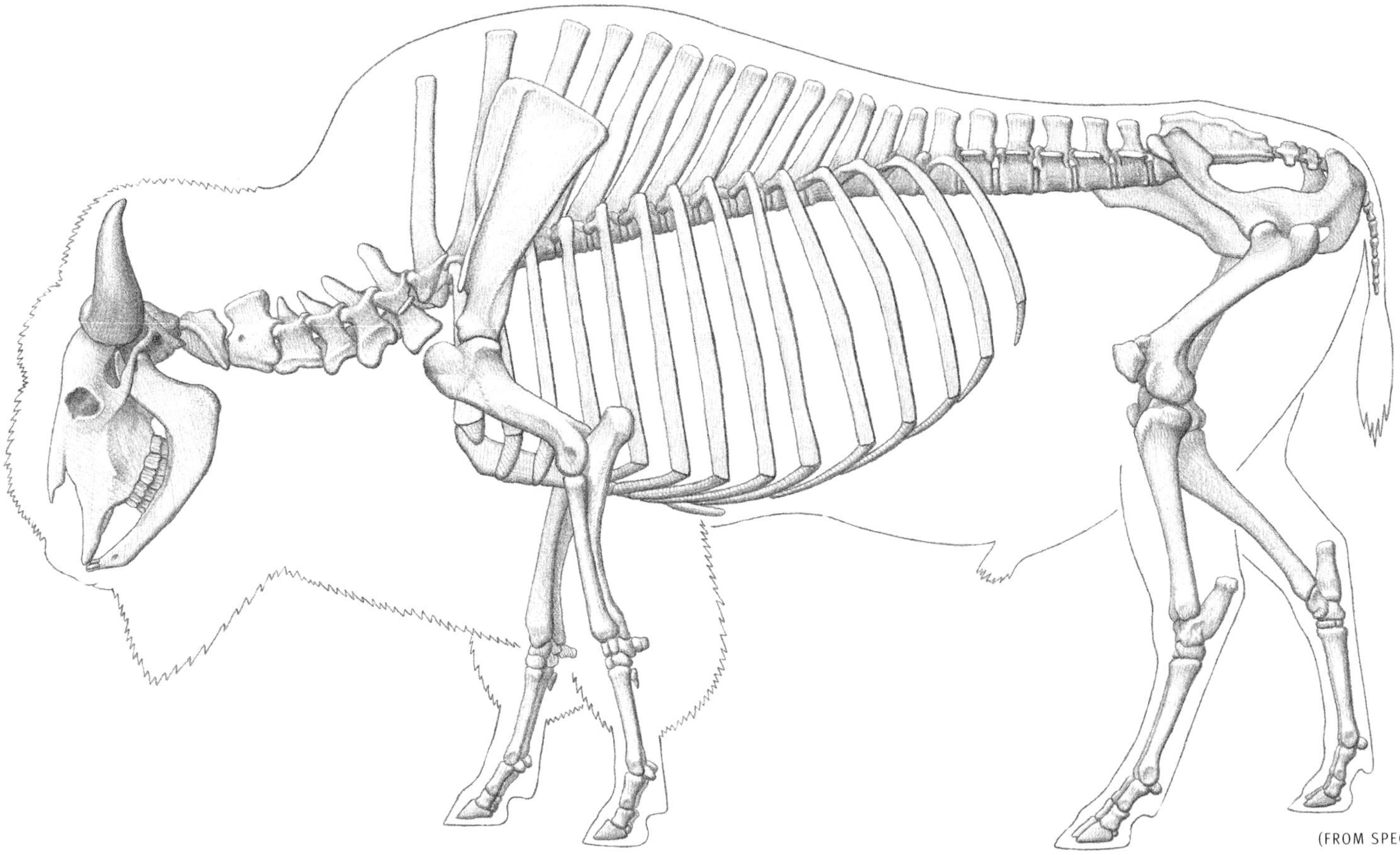

(FROM SPECIMENS)

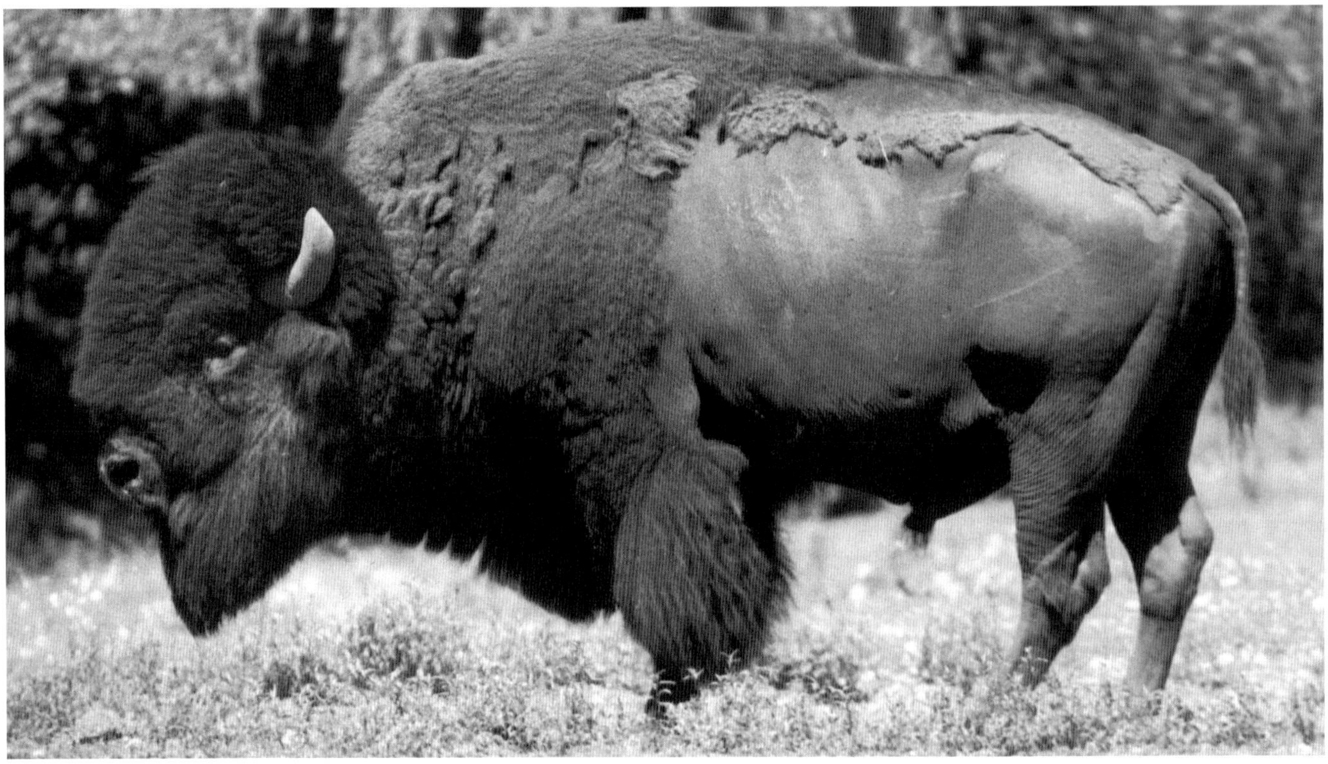

Bison bison (MALE)

American bison characteristics: Has very long spinous processes on thoracic vertebrae (especially between the shoulders). Four digits with hoofs per limb. Two central toes are large and weight-bearing; vestigial inner and outer toes, with hoofs, are very small and located higher on side of foot and to the rear (they do not articulate with the skeleton and do not touch the ground). Walks on toes. Front half of body develops permanent long hair, especially on the top of the skull, the chin, and the forearms). Rear half looses thick fur cover in the summer, so difference between hair length of front and rear portions of body is very pronounced in warm months, with a clear line of demarcation. Both sexes have horns.

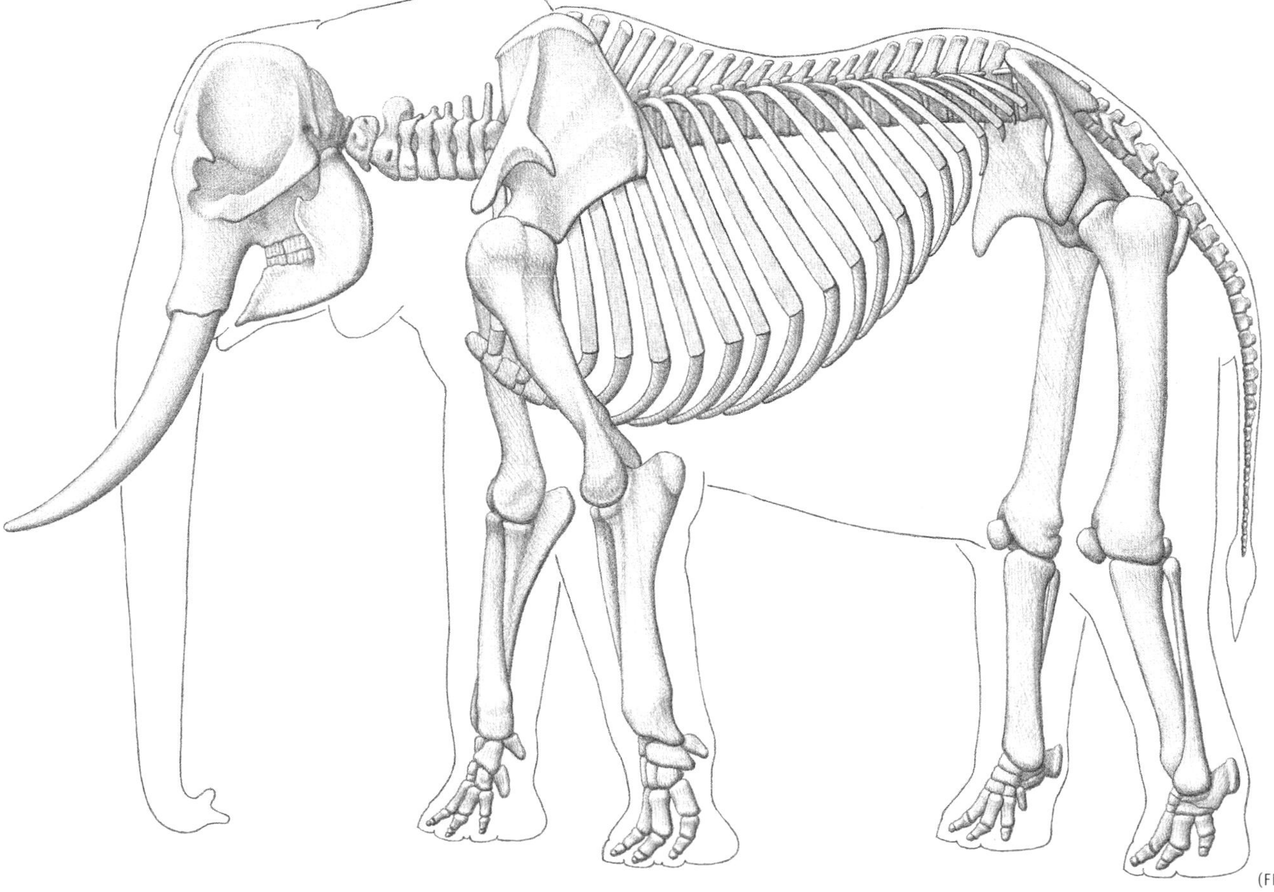

(FROM SPECIMEN PHOTOS)

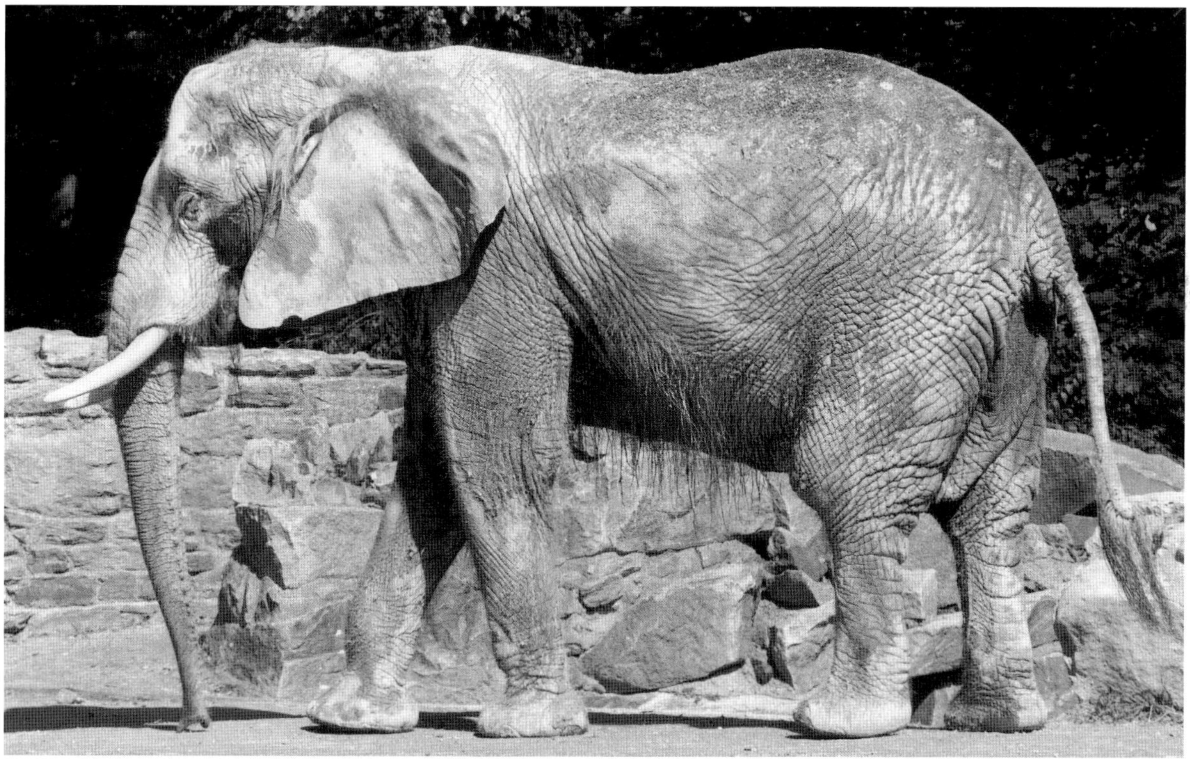

Loxodonta africana (FEMALE)

African elephant characteristics: Middle of back profile concave/low (convex/high in Indian). Nose extends into long, flexible, muscular trunk with nostrils and one prehensile finger-like projection at tip (two in Indian). Large skull; short nasal bones located high on skull (for attachment of trunk). Brain surrounded by thick, airy bone. Single rounded prominences on top of head (double in Indian). Upper incisors elongated into continuously growing tusks, in both male and female. Very large ears (larger than Indian). Short neck—cervical vertebrae compressed front to back. Rib cage extends to pelvis. Thick, pillar-like columnar limbs (bones in almost vertical straight line) and shoulder and hip sockets face downward, all to support massive body weight. Short feet. All feet have five digits—some inner and outer toes may be reduced and without hoofs. Both front and rear feet have an extra small, elongated bone (prepollex in front and prehallux in rear) just to the inside of the first digit. Front foot has four or five hoofs (five in Indian). Hind foot usually has three, four, or five hoofs (four or five in Indian). Thick elastic pad on sole of foot. Foot in life somewhat cylindrical or conical. When the animal is lying on belly, knee touches ground (femur directed downward); lower leg continues straight back. Long tail has wispy tuft of coarse hair.

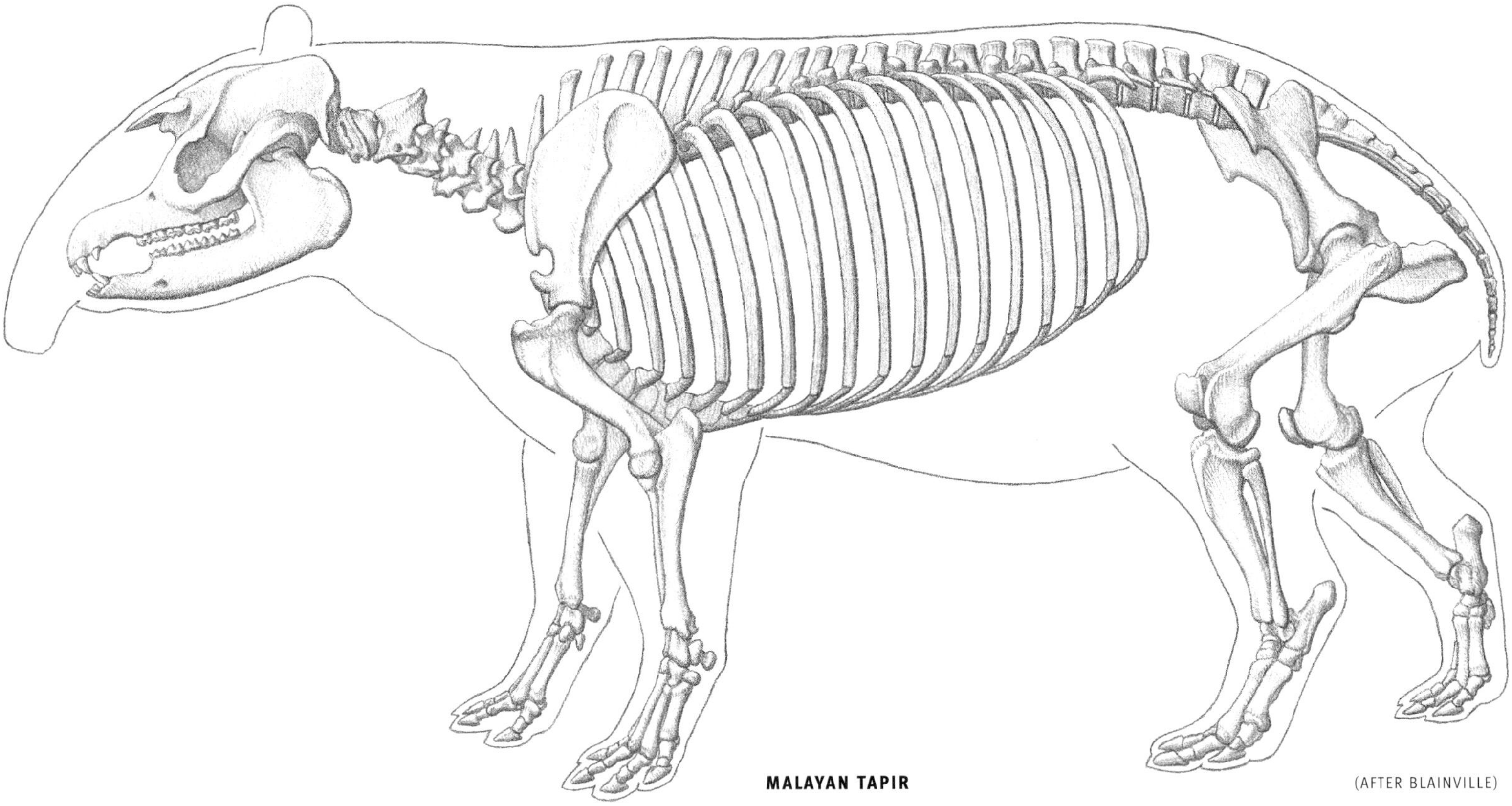

MALAYAN TAPIR

(AFTER BLAINVILLE)

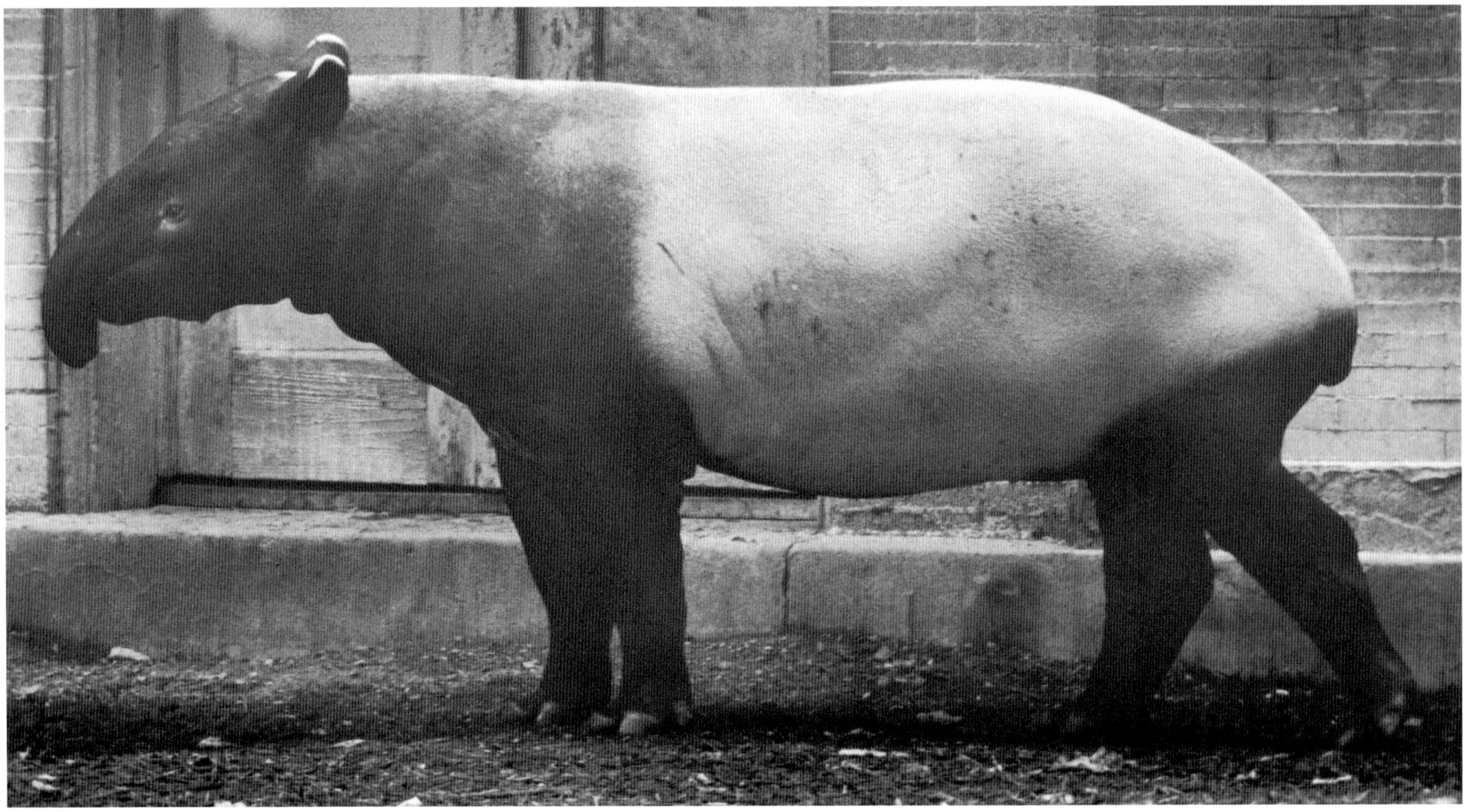

MALAYAN TAPIR
Tapirus indicus

Tapir characteristics: Elongated, movable snout. Nasal opening large on skull—nasal bones short and retracted for attachment of proboscis. Small eyes. Ears oval and erect. Pelvis oriented toward the vertical. Heavy, oval-shaped body (rear end pointed), with short limbs. Four digits on front limb; three on hind limb. Toes have hoofs. Walks on toes. Femur has projecting third trochanter on outer side of shaft for attachment of the gluteus superficialis muscle. Short tail. In same group as horses and rhinoceroses.

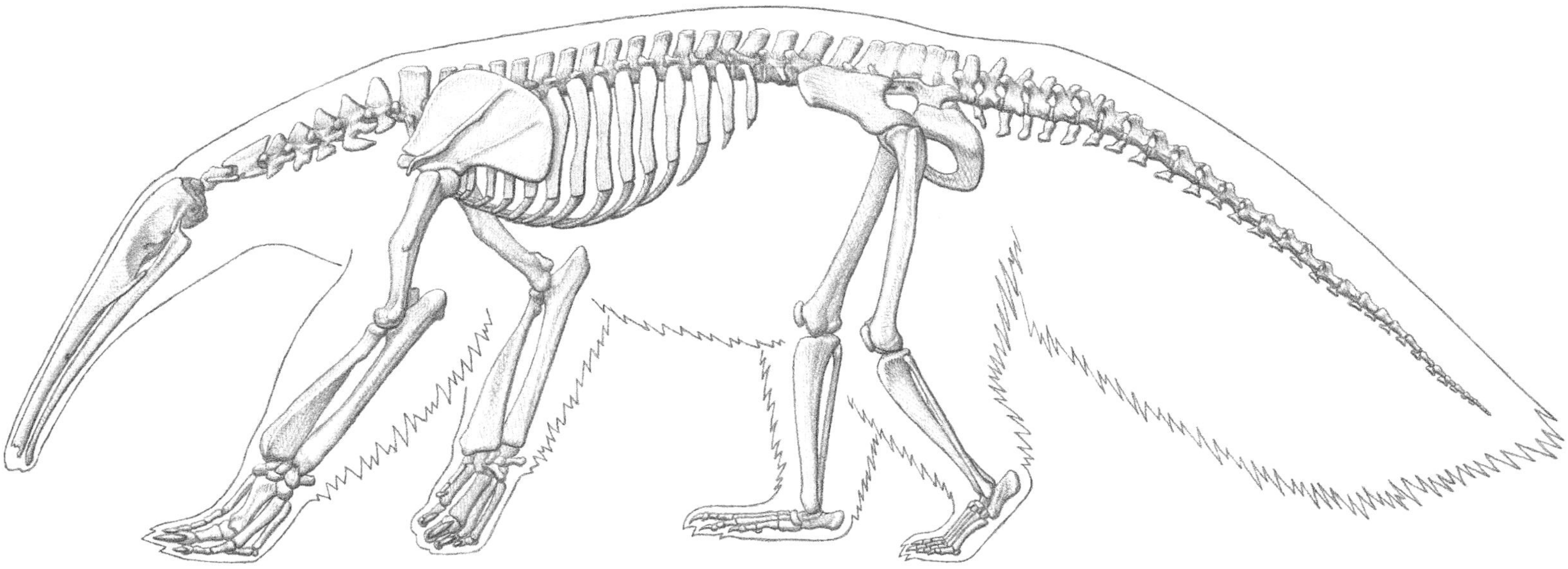

(FROM SPECIMENS; AFTER BLAINVILLE)

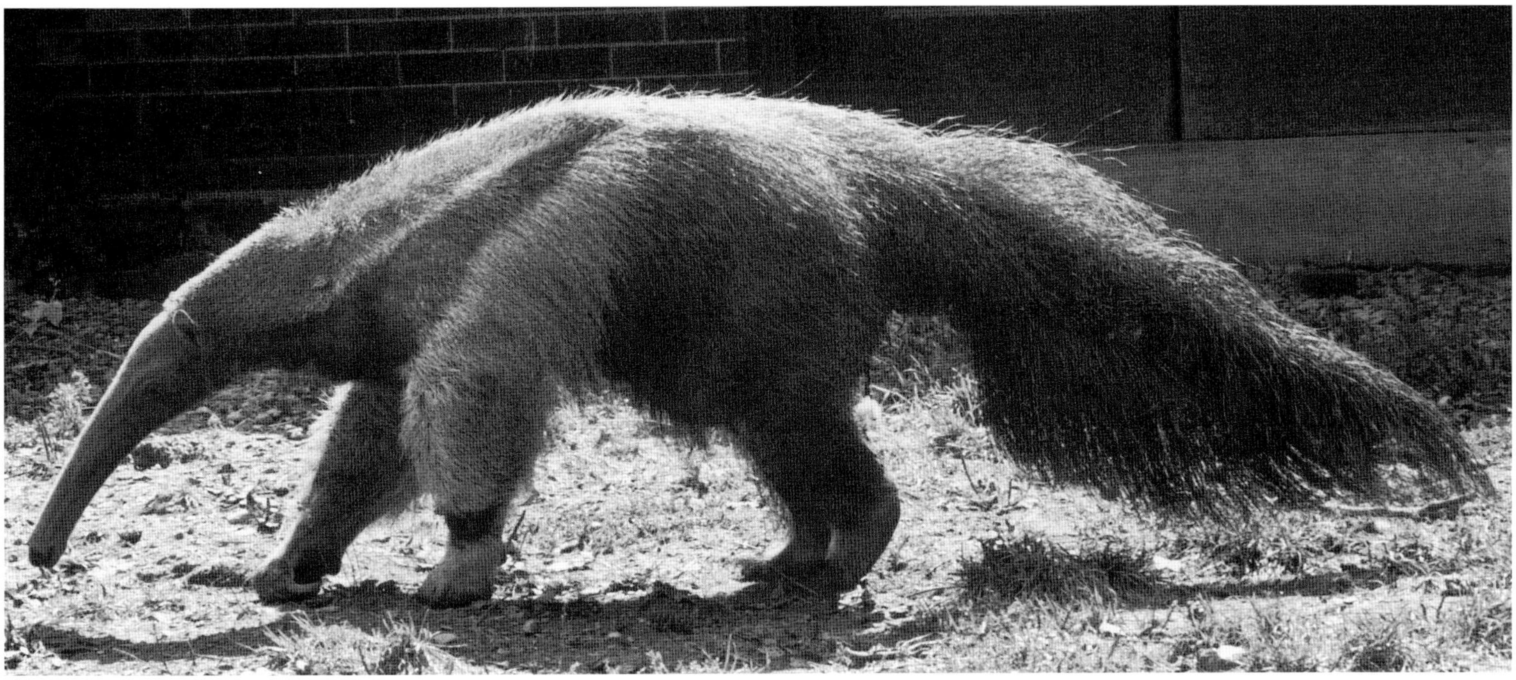

Myrmecophaga tridactyla

Giant anteater characteristics: Very elongated skull, no teeth. Jaw opens only slightly to allow long tongue to slide through small mouth. Small, rounded ears. Walks on the ends of the metacarpals of the hand, especially the outer metacarpals (the fingers and their claws are flexed inward) and on the sole of the foot. Five digits on hand with claws, except outer digit; middle digit has largest claw. Foot has five digits, all with small claws. Well developed medial epicondyle of lower end of humerus and olecranon of ulna (elbow). Narrow body; large, hairy tail.

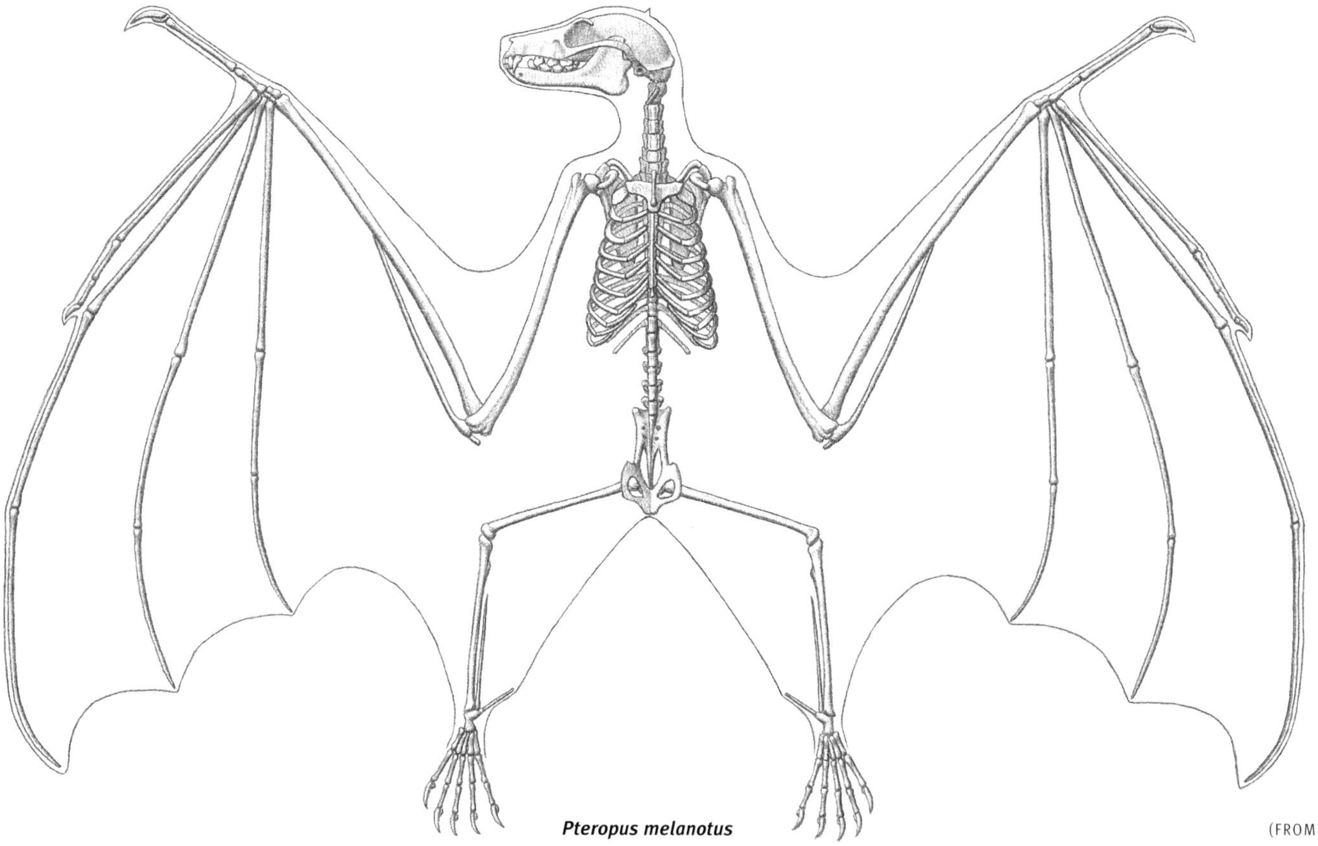

Pteropus melanotus

(FROM SPECIMEN)

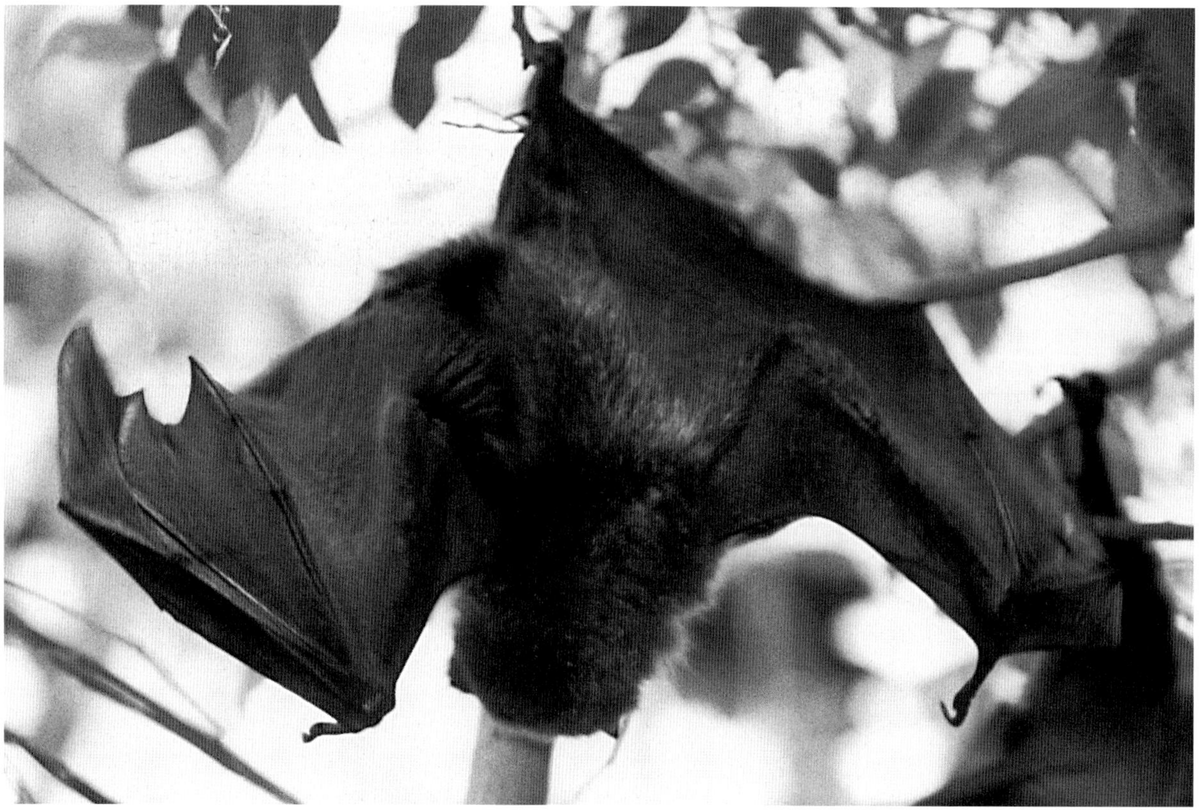

RODRIGUES FRUIT BAT

Pteropus rodricensis

Fruit bat characteristics: Slender, light bones. Forelimb, with very long bones, modified into wing; covered with skin membrane attached to the side of the body. Metacarpals of hand long and separated. Phalanges long. Short thumb with sharp claw. Has clavicle firmly connected to scapula and sternum. Keeled sternum for attachment of enlarged flight muscles. Very narrow pelvis. Leg rotated so knee faces outward and backward. Rear toes with sharp claws form hooks for hanging. Legs moved in unison with wings during flight. Five digits on each limb.

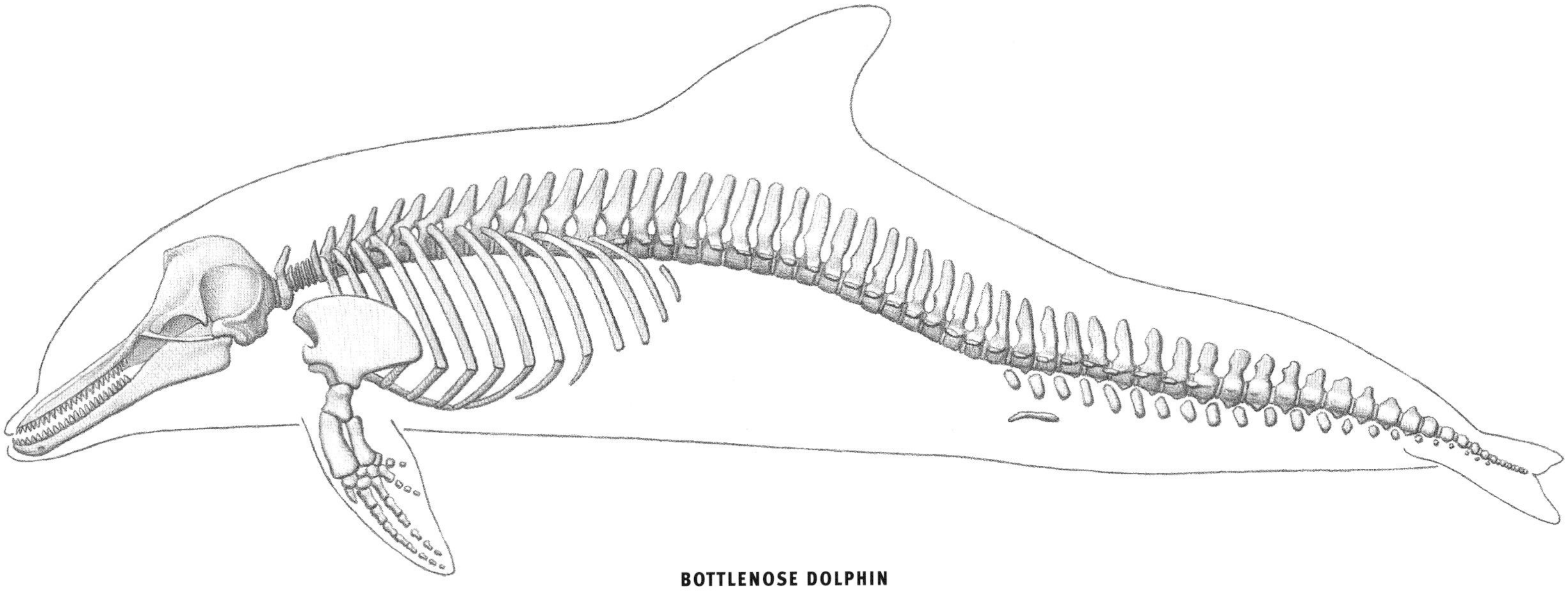

BOTTLENOSE DOLPHIN
Tursiops truncatus

(FROM SPECIMEN PHOTOS; AFTER ROMMEL)

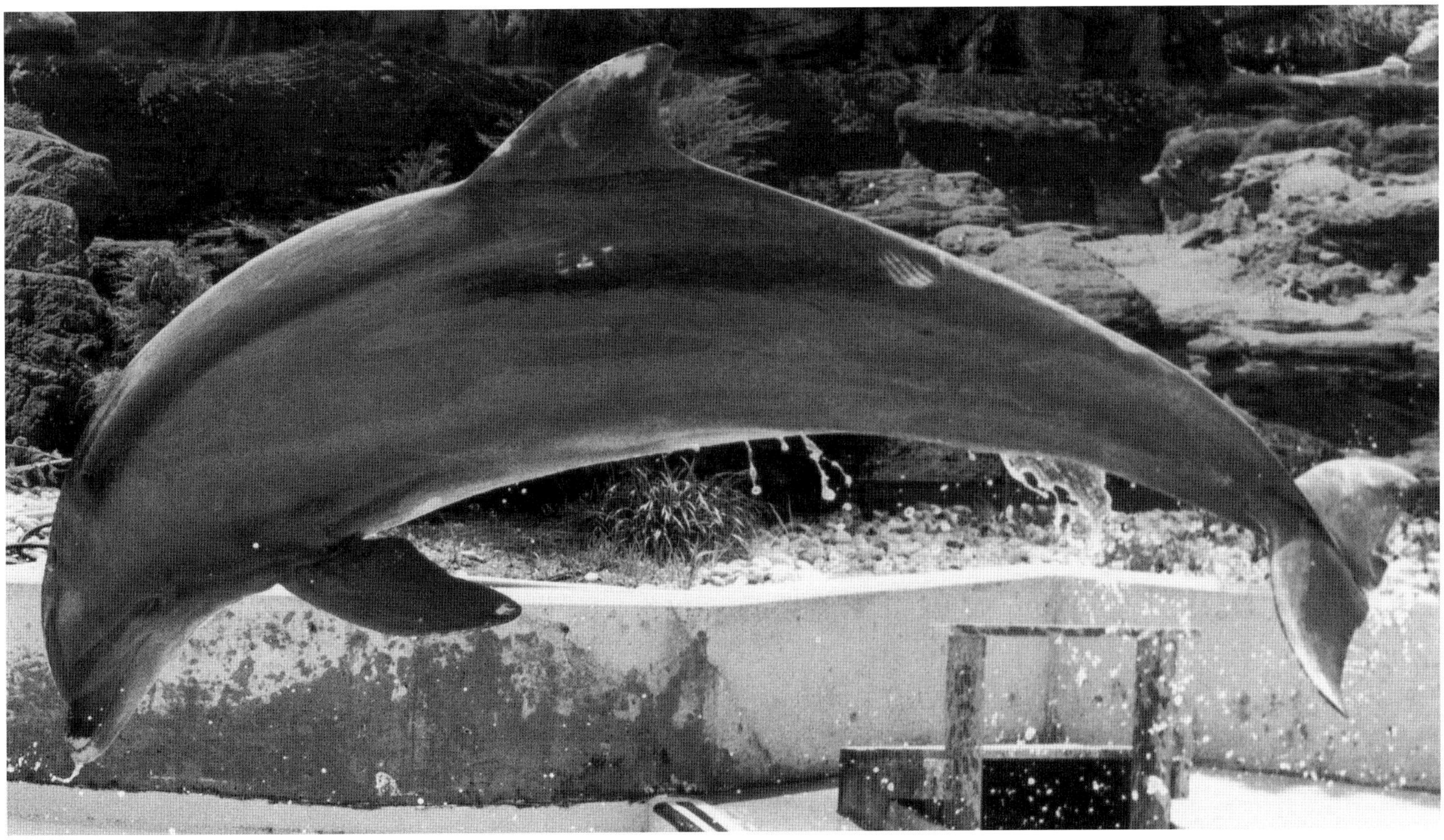

BOTTLENOSE DOLPHIN
Tursiops truncatus

Dolphin characteristics: Ultimate mammalian adaptation of streamlined body for full-time aquatic life. Very fast swimmers. Body covered with insulating blubber. Nasal bones and single external nostril (blowhole, which can be closed) reoriented rearward to top of head. No external ears. Large fatty swelling on forehead ("melon"). Dolphin has distinct beak separated from forehead (porpoise has rounded, blunt snout). Lower jaw extends slightly beyond upper jaw. Numerous teeth, atypical of mammals. Some neck vertebrae fused. Front limb evolved into a flat fin (flipper). No rear limb (retains two tiny vestigial pelvic bones suspended in the wall of abdomen for attachment of external reproductive organs). Tail flukes horizontal (vertical in fish); dorsal fin located at center of the back. Tail flukes and dorsal fin have no bony supports.

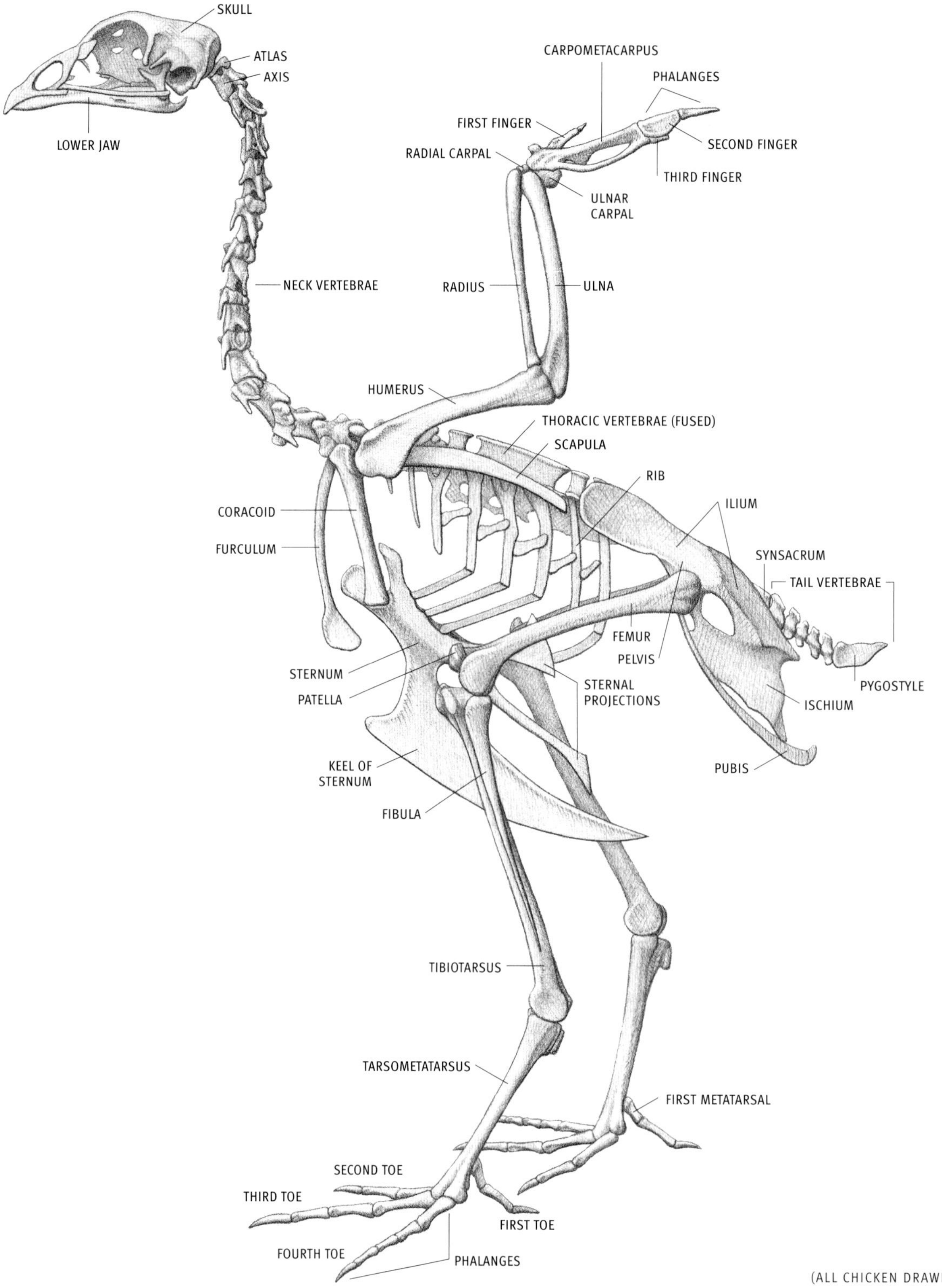

CHICKEN SKELETON
Gallus gallus

(ALL CHICKEN DRAWINGS FROM SPECIMENS)

Bird characteristics: Body always covered with feathers; feet (toes and usually tarsometatarsus) covered with scales (thickened skin). Aquatic birds have webbed toes. No teeth; horny beak.

Lightweight skeleton in flying birds (many hollow bones), with keel on sternum for attachment of flight muscles (pectoral muscles). No keel in large flightless birds (ostrich, emu, rhea). Completely bony ribs (no rib cartilage). Clavicles fused into single bone, the furculum (wishbone).

Numerous neck vertebrae (number varies by species) provide great neck flexibility. Some of the middle thoracic vertebrae fused in some species (chicken); posterior thoracic, all lumbar, and all sacral vertebrae fused into synsacrum, which in turn is fused to the pelvis. Short, flexible tail terminates in stout bone (pygostyle) for support of highly mobile long tail feathers.

Wing (arm) skeleton modified for flying (ostrich and penguins evolved from flying ancestors). Wrist joint automatically straightens when elbow joint is straightened; conversely, wrist joint automatically bends when elbow joint is bent. Individual hand and finger bones reduced in number and largely fused together for support of primaries (outer flight feathers). Three digits present; small third digit nonmovable. Short alular feathers attach to movable first digit. Secondaries (inner flight feathers) attach to rear edge of ulna.

Three toes point forward and one points backward in most species (e.g., chicken, hawk, crow), or two toes forward and two back (e.g., woodpecker, parrot). Ostrich has two toes per foot. Toes terminate with claws. Male chicken has bony spur covered with horny sheath on tarsometatarsus.

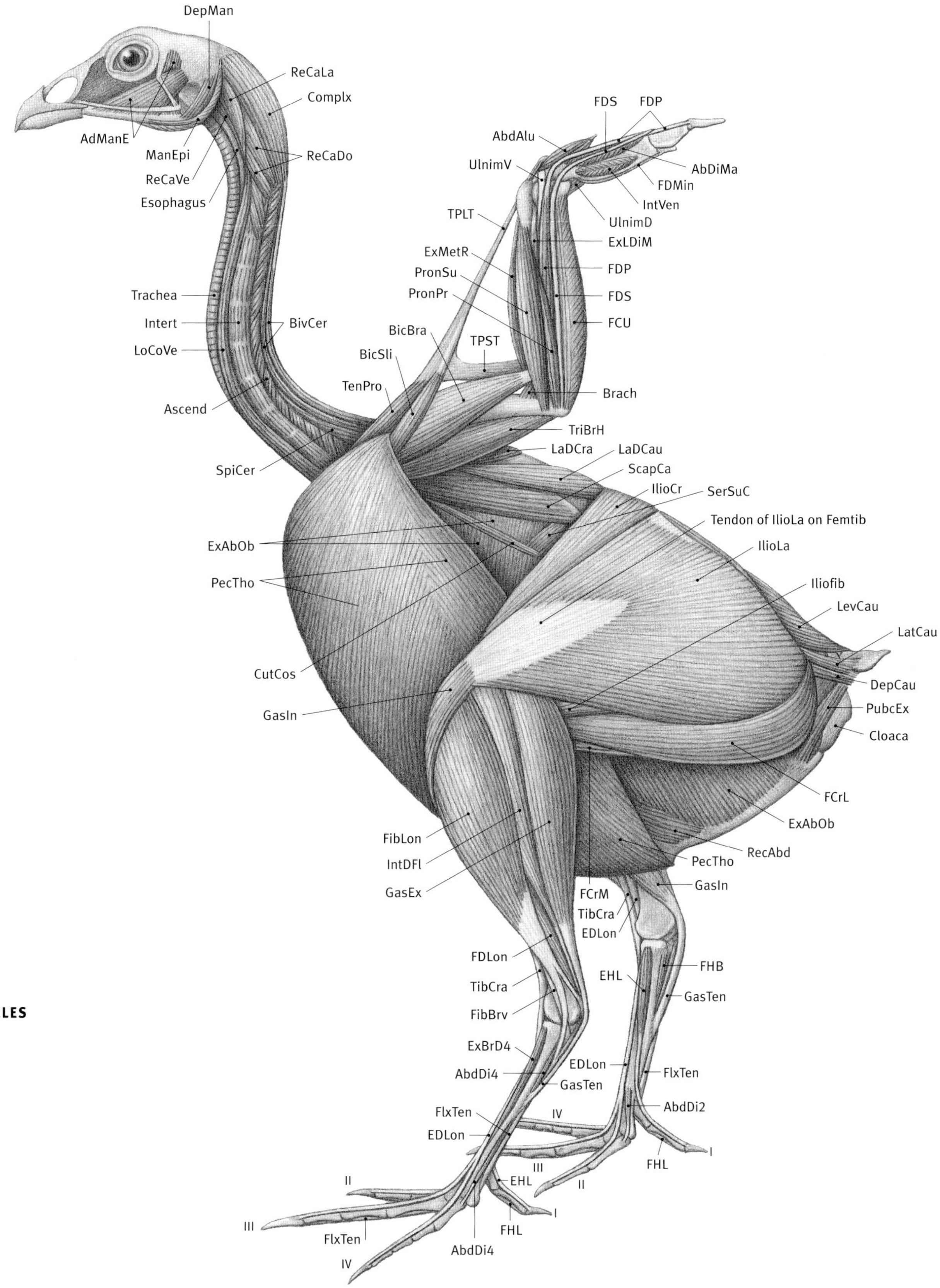

CHICKEN MUSCLES

AbdAlu *Abductor alulae;* **AbdDi2** *Abductor digiti II;* **AbdDi4** *Abductor digiti IV;* **AbDiMa** *Abductor digiti majoris;* **AdManE** *Adductor mandibulae externus;* **Ascend** *Ascendentes;* **BicBra** *Biceps brachii;* **BicSli** *Biceps slip;* **BivCer** *Biventer cervicis;* **Brach** *Brachialis;* **Complx** *Complexus;* **CutCos** *Cutaneus costohumeralis;* **DepCau** *Depressor caudae;* **DepMan** *Depressor mandibulae;* **EDLon** *Extensor digitorum longus;* **EHL** *Extensor hallucis longus;* **ExAbOb** *External abdominal oblique;* **ExBrD4** *Extensor brevis digiti IV;* **ExLDiM** *Extensor longus digiti majoris;* **ExMetR** *Extensor metacarpi radialis;* **FCrL** *Flexor cruris lateralis;* **FCrM** *Flexor cruris medialis;* **FCU** *Flexor carpi ulnaris;* **FDLon** *Flexor digitorum longus;* **FDMin** *Flexor digiti minoris;* **FDP** *Flexor digitorum profundus;* **FDS** *Flexor digitorum superficialis;* **Femtib** *Femorotibialis;* **FHB** *Flexor hallucis brevis;* **FHL** *Flexor hallucis longus;* **FibBrv** *Fibularis brevis;* **FibLon** *Fibularis longus;* **FlxTen** *Flexor tendons;* **GasEx** *Gastrocnemius, external head;* **GasIn** *Gastrocnemius, internal head;* **GasTen** *Gastrocnemius tendon;* **IlioCr** *Iliotibialis cranialis;* **Iliofib** *Iliofibularis;* **IlioLa** *Iliotibialis lateralis;* **IntDFl** *Intermediate digital flexors;* **Intert** *Intertransversarii;* **IntVen** *Interosseus ventralis;* **LaDCau** *Latissimus dorsi caudalis;* **LaDCra** *Latissimus dorsi cranialis;* **LatCau** *Lateralis caudae;* **LevCau** *Levator caudae;* **LoCoVe** *Longus colli ventralis;* **ManEpi** *Mandibularis epibranchialis;* **PecTho** *Pectoralis thoracis;* **PronPr** *Pronator profundus;* **PronSu** *Pronator superficialis;* **PubcEx** *Pubocaudalis externus;* **RecAbd** *Rectus abdominis;* **ReCaDo** *Rectus capitis dorsalis;* ReCaLa *Rectus capitis lateralis;* **ReCaVe** *Rectus capitis ventralis;* **ScapCa** *Scapulohumeralis caudalis;* **SerSuC** *Serratus superficialis caudalis;* **SpiCer** *Spinalis cervicis;* **TenPro** *Tensor propatagialis;* **TibCra** *Tibialis cranialis;* **TPLT** *Tensor propatagialis long tendon;* **TPST** *Tensor propatagialis short tendon;* **TriBrH** *Triceps brachii, humeral head;* **UlnimD** *Ulnimetacarpalis dorsalis;* **UlnimV** *Ulnimetacarpalis ventralis.*

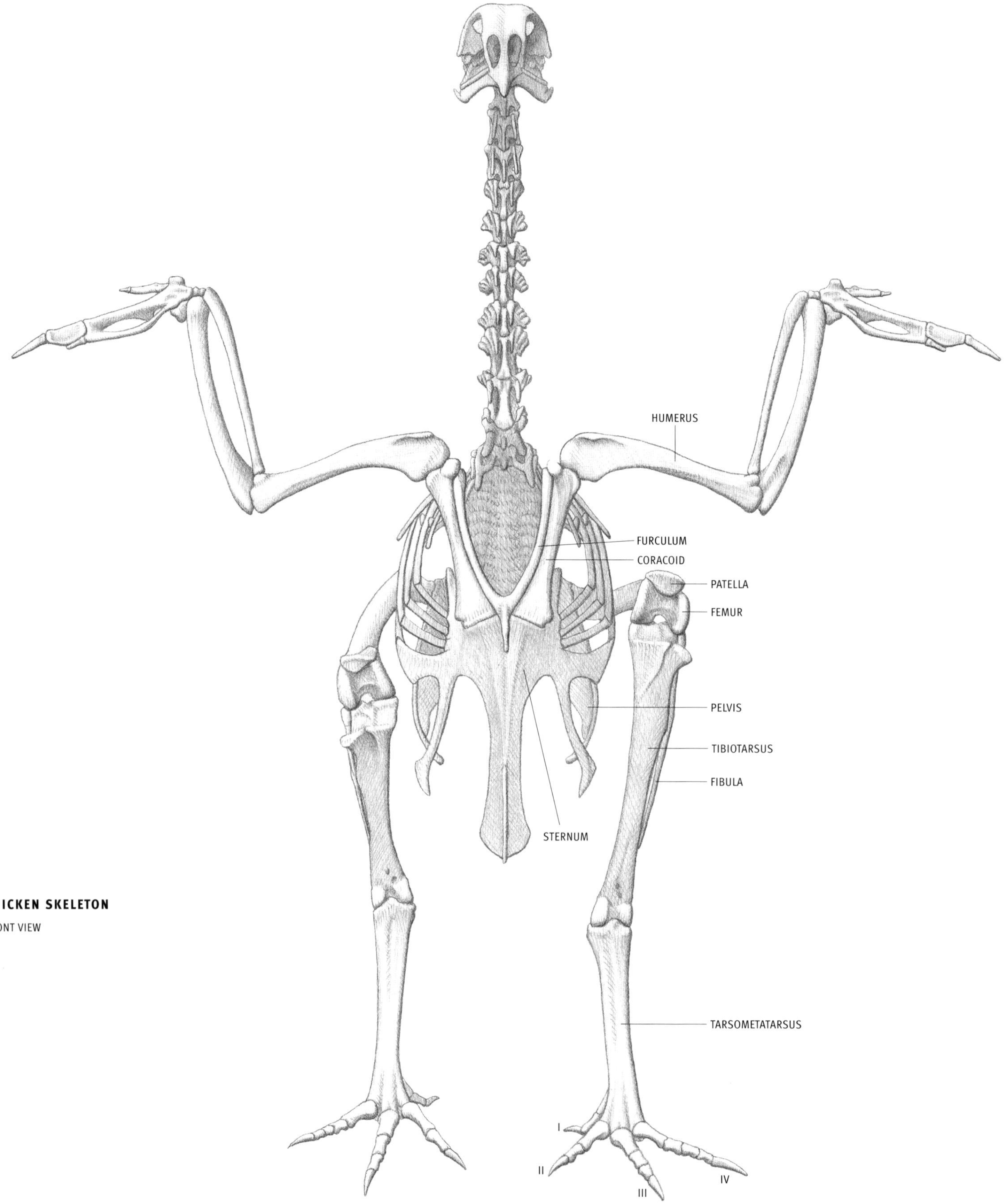

CHICKEN SKELETON

FRONT VIEW

AddAlu *Adductor alulae;* **AdManE** *Adductor mandibulae externus;* **BicBra** *Biceps brachii;* **BicSli** *Biceps slip;* **Brach** *Brachialis;* **Complx** *Complexus;* **DeltMa** *Deltoid major;* **DeltMi** *Deltoid minor;* **Ectep** *Ectepicondyloulnaris;* **EDC** *Extensor digitorum communis;* **EDLon** *Extensor digitorum longus;* **EHL** *Extensor hallucis longus;* **ELDM** *Extensor longus digiti majoris;* **ExBrAl** *Extensor brevis alulae;* **ExBrD3** *Extensor brevis digiti III;* **ExBrD4** *Extensor brevis digiti IV;* **ExLoAl** *Extensor longus alulae;* **ExMetR** *Extensor metacarpi radialis;* **ExMetU** *Extensor metacarpi ulnaris;* **FCU** *Flexor carpi ulnaris;* **FDMin** *Flexor digiti minoris;* **FibBrv** *Fibularis brevis;* **FibLon** *Fibularis longus;* **FlxTen** *Flexor tendons;* **GasIn** *Gastrocnemius, internal head;* **IlioCr** *Iliotibialis cranialis;* **IlioLa** *Iliotibialis lateralis;* **IntDor** *Interosseus dorsalis;* **Intert** *Intertransversarii;* **IntVen** *Interosseus ventralis;* **LoCoVe** *Longus colli ventralis;* **PecTho** *Pectoralis thoracis;* **ReCaDo** *Rectus capitis dorsalis;* **ReCaLa** *Rectus capitis lateralis;* **ScapCa** *Scapulohumeralis caudalis;* **Supcor** *Supracoracoid;* **TenPro** *Tensor propatagialis;* **TibCra** *Tibialis cranialis;* **TPLT** *Tensor propatagialis long tendon;* **TPST** *Tensor propatagialis short tendon;* **TriBrH** *Triceps brachii, humeral head;* **TriBrS** *Triceps brachii, scapular head;* **UlnimD** *Ulnimetacarpalis dorsalis.*

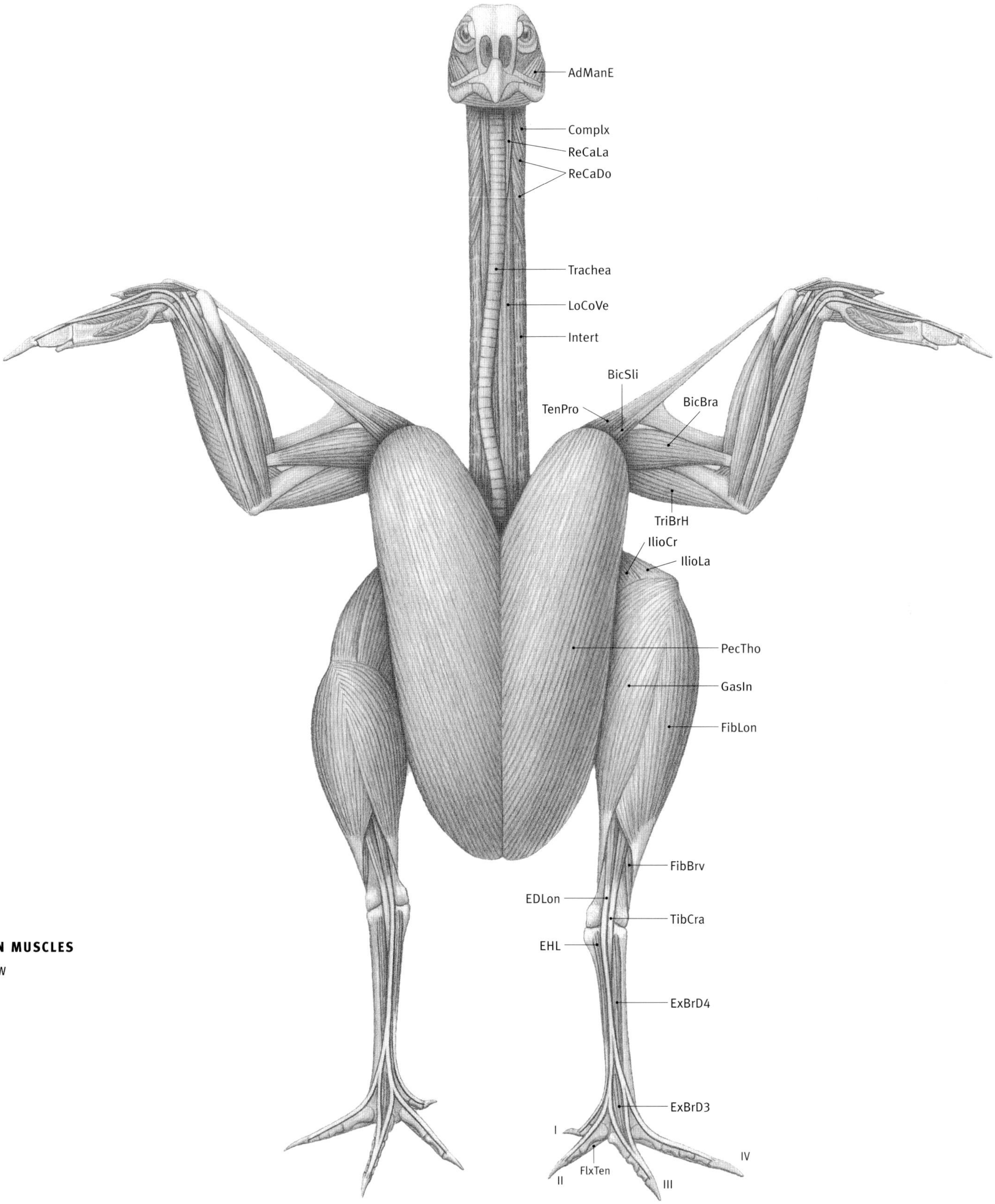

CHICKEN MUSCLES

FRONT VIEW

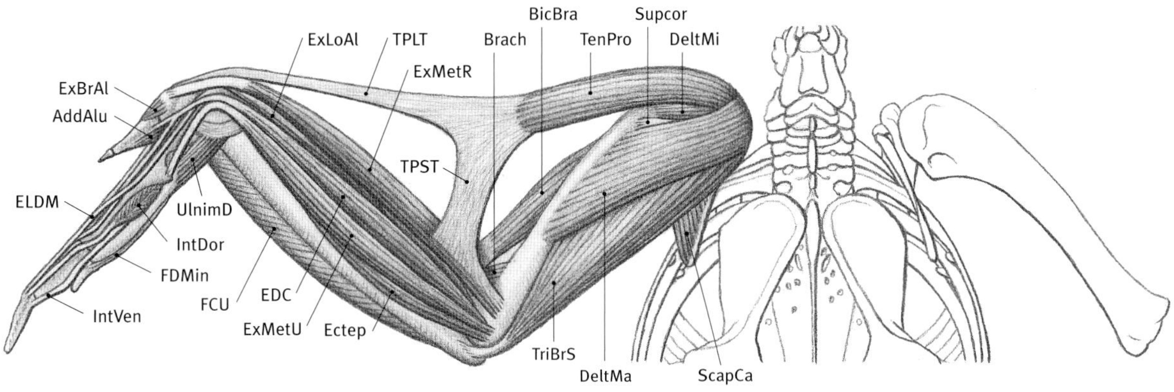

CHICKEN MUSCLES

LEFT WING

BACK VIEW

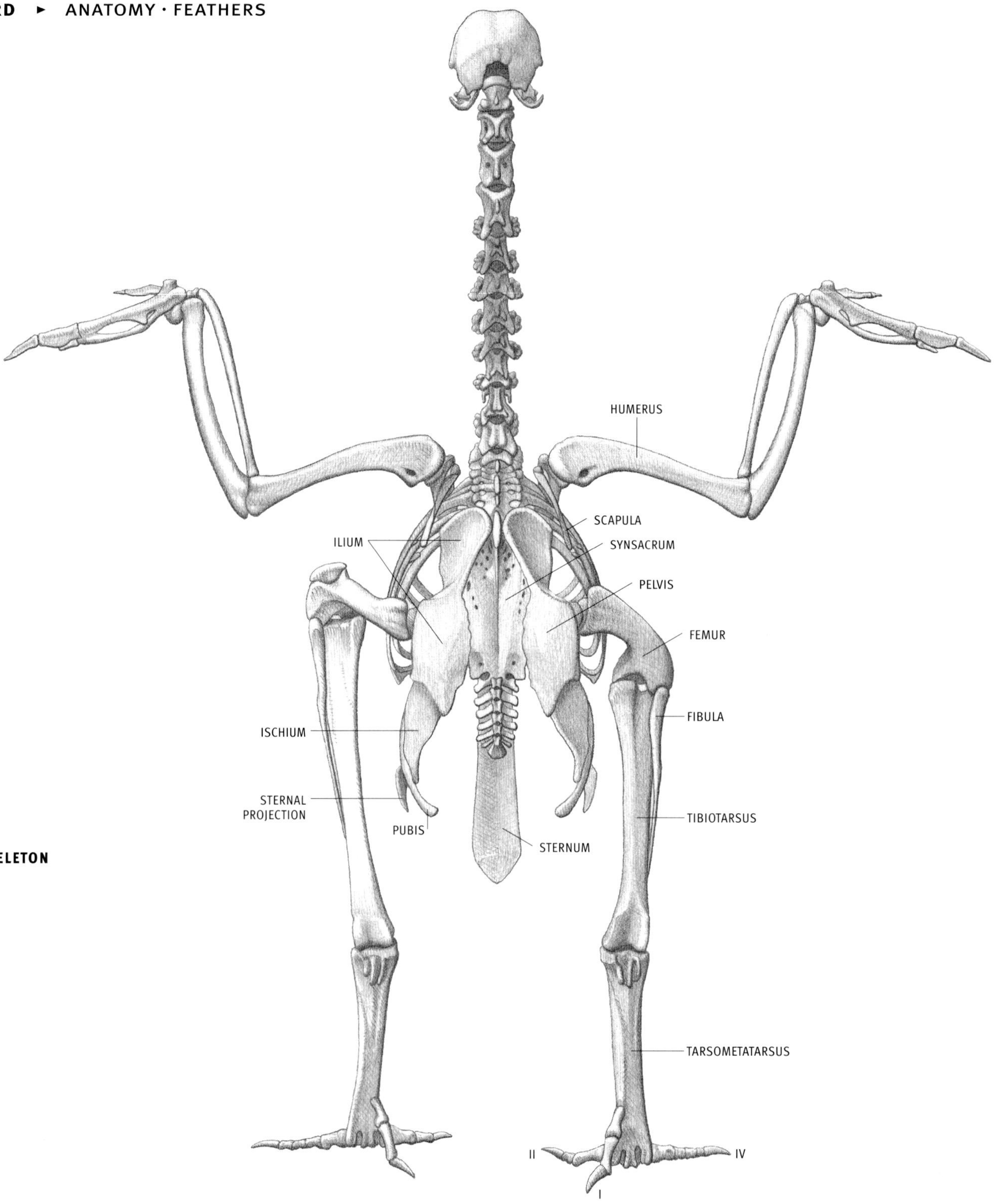

CHICKEN SKELETON

BACK VIEW

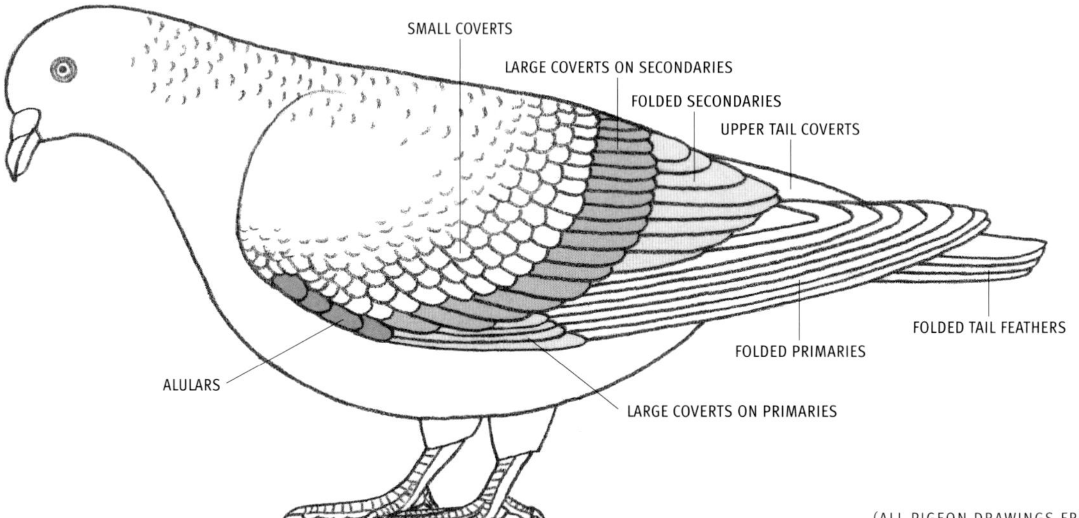

PIGEON

Columba livia

(ALL PIGEON DRAWINGS FROM SPECIMENS)

PIGEON WINGS

LEFT WING
TOP VIEW

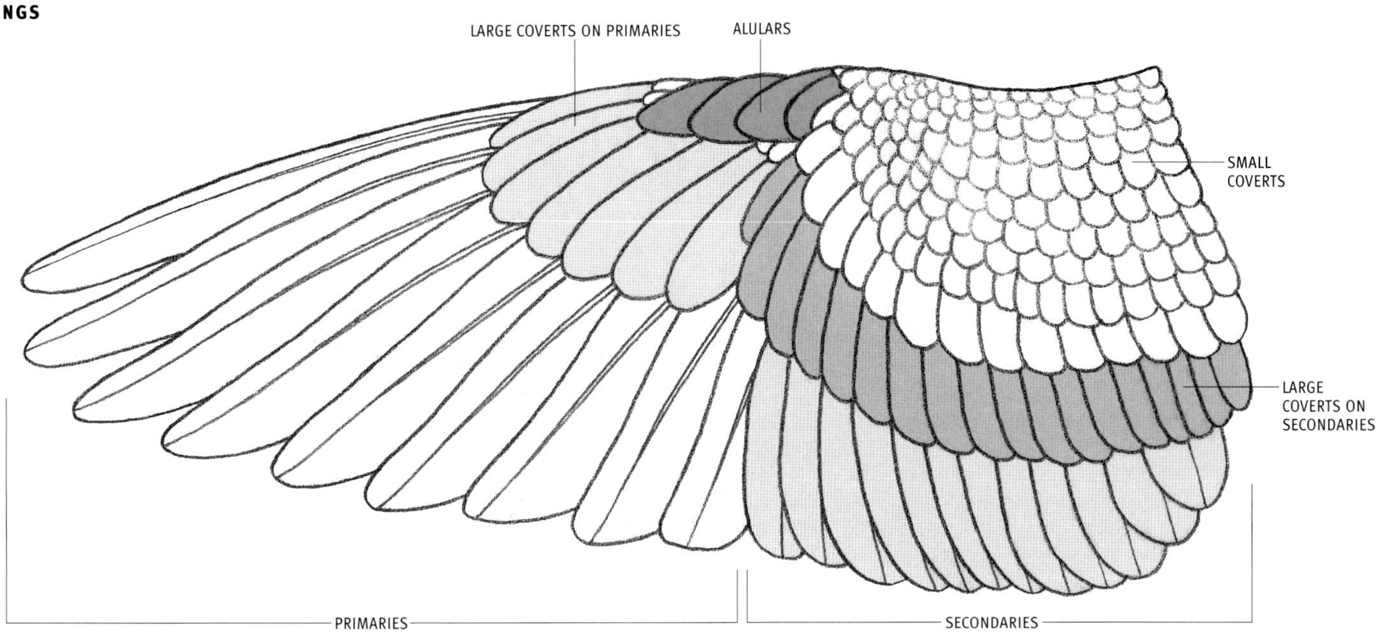

LEFT WING
TOP VIEW
COVERTS REMOVED

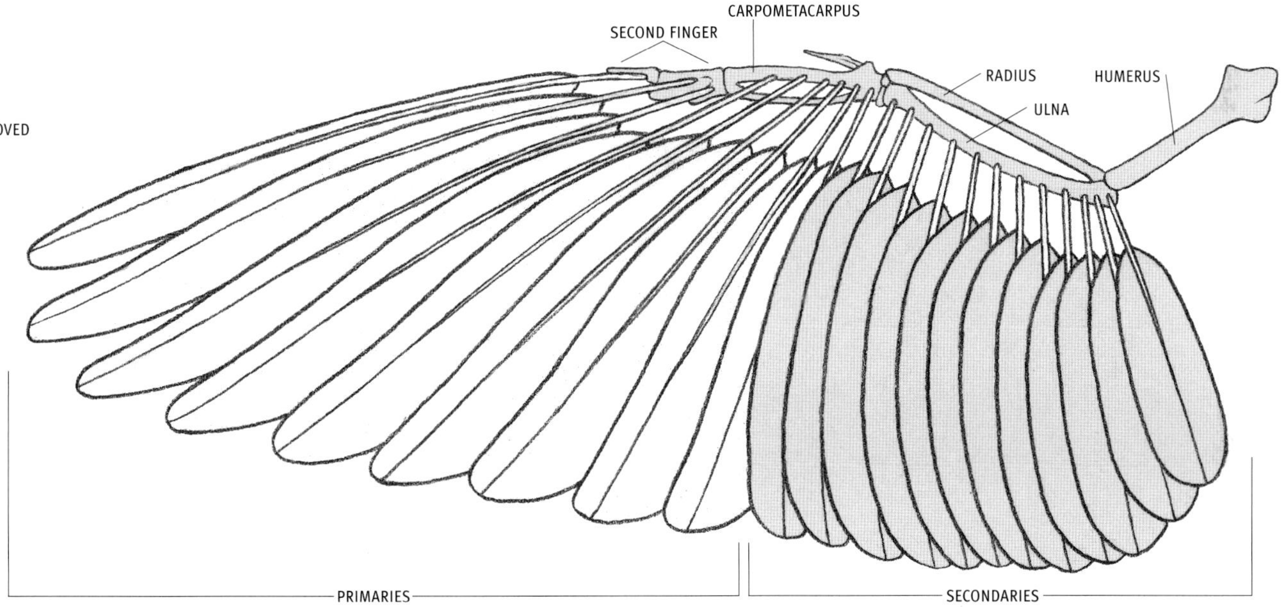

RIGHT WING
BOTTOM VIEW

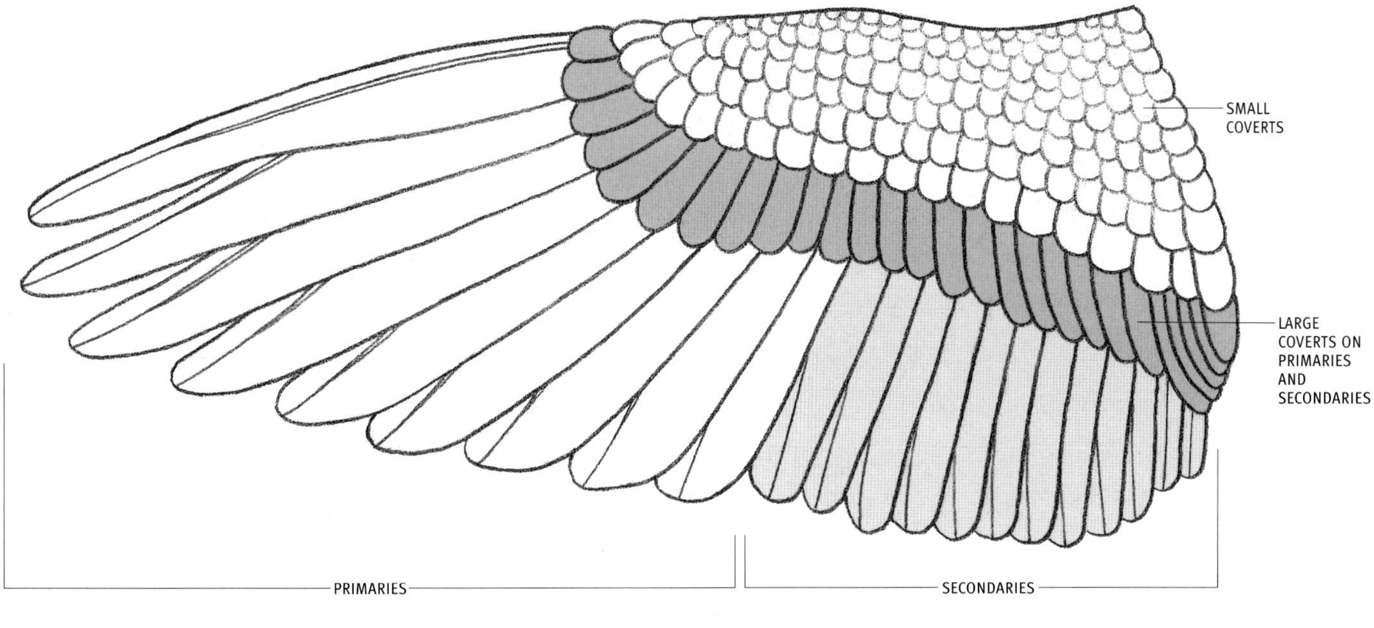

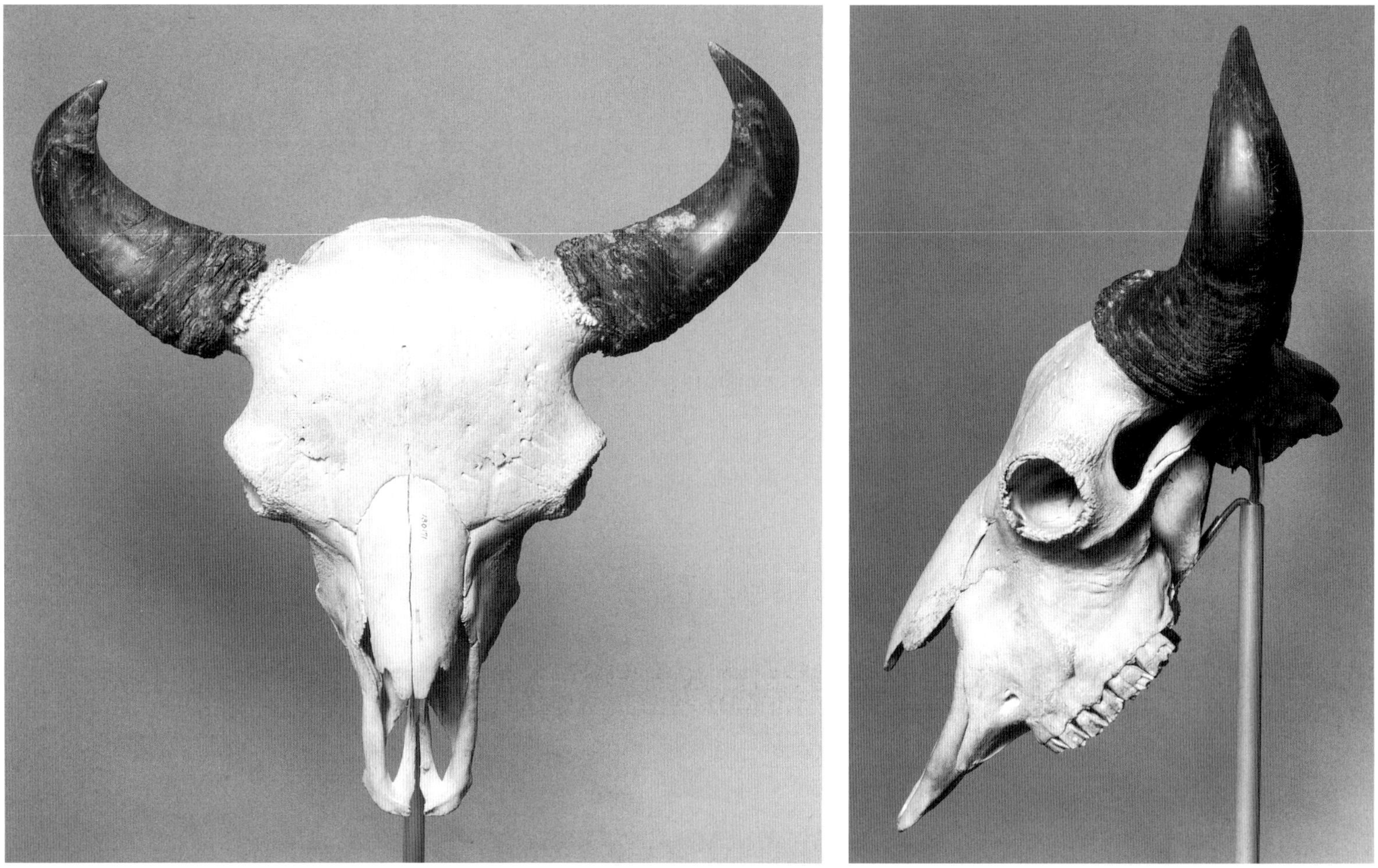

AMERICAN BISON (MALE)
Bison bison

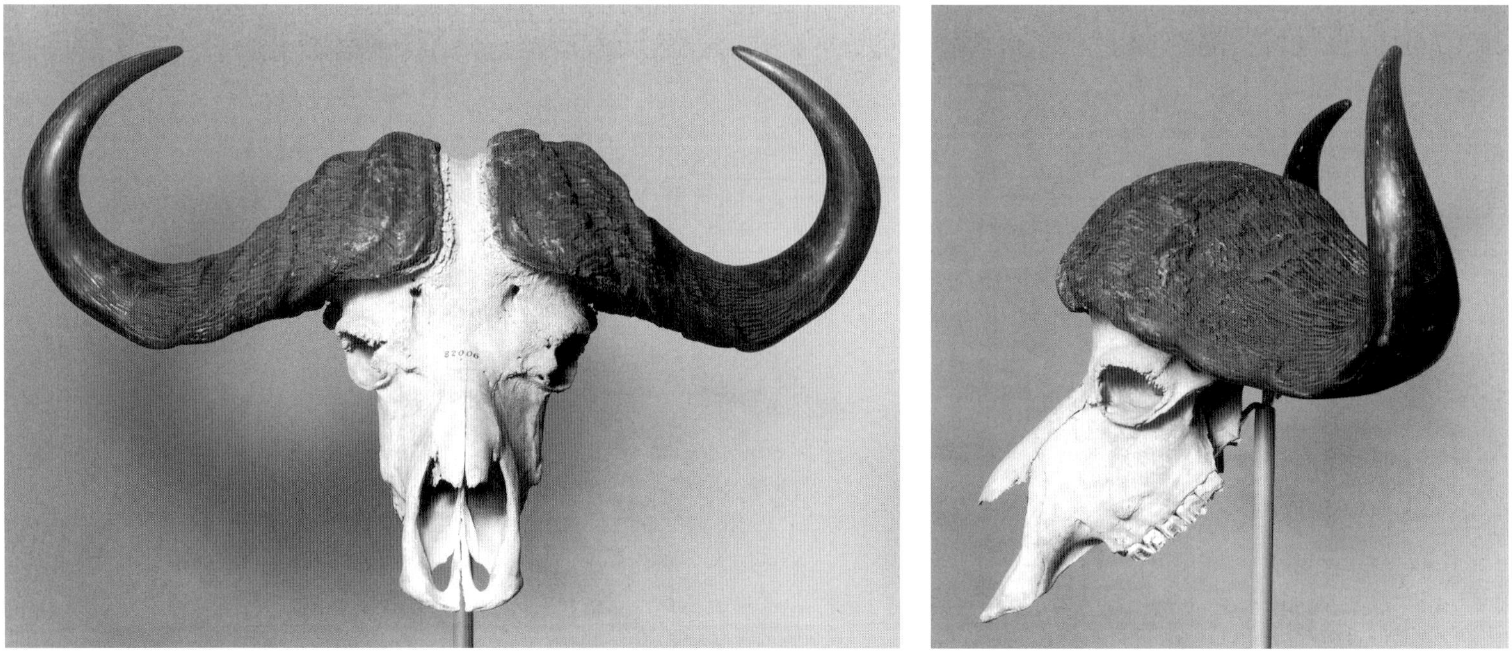

AFRICAN BUFFALO (MALE)
Syncerus caffer

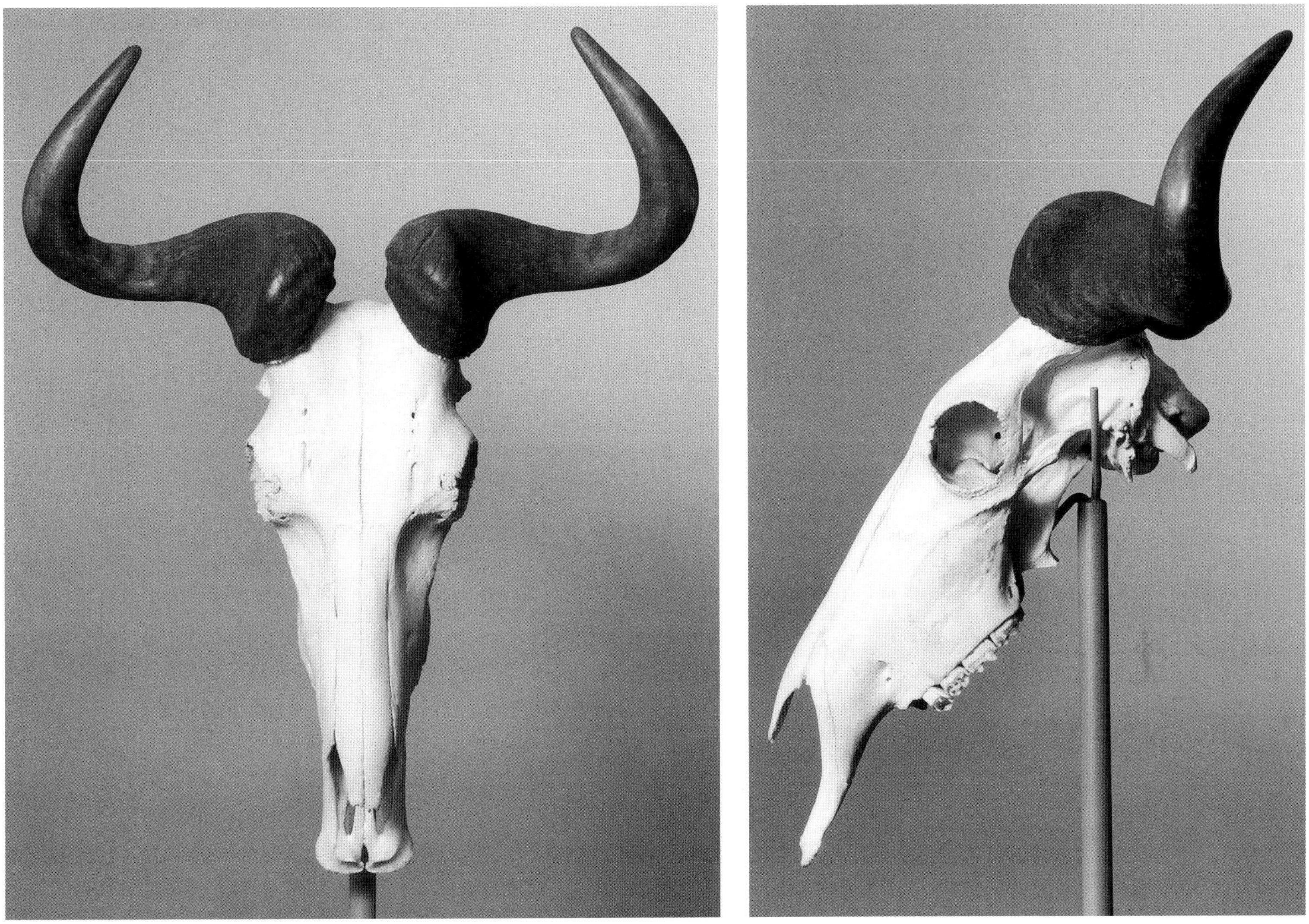

WHITE-BEARDED WILDEBEEST (MALE)
Connochaetes taurinus

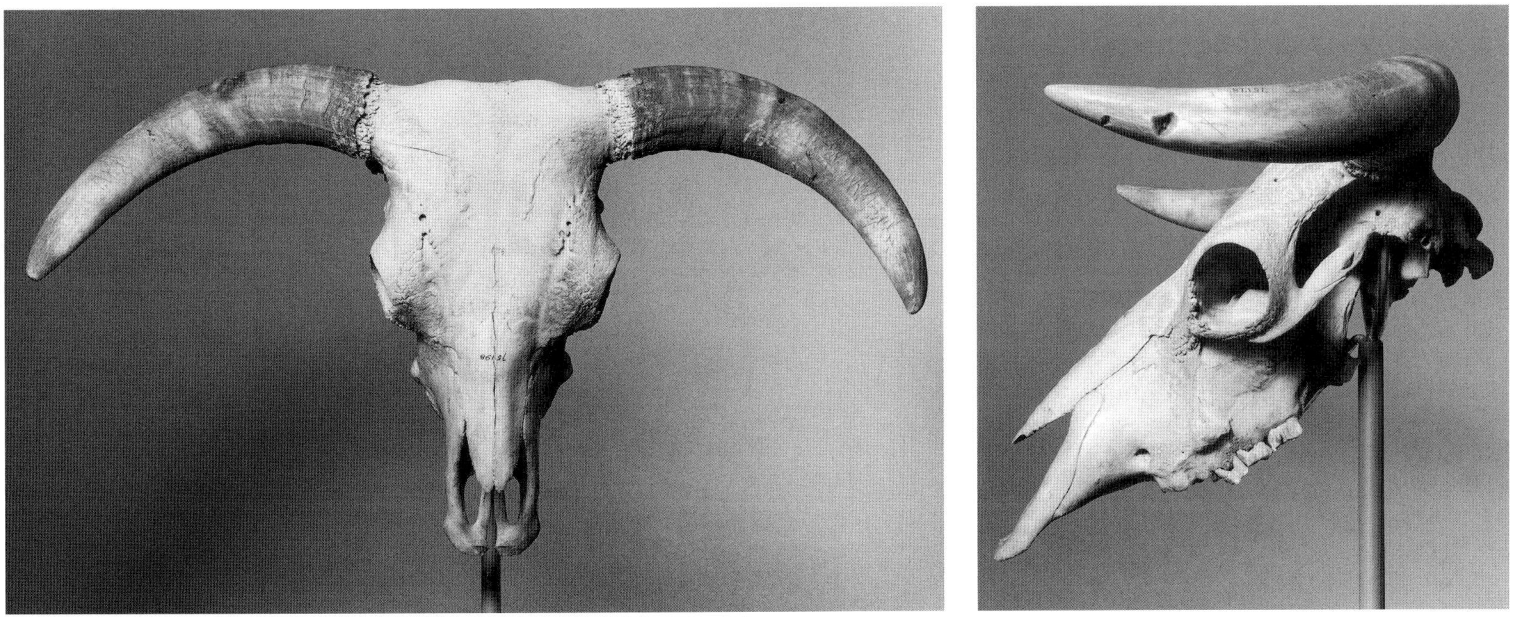

OX (MALE)
Bos taurus

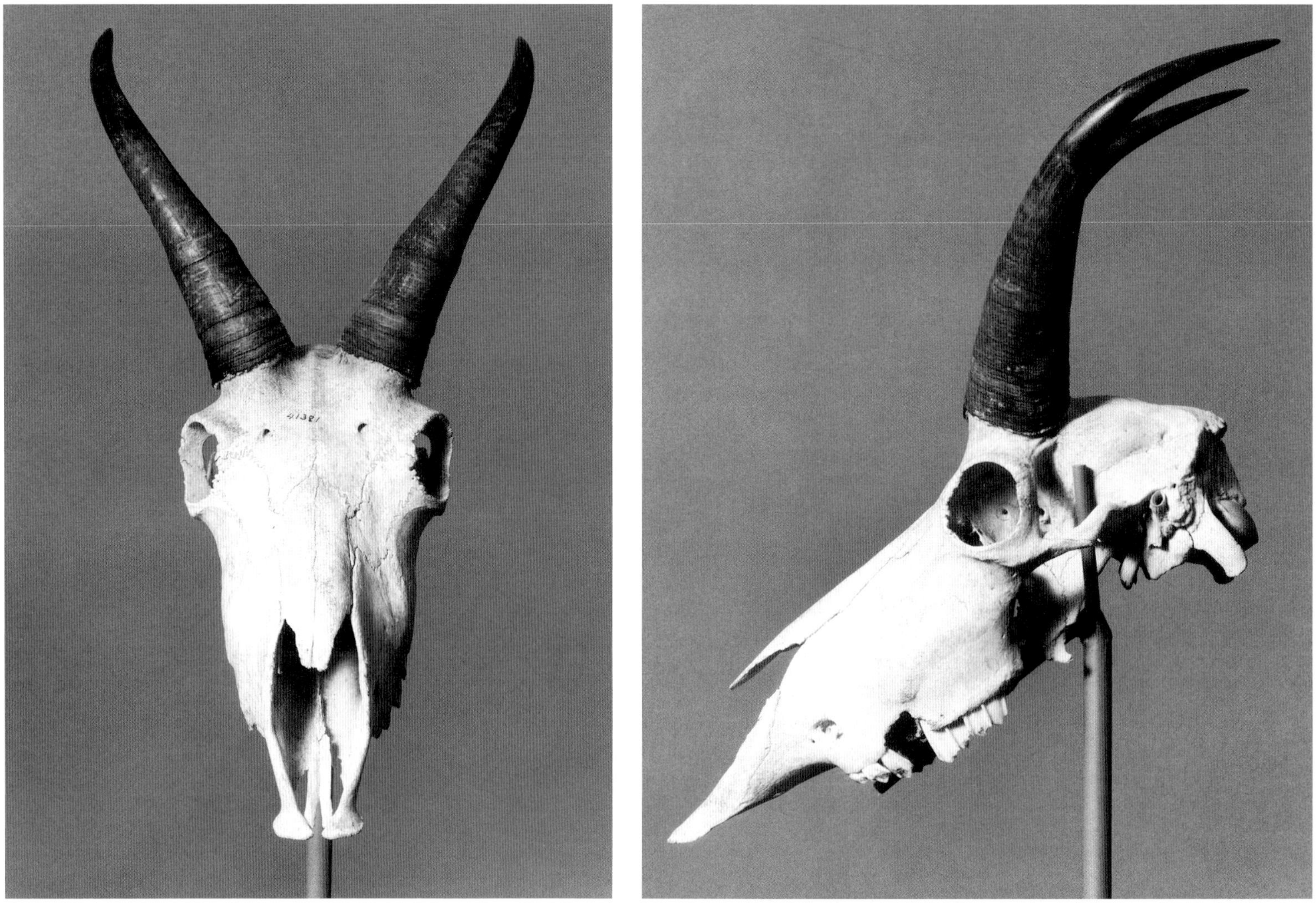

MOUNTAIN GOAT (MALE)
Oreamnos americanus

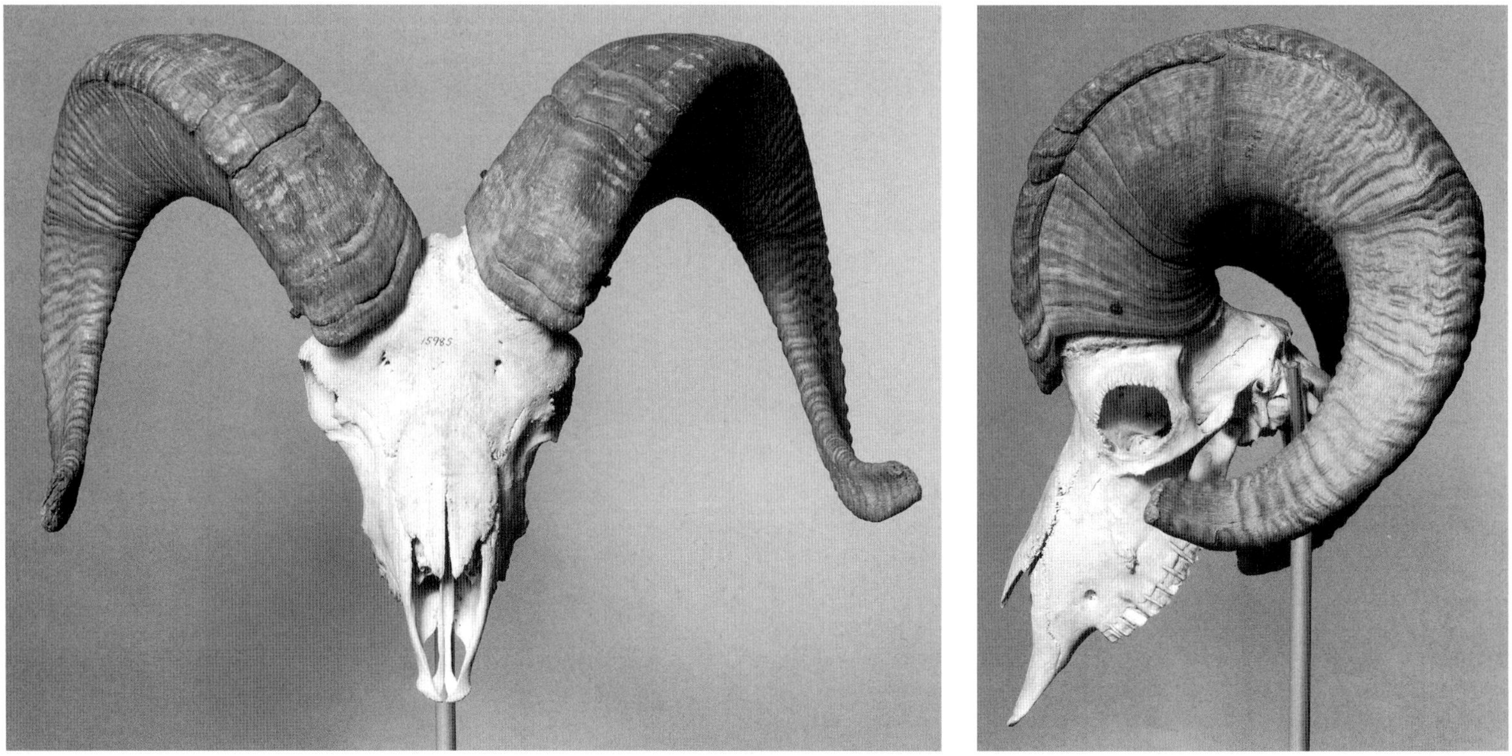

BIGHORN SHEEP (MALE)
Ovis canadensis

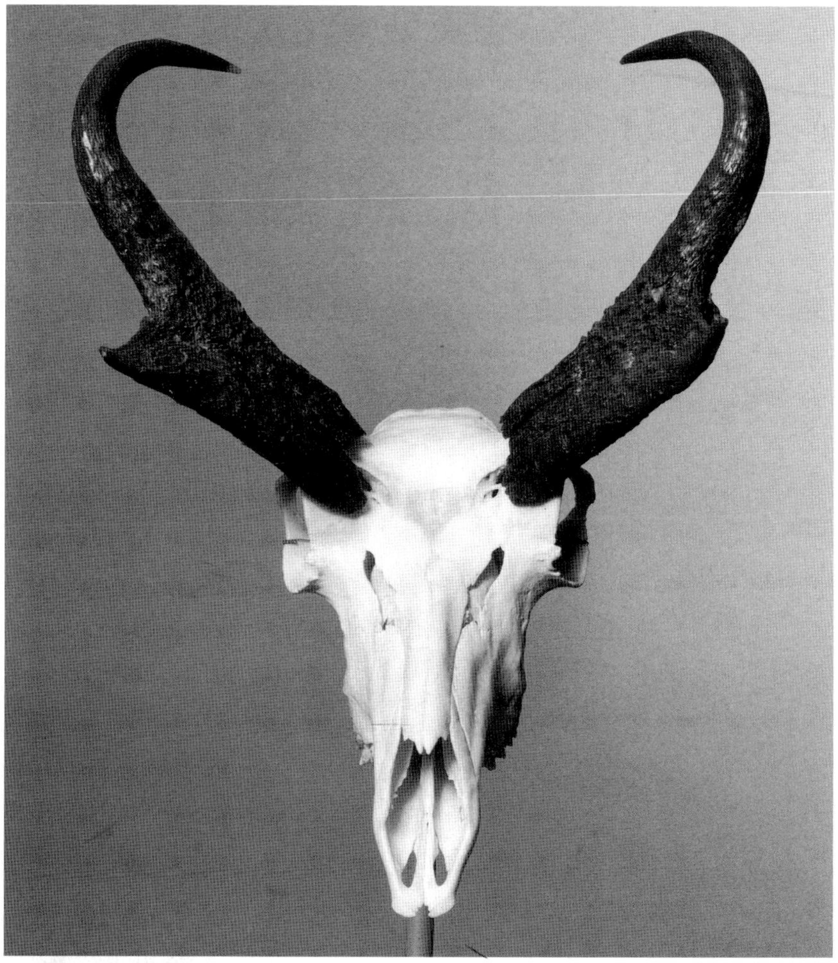

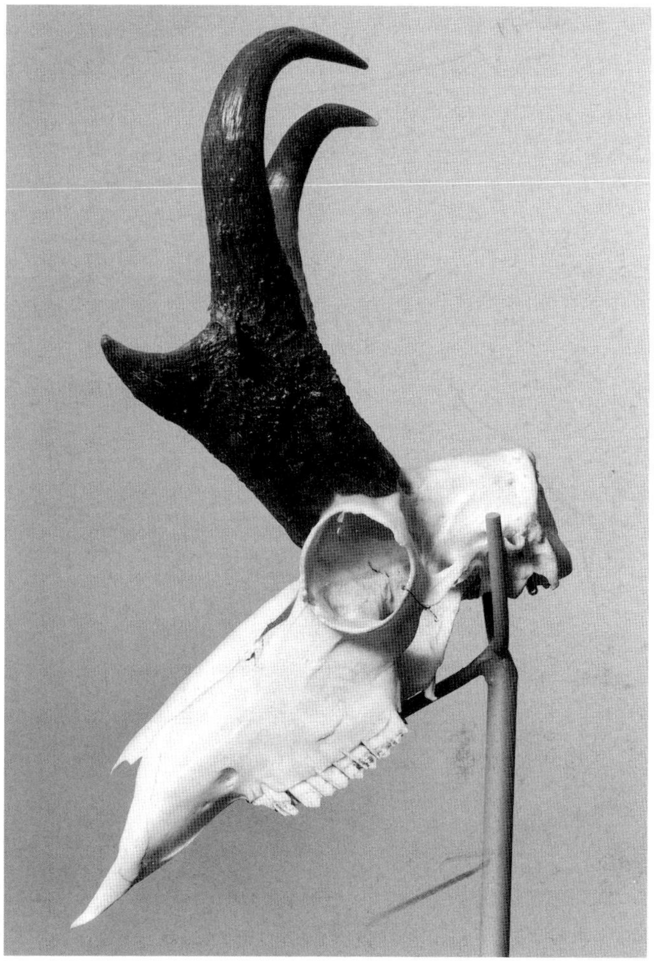

PRONGHORN ANTELOPE (MALE)
Antilocapra americana

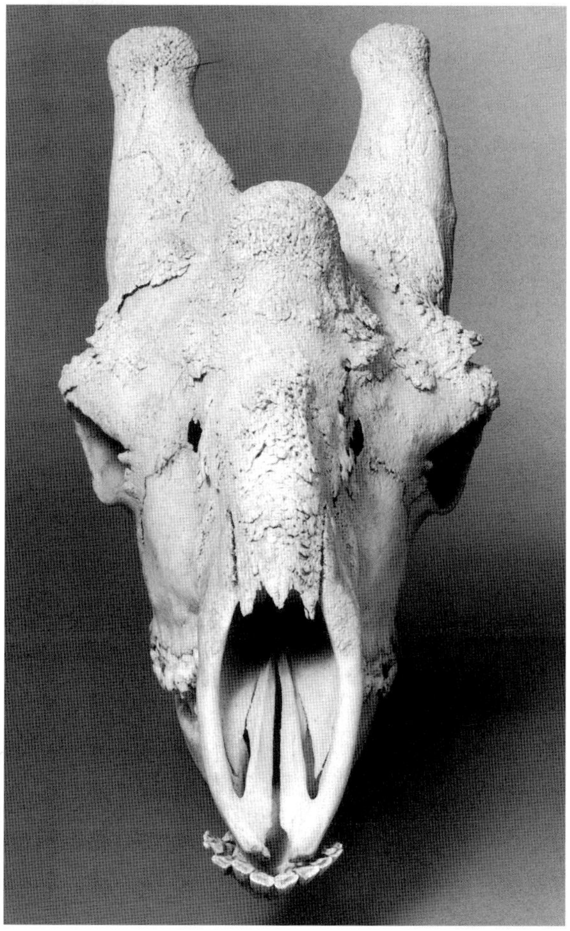

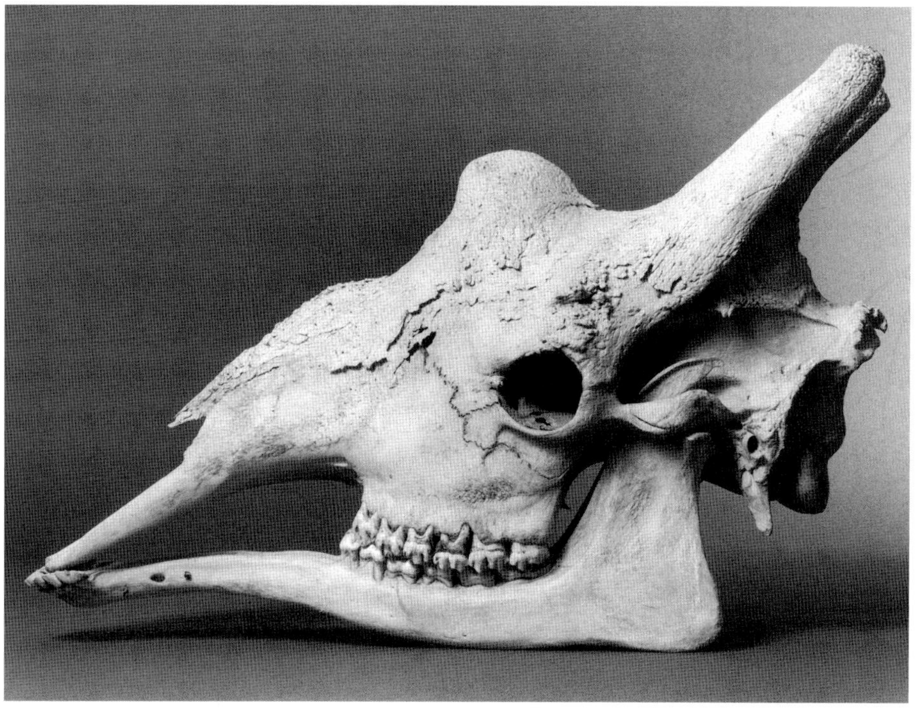

GIRAFFE (MALE)
Giraffa camelopardalis

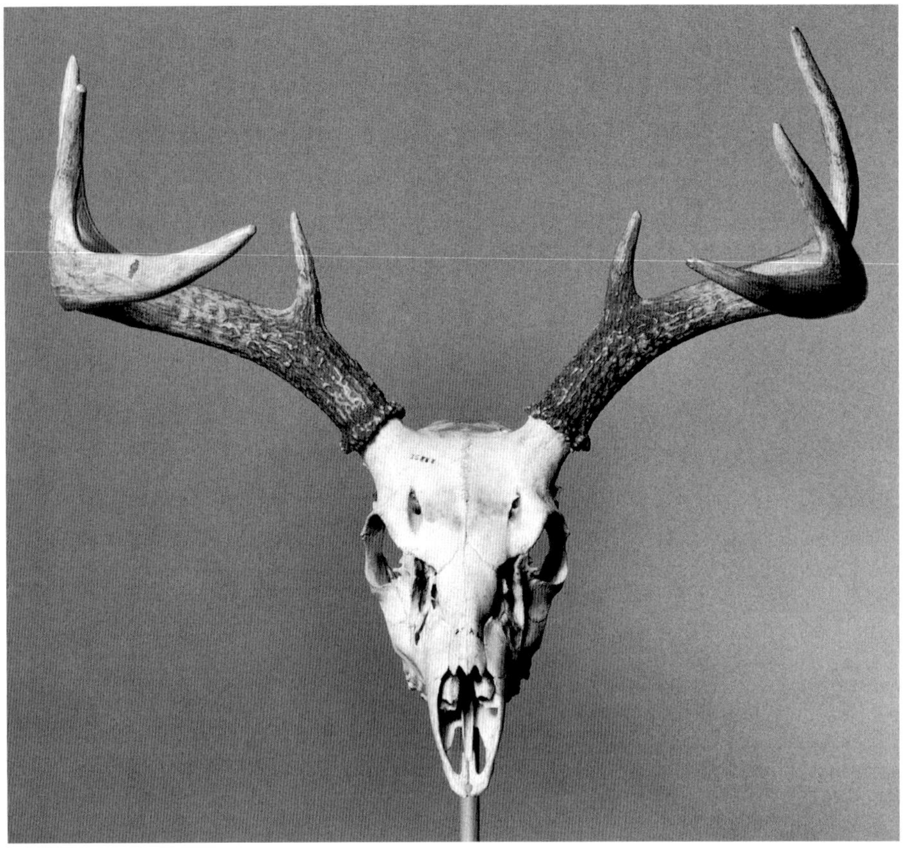
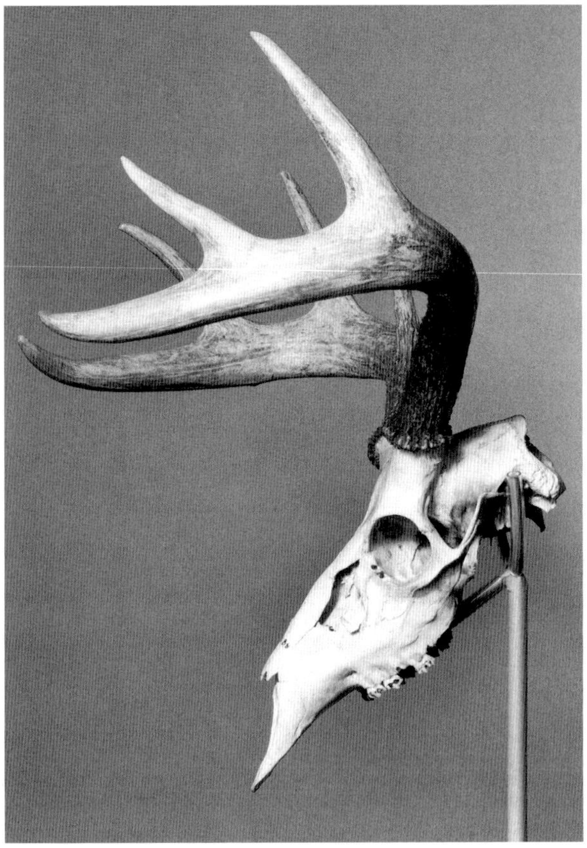

WHITE-TAILED DEER (MALE)
Odocoileus virginianus

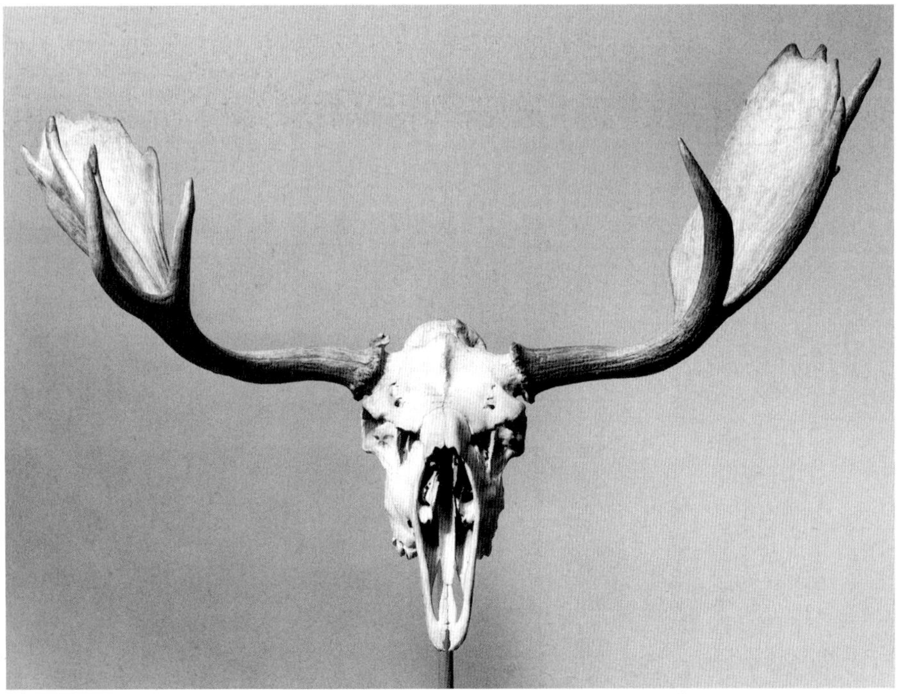
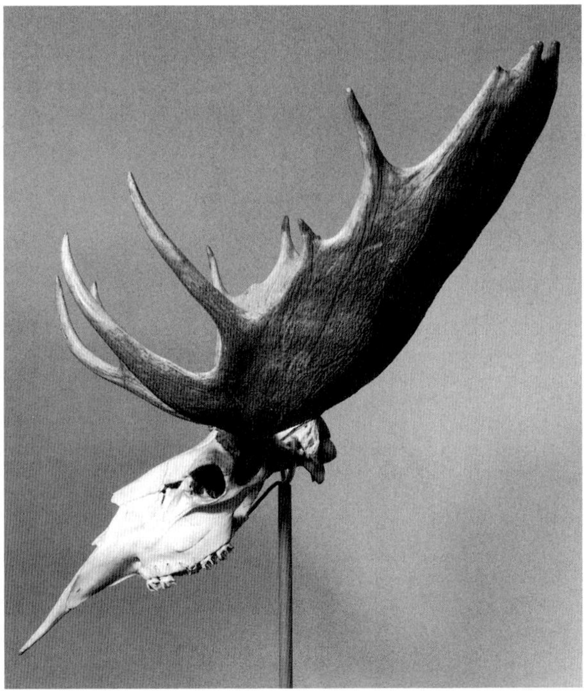

MOOSE (MALE)
Alces alces

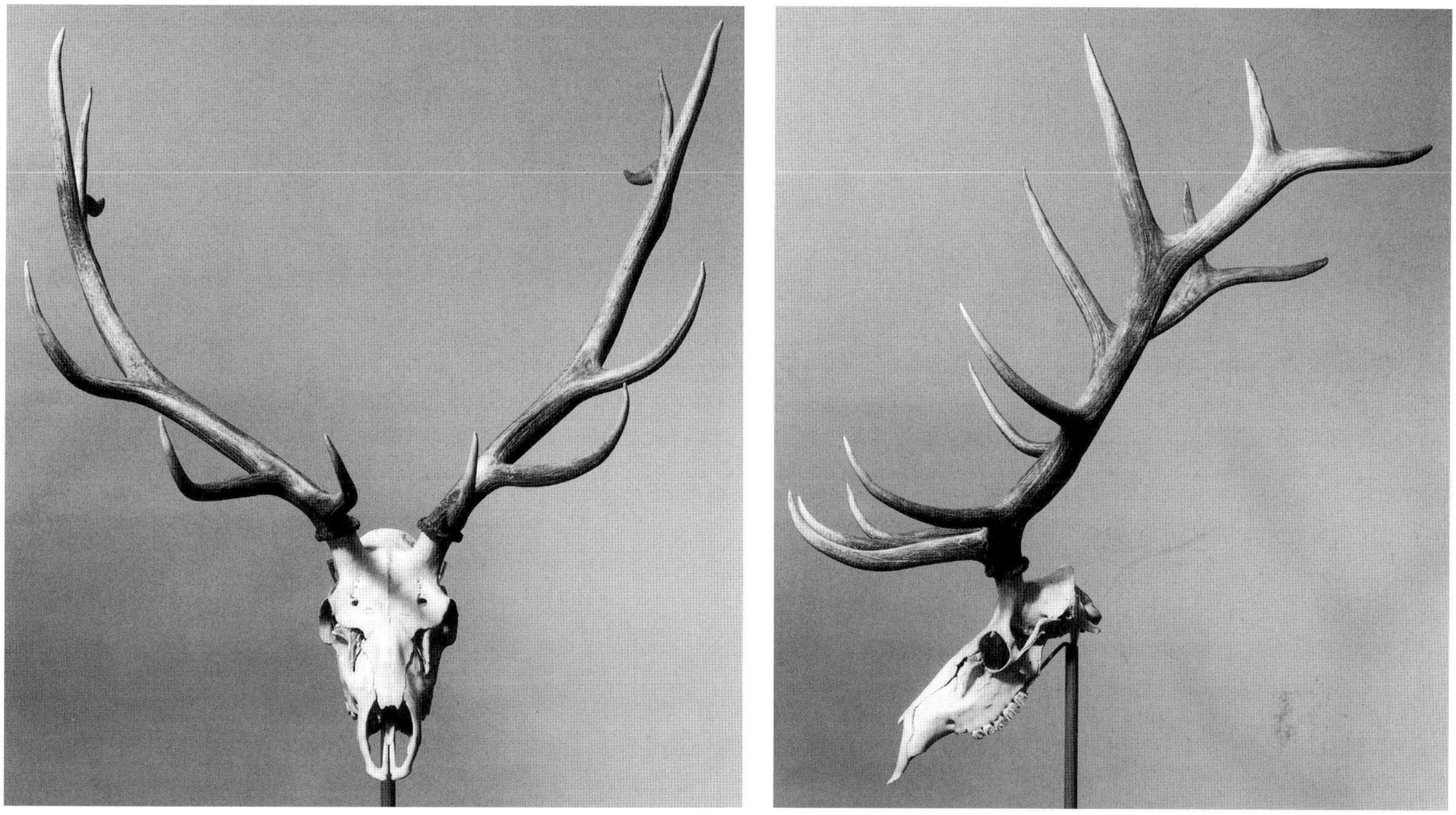

AMERICAN ELK (MALE)
Cervus canadensis

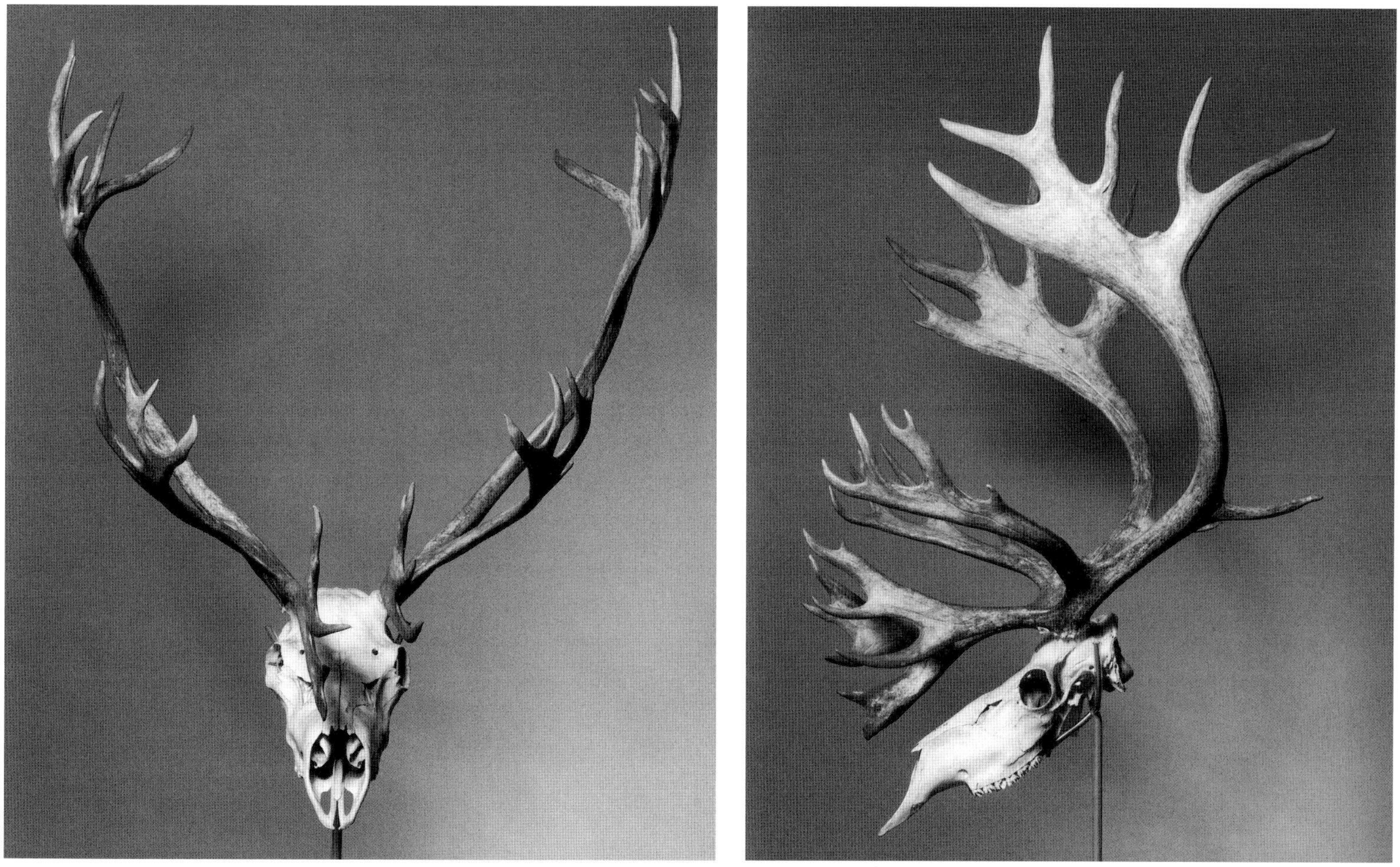

CARIBOU (MALE)
Rangifer tarandus

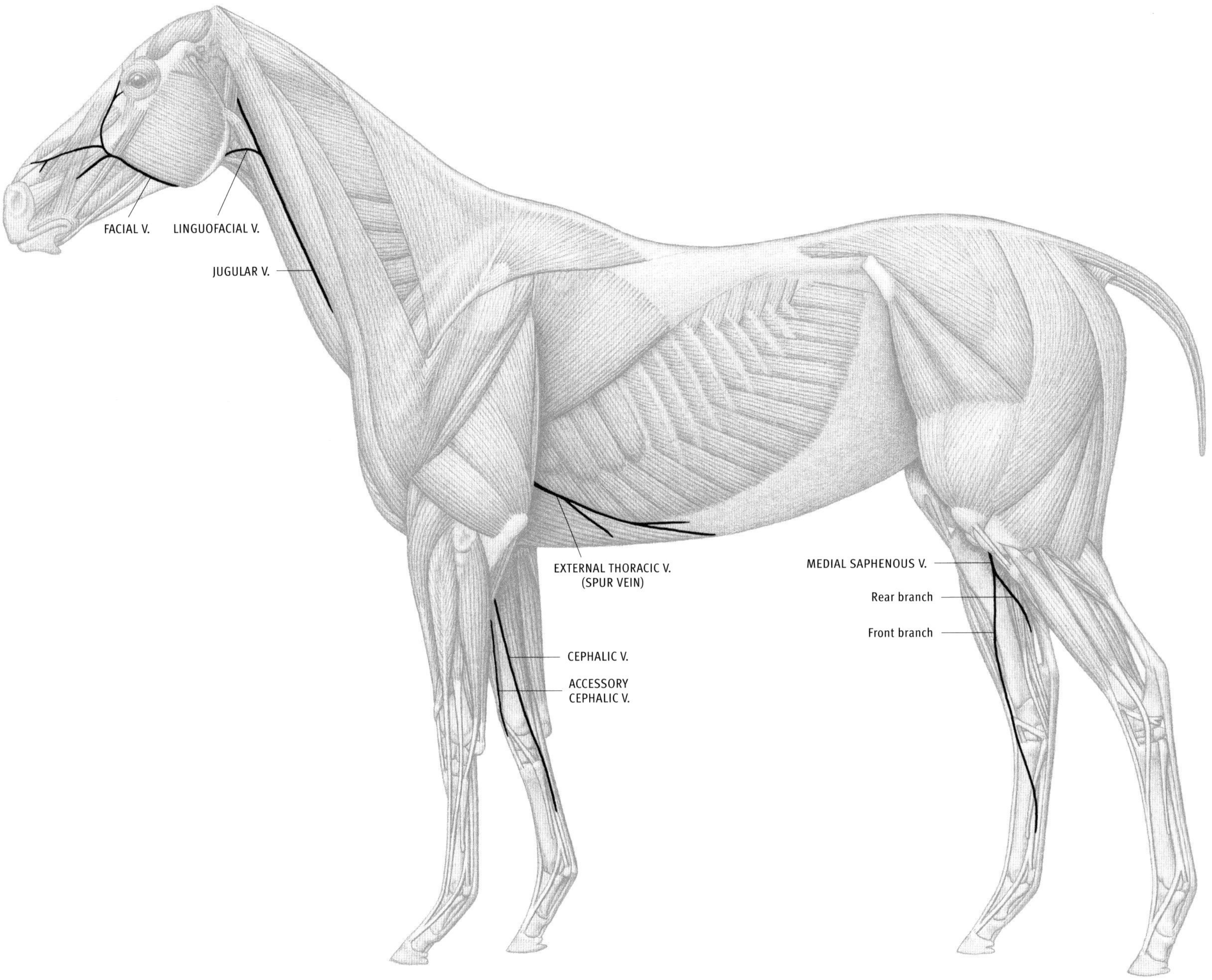

(AFTER ELLENBERGER; POPESCO)

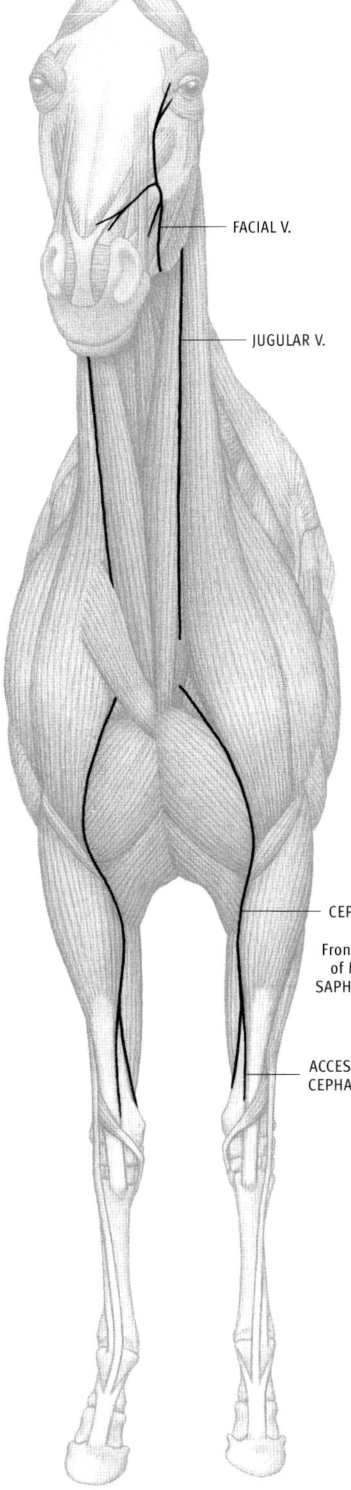

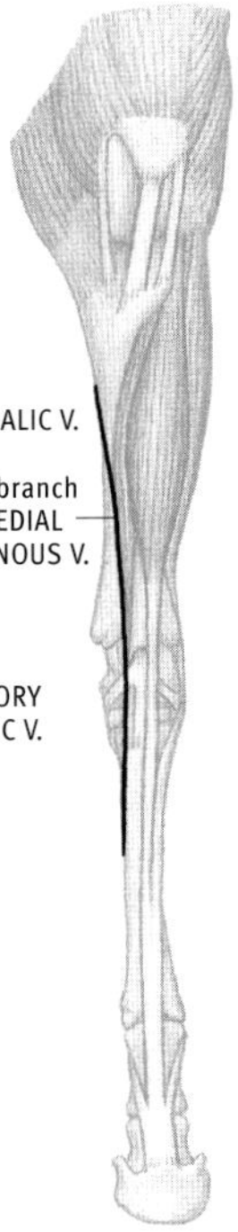

LEFT REAR LIMB
FRONT VIEW

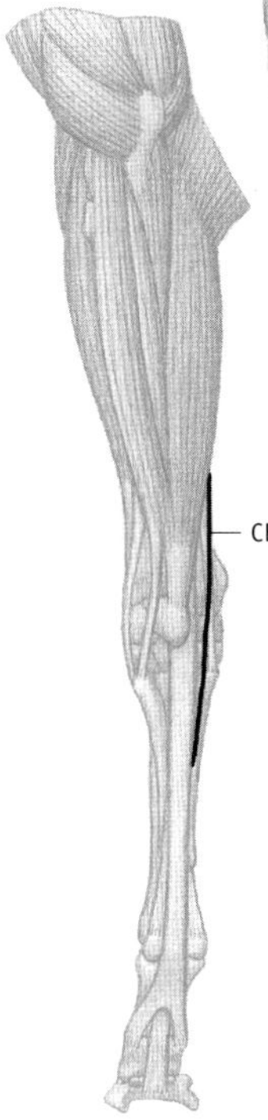

LEFT FRONT LIMB
REAR VIEW

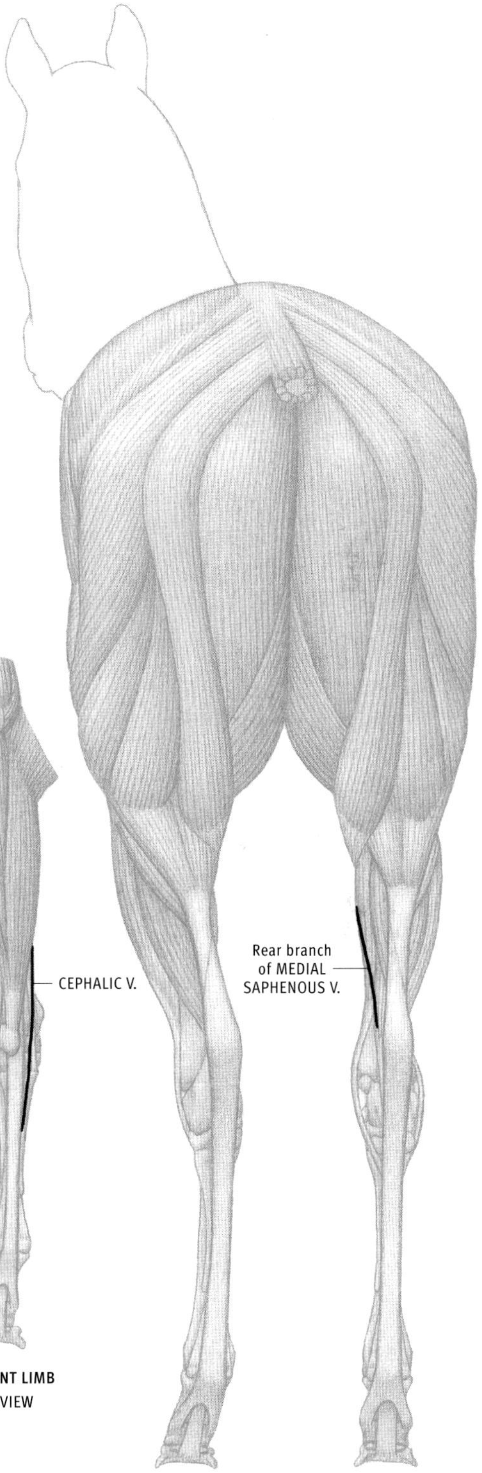

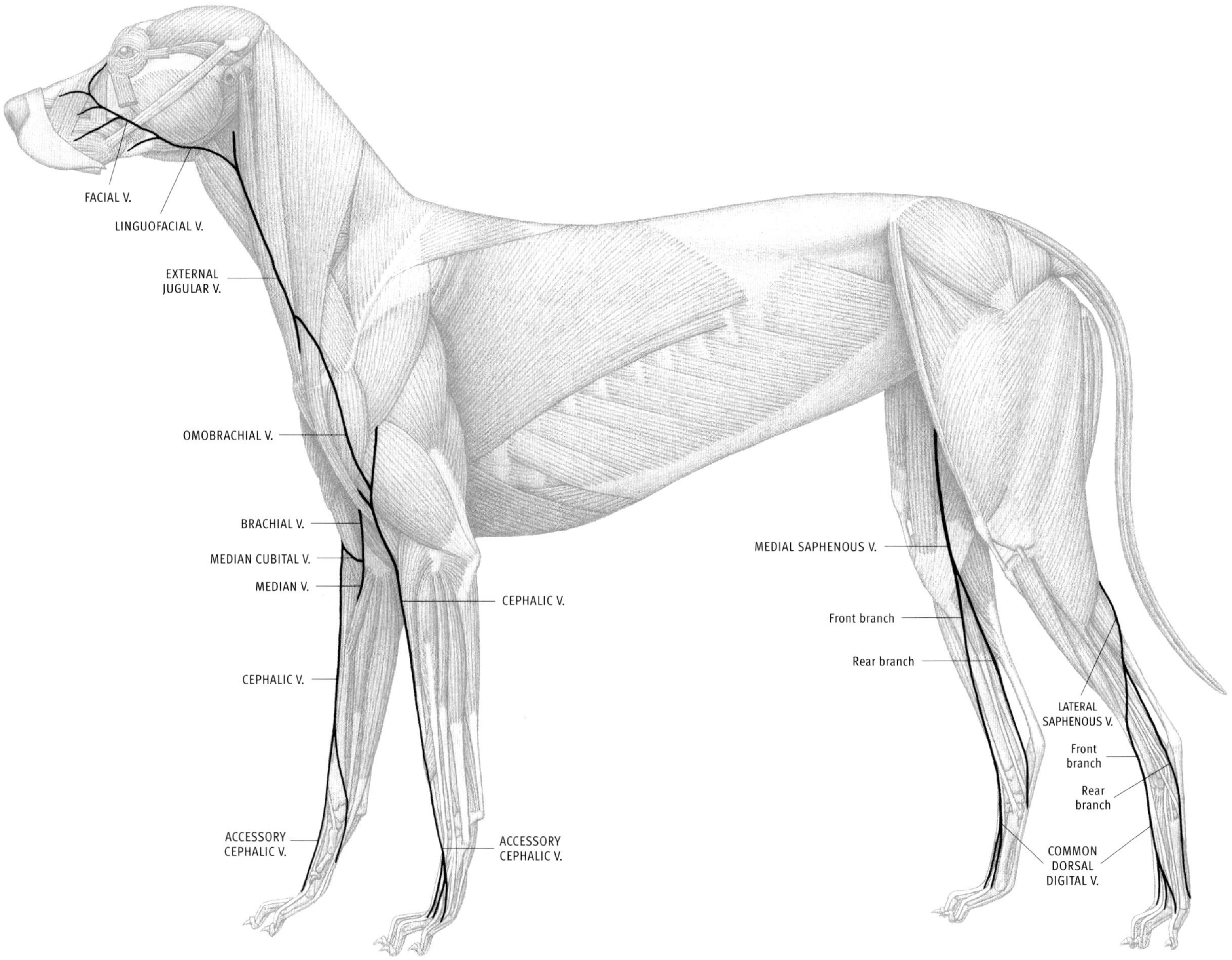

(AFTER ELLENBERGER; MILLER; POPESCO)

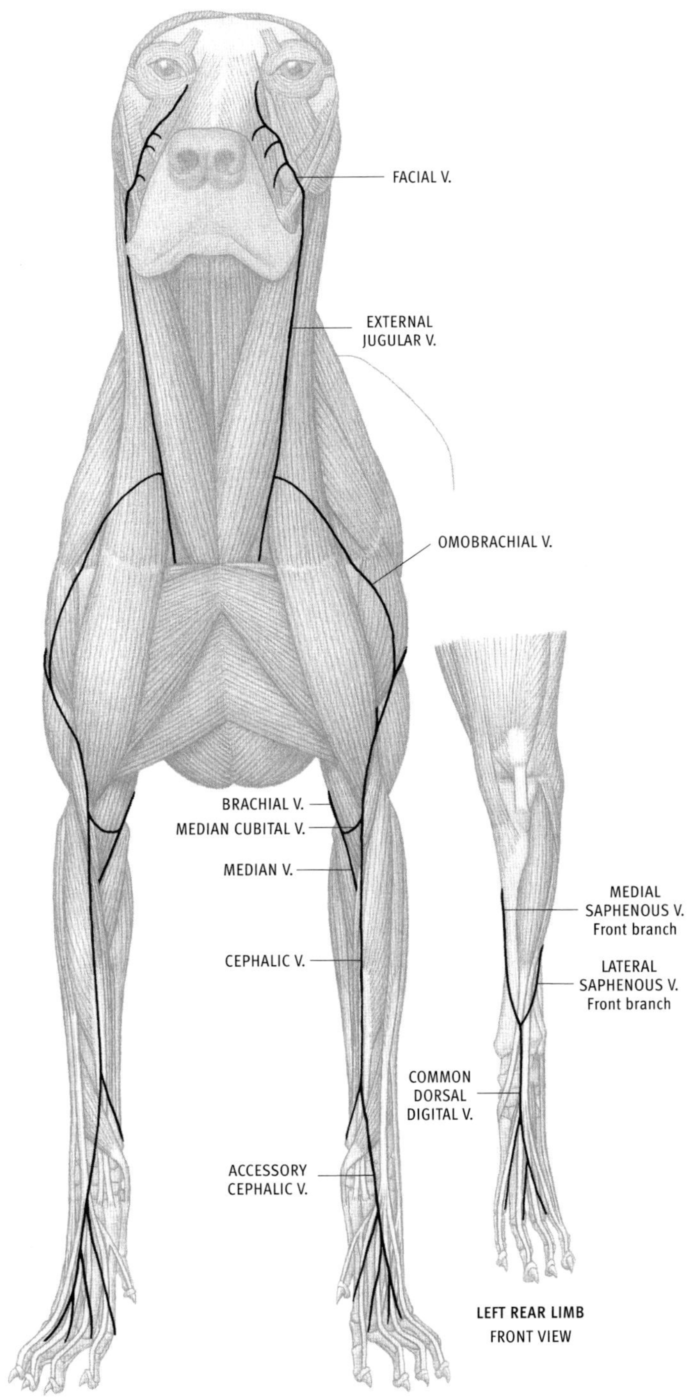

LEFT REAR LIMB
FRONT VIEW

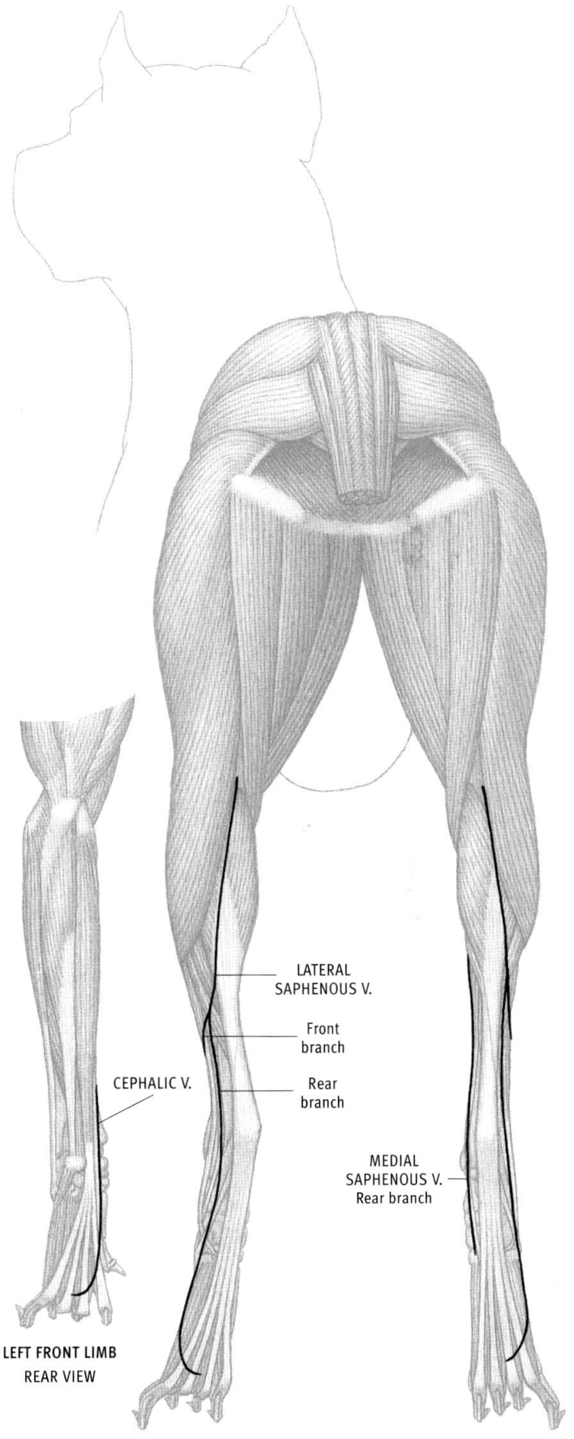

LEFT FRONT LIMB
REAR VIEW

PHOTOGRAPHY CREDITS

Skulls photographed by Eliot Goldfinger in the collection of the Department of Mammalogy at the American Museum of Natural History, New York: American bison, African buffalo, White-tailed deer, Caribou, Ox (neg. no. 603275); Bighorn sheep (neg. no. 603276); Mountain goat, Elk, Moose (neg. no. 603277).

COURTESY AMERICAN MUSEUM OF NATURAL HISTORY LIBRARY

Below: Eliot Goldfinger working on gorilla sculpture at the Philadelphia Zoo, 1983

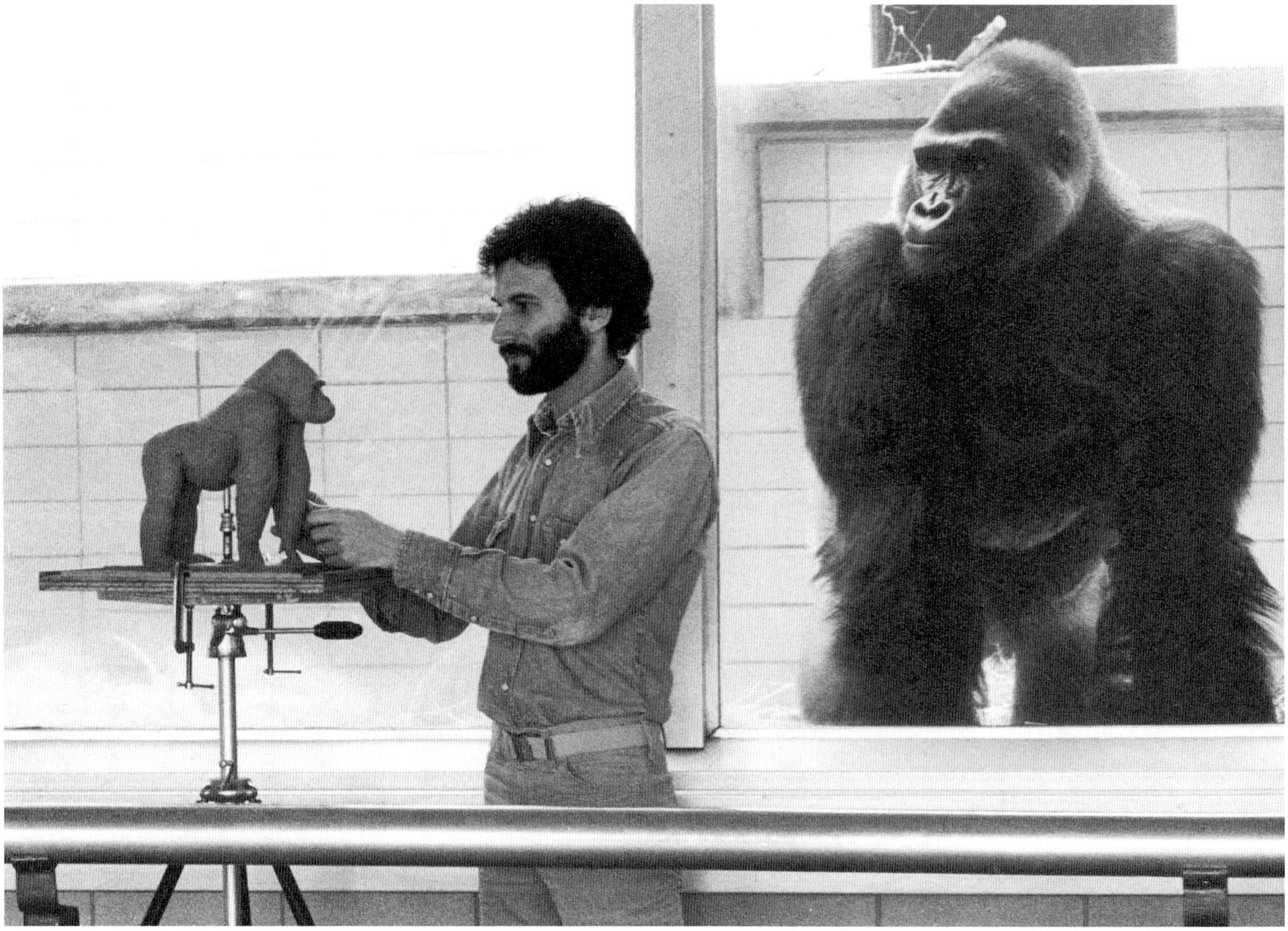

Photograph by Henry Galiano

BIBLIOGRAPHY

Anatomy for Artists

Adams, Norman, and Singer, Joe. 1979. *Drawing Animals.* New York: Watson Guptill. Beautiful pencil drawings by Adams of animals from life, conceptual diagrams, and anatomical drawings of the **elephant, bear, horse, ox, deer, sheep, chimpanzee, tiger, dog, and rabbit**.

Bammes, Gottfried. 1986. *Die Gestalt des Tieres* [The Structure of Animals]. Leipzig: Ravensburg. See below.

—— 1991. *Grosse Tieranatomie: Gestalt, Geschichte, Kunst* (Large Animal Anatomy: Structure, History, Art). Leipzig: Ravensburg. Both Bammes books cover comparative anatomy, mechanics, planar analysis of individual anatomical elements and overall animal bodies, and the translation of this information into art. This book shows numerous examples from the author's own artwork and works from art history.

Brown, Lewis S. 1948. *Horse Anatomy: A Handbook for Artists, Comprising the Study of the Proportion, Structure and Action of the Horse, as Compared to Man*. New York: Bridgman. Text and pencil drawings covering anatomy, surface form, and proportions of the common breeds of the **horse**; human and horse proportional comparisons; and movement. An excellent reference work with a touch of whimsy.

Calderon, W. Frank. 1936. *Animal Painting and Anatomy.* London: Seely, Service. Reprinted 1975, New York: Dover. Excellent work, with very descriptive text and beautifully drawn illustrations. Covers **domestic animals: horse, ox, dog** (minimal **cat**), with some comparisons to **humans**. A classic.

Ellenberger, W., Dittrich, H., and Baum, H. 1956. *An Atlas of Animal Anatomy for Artists,* 2nd ed. Lewis S. Brown, ed. New York: Dover. Based primarily on Ellenberger's *Handbuch der Anatomie der Tiere für Künstler.* 1901. Leipzig: Theodore Weicher, which consists of the most magnificently rendered plates; this is the classic animal anatomy work, covering the **horse, dog, lion, ox, deer,** and **goat**. Brown's edition contains additional plates from several sources, such as Stubbs (**horse**) and Cuvier (*q.v.*) (**monkey, seal, rabbit, bat,** among others) as well as a comprehensive annotated bibliography.

Goldfinger, Eliot. 1991. ***Human*** *Anatomy for Artists: The Elements of Form*. New York: Oxford. All muscles that create surface form are individually presented in various views. In sequence, the origin and insertion of a muscle is indicated on the skeleton in red, then the individual muscle is drawn on the skeleton, then all adjacent muscles of that region are shown, and finally a photo of the muscle, tensed and lit for maximum definition, completes the series. Also contains cross-sections, schematic diagrams, volumetric models, fat pads, facial muscles, and expressions.

Hamm, Jack. 1969. *How to Draw Animals.* New York: Grosset & Dunlap. An excellent book with an incredible amount of information. Author's pencil sketches, along with informative text, contain step-by-step drawing instructions and comparisons of numerous **wild** and **domestic animal** species. The book covers anatomy, proportion, simplified shapes, various poses, hair pattern, feet, gait, faces, facial features, and expression.

Knight, Charles R. 1959. *Animal Drawing: Anatomy and Action for Artists.* New York: Dover. Original title: *Animal Anatomy and Psychology for Artists and Laymen,* 1947. New York: McGraw-Hill. Many sketches from life (mammals, birds, reptiles, invertebrates), with various anatomical studies (**elephant, tiger, bear, camel, sea lion, gorilla**, etc.) and a substantial amount of text. Some anatomical drawings lack important specific details.

Lanteri, Edouard. 1965. *Modelling and Sculpture.* Vol. 3. New York: Dover. First published under the title *Modelling,* 1911. London: Chapman & Hall. Excellent instructions on how to sculpt the **horse, lion,** and **bull**. Includes much on their anatomy in numerous line drawings. Photographs of various stages of the sculptures of each species beautifully illustrate anatomical form.

Richer, Paul. 1920. *Nouvelle anatomie artistique du corps humain, II: Cours supérieur. Morphologie — La femme.* Paris: Plon. Artistic anatomy of the **human female**.

—— 1921. *Nouvelle anatomie artistique du corps humain, I: Cours pratique. Éléments d'anatomie l'homme.* Paris: Plon. Artistic anatomy of the **human male**.

—— 1971. *Artistic Anatomy.* New York: Watson-Guptill. Originally published in Paris as *Anatomie artistique*, 1890. One of the great text/atlases on **human** anatomy for artists.

Seton, Ernest Thomson. 1896. *Art Anatomy of Animals.* London: Macmillan. Reprinted 1977, Philadelphia: Running Press. Mediocre anatomical drawings of the **dog, horse, cat,** and **ox**. Nice proportional drawings. Some **bird** anatomy. Also contains fur and feather drawings, and some cross sections and gait.

Anatomical Works and Veterinary Textbooks

Anderson, R. J. 1883. A contribution to the anatomy of the **Indian elephant.** *Journal of Anatomy and Physiology*, vol. 17, 491–94. Three pages (no illustrations) with comments on Miall and Greenwood (*q.v.*), from his original dissection.

Ashdown, Raymond, and Done, Stanley. 1987. *Color Atlas of Veterinary Anatomy: Vol. 2, The Horse.* London: Mosley-Wolf. Excellent, clear dissections of the **horse**.

—— 1996. *Color Atlas of Veterinary Anatomy: Vol. 1, The Ruminants.* London: Mosley-Wolf. Excellent, clear dissections, mostly of **domestic cattle (cow)**.

Badoux, D. M. 1965. Some notes on the functional anatomy of *Macropus giganteus* Zimm, with general remarks on the mechanics of bipedal leaping. *Acta Anatomica,* vol. 63: 418–22. Very short paper on the muscles of the rear limb of the **kangaroo**.

Beddard, Frank E., and Treves, Frederick. 1889. On the anatomy of *Rhinoceros sumatrensis. Proceedings of the Zoological Society of London*, 7–25. Short descriptions of some of the muscles of the limbs, head, and neck of the **Sumatran rhinoceros**. Many important muscles are omitted. Contains several illustrations. A rare source of information on the seldom described rhino.

Bensley, B. A. 1945. *Practical Anatomy of the* ***Rabbit,*** 7th ed. Craigie, E. Horne, ed. Philadelphia: Blakiston. Small textbook, no illustrations of the muscles.

Blainville, H. M. Ducrotay de. 1839–46. *Ostéographie ou description iconographique comparée du squelette et du système dentaire des cinq classes d'animaux vertébrés récents et fossiles.* Paris: A. Bertrand, text: 4 vols.; atlas: 4 vols. The most magnificent work on animal skeletons ever published. Covers an enormous range of species, including **hippopotamus, lion, camel, Indian elephant, monkey, giraffe, tapir, giant anteater, squirrel, Indian rhino, monkeys**, etc. Some accuracy may be questionable, but the drawings are extraordinary.

Boas, J., and Paulli, S. 1908, 1925. *The Elephant's Head: Studies in the Comparative Anatomy of the Organs of the Head of the Indian Elephant and Other Mammals.* Copenhagen. Vol. 1, 1908: musculature in side view, 17 plates; vol. 2, 1925: skull, and sagittal sections of skull and musculature, 31 plates. Primarily the musculature of the head of the **Indian elephant**, based on a young specimen (older than three years). Also includes the head of the **camel**, **tapir**, **wild boar**, **elk**, **wolf**, and **horse**. Stunningly beautiful and accurate oversize plates in full color, with astonishing detail.

Campbell, Berry. 1936. The comparative myology of the fore-limb of the **hippopotamus**, **pig**, and **tapir**. *American Journal of Anatomy*, vol. 59, 201–47. Good description of the muscles, with several illustrations.

Craigie, E. Horne. 1966. *A Laboratory Guide to the Anatomy of the **Rabbit***. 2nd ed. Toronto: University of Toronto. Small manual with brief descriptions but no illustrations of the muscles. Derived from Bensley.

Crouch, James E. 1969. *Text-Atlas of Cat Anatomy*. Philadelphia: Lea & Febiger. Major work on the **cat**, with numerous, beautiful, line drawings.

Cuvier, George and Laurillard, C. L. c. 1850. *Anatomie comparée: recueil de planches de myologie*. Paris: Chez Dusacq. Magnificent, stunning, oversize volume. One of the most important major historical works on the musculature of mammals, covering the **Indian elephant, hippo, kangaroo, bear, rabbit, bat, seal, tapir, squirrel, orangutan**, etc. Some problems with inaccuracies and mislabeling; some muscle attachments are undefined and confusing. Contains superficial and deep muscles with numerous views.

Done, Stanley H., Goody, Peter C., Evans, Susan A., and Stickland, Neil C. 1996. *Color Atlas of Veterinary Anatomy:* Vol. 3, *The Dog & Cat*. London: Mosby-Wolf. Many color photographs of spectacular dissections next to labeled drawings, mostly of the **dog**, several of the **cat**. Also contains photos of the skeleton, radiographs, cross sections, and drawings of skeletal landmarks that can be felt just under the skin (alongside photos from life).

Eales, Nellie B. 1925–29. The anatomy of the head of a foetal **African elephant**, *Elephas africanus (Loxodonta africana)*. *Transactions of the Royal Society of Edinburgh*. This paper becomes part I in the series subsequently titled: *The anatomy of a foetal African elephant, Elephas africanus (Loxodonta africana)*. Vol. 54, 1925–26, pt. 1: Head, 491–51, 12 plates; vol. 55, 1927–28, pt. 2: Body muscles, 608–42, 5 plates; vol. 56, 1928–29, pt. 3: Contents of thorax & abdomen, skeleton, 202–46, 6 plates. Excellent and enjoyable text, describing the muscles, skeleton, and organs. Eales also discusses homologies of individual muscles to the muscles of other mammals, presents evolutionary relationships of elephants to other species, and compares fetal to adult, and African to Indian, elephants. Contains simplified line drawings.

Ellenberger, W., and Baum, H. 1893. *Topographische Anatomie des Pferdes*. Berlin: P. Parey. Excellent 3-volume work on the **horse**.

Evans, H. E., and Christensen, G. C., eds. 1979. *Miller's Anatomy of the Dog*. 2nd ed. Philadelphia: Saunders. Major work on the **dog**, with many halftone drawings and some line drawings of the muscles.

Field, Hazel E., and Taylor, Mary E. 1950. *An Atlas of Cat Anatomy*. Chicago: University of Chicago Press. An atlas of black-and-white dissection photos of the **cat**, with descriptions of the muscle attachments.

Getty, R., ed. 1975. *Sisson and Grossman's The Anatomy of the Domestic Animals*. 5th ed. Philadelphia: Saunders. Vol. 1: **Equine**, **Ruminant** (**ox** and **goat**); vol. 2: **Porcine** (**pig**), **Carnivore** (mostly **dog**, some **cat**), **Aves** (**birds**). Excellent; the standard veterinary textbook. Contains thorough, detailed descriptions of the skeleton and all the individual muscles. With numerous illustrations (many taken from Ellenberger), as well as some dissection photos.

Grassé, Pierre P., ed. 1971. *Traité de Zoologie*. Paris: Masson. Tome XVI: **Mammals**; fasc. 1: skeleton; fasc. 2: muscles; fasc. 3: muscles. Massive reference on diverse species, **wild** and **domestic**. No complete musculature drawings, only details of particular areas (head, limb, spine, etc.). Excellent bibliography; major reference source for this book.

Haughton, Samuel. 1867. On the muscular anatomy of the **rhinoceros**. *Proceedings of the Royal Irish Academy*, vol. 9, 515–24. Listing of the muscles of the limbs only, most with origins and insertions noted.

—— 1867. On the muscles of the marsupials. *Proceedings of the Royal Irish Academy,* 468–83. Listing of the muscles, and their attachments, of the **kangaroo**, with short descriptions of some of the muscles.

—— 1867. On the muscles of the Virginian **bear**. *Proceedings of the Royal Irish Academy*, vol. 9, 508–11. Four pages listing the weights of the muscles, with occasional mention of muscle attachments. No illustrations.

Hildebrand, Milton. 1974. *Analysis of Vertebrate Structure*. 2nd ed. New York: John Wiley. Very readable textbook on vertebrate structure, especially how the skeletons and muscles have evolved for running, jumping, digging, crawling, climbing, swimming, diving, flying, gliding, and feeding.

Macalister, Alexander. 1873. The anatomy of *Choeropsis liberiensis*. *Proceedings of the Royal Irish Academy,* series 2, vol. 1, 494–500. Brief descriptive text of the muscles, and their attachments, of the **pigmy hippopotamus**. Illustrations of the deep muscles of the forefoot and hind foot only.

—— 1873–74. The muscular anatomy of the **gorilla**. *Proceedings of the Royal Irish Academy*, vol. 1, 501–06. Some descriptions of the muscles, but mostly comparing the weights of various muscles, as well as comparisons with the chimpanzee.

Mariappa, D. 1986. *Anatomy and Histology of the Indian Elephant.* Oak Park, MI: Indira Publishing House. A contemporary description of the anatomy of the **Indian elephant**, with the names and configurations of the muscles and their attachments more closely allied to the musculature of the other mammals, which makes the anatomy much less confusing than earlier writers (among whom there is considerable disagreement). Line drawings are oversimplified and parts are unrealistic. Work based on four fetal specimens.

McLaughlin, Charles A. 1970. *Laboratory Anatomy of the **Rabbit***. Dubuque: Brown. Contains a listing of the muscles, their attachments and their functions, with five very simplified line drawings of the musculature.

Miall, L. C., and Greenwood, F. 1878. *Studies in Comparative Anatomy II: Anatomy of the **Indian Elephant***. London: Macmillan. Small book, same text as their *Journal of Anatomy* article, but with four plates, which include the front limb and proboscis.

—— 1878. The anatomy of the Indian elephant. *Journal of Anatomy and Physiology*, vol. 12, pt. 1, Muscles of the extremities, 261–87; pt. 2, Muscles of the head and trunk, 385–400. Excellent text on the muscles of the **Indian elephant**, based on a young female specimen; no illustrations.

Montané, Lucien, and Bourdelle, E. 1913–53. *Anatomie régionale des animaux domestiques*. Paris: Baillière. 4 vols. Vol. 1: **horse**; vol. 2: **ruminants**; vol. 3: **pig**; vol. 4: **dog** & **cat**. Standard veterinary book, in French. Contains several good cross sections.

Mori, Masaru. 1958. The skeleton and musculature of *Zalophus*. *Okajimas Folia Anatomica Japonica*, vol. 31, 203–84. Extensive text with line drawings throughout, plus four plates of photographs of individual bones, describing the California **sea lion**.

Murie, James. 1872. On the horns, viscera, and muscles of the **giraffe**. *The Annals and Magazine of Natural History*, vol. 9, 177–94. The text discusses only some of the muscles, but one of the plates is a wonderful full side view of the superficial muscles in very good detail, something rarely found.

—— 1872. On the Malayan tapir, *Rhinoceros sumatranus*. *Journal of Anatomy and Physiology*, vol. 6, 131–69. Contains an excellent plate of the side view of the superficial musculature of a **Malayan tapir**.

—— 1872, 1874. Descriptive anatomy of the **sea lion** *(Otaria jubata)*. *Transactions of the Zoological Society of London*, vol. 7, 1872, pt. 2: The muscles, 527–96; vol. 8, 1874, pt. 3: The skeleton, 501–600. Text and plates. Good descriptions of the musculature with excellent illustrations.

Nickel, Richard, Schummer, A., and Seiferle, E. 1968. *Lehrbuch der Anatomie der Haustiere*. Berlin: Parey. Vol. 1: *Bewegungsapparat* (Movement apparatus). Excellent volume on the skeleton and musculature of the **domestic mammals**. English translation is: *The Anatomy of the Domestic Animals*. Vol. 1: The Locomotor System of the Domestic Animals.

Orwoll, Sylfest O. 1940. The osteology and myology of the fox squirrel *(Sciurus niger rufiventer)*, the gray **squirrel** *(Sciurus carolinensis leucotis)*, and the red squirrel *(Tamiasciurus hudsonicus loquax)*. Doctoral thesis, Graduate School of Michigan State College. Brief descriptions with outline drawing of the individual bones of the skeleton; more extensive descriptions of all the muscles, with simplified, stylized line drawings.

Owen, Richard. 1841. Notes on the anatomy of the Nubian giraffe. *Transactions of the Zoological Society of London*, vol. 2, 232–34. Three pages (no illustrations) in this article discuss some of the muscles of the **giraffe**.

Pander, C. H., and D'Alton, J.W.E. 1821–28. *Die Vergleichende Osteologie*. Bonn. Beautiful engravings of articulated skeletons, surrounded by their outline in life; often awkward postures and outlines, accuracy questionable, some shockingly incorrect. Includes **hippo, Indian elephant, tapir, pig, lion giraffe, dromedary, monkey, sea lion, walrus, whale,** and **kangaroo.**

Parsons, F. G. 1896. On the anatomy of *Petrogale xanthopus*, compared with that of other kangaroos. *Proceedings of the Zoological Society of London*, 683–704. Anatomy of the **wallaby**, which is similar to the **kangaroo**.

Popesco, Peter. 1984. *Atlas of Topographical Anatomy of the Domestic Animals*. 4th ed. Philadelphia: Saunders. 3 vols. bound together. Major work, covering **bovine**, **sheep, goat, swine, horse**, and **dog**, with some attention to **cat** and **rabbit**. Very clear but highly stylized original illustrations in color; numerous cross sections.

Raven, Henry Cushier (and others). 1950. *The Anatomy of the **Gorilla***. New York: Columbia. Thorough work containing numerous excellent line drawings of the musculature. The skeleton drawings show the origins and insertions in two colors. Includes life-size fold-out drawings of the entire arm and leg.

Rommel, Sentiel A. 1990. Osteology of the bottlenose dolphin, 29–49. In Leatherwood, S., and Reeves, R., eds.: *The Bottlenose Dolphin*. New York: Academic Press. Thorough study of the skeleton of the bottlenose **dolphin**.

Schmaltz, Reinhold. 1905. *Atlas der Anatomie des Pferdes*. Berlin: R. Schoetz. Excellent, major 5-volume work on the **horse**.

Shepherd, Francis J. 1884. Short notes on the myology of the American black **bear** *(Ursus americanus)*. *Journal of Anatomy and Physiology*, vol. 18, 103–17. Good descriptions of the muscles; no illustrations.

Shindo, Tokuichi, and Mori, Masaru. 1956. Musculature of the Indian elephant. *Okajimas Folia Anatomica Japonica*, vol. 28, pt. 1, forelimb, 89–113; pt. 2, hind limb, 115–47; vol. 29, pt. 3, trunk, neck, and head, 17–41. Fairly extensive review of the muscles based on the author's dissections of two **Indian elephant** fetuses. The muscle attachments in the line drawings are often vague, with the points of attachment on the skeleton not defined—the muscles seem to end in space. Also, the orientation of regions of the body are not described, and with cut muscles pulled away, it is very difficult to figure out what region and which view is being presented. Many muscles are not labeled, and some labeled muscles are not mentioned in the text at all. A frustrating paper, with some good, specific information based on first-hand dissection.

Slijper, E. J. 1936. Die Cetaceen: Vergleichend—Anatomisch und Systematisch. *Capita Zoologica*, vol. 7. The anatomy of the **whale**, **dolphin** and **porpoise**.

Smuts, Malie M. S., and Bezuidenhout, A. J. 1987. *Anatomy of the Dromedary*. Oxford: Clarendon. Includes complete, in-depth descriptions of the skeleton and musculature of the **dromedary camel**, with numerous very clear illustrations.

Straus, William L., Jr. 1942. The structure of the crown-pad of the **gorilla** and of the cheek pad of the **orang-utan**. *Journal of Mammalogy*, vol. 23, 276–81. Description of the thick skin layers and the hair lying above the skull and head muscles that forms the crown of the gorilla.

Swindler, D. R., and Wood, C. D. 1982. *An Atlas of Primate Gross Anatomy: **Baboon, Chimpanzee,** and **Man***. Malabar: Krieger. Contains numerous drawings of the skeleton and musculature, comparing the same parts in the same views of the three species.

Walton, Elijah. 1865. *The Camel: Its Anatomy, Proportion and Paces*. London: Day & Son. A major monograph, in large folio size, partly in color, of the skeleton, surface musculature, and gait of the **dromedary camel**, with side, front, and rear views. Muscles not labeled, some not defined to their attachments. A major effort, but Smuts is much more useful.

Watson, M. 1874–75. Contributions to the anatomy of the **Indian elephant.** *Journal of Anatomy and Physiology*, vol. 8, 1874, pt. 3, 85–94; vol. 9, 1875, pt. 4. Muscles and blood vessels of the face and head. Good descriptions, no illustrations.

Way, Robert F., and Lee, Donald G. 1965. *The Anatomy of the **Horse**: A Pictorial Approach*. Philadelphia: Lippincott. Mediocre drawings of the musculature; good drawings of the origins and insertions of the muscles on the bones.

Windle, Bertram C. A. 1889. Notes on the limb myology of *Procyon cancrivorus* and of the *Ursidae*. *Journal of Anatomy and Physiology*, vol. 23, 81–89. Short paper basically on the **raccoon**, but with comparisons to the **bears**. No illustrations.

Windle, Bertram C. A., and Parsons, F. G. 1897–98. On the myology of terrestrial Carnivora. *Proceedings of the Zoological Society of London*, 1897, pt. 1: Muscles of the head, neck, and fore-limb, 370–409; 1898, pt. 2: Muscles of the hind limb and trunk, 152–86. A review of all the anatomical literature that preceded their paper, along with data from their own dissections. Good, short descriptions of the muscles. Several illustrations. Covers the **cat** and **dog families**, **bear**, and others.

—— 1898. On the anatomy of *Macropus rufus*. *Journal of Anatomy and Physiology,* vol. 32, 119–29. Short paper describing the muscles of the **kangaroo**.

—— 1901–03. On the muscles of the Ungulata. *Proceedings of the Zoological Society of London*, vol. 1, 1901, part 1: Muscles of the head, neck, and fore-limb, 656–704; vol. 2, 1903, part 2: Muscles of the hind-limb and trunk, 261–98. A review of all the anatomical literature that preceded their paper, along with data from their own dissections. Good, short descriptions of the muscles. Several illustrations. Covers the **hippo, pig, camel, deer, giraffe, cattle, goat, sheep, tapir, horse, rhinoceros, elephant,** and others.

Young, A. H. 1879. Note on the anatomy of the **Indian elephant**. *Journal of Anatomy and Physiology*, vol. 14, 289–91. Three pages (no illustrations) with comments on Miall and Greenwood's paper (*q.v.*).

Mammals

Kingdon, Jonathan. 1971–82. *East African Mammals, an Atlas of Evolution in Africa*. London: Academic Press. 3 vols., some with more than one part (total 7 books). An inspiring, massive work, by a single artist, describing, in text and numerous drawings, the natural history of the mammals of East Africa. Drawings range from quick sketches of animals in action and fur patterns to drawings of the skeleton and muscle dissections. Dissection drawings are not labeled and muscles are usually not drawn from beginning to end; attachments are undefined. Includes **hippo**, **cheetah**, **black** and **white rhino**, **lion**, **elephant**, **giraffe**, **hyena**, etc.

Lawler, Timothy E. 1979. *Handbook to the Orders and Families of Living Mammals*. 2nd ed. Eureka: Mad River Press. Classification of all the living mammals, with excellent overviews of their characteristics. Many simplified line drawings of skulls.

Papastavrou, Vassili. 1993. *Whale*. New York: Knopf. An Eyewitness Book, with numerous photographs of **whales**, **dolphins**, and **porpoises**, as well as a few other marine mammals. Also includes photographs of skulls and skeletons.

Redmond, Ian. 2000. *Gorilla, Monkey & Ape*. New York: Dorling Kindersley. An Eyewitness Book, with numerous photographs of **monkeys** and **apes**; also contains photographs of skeletons of orangutan, gorilla, and chimpanzee.

—— 1993. *Elephant.* New York: Knopf. An Eyewittness Book, loaded with captioned photographs. Contains a side view photo of an articulated adult female **African elephant** skeleton.

Reynolds, John E., Wells, R., and Eide, S. 2000. *The Bottlenose Dolphin: Biology and Conservation*. Gainsville: University Press of Florida. Contains a drawing of a bottlenose **dolphin** skeleton.

Sikes, Sylvia K. 1971. *The Natural History of the African Elephant.* New York: American Elsevier. Contains a side-view photo of an articulated **African elephant** skeleton.

Walker, Ernest P. 1968. *Mammals of the World.* 2nd ed. Baltimore: Johns Hopkins. 2 vols. Covers all the genera of **mammals** of the world, with numerous black-and-white photographs. Excellent reference on the natural history of mammals, describing surface appearance and dimensions, with some skeleton photos.

Birds

Chamberlain, Frank Wilbut. 1943. *Atlas of Avian Anatomy; Osteology, Arthrology, Myology.* East Lansing: Michigan State College, Agricultural Experiment Station, Memoir Bulletin 5. Illustration of articulated chicken skeleton in side-view, as well as individual bones, and numerous views of the musculature.

George, John C. and Berger, A. J. 1966. *Avian Myology*. New York: Academic Press. Good text, especially on the muscles of the pigeon.

Getty, R., ed. 1975. *Sisson and Grossman's The Anatomy of the Domestic Animals*. 5th ed. Philadelphia: Saunders. Vol. 2: Aves (birds). Excellent; the standard veterinary textbook. Contains thorough, detailed descriptions of the skeleton and all the individual muscles. Numerous illustrations.

Harvey, Elmer B., Kaiser, H. E., and Rosenberg, L. E. 1968. *An Atlas of the Domestic Turkey (Meleagris gallopavo); Myology and Osteology.* Washington, D.C.: U.S. Atomic Energy Commission. Excellent work on the turkey, with numerous illustrations.

Hudson, George E. and Lanzillotti, Patricia J. 1964. Muscles of the pectoral limb in galliform birds. *American Midland Naturalist,* vol. 71, 1–113. Good text and clear line drawings of the wing muscles of the chicken.

Hudson, George E., Lanzillotti, Patricia J., and Edwards, Glenn D. 1959. Muscles of the pelvic limb in galliform birds. *American Midland Naturalist,* vol. 61, 1–67. Good text and clear line drawings of the leg muscles of the grouse.

Lucas, Alfred Martin and Stettenheim, Peter R. 1972. *Avian Anatomy: Integument.* Washington, D.C.: U.S. Agricultural Research Service. Includes illustration of chicken musculature, side view, and numerous illustrations of the feather patterns.

Nickel, Richard, Schummer, A., Seiferle, E., et al. 1977. *Anatomy of the Domestic Birds.* Berlin: Parey. Good chapter on the skeleton; short chapter on the muscles, listing them with their attachments (no structural descriptions). Few muscle illustrations—includes rare front view of chicken.

Wray, Richard S. 1887. On some points on the morphology of the wings of birds. *Proceedings of the Zoological Society of London,* 343–57. Original paper on the arrangement of the wing feather groups. Also shows how the large flight feathers attach to the wing skeleton. Good illustrations.

Website: http://www.ups.edu/biology/museum/wingphotos.html. *Wing Photos*, Slater Museum of Natural History, University of Puget Sound, Tacoma, Washington. Numerous digital scans and photographs of bird wings, showing clear images of top and bottom of each wing. An amazing resource.

See also: Hildebrand; Knight; Muybridge; Parker; Seton.

Miscellaneous

Muybridge, Eadweard. 1979. *Muybridge's Complete Human and Animal Locomotion.* New York: Dover. Reprint of Muybridge's 1887 *Animal Locomotion*. Vol. 3 contains all animal photographic plates. Includes domestic and wild mammals in sequential photos of various phases of walking and running. Shows side-views, and occasionally front, rear, and three-quarter views. Also includes flying and flightless **birds**. Mammals include **horse**, **ox, pig, goat, dog, domestic cat, oryx, deer, elk, eland, antelope, bison, gnu, lion, tiger, jaguar, Indian elephant, dromedary, Bactrian camel, guanaco, raccoon, capybara, baboon, sloth,** and **kangaroo.**

Parker, Steve. 1988. *Skeleton*. New York: Knopf. An Eyewitness Book, with numerous skeleton photos, including **cat, hare, squirrel, monkey, bat** and **birds**.

Video

Dissection of the Giraffe Neck. 1998. Solounias, Nikos, and Eliot, David. Work in progress, 2002 personal communication. Dissection of the neck and shoulder of a mature female **giraffe** at the Memphis Zoo.

Form and Function in the Rhinoceros (Diceros). 1984. Rutgers State University of New Jersey. 20 mins., color video. Dissection of a **black rhino** at the American Museum of Natural History, primarily to weigh various muscle groups and study muscle mass placement on the skeleton (for comparison with the kudu—a long-limbed antelope). Individual muscles not separated.

Gait: Observing Dogs in Slow Motion. American Kennel Club. 36 mins., color video. Different types of locomotion and posture, both good and bad, in the various breeds of **dog**.

Locomotion of Four-Footed Animals. 1980. University of California. 15 mins., black-and-white video. Informative technical analysis of various forms of movement—walk, trot, pace, run, gallop, bound, hop, and pronk. Films of numerous animals (**elephant, rhino, deer, dog, horse, jack rabbit, okapi, cheetah,** etc.)

Thoroughbreds in Slow Motion. 1974. The Jockey Club. Lindberg Productions. 30 mins., color video. **Thoroughbred horses** filmed at races, ridden by jockeys, all in slow motion. Front, side, three-quarter, and rear views, showing very defined musculature of stunning animals, with close-ups of the limbs and the feet on impact. Mediocre video quality.

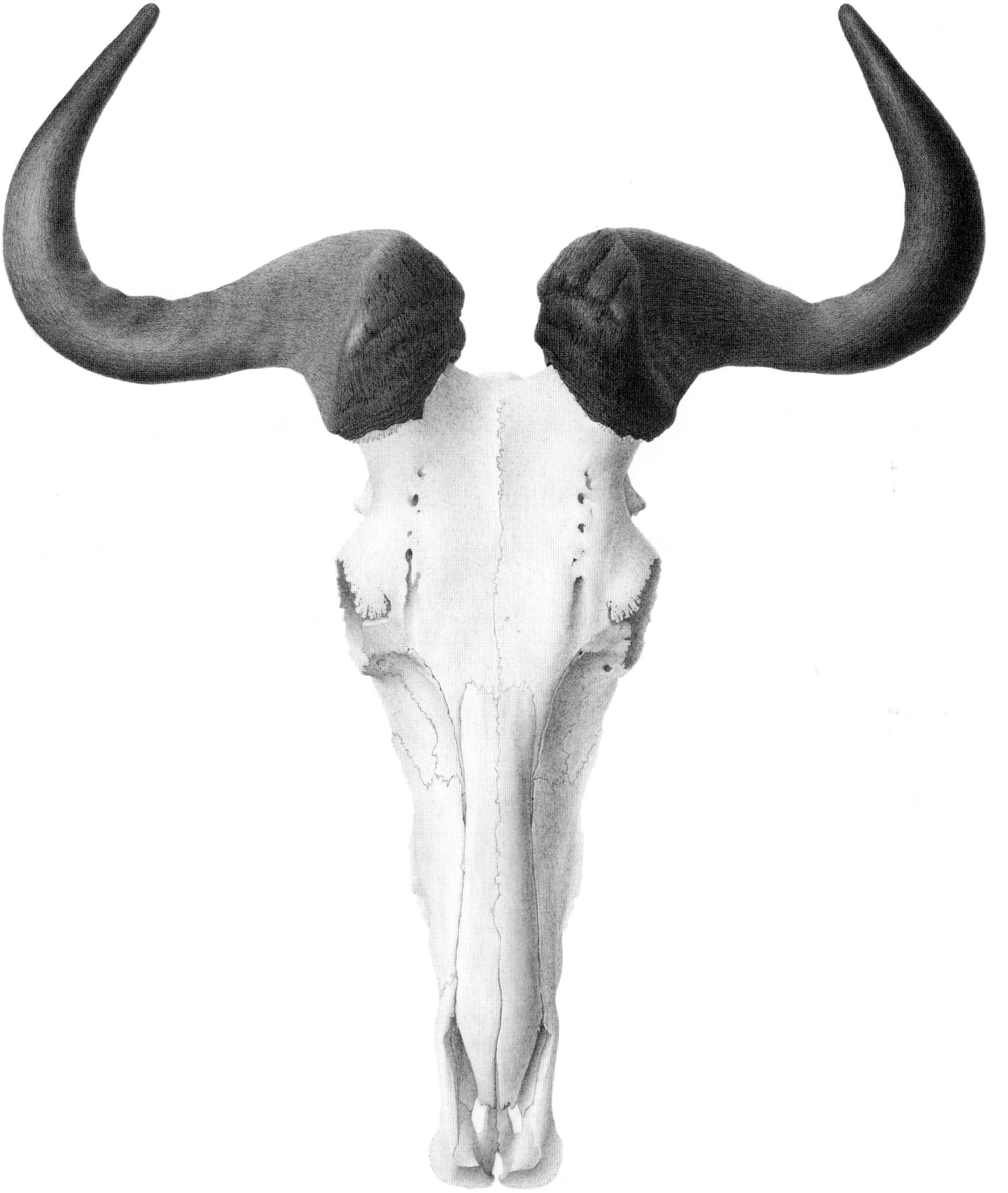

Wildebeest skull drawing, 1974. Pencil on paper
Image size: 13.5 x 11 inches

INDEX

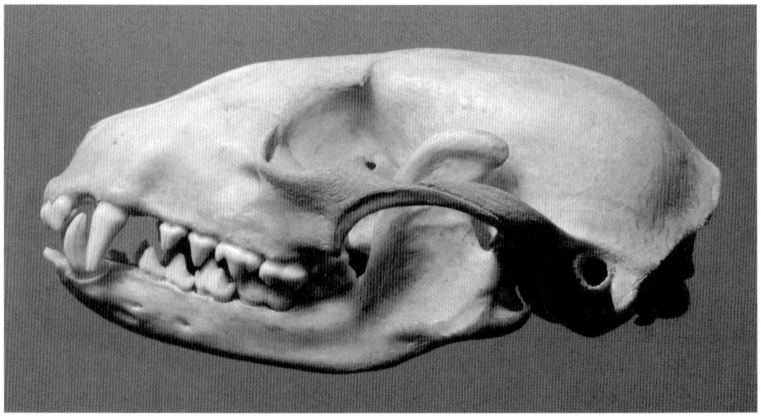

RACCOON
Procyon lotor

When I was twelve years old, I found a raccoon skull in the woods behind my house. Cleaning and studying this skull led to a passionate interest in form and function in nature. This has developed into a lifelong appreciation of the beauty of nature and a fascination with structure, evolution, and biodiversity. Ultimately, this translated into the exploration of how these forms in nature can be expressed in art. —*E.G.*